Software Engineering
Volume 2: The Supporting Processes
SECOND EDITION

TAKING
the
EXAM

with

Richard
Thayer

&

Mark
Christensen

Software Engineering
Volume 2: The Supporting Processes
SECOND EDITION

Edited by Richard H. Thayer and Mark J. Christensen

Foreword by Dixie Garr

Original contributions by

Richard H. Thayer

Ian Sommerville

IEEE

COMPUTER SOCIETY
http://computer.org

WILEY-INTERSCIENCE

A JOHN WILEY & SONS, INC., PUBLICATION

ISBN 0-7695-1557-6
Library of Congress Number 2002100878

Editorial production by Anne Jacobs
Cover art production by Joe Daigle/Studio Productions
Printed in the United States of America by The Printing House

Software Engineering:
Volume 2: The Supporting Processes
Table of Contents

Chapter 1. Software Engineering Supporting Processes

Chapter 2. Software Configuration Management
and Problem Resolution Processes

Chapter 3. Software Verification and Validation Processes

Chapter 4. Software Quality Assurance Process

Chapter 5. Software Reviews and Audits Processes

Chapter 6. Software Documentation Process

Chapter 7: Management Process

Chapter 8: Infrastructure Process

Chapter 9: Improvement and Training Processes

Appendix

Foreword
Software Engineering
Volume 2: The Supporting Processes

This is the second of two volumes published by the IEEE Computer Society to assist in preparation for the examination required to become a Certified Software Development Professional (CSDP). Like the first volume, it supports the Computer Society's position that the disciplined development of high-quality software requires a good development process, and that good, applicable standards are a key part of that process.

The first volume, *The Development Processes*, focuses on the primary processes of system analysis and design, plus software requirements, design, implementation (coding), testing, and maintenance. This second volume focuses on supporting and organizational life cycle processes, which include:

- Software configuration management process
- Software quality assurance process
- Validation and verification processes
- Reviews and audits processes
- Documentation process
- Problem solving process
- Management process
- Infrastructure process
- Improvement process
- Training process

These auxiliary processes have sometimes been viewed as less glamorous than the primary development processes. However, in my experience in being responsible for software quality as well as ultimate customer satisfaction and success, I realize that they are equally and critically important. It is these processes that have potential for great impact and attention paid can here have multifold return on investment. For example, the combination of project reviews and audits and software management has been shown to obviate much need later maintenance commitments. Software configuration management is absolutely indispensable in managing and fielding large, complex software products; without it, or if it is not done thoroughly and correctly, software components will not interoperate correctly and may not even be installable. Likewise software quality assurance is essential--a coordinated set of activities that are carried out throughout the software life cycle to ensure that high-quality software is being developed, rather than attempting to "test quality in" at the end of the development life cycle.

This volume is a new product, consisting of both original papers and highly regarded papers reprinted from authoritative sources.

I whole-heartedly support professional development, process improvement, and learning. These two Computer Society Tutorial volumes are an invaluable resource.

Dixie Garr
Vice President
Customer Success Engineering
Cisco Systems, Inc.

Preface
Volume 2: The Supporting Processes

The purpose of this tutorial is to provide within one source (two volumes) a considerable and useful proportion of software engineering technical knowledge. The papers selected and/or newly authored for this tutorial are tailored to provide sufficient coverage of software engineering issues to prepare the reader to take the IEEE Certified Software Development Professional (CSDP) examination.

The backbone for this publication is IEEE/EIA Standard 12207-1997, *Standard for Information Technology--- Software Life Cycle Processes.* This two-volume set covers (as defined in 12207) the process identified in Table 1.

Table 1: List of Software Engineering Processes

Volume 1	Volume 2	Volume 2
System requirements analysis	Documentation process	Management process
System architectural design	Configuration management process	Infrastructure process
Software requirements analysis	Quality assurance process	Improvement process
Software architectural design	Verification process	Training process
Software detailed design	Validation process	
Software implementation (coding)	Joint review process	
Software testing	Audit process	
Software maintenance	Problem resolution process	

We selected our tutorial papers based on the following characteristics:

- They defined and used similar terms to the CSDP exam

- They covered the state of the practice for the given topic thoroughly and evenly

- They avoid new, unproved concepts

- They do not try to sell one tool or concept over all others

- They are easy to read

- They are organized in a hierarchical manner (top-level concepts discussed first, second level concepts discussed next, and so forth)

- They avoid "gratuitous" mathematics

- They provide additional references

Our criteria are of course idealized. Even these "rules" can be violated if there is a good reason. In addition, to keep the whole tutorial under 500 pages, each article should be no longer than 10-12 journal pages.

The most current paper on a given topic was used. In a surprisingly large number of the basic specialty areas of software engineering, there were no recent, high-quality overview papers identified. It appears that, as a discipline matures, people no longer write overview papers. Therefore, some of these papers appear to be "old." Regardless of the year the article was written or published, these papers reflect the latest state of the practice in software engineering.

This tutorial was tailored to cover the CSDP exam specifications (see http://www.computer.org/certification) and the appropriate development processes. This particular volume covers:

- Chapter 1: Software Engineering Supporting Processes

- Chapter 2: Software Configuration Management and Problem Resolution Processes

- Chapter 3: Software Verification and Validation Processes

- Chapter 4: Software Quality Assurance Processes

- Chapter 5: Software Reviews and Audits Processes

- Chapter 6: Software Documentation Processes

- Chapter 7: Management Processes

- Chapter 8: Infrastructure Processes

- Chapter 9: Training and Improvement Processes

This tutorial also provides some abbreviated copies of the *IEEE Standards on Software Engineering* integrated within the appropriate chapter. This is an important addition since the CSDP examination includes and is centered on these standards.

- IEEE Std P730-2001, Standard for Software Quality Assurance Plans (new draft)

- IEEE Std 0828-1998 Standard for Software Configuration Management Plans

- IEEE Std 1012-1998 Standard for Software Verification and Validation

- IEEE Std 1028-1997 Standard for Software Reviews

- IEEE Std 1063-2001 Standard for Software User Documentation

- IEEE Std 1074-1997, Standard for Developing Software Life Cycle Processes

Other appropriate standards can be found at R.H. Thayer (ed..), *Software Engineering Project Management*, 2nd edition, IEEE Computer Society Press, Los Alamitos, CA, 1997. These standards are:

- IEEE Standard 1058-1998, Standard for Software Project Management Plans (paper by Fairley and Thayer)

- IEEE Standard 1062-1998, Recommended Practice for Software Acquisition

- *IEEE Standard 1540-2001, Standard for Software Life Cycle Processes—Risk Management*

An important note: these copies of the standards are incomplete and provide a condensed view of their engineering content. They cannot be used to cite conformance with the standards in a contractual situation. It is provided to provide the reader and CSDP test taker with a basic understanding of the contents of the IEEE standards.

However, these standards are an important part of this tutorial. These standards represent some of the "best practices" in software engineering. They also have the advantage of being in outline form, which should make them easier to understand, and perhaps remember.

Each chapter paraphrases from IEEE/EIA Standard12207.0-1997 to introduce the appropriate development or supporting process. As with the IEEE Software Engineering Standards themselves, these introductions represent condensed knowledge for the appropriate process.

This tutorial set (two volumes) is one of a set of tutorials on "software engineering" published by the IEEE Computer Society Press that are developed to support the CSDP test. Others include:

- R.H. Thayer (ed.), *Software Engineering Project Management*, 2nd edition, IEEE Computer Society Press, Los Alamitos, CA, 1997 (reprinted in 2001 to include the IEEE project management standards).

- R.H. Thayer and M. Dorfman (eds.), *Software Requirements Engineering*, 2nd edition, IEEE Computer Society Press, Los Alamitos, CA, 1997 (reprinted in 2001 to include the IEEE requirements standards).

- R.B. Hunter and R.H. Thayer (eds.), *Software Process Improvement*, IEEE Computer Society Press, Los Alamitos, CA, 2001 (includes the international and national process improvements standards and documents).

Acknowledgments

No successful endeavor has ever been done by one person alone. We would like to thank the people and organizations that supported us in this effort:

- Ellen Sander and Linda A. Minder, high-value copy editing and word processing

- Stephen B. Seidman, Chair, Computer Society Exam Preparation Committee

- Leonard L. Tripp, Chair, Computer Society Professional Practices Committee

- Robin B. Hunter, author of "Software Process Improvement"

- Ian Sommerville, author of "Documentation"

- The editors at the Computer Society Press.

We would like to thank Ms. Dixie Garr, Vice President, Cisco Systems, Inc., for taking the time to write the Forward for this book. Ms. Garr is a distinctive personality in Information Technology in the United States and an avid supporter of Software Engineering principles and processes. The reader can find additional information about Ms. Garr at http://www.forbes.com/2001/05/30/women2.html and "The Work Culture at Cisco Systems," Karen Mackey, editor, *IEEE Software*, November/December, 2000.

Richard H. Thayer, Ph.D.
Emeritus Professor of Software Engineering
California State University, Sacramento

Mark J. Christensen, Ph.D.
Independent Consultant
Chicago, Illinois

Contributors

Professor Ian Sommerville
Computing Department
Lancaster University
Lancaster LA1 4YR United Kingdom

Dr. Richard H. Thayer
Consultant (Project Management)
6540 Chiquita Way
Carmichael, CA 95608

Chapter 1

Software Engineering Supporting Processes

1. Introduction to IEEE/EIA Standard 12207.0-1996

IEEE/EIA Standard 12207.0-1996 establishes a common framework for software life cycle processes. The standard contains processes, activities and tasks that are to be applied during the acquisition of a system that contains software, a stand-alone software product, and software service during the supply, development, operation, and maintenance phases of software products.

The International Organization for Standardization (ISO) and the International Electrotechnical Commission (IEC) published ISO/IEC 12207, *Information Technology -- Software Life Cycle Processes*, in August 1995. IEEE/EIA Standard 12207.0 is an American version of the international standard. IEEE/EIA Standard 12207.0 consists of clarifications, additions, and changes accepted by the Institute of Electrical and Electronics Engineers (IEEE) and the Electronic Industries Association (EIA) during a joint project by the two organizations. IEEE/EIA Standard 12207.0 contains concepts and guidelines to foster better understanding and application of the standard. Thus, this standard provides industry a basis for software practices that is usable for both national and international businesses.

IEEE/EIA Standard 12207.0 may be used to:

- Acquire, supply, develop, operate, and maintain software.

- Support the above functions in the form of quality assurance, configuration management, joint reviews, audits, verification, validation, problem resolution, and documentation.

- Manage and improve the organization's processes and personnel.

- Establish software management and engineering environments based upon the life cycle processes as they are adapted and tailored to serve business needs.

- Foster improved understanding between customers and vendors and among the parties involved in the life cycle of a software product.

- Facilitate world trade in software.

IEEE/EIA Standard 12207-1996 is partitioned into three parts. The three parts are:

- IEEE/EIA Standard 12207.0-1996, *Standard for Information Technology -- Software Life Cycle Processes*: Contains ISO/IEC 12207 in its original form and six additional annexes (E through J): Basic concepts; Compliance; Life cycle process objectives; Life cycle data objectives; Relationships; and Errata. A unique IEEE/EIA foreword is included.

- IEEE/EIA Standard 12207.1-1997, Guide for ISO/IEC 12207, *Standard for Information Technology -- Software Life Cycle Processes -- Life cycle Data*: Provides additional guidance on recording life cycle data.

1

- IEEE/EIA P12207.2-1997, Guide for ISO/IEC 12207-1997, *Standard for Information Technology -- Software Life Cycle Processes -- Implementation Considerations*: Provides additions, alternatives, and clarifications to ISO/IEC 12207's life cycle processes as derived from U.S. practices.

2. Application of IEEE/EIA Standard 12207-1996

This paragraph lists the software life cycle processes that can be employed to acquire, supply, develop, operate, and maintain software products. IEEE/EIA Standard 12207 groups the activities that may be performed during the life cycle of software into five primary processes, eight supporting processes, and four organizational processes. One of the primary processes, *development*, is emphasized in this tutorial set.

2.1 Development processes

The *development process* contains the activities and tasks of the developer. The process contains the activities for requirements analysis, design, coding, integration, testing, and installation and acceptance related to software products. It may contain system related activities if stipulated in the contract. The developer performs or supports the activities in this process in accordance with the contract. The developer manages the development process at the project level following the *management process,* which is instantiated in this process. The developer next establishes an infrastructure under the process following the *infrastructure process*. Lastly, the developer tailors the process for the project; and manages the process at the organizational level following the *improvement* process and the *training* process.

This process consists of the following activities:

1. Process implementation
2. System requirements analysis
3. System architectural design
4. Software requirements analysis
5. Software architectural design
6. Software detailed design
7. Software coding and testing
8. Software integration
9. Software qualification testing
10. System integration
11. System qualification testing
12. Software installation
13. Software acceptance support.

This tutorial covers only seven of the above processes: system requirements analysis, design and software requirements, software architecture and detailed design, implementation (coding), testing and maintenance.8 are listed below

1. *System requirements analysis.* Describes the functions and capabilities of the system; business, organizational and user requirements; safety, security, human-factors engineering (ergonomics), interface, operations, maintenance requirements, design constraints and system measurements.

2. *System architectural design.* Identifies items of hardware, software, and manual-operations. All system requirements should be allocated among the items. Hardware configuration items, software configuration items, and manual operations are subsequently identified from these items.

3. *Software requirements analysis.* Establishes and documents software requirements including functional, performance, external interfaces, design constraints, and quality characteristics (see ISO/IEC Standard 9126 for details).

4. *Software architectural design.* Transforms software item requirements into an architecture that describes its top-level structure and identifies the software components. Each requirement for the software item is allocated to its corresponding software component and further refined to facilitate detailed design.

5. *Software detailed design.* Develops a detailed design for each software component of the software item. The software components are refined into lower levels containing software units that can be coded, compiled, and tested. All software requirements are allocated from the software components to software units.

6. *Software coding and unit testing.* Code and unit test each software configuration item.

7. *Software integration and testing.* Integrate the software units and software components into the software system. Perform qualification testing to ensure the final system meets the software requirements.

8. *Software maintenance.* Modification of a software product to correct faults, to improve performance or other attributes, or to adapt the product to a changing environment.

2.2 Supporting life cycle processes

The supporting life cycle processes consist of eight processes. A supporting process supports another process as an integral part with a distinct purpose and contributes to the success and quality of the software project. A supporting process is employed and executed, as needed, by another process. The supporting processes are:

1. *Documentation process.* Defines the activities for recording the information produced by a life cycle process.

2. *Configuration management process.* Defines the configuration management activities.

3. *Quality assurance process.* Defines the activities for objectively assuring that software products and processes are in conformance with their specified requirements and adhere to their established plans. *Joint reviews, audits, verification,* and *validation* may be used as techniques of *quality assurance.*

4. *Verification process.* Defines the activities (for the acquirer, the supplier, or an independent party) for verifying the software products and services in varying depth depending on the software project.

5. *Validation process.* Defines the activities (for the acquirer, the supplier, or an independent party) for validating the software products belonging to the software project.

6. *Joint review process.* Defines the activities for evaluating the status and products of a project. This process may be employed by any two parties, where one party (reviewing party) reviews another party (reviewed party) in a joint forum.

7. *Audit process.* Defines the activities for determining compliance with the requirements, plans, and contract. This process may be employed by any two parties, where one party (auditing party) audits the software products or activities of another party (audited party).

8. *Problem resolution process.* Defines a process for analyzing and removing the problems (including non-conformance), regardless of nature or source, which are discovered during the execution of development, operation, maintenance, or other processes.

2.3 Organizational life cycle processes

The organizational life cycle processes consist of four processes. These are employed by an organization to establish and implement an underlying structure composed of associated life cycle processes and personnel, then used to continuously improve the structure and processes. They are typically employed outside the realm of specific projects and contracts; however, lessons from such projects and contracts contribute to the improvement of the organization. The organizational processes are:

1. *Management process.* Defines the basic activities of management, including project management related to the execution of a life cycle process.

2. *Infrastructure process.* Defines the basic activities for establishing the underlying structure of a life cycle process.

3. *Improvement process.* Defines the basic activities that an organization (acquirer, supplier, developer, operator, maintainer, or the manager of another process) performs for establishing, measuring, controlling, and improving its life cycle process.

4. *Training process.* Defines the activities for providing adequately trained personnel.

3. Introduction to Tutorial

This tutorial (Volume 2 of the set) has been partitioned into chapters along the lines of the supporting and organizational processes of IEEE/EIA Standard 12207. (A description of the development processes can be found in Volume 1 of this tutorial set). In accordance with accepted practices, *verification* and *validation* and *reviews* and *audits* are combined into one chapter. *Problem resolution process* has been combined with *software configuration management,* primarily due to the dearth of publications on the subject. *Improvement* and *training* are included since both subjects are smaller in scope. All other supporting and organizational processes are isolated into separate chapters.

Each chapter is initiated with an introduction that introduces both the subject and the supporting papers and standards. Each introduction incorporates the appropriate clauses from IEEE/EIA Standard 12207. In general, there is one paper and one standard for each supporting process. However, there are some exceptions:

- The IEEE Computer Society did not develop a general *documentation process* standard. The most applicable standard is *IEEE Standard for Users Documentation*, which is included.

- The IEEE Computer Society did not develop a *problem resolution process* standard. Therefore, a standard is not provided.

- The software Review and Audits chapter contains two papers: one by John Marciniak discussing *reviews and audits* and the other by Frank Ackerman describing *software inspections*. These were included to provide adequate coverage of these areas.

- The standards for the management process can be found in a separate Computer Society Press tutorial, *Software Engineering Project Management*, 2nd edition, by Richard H. Thayer. Be sure to obtain the latest printing, dated 2001. The three standards included in the *Project Management* tutorial are:

  ➢ IEEE Standard 1058-1998, IEEE Standard for Software Project Management Plans (draft)

  ➢ IEEE Standard 1062-1998, IEEE Recommended Practice for Software Acquisition

  ➢ IEEE Standard 1540-2001, IEEE Standard for Software Life Cycle Processes— Risk Management.

- The last three operational processes -- infrastructure, improvement, and training -- do not have matching IEEE standards. However, papers describing these processes are provided.

4. Articles

A very short paper by Raghu Singh is included in this chapter, which provides additional information on IEEE/EIA Standard 12207-1997 and to provide credit to the standards working group for their efforts. Raghu Singh (IEEE Co-chair) and Perry DeWeese (EIA Co-chair) were chairs of the IEEE/EIA Standard 12207.0--1996 working group and Leonard Tripp (IEEE Co-chair) and Perry DeWeese (EIA Co-chair) were chairs of the IEEE/EIA Standard 12207.1–1997 working group.

The Software Life Cycle Processes standard

Raghu Singh
Space and Naval Warfare Systems Command

A new standard, Software Life Cycle Processes (ISO/IEC 12207), developed over the past six years, has recently been approved by JTC1 (Joint Technical Committee 1 of the International Organization for Standardization and the International Electrotechnical Commission). While software has been established as an integral part of scientific and business disciplines, environments for developing and managing software have proliferated without a common, uniform framework for the software life cycle. This standard provides such a framework, so that software practitioners can "speak the same language" when they create and manage software. Practitioners can use the framework to acquire, supply, develop, operate, and maintain software.

The processes

The new standard establishes a top-level architecture for the software life cycle, from concept definition to disposal. The architecture is built with a set of processes and interfaces between those processes. The processes are derived and identified on the basis of the principles of modularity and responsibility. Each process is placed under the responsibility of a party (or participant) in the software life cycle. The party uses the processes to fulfill its business purpose.

The 17 processes are grouped into three broad classes: primary, supporting, and organizational. The five primary processes are acquisition, supply, development, operation, and maintenance; they are the prime movers in the life cycle. The eight supporting processes are documentation, config-

---

LIFE CYCLE PROCESSES

Acquisition—The activities and tasks of the acquirer of software products and services. The acquirer may be the owner or a user.

Supply—The activities and tasks of the supplier providing development, operation, or maintenance service to the acquirer.

Development—The activities and tasks of the software developer. This developer may be required to perform or support system-level activities.

Operation—The activities and tasks of the operator of a system containing software.

Maintenance—The activities and tasks of the maintainer. This process uses the development process when software is modified.

Documentation—Used to record information produced by a life cycle process.

Configuration Management—Used to identify and baseline software (configuration) items; control their modification and release; record and report their status; and control their storage, handling, and delivery.

Quality Assurance—Assures independent and objective compliance of products and services and adherence of plans to contractual requirements. To prevent bias, the process is kept autonomous—that is, divorced from persons directly responsible for the products or services.

Verification—Used to verify an activity's products against requirements established by previous activities.

Validation—Used to determine whether the final product fulfills its specific intended use. (Verification and

Validation may be combined into one Verification and Validation Process or may be conducted by an independent party. In the latter situation, the processes are called Independent Verification Process, Independent Validation Process, or Independent Verification and Validation Process.)

Joint Review—Used by the reviewing and reviewed parties to jointly review technical status and progress.

Audit—Used by an auditor to assess an organization's products and tasks, but with emphasis on compliance with requirements and plans.

Problem Resolution—A closed-loop process for resolving problems and nonconformances, taking corrective actions, and reversing trends in those problems or nonconformances.

Management—Provides the generic activities and tasks for managing a software life cycle process. The management-related tasks of the primary processes and of some supporting processes are instantiations of this process.

Infrastructure—Used to establish and maintain the infrastructure needed for a life cycle process.

Improvement—Used to assess, measure, control, and improve a life cycle process.

Training—Used to acquire or develop personnel resources and skills.

Tailoring—A special, normative process used to tailor the standard to a particular project. This process itself, however, cannot be tailored.

November 1995

uration management, quality assurance, joint review, audit, verification, validation, and problem resolution. A supporting process supports another process with a distinct purpose. The four organizational processes are management, infrastructure, improvement, and training. An organization may use these processes at the corporate level to establish, implement, manage, and improve its life cycle processes.

Each process is defined in terms of its own constituent activities, and each of these is defined in terms of its constituent tasks. There are 74 activities and 224 tasks. A task is expressed as a requirement, a self-declaration, a recommendation, or a permissible action.

Attributes

The Software Life Cycle Processes standard establishes the necessary link between the software and its parent system, defining a narrow spectrum for the system life cycle and placing the software life cycle within it. Software is culled out of the system, designed and implemented, and integrated back into the system. Thus, software engineers participate in systems engineering.

The standard also implements TQM (total quality management) principles. It equips each process with a built-in "plan-do-check-act" cycle and appropriates quality-related tasks to each process.

Moreover, the standard is flexible in usage. An organization, a project, or the parties to an agreement can select appropriate processes, activities, and tasks to fulfill a particular business purpose. An organization can execute

The standard can be applied internally by an organization or contractually by two or more parties.

more than one process, and a process can be executed by more than one organization. And the standard can be applied internally by an organization or contractually by two or more parties. The tasks are expressed in contractual language. When applied solely within an organization or by an individual, the contractual language is interpreted as self-imposed tasks.

ISO/IEC 12207 is responsive to the rapidly evolving software technologies. It can be used with known software engineering models, methods, and environments. Moreover, it provides an acquirer an avenue for specifying a product or service, while encouraging the supplier to be creative in using appropriate technologies.

According to the standard, certain outputs from the processes are documented. However, the details of specific metrics and indicators and the formats for the outputs are left to the standard's users.

Finally, the standard permits compliance at the project and organizational levels. Appropriate processes, activities, and tasks are selected and tailored for a particular project's compliance. At the organizational level, as a condition of trade, a public declaration specifies a set of processes, activities, and tasks from the standard that suppliers to the organization comply with.

THE SOFTWARE LIFE CYCLE PROCESSES standard is not a substitute for systematic, disciplined management and engineering of software systems. The standard merely provides a framework within which the processes, activities, and tasks can be judiciously selected, planned, and executed. One key point to remember is that the standard contains only a set of well-defined building blocks (processes); the user of the standard must select, tailor, and assemble these processes appropriately and cost-effectively for the project or organization. However, the standard strongly recommends that such tailoring preserve the architecture, intent, and integrity of the standard.

Acknowledgments

This standard was developed under the sponsorship of Subcommittee 7 (Software Engineering) of the Joint Technical Committee 1 (Information Technology) of ISO and IEC. The working-group convener was James R. Roberts of the US (affiliated with Bell Communications Research) and the editor of the standard was the author of this article. The following countries participated in this standard's development: Australia, Brazil, Canada, Czech Republic, Denmark, Finland, France, Germany, Hungary, Ireland, Italy, Japan, Korea, The Netherlands, Spain, Sweden, the United Kingdom, and the United States.

A guidebook that will provide basic concepts and guidance on applying ISO/IEC 12207 is under development. For more information on this standard, contact Raghu Singh, Space and Naval Warfare Systems Command, SPAWAR 10-12, 2451 Crystal Dr. (CPK-5), Arlington, VA 22245-5200; e-mail singhr@smtp-gw.spawar.navy.mil.

Chapter 2

Software Configuration Management and Problem Resolution Processes

1. Introduction to Chapter

This chapter describes both the software configuration management process and the problem resolution process. Paragraph 2 describes the software configuration management process, and paragraph 3 describes the problem resolution process. Portions of this text are paraphrased from the introduction to IEEE Standard 828-1998 and IEEE/EIA Standard 12207.0-1996, Paragraphs 6.2 and 6.8. Paragraph 4 provides an overview and introduction to the papers contained in this chapter.

2. Software Configuration Management

(This text is paraphrased from the introduction to IEEE Standard 828-1998 and IEEE/EIA Standard 12207.0-1996, Paragraphs 6.2)

Software configuration management (SCM) is a formal engineering discipline that, as part of overall system configuration management, provides the methods and tools to identify and control software throughout its development and use. SCM activities include the identification and establishment of baselines; the review, approval, and control of changes; the tracking and reporting of such changes; the audits and reviews of the evolving software product; and the control of interface documentation and project suppliers (software developers).

SCM is the means through which the integrity and traceability of the software system are recorded, communicated, and controlled during both development and maintenance. SCM also supports reduction of overall software life cycle costs by providing a foundation for product and project measurement.

SCM constitutes good engineering practice for all software projects, whether phased development, rapid prototyping, or ongoing maintenance. The reliability and quality of software are enhanced by:

- Providing a structure for identifying and controlling documentation, code, interfaces, and databases to support all life cycle phases.

- Supporting a chosen development/maintenance methodology that fits the requirements, standards, policies, organization, and management philosophy.

- Producing management and product information concerning the status of baselines, change control, tests, releases, audits, etc.

2.1 Software configuration management process

The *Configuration Management Process* is a process of applying administrative and technical procedures throughout the software life cycle to: 1) identify, define, and baseline software items in a system 2) control modifications 3) release item; records and reporting item status and modification requests 4) ensure the completeness, consistency, and correctness of the items 5) control storage, handling, and delivery of the items.

This process consists of the following activities:

1. Configuration management plan

2. Configuration identification

3. Configuration control

4. Configuration status accounting

5. Configuration evaluation

6. Release management and delivery.

The *configuration management plan* describes the configuration management activities; procedures and schedule for performing these activities, the organization(s) responsible for performing these activities, and their relationship with other organizations, such as software development or maintenance. The plan is then documented and implemented. Note: the plan may be a part of the system configuration management plan.

A *configuration identification* scheme is established for the identification of software items and their versions to be controlled for the project. For each software configuration item and its versions, the following are identified - the documentation that establishes the baseline, the version references, and other identification details.

Configuration control performs the following tasks: identification and recording of change requests; analysis and evaluation of the changes; approval or disapproval of the request; and implementation, verification, and release of the modified software item. An audit trail exists, whereby each modification, the reason for the modification, and authorization of the modification can be traced. Lastly, a control and audit is performed of all accesses to the controlled software items that handle safety or security critical functions.

Configuration control is frequently under the control and management of the configuration control board. The *configuration control board* (frequently called the CCB) is composed of a group of people responsible for evaluating and approving or disapproving proposed changes to configuration items, and for ensuring implementation of approved changes [IEEE Standard 610.12-1990]. See also *problem resolution process* in Paragraph 2 below.

Configuration status accounting consists of the following task: the preparation of management records and status reports that show the status and history of controlled software items including baseline. Status reports should include the number of changes for a project, latest software item versions, release identifiers, the number of releases, and comparisons of releases.

Configuration evaluation is used to determine and ensure the functional completeness of the software items against their requirements and the physical completeness of the software items (whether their design and code reflect an up-to-date technical description).

Release management and delivery of software products and documentation should be formally controlled. Master copies of code and documentation are to be maintained for the life of the software product. The code and documentation that contain safety or security critical functions are handled, stored, packaged, and delivered in accordance with the policies of the organizations involved.

Configuration management is often grouped into formal and informal configuration management. *Formal configuration management* (also called external CM or baseline CM) is used to manage the configuration between the customer/user and the developer. CM is also frequently used to maintain the configuration after delivery and during the maintenance and operations phases of the life cycle. The configuration control board is the agency responsible for managing the configuration.

Informal configuration management (also called internal CM or developmental CM) is used for maintaining configuration control for products under development, such as plans, specifications, versions, test procedures and test results, and deliverable (but not yet delivered) documents. The project manager is the controlling authority while an individual called *the product support librarian* provides the accounting and auditing.

3. Problem Resolution Process

The problem resolution process is a process for analyzing and resolving the problems (including non-conformance), regardless of their nature or source, that are discovered during the execution of development, operation, maintenance, or other processes. The objective is to provide a timely, responsible, and documented means to ensure that all discovered problems are analyzed and resolved and trends are recognized. This process is frequently tied to *software configuration management* (configuration control).

This process consists of the following activities:

1. Process implementation

2. Problem resolution process.

3.1 Process implementation

- A *problem resolution process* is established for handling all problems (including non-conformance) detected in software products and activities. This activity is frequently under the direction and control of the *configuration control board*. The process should comply with the following requirements:

  - ➢ The process is closed-loop, ensuring that: all detected problems are promptly reported and entered into the problem resolution process. Action is initiated on problems and relevant parties are advised of the existence of the problem as appropriate. Causes are identified, analyzed, and, where possible, eliminated. Resolution and disposition are achieved. Status is tracked and reported, and records of the problems are maintained as stipulated in the contract.

  - ➢ The process contains a scheme for categorizing and prioritizing the problems. Each problem should be classified by the category and priority to facilitate trend analysis and problem resolution.

  - ➢ Analysis is performed to detect trends in the problems reported.

> Problem resolutions and dispositions are evaluated: to determine that problems have been resolved, adverse trends have been reversed, and changes have been correctly implemented in the appropriate software products and activities, and to determine whether additional problems have been introduced.

3.2 Problem resolution

Once problems (including non-conformance) have been detected in a software product or an activity, a problem report is prepared, describing each problem detected. The problem report is to be used as part of the closed-loop process described above, from detection of the problem, through investigation, analysis, and resolution of the problem and its cause, and later for trend detection across problems.

These reports are frequently sent to a controlling authority such as the CCB.

4. Overview of Papers

Although Bersoff's configuration management paper dates from 1984, it still provides the best overview of software configuration management (SCM). Ed Bersoff defines *configuration management* as the discipline of identifying the configuration of a system at discrete points in time for the purpose of systematically controlling changes to the configuration and maintaining the integrity and traceability of the configuration throughout the system life cycle. Configuration management tracks various artifacts developed during the lifetime of a software project through identification, control, audit, and status account of the various software development products.

Bersoff reminds us that controlling code is not enough. The documentation that enables us to use and operate the code must also be controlled. This paper also provides a lengthy description of the program support library (PSL). Bersoff discusses the major problems involved in deciding how to properly manage the software configuration: too much control is cumbersome; too little control invites disaster.

The second paper is an extract from IEEE Standard 828-1998, *Standard for Software Configuration Management Plans*, IEEE, Inc., New York, 1998. It provides a template for developing a software configuration management (SCM) plan. The standard provides the minimum required content for a Software Configuration Management Plan (SCMP) and the specific activities to be in undertaken in implementing a SCM system.

The reader is reminded again that this copy of the standard is incomplete and cannot be used to cite conformance with the standard in a contractual situation. It is intended to provide the reader and CSDP test taker with a basic understanding of the contents of the SCM standards and an outline of a SCM plan.

Elements of Software Configuration Management

EDWARD H. BERSOFF, SENIOR MEMBER, IEEE

Abstract—Software configuration management (SCM) is one of the disciplines of the 1980's which grew in response to the many failures of the software industry throughout the 1970's. Over the last ten years, computers have been applied to the solution of so many complex problems that our ability to manage these applications has all too frequently failed. This has resulted in the development of a series of "new" disciplines intended to help control the software process.

This paper will focus on the discipline of SCM by first placing it in its proper context with respect to the rest of the software development process, as well as to the goals of that process. It will examine the constituent components of SCM, dwelling at some length on one of those components, configuration control. It will conclude with a look at what the 1980's might have in store.

Index Terms—Configuration management, management, product assurance, software.

INTRODUCTION

SOFTWARE configuration management (SCM) is one of the disciplines of the 1980's which grew in response to the many failures of our industry throughout the 1970's. Over the last ten years, computers have been applied to the solution of so many complex problems that our ability to manage these applications in the "traditional" way has all too frequently failed. Of course, tradition in the software business began only 30 years ago or less, but even new habits are difficult to break. In the 1970's we learned the hard way that the tasks involved in managing a software project were not linearly dependent on the number of lines of code produced. The relationship was, in fact, highly exponential. As the decade closed, we looked back on our failures [1], [2] trying to understand what went wrong and how we could correct it. We began to dissect the software development process [3], [4] and to define techniques by which it could be effectively managed [5]-[8]. This self-examination by some of the most talented and experienced members of the software community led to the development of a series of "new" disciplines intended to help control the software process.

While this paper will focus on the particular discipline of SCM, we will first place it in its proper context with respect to the rest of the software development process, as well as to the goals of that process. We will examine the constituent components of SCM, dwelling at some length on one of those components, configuration control. Once we have woven our way through all the trees, we will once again stand back and take a brief look at the forest and see what the 1980's might have in store.

Manuscript received April 15, 1982; revised December 1, 1982 and October 18, 1983.

The author is with BTG, Inc., 1945 Gallows Rd., Vienna, VA 22180.

SCM IN CONTEXT

It has been said that if you do not know where you are going, any road will get you there. In order to properly understand the role that SCM plays in the software development process, we must first understand what the goal of that process is, i.e., where we are going. For now, and perhaps for some time to come, software developers are people, people who respond to the needs of another set of people creating computer programs designed to satisfy those needs. These computer programs are the tangible output of a thought process—the conversion of a thought process into a product. The goal of the software developer is, or should be, the construction of a product which closely matches the real needs of the set of people for whom the software is developed. We call this goal the achievement of "product integrity." More formally stated, product integrity (depicted in Fig. 1) is defined to be the intrinsic set of attributes that characterize a product [9]:

- that fulfills user functional needs;
- that can easily and completely be traced through its life cycle;
- that meets specified performance criteria;
- whose cost expectations are met;
- whose delivery expectations are met.

The above definition is pragmatically based. It demands that product integrity be a measure of the satisfaction of the real needs and expectations of the software user. It places the burden for achieving the software goal, product integrity, squarely on the shoulders of the developer, for it is he alone who is in control of the development process. While, as we shall see, the user can establish safeguards and checkpoints to gain visibility into the development process, the prime responsibility for software success is the developer's. So our goal is now clear; we want to build software which exhibits all the characteristics of product integrity. Let us make sure that we all understand, however, what this thing called software really is. We have learned in recent times that equating the terms "software" and "computer programs" improperly restricts our view of software. Software is much more. A definition which can be used to focus the discussion in this paper is that software is information that is:

- structured with logical and functional properties;
- created and maintained in various forms and representations during the life cycle;
- tailored for machine processing in its fully developed state.

So by our definition, software is not simply a set of computer programs, but includes the documentation required to define, develop, and maintain these programs. While this notion is not very new, it still frequently escapes the software

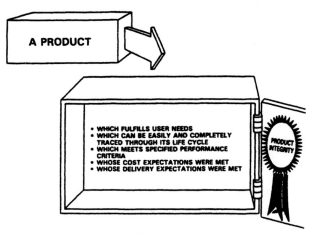

Fig. 1. Product integrity.

development manager who assumes that controlling a software product is the same as controlling computer code.

Now that we more fully appreciate what we are after, i.e., to build a software product with integrity, let us look at the one road which might get us there. We have, until now, used the term "developer" to characterize the organizational unit responsible for converting the software idea into a software product. But developers are, in reality, a complex set of interacting organizational entities. When undertaking a software project, most developers structure themselves into three basic discipline sets which include:

- project management,
- development, and
- product assurance.

Project management disciplines are both inwardly and outwardly directed. They support general management's need to see what is going on in a project and to ensure that the parent or host organization consistently develops products with integrity. At the same time, these disciplines look inside a project in support of the assignment, allocation, and control of all project resources. In that capacity, project management determines the relative allocation of resources to the set of development and product assurance disciplines. It is management's prerogative to specify the extent to which a given discipline will be applied to a given project. Historically, management has often been handicapped when it came to deciding how much of the product assurance disciplines were required. This was a result of both inexperience and organizational immaturity.

The development disciplines represent those traditionally applied to a software project. They include:

- analysis,
- design,
- engineering,
- production (coding),
- test (unit/subsystem),
- installation,
- documentation,
- training, and
- maintenance.

In the broadest sense, these are the disciplines required to take a system concept from its beginning through the development life cycle. It takes a well-structured, rigorous technical approach to system development, along with the right mix of development disciplines to attain product integrity, especially for software. The concept of an ordered, procedurally disciplined approach to system development is fundamental to product integrity. Such an approach provides successive development plateaus, each of which is an identifiable measure of progress which forms a part of the total foundation supporting the final product. Going sequentially from one baseline (plateau) to another with high probability of success, necessitates the use of the right development disciplines at precisely the right time.

The product assurance disciplines which are used by project management to gain visibility into the development process include:

- configuration management,
- quality assurance,
- validation and verification, and
- test and evaluation.

Proper employment of these product assurance disciplines by the project manager is basic to the success of a project since they provide the technical checks and balances over the product being developed. Fig. 2 represents the relationship among the management, development, and product assurance disciplines. Let us look at each of the product assurance disciplines briefly, in turn, before we explore the details of SCM.

Configuration management (CM) is the discipline of identifying the configuration of a system at discrete points in time for the purpose of systematically controlling changes to the configuration and maintaining the integrity and traceability of the configuration throughout the system life cycle. Software configuration management (SCM) is simply configuration management tailored to systems, or portions of systems, that are comprised predominantly of software. Thus, SCM does not differ substantially from the CM of hardware-oriented systems, which is generally well understood and effectively practiced. However, attempts to implement SCM have often failed because the particulars of SCM do not follow by direct analogy from the particulars of hardware CM and because SCM is a less mature discipline than that of hardware CM. We will return to this subject shortly.

Quality assurance (QA) as a discipline is commonly invoked throughout government and industry organizations with reasonable standardization when applied to systems comprised only of hardware. But there is enormous variation in thinking and practice when the QA discipline is invoked for a software development or for a system containing software components. QA has a long history, and much like CM, it has been largely developed and practiced on hardware projects. It is therefore mature, in that sense, as a discipline. Like CM, however, it is relatively immature when applied to software development. We define QA as consisting of the procedures, techniques, and tools applied by professionals to insure that a product meets or exceeds prespecified standards during a product's development cycle; and without specific prescribed standards, QA entails insuring that a product meets or

14

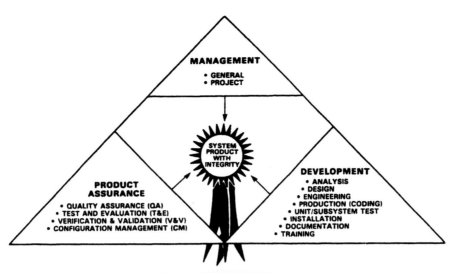

Fig. 2. The discipline triangle.

exceeds a minimum industrial and/or commercially acceptable level of excellence.

The QA discipline has not been uniformly treated, practiced or invoked relative to software development. First, very few organizations have software design and development standards that compare in any way with hardware standards for detail and completeness. Second, it takes a high level of software expertise to assess whether a software product meets prescribed standards. Third, few buyer organizations have provided for or have developed the capability to impose and then monitor software QA endeavors on seller organizations. Finally, few organizations have been concerned over precisely defining the difference between QA and other product assurance disciplines, CM often being subservient to QA or vice versa in a given development organization. Our definition of software given earlier suggests still another reason for the software QA discipline being in the same state as SCM so far as its universal application within the user, buyer, and seller communities. Software, as a form of information, cannot be standardized; only structures for defining/documenting software can be standardized. It follows that software development techniques can only be meaningfully standardized in relation to information structures, not information content.

The third of the four product assurance disciplines is validation and verification (V&V). Unlike CM and QA, V&V has come into being expressly for the purpose of coping with software and its development. Unlike QA, which prinicipally deals with the problem of a product's adherence to pre-established standards, V&V deals with the issue of how well software fulfills functional and performance requirements and the assurance that specified requirements are indeed stated and interpreted correctly. The verification part of V&V assures that a product meets its prescribed goals as defined through baseline documentation. That is, verification is a discipline imposed to ascertain that a product is what it was intended to be relative to its preceding baseline. The validation part of V&V, by contrast, is levied as a discipline to assure that a product not only meets the objectives specified through baseline documentation, but in addition, does the right job.

Stated another way, the validation discipline is invoked to insure that the end-user gets the right product. A buyer or seller may have misinterpreted user requirements or, perhaps, requirements have changed, or the user gets to know more about what he needs, or early specifications of requirements were wrong or incomplete or in a state of flux. The validation process serves to assure that such problems do not persist among the user, buyer, and seller. To enhance objectivity, it is often desirable to have an independent organization, from outside the developing organization, perform the V&V function.

The fourth of the product assurance disciplines is test and evaluation (T&E), perhaps the discipline most understood, and yet paradoxically, least practiced with uniformity. T&E is defined as the discipline imposed outside the development project organization to independently assess whether a product fulfills objectives. T&E does this through the execution of a set of test plans and procedures. Specifically in support of the end user, T&E entails evaluating product performance in a live or near-live environment. Frequently, particularly within the miliatry arena, T&E is a major undertaking involving one or more systems which are to operate together, but which have been individually developed and accepted as stand-alone items. Some organizations formally turn over T&E responsibility to a group outside the development project organization after the product reaches a certain stage of development, their philosophy being that developers cannot be objective to the point of fully testing/evaluating what they have produced.

The definitions given for CM, QA, V&V, and T&E suggest some overlap in required skills and functions to be performed in order to invoke these disciplines collectively for product assurance purposes. Depending on many factors, the actual overlap may be significant or little. In fact, there are those who would argue that V&V and T&E are but subset functions of QA. But the contesting argument is that V&V and T&E have come into being as separate disciplines because conventional QA methods and techniques have failed to do an adequate job with respect to providing product assurance, particularly for computer-centered systems with software components. Management must be concerned with minimizing the application of excessive and redundant resources to address the overlap of these disciplines. What is important is that all the functions defined above are performed, not what they are called or who carries them out.

THE ELEMENTS OF SCM

When the need for the discipline of configuration management finally achieved widespread recognition within the software engineering community, the question arose as to how closely the software CM discipline ought to parallel the extant hardware practice of configuration management. Early SCM authors and practitioners [10] wisely chose the path of commonality with the hardware world, at least at the highest level. Of course, hardware engineering is different from software engineering, but broad similarities do exist and terms applied to one segment of the engineering community can easily be applied to another, even if the specific meanings of those terms differ significantly in detail. For that reason, the elements of SCM were chosen to be the same as those for hardware CM. As for hardware, the four components of SCM are:

- identification,
- control,
- auditing, and
- status accounting.

Let us examine each one in turn.

Software Configuration Identification: Effective management of the development of a system requires careful definition of its baseline components; changes to these components also need to be defined since these changes, together with the baselines, specify the system evolution. A system baseline is like a snapshot of the aggregate of system components as they exist at a given point in time; updates to this baseline are like frames in a movie strip of the system life cycle. The role of software configuration identification in the SCM process is to provide labels for these snapshots and the movie strip.

A baseline can be characterized by two labels. One label identifies the baseline itself, while the second label identifies an update to a particular baseline. An update to a baseline represents a baseline plus a set of changes that have been incorporated into it. Each of the baselines established during a software system's life cycle controls subsequent system development. At the time it is first established a software baseline embodies the actual software in its most recent state. When changes are made to the most recently established baseline, then, from the viewpoint of the software configuration manager, this baseline and these changes embody the actual software in its most recent state (although, from the viewpoint of the software developer, the actual software may be in a more advanced state).

The most elementary entity in the software configuration identification labeling mechanism is the software configuration item (SCI). Viewed from an SCM perspective, a software baseline appears as a set of SCI's. The SCI's within a baseline are related to one another via a tree-like hierarchy. As the software system evolves through its life cycle, the number of

branches in this hierarchy generally increases; the first baseline may consist of no more than one SCI. The lowest level SCI's in the tree hierarchy may still be under development and not yet under SCM control. These entities are termed design objects or computer program components (see Fig. 3). Each baseline and each member in the associated family of updates will exist in one or more forms, such as a design document, source code on a disk, or executing object code.

In performing the identification function, the software configuration manager is, in effect, taking snapshots of the SCI's. Each baseline and its associated updates collectively represents the evolution of the software during each of its life cycle stages. These stages are staggered with respect to one another. Thus, the collection of life cycle stages looks like a collection of staggered and overlapping sequences of snapshots of SCI trees. Let us now imagine that this collection of snapshot sequences is threaded, in chronological order, onto a strip of movie film as in Fig. 4. Let us further imagine that the strip of movie film is run through a projector. Then we would see a history of the evolution of the software. Consequently, the identification of baselines and updates provides an explicit documentation trail linking all stages of the software life cycle. With the aid of this documentation trail, the software developer can assess the integrity of his product, and the software buyer can assess the integrity of the product he is paying for.

Software Configuration Control: The evolution of a software system is, in the language of SCM, the development of baselines and the incorporation of a series of changes into the baselines. In addition to these changes that explicitly affect existing baselines, there are changes that occur during early stages of the system life cycle that may affect baselines that do not yet exist. For example, some time before software coding begins (i.e., some time prior to the establishment of a design baseline), a contract may be modified to include a software warranty provision such as: system downtime due to software failures shall not exceed 30 minutes per day. This warranty provision will generally affect subsequent baselines but in a manner that cannot be explicitly determined *a priori*. One role of software configuration control is to provide the administrative mechanism for precipitating, preparing, evaluating, and approving or disapproving all change proposals throughout the system life cycle.

We have said that software, for configuration management purposes, is a collection of SCI's that are related to one another in a well-defined way. In early baselines and their associated updates, SCI's are specification documents (one or more volumes of text for each baseline or associated update); in later baselines and their associated updates, each SCI may manifest itself in any or all of the various software representations. Software configuration control focuses on managing changes to SCI's (existing or to be developed) in all of their representations. This process involves three basic ingredients.

1) Documentation (such as administrative forms and supporting technical and administrative material) for formally precipitating and defining a proposed change to a software system.

2) An organizational body for formally evaluating and

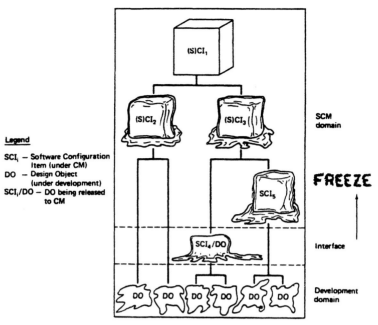

Fig. 3.   The development/SCM interface.

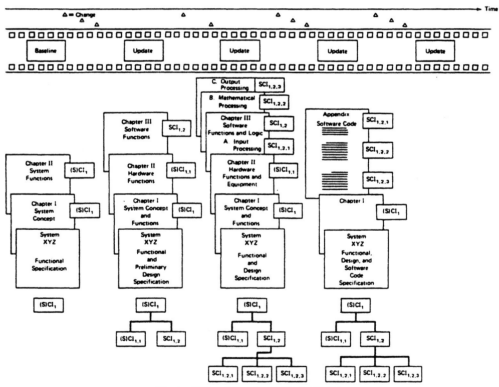

Fig. 4.   SCI evolution in a single document.

approving or disapproving a proposed change to a software system (the Configuration Control Board).

3) Procedures for controlling changes to a software system.

The Engineering Change Proposal (ECP), a major control document, contains information such as a description of the proposed change, identification of the originating organization, rationale for the change, identification of affected baselines and SCI's (if appropriate), and specification of cost and schedule impacts. ECP's are reviewed and coordinated by the CCB, which is typically a body representing all organizational units which have a vested interest in proposed changes.

Fig. 5 depicts the software configuration control process.

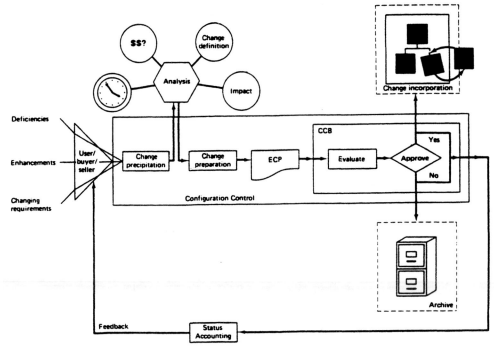

Fig. 5. The control process.

As the figure suggests, change incorporation is not an SCM function, but monitoring the change implementation process resulting in change incorporation is. Fig. 5 also emphasizes that the analysis that may be required to prepare an ECP is also outside the SCM purview. Note also from the figure how ECP's not approved by the CCB are not simply discarded but are archived for possible future reference.

Many automated tools support the control process. The major ones aid in controlling software change once the coding stage has been reached, and are generically referred to as program support libraries (PSL's). The level of support provided by PSL's, however, varies greatly. As a minimum, a PSL should provide a centralized and readily available repository for authoritative versions of each component of a software system. It should contain the data necessary for the orderly development and control of each SCI. Automation of other functions, such as library access control, software and document version maintenance, change recording, and document reconstruction, greatly enhance both the control and maintenance processes. These capabilities are currently available in systems such as SOFTOOL's change and configuration control environment (CCC).

A PSL supports a developmental approach in which project personnel work on a common visible product rather than on independent components. In those PSL's which include access controls, project personnel can be separately assigned read/write access to each software document/component, from programs to lines of code. Thus, all project personnel are assured ready access to the critical interface information necessary for effective software development. At the same time, modifications to various software components, whether sanctioned baselines or modules under development, can be closely controlled.

Under the PSL concept, the programmer operates under a well-defined set of parameters and exercises a narrower span of detailed control. This minimizes the need for explicit communication between analysts and programmers and makes the inclusion of new project personnel less traumatic since interface requirements are well documented. It also minimizes the preparation effort for technical audits.

Responsibility for maintenance of the PSL data varies depending on the level of automation provided. For those systems which provide only a repository for data, a secretary/librarian is usually responsible for maintaining the notebooks which will contain the data developed and used by project personnel and for maintenance of the PSL archives. More advanced PSL systems provide real time, on-line access to data and programs and automatically create the records necessary to fully trace the history of the development. In either case the PSL provides standardization of project recordkeeping, ensures that system documentation corresponds to the current system configuration, and guarantees the existence of adequate documentation of previous versions.

A PSL should support three main activities: code development, software management, and configuration control. Support to the development process includes support to design, coding, testing, documentation, and program maintenance along with associated database schema and subschema. A PSL provides this support through:

- storage and maintenance of software documentation and code,
- support to program compilation/testing,
- support for the generation of program/system documentation.

Support to the management of the software development process involves the storage and output of programming data such as:

- collection and automatic reporting of management data related to program development,

18

- control over the integrity and security of the data in the PSL,
- separation of the clerical activity related to the programming process.

PSL's provide support to the configuration control process through:

- access and change authorization control for all data in the library,
- control of software code releases,
- automatic program and document reconstruction,
- automatic change tracking and reporting,
- assurance of the consistency between documentation, code, and listings.

A PSL has four major components: internal libraries in machine-readable form, external libraries in hardcopy form, computer procedures, and office procedures. The components of a PSL system are interlocked to establish an exact correspondence between the internal units of code and external versions (such as listings) of the developing systems. This continuous correspondence is the characteristic of a PSL that guarantees ongoing visibility and identification of the developing system.

Different PSL implementations exist for various system environments with the specifics of the implementation dependent upon the hardware, software, user, and operating environment. The fundamental correspondence between the internal and external libraries in each environment, however, is established by the PSL librarian and computer procedures. The office procedures are specified in a project CM Plan so that the format of the external libraries is standard across software projects, and internal and external libraries are easily maintainable.

Newer PSL systems minimize the need for both office and computer procedures through the implementation of extensive management functionality. This functionality provides significant flexibility in controlling the access to data and allocating change authority, while providing a variety of status reporting capabilities. The availability of management information, such as a list of all the software structures changed to solve a particular Software Trouble Report or the details on the latest changes to a particular software document, provides a means for the control function to effectively operate without burdening the development team with cumbersome procedures and administrative paperwork. Current efforts in PSL refinement/development are aimed at linking support of the development environment with that of the configuration control environment. The goal of such systems is to provide an integrated environment where control and management information is generated automatically as a part of a fully supported design and development process.

Software Configuration Auditing: Software configuration auditing provides the mechanism for determining the degree to which the current state of the software system mirrors the software system pictured in baseline and requirements documentation. It also provides the mechanism for formally establishing a baseline. A baseline in its formative stages (for example, a draft specification document that appears prior to the existence of the functional baseline) is referred to as a "to-be-established" baseline; the final state of the auditing process conducted on a to-be-established baseline is a sanctioned baseline. The same may be said about baseline updates.

Software configuration auditing serves two purposes, configuration verification and configuration validation. Verification ensures that what is intended for each software configuration item as specified in one baseline or update is actually achieved in the succeeding baseline or update; validation ensures that the SCI configuration solves the right problem (i.e., that customer needs are satisfied). Software configuration auditing is applied to each baseline (and corresponding update) in its to-be-established state. An auditing process common to all baselines is the determination that an SCI structure exists and that its contents are based on all available information.

Software auditing is intended to increase software visibility and to establish traceability throughout the life cycle of the software product. Of course, this visibility and traceability are not achieved without cost. Software auditing costs time and money. But the judicious investment of time and money, particularly in the early stages of a project, pays dividends in the latter stages. These dividends include the avoidance of costly retrofits resulting from problems such as the sudden appearance of new requirements and the discovery of major design flaws. Conversely, failing to perform auditing, or constraining it to the later stages of the software life cycle, can jeopardize successful software development. Often in such cases, by the time discrepancies are discovered (if they are), the software cannot be easily or economically modified to rectify the discrepancies. The result is often a dissatisfied customer, large cost overruns, slipped schedules, or cancelled projects.

Software auditing makes visible to management the current status of the software in the life cycle product audited. It also reveals whether the project requirements are being satisfied and whether the intent of the preceding baseline has been fulfilled. With this visibility, project management can evaluate the integrity of the software product being developed, resolve issues that may have been raised by the audit, and correct defects in the development process. The visibility afforded by the software audit also provides a basis for the establishment of the audited life cycle product as a new baseline.

Software auditing provides traceability between a software life cycle product and the requirements for that product. Thus, as life cycle products are audited and baselines established, every requirement is traced successively from baseline to baseline. Disconnects are also made visible during the establishment of traceability. These disconnects include requirements not satisfied in the audited product and extraneous features observed in the product (i.e., features for which no stated requirement exists).

With the different point of view made possible by the visibility and traceability achieved in the software audit, management can make better decisions and exercise more incisive control over the software development process. The result of a software audit may be the establishment of a baseline, the redirection of project tasking, or an adjustment of applied project resources.

The responsibility for a successful software development project is shared by the buyer, seller, and user. Software auditing uniquely benefits each of these project participants. Appropriate auditing by each party provides checks and

19

balances over the development effort. The scope and depth of the audits undertaken by the three parties may vary greatly. However, the purposes of these differing forms of software audit remain the same: to provide visibility and to establish traceability of the software life cycle products. An excellent overview of the software audit process, from which some of the above discussion has been extracted, appears in [11].

Software Configuration Status Accounting: A decision to make a change is generally followed by a time delay before the change is actually made, and changes to baselines generally occur over a protracted period of time before they are incorporated into baselines as updates. A mechanism is therefore needed for maintaining a record of how the system has evolved and where the system is at any time relative to what appears in published baseline documentation and written agreements. Software configuration status accounting provides this mechanism. Status accounting is the administrative tracking and reporting of all software items formally identified and controlled. It also involves the maintenance of records to support software configuration auditing. Thus, software configuration status accounting records the activity associated with the other three SCM functions and therefore provides the means by which the history of the software system life cycle can be traced.

Although administrative in nature, status accounting is a function that increases in complexity as the system life cycle progresses because of the multiple software representations that emerge with later baselines. This complexity generally results in large amounts of data to be recorded and reported. In particular, the scope of software configuration status accounting encompasses the recording and reporting of:

1) the time at which each representation of a baseline and update came into being;

2) the time at which each software configuration item came into being;

3) descriptive information about each SCI;

4) engineering change proposal status (approved, disapproved, awaiting action);

5) descriptive information about each ECP;

6) change status;

7) descriptive information about each change;

8) status of technical and administrative documentation associated with a baseline or update (such as a plan prescribing tests to be performed on a baseline for updating purposes);

9) deficiencies in a to-be-established baseline uncovered during a configuration audit.

Software configuration status accounting, because of its large data input and output requirements, is generally supported in part by automated processes such as the PSL described earlier. Data are collected and organized for input to a computer and reports giving the status of entities are compiled and generated by the computer.

THE MANAGEMENT DILEMMA

As we mentioned at the beginning of this paper, SCM and many of the other product assurance disciplines grew up in the 1970's in response to software failure. The new disciplines were designed to achieve visibility into the soft-

ware engineering process and thereby exercise some measure of control over that process. Students of mathematical control theory are taught early in their studies a simple example of the control process. Consider being confronted with a cup of hot coffee, filled to the top, which you are expected to carry from the kitchen counter to the kitchen table. It is easily verified that if you watch the cup as you carry it, you are likely to spill more coffee than if you were to keep your head turned away from the cup. The problem with looking at the cup is one of overcompensation. As you observe slight deviations from the straight-and-level, you adjust, but often you adjust too much. To compensate for that overadjustment, you tend to overadjust again, with the result being hot coffee on your floor.

This little diversion from our main topic of SCM has an obvious moral. There is a fundamental propensity on the part of the practitioners of the product assurance disciplines to overadjust, to overcompensate for the failures of the development disciplines. There is one sure way to eliminate failure completely from the software development process, and that is to stop it completely. The software project manager must learn how to apply his resources intelligently. He must achieve visibility and control, but he must not so encumber the developer so as to bring progress to a virtual halt. The product assurers have a virtuous perspective. They strive for perfection and point out when and where perfection has not been achieved. We seem to have a binary attitude about software; it is either correct or it is not. That is perhaps true, but we cannot expect anyone to deliver perfect software in any reasonable time period or for a reasonable sum of money. What we need to develop is software that is good enough. Some of the controls that we have placed on the developer have the deleterious effect of increasing costs and expanding schedules rather than shrinking them.

The dilemma to management is real. We must have the visibility and control that the product assurance disciplines have the capacity to provide. But we must be careful not to overcompensate and overcontrol. This is the fine line which will distinguish the successful software managers of the 1980's from the rest of the software engineering community.

ACKNOWLEDGMENT

The author wishes to acknowledge the contribution of B. J. Gregor to the preparation and critique of the final manuscript.

REFERENCES

[1] "Contracting for computer software development—Serious problems require management attention to avoid wasting additional millions," General Accounting Office, Rep. FGMSD 80-4, Nov. 9, 1979.

[2] D. M. Weiss, "The MUDD report: A case study of Navy software development practices," Naval Res. Lab., Rep. 7909, May 21, 1975.

[3] B. W. Boehm, "Software engineering," *IEEE Trans. Comput.*, vol. C-25, pp. 1226–1241, Dec. 1976.

[4] *Proc. IEEE* (Special Issue on Software Engineering), vol. 68, Sept. 1980.

[5] E. Bersoff, V. Henderson, and S. Siegel, "Attaining software product integrity," *Tutorial: Software Configuration Management*, W. Bryan, C. Chadbourne, and S. Siegel, Eds., Los Alamitos, CA, IEEE Comput. Soc., Cat. EHO-169-3, 1981.

[6] B. W. Boehm *et al.*, *Characteristics of Software Quality*, TRW Series of Software Technology, vol. 1. New York: North-Holland, 1978.

[7] T. A. Thayer, *et al.*, *Software Reliability*, TRW Series of Software Technology, vol. 2. New York: North-Holland, 1978.

[8] D. J. Reifer, Ed., *Tutorial: Automated Tools for Software Eng.*, Los Alamitos, CA, IEEE Comput. Soc., Cat. EHO-169-3, 1979.

[9] E. Bersoff, V. Henderson, and S. Siegel, *Software Configuration Management*. Englewood Cliffs, NJ: Prentice-Hall, 1980.

[10] ——, "Software configuration management: A tutorial," *Computer*, vol. 12, pp. 6–14, Jan. 1979.

[11] W. Bryan, S. Siegel, and G. Whiteleather, "Auditing throughout the software life cycle: A primer," *Computer*, vol. 15, pp. 56–67, Mar. 1982.

[12] "Software configuration management," Naval Elec. Syst. Command, Software Management Guidebooks, vol. 2, undated.

21

IEEE Standard 828-1998
Software Configuration Management Plans

This standard was prepared by the Life Cycle Data Harmonization Working Group of the Software Engineering Standards Committee of the IEEE Computer Society. At the time this standard was approved, the working group consisted of the following members:

Leonard L. Tripp, *Chair*

Edward Byrne	Paul R. Croll	Perry DeWeese
Robin Fralick	Marilyn Ginsberg-Finner	John Harauz
Mark Henley	Dennis Lawrence	David Maibor
Ray Milovanovic	James Moore	Timothy Niesen
Dennis Rilling	Terry Rout	Richard Schmidt
Norman F. Schneidewind	David Schultz	Basil Sherlund
Peter Voldner	Ronald Wade	

Sponsored by

Software Engineering Standards Committee
of the IEEE Computer Society

Disclaimer: *This copy of the standards is incomplete and cannot be used to cite conformance with the standards in a contractual situation. Its purpose is to provide the reader and CSDP test taker with a basic understanding of the contents of the IEEE standards*

The Institute of Electrical and Electronic Engineering, Inc.
345 East 47th Street, New York, NY 10017-2394, USA

June 25, 1998

Table of Contents
IEEE Standard 828-1998
Software Configuration Management Plans

IEEE Standard for Software Configuration Management Plans

1. Overview

1.1 Scope

This standard establishes the minimum required contents of a Software Configuration Management (SCM) Plan (the Plan). It is supplemented by IEEE Std 1042-1987, which provides approaches to good software configuration management planning. This standard applies to the entire life cycle of critical software; e.g., where failure would impact safety or cause large financial or social losses. It also applies to noncritical software and to software already developed. The application of this standard is not restricted to any form, class, or type of software.

The Plan documents what SCM activities are to be done, how they are to be done, who is responsible for doing specific activities, when they are to happen, and what resources are required. It can address SCM activities over any portion of a software product's life cycle.

The content of the Plan is identified in Paragraph 4 of this standard. The required information is indicated by the words "shall" and "required." Additional optional information is also identified as appropriate. The user of this standard, however, is expected to expand and supplement the minimum requirements as necessary for the development environment, specific industry, organization, and project. Tailoring of a plan in conformance with this standard is described in Paragraph 5.

The primary users of this standard are assumed to be those planning SCM activities or performing SCM audits. In considering adoption of this standard, regulatory bodies should be aware that specific application of this standard may already be covered by one or more IEEE standards documents relating to quality assurance, definitions, or other matters (see IEEE Std 730-1998). It is not the purpose of this standard to supersede, revise, or amend existing standards directed to specific industries or applications.

2. References

The supporting references and citations pertaining to this standard can be found in the *Centralized IEEE Software Engineering Standards References* contained in this tutorial. These references provide additional information on software configuration management plans to assist in understanding and applying this standard.

3. Definitions

The definitions and acronyms pertaining to this standard can be found in the *Centralized IEEE Software Engineering Standards Glossary* contained in this tutorial. These are contextual definitions serving to augment the understanding of software configuration management plan activities as described within this standard.

The term "the Plan" is used throughout this standard to refer to the Software Configuration Management Plan.

4. The Software Configuration Management Plan

SCM planning information shall be partitioned into the six classes described in Table 1. The referenced subparagraphs of the standard provide the reader with detailed requirements for each class of information.

SCM planning information may be presented in any format, sequence, or location that is meaningful to the intended users of the Plan with the following restrictions:

a) A document with the title "Software Configuration Management Plan" shall exist either in stand-alone form or embedded in another project document;

b) This document shall contain all SCM planning information either by inclusion or by reference to other locations, such as other documents or automated systems; and

c) A format for this document shall be defined.

The writer of the Plan shall use the sequence of sections specified in Table 1 unless a different format has been defined in the Introduction of the Plan (see Paragraph 4.1).

4.1 Introduction

Introduction information provides a simplified overview of the SCM activities so that those approving, those performing, and those interacting with SCM can obtain a clear understanding of the Plan. The introduction shall include four topics: the purpose of the Plan, the scope, the definition of key terms, and references.

The purpose shall briefly address why the Plan exists and who the intended audience is.

The scope shall address SCM applicability, limitations, and assumptions on which the Plan is based. The following items shall be included:

a) Overview description of the software development project;

b) Identification of the software CI(s) to which SCM will be applied;

c) Identification of other software to be included as part of the Plan (e.g., support or test software);

d) Relationship of SCM to the hardware or system configuration management activities for the project;

e) The degree of formality, depth of control, and portion of the software life cycle for applying SCM on this project;

f) Limitations, such as time constraints, that applies to the Plan; and

g) Assumptions that might have an impact on the cost, schedule, or ability to perform defined SCM activities (e.g., assumptions of the degree of customer participation in SCM activities or the availability of automated aids).

Table 1 – SCM classes of information

Class of information	Description	Paragraph reference	Plan reference
Introduction	Describes the Plan's purpose, scope of application, key terms, and references	4.1	1
SCM management	(Who?) Identifies the responsibilities and authorities for accomplishing the planned activities	4.2	2
SCM activities	(What?) Identifies all activities to be performed in applying to the project	4.3	3
SCM schedules	(When?) Identifies the required coordination of SCM activities with the other activities in the project	4.4	4
SCM resources	(How?) Identifies tools and physical and human resources required for execution of the Plan	4.5	5
SCM plan maintenance	Identifies how the Plan will be kept current while in effect	4.6	6

Key terms shall be defined as they apply to the Plan in order to establish a common terminology among all users of the Plan.

All references in the Plan to policies, directives, procedures, standards, terminology, and related documents shall be uniquely identified to enable retrieval by users of the Plan.

4.2 SCM management

SCM management information describes the allocation of responsibilities and authorities for SCM activities to organizations and individuals within the project structure.

26

SCM management information shall include three topics: the project organization(s) within which SCM is to apply, the SCM responsibilities of these organizations, and references to the SCM policies and directives that apply to this project.

4.2.1 Organization

The organizational context, both technical and managerial, within which the planned SCM activities are to be implemented, shall be described. The Plan shall identify the following:

a) All organizational units that participate in or are responsible for any SCM activity on the project;

b) The functional roles of these organizational units within the project structure; and

c) Relationships between organizational units.

Organizational units may consist of a vendor and customer, a prime contractor and subcontractors, or different groups within one organization. Organization charts, supplemented by statements of function and relationships, can be an effective way of presenting this information.

4.2.2 SCM responsibilities

The allocation of SCM activities to organizational units shall be specified. For each activity listed within SCM activities (see Paragraph 4.3), the name of the organizational unit or job title to perform this activity shall be provided. A matrix that relates the organizations defined above to the SCM functions, activities, and tasks can be useful for documenting the SCM responsibilities.

For any review board or special organization established for performing SCM activities on this project, the Plan shall describe its:

a) Purpose and objectives;

b) Membership and affiliations;

c) Period of effectively;

d) Scope of authority; and

e) Operational procedures.

4.2.3 Applicable policies, directives, and procedures

Any external constraints placed on the Plan by other policies, directives, and procedures shall be identified. For each, its impact and effect on the Plan shall be stated.

4.3 SCM activities

SCM activities information identifies all functions and tasks required to manage the configuration of the software system as specified in the scope of the Plan. Both technical and managerial SCM activities shall be identified. General project activities that have SCM implications shall be described from the SCM perspective.

SCM activities are traditionally grouped into four functions: configuration identification, configuration control, status accounting, and configuration audits and reviews. The information requirements for each function are identified in Paragraphs 4.3.1 through 4.3.4.

Due to their high-risk nature, the requirements for interface control and subcontractor/vendor control activities are identified separately in Paragraphs 4.3.5 and 4.3.6.

4.3.1 Configuration identification

Configuration identification activities shall identify, name, and describe the documented physical and functional characteristics of the code, specifications, design, and data elements to be controlled for the project. The documents are acquired for configuration control. Controlled items may be intermediate and final outputs (such as executable code, source code, user documentation, program listings, databases, test cases, test plans, specifications, and management plans) and elements of the support environment (such as compilers, operating systems, programming tools, and test beds).

The Plan shall identify the project configuration items (CI) and their structures at each project control point. The Plan shall state how each CI and its versions are to be uniquely named and describe the activities performed to define, track, store, and retrieve CIs. Information required for configuration identification (see Figure 1) is specified in Paragraphs 4.3.1.1 through 4.3.1.3.

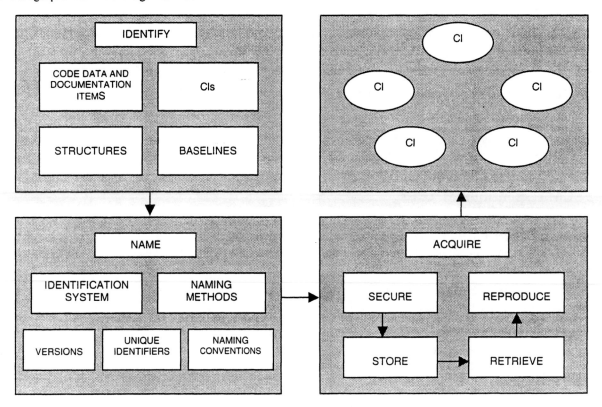

Figure 1 – Configuration identification processes

4.3.1.1 Identifying configuration items

The Plan shall record the items to be controlled, the project CIs, and their definitions as they evolve or are selected. The Plan shall also describe how the list of items and the structures are to be maintained for the project. As a minimum, all CIs that are to be delivered shall be listed.

Appropriate baselines shall be defined at control points within the project life cycle in terms of the following:

    a)   The event that creates the baseline;

    b)   The items that are to be controlled in the baseline;

    c)   The procedures used to establish and change the baseline; and

    d)   The authority required to approve changes to the approved baselined documents.

A means of identifying changes and associating them with the affected CIs and the related baseline shall be specified.

4.3.1.2 Naming configuration items

The Plan shall specify an identification system for assigning unique identifiers to each item to be controlled. It shall also specify how different versions of each are to be uniquely identified. Identification methods could include naming conventions and version numbers and letters.

The Plan shall describe the methods for naming controlled items for purposes of storage, retrieval, tracking, reproduction, and distribution. Activities may include version marking, labeling of documentation and executable software, serialization and altered item marking for executable code or data embedded on a microchip, and identification of physical packaging.

Subcontracted software, vendor proprietary software, and support software may require special identification schemes and labeling.

4.3.1.3 Acquiring configuration items

The Plan shall identify the controlled software libraries for the project and describe how the code, documentation, and data of the identified baselines are to be physically placed under control in the appropriate library. For each library the format, location, documentation requirements, receiving and inspection requirements, and access control procedures shall be specified.

The Plan shall specify procedures for the actual storage of documents and magnetic media, including the physical marking and labeling of items. Data retention periods and disaster prevention and recovery procedures may also be described.

Procedures shall describe how to retrieve and reproduce controlled items from library storage. These activities include verification of marking and labeling, tracking of controlled copies, and protection of proprietary and security information.

4.3.2 Configuration control

Configuration control activities request, evaluate, approve or disapprove, and implement changes to baselined CIs. Changes encompass both error correction and enhancement. The degree of formality necessary for the change process depends on the project baseline affected and on the impact of the change within the configuration structure.

For each project software library identified according to Paragraph 4.3.1.3, the Plan shall describe the change controls imposed on the baselined CIs. The Plan shall define the following sequence of specific steps:

    a)   Identification and documentation of the need for a change;

    b)   Analysis and evaluation of a change request;

    c)   Approval or disapproval of a request; and

    d)   Verification, implementation, and release of a change.

The Plan shall identify the records to be used for tracking and documenting this sequence of steps for each change. Any differences in handling changes based on the origin of the request shall be explicitly documented.

4.3.2.1 Requesting changes

The Plan shall specify the procedures for requesting a change to a baselined CI and the information to be documented for the request. As a minimum, the information recorded for a proposed change shall contain the following:

    a)   The name(s) and version(s) of the CIs where the problem appears;

    b)   Originator's name and organization;

    c)   Date of request;

    d)   Indication of urgency;

    e)   The need for the change; and

    f)   Description of the requested change.

Additional information, such as priority or classification, may be included to clarify the significance of the request and to assist in its analysis and evaluation. Other information, such as change request number, status, and disposition, may be recorded for change tracking.

4.3.2.2 Evaluating changes

The Plan shall specify the analysis required to determine the impact of the proposed change and the procedures for reviewing the results of the analysis. Changes should be evaluated according to their effect on the deliverable and their impact on project resources.

4.3.2.3 Approving or disapproving changes

The Plan shall identify each configuration control board (CCB) and its level of authority for approving proposed changes. A CCB may be an individual or a group. Multiple levels of CCBs may be specified, depending upon the degree of system or project complexity and upon the project baseline involved. When multiple CCBs are used, the Plan shall specify how the proper level is determined for a change request, including any variations during the project life cycle.

For any CCB utilized, the Plan shall indicate its level of authority and its responsibilities as defined in Paragraph 4.2.2.

4.3.2.4 Implementing changes

The Plan shall specify the activities for verifying and implementing an approved change. The information recorded for the completion of a change shall contain the following as a minimum:

a) The associated change request(s);

b) The names and versions of the affected items;

c) Verification date and responsible party;

d) Release or installation date and responsible party; and

e) The identifier of the new version.

Additional information, such as software fault metrics or identification of the supporting software used to implement the change, may be included.

The Plan shall also specify activities for release planning and control, e.g., coordinating multiple changes, reconfiguring the CIs, and delivering a new baseline.

4.3.3 Configuration status accounting

Configuration status accounting activities record and report the status of project CIs.

The Plan shall include information on the following:

a) What data elements are to be tracked and reported for baselines and changes?

b) What types of status accounting reports are to be generated and their frequency;

c) How information is to be collected, stored, processed, and reported; and

d) How access to the status data is to be controlled.

If an automated system is used for any status accounting activity, its function shall be described or referenced.

The following minimum data elements shall be tracked and reported for each CI: its initial approved version, the status of requested changes, and the implementation status of approved changes. The level of detail and specific data required may vary according to the information needs of the project and the customer.

4.3.4 Configuration audits and reviews

Configuration audits determine to what extent the actual CI reflects the required physical and functional characteristics. Configuration reviews are management tools for establishing a baseline.

The Plan shall identify the configuration audits and reviews to be held for the project. At a minimum, a configuration audit shall be performed on a CI prior to its release.

For each planned configuration audit or review, the Plan shall define the following:

a) Its objective;

b) The CIs under audit or review;

c) The schedule of audit or review tasks;

d) The procedures for conducting the audit or review;

e) The participants by job title;

f) Documentation required to be available for review or to support the audit or review;

g) The procedure for recording any deficiencies and reporting corrective actions; and

h) The approval criteria and the specific action(s) to occur upon approval.

4.3.5 Interface control

Interface control activities coordinate changes to the project CIs with changes to interfacing items outside the scope of the Plan. Hardware, system software and support software, as well as other projects and deliverables, should be examined for potential interfacing effects on the project.

The Plan shall identify the external items to which the project software interfaces. For each interface, the Plan shall define the following:

a) The nature of the interface;

b) The affected organizations;

c) How the interface code, documentation, and data are to be controlled; and

d) How the interface control documents are approved and released into a specified baseline.

For any CCB established to control interfaces, the Plan shall identify its responsibilities and procedures as specified in Paragraph 4.2.2.

4.3.6 Subcontractor/vendor control

Subcontractor/vendor control activities incorporate items developed outside the project environment into the project CIs. Included are software developed by contract and software acquired in its finished form. Special attention should be directed to these SCM activities due to the added organizational and legal relationships.

For both subcontracted and acquired software, the Plan shall define the activities to incorporate the externally developed items into the project CIs and to coordinate changes to these items with their development organizations.

For subcontracted software, the Plan shall describe the following:

a) What SCM requirements, including an SCM Plan, are to be part of the subcontractor's agreement?

b) How will the subcontractor be monitored for compliance?

c) What configuration audits and reviews of subcontractor items will be held?

d) How will external code, documentation, and data be tested, verified, accepted, and merged with the project software?

e) How will proprietary items be handled for security of information and traceability of ownership (e.g., copyright and royalties)?

f) How are changes to be processed, including the subcontractor's participation?

For acquired software, the Plan shall describe how the software will be received, tested, and placed under SCM; how changes to the supplier's software are to be processed; and whether and how the supplier will participate in the project's change management process. Acquired software can come from a vendor, a subcontractor, a customer, another project, or other source.

4.4 SCM schedules

SCM schedule information establishes the sequence and coordination for the identified SCM activities and for all events affecting the Plan's implementation.

The Plan shall state the sequence and dependencies among all SCM activities and the relationship of key SCM activities to project milestones or events. The schedule shall cover the duration of the Plan and contain all major milestones of the project related to SCM activities. SCM milestones shall include establishment of a configuration baseline, implementation of change control procedures, and the start and completion dates for a configuration audit.

Schedule information shall be expressed as absolute dates, as dates relative to either SCM or project milestones, or as a simple sequence of events. Graphic representation can be particularly appropriate for conveying this information.

4.5 SCM resources

SCM resource information identifies the software tools, techniques, equipment, personnel, and training necessary for the implementation of the specified SCM activities.

SCM can be performed by a combination of software tools and manual procedures. Tools can be SCM-specific or embedded in general project aids; they can be standard organizational resources or ones specially acquired or built for this project. Tools can be applied to library structure and access control; documentation development and tracking; code control; baseline system generation; change processing, communication and authorization; change/problem tracking and status reporting; archiving, retention, and retrieval of controlled items; or the SCM planning process itself.

For each type of SCM activity identified, the Plan shall specify what tools, techniques, equipment, personnel, and training are required and how each resource will be provided or obtained.

For each software tool, whether developed within the project or brought in from outside the project, the Plan shall describe or reference its functions and shall identify the configuration controls to be placed on the tool.

4.6 SCM plan maintenance

SCM plan maintenance information identifies the activities and responsibilities necessary to ensure continued SCM planning during the life cycle of the project. The Plan shall state the following:

a) Who is responsible for monitoring the Plan?

b) How frequently are updates to be performed?

c) How are changes to the Plan to be evaluated and approved?

d) How are changes to the Plan to be made and communicated?

The Plan should be reviewed at the start of each project software phase, changed accordingly, and approved and distributed to the project team.

If the Plan has been constructed with detailed procedures documented elsewhere in appendixes or references, different maintenance mechanisms for those procedures may be appropriate.

5. Tailoring of the Plan

This standard permits significant flexibility in preparing an SCM Plan. A successful Plan reflects its project environment. It should be written in terms familiar to its users and should be consistent with the development and procurement processes of the project.

To conform to the requirements set forth in other applicable standards or to accommodate local practices, a Plan may be tailored upward, to add information, or tailored to use a specified format. The Plan may also be tailored downward, omitting information required by this standard, when specific standard requirements are identified as not applicable to this project.

5.1 Upward tailoring

Some information requirements applicable to a particular project may not be stated in this standard due to its scope of establishing the minimum required contents of an SCM Plan. If additional requirements are applicable to the project, the Plan shall so state these additions as part of the Introduction and indicate the reason for their insertion. A cost-benefits analysis should be completed for each additional requirement. Requirements that are additional should be agreed upon by all affected project functions and the parties responsible for approval of the plan.

5.2 Downward tailoring

Some information requirements stated in this standard may not apply to a particular project due to the project's limited scope, low complexity, or unusual environment. If a requirement is not applicable to the project, the Plan shall so state this deletion as part of the Introduction and indicate the reason for removal. Requirements that are inapplicable should be agreed upon by all affected project functions and all parties responsible for approval of the Plan.

The Plan shall omit none of the six major classes of information. Detailed information may be omitted as indicated above but within the limits of the consistency criteria stated in Paragraph 6.

If certain information has not been decided on or is unavailable at the time the Plan is initially approved, the Plan shall mark those areas or sections as "to be determined" and shall indicate, as part of Plan maintenance, information on how and when further information will be provided.

5.3 Format

The information may be presented in the Plan in any sequence or presentation style deemed suitable for the Plan's users. To achieve consistency and convenience within a single organization or industry segment, a standard format for SCM plans is desirable and appropriate. To customize this standard for a particular group of users, a supplement to the standard specifying Plan structure and standard terminology may be used.

6. Conformance to the standard

An SCM Plan shall satisfy the criteria in Paragraphs 6.1 through 6.4 in order to conform to this standard.

6.1 Minimum information

The Plan shall include the six classes of SCM information identified in Paragraph 4: introduction, management, activities, schedules, resources, and plan maintenance. Within each class, all of the required information stated in Paragraph 4 of this standard, as indicated by the words "shall" and "required," shall be documented within the Plan. If certain required information is not applicable, the reasons shall be so stated. If a sequence of information other than the sequence of this standard is used, an explicit cross-reference between the Plan and the standard shall be provided.

6.2 Presentation format

One document, section title, or such reference shall exist that is specifically labeled "Software Configuration Management Plan." Within this document, each of the six classes of information shall be included. While the information may be provided in a number of presentation styles, the requirement is to provide all Plan information and references in a single document.

6.3 Consistency criteria

The documented information shall satisfy the following consistency criteria:

a) All activities defined in the Plan (see Paragraphs 4.3.1 through 4.3.6) shall be assigned to an organizational unit (see Paragraph 4.2.2).

b) All activities defined shall have resources identified to accomplish the activities (see Paragraph 4.5).

c) All CIs identified in the Plan (see Paragraph 4.3.1) shall have defined processes for baseline establishment and change control (see Paragraph 4.3.2).

6.4 Conformance declaration

If the preceding criteria are met, then the conformance of any SCM planning documentation with this standard may be stated accordingly: "This SCM Plan conforms with the requirements of IEEE Std 828-1998."

Chapter 3

Software Verification and Validation Processes

1. Introduction to Chapter

This chapter describes both the software verification and validation processes. Paragraph 2 describes the verification process, and Paragraph 3 describes the validation process. Portions of this text are paraphrased from IEEE/EIA Standard 12207.0-1996, Paragraphs 6.4 and 6.5. Paragraph 4 provides an overview and introduction to the papers contained in this chapter.

2. Software Verification Process

The software *verification process* is a process for determining whether the software products of an activity fulfill the requirements or conditions imposed on them in the previous activities. For cost and performance effectiveness, verification should be integrated, as early as possible, with the process (such as supply, development, operation, or maintenance) that employs it. Components of this process may include analysis, review, and testing.

This process may be executed with varying degrees of independence. The degree of independence ranges from the same person or a different person in the same organization to a person in a different organization with varying degrees of separation. An independent verification process exists if the process is executed by an organization independent of the supplier, developer, operator, or maintainer.

2.1 List of activities

This process consists of the following activities:

1. Process implementation

2. Software verification.

2.2 Process implementation

This activity consists of the following tasks:

- A determination is made if the project warrants a verification effort and by the degree of organizational independence of the required effort. The project requirements are analyzed for criticality. Criticality may be gauged in terms of:

  ➢ The potential of an undetected error in a system or software requirement for causing death or personal injury, mission failure, or financial or catastrophic equipment loss or damage.

  ➢ The maturity of and risks associated with the software technology to be used.

  ➢ Availability of funds and resources.

- If the project warrants a verification effort, a verification process is established to verify the software product.

- If the project warrants an independent verification effort, a qualified organization responsible for conducting the verification is selected. This organization is assured the independence and authority to perform the verification activities.

- Target life cycle activities and software products requiring verification are determined based upon the scope, magnitude, complexity, and critical analysis listed above. Verification activities and tasks including associated methods, techniques, and tools for performing the tasks, are selected for the target life cycle activities and software products.

- A verification plan is developed and documented based upon the verification tasks as determined. This plan addresses the life cycle activities and software products subject to verification, the required verification tasks for each life cycle activity and software product, and related resources, responsibility, and schedules. The plan also addresses procedures for forwarding verification reports to the acquirer and other involved organizations.

- The verification plan is then implemented. Problems and non-conformance detected by the verification effort are entered into the *problem resolution process*. This process should resolve all problems and non-conformance. Results of the verification activities are made available to the acquirer and other involved organizations.

2.3 Software verification

This activity consists of the following tasks:

- *Contract verification*. The contract is verified according to the criteria listed below:

  - The supplier has the capability to satisfy the requirements.

  - The requirements are consistent and cover user needs.

  - Adequate procedures are stipulated for handling changes to requirements and escalating problems.

  - Procedures and their extent for interface and cooperation among the parties are stipulated, including ownership, warranty, copyright, and confidentiality.

  - Acceptance criteria and procedures are stipulated in accordance with requirements.

- *Process verification*. This process is verified according to the criteria listed below:

  - Project planning requirements are adequate and timely.

  - Processes selected for the project are adequate, implemented, executed as planned, and compliant with the contract.

- ➢ The standards, procedures, and environments are adequate for the project's processes.

- ➢ The project is staffed and personnel trained as required by the contract.

- *Requirements verification*. The requirements are verified according to the following criteria:

  - ➢ The system requirements are consistent, feasible, and testable.

  - ➢ The system requirements have been appropriately allocated to hardware items, software items, and manual operations according to design criteria.

  - ➢ The software requirements are consistent, feasible, testable, and accurately reflect system requirements.

  - ➢ The software requirements related to safety, security, and criticality are correct as shown by suitably rigorous methods.

- *Design verification*. Design is verified by the following criteria:

  - ➢ The design is correct and consistent with and traceable to requirements.

  - ➢ The design implements proper sequence of events, inputs, outputs, interfaces, logic flow, allocation of timing and sizing budgets, and error definition, isolation, and recovery.

  - ➢ Design is selected from requirements.

  - ➢ The design correctly implements safety, security, and other critical requirements as shown by suitably rigorous methods.

- *Code verification*. All code is verified according to the criteria listed below:

  - ➢ The code is traceable to design and requirements, testable, correct, and compliant with requirements and coding standards.

  - ➢ The code implements proper event sequence, consistent interfaces, correct data and control flow, completeness, appropriate allocation timing and sizing budgets, and error definition, isolation, and recovery.

  - ➢ Selected code can be derived from design or requirements.

  - ➢ The code correctly implements safety, security, and other critical requirements as shown by suitably rigorous methods.

- *Integration verification*. Integration is verified through consideration of the following criteria:

37

> The software components and units of each software item have been completely and correctly integrated into the software item.

> The hardware items, software items, and manual operations of the system have been completely and correctly integrated into the system.

> The integration tasks have been performed in accordance with an integration plan.

- *Documentation verification.* Documentation is verified by the following criteria:

> The documentation is adequate, complete, and consistent.

> Documentation preparation is timely.

> Configuration management of documents follows specified procedures.

3. Software Validation Process

The *software validation process* is a process for determining whether the requirements and the final, as-built system or software product fulfills its specific intended use. Validation may be conducted in earlier stages. This process may be conducted as a part of the *software acceptance support*. This process may also be executed with varying degrees of independence. The degree of independence may range from the same person or a different person in the same organization to a person in a different organization with varying degrees of separation. A case, in which the process is executed by an organization independent of the supplier, developer, operator, or maintainer, is called an *independent validation process*.

3.1 List of activities

This process consists of the following activities:

1. Process implementation

2. Software validation.

3.2 Process implementation.

This activity consists of the following tasks:

- A determination shall be made if the project warrants a validation effort and the degree of organizational independence of the effort required.

- If the project warrants a validation effort, a validation process is established to validate the system or software product. Validation tasks are selected from those defined below, including associated methods, techniques, and tools for performing the tasks.

- If the project warrants an independent effort, a qualified organization responsible for conducting the effort is selected. The conductor is assured of the independence and authority to perform the validation tasks.

- A validation plan is developed and documented. The plan includes, but is not limited to, the following:

    ➤ Items subject to validation

    ➤ Validation tasks to be performed

    ➤ Resources, responsibilities, and schedules for validation

    ➤ Procedures for forwarding validation reports to the acquirer and other parties.

- The validation plan is then implemented. Problems and non-conformance detected by the validation effort are entered into the *problem resolution process* that resolves all problems and non-conformance. Results of the validation activities are made available to the acquirer and other involved organizations.

3.3 Software validation. This activity consists of the following tasks:

- Preparation of selected test requirements, test cases, and test specifications for analyzing test results.

- Ensurance that these test requirements, test cases, and test specifications reflects the particular requirements for the specific intended use.

- Conducting the following software tests:

    ➤ Testing with stress, boundary, and singular inputs

    ➤ Testing the software product for its ability to isolate and minimize the effect of errors; that is, graceful degradation upon failure, request for operator assistance upon stress, boundary, and singular conditions

    ➤ Testing representative users who can successfully achieve their intended tasks using the software product.

- Validating that the software product satisfies its intended use.

- Testing the software product as appropriate in selected areas of the target environment.

4. Overview of Papers

The first paper discussing software verification and validation is a revision and update of the US National Institute of Standards and Technology (NIST) Special Publication 500-165. Both the NIST publication and the new paper were written by Roger Fujii and Dolores Wallace. This paper describes software V&V, its objectives and recommended tasks, and provides guidance for selecting techniques to perform the task. It explains the differences between V&V and quality assurance, and how development, quality assurance, V&V, and other software engineering practitioners can use V&V techniques to produce quality software.

Verification

The second paper is extracted from IEEE Standard 1012-1998, *Standard for Software Verification and Validation,* IEEE, Inc., New York, 1998, which defines the software verification and validation (V&V) processes. This standard determines whether development products of a given activity conform to the requirements of that activity, and whether the selected software satisfies its intended use and user needs. This determination may include analysis, evaluation, review, inspection, assessment, and testing of software products and processes. The V&V

Validation

processes assess the software in the context of the system, including the operational environment, hardware, interfacing software, operators, and users.

This standard is longer than others in this volume because it deals with the activity rather than merely the plan for the activity.

The reader is again reminded that this copy of the standard is incomplete and cannot be used to cite compliance with the standard in a contractual situation. It is intended to provide the reader and CSDP test taker with a basic understanding of the contents of the V&V standards and an outline of a V&V plan.

Software Verification and Validation (V&V)

Roger U. Fujii

Logicon, Incorporated
222 West Sixth Street
San Pedro, CA 90733-0471

Dolores R. Wallace

National Computer Systems Laboratory
National Institute of Standards and Technology
Gaithersburg, MD 20899

Abstract

Software engineering standards tie together to provide a strong framework for ensuring quality computer systems. Standards for software verification and validation (V&V), a systems engineering approach to ensure quality software, support the requirements of standards for project management and quality assurance. When used together, they contribute to safe, secure, reliable, and maintainable computer systems.

This report describes software V&V, its objectives, recommended tasks, and guidance for selecting techniques to perform the tasks. It explains differences between V&V and quality assurance, and how development, quality assurance, V&V, and other software engineering practitioners can use V&V techniques to produce quality software. While two studies of V&V's cost-effectiveness have different conclusions, an analysis of the parameters of those studies suggests that the benefits of V&V outweigh the costs associated with it.

This report describes six existing software engineering standards for software verification and validation. A description is provided on which standards contain guidance for scoping the V&V effort, planning the V&V effort, and managing the V&V effort.

1. Introduction

The purpose of this paper is to provide a brief introduction to Software Verification and Validation (V&V). Traditionally, software V&V is defined as a systems engineering methodology to ensure that quality (that is, emphasizing correctness, reliability, and usability) is built into the software during development. The analysis and test activities performed by V&V evaluate and assess the software products and development processes during each software life cycle phase in parallel with, not after the completion of, the development effort. This evaluation and assessment provides early identification of errors, assessment of software performance, compliance with requirements, identification of program risks, and assessment of the quality of development processes and products. Because software is becoming an integral part of linking the system together, V&V ensures that the examined software performs correctly within the system context (that is, system performance, system stimuli and operating environment, user features across the system, among others).

Software V&V is complementary to and supportive of quality assurance, project management, systems engineering, and development. V&V utilizes unique V&V techniques in addition to well-proven techniques used by these other complementary development functional groups. V&V uses these techniques to (1) unravel the details of the software product or process; (2) examine each individual detail piece to determine its correctness; and (3) determine completeness, correctness, and other quality attributes when the pieces are viewed as a whole from an unbiased persepective. Figure 1 illustrates how V&V activities supports the other functional groups (that is, development, systems engineering, and quality assurance) of the development effort.

By examining the software in detail and assessing the detailed pieces against the total system requirements, software V&V attacks two of the major contributors to software failures: (1) incorrect or missing requirements (lack of understanding the problem to be solved by software); and (2) poor organization in software architecture and failure to plan effectively (managing information complexity). Our modern software paradigms and techniques can assist in deal-

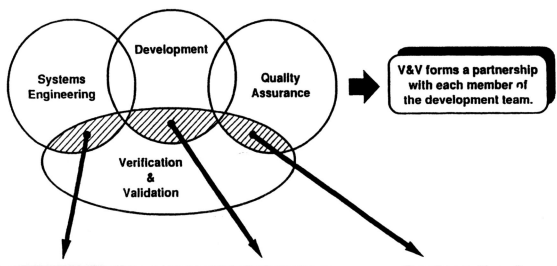

Figure 1. Relationship of V&V to the development team

ing with these causes of primary software failures, and software V&V in particular is a powerful technique to address these types of failures.

In the remainder of the paper, the primary V&V techniques used in life cycle phase will be described. A section of the paper will describe a selction of standards on software V&V that are representative of the currect standards used by United States Federal agencies, industries, and academia.

2. Overview Of Software Verification and Validation

In 1961, a software error caused the destruction of a Mariner payload on board a radio-controlled Atlas booster. The Atlas guidance software had used incorrect radar data to compute navigation and steering commands. The cause was a simple programming error of misusing a hyphen on previous data rather than on the corrected, extrapolated data.

This simple but expensive error led the Air Force to require independent review of the guidance equations and software implementation of all future mission-critical space launches. This need to ensure software quality and to have high confidence in the correct performance of the system gave birth to the methodology of software verification and validation. At a time when missile guidance theories and computer technologies were still in their infancy and many

unknowns were yet to be solved, software V&V proved highly successful in providing the independent assessment of the proposed technical solution's correctness. Through early identification and correction of errors, V&V also succeeded in developing higher confidence in the system. Program managers made better decisions because they now had the technical insight and advanced notice of risk-prone areas to make informed decisions. Since then, software V&V has become a powerful risk management tool.

As these and other benefits of V&V became apparent in improved software quality, including safety and security, complex information systems outside the Department of Defense began using the V&V methodology. Today, the methodology has proliferated throughout the Department of Defense (DOD) services, the Federal Aviation Administration, and the National Aeronautics and Space Administration, as well as medical and nuclear power industries. The history of the growth of V&V is shown in Figure 2; some agencies, like the Food and Drug Administration, are presently deciding how to incorporate V&V requirements into their policies and procedures regarding medical devices.

In many cases, V&V is governed by standards establishing software development, project management, and software quality assurance requirements. Government and industry began to develop V&V standards because managers needed a specification of

42

INITIAL RELEASE	STANDARD/REGULATION
AFR 122-9/-10 1970	"Design Certification Program for Nuclear Weapon System Software and Firmware" for Air Force nuclear weapon systems software (mandatory)
AFR 800-14 1975	"Acquisition Management: Acquisition and Support Procedures for Computer Resources in Systems" for acquisition of major Air Force embedded computer systems
MIL-STD-1679 1978	"Software Development" for Navy systems
JCMPO INST 8020.1 1981	"Safety Studies, Reviews, and Evaluation Involving Nuclear Weapon Systems" for Navy nuclear cruise missile weapon systems software (mandatory)
ANSI/IEEE - ANS 7.4.3.2 1982	"Application Criteria for Programmable Digital Computer Systems in Safety Systems of Nuclear Power Generating Stations" for Nuclear power generation embedded software
FIPSPUB101 1983	"Guideline for Lifecycle Validation, Verification, and Testing of Computer Software" for general guidance to computer software industry
DoD-STD-2167A and 2168 1985-1988	"Defense System Software Development: Quality Program" for development of DoD mission critical computer system software
ANSI/IEEE-STD 1012 1986	"Standard for Software Verification and Validation Plans" for any software development
NASA SMAP GUIDEBOOKS 1986	"Software Verification and Validation for Project Managers" for software intensive systems for NASA
FIPSPUB132 1987	"Guideline for Software Verification and Validation Plans" for uniform and minimum requirements of V&V; adopts ANSI/IEEE 1012
ANSI/ANS 10.4 1987	"Guidelines for V&V of Scientific and Engineering Computer Programs for the Nuclear Industry" for scientific and engineering programs (R&D) for nuclear power industry
ARMY REG 50-4 1988	"Software Studies and Reviews of Nuclear Weapon Systems" for Army nuclear weapon system software
AFSCP 800-5 1988	"Software Independent Verification and Validation" for Air Force systems with potential to cause death, system loss, more than $550K damage to equipment, or severe illness/injury
FAA STD 0-26 (DRAFT) —	"National Aerospace System Software Development" for national airspace system-advanced automation system
FDA XXX —	"Reviewer Guidance for Computer Controlled Medical Devices" for computer controlled medical devices.

Figure 2. History of V&V standards

this methodology for contract procurements and for monitoring the technical performance of V&V efforts.

2.1. Objectives of V&V

Software V&V comprehensively analyzes and tests software during all stages of its development and maintenance in parallel with the development process to

- determine that it performs its intended functions correctly,
- ensure that it performs no unintended functions, and
- measure and assess the quality and reliability of software.

As a systems engineering discipline, software V&V also assesses, analyzes, and tests the software on how it interfaces with, influences the performance of, or reacts to stimuli from the system elements. These systems elements include the following:

- hardware including all hardware directly or indirectly influenced by the software,
- users that interface with the software or other system components,
- external software linked to the system,
- and system environment (such as stimuli, inputs, operating conditions).

A software error needs the system elements to be present for the error to cause an effect. Software performing correctly in one set of conditions or system environment could fail under different system stimuli. Therefore, in order to determine software correctness, software V&V must always consider the system when performing V&V analysis and testing. When performed in parallel with software development, V&V yields several benefits:

- uncovers high risk errors early, giving the design team time to evolve a comprehensive solution rather than forcing them into a make-shift fix to accommodate software deadlines.

- evaluates the correctness of products against system and software requirements.

- provides management with in-depth technical visibility into the quality and progress of the development effort that is continuous and comprehensive, not just at major review milestones (which may occur infrequently).

- provides the user an incremental preview of system performance, with the chance to make early adjustments.

- provides decision criteria for whether or not to proceed to the next development phase.

2.2 Responsibilities of V&V Versus Other Groups

While the techniques of V&V may be applied by anyone involved in software development and maintenance, a comprehensive V&V effort is often administered by a specific group. Similarly, a project may have developers who are from the end-user organization or who may be contractors or subcontractors. Other groups may be quality assurance, configuration management, and data management. The organizational structure of a project depends on many characteristics (for example, size, complexity, purpose of the software, corporate culture, project standards, contractual requirements). Often these groups are separate, but in many instances, especially for small projects, the structure is not as diverse. On these projects, the functions described in this section must still be performed but may be distributed differently.

A functional view demonstrates how V&V and other groups complement their software quality responsibilities. The software development group builds the software product to satisfy the established quality and performance requirements. The group relies on its quality assurance group, systems engineering, requirements analysts, designers, program-

mers, testers, data and configuration management specialists, documentation specialists, and others.

The quality assurance group verifies that the development process and products conform to established standards and procedures. Via reviews, audits, inspections, and walk-throughs, it acts as a formal check and balance to monitor and evaluate software as it is being built. The software systems engineering group ensures that the software product satisfies system requirements and objectives. It uses techniques such as simulations to gain reasonable assurance that system requirements are satisfied.

The configuration and data management groups monitor and control the software program versions and data during its development, using such techniques as formal audits, change control records, traceability of requirements, and sign-off records. The user group must provide assurance that the software product satisfies user requirements and operational needs. Typically, it uses techniques such as formal design reviews and acceptance testing.

Like software systems engineering, the V&V group is responsible for verifying that the software product at each life cycle phase satisfies software quality attributes and that the software product at each phase satisfies the requirements of the previous phase. In addition, V&V is responsible for validating that the software satisfies overall system requirements and objectives. The activities are directed at the software, but V&V must consider how the software interacts with the rest of the system, including hardware, users, other software, and with other external systems. V&V maintains its own configuration and data management functions on programs, data, and documentation received from the development organization to assure V&V discrepancy reports are against controlled documents and to repeat V&V tests against controlled software releases. V&V responsibilities may vary for different projects; some examples are provided in Section 2.3.

V&V documentation, evaluation, and testing are different from those conducted by other groups. The quality assurance group reviews documents for compliance to standards. V&V performs a check on the technical correctness of the document contents. V&V may perform in-depth evaluation by such activities as rederiving the algorithms from basic principles, computing timing data to verify response time requirements, and developing control flow diagrams to identify missing and erroneous requirements. V&V may suggest, if appropriate, alternative approaches. V&V testing is usually separate from the development group's testing. In some cases, V&V may use development test plans and results and supplement them with additional tests.

2.3 Organizing a V&V Effort

A major influence on the responsibilities of V&V, and its relationship to other groups, is to whom V&V reports. Four methods of organizing a V&V effort are described: independent; embedded in the development system engineering group; embedded in the development quality assurance group; and embedded in the user group.

The traditional approach is that the V&V group is independent of the development group and is called *independent V&V* or *IV&V*. As IV&V, the V&V group reports directly to the system program manager, often the acquisition organization, who manages the separate development and IV&V teams. In this relationship, the V&V organization establishes formal procedures for receiving software releases and documentation from the development team. V&V sends all evaluation reports and discrepancy reports to both the program manager and development group. To maintain an unbiased technical viewpoint, V&V may selectively use results or procedures from the quality assurance or systems engineering groups.

The V&V tasks are oriented toward engineering analysis (for example, algorithm analysis, control/data flow analysis) and comprehensive testing (such as simulation). The objective is to develop an independent assessment of the software quality and to determine whether the software satisfies critical system requirements. Advantages of this approach are detailed analysis and test of software requirements; an independent determination of how well the software performs; and early detection of high-risk software and system errors. Disadvantages are higher cost to the project and additional development interfaces.

When the V&V group is embedded in development's systems engineering group, the V&V tasks are to review the group's engineering analyses (for instance, algorithm development, sizing/timing) and testing (like test evaluation or review of the adequacy of the development test planning document). In some instances, the V&V organization may be the independent test team for the systems engineering group, sharing some test data generated by the systems engineering group. V&V's results are reviewed and monitored by the systems engineering and quality assurance groups. An independent V&V group reporting to the systems engineering group is another alternative. Advantages to using systems engineering personnel in the V&V tasks are minimum cost impact to the project; no system learning for the staff; and no additional development interfaces. A disadvantage is the loss of engineering analysis objectivity.

When the V&V group is embedded in the development's quality assurance group, its tasks take on a monitoring, auditing, and reviewing content (for example, audit performance, audit support, test witnessing, walk-through support, documentation review). In these tasks, the V&V group is part of quality assurance and maintains its relationship to systems engineering and other development groups in the same manner as quality assurance. The main advantages of embedding V&V as part of quality assurance are low cost to the project and bringing V&V analysis capabilities into reviews, audits, and inspections. A disadvantage is the loss of an independent software systems analysis and test capability.

When the V&V group is embedded in the user group, its tasks are an extension of the users' responsibilities. The tasks consist of configuration management support of development products, support of formal reviews, user documentation evaluation, test witnessing, test evaluation of the development test planning documents, and user testing support (for example, user acceptance testing and installation and checkout testing).

As an extension of the user group, the V&V group would receive formal software product deliverables and provide comments and data to the development project management that distributes the information to its own development team. An advantage of this approach is the strong systems engineering and user perspective that can be brought to bear on the software product during development. Main disadvantages are loss of detailed analysis and test of incremental software products (since these typically are not formal deliverables) and error detection and feedback to the development team constrained by the frequency of formal product deliverables. If the user group has an IV&V group reporting to it, then the disadvantages can be overcome. However, in this instance, the project incurs the disadvantage of having an additional development interface.

2.4 Applying V&V to a Software Life Cycle

The minimum recommended V&V tasks that are required by the ANSI/IEEE Standard for Software Verification and Validation Plans (SVVP) [1] for the development phases are shown in Figure 3. They are considered effective and applicable to all types of software applications. Tailoring V&V for a specific project is accomplished by adding tasks to the minimum set or, when appropriate, deleting V&V tasks. Figures 4a and 4b list additional V&V tasks in the life cycle phase where they most likely can be applied, and considerations that one might use to assign the tasks to V&V. The SVVP standard requires V&V management tasks spanning the entire software life cycle and V&V tasks for operations and maintenance.

PHASE	TASKS	KEY ISSUES
Concept	Concept-documentation evaluation	Satisfy user needs; constraints of interfacing systems
Requirements Definition	Traceability analysis	Trace of requirements to concept
	Requirements validation	Correctness, consistency, completeness, accuracy, readability, and testability; satisfaction of system requirements
	Interface analysis	Hardware, software, and operator interfaces
	Begin planning for V&V system testing	Compliance with functional requirements; performance at interfaces; adequacy of user documentation; performance at boundaries
	Begin planning for V&V acceptance testing	Compliance with acceptance requirements
Design	Traceability analysis	Trace of design to requirements
	Design evaluation	Correctness; design quality
	Interface analysis	Correctness; data items across interface
	Begin planning for V&V component testing	Compliance to design; timing and accuracy; performance at boundaries
	Begin planning for V&V integration testing	Compliance with functional requirements; timing and accuracy; performance at stress limits
Implementation	Traceability analysis	Trace of source code to design
	Code evaluation	Correctness; code quality
	Interface analysis	Correctness; data/control access across interfaces
	Component test execution	Component integrity
Test	V&V integration-test execution	Correctness of subsystem elements; subsystem interface requirements
	V&V system-test execution	Entire system at limits and user stress conditions
	V&V acceptance-test execution	Performance with operational scenarios
Installation and Checkout	Installation-configuration audit	Operations with site dependencies; adequacy of installation procedure
	V&V final report generation	Disposition of all errors; summary of V&V results

4/89-0036-SMV-6480

Figure 3. Minimum set of recommended V&V tasks

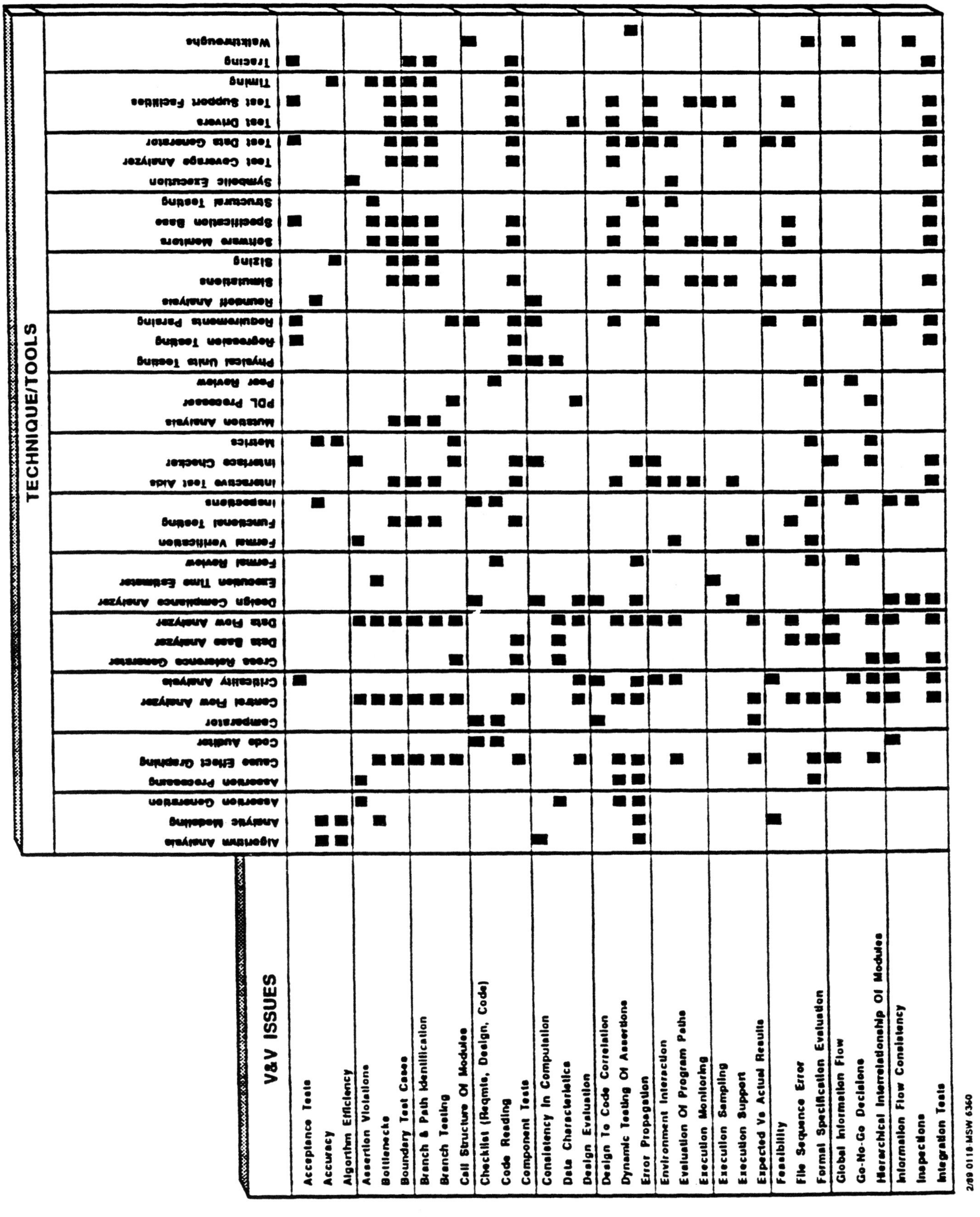

TECHNIQUE/TOOLS

V&V ISSUES

Acceptance Tests
Accuracy
Algorithm Efficiency
Assertion Violations
Bottlenecks
Boundary Test Cases
Branch & Path Identification
Branch Testing
Call Structure Of Modules
Checklist (Reqmts, Design, Code)
Code Reading
Component Tests
Consistency In Computation
Data Characteristics
Design Evaluation
Design To Code Correlation
Dynamic Testing Of Assertions
Error Propagation
Environment Interaction
Evaluation Of Program Paths
Execution Monitoring
Execution Sampling
Execution Support
Expected Vs Actual Results
Feasibility
File Sequence Error
Formal Specification Evaluation
Global Information Flow
Go-No-Go Decisions
Hierarchical Interrelationship Of Modules
Information Flow Consistency
Inspections
Integration Tests

Algorithm Analysis
Analytic Modeling
Assertion Generation
Assertion Processing
Cause Effect Graphing
Code Auditor
Comparator
Control Flow Analyzer
Criticality Analysis
Cross Reference Generator
Data Base Analyzer
Data Flow Analyzer
Design Compliance Analyzer
Execution Time Estimator
Formal Review
Formal Verification
Functional Testing
Inspections
Interactive Test Aids
Interface Checker
Metrics
Mutation Analysis
PDL Processor
Peer Review
Physical Units Testing
Regression Testing
Requirements Parsing
Roundoff Analysis
Simulations
Sizing
Software Monitors
Specification Base
Structural Testing
Symbolic Execution
Test Coverage Analyzer
Test Data Generator
Test Drivers
Test Support Facilities
Timing
Tracing
Walkthroughs

Figure 4a. Cross-reference of V&V issues to V&V techniques/tools (part 1)

47

2/89 0118-MSW 6350

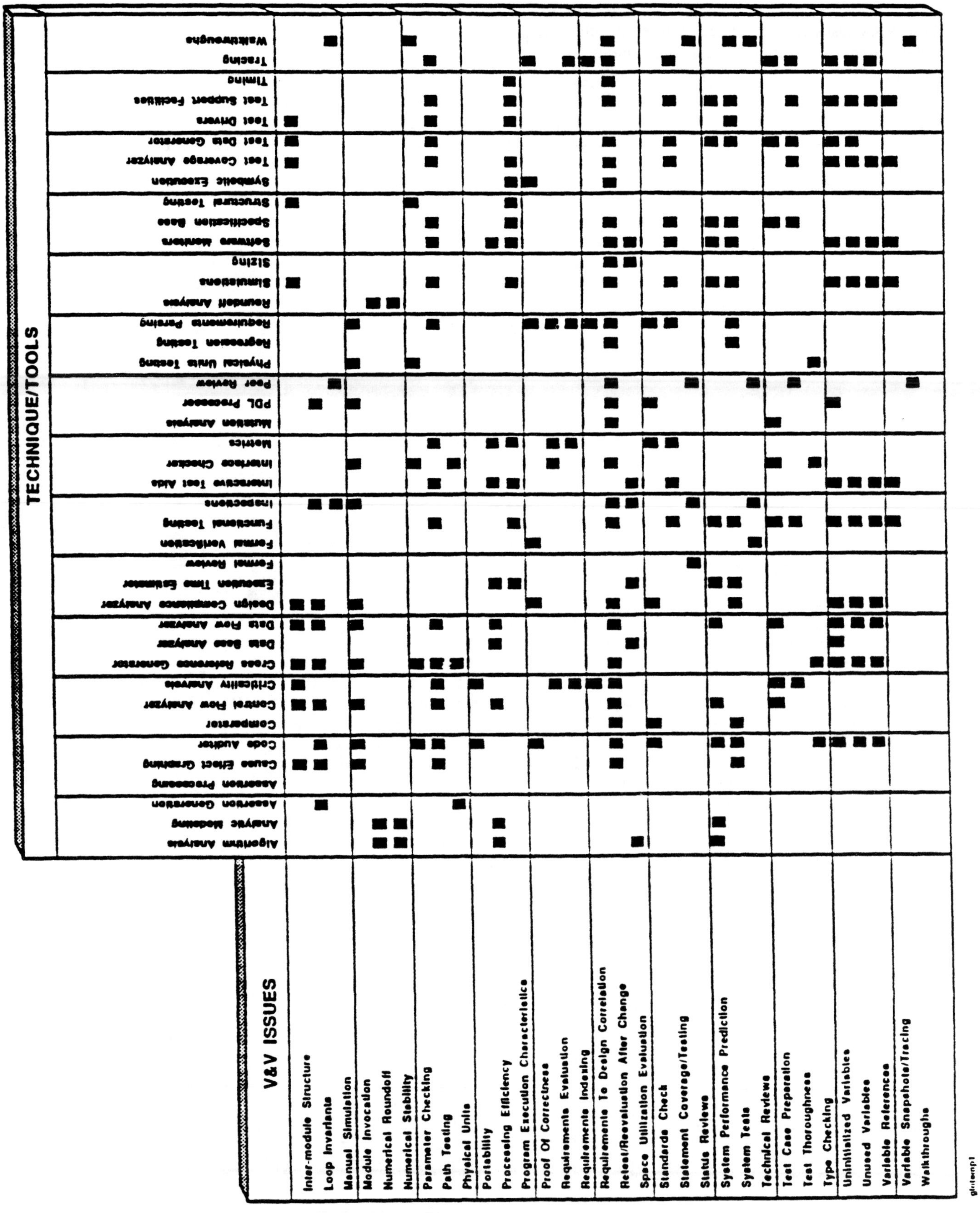

TECHNIQUE/TOOLS

Walkthroughs
Tracing
Timing
Test Support Facilities
Test Drivers
Test Data Generator
Test Coverage Analyzer
Symbolic Execution
Structural Testing
Specification Base
Software Monitors
Sizing
Simulations
Roundoff Analysis
Requirements Parsing
Regression Testing
Physical Units Testing
Peer Review
PDL Processor
Mutation Analysis
Metrics
Interface Checker
Interactive Test Aids
Inspections
Functional Testing
Formal Verification
Formal Review
Execution Time Estimator
Design Compliance Analyzer
Data Flow Analyzer
Data Base Analyzer
Cross Reference Generator
Criticality Analysis
Control Flow Analysis
Comparator
Code Auditor
Cause Effect Graphing
Assertion Processing
Assertion Generation
Analytic Modeling
Algorithm Analysis

V&V ISSUES

Inter-module Structure
Loop Invariants
Manual Simulation
Module Invocation
Numerical Roundoff
Numerical Stability
Parameter Checking
Path Testing
Physical Units
Portability
Processing Efficiency
Program Execution Characteristics
Proof Of Correctness
Requirements Evaluation
Requirements Indexing
Requirements To Design Correlation
Retest/Reevaluation After Change
Space Utilization Evaluation
Standards Check
Statement Coverage/Testing
Status Reviews
System Performance Prediction
System Tests
Technical Reviews
Test Case Preparation
Test Thoroughness
Type Checking
Uninitialized Variables
Unused Variables
Variable References
Variable Snapshot/Tracing
Walkthroughs

gl+tempt

Figure 4b. Cross-reference of V&V issues to V&V techniques/tools (part 2).

These V&V tasks can be applied to different life cycle models simply by mapping traditional phases to the new model. Examples include variations of the traditional waterfall, Boehm's spiral development [2], rapid prototyping, or evolutionary development models [3]. The V&V tasks are fully consistent with the ANSI/IEEE standard for software life cycle processes [4]. The SVVP standard specifies minimum input and output requirements for each V&V task; a V&V task may not begin without specific inputs, and is not completed until specific outputs are completed.

2.4.1 Management of V&V

Management tasks for V&V span the entire life cycle. These tasks are to plan the V&V process; coordinate and interpret performance and quality of the V&V effort; report discrepancies promptly to the user or development group; identify early problem trends and focus V&V activities on them; provide a technical evaluation of the software performance and quality at each major software program review (so a determination can be made of whether the software product has satisfied its requirements well enough to proceed to the next phase); and assess the full impact of proposed software changes. The output of the V&V activities consists of the Software Verification and Validation Plan (SVVP), task reports, phase summary reports, final report, and discrepancy report.

Major steps in developing the V&V plan are as follows:

- Define the quality and performance objectives (for example, verify conformance to specifications, verify compliance with safety and security objectives, assess efficiency and quality of software, and assess performance across the full operating environment).

- Characterize the types of problems anticipated in the system and define how they would show up in the software.

- Select the V&V analysis and testing techniques to effectively detect the system and software problems.

The plan may include a tool acquisition and development plan and a personnel training plan. The SVVP is a living document, constantly being revised as knowledge accumulates about the characteristics of the system, the software, and the problem areas in the software.

An important V&V management activity is to monitor the V&V technical progress and quality of results. At each V&V phase, planned V&V activities are reviewed and new tasks are added to focus on the critical performance/quality functions of the software and its system. The monitoring activity conducts formal reviews of V&V discrepancy reports and technical evaluation results to provide a check of their correctness and accuracy. V&V studies (reference) have shown that responding to discrepancy reports and V&V evaluation reports consumes the largest portion of a development group's interface time with the V&V group.

Boehm and Papaccio [5] report that the Pareto analysis, that is, 20 percent of the problems cause 80 percent of the rework costs, applies to software; they recommend that V&V "focus on identifying and eliminating the specific high-risk problems to be encountered by a software project." Part of the V&V management activities is to define and use methods to address these problems of rework and risk management. One method of providing early delivery of information is to have the development team deliver incremental documents (for example, draft portions) and "software builds" to V&V. A software build represents a basic program skeleton containing portions of the full software capabilities. Each successive build integrates additional functions into the skeleton, permitting early software deliveries to V&V in an orderly development process. Based on discrepancy or progress reports, software program management can make the technical and management decisions to refocus the V&V and development team onto the program's specific problem areas of the software.

Criticality analysis, a method to locate and reduce high-risk problems, is performed at the beginning of a project. It identifies the functions and modules that are required to implement critical program functions or quality requirements (such as safety and security). The steps of the analysis are:

- Develop a block diagram or control-flow diagram of the system and its software. Each block or control flow box represents a system or software function (module).

- Trace each critical function or quality requirement through the block or control flow diagram.

- Classify all traced software functions (modules) as critical to either the proper execution of critical software functions or the quality requirements.

- Focus additional analysis on these traced software functions (modules).

- Repeat criticality analysis for each life cycle phase to observe whether the implementation details shift the emphasis of the criticality.

The criticality analysis may be used along with the cross-reference matrix of Figure 4 to identify V&V techniques to address high-risk concerns.

2.4.2 Concept Definition Evaluation

In this phase, the principal V&V task is to evaluate the concept documentation to determine whether the defined concept satisfies user needs and project objectives (for example, statement of need, project initiation memo) in terms of system performance requirements, feasibility (for example, overestimation of hardware capabilities), completeness, and accuracy. The evaluation also identifies major constraints of interfacing systems and constraints/limitations of the proposed approach and assesses the allocation of system functions to hardware and software, where appropriate. The evaluation assesses the criticality of each software item defined in the concept.

Most of the techniques in the cross-reference matrix of Figure 4 are described in a publication from the National Institute of Standards and Technology (formerly the National Bureau of Standards), the National Bureau of Standards Special Publication 500-93, "Software Validation, Verification, and Testing Technique and Tool Reference Guide" [6]. In Figure 4, the techniques are mapped against specific V&V issues [7] which they address.

While the use of the cross-reference matrix for selecting V&V techniques and tools is applicable to all phases, its use is illustrated in this report only for examining how concept feasibility is determined. Of several techniques for determining feasibility of a software concept and architecture, those most commonly used are requirements parsing, analytic modeling, and simulation. These give the V&V analyst a way to parse the desired performance requirements from other concept data; analytically model the desired performance; and, by creating a simulation of the proposed operating environment, execute test data to determine whether the resulting performance matches the desired performance. Criticality analysis is especially useful during concept definition to identify the critical functions and their distribution within the system architecture. Test data generation defines the performance limits of the proposed system concept; the predicted performance can be verified by using the simulation to execute the test scenario.

2.4.3 Requirements Analysis

Poorly specified software requirements (for example, incorrect, incomplete, ambiguous, or not testable) contribute to software cost overruns and problems with reliability due to incorrect or misinterpreted requirements or functional specifications. Software often encounters problems in the maintenance phase because general requirements (such as maintainability, quality, and reusability) were not accounted for during the original development. The problem of outdated requirements is intensified by the very complexity of the problems being solved (which causes uncertainty in the intended system performance requirements) and by continual changes in requirements to incorporate new technologies. V&V tasks verify the completeness of all the requirements.

The most commonly used V&V tasks for requirements analysis are control flow analysis, data flow analysis, algorithm analysis, and simulation. Control and data flow analysis are most applicable for real-time and data-driven systems. These flow analyses transform logic and data requirements text into graphic flows that are easier to analyze than the text. PERT, state transition, and transaction diagrams are examples of control flow diagrams. Algorithm analysis involves rederivation of equations or evaluation of the suitability of specific numerical techniques. Simulation is used to evaluate the interactions of large, complex systems with many hardware, user, and other interfacing software components.

Another activity in which V&V plays an important role is test management. V&V looks at all testing for the software system and ensures that comprehensive testing is planned. V&V test planning begins in the requirements phase and spans almost the full range of life cycle phases. Test planning activities encompass four separate types of testing—component, integration, system, and acceptance testing. The planning activities result in documentation for each test type consisting of a test plan, test design, test case, and test procedure documents.

Component testing verifies the design and implementation of software units or modules. Integration testing verifies functional requirements as the software components are integrated, directing attention to internal software interfaces and external hardware and operator interfaces. System testing validates the entire software program against system requirements and software performance objectives. V&V system tests validate that the software executes correctly in a simulated system environment. They do not duplicate or replace the user and development team's responsibilities of testing the entire system requirements (for example, those pertaining to hardware, software, and users).

Acceptance testing validates the software against V&V acceptance criteria, defining how the software should perform with other completed software and hardware. One of the distinctions between V&V system and acceptance testing is that the former uses a laboratory environment in which some system features are simulated or performed by nonoperational hardware or software, and the latter uses an operational environment with final configurations of other system hardware and software. V&V acceptance testing usually consists of tests to demonstrate that the software will execute as predicted by V&V system testing in the operational environment. Full acceptance testing is the responsibility of the user and the development systems engineering group.

2.4.4 Design Evaluation

The minimum set of design phase V&V tasks—traceability, interface analysis, and design evaluation—assures that (1) requirements are not misrepresented or incompletely implemented, (2) unintended requirements are not designed into the solution by oversight or indirect inferences, and (3) requirements are not left out of the design. Design errors can be introduced by implementation constraints relating to timing, data structures, memory space, and accuracy, even though the basic design satisfies the functional requirements.

The most commonly used V&V tasks are algorithm analysis, database analysis, timing/sizing analysis, and simulation. In this phase, algorithm analysis examines the correctness of the equations or numerical techniques as in the requirements analysis phase, but also examines truncation and round-off effects, numerical precision of word storage and variables (for example, single- versus extended-precision arithmetic), and data-typing influences. Database analysis is particularly useful for programs that store program logic in data parameters. A logic analysis of these data values is required to determine the effect these parameters have on program control. Timing/sizing analysis is useful for real-time programs having response time requirements and constrained memory execution space requirements.

2.4.5 Implementation (Code) Evaluation

Clerical and syntactical errors have been greatly reduced through use of structured programming and reuse of code, adoption of programming standards and style guides, availability of more capable computer languages, better compiler diagnostics and automated support, and, finally, more knowledgeable programmers. Nevertheless, problems still occur in translating design into code and can be detected with some V&V analyses.

Commonly used V&V tasks are control flow analysis, database analysis, regression analysis, and sizing/timing analysis. For large code developments, control flow diagrams showing the hierarchy of main routines and their subfunctions are useful in understanding the flow of program control. Database analy-

sis is performed on programs with significant data storage to ensure that common data and variable regions are used consistently between all call routines; data integrity is enforced and no data or variable can be accidentally overwritten by overflowing data tables; and data typing and use are consistent throughout all program elements.

Regression analysis is used to reevaluate requirements and design issues whenever any significant code change is made. This technique ensures project awareness of the original system requirements. Sizing/timing analysis is done during incremental code development and compared against predicted values. Significant deviations between actual and predicted values is a possible indication of problems or the need for additional examination.

Another area of concern to V&V is the ability of compilers to generate object code that is functionally equivalent to the source code, that is, reliance on the correctness of the language compiler to make data-dependent decisions about abstract, programmer-coded information. For critical applications, this problem is solved by validating the compiler or by validating that the object code produced by the compiler is functionally equivalent to the source.

Other tasks indicated in Figure 4 for code evaluation are walk-throughs, code inspections, and audits. These tasks occur in interactive meetings attended by a team that usually includes at least one member from the development group. Other members may belong to the development group or to other groups involved in software development. The duration of these meetings is usually no more than a few hours in which code is examined on a line-by-line basis.

In these dynamic sessions, it may be difficult to examine the code thoroughly for control logic, data flow, database errors, sizing, timing and other features that may require considerable manual or automated effort. Advance preparation for these activities may be necessary and includes additional V&V tasks shown in Figure 4. The results of these tasks provide appropriate engineering information for discussion at meetings where code is evaluated. Regardless of who conducts or participates in walk-throughs and inspections, V&V analyses may be used to support these meetings.

2.4.6 Testing

As already described, V&V test planning is a major portion of V&V test activities and spans several phases. A comprehensive test management approach to testing recognizes the differences in objectives and strategies of different types of testing. Effective testing requires a comprehensive understanding of the system. Such understanding develops from systematically analyzing the software's concept, requirements, design, and code. By knowing internal software details, V&V testing is effective at probing for errors and weaknesses that reveal hidden faults. This is considered structural, or white-box, testing. It often finds errors for which some functional, or black-box, test cases can produce the correct output despite internal errors.

Functional test cases execute part or all of the system to validate that the user requirement is satisfied; these test cases cannot always detect internal errors that will occur under special circumstances. Another V&V test technique is to develop test cases that violate software requirements. This approach is effective at uncovering basic design assumption errors and unusual operational use errors. In general, the process of V&V test planning is as effective in detecting errors as test executions.

The most commonly used optional tasks are regression analysis and test, simulation, and user document evaluation. User document evaluation is performed for systems having an important operator interface. For these systems, V&V reviews the user documentation to verify that the operating instructions are consistent with the operating characteristics of the software. The system diagnostic messages and operator recovery procedures are examined to ensure their accuracy and correctness with the software operations.

2.4.7 Installation and Checkout Activities

During installation and checkout, V&V validates that the software operates correctly with the operational hardware system and with other software, as specified in the interface specifications. V&V may verify the correctness and adequacy of the installation procedures and certify that the verified and validated software is the same as the executable code delivered for installation. There may be several installation sites with site-dependent parameters. V&V verifies that the program has been accurately tailored for these parameters and that the configuration of the delivered product is the correct one for each installation.

Optional V&V tasks most commonly used in this phase are regression analysis and test, simulation, and test certification. Any changes occurring from installation and test are reviewed using regression analysis and test to verify that our basic requirement and design assumptions affecting other areas of the program have not been violated. Simulation is used to test operator procedures and to help isolate any installation problems. Test certification, especially in critical software systems, is used to demonstrate that the delivered software product is identical to the software product subjected to V&V.

2.4.8 Operations and Maintenance Evaluation and Test

For each software change made in the operations and maintenance phase, all life cycle phase V&V activities of Figure 3 are considered and possibly repeated to ensure that nothing is overlooked. V&V activities are added or deleted to address the type of software change made. In many cases, an examination of the proposed software change shows that V&V needs to repeat its activities on only a small portion of the software. Also, some V&V activities such as concept documentation evaluation require little or no effort to verify a small change. Small changes can have subtle but significant side effects in a software program.

If V&V is not done in the normal software development phase, then the V&V in the maintenance phase must consider performing a selected set of V&V activities for earlier life cycle phases. Some of the activities may include generating requirements or design information from source code, a process known as reverse engineering. While costly and time-consuming, it is necessary when the need exists for a rigorous V&V effort.

2.5 Effectiveness of V&V

The effectiveness of V&V varies with project size and complexity, and V&V staff experience. Two study results are provided as follows:

Radatz's 1981 study [8] for Rome Air Development Center reported V&V effectiveness results for four large IV&V projects ranging from 90K to 176K lines of code. The projects were real-time command and control, missile tracking, and avionics programs and a time-critical batch trajectory computation program. The projects varied from 2.5 to 4 years to develop. Two projects started V&V at the requirements phase, one at the code phase, and one at testing. The V&V organization used a staff of 5 to 12 persons per project.

In 1982, McGarry [9] reported on three small projects at the Software Engineering Laboratory (SEL) at NASA Goddard Space Flight Center. Three flight dynamics projects ranging in size from 10K to 50K lines of code were selected. V&V was involved in requirements and design verification, separate system testing, and validation of consistency from start to finish. The V&V effort lasted 18 months and used a staff averaging 1.1, peaking at 3, persons.

Based on these studies, some positive effects of V&V on a software project include:

Radatz Study	McGarry Study
• Errors were detected early in the development—50 percent to 89 percent detected before development testing began. • Large number of discrepancies were reported (total 1,259) on average of over 300 per program.	• Rates of uncovering errors early in the development cycle were better.
• V&V found an average 5.5 errors per thousand lines of code.	• V&V found 2.3 errors per thousand lines of code.
• Over 85 percent of the errors affected reliability and maintainability.	• Reliability of the software was no different from other SEL projects.
• Effect on programmer productivity was very positive—total savings per error of 1.3 to 6.1 hours.	• Productivity of the development teams was the lowest of any SEL project (due to the V&V interface).
• The largest savings amounted to 92–180 percent of V&V costs.	• Cost rate to fix all discovered errors was no less than in any other SEL project.

- Better quality (for example, complete, consistent, readable, testable) and more stable requirements.
- More rigorous development planning, at least to interface with the V&V organization.
- Better adherence by the development organization to programming language and development standards and configuration management practices.
- Early error detection and reduced false starts.
- Better schedule compliance and progress monitoring.
- Greater project management visibility into interim technical quality and progress.
- Better criteria and results for decision-making at formal reviews and audits.

Some negative effects of V&V on a software development project include:

- Additional project cost of V&V (10–30 percent).
- Additional interface involving the development team, user, and V&V organization (for example, attendance at V&V status meeting, anomaly resolution meeting).
- Lower development staff productivity if programmers and engineers spend time explaining the system to V&V analysts and resolving invalid anomaly reports.

Some steps can be taken to minimize the negative effects and to maximize the positive effects of V&V. To recover much of the V&V costs, V&V is started early in the software requirements phase. The interface activities for documentation, data, and software deliveries between developer and V&V groups should be considered as an inherently necessary step required to evaluate intermediate development products. This is a necessary by-product of doing what's right in the beginning.

To offset unnecessary costs, V&V must organize its activities to focus on critical areas of the software so that it uncovers critical errors for the development group and thereby results in significant cost savings to the development process. To do this, V&V must use its criticality analysis to identify critical areas and it must scrutinize each discrepancy before release to ensure that no false or inaccurate information is released to prevent the development group from wasting time on inaccurate or trivial reports.

To eliminate the need to have development personnel train the V&V staff, it is imperative that V&V select personnel who are experienced and knowledgeable about the software and its engineering application. When V&V engineers and computer scientists reconstruct the specific details and idiosyncracies of the software as a method of reconfirming the correctness of engineering and programming assumptions, they often find subtle errors. They gain detailed insight into the development process and an ability to spot critical errors early. The cost of the development interface is minimal, and at times nonexistent, when the V&V assessment is independent.

3. Standards and Guidelines For Planning and Managing V&V

The documents in Figure 5 establish guidelines for planning and managing a V&V effort. Their activities produce information that satisfies the life cycle requirements of standards governing projects. They have the following features:

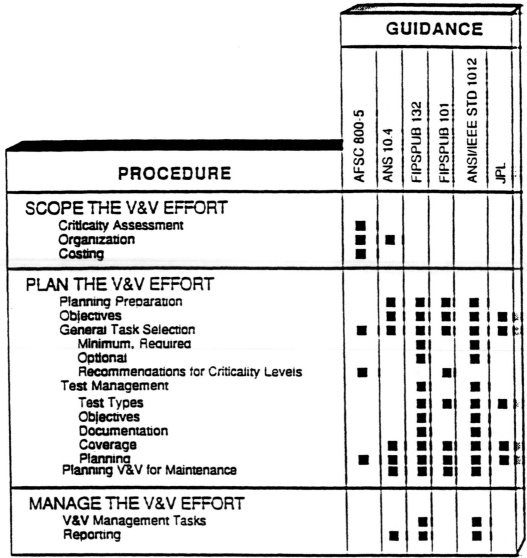

Figure 5. Planning V&V with guidance from V&V documents

4/89-0040-SMV-6480

- Require V&V to determine how well evolving and final software products comply with their requirements.
- Permit users to select specific techniques to satisfy their application needs.
- Identify a broad spectrum of V&V analysis and test activities.

Brief descriptions of each document follow:

The NIST issued the Federal Information Processing Standards Publication "Guideline for Lifecycle Validation, Verification and Testing," in 1983 [10]. This document was followed in 1987 with the "Guideline for Software Verification and Validation Plans," [11] which adopted the ANSI/IEEE standard for V&V planning [1]. Reference to the guideline, FIPSPUB 132, includes reference to the ANSI/IEEE specifications.

FIPSPUB 101 permits performance of V&V activities by developers, the same organization, or some independent group [10]. FIPSPUB 132 /IEEE 1012 does not require independence; it does require the SVVP to "define the relationship of V&V to other efforts such as development, quality assurance, configuration or data management, or end user" [1,11]. Internal and external lines of communication to V&V must be defined; V&V could occur independently or within one of the other efforts.

The Air Force pamphlet, "AFSC /AFLCP 800-5 Software Independent Verification and Validation," [12] is concerned only with software IV&V. It describes V&V activities typically performed by an independent V&V group separate from the developer's quality assurance group required by DOD-STD-2167A Standard, "Defense System Software Development" [13]. The AF pamphlet provides the criteria for selecting an independent V&V group.

The V&V activities of "Guidelines for the Verification and Validation of Scientific and Engineering Computer Programs for the Nuclear Industry," ANS 10.4, [14] may be performed by the program developer, as a task separate from development, or by an IV&V agent. The guideline contains an example of a division of V&V responsibilities.

The "Independent Verification and Validation of Computer Software: Methodology" from the Jet Propulsion Laboratory (JPL) [15] states that V&V activities should be performed independently of the development organization to ensure effectiveness and integrity of the V&V effort. The document allows flexibility in selecting the extent of the detailed V&V effort it describes.

4. Summary

Software V&V is a proven systems engineering discipline for generating correct and quality software. In addition to early error detection and correction benefits, software V&V has become a powerful risk management tool by providing the detailed technical insight into the "true" performance of the software. All software V&V is performed with a system perspective to ensure that the software is solving the "right problem."

Acknowledgments

The following people have provided substantive guidance to the authors through their reviews of this report: Dr. William Bryan, Grumman Data Systems; Fletcher Buckley, General Electric Company; Taz Daughtrey, Babcock and Wilcox; Dr. Herbert Hecht, SoHar, Incorporated; Tom Kurihara, Department of Defense; Dr. Jerome Mersky, Logicon, Incorporated; George Tice, Mentor Graphics Corporation; Dr. Richard Thayer, California State University–Sacramento, and Dr. N. Pat Wilburn, Columbia Software.

References

[1] ANSI/IEEE Std.1012-1986, "Standard for Software Verification and Validation Plans," IEEE, Inc., New York, NY, Nov. 1986.

[2] Boehm, B.W., "A Spiral Model of Software Development and Enhancement," *Computer*, May 1988, pp. 61–72.

[3] Davis, A.M., E.H. Bersoff, and E.R. Comer, "A Strategy for Comparing Alternative Software Development Life Cycle Models," *IEEE Trans. Software Eng.*, Vol. 14, No. 10, Oct. 1988, pp. 1453-1461.

[4] ANSI/IEEE 1074-1991, "Standard for Software Life Cycle Processes," IEEE, Inc., New York, NY.

[5] Boehm, B.W., and P.N. Papaccio, "Understanding and Controlling Software Costs," *IEEE Trans. Software Eng.*, Oct. 1988.

[6] Powell, P.B., "Software Validation, Verification and Testing Technique and Tool Reference Guide," *National Bureau of Standards Special Publication 500-93*, National Institute of Standards and Technology, Gaithersburg, MD 20899, 1982.

[7] Adrion, W.R., M.A. Branstad, and J.C. Cherniavsky, "Validation, Verification, and Testing of Computer Software," *ACM Computing Surveys*, Vol. 14, No. 2, June 1982.

[8] Radatz, J.W., "Analysis of IV&V Data," RADC-TR-81-145, Logicon, Inc., Rome Air Development Center, Griffiss AFB, NY, June 1981.

[9] McGarry, F., and G. Page, "Performance Evaluation of an Independent Software Verification and Integration Process," NASA Goddard, Greenbelt, MD, SEL 81-110, September 1982.

[10] "Guideline for Lifecycle Validation, Verification and Testing of Computer Software," FIPSPUB101, National Institute of Standards and Technology, Gaithersburg, MD 20899, 1983.

[11] "Guideline for Software Verification and Validation Plans," FIPSPUB132, National Institute of Standards and Technology, Gaithersburg, MD 20899, 1987.

[12] AFSC/AFLCP 800-5 Air Force Systems Command and Air Force Logistics Command Software Independent Verification and Validation, Washington, DC, 22 May 1988.

[13] DoD-Std-2167A Military Standard Defense System Software Development, AMSC No. 4327, Department of Defense, Washington, DC, Feb. 29, 1988.

[14] ANSI/ANS-10.4-1987, "Guidelines for the Verification and Validation of Scientific and Engineering Computer Programs for the Nuclear Industry," American Nuclear Society, La Grange Park, IL 1987.

[15] Blosiu, J.O., "Independent Verification and Validation of Computer Software: Methodology," National Aeronautics and Space Administration, Jet Propulsion Laboratory, Pasadena, Calif., JPL D-576, Feb. 9, 1983.

IEEE Standard 1012-1998
Software Verification and Validation

Abstract: Uniform, minimum acceptable requirements for preparation and content of Software Quality Assurance Plans (SQAPs) are provided. This standard applies to the development and maintenance of critical software. For noncritical software, or for software already developed, a subset of the requirements of this standard may be applied.

This standard was prepared by the Life Cycle Data Harmonization Working Group of the Software Engineering Standards Committee of the IEEE Computer Society. At the time this standard was approved, the working group consisted of the following members:

Leonard L. Tripp, *Chair*

Edward Byrne	Paul R. Croll	Perry DeWeese
Robin Fralick	Marilyn Ginsberg-Finner	John Harauz
Mark Henley	Dennis Lawrence	David Maibor
Ray Milovanovic	James Moore	Timothy Niesen
Dennis Rilling	Terry Rout	Richard Schmidt
Norman F. Schneidewind	David Schultz	Basil Sherlund
Peter Voldner	Ronald Wade	

Sponsored by

Software Engineering Standards Committee
of the IEEE Computer Society

The Institute of Electrical and Electronic Engineering, Inc.
345 East 47th Street, New York, NY 10017-2394, USA

October 20, 1998

Table of Contents

IEEE Standard 1012-1998
Software Verification and Validation

IEEE Standard for Software Verification and Validation

1. Overview

Software verification and validation (V&V) processes determine whether development products of a given activity conform to the requirements of that activity, and whether the software satisfies its intended use and user needs. This determination may include analysis, evaluation, review, inspection, assessment, and testing of software products and processes. V&V processes assess the software in the context of the system, including the operational environment, hardware, interfacing software, operators, and users.

This V&V standard is a process standard that addresses all software life cycle processes, including acquisition, supply, development, operation, and maintenance. This standard is compatible with all life cycle models. Not all life cycle models use all of the life cycle processes listed in this standard.

The user of this standard may invoke those software life cycle processes and the associated V&V processes that apply to the project. A description of the software life cycle processes may be found in ISO/IEC 12207 [ISO/IEC 12207: 1995].

1.1 Purpose

The purpose of this standard is to:

a) Establish a common framework for V&V processes, activities, and tasks in support of all software life cycle processes, including acquisition, supply, development, operation, and maintenance processes;

b) Define the V&V tasks, required inputs, and required outputs;

c) Identify the minimum V&V tasks corresponding to software integrity levels using a four-level scheme; and

d) Define the content of a Software V&V Plan (SVVP).

1.2 Field of application

This standard applies to software being developed, maintained, and reused. The term *software* also includes firmware, microcode, and documentation.

Software is a key component that contributes to system behavior and performance. This relationship requires that software V&V processes must take software interactions with all system components into consideration. The user of this standard should consider V&V as part of the software life cycle processes defined by industry standards such as ISO/IEC 12207 [ISO/IEC 12207: 1995], IEEE Std 1074-1997 [IEEE Std 1074-1997], or IEEE/EIA Std 12207.0-1996 [IEEE/EIA 12207.0-1996].

1.3 V&V objectives

V&V processes provide an objective assessment of software products and processes throughout the software life cycle. This assessment demonstrates whether the software requirements and system requirements (e.g., those allocated to software) are correct, complete, accurate, consistent, and testable. Other objectives of performing V&V are to:

a) Facilitate early detection and correction of software errors;

b) Enhance management insight into process and product risk; and

c) Support the software life cycle processes to ensure compliance with program performance, schedule, and budget requirements.

The verification process provides supporting evidence that the software and its associated products:

a) Comply with requirements (e.g., for correctness, completeness, consistency, accuracy) for all life cycle activities during each life cycle process (acquisition, supply, development, operation, and maintenance);

b) Satisfy standards, practices, and conventions during life cycle processes; and

c) Establish a basis for assessing the completion of each life cycle activity and for initiating other life cycle activities.

The validation process provides supporting evidence that the software satisfies system requirements allocated to software, and solves the right problem (e.g., correctly models physical laws, or implements system business rules).

V&V support primary life cycle processes. V&V processes are most effective when conducted in parallel with software development processes; otherwise, V&V objectives may not be realized. In this standard, V&V processes are discussed together because the V&V activities and tasks are interrelated and complementary. In some circumstances, the verification process may be viewed as a process separate from the validation process. The V&V task criteria described in Table 1 uniquely define the compliance requirements for V&V processes

1.4 Organization of the standard

This standard is organized into paragraphs (Paragraphs 1 through 7), tables (Tables 1 through 3), and figures (Figures 1 through 3). Paragraph 1, Figures 1, 2, and 3, and Table 3 contain informative material that provides illustrations, examples, and process flow diagrams useful in understanding and using this standard. Paragraphs 2, 3, 4, 5, 6, and 7 and Tables 1 and 2 contain the mandatory V&V requirements for this standard. *Tables 1, 2, and 3 can be found in the complete version of this standard. They were too large to be contained here.*

Paragraph 2 lists normative references. Paragraph 3 provides a definition of terms, abbreviations, and conventions. Paragraph 4 explains the concept of using software integrity levels for determining the scope and rigor of V&V processes. Paragraph 5 describes each primary software life cycle process and lists the V&V activities and tasks associated with the life cycle process. Paragraph 6 describes the V&V reporting, administrative, and documentation requirements. Paragraph 7 outlines the content of a Software Verification and Validation Plan (SVVP).

Tables 1, 2, and 3 are the focal point of this standard, containing detailed V&V process, activity, and task requirements. Table 1 provides V&V task descriptions, inputs, and outputs for each life cycle process. Table 2 lists minimum V&V tasks required for different software integrity levels. Table 3 provides a list of optional V&V tasks and their suggested applications in the life cycle. These optional V&V tasks may be added to the minimum V&V tasks to tailor the V&V effort to project needs and application specific characteristics.

Figure 1 provides an example of an overview of the V&V inputs, outputs, and minimum V&V tasks for the highest software integrity level (Integrity Level 4). Figure 2 provides guidelines for scheduling V&V test planning, execution, and verification activities. An example of a phased life cycle model was used in Figures 1 and 2 to illustrate a mapping of the ISO/IEC 12207 life cycle processes to the V&V activities and tasks described in this standard.

This standard implements the V&V framework using the terminology of process, activity, and task. Figure 3 illustrates how the V&V processes are subdivided into activities, which in turn have associated tasks. Hereafter, the term *V&V effort* is used to refer to the framework of the V&V processes, activities, and tasks.

1.5 Audience

The audience for this standard is software suppliers, acquirers, developers, maintainers, V&V practitioners, operators, and managers in both the supplier and acquirer organizations.

1.6 Compliance

The word *shall* identify mandatory requirements to claim compliance with this standard. The words *should* or *may* indicate optional tasks that are not required to claim compliance to this standard.

Any software integrity level scheme may be used with this standard. The software integrity level scheme used in this standard is not mandatory, but rather, establishes the minimum V&V tasks for the referenced software integrity scheme. To demonstrate compliance to this standard whenever different software integrity schemes are used, the user should map the project-specific software integrity scheme to the integrity scheme used in this standard. This mapping establishes the minimum V&V tasks that should be assigned to the project. Compliance with this standard requires that this mapping and the associated minimum V&V tasks be documented in the SVVP.

Not all V&V efforts are initiated at the start of the life cycle process of acquisition and continued through the maintenance process. If a project uses only selected life cycle processes, then compliance with this standard is achieved if the minimum V&V tasks are implemented for the associated life cycle processes selected for the project.

As in all cases, the minimum V&V tasks are defined by the software integrity level assigned to the software. For life cycle processes that are not used by the project, the V&V requirements and tasks for those life cycle processes are optional V&V tasks invoked as needed at the discretion of the project. Specific software development methods and technologies (such as automated code generation from detailed design) may eliminate development steps or combine several development steps into one. Therefore, a corresponding adaptation of the minimum V&V tasks is permitted.

When this standard is invoked for existing software and the required V&V inputs are not available, then V&V tasks may use other available project input sources or may reconstruct the needed inputs to achieve compliance with this standard.

1.7 Disclaimer

This standard establishes minimum criteria for V&V processes, activities, and tasks. The implementation of these criteria does not, however, automatically ensure compliance to system or mission objectives, or prevent adverse consequences (e.g., loss of life, mission failure, loss of system safety or security, financial or social loss). Compliance with this standard does not absolve any party from any social, moral, financial, or legal obligations.

1.8 Limitations

None.

2. References

The supporting references and citations pertaining to this standard can be found in the *Centralized IEEE Software Engineering Standards References* contained in this tutorial. These references provide additional information on software verification and validation to assist in understanding and applying this standard.

3. Definitions

The definitions and acronyms pertaining to this standard can be found in the *Centralized IEEE Software Engineering Standards Glossary* contained in this tutorial. These are contextual definitions serving to augment the understanding of software verification and validation activities as described within this standard. Additional relevant terms are defined in IEEE Std 610.12-1990.

4. V&V software integrity levels

4.1 Software integrity levels

Software exhibits different criticality based upon its intended use and application of the system to critical or noncritical uses. Some software systems affect critical, life-sustaining systems, while other software systems are noncritical, standalone research tools. Software criticality is a description of the intended use and application of a system. This standard uses a software integrity level approach to quantify software criticality. Software integrity levels denote a range of software criticality values necessary to maintain risks within acceptable limits. These software properties may include safety, security, software complexity, performance, reliability, or other characteristics. Critical, high-integrity software typically requires a larger set and more rigorous application of V&V tasks.

For planning the V&V processes, software integrity levels are generally assigned early in the development process, preferably during the system requirements analysis and architecture design activities. The software integrity level can be assigned to software requirements, functions, group of functions, or software components or subsystems. The assigned software integrity levels may vary as the software evolves. Design, coding, procedural, and technology implementation features selected by the development organization can raise or lower the software criticality and the associated software integrity levels assigned to the software. Risk mitigation approaches acceptable to the acquirer also may be used to reduce software criticality, thus allowing the selection of a lower integrity level. The software integrity level assignment is continually updated and reviewed by conducting the V&V criticality analysis task throughout the software development process.

This standard does not mandate the use of the software integrity scheme referenced in this standard. The user of this standard may select any software integrity scheme (such as from existing standards) that defines the requirements for assigning software integrity levels. The software integrity levels established for a project result from agreements among the acquirer, supplier, developer, and independent assurance authorities (e.g., a regulatory body or responsible agency). The V&V effort shall specify a software integrity scheme if one is not already defined. This

61

standard shall use the following four-level software integrity scheme listed in Table 4 as a method to define the minimum V&V tasks that are assigned to each software integrity level:

Table 4: Four Level Software Integrity Scheme

Criticality	Description	Level
High	Selected function affects critical performance of the system.	4
Major	Selected function affects important system performance.	3
Moderate	Selected function affects system performance, but workaround strategies can be implemented to compensate for loss of performance.	2
Low	Selected function has noticeable effect on system performance but only creates inconvenience to the user if the function does not perform in accordance with requirements.	1

To identify the minimum V&V tasks that apply to a different selected software integrity level scheme, the user of the standard shall map this standard's software integrity scheme and associated minimum V&V tasks to their selected software integrity level scheme. The mapping of the software integrity level scheme and the associated minimum V&V tasks shall be documented in the SVVP.

This standard does not apply to those portions of the software for which none of the software integrity criteria apply (e.g., those software portions below Level 1). The basis for assigning software integrity levels to software components shall be documented in a V&V Task Report and V&V Final Report.

The integrity level assigned to reusable software shall be in accordance with the integrity level scheme adopted for the project, and the reusable software shall be evaluated for use in the context of its application.

The V&V processes are tailored to specific system requirements and applications through the selection of a software integrity level with its corresponding minimum V&V tasks and the addition of optional V&V tasks. The addition of optional V&V tasks allows the V&V effort to address application specific characteristics of the software.

5. V&V processes

V&V processes support the management process (Paragraph 5.1), acquisition process (Paragraph 5.2), supply process (Paragraph 5.3), development process (Paragraph 5.4), operation process (Paragraph 5.5), and maintenance process (Paragraph 5.6). The minimum V&V activities and tasks supporting the above processes are referenced in the following subparagraphs and defined in Table 1. This paragraph's subtitles are the same as subtitles in Table 1 to correlate the requirements of the following subparagraphs with Table 1 tasks.

The V&V effort shall comply with the task descriptions, inputs, and outputs as described in Table 1. The V&V effort shall perform the minimum V&V tasks as specified in Table 2 for the assigned software integrity level. If the user of this standard has selected a different software integrity level scheme, then the mapping of that integrity level scheme to Table 2 shall define the minimum V&V tasks for each of the user's software integrity levels.

Not all software projects include each of the life cycle processes listed above. To be in compliance with this standard, the V&V processes shall address all those life cycle processes used by the software project.

Some V&V activities and tasks include analysis, evaluations, and tests that may be performed by multiple organizations (e.g., software development, project management, quality assurance, V&V). For example, risk analysis and hazard analysis are performed by project management, the development organization, and the V&V effort. The V&V effort performs these tasks to develop the supporting basis of evidence showing whether the software product satisfies its requirements. These V&V analyses are complementary to other analyses and do not eliminate or replace the analyses performed by other organizations. The degree to which these analyses efforts are coordinated with other organizations shall be documented in the organizational responsibility section of the SVVP.

The user of this standard shall document the V&V processes in the SVVP and shall define the information and

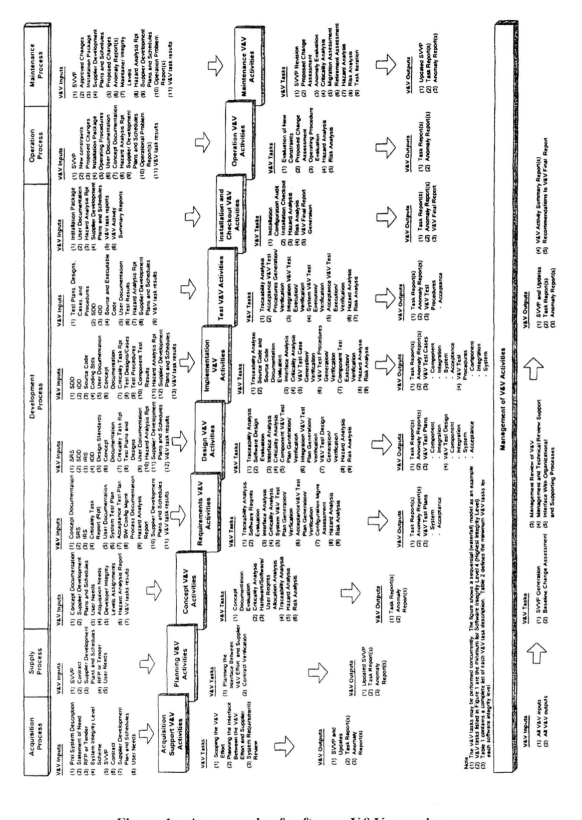

Figure 1 – An example of software V&V overview

63

facilities necessary to manage and perform these processes, activities, and tasks, and to coordinate those V&V processes with other related aspects of the project. The results of V&V activities and tasks shall be documented in task reports, activity summary reports, anomaly reports, V&V test documents, and the V&V Final Report.

5.1 Process: management

The management process contains the generic activities and tasks, which may be employed by any party that manages its respective processes. The management tasks are to 1) prepare the plans for execution of the process, 2) initiate the implementation of the plan, 3) monitor the execution of the plan, 4) analyze problems discovered during the execution of the plan, 5) report progress of the processes, 6) ensure products satisfy requirements, 7) assess evaluation results, 8) determine whether a task is complete, and 9) check the results for completeness.

5.1.1 Activity: management of V&V

The Management of V&V activity is performed in all software life cycle processes and activities. This activity continuously reviews the V&V effort, revises the SVVP as necessary based upon updated project schedules and development status, and coordinates the V&V results with the developer and other supporting processes such as quality assurance, configuration management, and reviews and audits. The Management of V&V assesses each proposed change to the system and software, identifies the software requirements that are affected by the change, and plans the V&V tasks to address the change. For each proposed change, the Management of V&V assesses whether any new hazards or risks are introduced in the software, and identifies the impact of the change to the assigned software integrity levels. V&V task planning is revised by adding new V&V tasks or increasing the scope and intensity of existing V&V tasks if software integrity levels or hazards or risks are changed. The Management of V&V activity monitors and evaluates all V&V outputs. Through the use of V&V metrics and other qualitative and quantitative measures, this V&V activity develops program trend data and possible risk issues that are provided to the developer and acquirer to effect timely notification and resolution. At key program milestones (e.g., requirements review, design review, test readiness), the Management of V&V consolidates the V&V results to establish supporting evidence whether to proceed to the next set of software development activities. Whenever necessary, the Management of V&V determines whether a V&V task needs to be re-performed as a result of developer changes in the software program.

The V&V effort shall perform, as appropriate for the selected software integrity level, the minimum V&V tasks for Management of V&V from the following list:

a) Task: Software Verification and Validation Plan (SVVP) Generation;

b) Task: Baseline Change Assessment;

c) Task: Management Review of V&V;

d) Task: Management and Technical Review Support; and

e) Task: Interface With Organizational and Supporting Processes.

5.2 Process: acquisition

The acquisition process begins with the definition of the need (e.g., statement of need) to acquire a system, software product, or software service. The process continues with the preparation and issuance of a request for proposal (e.g., bid request, tender), selection of a supplier, and management of the acquisition process through to the acceptance of the system, software product, or software service. The V&V effort uses the acquisition process to scope the V&V effort, plan interfaces with the supplier and acquirer, and review the draft systems requirements contained in the request for proposal.

5.2.1 Activity: acquisition support V&V

The Acquisition Support V&V activity addresses project initiation, request for proposal, contract preparation, supplier monitoring, and acceptance and completion.

The V&V effort shall perform, as appropriate for the selected software integrity level, the minimum V&V tasks for Acquisition Support V&V from the following list:

a) Task: Scoping the V&V Effort;

b) Task: Planning the Interface Between the V&V Effort and Supplier; and

c) Task: System Requirements Review.

5.3 Process: supply

The supply process is initiated by either a decision to prepare a proposal to answer an acquirer's request for proposal or by signing and entering into a contract with the acquirer to provide the system, software product, or software service. The process continues with the determination of procedures and resources needed to manage the project, including development of project plans and execution of the plans through delivery of the system, software product, or software service to the acquirer. The V&V effort uses the supply process products to verify that the request for proposal requirements and contract requirements are consistent and satisfy user needs. The V&V planning activity uses the contract requirements, including program schedules, to revise and update the interface planning between the supplier and acquirer.

5.3.1 Activity: planning V&V

The Planning V&V activity addresses the initiation, preparation of response, contract, planning, execution and control, review and evaluation, and delivery and completion activities.

The V&V effort shall perform, as appropriate for the selected software integrity level, the minimum V&V tasks for Planning V&V from the following list:

a) Task: Planning the Interface Between the V&V Effort and Supplier; and

b) Task: Contract Verification.

5.4 Process: development

The development process contains the activities and tasks of the developer. The process contains the activities for requirements analysis, design, coding, integration, testing, and installation and acceptance related to software products. The V&V activities verify and validate these software products. The V&V activities are organized into Concept V&V, Requirements V&V, Design V&V, Implementation V&V, Test V&V, and Installation and Checkout V&V.

5.4.1 Activity: concept V&V

The Concept V&V activity represents the delineation of a specific implementation solution to solve the user's problem. During the Concept V&V activity, the system architecture is selected, and system requirements are allocated to hardware, software, and user interface components. The Concept V&V activity addresses system architectural design and system requirements analysis. The objectives of V&V are to verify the allocation of system requirements, validate the selected solution, and ensure that no false assumptions have been incorporated in the solution.

The V&V effort shall perform, as appropriate for the selected software integrity level, the minimum V&V tasks for Concept V&V from the following list:

a) Task: Concept Documentation Evaluation;

b) Task: Criticality Analysis;

c) Task: Hardware/Software/User Requirements Allocation Analysis;

d) Task: Traceability Analysis;

e) Task: Hazard Analysis; and

f) Task: Risk Analysis.

5.4.2 Activity: requirements V&V

The Requirements V&V activity defines the functional and performance requirements, interfaces external to the software, qualification requirements, safety and security requirements, human factors engineering, data definitions, user documentation for the software, installation and acceptance requirements, user operation and execution requirements, and user maintenance requirements. The Requirements V&V activity addresses software requirements analysis. The objectives of V&V are to ensure the correctness, completeness, accuracy, testability, and consistency of the requirements.

The V&V effort shall perform, as appropriate for the selected software integrity level, the minimum V&V tasks for

Requirements V&V from the following list:

a) Task: Traceability Analysis;

b) Task: Software Requirements Evaluation;

c) Task: Interface Analysis;

d) Task: Criticality Analysis;

e) Task: System V&V Test Plan Generation and Verification;

f) Task: Acceptance V&V Test Plan Generation and Verification;

g) Task: Configuration Management Assessment;

h) Task: Hazard Analysis; and

i) Task: Risk Analysis.

5.4.3 Activity: design V&V

In the Design V&V activity, software requirements are transformed into an architecture and detailed design for each software component. The design includes databases and interfaces (external to the software, between the software components, and between software units). The Design V&V activity addresses software architectural design and software detailed design. The objectives of V&V are to demonstrate that the design is a correct, accurate, and complete transformation of the software requirements and that no unintended features are introduced.

The V&V effort shall perform, as appropriate for the selected software integrity level, the minimum V&V tasks for Design V&V from the following list:

a)   Task: Traceability Analysis;

b)   Task: Software Design Evaluation;

c)   Task: Interface Analysis;

d)   Task: Criticality Analysis;

e)   Task: Component V&V Test Plan Generation and Verification;

f)   Task: Integration V&V Test Plan Generation and Verification;

g)   Task: V&V Test Design Generation and Verification;

h)   Task: Hazard Analysis; and

i)   Task: Risk Analysis.

5.4.4 Activity: implementation V&V

The Implementation V&V activity transforms the design into code, database structures, and related machine executable representations. The Implementation V&V activity addresses software coding and testing. The objectives of V&V are to verify and validate that these transformations are correct, accurate, and complete.

The V&V effort shall perform, as appropriate for the selected software integrity level, the minimum V&V tasks for Implementation V&V from the following list:

a)   Task: Traceability Analysis;

b)   Task: Source Code and Source Code Documentation Evaluation;

c)   Task: Interface Analysis;

d)   Task: Criticality Analysis;

e)   Task: V&V Test Case Generation and Verification;

f)   Task: V&V Test Procedure Generation and Verification;

g)   Task: Component V&V Test Execution and Verification;

h)   Task: Hazard Analysis; and

i) Task: Risk Analysis.

5.4.5 Activity: test V&V

The Test V&V activity covers software testing, software integration, software qualification testing, system integration, and system qualification testing. The Test V&V activity and its relationship to the software life cycle is shown in Figure 2. The objectives of V&V are to ensure that the software requirements and system requirements allocated to software are satisfied by execution of integration, system, and acceptance tests.

For software integrity Levels 3 and 4, the V&V effort shall generate its own V&V software and system test products (e.g., plans, designs, cases, procedures), execute and record its own tests, and verify those plans, designs, cases, procedures, and test results against software requirements. For software integrity Levels 1 and 2, the V&V effort shall verify the development process test activities and products (e.g., test plans, designs, cases, procedures, and test execution results).

The V&V effort shall perform, as appropriate for the selected software integrity level, the minimum V&V tasks for Test V&V from the following list:

a) Task: Traceability Analysis;

b) Task: Acceptance V&V Test Procedure Generation and Verification;

c) Task: Integration V&V Test Execution and Verification;

d) Task: System V&V Test Execution and Verification;

e) Task: Acceptance V&V Test Execution and Verification;

f) Task: Hazard Analysis; and

g) Task: Risk Analysis.

5.4.6 Activity: installation and Checkout V&V

The Installation and Checkout V&V activity is the installation of the software product in the target environment and the acquirer's acceptance review and testing of the software product. The Installation and Checkout V&V activity addresses software installation and software acceptance support. The objectives of V&V are to verify and validate the correctness of the software installation in the target environment.

The V&V effort shall perform, as appropriate for the selected software integrity level, the minimum V&V tasks for Installation and Checkout V&V from the following list:

a) Task: Installation Configuration Audit;

b) Task: Installation Checkout;

c) Task: Hazard Analysis;

d) Task: Risk Analysis; and

e) Task: V&V Final Report Generation.

5.5 Process: operation

The operation process covers the operation of the software product and operational support to users. The Operation V&V activity evaluates the impact of any changes in the intended operating environment, assesses the effect on the system of any proposed changes, evaluates operating procedures for compliance with the intended use, and analyzes risks affecting the user and the system.

5.5.1 Activity: operation V&V

The Operation V&V activity is the use of the software by the end user in an operational environment. The Operation V&V activity addresses operational testing, system operation, and user support. The objectives of V&V are to evaluate new constraints in the system, assess proposed changes and their impact on the software, and evaluate operating procedures for correctness and usability. The V&V effort shall perform, as appropriate for the selected software integrity level, the minimum V&V tasks for Operation V&V from the following list:

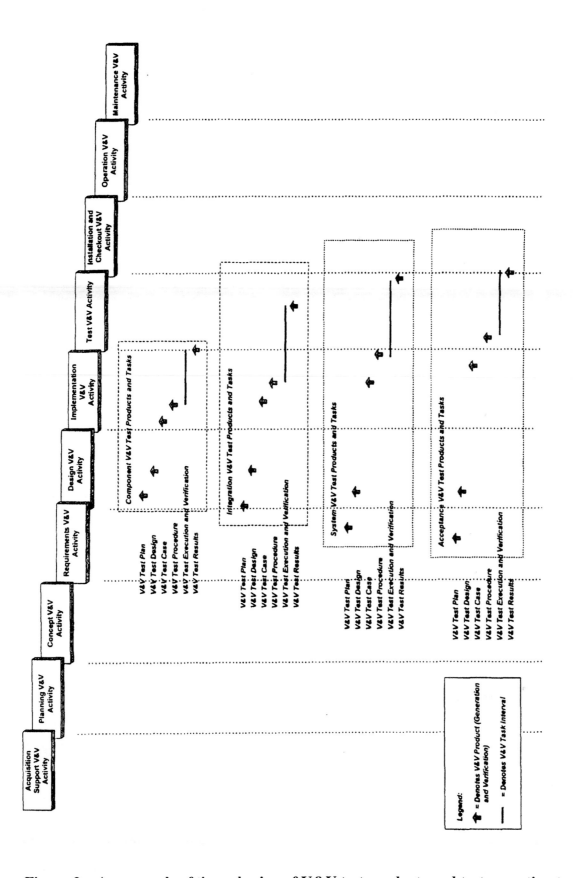

Figure 2—An example of time phasing of V&V test products and test execution tasks

a) Task: Evaluation of New Constraints;

b) Task: Proposed Change Assessment;

c) Task: Operating Procedures Evaluation;

d) Task: Hazard Analysis; and

d) Task: Risk Analysis.

5.6 Process: maintenance

The maintenance process is activated when the software product undergoes modifications to code and associated documentation caused by a problem or a need for improvement or adaptation. The Maintenance V&V activity addresses modifications (e.g., enhancements, additions, deletions), migration, or retirement of the software during the operation process.

Modifications of the software shall be treated as development processes and shall be verified and validated as described in Paragraph 5.1 (management process), and Paragraph 5.4 (development process) of this standard. Software integrity level assignments shall be assessed during the maintenance process. The software integrity level assignments shall be revised as appropriate to reflect the requirements of the maintenance process. These modifications may be derived from requirements specified to correct software errors (e.g., corrective), to adapt to a changed operating environment (e.g., adaptive), or to respond to additional user requests or enhancements (e.g., perfective).

5.6.1 Activity: maintenance V&V

The Maintenance V&V activity covers modifications (e.g., corrective, adaptive, and perfective), migration, and retirement of software. Migration of software is the movement of software to a new operational environment. For migrating software, the V&V effort shall verify that the migrated software meets the requirements of Paragraph 5.4 through Paragraph 5.5. The retirement of software is the withdrawal of active support by the operation and maintenance organization, partial or total replacement by a new system, or installation of an upgraded system.

If the software was verified under this standard, the standard shall continue to be followed in the maintenance process. If the software was not verified under this standard and appropriate documentation is not available or adequate, the V&V effort shall determine whether the missing or incomplete documentation should be generated. In making this determination of whether to generate missing documentation, the minimum V&V requirements of the assigned software integrity level should be taken into consideration.

The Maintenance V&V activity addresses problem and modification analysis, modification implementation, maintenance review/acceptance, migration, and software retirement. The objectives of V&V are to assess proposed changes and their impact on the software, evaluate anomalies that are discovered during operation, assess migration requirements, assess retirement requirements, and re-perform V&V tasks.

The V&V effort shall perform, as appropriate for the selected software integrity level, the minimum V&V tasks for Maintenance V&V from the following list:

a) Task: SVVP Revision;

b) Task: Proposed Change Assessment;

c) Task: Anomaly Evaluation;

d) Task: Criticality Analysis;

e) Task: Migration Assessment;

f) Task: Retirement Assessment;

g) Task: Hazard Analysis;

h) Task: Risk Analysis; and

i) Task: Task Iteration.

6. Software V&V reporting, administrative, and documentation requirements

6.1 V&V reporting requirements

V&V reporting occurs throughout the software life cycle. The SVVP shall specify the content, format, and timing of all V&V reports. The V&V reports shall constitute the Software Verification and Validation Report (SVVR). The V&V reports shall consist of required V&V reports (e.g., V&V Task Reports, V&V Activity Summary Reports, V&V Anomaly Reports, and V&V Final Report). The V&V reports may also include optional reports. Reporting requirements are described in Paragraph 7.6 of this standard.

6.2 V&V administrative requirements

The SVVP describes the V&V administrative requirements that support the V&V effort. These V&V administrative requirements shall consist of the following:

a) Anomaly Resolution and Reporting;

b) Task Iteration Policy;

c) Deviation Policy;

d) Control Procedures; and

e) Standards, Practices, and Conventions.

V&V administrative requirements are described in Paragraph 7.7 of this standard.

6.3 V&V documentation requirements

6.3.1 V&V test documentation

V&V Test documentation requirements shall include the test plans, designs, cases, procedures, and results for component, integration, system, and acceptance testing. The V&V test documentation shall comply with project-defined test document purpose, format, and content (e.g., see IEEE Std 829-1983 [IEEE STD 829-1983]). The V&V task descriptions for component, integration, system, and acceptance testing are described in Table 1.

6.3.2 SVVP documentation

The V&V effort shall generate an SVVP that addresses the topics described in Paragraph 7 of this standard. If there is no information pertinent to a topic, the SVVP shall contain the phrase, "This topic is not applicable to this plan," with an appropriate reason for the exclusion. Additional topics may be added to the plan. If some SVVP material appears in other documents, the SVVP may repeat the material or make reference to the material. The SVVP shall be maintained throughout the life of the software.

The SVVP shall include the V&V documentation requirements defined in Paragraph 6.1, 6.2, and 6.3.1.

7. SVVP outline

The SVVP shall contain the content as described in Paragraphs 7.1 through 7.8 of this standard. The user of this standard may adopt any format and section numbering system for the SVVP. The SVVP section numbers listed in this standard are provided to assist the readability of this standard and are not mandatory to be in compliance with this standard.

An example SVVP outline is shown in the boxed text in Table 5.

7.1 (SVVP Section 1) Purpose

The SVVP shall describe the purpose, goals, and scope of the software V&V effort, including waivers from this standard. The software project for which the Plan is being written and the specific software processes and products covered by the software V&V effort shall be identified.

7.2 (SVVP Section 2) Referenced documents

The SVVP shall identify the compliance documents, documents referenced by the SVVP, and any supporting documents supplementing or implementing the SVVP.

7.3 (SVVP Section 3) Definitions

The SVVP shall define or reference all terms used in the SVVP, including the criteria for classifying an anomaly as a critical anomaly. All abbreviations and notations used in the SVVP shall be described.

Table 5: Software V&V Plan Outline (example)

1. Purpose
2. Referenced Documents
3. Definitions
4. V&V Overview
   4.1 Organization
   4.2 Master Schedule
   4.3 Software Integrity Level Scheme
   4.4 Resources Summary
   4.5 Responsibilities
   4.6 Tools, Techniques, and Methods
5. V&V Processes
   5.1 Process: Management
      5.1.1 Activity: Management of V&V
   5.2 Process: Acquisition
      5.2.1 Activity: Acquisition Support V&V
   5.3 Process: Supply
      5.3.1 Activity: Planning V&V
   5.4 Process: Development
      5.4.1 Activity: Concept V&V
      5.4.2 Activity: Requirements V&V
      5.4.3 Activity: Design V&V
      5.4.4 Activity: Implementation V&V
      5.4.5 Activity: Test V&V
      5.4.6 Activity: Installation and Checkout V&V
   5.5 Process: Operation
      5.5.1 Activity: Operation V&V
   5.6 Process: Maintenance
      5.6.1 Activity: Maintenance V&V
6. V&V Reporting Requirements
7. V&V Administrative Requirements
   7.1 Anomaly Resolution and Reporting
   7.2 Task Iteration Policy
   7.3 Deviation Policy
   7.4 Control Procedures
   7.5 Standards, Practices, and Conventions
8. V&V Documentation Requirements

7.4 (SVVP Section 4) V&V overview

The SVVP shall describe the organization, schedule, software integrity level scheme, resources, responsibilities, tools, techniques, and methods necessary to perform the software V&V.

7.4.1 (SVVP Section 4.1) Organization

The SVVP shall describe the organization of the V&V effort, including the degree of independence required. The SVVP shall describe the relationship of the V&V processes to other processes such as development, project management, quality assurance, and configuration management. The SVVP shall describe the lines of communication within the V&V effort, the authority for resolving issues raised by V&V tasks, and the authority for approving V&V products.

7.4.2 (SVVP Section 4.2) Master schedule

The SVVP shall describe the project life cycle and milestones. It shall summarize the schedule of V&V tasks and task results as feedback to the development, organizational, and supporting processes (e.g., quality assurance and configuration management). V&V tasks shall be scheduled to be re-performed according to the task iteration policy.

If the life cycle used in the SVVP differs from the life cycle model in this standard, this section shall describe how all requirements of the standard are satisfied (e.g., by cross-referencing to this standard).

7.4.3 (SVVP Section 4.3) Software integrity level scheme

The SVVP shall describe the agreed upon software integrity level scheme established for the system and the mapping of the selected scheme to the model used in this standard. The SVVP shall document the assignment of software integrity levels to individual components (e.g., requirements, detailed functions, software modules, subsystems, or other software partitions), where there are differing software integrity levels assigned within the program. For each SVVP update, the assignment of software integrity levels shall be reassessed to reflect changes that may occur in the integrity levels as a result of architecture selection, detailed design choices, code construction usage, or other development activities.

7.4.4 (SVVP Section 4.4) Resources summary

The SVVP shall summarize the V&V resources, including staffing, facilities, tools, finances, and special procedural requirements (e.g., security, access rights, and documentation control).

7.4.5 (SVVP Section 4.5) Responsibilities

The SVVP shall identify an overview of the organizational element(s) and responsibilities for V&V tasks.

7.4.6 (SVVP Section 4.6) Tools, techniques, and methods

The SVVP shall describe documents, hardware and software V&V tools, techniques, methods, and operating and test environment to be used in the V&V process. Acquisition, training, support, and qualification information for each tool, technology, and method shall be included.

Tools that insert code into the software shall be verified and validated to the same rigor as the highest software integrity level of the software. Tools that do not insert code shall be verified and validated to assure that they meet their operational requirements. If partitioning of tool functions can be demonstrated, only those functions that are used in the V&V processes shall be verified to demonstrate that they perform correctly for their intended use.

The SVVP shall document the metrics to be used by V&V, and shall describe how these metrics support the V&V objectives.

7.5 (SVVP Section 5) V&V processes

The SVVP shall identify V&V activities and tasks to be performed for each of the V&V processes described in Paragraph5 of this standard, and shall document those V&V activities and tasks. The SVVP shall contain an overview of the V&V activities and tasks for all software life cycle processes.

7.5.1 (SVVP Sections 5.1 through 5.6) "Software life cycle"

The SVVP shall include Sections 5.1 through 5.6 for V&V activities and tasks as shown in SVVP Outline in the boxed text.

The SVVP shall address the following eight topics for each V&V activity:

a) *V&V Tasks.* The SVVP shall identify the V&V tasks to be performed. Table 1 describes the minimum V&V tasks, task criteria, and required inputs and outputs. Table 2 specifies the minimum V&V tasks that shall be performed for each software integrity level.

   The minimum tasks for software integrity Level 4 are consolidated in graphic form in Figure 1.

   Optional V&V tasks may also be performed to augment the V&V effort to satisfy project needs. Optional V&V tasks are listed in Table 3. The list in Table 3 is illustrative and not exhaustive. The standard allows for optional V&V tasks to be used as appropriate.

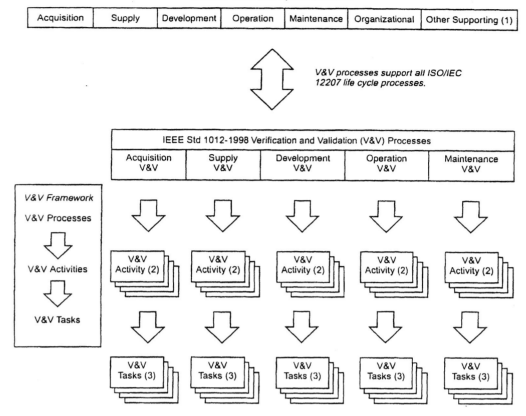

ISO/IEC 12207 Life Cycle Processes

| Acquisition | Supply | Development | Operation | Maintenance | Organizational | Other Supporting (1) |

V&V processes support all ISO/IEC 12207 life cycle processes.

IEEE Std 1012-1998 Verification and Validation (V&V) Processes

| Acquisition V&V | Supply V&V | Development V&V | Operation V&V | Maintenance V&V |

V&V Framework

V&V Processes

V&V Activities

V&V Tasks

V&V Activity (2)

V&V Tasks (3)

NOTES:

1 — "Other Supporting Processes" consist of "Documentation," "Configuration Management," "Quality Assurance," "Joint Review," "Audit," and "Problem Resolution."

2 — Management of V&V activity is concurrent with all V&V activities.

3 — The task description, inputs, and outputs of all V&V tasks are included in Table 1.

Figure 3—Framework of V&V processes, activities, and tasks hierarchy

Some V&V tasks are applicable to more than one software integrity level. The degree of rigor and intensity in performing and documenting the task should be commensurate with the software integrity level. As the software integrity level decreases, so does the required scope, intensity, and degree of rigor associated with the V&V task. For example, a hazard analysis performed for software integrity Level 4 software might be formally documented and consider failures at the module level; a hazard analysis for software integrity Level 3 software may consider only significant software failures and be documented informally as part of the design review process.

Testing requires advance planning that spans several development activities. Test documentation and its occurrence at specific processes in the life cycle are shown in Figures 1 and 2.

b) *Methods and Procedures.* The SVVP shall describe the methods and procedures for each task, including on-line access, and conditions for observation/evaluation of development processes. The SVVP shall define the criteria for evaluating the task results.

c) *Inputs.* The SVVP shall identify the required inputs for each V&V task. The SVVP shall specify the source and format of each input. The inputs required for the minimum V&V tasks are identified in Table 1. Other inputs may be used. For any V&V activity and task, all of the required inputs from preceding activities and tasks may be used but for conciseness, only the primary inputs are listed in Table 1.

d) *Outputs.* The SVVP shall identify the required outputs from each V&V task. The SVVP shall specify the purpose, format, and recipients of each output. The required outputs from each of the V&V tasks are identified in Table 1. Other outputs may be produced.

The outputs of the Management of V&V and of the V&V tasks shall become inputs to subsequent processes and activities, as appropriate.

e) *Schedule.* The SVVP shall describe the schedule for the V&V tasks. The SVVP shall establish specific milestones for initiating and completing each task, for the receipt and criteria of each input, and for the delivery of each output.

f) *Resources.* The SVVP shall identify the resources for the performance of the V&V tasks. The SVVP shall specify resources by category (e.g., staffing, equipment, facilities, travel, and training.).

g) *Risks and Assumptions.* The SVVP shall identify the risks (e.g., schedule, resources, or technical approach) and assumptions associated with the V&V tasks. The SVVP shall provide recommendations to eliminate, reduce, or mitigate risks.

h) *Roles and Responsibilities.* The SVVP shall identify the organizational elements or individuals responsible for performing the V&V tasks.

7.6 (SVVP Section 6) V&V Reporting requirements

V&V reporting shall consist of Task Reports, V&V Activity Summary Reports, Anomaly Reports, and the V&V Final Report. Task report(s), V&V activity summary report(s), and anomaly report(s) are provided as feedback to the software development process regarding the technical quality of each software product and process.

V&V reporting may also include optional reports such as special study reports. The format and grouping of the V&V reports are user defined. The required V&V reports shall consist of the following:

a) *Task Reports.* V&V tasks shall document V&V task results and status, and shall be in a format appropriate for technical disclosure. Examples of Task Reports include the following:

1) Anomaly Evaluation;

2) Baseline Change Assessment;

3) Concept Documentation Evaluation;

4) Configuration Management Assessment;

5) Contract Verification;

6) Criticality Analysis;

7) Evaluation of New Constraints;

8) Hardware/Software/User Requirements Allocation Analysis;

9) Hazard Analysis;

10) Installation Checkout;

11) Installation Configuration Audit;

12) Interface Analysis;

13) Migration Assessment;

14) Operating Procedures Evaluation;

15) Proposed Change Assessment;

16) Recommendations;

17) Review Results;

18) Risk Analysis;

19) Software Design Evaluation;

20) Software Integrity Levels;

21) Software Requirements Evaluation;

22) Source Code and Source Code Documentation Evaluation;

23) System Requirements Review;

24) Test Results; and

25) Traceability Analysis.

b) *V&V Activity Summary Reports.* An Activity Summary Report shall summarize the results of V&V tasks performed for each of the following V&V activities: Acquisition Support, Planning, Concept, Requirements, Design, Implementation, Test, and Installation and Checkout. For the Operation activity and Maintenance activity, V&V Activity Summary reports may be either updates to previous V&V activity summary reports or separate documents. Each V&V Activity Summary Report shall contain the following:

1) Description of V&V tasks performed;

2) Summary of task results;

3) Summary of anomalies and resolution;

4) Assessment of software quality;

5) Identification and assessment of technical and management risks; and

6) Recommendations.

c) *Anomaly Report.* An Anomaly Report shall document each anomaly detected by the V&V effort. Each anomaly shall be evaluated for its impact on the software system and assessed as to whether it is a critical anomaly (e.g., IEEE Std 1044-1993 [IEEE STD 1044-1993]). The scope and application of V&V activities and tasks shall be revised to address the causes of these anomalies and risks. Each Anomaly Report shall contain the following:

1) Description and location in document or code;

2) Impact;

3) Cause of the anomaly and description of the error scenario;

4) Anomaly criticality level; and

5) Recommendations.

d) *V&V Final Report.* The V&V Final Report shall be issued at the end of the Installation and Checkout activity or at the conclusion of the V&V effort. The V&V Final Report shall include the following:

1) Summary of all life cycle V&V activities;

2) Summary of task results;

3) Summary of anomalies and resolutions;

4) Assessment of overall software quality;

5) Lessons learned/best practices; and

6) Recommendations.

Optional reports may include the following:

a) *Special Studies Reports.* These reports shall describe any special V&V studies conducted during the software life cycle. The title of the report may vary according to the subject matter. The reports shall document the results of technical and management tasks and shall include the following:

1) Purpose and objectives;

2) Approach; and

3) Summary of results.

b) *Other Reports.* These reports shall describe the results of tasks not defined in the SVVP. The title of the report may vary according to the subject matter. These other task reports may include, for example, quality assurance results, end user testing results, safety assessment report, or configuration and data management status results.

7.7 (SVVP Section 7) V&V administrative requirements

Administrative V&V requirements shall describe anomaly resolution and reporting, task iteration policy, deviation policy, control procedures, and standards, practices, and conventions.

7.7.1 (SVVP Section 7.1) Anomaly resolution and reporting

The SVVP shall describe the method of reporting and resolving anomalies, including the criteria for reporting an anomaly, the anomaly report distribution list, and the authority and time lines for resolving anomalies. The section shall define the anomaly criticality levels. Classification for software anomalies may be found in IEEE Std 1044-1993 [IEEE STD 1044-1993].

7.7.2 (SVVP Section 7.2) Task iteration policy

The SVVP shall describe the criteria used to determine the extent to which a V&V task shall be repeated when its input is changed or task procedure is changed. These criteria may include assessments of change, software integrity level, and effects on budget, schedule, and quality.

7.7.3 (SVVP Section 7.3) Deviation policy

The SVVP shall describe the procedures and criteria used to deviate from the Plan. The information required for deviations shall include task identification, rationale, and effect on software quality. The SVVP shall identify the authorities responsible for approving deviations.

7.7.4 (SVVP Section 7.4) Control procedures

The SVVP shall identify control procedures applied to the V&V effort. These procedures shall describe how software products and V&V results shall be configured, protected, and stored.

These procedures may describe quality assurance, configuration management, data management, or other activities if they are not addressed by other efforts. The SVVP shall describe how the V&V effort shall comply with existing security provisions and how the validity of V&V results shall be protected from unauthorized alterations.

7.7.5 (SVVP Section 7.5) Standards, practices, and conventions

The SVVP shall identify the standards, practices, and conventions that govern the performance of V&V tasks including internal organizational standards, practices, and policies.

7.8 (SVVP Section 8) V&V documentation requirements

The SVVP shall define the purpose, format, and content of the test documents. A description of the format for these test documents may be found in IEEE Std 829-1983 [IEEE STD 829-1983]. If the V&V effort uses test documentation or test types (e.g., component, integration, system, acceptance) different from those in this standard, the software V&V effort shall show a mapping of the proposed test documentation and execution to the test items defined in this standard. Test planning tasks defined in Table 1 shall be implemented in the test plan, test design(s), test case(s), and test procedure(s) documentation.

The SVVP shall describe the purpose, format, and content for the following V&V test documents:

a) Test Plan;

b) Test Design;

c) Test Cases;

d) Test Procedures; and

e) Test Results.

All V&V results and findings shall be documented in the V&V Final Report.

Chapter 4

Software Quality Assurance Process

1. Introduction to Chapter

This chapter describes the software quality assurance processes. Portions of this text are paraphrased from IEEE/EIA Standard 12207.0-1996, Paragraphs 6.3. Paragraph 2 provides an overview and introduction to the papers contained in this chapter.

1.1 Software quality assurance

The *software quality assurance (SQA)* process is a process for providing adequate assurance that the software products and processes in the project life cycle conform to their specified requirements and adhere to their established plans. To be unbiased, quality assurance needs to have organizational freedom and authority from persons directly responsible for developing the software product or executing the process within the project. Quality assurance may be internal or external, depending upon whether evidence of product or process quality is demonstrated to the management of the supplier or the acquirer. Quality assurance may make use of the results of other supporting processes, such as *verification, validation, joint reviews, audits,* and *problem resolution.* The SQA process consists of the following activities:

1. Process implementation

2. Product assurance

3. Process assurance

4. Assurance of quality systems.

1.2 SQA process implementation

- A quality assurance process tailored to the project is established. The objectives of the quality assurance process are to assure that the software products and the processes employed for providing those software products comply with their established requirements and adhere to their established plans.

- The quality assurance process is coordinated with the related *verification* and *validation* (V&V), *joint review*, and *audit processes.*

- A plan for conducting the quality assurance process activities and tasks is developed, documented, implemented, and maintained for the life of the contract. The plan should include the following:

  ➢ Quality standards, methodologies, procedures, and tools for performing the quality assurance activities (or their references in the organization's official documentation)

  ➢ Procedures for contract review and coordination

> Procedures for identification, collection, filing, maintenance, and deposition of quality records

> Resources, schedule, and responsibilities for conducting the quality assurance activities

> Selected activities and tasks from supporting processes, such as *verification* and *validation* (V&V), *joint review*, *audit* and *problem resolution.*

- Scheduled and on-going quality assurance activities and tasks are then executed. When problems or non-conformance with contract requirements are detected, they are documented to serve as input to the *problem resolution process.* Records of these activities and tasks, their execution, problems, and problem resolutions are prepared and maintained.

- Records of quality assurance activities and tasks are made available to the acquirer as specified in the contract.

- Persons responsible for assuring compliance with the contract requirements have the organizational freedom, resources, and authority to permit objective evaluations and to initiate, affect, resolve, and verify problem resolutions.

1.3 Software product assurance

- Assure that all plans required by the contract are documented, comply with the contract, are mutually consistent, and are being executed as required.

- Ensure that software products and related documentation comply with the contract and adhere to the plans.

- In preparation for the delivery of software products, assure that contractual requirements are fully satisfied and that requirements are acceptable to the acquirer.

1.4 Software process assurance

- Assurance that those software life cycle processes (supply, development, operation, maintenance, and supporting processes including quality assurance) employed for the project comply with the contract and adhere to the plans.

- Assurance that the internal software engineering practices, development environment, test environment, and libraries comply with the contract.

- Applicable prime-contract requirements are to be passed down to the subcontractor. The subcontractor's software products satisfy prime-contract requirements.

- The acquirer and other parties are provided the required support and cooperation in accordance with the contract, negotiations, and plans.

- Software product and process measurements are in accordance with established standards and procedures.

- The assigned staff has the skill and knowledge necessary to meet the requirements of the project and receive any necessary training.

Software assurance of quality systems are assured in accordance with the clauses of ISO 9001 as specified in the contract.

2. Overview of Papers

The first paper on software quality assurance by Patricia Hurst, a consultant from Virginia, is an original article in the first *Software Engineering* tutorial.[1] Hurst reviews the history of software quality assurance (SQA) and its role in software development. She provides a number of reasons for developers to practice good SQA, ranging from a moral obligation to develop a high-quality product to the pressures of competition. Using current worldwide initiatives in software quality improvement, she provides two definitions of SQA, one comparatively narrow and the other broad.

Next, Hurst describes those SQA functions carried out across an entire development organization as well as on a particular project. Finally, she reviews how a software developer would organize and carry out the SQA functions. She also notes that an effective program of software quality assurance has proven to be cost-effective in many environments.

The second paper is extracted from IEEE Standard 730-1998, *Standard for Software Quality Assurance Plans,* IEEE, Inc., New York, 1998. A minimum acceptable requirement for preparation and content of software quality assurance (SQA) plans is detailed. The outline is primarily provided for the development and maintenance of critical software. For less critical software, a subset of this standard may apply.

The reader is again reminded that this copy of the standard is incomplete and cannot be used to cite conformance with the standard in a contractual situation. It is intended to provide the reader and CSDP test taker with a basic understanding of the contents of the SQA standards and an outline of a SQA plan.

---

1. Dorfman, Merlin, and R.H. Thayer, *Software Engineering,* IEEE Computer Society Press, Los Alamitos, CA 1997.

Software Quality Assurance: A Survey of an Emerging View

Patricia W. Hurst

Consultant

Charlottesville, VA

Abstract

Since the mid 1980s, the term "quality assurance" has assumed increasing importance in the software development industry. The once accepted practice of relying on back-end testing to assure quality is fading with the recognition that quality must be addressed from conception, through development, and throughout the maintenance activities. Quality programs are being organized and implemented by many organizations using the Capability Maturity Model developed by the Software Engineering Institute for guidance. This survey article provides a historical perspective and rationale for quality assurance, discusses U. S. and international initiatives to improve quality, defines an emerging view of quality assurance as a subset of a broader Quality Management concern, defines the functions required for a Quality Management program, and presents an organizational structure to support these functions.

INTRODUCTION

Since the mid 1980s, the term "quality assurance" has assumed increasing importance in the software development industry. It is being recognized that quality must be addressed throughout the software life cycle in order to supply software products which meet the needs of our society and its consumers. The once accepted practice of relying on back-end testing of the product to assure quality is fading with the recognition that quality must be addressed from conception, through development, and throughout the maintenance activities.

This recognition has not been sudden, but has emerged over the decades since software was first produced in the 1940s. This emergence has occurred as many software products and systems have repeatedly failed to meet expectations in terms of costs, schedules, functionality, and corrective maintenance. These failed expectations have continued in spite of numerous improvements in platforms, operating systems, languages, development methodologies, computer-aided software engineering (CASE) tools, and management practices. The industry has diligently searched for a "silver bullet" to eliminate the nightmares experienced by developers. However, the community is learning, as has virtually every other area of engineering, that advances in quality and productivity do not occur simply through new technologies. Rather, improvement requires attention to the processes used to develop and maintain software products.

This survey article provides a historical perspective and rationale for quality assurance, discusses U. S. and international initiatives to improve quality, defines an emerging view of quality assurance as a subset of a broader Quality Management concern, defines the functions required for a Quality Management program, and presents an organizational structure to support these functions.

BACKGROUND

From a historical perspective, the early years through the 1960s can be viewed as the functional era of software engineering, the 1970s as the schedule era, and the 1980s as the cost era [5]. In the late 1960s, the focus began to shift from the singular issue of "what functions should the software perform," to the broader recognition that software was expensive, of insufficient quality, hard to schedule, and difficult to manage. Thus, the focus in the 1970s was placed on planning and controlling of software projects. Life-cycle models which defined development phases were introduced and project planning and tracking procedures emerged. In the 1980s, information technology spread through every facet of our institutions and became available to individuals as well. Driven by competition, issues of productivity became more significant and various models used for estimating costs were developed by organizations in industry and academia. In the mid 1980s, quality issues emerged and have subsequently increased in importance. The decade of the 1990s is already being characterized as the "quality era" [34]. As society's dependence on software increases and technology provides for expanding functionality, the demand for quality intensifies. For vendors of software to compete in the marketplace at home and abroad, quality is becoming more of a necessity. In this decade, quality has become a key issue in how software is conceived, developed and maintained for the broad and diverse customer base.

With this focus on quality, the software industry is recognizing that producing quality products requires a concern for not only quality of product but quality of process as well. In a 1987 article, "No Silver Bullet" [8], Brooks argued that the difficulties of software development are inevitable for they arise not from accident, but from software's inescapable essence — the complexity of interlocking constructs. Indeed, for 25 years, software engineers have sought methods which they hoped would provide a technological "fix" for the software crisis. Although small improvement can be made by the use of specific methods, there is little empirical evidence to support the hypothesis that such fixes can radically improve the way we develop software systems [21]. While attention to quality issues may not slay the dragon of software complexity and satisfy Brook's yardstick for a technological breakthrough of a tenfold improvement in quality or productivity, or both, there is growing evidence that it can provide a significant step in that direction. Several companies [11, 16, 17, 28, 54, 56] have reported increases in quality and productivity by focusing on improving the quality of their development processes.

RATIONALE

There are many reasons for wanting to improve software processes and quality. These include a moral obligation, customer satisfaction, cost effectiveness, predictability, application demand, and international competition.

Moral obligation. The increasing reliance on software in life-critical systems morally obligates the producers to provide products that are reliable in performing their needed functions and can be counted on to do no harm. The realities of software fragility are evident in critical systems that we build. As examples [36], a Patriot missile timing error may have contributed to the deaths of 28 soldiers in Dhahran during the Gulf War and software has been suspect in the Therac-25 radiation-therapy machine which has been implicated in at least two deaths.

Customer satisfaction. From the customer's view, quality is conformance to expectations and requirements. Customers today often have multiple sources from which to select products or services; they are increasingly demanding more assurances that their expectations will be met.

Cost effectiveness. With the increase in size and complexity of software systems, the costs have correspondingly increased. With the decrease in hardware costs over the years, the cost of labor has become a major contributor to development costs. Improved development processes are needed to make more efficient use of personnel resources.

Predictability. The need for better predictability of costs, schedules and product quality is driven by customer demands and cost concerns. For example, a Federal Aviation Administration (FAA) project to develop new workstation software for air-traffic controllers was reported in 1994 to be bug-infested and running five years late accompanied by $1 billion over budget [23]. A 1994 survey by IBM's Consulting Group [23] of leading companies that developed large distributed systems showed that 55% of the projects cost more than expected, 68% overran their schedules and 88% had to be substantially redesigned.

Application demand. The demands for software continue to increase in terms of size, complexity, and new domains. Modern, windows-based commercial products average 100,000 lines of code (LOC) [33]. Operating and data-base management systems often exceed one million LOC and complex telephone switching systems are up to 10 million LOC [37]. Because hardware capabilities rapidly advance, an order of magnitude growth in system size every decade is expected for many industries. Such growth in system size is stressing our cultural tradition founded in the prowess of the individual programmer.

International competition. The 21st century will be very competitive for software vendors in the global marketplace. Software is a labor intensive activity. Third world countries, with low wage earners, looking to "leap frog" into the technological age have discovered that software can be key to a competitive strategy for their future. Past practices that enabled U. S. software producers to achieve supremacy will not suffice and bold steps are needed to ensure that our software industry will not fall to foreign competition. Other industries such as automotive, steel, and consumer

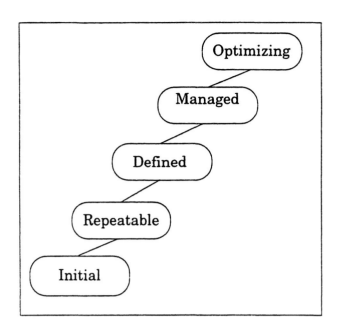

Figure 1. SEI Capability Maturity Model

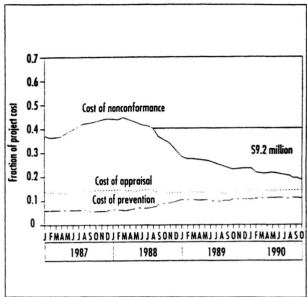

Figure 2. Raytheon's Savings Due to Rework

electronics faced the same challenge and in their hesitation to change, lost marketshare. The challenge for the software industry will be to provide customer satisfaction at a competitive price.

QUALITY IMPROVEMENT INITIATIVES

A movement to improve software development emerged in the mid 1980s. Shortcomings in managing development and maintenance processes were recognized as prime inhibitors of growth in software productivity and quality. This movement focused on the underlying foundation of development efforts — a foundation composed of people, tasks, tools, methods, and a well-defined and documented process. Several initiatives to provide the needed foundation have been undertaken.

Software Engineering Institute. In November 1986, the Software Engineering Institute (SEI) began developing a process-maturity framework that would help developers improve their software process. This work has evolved into the Capability Maturity Model (CMM) Version 1.1 [44] which presents recommended practices in a number of key process areas that have been shown to enhance the software development and maintenance capability of an organization. The CMM provides a rating scale composed of five maturity levels as shown in Figure 1. It is based on the principles of incremental and continuous process improvement espoused by Walter Shewart, W. Edwards Deming, Joseph Juran, and Philip Crosby.

Many organizations in the U. S. are using the SEI model as a catalyst for change. For example, the Air Force has mandated that all of its software development organizations must reach Level 3 of the CMM by 1998 [23]. A similar directive has been issued by the Navy and NASA is considering such a policy [23]. Industry organizations using the CMM include large and small companies.

Improvement efforts have shown that the return on investment is high and published results demonstrate this cost effectiveness. Results from a two-year effort to progress to Level 3 at the Software Engineering Division of Hughes Aircraft [28] indicate a $2 million per year savings. Intangible benefits cited include increased pride in work, quality of work life, and in general, fewer problems. Raytheon achieved similar results over a three-year improvement effort that took the Equipment Division from a Level 2 to a Level 3 [17]. Their analysis, as shown in Figure 2, indicates that $9.2 million was saved by reducing rework on a base of nearly $115 million in development costs. During the past several years, Computer Sciences Corporation has experienced about a 20% annual increase in productivity and quality [11]. This is a result of applying the SEI approach as well as other ongoing improvement activities. Procase Corporation, a smaller company which is a producer of CASE tools, progressed from a Level 1 to a Level 2 over an 18-month period [54]. The company is now shipping releases close to a 6-month cycle compared with a previous 30-month cycle.

The CMM represents a broad consensus of the software community on best practices and is providing guidance for many organizational software process-improvement efforts.

ISO 9000-3. Another method for assessing the ability of an organization to produce software with predictability and quality is *ISO 9000-3, Guidelines for the Application of ISO 9001 to the Development, Supply, and Maintenance of Software*, which is part of the ISO 9000 series of standards published by the International Standards Organization (ISO) [2]. These standards describe the requirements for various types of companies and organizations doing business in the European Community.

BOOTSTRAP. BOOTSTRAP [35], a project under the auspices of the European Strategic Programme for Research in Information Technology (ESPRIT), applied the SEI model to the European software industry. Although the CMM maturity levels are still recognizable, the assessment methodology yields more detailed capability profiles of organizations and projects. As of 1993, 90 projects in 37 organizations had been assessed with results showing that 73% of the organizations were at Level 1 with the remainder at Level 2.

SPICE. In 1993, the International Standards Group for Software Engineering sponsored the Software Process Improvement and Capability dEtermination (SPICE) project which has been endorsed by the international community [18]. Its objective is to develop an international standard for software process assessment by building on the best features of existing software assessment methods such as the SEI model.

Other Models. Other improvement models have been developed and used by large companies, such as Hewlett-Packard's Software Quality and Productivity Analysis (SQPA) [25]. Models have also been developed as an adjunct to consulting services, such as those offered by R. S. Pressman & Associates, Inc., Howard Rubin & Associates, and Capers Jones through Software Productivity Research, Inc.

QUALITY ASSURANCE DEFINITION

Over a decade ago, Buckley [9] stated, "You can wander into any bar in town and get into a fight over quality assurance." This is still true. There are various definitions of quality assurance and related concepts. Definitions provided by the IEEE [32] and by the CMM [44] are as follows:

IEEE Definition 1. A planned and systematic pattern of all actions necessary to provide adequate confidence that an item or product conforms to established technical requirements.

IEEE Definition 2. A set of activities designed to evaluate the process by which products are developed or manufactured.

CMM Definition of Purpose. The purpose of quality assurance is to provide management with appropriate visibility into the process being used by the software project and of the products being built.

The first IEEE definition is very broad in scope and includes plans and subsequent actions taken by a project's development personnel as well as by others in organizational support roles. Such plans address areas such as project planning and tracking, development process models, deliverable and in-process documentation, reviews and audits, requirements management, configuration management, verification and validation procedures, and training. The *IEEE Standard for Software Quality Assurance Plans* [31] provides the contents of such a comprehensive plan.

The second IEEE definition of quality assurance and the CMM definition of its purpose are similar and narrower in scope. The key phrases are "to evaluate" and to provide "appropriate visibility into" the process being used to develop the software products. These definitions imply an oversight function concerned with assuring that defined processes are in place for the development and support activities required to produce a quality product and with assuring that these processes are being complied with.

To bridge this chasm between the broad and the narrow definitions, terms such as "Quality Management" and "Quality Program" are being used to encompass the broad spectrum of quality-oriented activities while the term "Quality Assurance" is applied to the oversight function. The terms are in a state of evolution and are being influenced by the increasing popularity of the CMM among developer organizations.

In the remainder of this paper, the terms Quality Management (QM) and Quality Assurance (QA) will be used in conformance with this emerging new view.

QUALITY MANAGEMENT FUNCTIONS

Quality Management is concerned with quality-related activities across the spectrum of a software development organization. Since consistency is needed

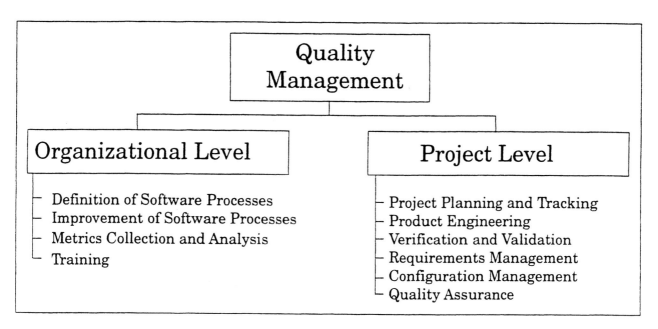

Figure 3. Primary Quality Management Functions

both for reliable prediction of schedules, costs, and product quality and for improvement over time, a primary goal is to provide for consistency across a multitude of individual software projects. This applies to the various processes and methodologies used by the various projects. Thus, QM must address quality functions at two levels, the organizational and the project levels. The organizational-level functions include those necessary to define and support the processes and methodologies which will be used by individual projects within the organization. The project-level functions include those necessary to carry out the defined processes, using the defined methodologies, for a specific project. The primary functions addressed by QM are shown in Figure 3.

Organizational Level Functions

Primary functions at the organizational level include definition and improvement of software development processes, metrics collection and analysis, and training.

Definition of Software Development Processes. This function is to define and document the processes which development projects will follow. These processes encompass the activities, procedures, documentation, and standards required to carry out the QM functions shown at the project level.

Software process models are at the heart of improving the way software is developed and thus the quality of the resultant products. While a life-cycle model, such as the waterfall, spiral, or evolutionary, defines the

high-level activities for the development effort, a process model is a more detailed decomposition and is usually displayed as a network of activities.

A software process model defines the various development activities which must be performed. For each activity, the model defines information or documents which must be available for the activity to occur, work-products that are produced, standards that must be met, methodologies and tools that must be used, verification and validation procedures that will be applied, configuration management activities that will be applied, and quality assurance activities that will be applied. Thus, a process model integrates the various quality management activities appropriate for a project.

Automated support is available for modeling and enacting a defined process. These tools aid in ensuring that the personnel participating on a project follow the defined process. A description of several tools is given in [52]. Examples include Process Weaver from Cap Gemini, InConcert from Xsoft Inc., and Process Engineer from Learmonth & Burchett Management Systems.

Procedures and standards apply to various products during a project's life. Document templates are typically developed for deliverable and non-deliverable work-products such as the project plan, the requirement specifications, user and operator manuals, various design documents, and test plans. Documents which contains descriptions of the processes and procedures

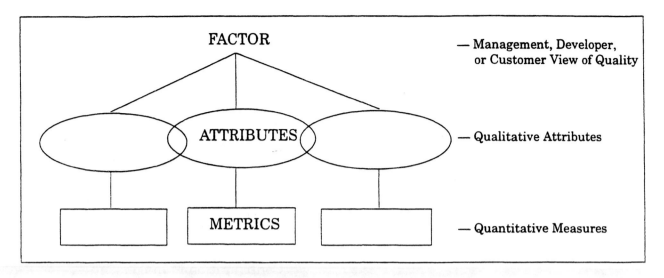

FACTOR — Management, Developer, or Customer View of Quality

ATTRIBUTES — Qualitative Attributes

METRICS — Quantitative Measures

Figure 4. Software Metrics Framework

to be followed on individual projects, such as for configuration management, verification and validation, and quality assurance activities, are also required. Coding standards include expectations and restrictions on items such as descriptive comments, programming languages, control structures, data structures, naming conventions, source-code size, and operating system interfaces.

Defined processes are used, perhaps with tailoring, by individuals on specific projects to guide them in performing their work according to expectations.

Improvement of Software Development Processes. Improving development processes requires evaluating the current processes being used and products produced, identifying areas that are weak, and modifying the defined processes in these areas. It also includes follow-up evaluation to ensure that the modifications are indeed improving productivity and/or product quality.

Metrics Collection and Analysis. Software metrics play an important role in evaluating and improving the development processes and the software products. Such improvement results in increased productivity and quality, and reduced cycle time, all of which improve a company's competitiveness. Although there are a number of successful metrics programs in industry [16, 24, 25, 38, 48, 59], only about 25% of application development organizations have a formal metrics program [59]. Implementation of metrics is a complex issue as indicated in a survey by Howard Rubin & Associates, as mentioned in [39], that reported two out of three measurement efforts either failed or were discontinued after two years.

An example of a successful metrics program is found within Motorola. Their six sigma program has a quality goal of no more than 3.4 defects per million lines of code. One Motorola Division achieved a 50X reduction in released-software defect density within 3.5 years [16].

An example of a small software group that has benefited from a measurement program is from Eastman Kodak Company [56]. Since 1990, the group has measured the time spent in different work phases on development and maintenance projects. Distribution trends have been used to set quantitative improvement goals, identify opportunities that can increase productivity, and develop heuristics to assist with estimating new projects. The focus has been on improving up-front activities such as requirements analysis, instituting design and code inspections, and formalizing software quality assurance practices. A notable result has been a reduction in the corrective maintenance effort from 13.5% to a steady state of less than 2%.

Metrics can be classified into two broad categories — process metrics and product metrics. Process metrics can be used to improve the development and maintenance processes. Examples include defects associated with testing and inspections, defect containment efficiency, and labor consumed. Product metrics can be used to improve the software and its associated products. Examples include complexity of the design, the size of the source code, and the usability of the documentation produced.

A popular approach to defining product metrics is through a hierarchical framework [51, 53]. A three-level framework is shown in Figure 4. The first level

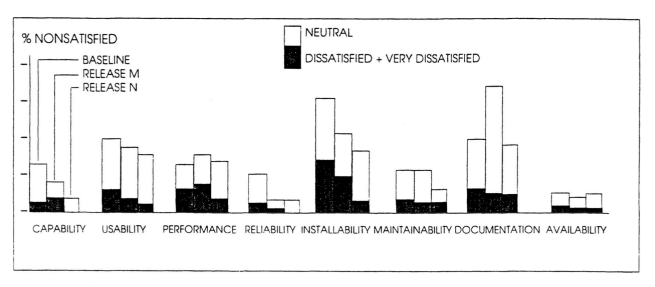

Figure 5. Monitoring Software Quality in Terms of Customer Satisfaction

establishes high-level quality factors; the second identifies the software attributes which define the factor; and the third identifies the metrics which can be used to measure the degree of presence of each attribute, and thus the quality factor. For example, the quality factor "maintainability" may be decomposed into three attributes: consistency, simplicity and modularity; the attribute simplicity may be decomposed into metrics describing the LOC and the maximum loop-nesting level for a module. The framework can be used for individual modules or for a system to enforce standards and to measure deviations from quality goals. Commonly accepted quality factors include correctness, reliability, efficiency, integrity, usability, maintainability, testability, flexibility, portability, reusability, and interoperability [46]. The concept of a metrics framework is supported by several commercial packages such as Logiscope marketed by Verilog, Inc.

Another example of quality factors, with focus on customer satisfaction/dissatisfaction, is found in the CUPRIMDA model used by IBM's AS/400 Division as part of a corporate strategy of market-driven quality (MDQ) [34]. CUPRIMDA is an acronym for eight quality factors as shown in Figure 5. Each factor is defined through a set of metrics and used to measure products across different releases and against benchmarked competitors. This information is used to improve the process and as a result, the product, in areas contributing to low customer satisfaction.

In a similar way of measuring customer satisfaction, the Hewlett-Packard Company focuses on FURPS (functionality, usability, reliability, performance, and supportability) [24, 25]. Similar dimensions of quality

are used by other companies.

A useful approach for developing a set of metrics is provided by the "goal/question/metric" paradigm [3, 4]. It is well described by Grady[25]: "The basic principle behind the paradigm is that each organization or project has a set of goals. For each goal there is a set of questions that you might ask to help you understand whether you are achieving your goal. Many of these questions have answers that can be measured. To the extent that the questions are a complete set, and to the extent the metric data satisfactorily answers the questions, you can measure whether you are meeting goals." The relationships among goals, questions, and metrics are shown in Figure 6. This approach was used in brainstorming sessions by the Hewlett-Packard's Software Metrics Council as an initial step in defining a set of software maintenance metrics [25]. As such, the "metrics" were not precisely defined but provided a platform for further discussion, feedback and refinement. An example follows:

Goal: Minimize Engineering Effort and Schedule

Question: Where are the resources going and where are the worst rework loops in the process?

Metrics: Engineering months by product/component/activity.

Increasingly, a metrics program is being viewed by industry and government organizations as a powerful tool for improving the quality of products and processes in software development. The IEEE has developed standards for productivity metrics [30] and software

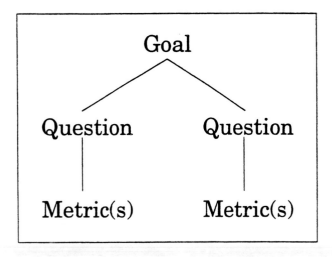

Figure 6. Goal/Question/Metric Paradigm

quality metrics [29]. The Department of Defense (DoD) is developing a software-metrics database which is to become a national repository for all DoD organizations, on both in-house and contracted projects, and for others who choose to contribute [40]. An Air Force policy requires software-intensive programs, whether embedded, command and control, or management information systems, to have a metrics program which collects the core attributes of size, effort, schedule, quality and rework [40].

Metrics programs are well supported by vendor tools. Software Productivity Research provides Checkpoint for estimating staffing and quality levels. Industry baselines for productivity and quality measures are provided through products such as SLIM from Quantitative Software Management and several from Howard Rubin & Associates. McCabe & Associates provides a toolset to support the analysis of software structure.

A comprehensive metrics training program is provided through METKIT, a product produced by an ESPRIT project [1]. The industrial package consists of 18 modules, a computer-aided instruction system, and a textbook [21].

Training. For a viable quality program, the organization needs to provide for training of personnel in their processes, standards, and metrics program. Management, technical and support staff who are to be involved in the project-level activities should be included.

Project Level Functions

The primary functions at the project level are implementations of the defined processes established by the organization as standards to be followed by all software projects within the organization. These functions include project planning and tracking, product engineering, verification and validation, requirements management, configuration management, and quality assurance.

Project Planning and Tracking. Project planning is performed at the beginning of a project and includes defining the work to be performed, estimating resources required, and producing a schedule. The planning process itself adheres to the process defined at the organization level and the resultant plan should incorporate processes defined for the other project-level functions described below. Tailoring of the defined processes may be necessary for a specific project and is performed during the planning phase. The project tracking functions involve assessing the status of the work and work-products as the project progresses, evaluating adherence to the plan, and taking action to correct any deviation.

Product Engineering. Product engineering involves following the defined software process model, with the appropriate methods and tools, to develop the software and associated products. Activities defined by product engineering include requirements analysis, design, implementation, and testing.

Verification and Validation (V&V). V&V is "the process of determining whether the requirements for a system or component are complete and correct, the products of each development phase fulfill the requirements or conditions imposed by the previous phase, and the final system or component complies with specified requirements" [32]. This process should be integrated into the software process model and includes "gate-keeping" activities at each process step to ensure freedom from defects and compliance with standards and requirements. Example activities include producing traceability matrices, holding technical reviews and inspections, and performing unit, integration and system testing. Reviews and inspections are particularly important V&V activities.

The idea of software reviews has been around almost as long as software. Babbage and von Neumann regularly asked colleagues to examine their programs [22]. By the 1970s, various review methods had emerged and were called walkthroughs, structured walkthroughs, and code inspections. Petroski, in his text *To Engineer is Human* [47] states that "it is the essence of modern engineering not only to be able to check one's own work, but also to have one's work checked and to be able to check the work of others." The value of reviews is based on the fact that the cost of fixing a defect rises dramatically the later it is found in the development cycle. Reviews of requirements, design, and code allow early detection of defects and thus, lower costs.

Over the years, many companies have reported their experiences with inspections [19, 50, 58]. At Bell-Northern Research, code inspections uncovered approximately 80% of all defects on an ultralarge project of 2.5 million lines of code [50].

Requirements Management (RM). Software requirements are essential for proper planning of software development activities. Requirements management includes ensuring that requirements are well defined, agreed to by appropriate parties, used for project planning, and modified according to a defined procedure. The modification procedure must ensure that later changes are incorporated properly and that project plans are updated accordingly. If appropriate, the requirements may be placed under the full rigor of formal configuration management.

Configuration Management (CM). The purpose of CM [44] is to "establish and maintain the integrity of the products of the software project throughout the project's software life cycle." This involves identifying the software work products — called configuration items — to be placed under CM control and providing the technical and administrative procedures required to ensure that approved baselined versions exist at specific points during the project, that changes are incorporated in a defined manner, and that the status of configurations items are accounted for. Examples of work products that may be designated as configuration items include the project plan, the requirements, the architectural design, the source code, and the user manual.

CM has been addressed by many organizations [41]. About 80% of organizations examined in one survey have well-developed mechanisms for controlling changes to requirements, design, and code. There are a number of automated tools, which support elements of CM, especially for source code. Examples include Digital Equipment Corporation's VMS, Softool Corporation's CCC, and Expertware Inc.'s CMVision. However, many CM tools were developed on mainframe machines and few fully support the needs required in distributed client-server environments [10].

Quality Assurance. QA, as noted previously, is an oversight function providing assurance that all processes defined in the project plan are followed. Thus, QA ensures that all product engineering, V&V, RM and CM activities are carried out as planned and that work products conform to standards. QA also assures that the project plan itself was developed according to defined procedures and meets the standards for the organization. QA functions are performed through a series of reviews, audits, and consultations.

QA reviews ensure documented processes are followed and that planned activities such as project reviews and inspections are held. QA personnel may attend technical and management reviews and may attend work-product inspections. Their presence, however, is not as a technical contributor with responsibility for detecting technical-content errors. Their presence is to observe that the meeting processes are being implemented as planned and to note deviations. For example, they may note that the moderator of a code inspection did not distribute materials in advance and that the inspectors are not prepared. They may also evaluate effectiveness of the meeting procedures and make recommendations for change. QA personnel may perform reviews to ensure proper records, status-accounting reports, and other physical documents are present and are being used as planned. For example, QA may periodically review the project manager's records to ensure that monthly reports, inspection meeting reports, and testing reports are being produced, distributed and saved according to procedures. QA may also review CM records to ensure that monthly reports are being produced, distributed and saved according to procedures.

QA may audit a variety of work products for which standards have been established. This includes auditing of deliverable work-products such as code and manuals prior to delivery. Similar to attending reviews, their purpose is not to detect technical-content errors but to ensure that all items are present, that all standards are complied with, and that all activities, such as completion of test-traceability matrices, have been completed prior to delivery. QA may also review non-deliverable work-products, such as design documents and test plans, for standards compliance.

QA personnel provide consulting services throughout the project life from initial planning through final product delivery. This includes advising the project management on implementing and tailoring the organizational processes and standards as well as advising on corrective actions required to eliminate discrepancies detected during reviews and audits.

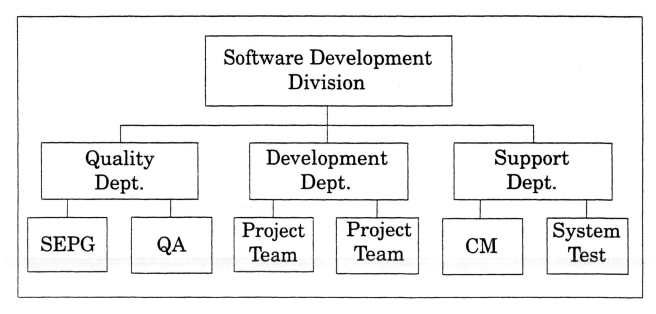

Figure 7. Organizational Structure Supporting Quality Management Activities

An important part of the QA function is reporting to project management and to senior management regarding the status of project adherence to defined processes as described in the project plan. Noncompliance issues that cannot be resolved within the software project are addressed by senior management.

The QM functions defined at the organizational and project levels provide a comprehensive set of well-integrated processes needed for prediction and control of project costs and schedule and of product quality.

QUALITY MANAGEMENT ORGANIZATION

The organization of personnel and other resources required to carry out the development and QM functions is a critical element of success in implementing a quality program. The organizational structure used to define roles and responsibilities of personnel can vary depending on the resources, skills, and culture inherent in the organization itself. The structure presented in this section is a composite based on the author's experience as an instructor and consultant for organizations seeking to institute a QM program, and thus, is intended as a representative structure. The structure is shown in Figure 7. Some alternatives are described in the text.

Software Engineering Process Group (SEPG). The SEPG is responsible for capturing, documenting, maintaining and disseminating the organization's software process activities. The SEI's CMM requires

an SEPG, or similar group, for Level 3 [44]. In the context of this paper, the SEPG performs the functions defined at the organizational level, which include definition and improvement of software development processes, metrics collection and analysis, and training.

Many software development organizations are in the early stage of implementing QM functions with primary focus on definining the various processes required. As such, the SEPG may not be considered a permanent organizational entity with traditional line management as shown, but instead may report to a "Steering Committee" composed of managers who will implement the defined procedures on software projects. The Steering Committee would include the division and department managers and the project team, QA, CM, and Test managers. In this early stage, "working groups" are created to define and document a specific process(es) which will become the organizational standard. For example, a requirements working group would be responsible for defining and documenting the process to be followed by individual projects for requirements management. The working groups report to the SEPG. The SEPG and the working groups are typically staffed with software development personnel on a part- or full-time basis.

Quality Assurance (QA). The QA group is responsible for assuring defined processes are followed by those organizational entities carrying out the project-level QM function. Thus, the QA group performs those QA functions defined at the project level which include reviews, audits, and consultations.

90

The QA organization is staffed with personnel who have in-depth knowledge of the processes for which they are providing oversight; thus, experience in software engineering is a desirable pre-requisite. The organization may have part- or full-time staff positions and may rotate software engineers into QA positions for a period of time.

Project Team. The project team includes the software project manager and software engineers who develop the software and related products. This group performs all project-level QM functions except for QA functions. The project manager is responsible for project planning and tracking and software engineers are responsible for product engineering, verification and validation (other than system testing), and requirements management.

Configuration Management (CM). The CM group performs the configuration management activities for all projects in the organization. It is not uncommon in small development organizations, however, for the project team to perform these functions for a specific project.

System Test. The system test group is responsible for the independent V&V activity of testing the complete system prior to delivery. It is not uncommon in small development organizations, however, for the project team to perform these functions for a project.

SUMMARY

The future prospects for improvement in software quality appear promising. Quality Management programs are being organized and implemented by many development organizations using the Capability Maturity Model developed by the Software Engineering Institute for guidance. Quality Assurance as an entity of Quality Management is emerging as an important oversight function to ensure that documented processes are being followed and that they are effective. Organizations such as Hughes Aircraft, Motorola, Raytheon, and IBM have shown that improvements in quality and productivity go hand-in-hand in the field of software development, as has been shown in other industries such as manufacturing. The technologies needed for improvement are defined and available to organizations through methodologies and supporting tools. Quality initiatives by industry and by government agencies provide strong incentives for a change in culture from the ad-hoc development processes of the past decades to a more defined structure for the future. Only through a focus on quality issues can the U. S. software industry maintain its supremacy and meet the challenges of the competitive 21st century.

REFERENCES

1. Ashley, Nicholas, "METKIT: Training in How to Use Measurement as a Software Management Tool," *Software Quality Journal*, 3, 1994, pp. 129-136.
2. Bamford, Robert and Deibler, William, "Comparing, Contrasting ISO 9001 and the SEI Capability Maturity Model," *IEEE Computer*, October 1993, pp. 68-70.
3. Basili, V. R. and Weiss, D. M., "A Methodology for Collecting Valid Software Engineering Data," *IEEE Transactions on Software Engineering*, Vol. SE-10, No. 6, November 1984.
4. Basili, V. R. and Rombach, H. D., "Tailoring the Software Process to Project Goals and Environments," *IEEE Proceedings of the Ninth International Conference on Software Engineering*, Monterey, CA, April 1987.
5. Basili, V.R. and Musa, J. D., "The Future Engineering of Software: A Management Perspective," *IEEE Computer*, Vol. 24, No. 9, September 1991, pp. 90-96.
6. Basili, Victor *et al*, "Technology Transfer at Motorola," *IEEE Software*, March 1994, pp. 70-76.
7. Brooks, F. P., *The Mythical Man-Month*, Addison-Wesley, 1975.
8. Brooks, Fred, "No Silver Bullet: Essence and Accidents of Software Engineering," *IEEE Computer*, April 1987.
9. Buckley, Fletcher J., "Software Quality Assurance," *IEEE Transactions on Software Engineering*, January 1984, pp. 36-41.
10. Buckley, Fletcher J., "Implementing a Software Configuration Management Environment," *IEEE Computer*, February 1994, pp. 56-61.
11. Card, David, "The SEI Software Process Improvement Approach: A Case Study," *Software Engineering Strategies*, November/December 1993, pp. 7-14.
12. Crosby, P. B., *Quality is Free: The Art of Making Quality Certain*, McGraw-Hill, 1979.
13. Crosby, Philip, *Quality Without Tears*, McGraw-Hill, 1984.
14. Curtis, B. and Paulk, M., "Creating a Software Process Improvement Program," *Information and Software Technology*, June/July, 1993, pp. 381-386.
15. Cusumano, Michael, *Japan's Software Factories: A Challenge to U. S. Management*, M.I.T. Press, 1991.
16. Daskalantonakis, Michael, "A Practical View of Software Measurement and Implementation Experiences within Motorola, *IEEE Transactions on Software Engineering*, November 1992, pp. 998-1010.
17. Dion, Raymond, "Elements of a Process-Improvement Program," *IEEE Software*, July 1992, pp. 83-85.
18. Dorling, A., "SPICE: Software Process Improvement and Capability dEtermination," *Information and Software Technology*, June/July 1993, pp. 404-406.
19. Ebenau, Robert G., "Predictive Quality Control with Software Inspections," *CrossTalk*, June 1994, pp. 9-16.
20. Fenton, Norman, *Software Metrics: A Rigorous Approach*, Chapman & Hall, 1991.
21. Fenton, Norman, "How Effective Are Software Engineering Methods?" *The Journal of Systems and Software*, 22, 1993, pp. 141-146.
22. Freedman, D. P. and Weinberg, G. M., "Reviews, Walkthroughs, and Inspections," *IEEE Transactions on Software Engineering*, January 1984.

23. Gibbs, W. Wayt, "Software's Chronic Crisis," *Scientific American*, September 1994, pp. 86-95.

24. Grady, R. B. and Caswell, D. L., *Software Metrics: Establishing a Company-wide Program*, Prentice-Hall, 1986.

25. Grady, Robert B., *Practical Software Metrics for Project Management and Process Improvement*, Prentice-Hall, 1992.

26. Hausler, P. A., Linger, R. C., and Trammell, C. J., "Adopting Cleanroom Software Engineering With a Phased Approach," *IBM Systems Journal*, Vol. 33, No. 1, 1994, pp. 89-109.

27. Humphrey, Watts, *Managing the Software Process*, Addison-Wesley, 1989.

28. Humphrey, W., Snyder, T. and Willis, R., "Software Process Improvement at Hughes Aircraft," *IEEE Software*, July 1991.

29. *IEEE Standard for a Software Quality Metrics Methodology*, IEEE Std 1061-1992, IEEE, 1992.

30. *IEEE Standard for Software Productivity Metrics*, IEEE Std 1045-1992, IEEE, 1992.

31. *IEEE Standard for Software Quality Assurance Plans*, IEEE 730-1989, IEEE, 1989.

32. *IEEE Standard Glossary of Software Engineering Terminology*, Std 610.12-1990, IEEE, 1990.

33. Jones, Capers, "Determining Software Schedules," *IEEE Computer*, February 1995, pp. 73-75.

34. Kan, S. H., Basili, V. R., and Shapiro, L. N., "Software Quality: An Overview from the Perspective of Total Quality Management," *IBM Systems Journal*, Vol. 33, No. 1, 1994, pp. 4-19.

35. Kuvaja, Pase and Bicego, Adriana, "BOOTSTRAP — a European Assessment Methodology", *Software Quality Journal*, 3, 1994, 99 117-127.

36. Lutz, Michael, "Complex Software: Unsafe at any Level," *IEEE Software*, November 1994, pp. 110-111.

37. Marciniak, John J., Editor-in-Chief, "Quality Assurance", *Encyclopedia of Software Engineering*, Volume 2, John Wiley & Sons, 1994, pp. 941-958.

38. McGarry, F. E., "Results of 15 Years of Measurement in the SEL," *Proceedings: Fifteenth Annual Software Engineering Workshop*, NASA/Goddard Space Flight Center, November, 1990.

39. Miluk, G. "Cultural Barriers to Software Measurement," *Proceedings: First International Conference on Applications of Software Measurement*, November 1990.

40. Mosemann, Lloyd K., "Predictability", *Crosstalk*, August 1994, pp. 2-6.

41. Oliver, Paul, "Using a Process Assessment to Improve Software Quality," *Software Engineering Strategies*, March/April, 1993, pp. 14-20.

42. Over, James, "Motivation for Process-Driven Development," *Crosstalk*, January 1993, pp. 17-24.

43. Parnas, E. W. and Weiss, D. M., "Active Design Reviews: Principles and Practices," *Proceedings of ICSE '85* (London, England, Aug. 28-30), IEEE Computer Society, 1985, pp. 132-136.

44. Paulk, Mark C. *et al.*, *Capability Maturity Model for Software, Version 1.1*, CMU/SEI-93-TR-24, Software Engineering Institute, 1993.

45. Paulk, Mark *et al.*, "Capability Maturity Model, Version 1.1," *IEEE Software*, July 1993, pp. 18-26.

46. Perry, William, "Quality Concerns in Software Development," *Information Systems Management*, Spring 1992, pp. 48-52.

47. Petroski, Henry, *To Engineer is Human*, St. Martin's Press, 1985.

48. Pfleeger, S. L., Fitzgerald, J. C., and Porter, A., "The CONTEL Software Metrics Program," *Proceeding: First International Conference on Applications of Software Measurement*, November, 1990.

49. Pressman, Roger, "Assessing Software Engineering Practices for Successful Technology Transition," *Software Engineering Strategies*, 1992, pp. 6-14.

50. Russell, Glen W., "Experience with Inspections in Ultralarge-Scale Developments," *IEEE Software*, January 1991, pp. 25-30.

51. Schulmeyer, G. Gordon and McManus, James I., *Handbook of Software Quality Assurance*, Van Nostrand Reinhold, 1987.

52. Sharon, David and Bell, Rodney, "Tools that Bind: Creating Integrated Environments," *IEEE Software*, March 1995, pp. 76-85.

53. *Specification of the Software Quality Attributes, Vol. 1, 2, and 3*, RADC-TR-85-37, Rome Laboratories, 1985.

54. Sudlow, Bill, "Moving from Chaos to SEI Level 2", *Software Development*, December 1994, pp. 37-40.

55. *The Project Management Body of Knowledge*(Draft), Project Management Institute, August 1994.

56. Weigers, Karl, "Lessons from Software Work Effort Metrics," *Software Development*, October 1994, pp. 37-47.

57. Weinberg, Gerald and Freedman Daniel, *Handbook of Walkthorughs, Inspections, and Technical Reviews, Third Ed.*, Dorset House, 1990.

58. Weller, Edward F., "Lessons from Three Years of Inspection Data," *IEEE Software*, September 1993, pp. 38-45.

59. Yourdon, Ed, "Software Metrics," *Application Development Strategies*, Vol. VI, No. 11, November 1994, pp. 1-16.

ABOUT THE AUTHOR

PATRICIA W. HURST is a consultant to corporations and government agencies specializing in software process improvement based on the CMM. She has worked onsite at Fortune 100 corporations in successful efforts to reach Level 2. She has given seminars and workshops nationally and internationally on various software engineering topics such as quality assurance, project management, requirements management and risk management. She has authored articles for a variety of publications and presented papers at national conferences. She is author of *Software Quality Assurance: Control, Metrics and Testing*, a course published by Technology Exchange Company, Reading, MA.

IEEE Standard 730-2001
Software Quality Assurance Plans

Abstract. The standard specifies the format and content of software quality assurance plans. It meets the IEEE/EIA Standard 12207.1-1997 requirements for such plans.

The authors of this revision of the standards are:

Robert Shillato, *Chairperson*

Ron Dean   John Horch   David Schultz

Sponsored by

Software Engineering Standards Committee
of the IEEE Computer Society

The Institute of Electrical and Electronic Engineering, Inc.
345 East 47th Street, New York, NY 10017-2394, USA

October 5, 2001

Table of Contents
IEEE Standard 730-2001
Software Quality Assurance Plans

IEEE Standard for Software
Quality Assurance Plans

1. Overview

1.1 Scope

This standard applies to the development of Software Quality Assurance Plans (SQAP). The existence of this standard should not be construed to prohibit additional content in a SQAP. An assessment should be made for the specific software item to assure adequacy of coverage. Where this standard is invoked for an organization or project engaged in producing several software items, the applicability of the standard should be specified for each of the software items.

Although this document does not require the use of IEEE/EIA Standard 12207.0 and 12207.1, it is consistent with those two standards. The SQAP meeting the requirements of this standard will be in compliance with the SQAP information item of IEEE/EIA 12207.1.

1.2 Purpose

The purpose of this standard is to provide uniform, minimum acceptable requirements for preparation and content of Software Quality Assurance Plans.

In considering adoption of this standard, regulatory bodies should be aware that specific application of this standard may already be covered by one or more IEEE or ANSI standards documents relating to quality assurance, definitions, or other matters. It is not the purpose of this document to supersede, revise, or amend existing standards directed to specific industries or applications.

1.3 Conformance to this standard

Content conformance to this standard can be claimed when all requirements (indicated by "shall") are carried out as defined in this standard. Format conformance to this standard can be claimed if the resulting SQAP is in the format specified in Paragraph 4. The word "shall" is used to express a requirement, "should" to express a recommendation, and "may" to express alternative or optional methods of satisfying a requirement.

2. References

The supporting references and citations pertaining to this standard can be found in the *Centralized IEEE Software Engineering Standards References* contained in this tutorial. These references provide additional information on software quality assurance plans to assist in understanding and applying this standard.

3. Definitions

The definitions and acronyms pertaining to this standard can be found in the *Centralized IEEE Software Engineering Standards Glossary* contained in this tutorial. These are contextual definitions serving to augment the understanding of software quality assurance plan activities as described within this standard.

4. Software quality assurance plan

The Software Quality Assurance Plan shall include the sections listed below to be in conformance with this standard. The sections shall be ordered in the described sequence, or if the sections are not ordered in the described sequence, a table shall be provided at the end of the SQAP that provides a cross-reference from the lowest subsection of the standard to the that portion of the SQAP where the material is provided. If there is no information pertinent to a section, the following shall appear below the section heading, "This section is not applicable to this plan," together with the appropriate reasons for the exclusion.

The first page of the SQAP shall include the date of issue, the status of the document, and the identification of the issuing organization. The SQAP sections shall be:

a) Purpose;

b) Reference documents;

c) Management;

d) Documentation;

e) Standards, practices, conventions, and metrics;

f) Software reviews;

g) Test;

h) Problem reporting and corrective action;

i) Tools, techniques, and methodologies;

j) Software code control;

k) Media control;

l) Supplier control;

m) Records collection, maintenance, and retention;

n) Training;

o) Risk management;

p) Glossary; and

q) SQAP change procedure and history.

Additional sections may be added as required.

Some of the material may appear in other documents. If so, then reference to these documents should be made in the body of the SQAP. In any case, the contents of each section of the plan shall be specified either directly or by reference to another document.

The SQAP shall be approved by the manager of each unit of the organization having responsibilities defined within this SQAP or their designated representatives.

Details for each section of the SQAP are described in Paragraph 4.1 through Paragraph 4.17 of this standard. [IEEE Std 730.1-1995]

4.1 Purpose (Section 1 of the SQAP)

This section shall delineate the specific purpose and scope of the particular SQAP. It shall list the name(s) of the software items covered by the SQAP and the intended use of the software. It shall state the portion of the software life cycle covered by the SQAP for each software item specified.

4.2 Reference documents (Section 2 of the SQAP)

This section shall provide a complete list of documents referenced elsewhere in the text of the SQAP. Included in this list shall be the documents that were used in developing the SQAP, including policies or laws that give rise to the need for this plan, as well as other plans or task descriptions that elaborate details of this plan. The version of each document shall be included in the list.

4.3 Management (Section 3 of the SQAP)

This section shall describe the project's organization, its tasks, and its roles and responsibilities. [IEEE Std 1058-1998]

4.3.1 Organization

This paragraph shall depict the organizational structure that influences and controls the quality of the software. This shall include a description of each major element of the organization together with the delegated responsibilities. The amount of organizational freedom and objectivity to evaluate and monitor the quality of the software, and to verify problem resolutions shall be clearly described and documented. In addition, the organization responsible for preparing and maintaining the SQAP shall be identified.

4.3.2 Tasks

This paragraph shall describe (a) that portion of the software life cycle covered by the SQAP, (b) the tasks to be performed, (c) the entry and exit criteria for each task, and (d) the relationships between these tasks and the planned major check-points. The sequence and relationships of tasks, and their relationship to the project management plan master schedule, shall be indicated. If a project management plan exists, this information may also be included in that document.

4.3.3 Roles and responsibilities

This paragraph shall identify the specific organizational elements that will make each major decision and that will perform each task.

4.3.4 Quality assurance estimated resources

This paragraph shall provide the estimate of resources and the costs to be expended on quality assurance and quality control tasks. If a project management plan exists, this information may be included in that document and just referenced in the SQAP.

4.4 Documentation (Section 4 of the SQAP)

4.4.1 Purpose

This section shall perform the following functions:

a) Identify the documentation governing the development, verification and validation, use, and maintenance of the software.

b) List which documents are to be reviewed or audited for adequacy. For each document listed, identify the review or audit to be conducted and the criteria by which adequacy is to be confirmed, with reference to Section 6 of the SQAP.

4.4.2 Minimum documentation requirements

To ensure that the implementation of the software satisfies the technical requirements, the following documentation is required as a minimum: (Note: Names of various artifacts listed below use the terminology contained in ISO 12207.1. The content of these documents may be included in other documents as long as traceability to the required information is maintained; e.g., a reference in that section of the document or a traceability table.). [IEEE/EIA 12207.0-1997]

4.4.2.1 Software requirements description (SRD)

The SRD shall specify requirements for a particular software product, program, or set of programs that perform certain functions in a specific environment. The SRD may be written by the supplier (internal or external), the customer, or by both. The SRD shall address the basic issues of functionality, external interfaces, performance, attributes, and design constraints imposed on implementation. Each requirement shall be uniquely identified and defined such that its achievement is capable of being objectively verified and validated. [IEEE Std 830-1998]

4.4.2.2 Software design description (SDD)

The SDD shall depict how the software will be structured to satisfy the requirements in the SRD. The SDD shall describe the components and subcomponents of the software design, including databases and internal interfaces. The SDD may be prepared first as the Architecture Design (also sometimes referred to as the top-level SDD) and shall be subsequently expanded to produce the detailed SDD. [IEEE Std 1016-1998]

4.4.2.3 Test or verification and validation plans

Software test or verification and validation processes are used to determine if developed software products conform to their requirements, and whether the software products fulfill the intended use and user expectations. This includes analysis, evaluation, review, inspection, assessment, and testing of the software products and the processes that produced the products. Also, the software testing, verification, and validation processes apply when integrating purchased or customer-supplied software products into the developed product.

Document the testing or verification and validation tasks in a specific plan for each specific process executed. Each plan defines the testing or verification and validation tasks and required inputs and outputs needed to maintain the appropriate software integrity level. It also provides a means of verifying the implementation of the requirements of the SRD in the design as expressed in the SDD and in the testing as expressed in the project's test documentation. [IEEE Std 829-1998], [IEEE Std 1008-1987], [IEEE Std 1012-1998]

4.4.2.4 Software verification results report (SVRR) and test or validation results report (TVRR)

The SVRR shall describe the results of the software verification activities conducted according to the Verification Plan. The TVRR shall describe the results of the software test or validation carried out according to the Test or Validation Plan.

4.4.2.5 User documentation

User documentation guides the users in installing, operating, managing, and maintaining (does not apply when modifying software source code) software products. The documentation shall describe the data control inputs, input sequences, options, program limitations, and all other essential information for the software product. All error messages shall be identified and described. All corrective actions to correct the errors causing the error messages shall be described. The documentation is applicable to embedded software; however, that portion of the embedded software that has no direct user interaction is exempt from this requirement. [IEEE Std 1063-1987]

4.4.2.6 Software configuration management plan (SCMP)

The SCMP shall document what software configuration management (SCM) activities shall be accomplished, how they shall be accomplished, who is responsible for specific tasks, the schedule of events, and what resources will be utilized. Part of the plan includes documenting how the release and delivery of the product is managed. The plan can address SCM tasks over any portion of the product's development life cycle. At a minimum, the plan should address the SCM tasks that apply to the portion of the life cycle covered by the SQAP. [IEEE Std 828-1998]

4.4.3 Other documentation

Identify other documents applicable to the software development project and software product that may be required. Other documentation may include the following:

(Note: Names of various artifacts listed below use the terminology contained in ISO 12207.1. [IEEE/EIA 12207.0-1997])

a) Development Process Plan;

b) Software Development Standards Description;

c) Software Engineering Methods/Procedures/Tools Description;

d) Project Management Plan; and

e) Maintenance Plan.

4.5 Standards, practices, conventions, and metrics (Section 5 of the SQAP)

4.5.1 Purpose

This section shall:

a) Identify the standards, practices, conventions, statistical techniques to be used, quality requirements, and metrics to be applied. Product and process measures shall be included in the metrics used and may be identified in a separate measurement plan. [IEEE Std 1045-1992], [IEEE Std 1058-1998]

b) State how conformance with these items is to be monitored and assured.

4.5.2 Content

The subjects covered shall include the basic technical, design, and programming activities involved, such as documentation, variable and module naming, programming, inspection, and testing. As a minimum, the following information shall be provided: [IEEE Std 982.1-1988], [IEEE Std 982.2-1988]

a) Documentation standards;

b) Design standards;

c) Coding standards;

d) Commentary standards;

e) Testing standards and practices; and

f) Selected software quality assurance product and process metrics.

4.6 Software reviews (Section 6 of the SQAP)

4.6.1 Purpose

This section shall: [IEEE Std 1028.1-1997]

a) Define the software reviews to be conducted. They may include managerial reviews, acquirer-supplier reviews, technical reviews, inspections, walk-throughs, and audits.

b) List the schedule for software reviews as they relate to the software project's schedule.

c) State how the software reviews shall be accomplished.

d) State what further actions shall be required and how they shall be implemented and verified.

4.6.2 Minimum requirements

As a minimum, the following software reviews shall be conducted:

4.6.2.1 Software specification review (SSR)

The SSR is held to assure the adequacy of the requirements stated in the SRD.

4.6.2.2 Architecture design review (ADR)

The ADR is held to evaluate the technical adequacy of the preliminary design (also known as top-level design) of the software as depicted in the preliminary software design description.

4.6.2.3 Detailed design review (DDR)

The DDR is held to determine the acceptability of the detailed software designs as depicted in the detailed software design description in satisfying the requirements of the SRD.

4.6.2.4 Software verification and validation plan review (SVVPR)

The SVVPR is held to evaluate the adequacy and completeness of the verification and validation methods defined in the Software Verification and Validation Plan.

4.6.2.5 Functional audit

This audit is held prior to the software delivery to verify that all requirements specified in the SRD have been met.

4.6.2.6 Physical audit

This audit is held to verify internal consistency of the software, its documentation, and its readiness for release.

4.6.2.7 In-Process audits

In-process audits of samples of the design are held to verify the consistency of the design, including:

a) Code versus design documentation;

b) Interface specifications (hardware and software);

c) Design implementations versus functional requirements; and

d) Functional requirements versus test descriptions.

4.6.2.8 Managerial reviews

Managerial reviews are held periodically to assess the execution of all of the actions and the items identified in the SQAP. These reviews shall be held by an organizational element independent of the unit being reviewed, or by a qualified third party. This review may require additional changes in the SQAP itself.

4.6.2.9 Software configuration management plan review (SCMPR)

The SCMPR is held to evaluate the adequacy and completeness of the configuration management methods defined in the SCMP.

4.6.2.10 Post-Implementation review

This review is held at the conclusion of the project to assess the development activities implemented on that project and to provide recommendations for appropriate actions.

4.6.3 other

Other reviews and audits may include the user documentation review (UDR). This review is held to evaluate the adequacy (e.g., completeness, clarity, correctness, and usability) of the User Documentation.

4.7 Test (Section 7 of the SQAP)

This section shall identify all the tests not included in the Software Verification and Validation Plan for the software covered by the SQAP and shall state the methods to be used. If a separate test plan exists it should be referenced.

4.8 Problem reporting and corrective action (Section 8 of the SQAP)

This section shall:

a) Describe the practices and procedures to be followed for reporting, tracking, and resolving problems or issues identified in both software items and the software development and maintenance process.

b) State the specific organizational responsibilities concerned with their implementation.

4.9 Tools, techniques, and methodologies (Section 9 of the SQAP)

This section shall identify the software tools, techniques, and methods used to support SQA processes. For each, this section shall state their intended use, applicability or circumstances under which they are to be used or not to be used, and limitations.

4.10 Software code control (Section 10 of the SQAP)

This section shall define the methods and facilities used to maintain, store, secure, and document controlled versions of the identified software during all phases of the software life cycle. This may be implemented in conjunction with a computer program library. This may be provided as a part of the SCMP. If so, an appropriate reference shall be made thereto.

4.11 Media control (Section 11 of the SQAP)

This section shall state the methods and facilities to be used to (a) identify the media for each computer product and the documentation required to store the media, including the copy and restores process, and (b) protect computer program physical media from unauthorized access or inadvertent damage or degradation during all phases of the software life cycle. This may be provided as a part of the SCMP. If so, an appropriate reference shall be made thereto.

4.12 Supplier control (Section 12 of the SQAP)

This section shall state the provisions for assuring that software provided by suppliers meets established requirements. In addition, this section shall state the methods that will be used to assure that the software supplier receives adequate and complete requirements. For previously developed software, this section shall state the methods to be used to assure the suitability of the product for use with the software items covered by the SQAP. For software that is to be developed, the supplier shall be required to prepare and implement a SQAP in accordance with this standard. This section shall also state the methods to be employed to assure that the suppliers comply with the requirements of this standard. If software is to be developed under contract, then the procedures for contract review and update shall be described.

4.13 Records collection, maintenance, and retention (Section 13 of the SQAP)

This section shall identify the SQA documentation to be retained, shall state the methods and facilities to be used to assemble, file, safeguard, and maintain this documentation, and shall designate the retention period.

4.14 Training (Section 14 of the SQAP)

This section shall identify the training activities necessary to meet the needs of the SQAP.

4.15 Risk management (Section 15 of the SQAP)

This section shall specify the methods and procedures employed to identify, assess, monitor, and control areas of risk arising during the portion of the software life cycle covered by the SQAP. If safety considerations are involved, then this section shall specify the methods and procedures employed to assure safe operation.

4.16 Glossary

This section shall contain a glossary of terms unique to the SQAP or, if a project management plan exists, reference its glossary.

4.17 SQAP change procedure and history

This section shall contain the procedures for modifying the SQAP and maintaining a history of the changes.

Chapter 5

Software Reviews and Audits Processes

1. Introduction to Chapter

This chapter describes both the software reviews and audits processes. Paragraph 2 describes the review process, and Paragraph 3 describes the audit process. Portions of this text are paraphrased from IEEE/EIA Standard 12207.0-1996, Paragraphs 6.6 and 6.7. Paragraph 4 provides an overview and introduction to the papers contained in this chapter.

2. Joint review process

The *joint review process* (also known as *milestone reviews*) is a process for evaluating the status and products of a project activity as appropriate. Joint reviews include both project management and technical levels and are held throughout the life of the contract. This process may be employed by any two parties, in which one party (reviewing party) reviews another party (reviewed party). This process consists of the following activities:

1. Process implementation

2. Project management reviews

3. Technical reviews.

2.1 Process implementation

- Periodic reviews are held at predetermined milestones as specified in the project plan(s). *Ad hoc* reviews should be called when deemed necessary by either party.

- All resources required to conduct the reviews are agreed upon by the parties. These resources include personnel, location, facilities, hardware, software, and tools.

- The parties should agree on the following items at each review: meeting agenda, software products (results of an activity) and problems to be reviewed; scope and procedures; and entry and exit criteria for the review.

- Problems detected during the reviews are recorded and entered into the *problem resolution process* as required.

- The review results are documented and distributed. The reviewing party will acknowledge to the reviewed party the adequacy (for example, approval, disapproval, or contingent approval) of the review results.

- The parties shall agree on the outcome of the review and any action item responsibilities and closure criteria.

2.2 Project management reviews

- Project status is evaluated relative to the applicable project plans, schedules, standards, and guidelines. The outcome of the review should be discussed between the two parties and include provisions for the following:

  - ➤ Ensure activities progress according to plan, based on an evaluation of the activity or software product status

  - ➤ Maintain global control of the project through adequate allocation of resources

  - ➤ Change project direction or determine the need for alternate planning

  - ➤ Evaluate and manage the risk issues that may jeopardize the success of the project.

2.3 Technical reviews

This activity consists of the following task:

- Technical reviews are held to evaluate the software products or services under consideration and to provide evidence that:

  - ➤ They are complete.

  - ➤ They comply with their standards and specifications.

  - ➤ Changes to them are properly implemented and affect only those areas identified by the *configuration management process*.

  - ➤ They are adhering to applicable schedules.

  - ➤ They are ready for the next activity.

  - ➤ The development, operation, or maintenance is being conducted according to the plans, schedules, standards, and guidelines of the project.

3. Audit Process

The audit process is a process for determining compliance with the requirements, plans, and contract as appropriate. This process may be employed by any two parties, in which one party (auditing party) audits the software products or activities of another party (audited party). This process consists of the following activities:

1. Process implementation

2. Audit.

3.1 Process implementation

- Audits are held at predetermined milestones as specified in the project plan(s).

- Auditing personnel do not have any direct responsibility for the software products and activities they audit.

- All resources required to conduct the audits are agreed upon by the parties. These resources include supporting personnel, location, facilities, hardware, software, and tools.

- The parties should agree on the following items at each audit: agenda; software products (and results of an activity) to be reviewed; audit scope and procedures; and entry and exit criteria for the audit.

- Problems detected during the audits are recorded and entered into the *problem resolution process* as required.

- After completing an audit, the audit results are documented and provided to the audited party. The audited party acknowledges to the auditing party any problems found in the audit and related problem resolutions planned.

- The parties shall agree on the outcome of the audit and any action item responsibilities and closure criteria.

3.2 Audit

- Audits are conducted to ensure that:

  ➢ As-coded software products (such as a software item) reflect the design documentation.

  ➢ The acceptance review and testing requirements prescribed by the documentation are adequate for acceptance of the software products.

  ➢ Test data comply with the specifications.

  ➢ Software products were successfully tested and meet their specifications.

  ➢ Test reports are correct and discrepancies between actual and expected results have been resolved.

  ➢ User documentation complies with standards as specified.

  ➢ Activities have been conducted according to applicable requirements, plans, and contract.

  ➢ The cost and schedules adhere to the established plans.

4. Overview of Papers

The first paper in this chapter is a paper by John Marciniak from the predecessor of this tutorial [1]. This revised paper updates Marciniak's article of the same title in the *Encyclopedia of Software Engineering* [2]. Marciniak was chief editor for the encyclopedia. In this paper, Marciniak describes a review as a process during which a work product or a set of work products is presented to project personnel, managers, users, customers, and/or interested parties for consent or approval. Types of reviews include *audits, peer reviews, design reviews, formal qualification reviews, requirements reviews* and *test reviews.* A definition is provided for each of these review types.

Marciniak also defines two categories of reviews: *formal reviews,* which are required by contract commitment, and *informal reviews,* which, although not contractually required, are held due to their perceived benefits. He also integrates reviews, audits, walkthroughs, and inspections into the software development life cycle, illustrating when a given review might be held as well as the impact this review has on the life cycle and its products. He does not describe the activities of an *inspection,* only those of a *walkthrough.*

The second article is a paper by Frank Ackerman, describing software inspections. Inspections are undoubtedly one of the most effective tools available to the software engineering practitioner to assure a quality software system. Software inspections were developed and described by Michael Fagan [3], who worked for IBM in the 1970s. Essentially, software inspections are a form of peer review (like walkthroughs), which use the ability of individuals, not under pressure, willing to discuss freely the work being done to find errors in a software artifact.

Ackerman's paper provides a description of an inspection, the steps that the team must go through to ensure a quality inspection, a description of the people involved in a software inspection, and the benefits and results of a good software inspection. Ackerman also shows that properly applied software inspections are cost-effective through early detection of software errors.

The third article is extracted from IEEE Standard 1028-1998, IEEE *Standard for Software Reviews.* IEEE, Inc., New York, 1998. This standard defines five types of software reviews, together with procedures required for the execution of each review type. This standard is concerned only with the reviews; it does not define procedures for determining the necessity of a review, nor does it specify the disposition of the review results. Review types include management reviews, technical reviews, inspections, walk-throughs, and audits.

The reader is again reminded that this copy of the standard is incomplete and cannot be used to cite compliance with the standard in a contractual situation. It is intended to provide the reader and CSDP test taker with a basic understanding of the contents of the standard.

1. Dorfman, Merlin, and R.H. Thayer, *Software Engineering*, IEEE Computer Society Press, Los Alamitos, CA 1997.

2. Marciniak, John J., Editor-in-Chief, *Encyclopedia of Software Engineering*, 2 Vols., John Wiley, New York, 1994.

3. Fagan, M.E., "Design and Code Inspections to Reduce Errors in Program Development," *IBM Systems Journal*, Vol. 15, No. 3, 1976, pp. 182-211.

Reviews and Audits

John J. Marciniak
Kaman Sciences Corporation

Reviews and audits are valuable tools used in software development projects, as well as in systems development. The distinction between software management and systems management, as well as software engineering and systems engineering, is becoming blurred as "systems" development involves an increasing integration of these disciplines. One example is in reengineering projects where the trade-off between new software development is intrinsically related to the development or use of new hardware. The economics of reengineering projects dictate the acquisition approach and the degree of hardware and software development. The types of reviews discussed apply equally to the total system environment; however, their genesis is in software development. Some of these review types will vary in area of application while others such as the Formal Inspection, are more pertinent to the practice of software development.

Reviews come in different forms and names. Some of these are: formal reviews, inspections, audits, and walk-throughs. In each of these categories, the terms have different connotation and meaning. For example, general management reviews include project reviews and management oversight. Irrespective of the use or purpose, the form of the review is most important. Thus, one has to distinguish between the review as a practice and its use in practice.

The most common characteristics that distinguish review forms are: purpose, scope, and method. It is the purpose of this article to introduce these forms, explain the basic differences between them, and provide insight in how they are applied in software development practice. In general the purpose and scope of the review will determine the method used and the degree of formality applied. In Table 1 we depict these general characteristics.

The scope of a review may range from the entire project to a review of the design, or a single document such as the users' guide. In general, the scope of a review does not appreciably affect the review procedure, only the impact that it has on the level and area of application. The purpose of a review may range from an audit or inspection of a specific product, to an assessment or completion of a development milestone. For example, to determine the adequacy of a design specification, an inspection may be used. To determine the status of the progress of development at various milestones such as the completion of software design, management reviews or walk-throughs may be used. The method may vary from free form, or informal, to a specific methodology such as formal inspections. A free-form, or less formal procedure, may be used in technical interchange meeting (TIMs), while a formal inspection may be applied to assess the status of a specific product at the various points in its development.

Definitions

According to the *IEEE Standard Glossary of Software Engineering Terminology* (IEEE, 1990a), a review is

> A process or meeting during which a work product, or a set of work products, is presented to project personnel, managers, users, customers, or other interested parties for comment or approval. Types include code review, design review, formal qualification review, requirements review, and test readiness review.

This is the most general form and, as we shall see, is focused and customized depending on the specific purpose of the review.

Reviews are further classified according to formality. A formal review is typically one that is required by a contract commitment that is usually invoked through the application of a standard such as military standard 498 (MIL-STD-498), which are often more prevalent in government acquisition projects. The implication is that it is a contractual milestone witnessed by the customer or acquirer of the system, and normally denotes the completion of certain activities such as detailed design or system testing and results in a development or formal baseline for continued development of the software system.

Table 1. Review Characteristics

Type	Scope	Purpose	Method
Reviews	Usually broad	Project progress assessment of milestone completion	Ad hoc
Walk-throughs	Fairly narrow	Assess specific development products	Static analysis of products
Inspections	Narrow	Assess specific development products	Noninteractive, fairly procedural
Audits	Narrow to broad	Check processes and products of development	Formal, mechanical and procedure

In another perspective, Freedman and Weinberg use the following criteria to classify a formal review: (Freedman, 1990a)

1. A written report on the status of the product reviewed—a report that is available to everyone involved in the project, including management;

2. Active and open participation of everyone in the review group, following some traditions, customs, and written rules as to how such a review is to be conducted;

3. Full responsibility of all participants for the quality of the review—that is, for the quality of the information in the written report.

One can see that, from this description, the criteria shifts to certain responsibilities for the review participants as opposed to the contract vehicle.

As we see, there are different views as to the formality of the review. In contradistinction, informal reviews are those that are held which are not contractually required, or less formal from the perspective of Freedman and Weinberg, such as technical interchange meetings. The procedures applied for both formality types are similar, the principal difference being the rigor applied in the conduct of the review, for example, formal management of minutes.

There are other types of review classifications. For example, there are internal management reviews. (Marciniak, 1990) These may be periodic reviews of the project by senior management within the developing organization to assess progress or special reviews based on specific issues such as the impact of the development on other market areas. In the latter, management uses the review to provide general awareness of the direction of the project in order to take advantage of the resulting product in other market areas or to avoid conflict with other company projects.

Another major classification of reviews is the peer review. Peer reviews are usually walk-throughs, inspections, and round-robin reviews (Freedman, 1990b). The common characteristic of a peer review is that it is conducted by peers. A walk-through is normally a peer review; however, in many cases it is conducted with participants who are nonpeers. These reviews are normally confined to a single product such as a segment of the design, or a code unit, or component. The definitions of these reviews follows.

A Walk-through is

A static analysis technique in which a designer or programmer leads members of the development team and other interested parties through a segment of documentation or code, and the participants ask questions and make comments about possible errors, violation of development standards, and other problems. (IEEE, 1990b)

Walk-throughs are sometimes referred to as structured walk-throughs (not to be confused with formal inspections, see below); however, according to Freedman and Weinberg they are one and the same (Freedman, 1990c). A walk-through is probably the most common review technique in a software project, and the method will vary based on individual implementation.

A special form of a walk-through is the Formal Inspection. The Formal Inspection was developed at IBM (Fagan, 1976) and is often referred to simply as Fagan Inspections. A principal distinguishing factor between a walk-through and a formal inspection is that the formal inspection is led by a moderator independent of the person responsible for the product, while the walk-through is led by a reader or presenter who may be the developer of the product.

In a formal inspection the collection of anomalies is carefully structured to capture statistical evidence of the effort. A formal inspection should not be confused with an inspection. The choice of the term is perhaps unfortunate as the formal inspection is a type of walk-through rather than an inspection. Hollocker discusses the procedures used for Formal Inspections; however, chooses to use the words "Software Inspection." (Hollocker, 1990)

Inspection

An inspection is

A static analysis technique that relies on visual examination of development products to detect errors, violations of developing standards, and other problems. Types include code inspection; design inspections. (IEEE, 1990c)

Freedman and Weinberg define inspection as "a method of rapidly evaluating material by confining attention to a few selected aspects, one at a time" (Freedman, 1990d). The inspection is carried out in an noninteractive manner, usually by a party that is detached from the developer.

The difference between inspections and audits is not obvious, and perhaps the difference is not pertinent. The differences are stated in Evans (Evans, 1987a).

An inspection normally has a narrow focus evaluating only a segment of the project environment. The inspection structure is very rigid and the evaluation criteria are predetermined based on a model of acceptability.

An audit may also have a narrow focus, but, in most cases, is use to evaluate the broader aspects of the project environment. Besides checking individual segments of the project infrastructure against plans, audits may evaluate the interrelationships between segments of the infrastructure. When assessing the implementation attributes, audits tend to be more "freewheeling" allowing the auditor to pursue paths not necessarily included in the initial audit.

Another view put forth in Evans, focuses on interaction (Evans 1987b). An audit is normally more interactive in that the auditor communicates with the project staff. In an inspection, the inspector uses a rigid set of guidelines or a checklist to assess the degree of compliance with the checklist or guidelines. In either event, the important thing is to focus on the purpose of the procedure, then apply the mechanism that is more appropriate for the project.

Audits

An audit is much like an inspection; however, as indicated above, it tends to be of a broader nature and involve interactions with the project staff.

In the general form an audit is

An independent examination of a work product or set of work products to assess compliance with specifications, standards, contractual agreements, or other criteria. (IEEE, 1990d)

The IEEE defines two specific forms of audits, the Functional Configuration Audit (FCA) and the Physical Configuration Audit (PCA).

A functional configuration audit (FCA) is

An audit conducted to verify that the development of a configuration item has been completed satisfactorily, that the item has achieved the performance and functional characteristics specified in the functional or allocated configuration identification, and that its operational and support documents are complete and satisfactory. (IEEE, 1990e)

A physical configuration audit (PCA) is

An audit conducted to verify that a configuration item, as built, conforms to the technical documentation that defined it. (IEEE, 1990f)

These two audits are formal audits because they are required by the contractual instruments that govern the development project. If there were no contractual instrument, the eventual user would still conduct a form of the above to verify the product. A simple example is buying an automobile. When the automobile is ordered, a spec sheet or contract is normally filled out calling for items such as fog lights and radios. A functional audit would verify that the radio performs, for example, that it plays the bands specified, while a physical audit would verify that the type of radio ordered is the one that is actually delivered with the automobile.

There are other types of audits that are conducted during the development process. For example, there are quality assurance audits that audit a particular process of development such as the conduct of reviews and walk-throughs. There are configuration management audits that audit the processes of configuration management. The distinguishing factor in these types of audits is that they are carried out by the function with that specific responsibility. For example, a software quality assurance (SQF) audit is carried out by the software quality assurance function, and it is based on SQA plans and procedures.

Application in the life cycle

Reviews, audits, walk-throughs, and inspections are used to provide assessment of the progress, processes used, and products of the project. The program management plan, or software development plan, will normally specify the types of reviews used and the methods that are applied in their use. Certain reviews, as mentioned above, will be dictated by contract requirements, usually through the use of development standards such as IEEE Std 1498 (IEEE, 19XX). In Figure 1 we show a typical waterfall life cycle with examples of system development reviews and audits.

There are three parts to a review: the planning phase, the review conduct, and the post review phase. All are important to any successful review. The elimination or neglect of any of the phases will jeopardize a successful review.

In the planning phase, the actions generally include stating the purpose of the review, arranging for participants, ensuring that review materials are provided for their inspection well prior to the conduct of the review, making physical arrangements for the location and support required, and preparing an agenda. During the conduct of the review, it is important to follow the agenda in a disciplined manner. Generally speaking, the purpose of the review conduct is not to fix problems that are identified, but, to identify them and assign action for their resolution. Reviews can very easily get contentious so it is important to ensure that a moderator or review leader maintains control of the proceedings. A recorder or scribe has to be assigned to transcribe the proceedings into recorded form for the purpose of preparing a record of the review and a postreview action list. The postreview period can be flexible depending on the actions required. These are normally followed to completion by management and reported on at the next review. It is possible that another review may be required if the review results are unsatisfactory. Naturally, this could result in some project impact, usually of schedule and cost.

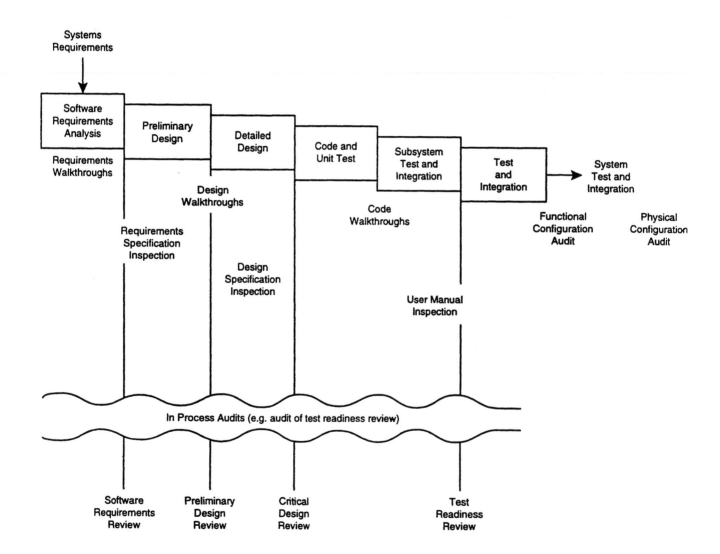

Figure 1. Reviews in the software life cycle

110

Management Reviews

Objective. A management review is a formal management-team evaluation of a project-level plan or a project's status relative to such a plan. The review team communicates progress, coordinates the decision making within their span of control, and provides recommendations for:

- Making activities progress according to plan, based on an evaluation of product development status
- Changing project direction or identifying the need for alternative planning
- Maintaining global control of the project through adequate allocation of resources

Moreover, to further tailor this review process for an individual project milestone, specific objectives are to be identified in a "Statement of Objectives" made available before the review meeting. The management review concept can be applied to new development or to maintenance activities. It can also be useful in managing process improvement projects.

People and Their Agendas. Roles for the management review include:

- Leader
- Reporter
- Team member

The review leader is responsible for the administrative tasks pertaining to the review, for assuring that the review is conducted in an order manner, and for issuing any minutes or reports. The reporter is responsible for having the project status and all supporting documentation available for distribution before the meeting. This individual is also responsible for documenting the findings, decisions, and recommendations of the review team.

When to Hold a Management Review. Typically, the project planning documents (for example, Software Quality Assurance Plan, Software Development Plan, or Software Verification and Validation Plan) establish the need for conducting specific management reviews. As stated in these plans, a management review can be initiated by the completion of a project phase or specific software deliverable (for example, a planning document, a requirements specification, or a design document). Moreover, management reviews not required by plan may occur, as needed, to deal with any unscheduled events or contingencies.

A selected review leader establishes or confirms a statement of objectives for the meeting and verifies that any appropriate software deliverables and any other documents or reports available are sufficiently complete to support the review objectives. In addition to any applicable reference material supplied by project management, or requested by the review leader, these would include:

- A Statement of Objectives for the management review and its agenda
- Current project schedule, resource, and cost data
- Pertinent reports (for example, managerial review reports, technical review reports, or audit reports) from other reviews and/or audits already completed
- Software deliverable status or current disposition

Procedures. The review leader, having identified the team, schedules facilities for the meeting and distributes any materials needed by the review team for advanced preparation (for example, statement of objectives, agenda, or presentation requirements). In addition, the review leader might consider requesting that a project representative conduct an overview session for the review team. This overview can occur as part of the examination meeting or as a separate meeting. The management review process is considered complete when all issues identified in the review "Statement of Objectives" have been addressed and the management review report has been issued. Project management typically tracks any action items through to resolution. If a re-review is required. it would provide confirmation of action item completion.

Output. The Management Review Report identifies:

- The project being reviewed and the team that participated in that review
- Inputs to the review
- Review objectives
- Action item ownership, status, and tracking responsibility
- Project status and a list of issues that must be addressed for the project to meet its milestone
- Recommendations regarding any further reviews and audits, and a list of additional information and data that must be obtained before they can be executed

The Walk-through

Objective. The walk-through process has much in common with both the general technical review process and the inspection process. It, too, is used to evaluate a specific software element and provide evidence that the software element satisfies its specifications and conforms to applicable standards. Its statement of objectives includes software element specific objectives. They also exist in the form of a checklist that varies with the product being presented. Objectives typically do not pertain to any additional constraints on the walk-through process.

Distinctions from other review processes, however, are established by unique objectives. The following always appear in the Statement of Objectives for the application of the walk-through process:

- Detect, identify, and describe software element defects
- Examine alternatives and stylistic issues
- Provide a mechanism that enables the authors to collect valuable feedback on their work, yet allows them to retain the decision-making authority for any changes

People and Their Agendas. Roles for the walk-through are similar to those for other review processes, with one important distinction. The leader responsible for conducting a specific walk-through, handling the administrative tasks pertaining to the walk-through, and ensuring that the walk-through is conducted in an orderly manner is usually the author.

The scribe is responsible for writing down all comments made during the walk-through that pertain to errors found, questions of style, omissions, contradictions, suggestions for improvement, or alternative approaches.

Each team member is responsible for reviewing any input material prior to the walk-through and participating during the walk-through to ensure that it meets its objective. Roles may be shared among the walk-through members.

When to Hold the Walk-through Meeting. The need for conducting walk-throughs, as with all product reviews, can be established either by local practice or in planning documents. Completion of a specific software element can trigger the walkthrough for the element. Additional walk-throughs can be conducted during development of the software element at the request of the author or management from various functional areas. A walk-through is conducted when the author indicates readiness.

Procedures. *Planning.* During the planning process phase the author:

- Identifies the walk-through team
- Schedules the meeting and selects the meeting place
- Distributes all necessary input materials to the participants, allowing for adequate preparation time

Overview. An overview presentation is made by the author as part of the walk-through meeting. Before that meeting, however, individual preparation is still required.

Preparation. During the preparation phase participants review the input material that was distributed to them and prepare a list of questions and issues to be brought up during the walk-through.

Examination. During the walk-through meeting:

- The author makes an overview presentation of the software element
- The author "walks through" the specific software element so that members of the walk-through team may ask questions or raise issues about the software element, and/or make notes documenting their concerns
- The scribe writes down comments and decisions for inclusion in the walk-through report

At the completion of the walk-through, the team may recommend a follow-up walk-through that follows the same process and would, at a minimum, cover areas changed by the author. The walk-through process is complete when the entire software element has been walked through in detail and all deficiencies, omissions, efficiency issues, and suggestions for improvement have been noted. The walk-through report is issued, as required by local standards.

Output. The walk-through report contains:

- Identification of the walk-through team
- Identification of the software element(s) being examined
- The statement of objectives that were to be handled during this walk-through meeting
- A list of the noted deficiencies, omissions, contradictions, and suggestions for improvement

- Any recommendations made by the walk-through team on how to dispose of deficiencies and unresolved issues. If follow-up walk-throughs are suggested, that should be mentioned in the report as well

Formal Inspections

Objective. A formal inspection, as stated earlier, is a variant of the procedure used for a structured walk-through. The differences are described in the following procedure and contrasted with the above procedures for a walk-through.

The objective of the formal inspection is to detect defects in the product being inspected by comparison with a checklist that typifies the types of defects that are common to the type of product being inspected. These are recorded and a statistical report is prepared so that evidential data is compiled. These data are used: to compare the product at this stage of development with later stages; compile a basis for statistical measure of the product; and to build an experience base to be used for other products in the same or similar projects.

People and Their Agendas. The roles in a formal inspection include a moderator, participants or inspectors, the preparer or developer of the product, and a recorder. The moderator is normally a peer who is selected for his/her technical expertise with the type of material. This person should be someone who is from outside the project. The participants are peers of the preparer and normally from the project staff to ensure that they are familiar with the project from a technical point of view.

Procedures. Prior to the inspection, the moderator makes arrangements for the inspection based on similar procedures used for a walk-through. The materials to be inspected, the checklists to be used, and the facilities where the inspection is to be located are all planning functions that need to be accomplished. The moderator controls the inspection process by walking through the code or design in a step-by-step manner. The peers comment on the product and these are recorded by the recorder.

It is important to identify the checklist that will be used and ensure that the recorder understands his/her duties with respect to recording the results. The checklist, which is the basis for the inspection, is composed of the common types of defects that are found in the product. For example, in a code inspection the following types of defects may be listed in the checklist (Vliet, 1993):

1. wrongful use of data: uninitialized variables, array index out of bounds, dangling pointers, and so forth;

2. faults in declarations, such as the use of undeclared variables, or the declaration of the same name in nested blocks;

3. faults in computations; division by zero, overflow, wrong use of variables of different types in one and the same expression, faults caused by an erroneous conception of operator priorities, etc.;

4. faults in relational expressions, such as using an incorrect operator, or an erroneous conception of priorities of Boolean operators;

5. faults in control flow, such as infinite loops, or a loop that gets executed n+1 or n-1 times rather than n;

6. faults in interfaces, such as an incorrect number of parameters, parameters of the wrong type, or an inconsistent use of global variables.

When to Hold the Formal Inspection Meeting. Inspections are regularly scheduled in accordance with project plans based on the status of a product. For example, periodic inspections of the product could be conducted at the preliminary design, detailed design, and implementation or code completion.

Output. The result of the inspection is a list of the defects that are found. Defects may be categorized according to severity. The defects are corrected after the inspection and the results are checked by the moderator. A reinspection may be called for if the product is deemed unsatisfactory to proceed.

Audits

Objective. Audits, performed in accordance with documented plans and procedures, provide an independent confirmation that product development and process execution adhere to standards, guidelines, specifications, and procedures. Audit personnel use objective audit criteria (for example, contracts and plans; standards, practices and conventions: or requirements and specifications) to evaluate:

- Software elements
- The processes for producing them
- Projects
- Entire quality programs

People and Their Agendas. It is the responsibility of the audit team leader to organize and direct the audit and to coordinate the preparation and issuance of the audit report. The audit team leader is ultimately responsible for the proper conduct of the audit and its reports, and makes sure that the audit team is prepared.

The entity initiating the audit is responsible for authorizing the audit. Management of the auditing organization assumes responsibility for the audit and the allocation of the necessary resources to perform the audit.

Those whose products and processes are being audited provide all relevant materials and resources and correct or resolve deficiencies cited by the audit team.

When to Audit. The need for an audit is established by one of the following events:

- A special project milestone, calendar date, or other criterion has been met and, as part of its charter, the auditing organization is to respond by initiating an audit.

- A special project milestone has been reached. The audit is initiated per earlier plans (for example, the Software Quality Assurance Plan, or Software Development Plan). This includes planned milestones for controlling supplier development.

- External parties (for example, regulatory agencies or end users) require an audit at a specific calendar date or project milestone. This may be in fulfillment of a contract requirement or as a prerequisite to contractual agreement.

- A local organizational element(s)(for example, project management, functional management, systems engineering, or internal quality assurance/control) has requested the audit, establishing a clear and specific need.

Perhaps the most important inputs required to assure the success of the audit are the purpose and scope of the audit. Observations and evaluations performed as part of the audit require objective audit criteria, such as contracts requirements, plans, specifications, procedures, guidelines, and standards. The software elements and processes to be audited need to be made accessible, as do any pertinent histories. Background information about the organization responsible for the products and processes being audited (for example, organization charts) are critical for both planning and execution of the audit.

Procedures. The auditing organization develops and documents an audit plan for each audit. This plan should, in addition to restating the audit scope, identify the:

- Project processes to be examined (provided as input) and the time frame for audit team observations

- Software to be examined (provided as input) and their availability where sampling is used, a statistically valid sampling methodology is used to establish selection criteria and sample use

- Reporting requirements (that is, results report, and, optionally, the recommendations report with their general format and distribution defined), whether recommendations are required or excluded should be explicitly stated

- Required follow-up activities

- Activities, elements, and procedures necessary to meet the scope of the audit

- Objective Audit Criteria that provide the basis for determining compliance (provided as input)

- Audit Procedures and Checklists

- Audit Personnel requirements (for example, number, skills, experience, and responsibilities)

- Organizations involved in the audit (for example, the organization whose products and processes are being audited)

- Date, time, place, agenda, and intended audience of "overview" session (optional)

The audit team leader prepares an audit team having the necessary background and (when allowed) notifies the involved organizations, giving them a reasonable amount of advance warning before the audit is performed. The notification should be written to include audit scope, the identification processes and products to be audited, and the auditors' identity.

An optional overview meeting with the audited organization is recommended to "kick off" the examination phase of the audit. The overview meeting, led by the audit team leader, provides:

- Overview of existing agents (for example, audit scope, plan and related contracts)

- Overview of production and processes being audited

- Overview of the audit process, its objectives, and outputs
- Expected contributions of the audited organization to the audit process (that is, the number of people to be interviewed, meeting facilities, et cetera)
- Specific audit schedule

The following preparations are required by the audit team:

- Understand the organization: It is essential to identify functions and activities performed by the audited organization and to identify functional responsibility
- Understand the products and processes: It is a prerequisite for the team to learn about the products and processes being audited through readings and briefings
- Understand the Objective Audit Criteria: It is important that the audit team become familiar with the objective and criteria to be used in the audit
- Prepare for the audit report: It is important to choose the administrative reporting mechanism that will be used throughout the audit to develop the report that follows the layout identified in the audit plan
- Detail the audit plan: Choose appropriate methods for each step in the audit program

In addition, the audit team leader makes the necessary arrangements for:

- Team orientation and training
- Facilities for audit interviews
- Materials, documents, and tools required by the audit procedures
- The software elements to be audited (for example, documents, computer files, personnel to be interviewed)
- Scheduling interviews

Elements that have been selected for audit are evaluated against the Objective Audit Criteria. Evidence is examined to the depth necessary to determine if these elements comply with specified criteria.

An audit is considered complete when:

- Each element(s) within the scope of the audit has been examined

- Findings have been presented to the audited organization
- Response to draft findings have been received and evaluated
- Final findings have been formally presented to the audited organization and initiating entity
- The audit report has been prepared and submitted to recipients designated in the audit plan
- The recommendation report, if required by plan, has been prepared and submitted to recipients designated in the audit plan
- All of the auditing organization's follow-up actions included in the scope (or contract) of the audit have been performed.

Output. Following a standard framework for audit reports, the draft and final audit reports contain:

- Audit Identification: Report title, audited organization, auditing organization, and date of the audit
- Scope: Scope of the audit, including an enumeration of the standards, specifications, practices, and procedures constituting the Objective Audit Criteria against which the audit of the software elements and processes were conducted
- Conclusions: A summary and interpretation of the audit findings, including the key items of nonconformance
- Synopsis: A listing of all the audited software elements and processes, and associated findings
- Follow-up: The type and timing of audit follow-up activities

Additionally, when stipulated by the audit plan, recommendations are provided to the audited organization, or the entity that initiated the audit. Recommendations are reported separately from results.

Comments and issues raised by the audited organization must be resolved. The final audit report should then be prepared, approved, and issued by the audit team leader to the organizations specified in the audit plan.

Inspections

Inspections are limited forms of an audit. The procedures for conducting an inspection are similar to an audit except that they are limited due to the focus of the inspection.

Future directions

As previously mentioned, the use of reviews and audits in the software development business is becoming more blurred because of the concentration on a systems perspective. Thus, we will see more emphasis on systems engineering. This will not change the mechanisms or practices that are used. They will be applied, however, in more of a systems management and engineering context. Thus, the use of specific review procedures will be more broadly applied in the development or acquisition of the system.

One trend that we currently see is the use of more interactive techniques. A walk-through is an interactive procedure. The moderator or inspector, participants, recorder—all communicate as the product is being "walked through". As systems development becomes more dynamic, as we already see in Web development, electronic techniques will enhance this procedure. It is possible to have an on-line review conducted across geographic distances. It is even possible to make dynamic changes to products as the capability to do so advances (for example, in the development of a home page as an element of Web site development). If a product such as a document is being reviewed, changes to it can be accomplished in real time. This will place more emphasis on the rigor or formality required of the process to properly control and account for changes. Configuration management will take on a real-time (and more dramatic) meaning in this environment.

Another trend that is quite possible is the more prevalent use of formal inspections. It has already been demonstrated that this technique has great benefit to the development of software. As software engineering progresses in maturity, there will be more emphasis on the attainment of specific attributes of the product. We should be able to relate the attainment software quality factors such as reliability, usability, and complexity described by the work of McCall and Bowen directly to the product (Vincent, 1988). Thus, the coupling or relationship of these factors to the product will be a more measured one. This will afford the quantifiable prediction of quality, and control of the product in order to meet these predictions. The implication is that checklists, based on experiential data associated with the attainment of specific quality attributes, will be more widely used.

Summary

The different types of reviews used in a software development process range from informal technical reviews to formal reviews such as the FCA. The types and number of reviews are largely determined by the complexity and size of the project. In a project that is internal to an organization, reviews tend to be more informal compared to a project that is under contract. Normally, the number and types of reviews will be detailed in management plans with specific methods left to a procedures and standards handbook.

Although there are different reasons for conducting reviews, the principal purpose is to assess the progress or integrity of a process or product. Reviews are also important for gathering data. The systematic collection of data is essential for assessing the process in order to support process improvement programs as well as developing experiential data for applying to new projects. These data can support the prediction of various activities such as the quality of products through comparisons of previous data collected on prior projects.

Thus, reviews of all sorts provide a basic performance and assessment technique that bridges the individual project, and even the organization. They are the essential performance technique in software development practice.

Portions of this article have been excised from Software Reviews and Audits, Charles Hollocker, John Wiley & Sons, New York, N.Y., 1990.

References

M. Evans and J. Marciniak, *Software Quality Assurance and Management*, John Wiley & Sons, New York, N.Y., 1987a, p. 115; 1987b, p. 229.

Michael Fagan, "Design and Code Inspection to Reduce Errors in Program Development," *IBM Systems J.*, Vol. 15, No. 3, 1976.

Daniel P. Freedman and Gerald M. Weinberg, *Walkthroughs, Inspections, and Technical Reviews*, Dorset House, New York, N.Y., Third Ed., 1990a, pp. 10–11; 1990b, p. 232; 1990c, p. 232; 1990d, p. 239.

Charles Hollocker, *Software Reviews and Audits*, John Wiley & Sons, New York, N.Y., 1990, pp. 44–48.

IEEE Std 610.12-1990, *Standard Glossary of Software Engineering Terminology*, IEEE, New York, N.Y., 1990a, p. 64;. 1990b, p. 81; 1990c, p. 40; 1990d, p. 11; 1990e, p. 35; 1990f, p. 55.

IEEE Std 1498, IEEE, New York, N.Y.

John J. Marciniak and Donald J. Reifer, *Software Acquisition Management*, John Wiley & Sons, New York, N.Y., 1990, p. 26.

Mil-Std-498, "Software Development and Documentation," Department of Defense, 1994.

J. Vincent, A. Waters, and J. Sinclair, *Software Quality Assurance*, Prentice-Hall, Englewood Cliffs, N.J., Vol. 1, 1988, pp. 11–28.

Software Inspections and the Cost Effective Production of Reliable Software

A. Frank Ackerman*

Institute for Zero Defect Software
San Jose, California

Software inspections were first defined for IBM by M. E. Fagan in 1976 [FGN76]. Since that time they have been used within IBM [DBN81] and other organizations [PEL82]. An IEEE software engineering standard covering inspections was approved in 1988 [IEEE88]. This paper describes software inspections as they were used in a large telecommunications R&D organization, and the technology transfer program that was used for their effective implementation. It also describes the placement of software inspections within the overall development process, and discusses their use in conjunction with other verification and validation techniques.

1. Introduction

The routine production of software products of high reliability produced within budget and on schedule continues to be an elusive goal. The root cause of the difficulty is that although software development can be conceptualized as an industrial process [FGN76], most of the individual steps of this process must be performed by individual "intellectual artisans." The scope of an artisan's work is inherently difficult to bound, the techniques employed can not be specified precisely, and the quality of the resulting products is variable. By contrast, in a well-organized industrial process, each individual operation is clearly delineated, the techniques employed are clearly defined, and the whole process can be managed in such a way that it predictably produces products of specified quality. Software inspections, as defined in this paper, were first employed by M.E. Fagan in 1974 at the IBM Corporation as a method for reducing variability in the quality of individual operations in a software development process. Inspections also facilitated tighter, more rational process control [FGN76].

This paper is based on the results of a software engineering technology transfer program to implement software inspections at a large telecommunications R&D organization. Used for more than two years on a wide variety of applications, the program trained more than 2,400 software developers and managers in 40 different projects. The current evaluation of such programs is that software inspections can indeed produce the quality and productivity benefits claimed by M.E. Fagan, but that the implementation of software inspections within a development organization is a challenging task. This task requires not only a sound understanding of software development technology, but also a keen appreciation of the behavior and motivation of individual developers and the organizational culture in which these individuals work.

Sections 2, 3, and 4 of this paper describes software inspections and how they can be used to improve the industrial production of software products. Section 5 discusses the relationship of software inspections to other verification tasks. Section 6 describes a method for implementing software inspections within development organizations.

2. Software Inspections Overview

Software inspections are designed to address the three major tasks of process management: planning, measurement, and control. For software development, the corresponding tasks are (1) the definition of a software development process as a clearly defined series of individual operations, (2) the collection of quantitative quality data at different points in the process, and (3) the use of this data for improving the process.

The individual operations within a complete development process can be delineated by specifying explicit exit criteria to be met by the work products produced by each operation. The process can then be "thought of as a continuous process during which sequential sets of exit criteria are satisfied, the last set in the entire series requiring a well-defined end product" [FGN76]. For example, the exit criteria for the completion of module coding might be: compilation with no faults, no warnings from a portability checker, and no violations from a standards checker.

---

* This paper is adapted from an earlier paper, "Software Inspections and the Industrial Production of Software," by the author, Priscilla J. Fowler, and Robert G. Ebenau, which appeared in *Software Validation*, H.I. Hausen, ed., Elsevier, Amsterdam, 1984, pp. 13–40.

117

DATE: UNIT:

MODERATOR: TYPE:

INSPECTORS: AMOUNT:

DISPOSITION:

OVERVIEW: ESTIMATED REWORK COMPLETION:

PREPARATION: ESTIMATED REWORK EFFORT:

MEETING: ACTUAL REWORK EFFORT:

	DEFECTS THIS OPERATION				DEFECTS IN PRIOR OPERATION			
	M	W	E	TOTAL	DOCU-MENT	ERROR TYPE	ERROR CLASS	MR/STR NUMBER
IF: INTERFACE								
DA: DATA								
LO: LOGIC								
IO: INPUT/OUTPUT								
PF: PERFORMANCE								
FN: FUNCTIONALITY								
HF: HUMAN FACTORS								
ST: STANDARDS								
DC: DOCUMENTATION								
SN: SYNTAX								
TE: TEST ENVIRONMENT								
TC: TEST COVERAGE								
OT: OTHER								
TOTAL								

M = MISSING   W = WRONG   E = EXTRA

Figure 1. Software inspection data

The operations which make up a particular development process, and the exit criteria which define their completion, are dependent on the particular application, the development techniques being used, and the culture of the organization. The only essential requirements are that the criteria be explicit, unambiguous, and verifiable.

One of the mechanisms used to collect quantitative quality data at defined points in the development process is a software inspection. A software inspection is a group review process that is used to detect and correct defects in a software work product. It is a formal, technical activity that is performed by the work product author and a small peer group on a limited amount of material. It produces a formal, quantitative report on the resources expended and the results achieved.

Software inspections are often compared to walk-throughs [YRD78] and indeed there are many similarities. But there are major differences in focus and intent. Walk-throughs are generally considered to be a developer technique that can be used by individuals to improve the quality of their work. Inspections, on the other hand, are intended to be a process management tool that will not only improve the quality of individual work products, but will also produce data that can be used for rational, quantitative decision-making. Thus, within each development process, software inspections must be formally and rigorously defined and they must be executed according to specification. More details on software inspections are provided in the next section.

An example of the data collected for an individual software inspection is shown in Figure 1.[1] The use of these data for process control is illustrated in Figure 2. In Figure 2, inspection data is shown as being used in three different ways: feed-back, feed-forward, and feed-into. For example, a series of design inspections might reveal an unexpectedly high percentage of data definition defects that could indicate a need for better

---

[1] Figure 1 uses the term "defects" rather than "errors," which is the term used by Fagan [FGN76]. The reason for this change of terminology is to be consistent with IEEE Std 729-1983, *IEEE Standard Glossary of Software Engineering Terminology*. All the terms used in this paper are consistent with this standard unless otherwise noted.

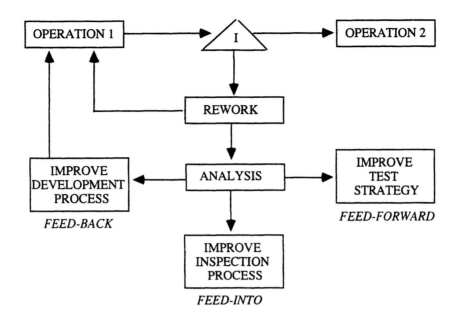

Figure 2. The use of inspection data

control of documentation for data layouts, that is, a need for a process adjustment to assure higher quality in subsequent work products. Information feed-forward can provide intelligence on treatment adjustments for individual work products. For example, a work product that was found to have an unusually high percentage of logic defects could be subjected to more rigorous testing.

The third use of inspection data (feed-into) can provide effectiveness and quality data about the inspection operations themselves. (For example, Are work products being examined carefully? are inspectors sufficiently prepared? and so on.) The collection and analysis of inspection data in conjunction with other process measures, such as reports on quality and productivity from testing operations, allows individual inspection operations to be adjusted for overall effectiveness. Thus, used properly, software inspections are self-regulating. They have repeatedly proven to be an effective method for improving both quality and productivity.

In his paper, Fagan reports on the effectiveness of software inspections applied to the development of a moderately complex component of a large operating system [FGN76]. Software inspections were held on detail designs, on cleanly compiled code, and at the completion of unit test. The result was a 23 percent productivity improvement and a 38 percent quality improvement, when compared with the development of a similar component that used walk-throughs.

In a trial of software inspections on a time-sharing system component upgrade at a large telecommunications R&D organization, software inspections were held on 1,482 noncommentary lines of source code after clean compile and some unit testing. The results were that 32 failures were detected by inspections with a total documented expenditure of 116 staff hours. The product (which altogether contained 8,940 lines of old, new, and changed code) was then subjected to system test, which detected 21 failures with an estimated expenditure of 162 staff hours.

3. Software Inspection Specifics

The Software Inspection Process. Each software inspection is itself a five or six-step process that is carried out by a designated moderator, by the author of the work product being inspected, and by at least one other peer inspector. The six steps are:

- Planning
- Overview
- Preparation
- Meeting
- Rework
- Follow-up

119

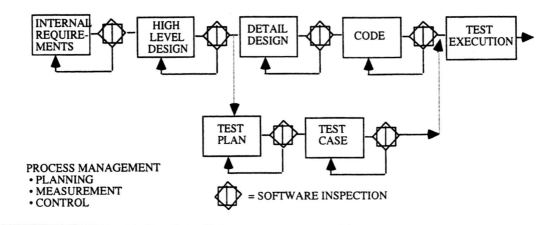

PROCESS MANAGEMENT
• PLANNING
• MEASUREMENT
• CONTROL

◈ = SOFTWARE INSPECTION

Figure 3. Software development process

Planning for an inspection begins when an author's work product meets the entry criteria established for this type of inspection. The first step is to select a moderator—a peer developer responsible for carrying out the inspection. A moderator may be selected by the author or a first-line manager from among a pool of qualified developers, or may be selected from an independent group with overall responsibility for the conduct of inspections for that organization. Since the moderator has overall responsibility for the inspection, including the final decision on the work product's disposition at the end of the inspection, it is important that he or she be as objective as possible. One way to ensure this is to specify that the moderator not be a member of a group that has direct production responsibility for the work product being inspected.

The moderator's first task is to meet with the author and to verify that the work product to be inspected meets the entry criteria for this type of inspection. When the work product meets these criteria, the next step is to decide whether or not to hold an overview, to select the other inspectors, and to schedule the overview and the meeting.

A software inspection overview is a presentation that is made to provide inspectors with any background information they may need in order to properly inspect the author's work product. Typically, an overview is given by an author, and it often covers material pertinent to a number of inspections. For example, for the time-sharing system component cited above, a single overview of the whole system was held for all prospective inspectors before beginning any of the individual inspections.

Another use of an overview is to provide a tutorial session on a specialized design or implementation technique that is used in the work product to be inspected, for example, a specialized enqueue and dequeue technique for synchronizing independent processes. The purpose of the overview is educational; the only inspection data collected during this step are the author's preparation time and the time the author and the inspectors spend at the overview presentation.

Preparation for a software inspection is an individual activity. The author prepares by collecting all the material required for this inspection and by completing an Inspection Profile Form (see Form 1 at the end of this paper). The other inspectors prepare by studying the work product to be inspected and by completing an Inspection Preparation Log (see Form 2). The purpose of individual preparation is to develop an understanding of the work product and to note places where this understanding is incomplete, or where the work product appears to have defects. Obvious defects are noted during this step, but detailed analysis and classification of defects is deferred to the inspection meeting.

The inspection meeting is conducted by the moderator. There is an established agenda that consists of:

- Introduction
- Establishing preparedness
- Examining the material and recording defects
- Reviewing defect list
- Determining disposition
- Debriefing.

During the introduction, the moderator introduces the inspectors and the material to be examined and states the purpose of the meeting. Preparedness is established by having each inspector report his or her preparation time as entered on the Inspection Preparation Log. The moderator sums these times for entry on the Inspection Management Report (see Form 3). If the moderator feels that preparation has been insufficient for an effective meeting, he or she may postpone the meeting.

Examining the material and recording defects are the major activities of an inspection meeting. At the meeting, one of the inspectors takes the role of reader and paces the group through the material by paraphrasing each "line" or section of the material aloud for the group. As the reader proceeds through the material in what he or she has selected as the most effective sequence for defect detection, the inspectors (including the reader) interrupt with questions and concerns. Each of these is either handled immediately or tabled. Whenever the group agrees, or the moderator rules, that a defect has been detected, the recorder for that inspection notes the location, description, class, and type on the Inspection Defect List (Form 4). (The role of recorder can be assumed by the moderator or any other inspector other than the author.)

After the reading and recording of defects, the moderator has the recorder review the Defect List to make sure that all defects have been recorded and correctly classified. After this is done, the inspectors determine the disposition of the material: "meets," "rework," or "re-inspect." The disposition of "meets" is given when the work product as inspected meets the exit criteria (or needs only trivial corrections) required for that type of inspection. The disposition of "re-inspect" is given when rework will change the work product in a substantial way.

Since an inspection meeting is to determine and record defects in a peer's work product, there is always the potential that interpersonal tension will develop during the meeting. An experienced moderator will note this and after the meeting initiate a suitable "debriefing exercise" to give these tensions opportunity for safe release. The debriefing exercise that we teach in our inspections training classes simply gives each participant an opportunity to briefly share his or her experience of the meeting in a supportive atmosphere.

Our experience with the interpersonal aspect of inspections is that problems in this area can be significant when inspections are initially introduced in a . project, but they tend to disappear as inspections become a routine procedure. The two-day workshop we give to all inspectors considers the interpersonal problems associated with the use of inspections

throughout the course and the final lecture deals with this area exclusively. Given this training, our experience is that most groups are able to handle any initial start-up problems without undue difficulty.

From the above description, it may appear that an inspection meeting is a formidable affair. It is not. The formality of the agenda, the assigned rules, the specified defect classification, and the limited purpose of the meeting all serve to create an effective meeting in which all the participants know what is to be done, and how to do it. With a modicum of training (described in a subsequent section), a synergistic team effort develops during the meeting that produces a result superior to the sum of what could be accomplished by isolated individual efforts. The meeting often develops the spirit of a detective drama because each participant's remarks provide clues in a vigorous effort to detect defects.

Inspection rework is performed by the author. It consists simply of correcting the defects noted in the Inspection Defect List.

The follow-up step is the responsibility of the moderator. It consists of verifying the corrections made during rework and completing the Inspection Management Report and the Inspection Defect Summary Report (Form 5).

Figure 4 gives a schematic of the overall process. Rework, and/or Follow-up may be skipped if the disposition is "meets."

Software Inspection Roles. Routine, effective, and hassle-free execution of an inspection process is facilitated by recognizing the specific inspection roles mentioned above. The following table provides a brief summary of the roles in an inspection.

Author	the producer (or current owner) of the subject work product
Moderator	an inspector responsible for organizing, executing, and reporting a software inspection
Reader	an inspector who guides the examination of the work product at the meeting
Recorder	an inspector who enters all the defects found during the meeting on the Inspection Defect List (Form 4)
Inspector	a member of an inspection team other than the author. Often chosen to represent a specific development role: designer, tester, technical writer, for example

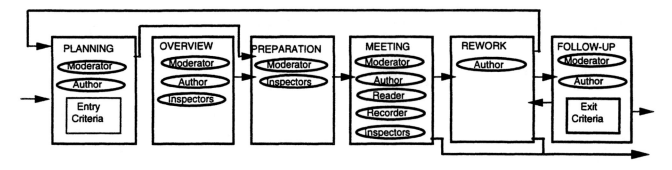

Figure 4. Software inspection process

In Figure 4 each role is associated with the step in which it participates.

Software Inspections As A Process Control Tool. As described in the previous section, the use of software inspections as a process control tool requires that they be employed at specified points throughout the development process. Figure 3 provides an example of a development process with software inspections being applied to internal requirements, high-level design, detail design, coding, test plans, and test cases. Within a development process each of these inspections is defined by specifying:

- Entry criteria
- Exit criteria
- Recommended participants
- Defect classifications
- Defect detection strategies.

Entry criteria are the pro-form conditions that a work product must meet before it is considered ready for inspection. These generally include the development operation exit criteria that would apply if an inspection were not specified for that operation, but they also include requirements for an effective inspection. For example, the entry criteria for a code inspection would require a clean compile, but it would also specify that the material to be inspected have visible line numbers and that the pertinent requirements, design, and change information be included as part of the inspection package.

Exit criteria are the completion conditions for an inspection. Typically, these are the correction of all detected defects and the documentation of any uncorrected defects in the project problem-tracking system.

Since a software inspection is a cooperative process that relies on group synergy, the selection of participants is an important issue. At inspections held early in the development process, for example, at

requirements or high-level design, both the user and system test viewpoints should be represented, as well as that of the developers responsible for implementation. The representation of all of these points of view will sometimes require inspection teams as large as seven or eight. At inspections held later in the development process, for example, code inspections, teams of three or four developers concerned only with detail design, coding, and unit test are effective [BCK81].

Strategies for detecting defects depend on the type of inspection, the kind of material, and the defect categories. In Fagan's implementations [FGN76], the inspectors are provided with checklists keyed to the defect types. In our implementations we have stressed "understanding" during preparation rather than defect detection. So a checklist organized by defect type is not appropriate. What we are now tending to provide are "preparation guidelines" that are keyed to the organization of the material being inspected. For example, for high-level designs it is important to verify that the functionality being specified in the design is in one-to-one correspondence with the requirements. Hence a high-level design preparation guideline might provide useful questions to be asked of each part of each subprogram and module design to check for this correspondence.

As described in the previous section, defect counts are used as process control data. Thus, the precise classification of defects is an essential part of the specification of each type of inspection. For software inspections, a defect is defined to be noncompliance with a product specification or document standard. Thus, as shown in Figure 1, defects are categorized by type and class. The classes, as defined by Fagan, are M="missing", E="extra," and W="wrong" [FGN76]. "Missing" is used for material that is called for in the specification or the standard, but is absent. "Extra" is used for material that exceeds the specification or the standard. "Wrong" is used for material that should be present, and is present, but contains a flaw.

Defect-type classifications depend on the nature of the material being inspected and on the specific development process. It should be possible to classify any defect easily and unambiguously during an inspection meeting. Furthermore, the resulting defect counts, when taken over time, should yield useful process control information. The thirteen defect types listed in Figure 1 form a generic set that has been used as a starting point with many different development projects. The appropriate types for each kind of inspection are selected from these thirteen and given definitions that apply to a particular inspection for a given project. An example of this kind of tailoring is given in Figure 5. An example of the kind of material inspected for these particular defects is given in Figure 6.

Other Aspects of the Use of Software Inspections. My experience with the implementation of software inspections in many development organizations is that the introduction of this technique often provides additional benefits beyond the measurable improvements in productivity and quality. One of the motivations in establishing software inspections as a standard part of a development process is that the use of inspections makes a frequently opaque operation more visible. Unlike a number of other software engineering techniques, software inspections are adaptable enough to be effective with primitive methodologies.

Every software project must produce code, and it is always possible to define an initial set of useful error types and detection strategies for a code inspection. Hence, about the only project for which inspections cannot be applied to at least the code is a project where the individual code modules are very large (greater than 500 lines) and are so badly structured that they cannot be partitioned. In my experience I have found that the use of the basic notions of structured programming is widespread so the occurrence of large, unstructured modules is rare.

When it is clear to the developers that their management supports their use of inspections as a technique for making improvements in quality and productivity, the experience of performing code inspections leads rapidly into consideration of other software engineering techniques. In many projects the precision of the inspection process points out the usefulness of a separate requirements document, and this in turn can lead to a better understanding of the usefulness of design documentation. Furthermore, when some of these other techniques are implemented, the data collected by inspections can be used to quantify the quality improvements achieved by these techniques.

Performance (PF)
- There is a plausible argument that the component will not meet the performance objectives stated in the requirements.

Data (DA)
- Missing or extra item in an Input, Output, or Update section.
- Incorrect or missing data type in an Input, Output, or Update section.

Interface (IF)
- Missing or extra routine call in a Processing section.
- An incorrect Invocation section.

Functionality (FN)
- In a Processing section a step is missing, extra, or erroneous.
- In a Processing section logical conditions are missing, extra, or erroneous.

Documentation (DC)
- The content of a Description section is. incomplete or misleading.
- The description of a data item is ambiguous.
- A processing step is not clearly described.

Standard (ST)
- An applicable standard in the Project Standards Manual is violated.

Syntax (SN)
- A defect in grammar, punctuation, or spelling.

Other (OT)
- A defect that does not fall under any of the types given above.

Figure 5. Example of High-Level Design Inspection Defect Types

SUBPROGRAM: prcl

TITLE: Print in columns

DESCRIPTION: This subprogram formats an input file into a columnized output file.

INPUTS:

-l	optional length command
-k	optional number of columns
-w	optional page width command
filename	input file

UPDATES: N/A

OUTPUTS:

Formatted output	listed to standard output file
Error message	to standard error file
Status	process status code

PROCESSING:

1. Formats input file into **k** columns per page on standard output.

2. If error detected sends error message to standard error file.

3. Return status code of 0 for normal exit or 1 for error exit.

INVOCATION: Called form the shell using the following format:
    prcl [-linteger] [-kinteger] [-winteger] filename

Figure 6. Example of High-Level Design Specification

The process of inspecting all the work products produced by a given development operation exposes the development group as a whole to both good and bad examples. The inspection both develops and enforces group norms for quality workmanship. Participating in inspections thus eliminates much of the ambiguity about what is expected of each developer. Participating in inspections also spreads detail technical information around. This is especially important in projects where much of the essential information isn't formally written down. Finally, although project management is strongly warned against formally using detailed inspection data for personnel evaluation, the process does provide individuals with an objective means for dynamically assessing the quality of their work. For example, if I know the overall project defect rate for detail designs, I can use that information to motivate improvements in my own work, while also realizing that the inspection process will correct my mistakes before they become public.[2]

4. Software Inspections Data and Process Control

The collection and analysis of data is the essential feature that sets software inspections apart from other peer review techniques, for example, walk-throughs as described by Yourdon [YRD78].

The first use of inspection data is made by the first-line manager. The inspection disposition of "meets," "rework," or "reinspect," and the estimated effort and dates for rework provide essential process scheduling information. If the amount of rework is extensive, and scheduling constraints are tight, the manager may need to negotiate a reduction in the amount of functionality to be delivered. Some of the defects can then be documented with trouble reports so that they can be addressed during the next development cycle, and the rework limited to the corrections that can be made without impacting the scheduled delivery to the next operation.

---

[2] At the completion of one trial of inspections at IBM [IBM77], a study was made of individual defect rates. During the course of the

project defect rates decreased for all the developers. The software inspection process has the potential for enhancing professional growth and increasing job satisfaction.

The next use of inspection data is made by the developers or verifiers who receive the work product at later stages in the process. The Inspection Defect Summary Report[3] is essentially an "intelligence" report on the state of the work product at the time it was inspected. Although these defects are normally corrected during the rework step, the data nonetheless points to potential weak spots in the product.

The data on the amount of material inspected, the amount of inspector preparation, and the speed with which the material was examined during the meeting can be used by a quality assurance function to assess the effectiveness of an inspection. In a study performed by F.O. Buck at IBM [BCK81], it was found that inspection preparation and examination rates during the meeting were significant predictors of an effective inspection. For example, during the course of one development project inspection teams that inspected design and code at, or less than, the recommended rate found more than 100 percent more defects per thousand lines of code than did teams that exceeded this recommended rate. Furthermore, for a series of 106 inspections held as part of an inspection training effort, it was found that unless a team prepared for the recommended amount of time, it would, on the average, inspect faster, (less effectively) than the recommended rate.

The determination of recommended inspection and preparation rates is a quality assurance responsibility. The optimal rate depends on the type of material and the application. For code the initial recommendation is to plan for a rate of 100 lines of code per hour. This recommendation is derived from the study by Buck [BCK81] and has been substantiated in experience. For straightforward application code, some of our projects are reporting higher rates. On the other hand, for inspections of performance sensitive microcode, one project reported a rate of 40 lines of code per hour. Within each project, the reported rates should be scrutinized by quality assurance by studying the number and kinds of defects uncovered at different rates for similar workproducts.

The above are all examples of the immediate use of data from individual inspections. When inspection data are accumulated over time, summarized, and used in conjunction with other process data, rational, real-time control of a software development process becomes a possibility. For example, one of the standard inspection reports is the normalized distribution of the types of defects detected at each inspection point during designated time periods (Figure 7).

When a report such as this shows that a particular process is experiencing higher than normal defect percentages during initial development increments, it may be possible to remedy the problem and improve the quality of subsequent workproducts. For example, the sample report in Figure 7 shows that about one in every four defects is a documentation problem, an unexpectedly high percentage for this type of inspection. Perhaps the documentation standards for this work product are confusing; perhaps some of the developers need additional training in the application of these standards. At any rate, the inspection report has indicated the need for further investigation and remedy.

By comparing the defect detection and correction efficiencies between different inspection points and testing points, project management can make informed decisions for optimizing a development process overall. For example, in [DBN81], J.A. Dobbins and R.D. Buck report that an analysis of inspection data in their organization led to a shift in emphasis from code inspections to design inspections. They also report that an analysis of test reports led to the realization that an additional interface inspection needed to be added to their development process.

5. Software Inspections and Other Verification Techniques

As discussed above, software inspections are a process control tool, and are thus designed to work in cooperation with any other technique employed during a development process. In particular, the above discussion assumes that a development process employing software inspections will also employ testing,[4] reviews, and audits. Proof-of-correctness techniques are currently not widely used for the industrial production of software, but as argued by R.A. De Millo, et al., [DML79] a proof is a social process, not a formal one, and hence the use of proof techniques is also compatible with the use of software inspections.

---

[3] The Inspection Defect List (Form 4) is private to the inspection team. It is only used during the meeting to collect raw data and during follow-up. The data contained on the Defect List is sumarized by the moderator on the Inspection Defect Summary Report (Form 5).

---

[4] "Testing" refers to the process of exercising or evaluating a system or system component by automated (not manual) means to verify that it satisfies specified requirements or to identify differences between expected and actual results.

Defect Type	Defect Category			Total Defect	Defect %
	Missing	Wrong	Extra		
IF (Interface)	5	17	1	23	6.6
DA (Data)	3	21	1	25	7.2
LO (Logic)	32	40	14	77	24.8
IO (Input/Output)	7	9	3	19	5.5
PF (Performance)	0				
FN (Functionality)	5	7	2	14	4.0
HF (Human Factors)	3	2	5	10	2.9
ST (Standards)	25	24	3	52	14.9
DC (Documentation)	37	51	10	92	28.1
SN (Syntax)	4	9	1	14	4.0
TE (Test Environment)	0				
TC (Test Coverage)	0				
OT (Other)	2	5		7	2.0
	123	185	40	348	100.0

Figure 7. Software Inspection Summary Report. (Simulated Data)

Testing and software inspections both have the same purpose, that is, to discover defects [MRS79]. Within a given software development process, they play complementary and supporting roles. The first thing to note in discussing the relationship of software inspections and testing is that software inspections may be employed early in the development process while testing, since it requires executable units of code, cannot complete until these units have been specified, designed, and compiled. Since the cost of detecting and correcting defects in a software product rises exponentially as one proceeds through the development process [BHM76], the use of inspections as an adjunct to testing can often result in cost savings. To fully understand the relationship between inspections and testing, it is necessary to distinguish the different kinds of testing that are performed in the course of developing a software product. Below we discuss the relationship between unit testing, system testing, and software inspections.

In unit testing, an individual unit of program production (a function, or a collection of functions) is subjected to detailed testing to discover if there are any input combinations that will cause the unit to behave in an unexpected manner, or to produce incorrect results. Since it is practically impossible to test all input combinations, the art of unit testing is that of specifying a limited set of inputs that will most likely reveal defects. One of the concepts used for the specification of such input sets is that of code coverage, for example, that all statements be executed or all branches be executed. In practice, it is extremely difficult to specify input sets that give 100 percent branch coverage; but detailed design and code inspections are a line-by-line examination of designs and code, and

hence provide 100 percent coverage because all branches are considered. For processes where data is being collected on the relative effort and effectiveness of unit testing and software inspections, rational judgments can be made on which to use, or how they should be combined.

For system testing, the situation is different because this operation exercises many units (including the entire system) and thus provides an opportunity for defect detection beyond the scope of the inspection of individual units. However, there is still a use for inspections in this area. For example, in one case cited above [DBN81], the detection of a large number of interface defects during a test operation led to the creation of a special interface inspection to detect and correct these defects prior to this testing operation. The overall result was an improvement in productivity. The reason for this is that one inspection may find a number of errors that are then corrected all at once, while testing tends to find and correct defects one by one.

A further use of software inspections in relation to testing is in the use of test plan and test case inspections [LRS75]. The purpose of these inspections is to improve the effectiveness of the test operation by improving the defect detection potential of the tests. An application of test plan and test case inspections at IBM reported that the number of test cases was increased by 30 percent, but that the overall result was an 85 percent improvement in test productivity [EBN81].

By definition, software inspections are a small peer group process whose purpose is the detection and correction of defects. When development work products must be examined by larger groups, or by management, software inspections do not apply. Nor do they apply when the purpose of the examination is other than defect detection, for example, the consideration of architectural or design alternatives. Each of these cases calls for procedures specifically designed to achieve the desired objectives.

The proper design and execution of various kinds of review procedures is beyond the scope of this paper, but we can make some suggestions on the use of reviews in relationship to inspections. Where it is the case that the purpose of a manual examination of a work product is strictly to detect and correct defects, then inspections have been shown to be superior to other review procedures [FGN76], and in addition, they provide data for process management. Of course, in order to detect defects in a work product there must be a clear understanding of the product specifications and document standards.

Often the use of a special review procedure will be dictated by considerations other than verification, and the question then arises as to whether the review subsumes the defect detection and correction function of an inspection, or whether an inspection should be held in addition to the review. In general, the answer to this question is that if it appears that an inspection might be of benefit, then the inspection can be implemented and the resulting inspection data can then decide the question.

Audits by definition[5] involve an agent external to the process being examined. Except for special cases, for example, the auditing of financial software by outside auditors, auditing of software development work products is not an efficient verification technique because it involves the duplication of technical expertise within an auditing function.

Procedural audits are another matter. In the case of software inspections, it is assumed that a quality assurance function has responsibility for auditing inspection procedures to ensure (1) that the procedures are being performed as specified, and (2) that the procedures, when faithfully executed, are producing the intended results in quality and productivity. In this application of audits, inspection reports become input to the audit operation.

Where formal verification techniques, such as Dijkstra's discipline of programming [DJK76], are being utilized as part of the design and implementation operations, software inspections are a natural choice for a peer examination technique. Where automatic verifiers are used in a development process, the situa-

tion is similar to that in which a compiler is employed. The compiler is assumed to operate correctly, and the problem is that of saying the right things in the higher level language. Software inspections can be applied to the verification of correctness conditions just as they are to compiler input.

Walk-throughs, as described in [IEEE88], are often compared to inspections. The essential differences between inspections and walk-throughs are: (1) walk-throughs are not a formally documented and implemented development process, (2) walk-throughs do not create quality records that can be used for process improvement, (3) walk-throughs do not create quality records that provide evidence that detected defects have been corrected and the corrections verified.

Terminology is not the issue here. A software development work product verification process that does not have the three characteristics just listed does not satisfy the requirements of ISO 9001; more is required. Furthermore, a process that can be managed and relied on throughout the life of an organization is needed. Walk-throughs, as the term is used here, do not meet these requirements.

6. A Software Inspection Implementation Program

The Development and Training Environment. Installing software inspections as an effective technique in a development organization can be a difficult job since it involves changing the behavior of a whole organization. The required behavior changes are not large, but they must be coordinated between the developers, first-level management, project management, and software quality assurance. In addition, for long-running projects, the changes must be planned and executed within existing scheduling constraints.

This section describes a comprehensive inspections implementation program that was carried out in the early eighties at a large telecommunications R&D organization. Similar programs have since been used in many other organizations for the successful installation of effective inspection processes.

In the subject organization each project was an independent organizational entity. The management of each project had the responsibility for choosing the appropriate means of achieving project objectives, and a wide variety of approaches were employed. The approach that was selected depended largely on the past experience of the managers and senior developers. Tools, techniques, and procedures were borrowed freely between projects, but generally they were tailored, or reimplemented to fit the project's perception of its needs.

---

[5] IEEE-Std-729, op cit, gives two definitions. The first is "an independent review for the purpose of assessing compliance."

Within the subject organization, the systems training department had the responsibility for providing software engineering training in subject matter that was applicable to a number of different projects. For example, it provided training in the use of the Unix operating system, the C language, microprocessor application design, data communications, and so on.

Within the systems training department, the system development technology group had responsibility for developing and delivering training in software engineering methodologies that could be utilized by a variety of application areas regardless of the specific implementation techniques being utilized. Figure 8 shows the subject matter covered by this group's curriculum.

During the course of developing the software inspections program within this curriculum, it became apparent that if this training program wanted to use actual, effective implementations of software inspections on individual projects as its measure of success, it would have to take a novel approach. The approach that was developed was called *consultative training*

and became the group's primary method of software engineering technology transfer. Consultative training utilized a project-oriented view of the subject matter of software engineering, as shown in Figure 9 [EMR83].

Software Inspection Program Design Concepts. For software inspections, the application of the consultative training concept resulted in the following program design concepts:

- The software inspections program was focused on entire software projects, as opposed to traditional training focused on individual developers. Within Bell Laboratories, individual software projects normally correspond with a single organizational element, for example, a group or a department, and hence this approach allowed us to work in concert with project management as well as the developers. It also allowed us to schedule the various implementation steps at the project's convenience.

THE SOFTWARE ENGINEERING CURRICULUM

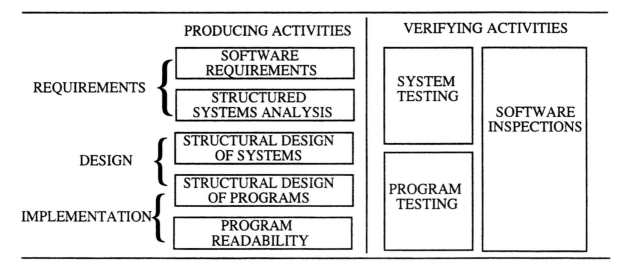

Figure 8. Our original software engineering curriculum

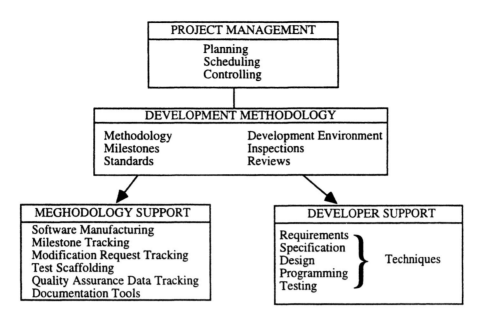

Figure 9. Project-Oriented View of Software Engineering

- Within each project, our major concern was with motivating and training developers and first-line managers. We obtained the support of upper management and coordinated the program with them, but we avoided a top-down approach. Our assumption was that effective behavioral change cannot be dictated from above.[6]

- We employed formal classroom training as a major part of our program, but we also provided direct consulting. We assisted projects in selecting the appropriate inspection points within their existing methodology, and we helped specify the entry and exit criteria, defect types and detection strategies, and the recommended participants. As part of this effort we supplied each project with first drafts of a Project Inspection Manual that contained our initial suggestions for the specification of each type of inspection the project would use. This manual also contained inspection data collection forms tailored to the project's needs.

- We entered into an ongoing relationship with each client project and provided whatever assistance was appropriate when problems arose. In particular, we performed evaluation and review activities to determine whether the project was in fact following its procedures, whether these procedures were in fact producing the desired results, and whether the overall perception of the developers and first-line managers was that inspections were making a positive contribution to their project.

- In order to make our formal classroom training directly applicable to an individual project, we separated the teaching and exercise material into two classes: (1) that which taught principles and techniques generic to any application of software inspections, and (2) that which considered aspects that could be specialized for a particular project. This meant, for example, that we could apply the project's own definitions of defect types and detection strategies against class exercise material developed from actual project work products.

- Wherever possible, software inspections were introduced into a project on a trial basis. A trial allowed a shakedown of the software inspection procedures in the project environment, and also allowed the project to directly experience the benefits of inspections before making a full-scale commitment.

---

[6] This is no longer an assumption. In the few instances where we violated this principle, we were emphatically taught its general validity.

Software Inspections Program Implementation. To implement the concepts just discussed above we designed the six-step program shown in Figure 10. This formal approach to the delivery of this program allowed us to keep track of each project's progress through its implementation plan. It also helped us manage and allocate our own resources among the constantly changing needs of our clients, and it at times provided a structure for charging for our services. This six-step program also served to make clear to each project what its responsibilities were during each step of the program. Each of these six steps is described below.

1. *Software Inspections Overview*. The overview was a presentation to managers and key developers on a project. It introduced the software inspections technique, discussed how it would be carried out, what the expected benefits would be, what the costs would be, and what project resources would be required for implementation. At the conclusion of this presentation, the project decided whether or not it wished to proceed with a software inspections implementation program at that time and, if it did, who on the project would have responsibility for initiating the effort.

2. *Needs-Assessment*. The needs-assessment activity consisted of meeting with the project members who were assigned to initiate the program, and one or two members of the software inspection program staff. Project members first presented an overview of the project, including the nature of the application, project resources and schedules, and the development environment. Project members and the software inspections program staff

then determined training requirements and schedules, project development phase demarcations with appropriate software inspection types, and a schedule and participants for the trial use of software inspections. The trial period was designed to correspond to some part of the project's development cycle so that any defect data from the project's normal quality assurance procedures could be used later in evaluating the use of software inspections on that project. A software inspections coordinator, who would have responsibility for the project's inspection program, and who interfaced with the inspection program staff was designated by project management.

3. *Implementation Support*. The classroom training on inspections was most effective when there was sufficient time in the project's inspection implementation schedule to prepare (1) an initial draft of the project's software inspections manual and (2) practice inspection material based on an actual project work product. These materials were produced through a joint effort between the software inspections staff and the project's software inspections coordinator. This effort supplemented the inspections staff's understanding of inspections in general with essential information about the project's specific environment. The inspections staff involvement in turn overcame the project's lack of expertise and, more subtly, provided an outside impetus toward completing work that was not directly related to the immediate development schedule. The inspections staff involvement also provided the coordinator with psychological support—the coordinator, after all, must deal directly with his or her colleagues' resistance to changes in project procedures.

COURSE/ACTIVITY	AUDIENCE	PURPOSE	LENGTH
1. Software Inspections Overview	Project Management Key Developers	To provide decision base	½ Day class
2. Software Inspections Needs Assessment	Project Management Key Developers	To plan project use of process	½–1 Day consulting
3. Implementation	Inspections Coordinator	Design and document project process	1–2 Days support
4. Software Inspections Workshop	Project Development Groups	To provide developer training	2 Day class
5. Software Inspections Management Seminar	Project Management	To provide management training	½ Day class
6. Software Inspections Review and Evaluation	Project Management Key Developers	To "tune" the process	Interview as needed

Figure 10. The Bell Labs Software Inspections Program

4. *Developer Workshop.* The developer workshop taught the steps needed to prepare for, participate in, and lead an inspection. A major section of the workshop was a full-scale practice inspection that inspected the project material especially prepared for this purpose, and that utilized draft copies of the project's inspections manual. This exercise thus not only provided the developers with experience in the inspection technique generally, but it also gave them a chance to trial the specific procedures that would be used on their project, and a chance to offer their own suggestions for improving these procedures. The workshop concluded with a discussion of project implementation considerations by the software inspections coordinator who worked with the training staff to tailor the program to the project.

5. *Management Seminar.* In the initial implementation period of inspections on a project, the inspections staff sought to maximize the involvement of the developers on whom the success of the technique ultimately depended and to minimize involvement by management. Once inspections began to take hold, however, there was a need to provide management with additional information. In fact, project management ultimately has a key role to play in a successful project implementation of inspections. This role was discussed with the developers in the workshop, and skepticism about whether or not management will play its role properly was blunted by the inspections staff's commitment to bring the developers' concerns directly to the management. For small projects, this could be handled informally; for large projects, a half-day seminar was used for this purpose.

6. *Evaluation and Review.* At the conclusion of a trial, and at appropriate intervals thereafter, a project should review its software inspection procedures to determine what changes, if any, should be made in its procedures. In this step, the software inspections program staff evaluated the project's inspection process using project inspection data, direct observation of inspection meetings, and formal interviews with participating developers and their first-level managers. The collected data was then evaluated and presented, along with recommendations for improvements, to the project's software inspections coordinator and to interested developers and managers.

The results of this program were positive. Of the 42 projects that participated in the program by the middle of 1984, 25 were using inspections as an established part of their development process, 4 were trailing inspections, and 5 had training scheduled. The remaining 8 projects did not immediately continue the program for a variety of reasons: one project did not follow the training with the necessary implementation resources, in another the supervisor sabotaged the process by attending inspection meetings, and so on. The review and evaluation step described above was completed for 6 projects.

Data for one completed evaluation was obtained from a series of 40 interviews with developers and project management, from inspection records, and by direct observation. The results were that:

- inspections were being consistently used;
- the developers and managers were enthusiastic and supportive of the inspection process; and
- more than 90 percent of those interviewed felt that inspections increased product quality and enhanced developer growth, with a majority perceiving no delay in production schedules as a result of using inspections.

These results have been corroborated by other studies and by less formal project evaluations. The bottom line is that this approach to the implementation of software inspections is effective. However, there were still some problems:

Timing and Initial Implementation. The least effective software inspection is the code inspection since it can find errors only after the completion of requirements, design, and coding. Yet one large project chose to restrict the initial application of inspections to code because they had just implemented a new methodology that contained detailed procedures for design reviews. Had we been able to start our work with this project a few months sooner, most likely we would have been able to convince them to use design inspections rather than reviews. Our philosophy has been to work with whatever opportunities have presented themselves to us and to let the effectiveness of the inspection technique speak for itself over the long haul

Data Collection and Analysis. Most projects agree in theory with the need to collect and analyze data on the effectiveness of the inspection process. They understand the potential benefits from having the data: immediate and well-documented results from software inspection meetings; indication of troublesome areas in system implementation in time for preventive measures, such as redesign or more thorough testing; and measures of the costs of the inspection process versus other defect detection and correction methods. However, few projects as yet are willing to invest in other than the most minimal of data collection and analysis efforts. Fear of misuse of the information is one problem. Another is limited staff for doing the work involved. One answer is more mechanized support for data collection and analysis, and then more specific procedures for how to use the results.

Management Support. Management support is key to the success of any new technique. If a sustained commitment to spending the resources required is not maintained, failure is certain, and much effort will be wasted. A well-defined trial use of software inspections helps give management a good measure of the benefits and costs of using software inspections in their particular projects.

Continued success is possible, however, only when management uses inspections in a way that is consistent with other project objectives and with developer expectations. One failure we experienced was the direct result of the management's lack of proper support and encouragement for developers in implementing this process.

7. Conclusions

Software inspections have been shown [FGN76] [IBM77] [PEL82] [MCK81] [EBN81a] to be an efficient and effective method for improving project productivity and product quality in a wide variety of industrial software development environments. Software inspections can be effectively employed together with testing, product reviews, procedural audits, and formal verification techniques. The successful installation of software inspections within ongoing projects is complex, but well-conceived and supported programs have been successful in numerous development organizations.

References

[ACK82] Ackerman, A.F., Ackerman, A.S., and Ebenau, R.G., "A Software Inspections Training Program," *Proc. COMPSAC 82* IEEE Computer Society Press, Los Alamitos, Calif., 1982, pp. 443–444.

[BCK81] Buck, F.O., "Indicators of Quality Inspection," IBM Technical Report TR21.802, Systems Communications Division, Kingston, N.Y., 1981.

[BHM76] Boehm, B.W., "Software Engineering," *IEEE Trans. Computers*, Dec. 1976, pp. 1,226–1,241.

[DML79] DeMillo, R.A., Lipton, R.J., and Perles, A.J., "Social Processes and Proofs of Theories and Programs," *Comm. ACM*, Vol. 22, No. 5, 1979, pp. 271–280.

[DBN81] Dobbins, J.A. and Buck, R.D., "Software Quality in the 80's," *Proc. Trends and Applications Symp.*, IEEE Computer Society Press, Los Alamitos, Calif., 1981, pp. 31–37.

[DJK76] Dijkstra, E.W., *A Discipline of Programming*, Prentice-Hall, Englewood Cliffs, N.J., 1976.

[EBN81] Ebenau, R.G., Private communication

[EBN81a] Ebenau, R.G., "Inspecting For Software Quality," *Proc. 2nd Nat'l Symp. EDP Quality Assurance*, 1981, DPMA Education Foundation, produced by U. S. Professional Development Institute, Inc., 12611 Davon Drive, Silver Spring, Md. 20904

[EMR83] Emerson, T.J., et al., "Training For Software Engineering Technology Transfer," *Workshop on Software Engineering Technology*, IEEE Computer Society Press, Los Alamitos, Calif., 1983, pp. 34–41.

[FGN76] Fagan, M.E., "Design and Code Inspections to Reduce Errors in Program Development," *IBM System J.*, Vol. 15, No. 3, 1976.

[IBM77] "Inspections in Application Development—Introduction and Implementation Guidelines," IBM publication GC20-2000, July 1977, IBM Technical Publications, Department 824, 1133 Westchester Avenue, White Plains, N.Y. 10604

[IEEE88] IEEE, ANSI/IEEE Std 1028-1988, Standard for Software Reviews and Audits.

[LRS75] Larson, R.R., "Test Plan and Test Case Inspection Specifications," Technical Report TR21.586, April 4, 1975, IBM Corporation, Kingston, N.Y.

[MCK81] McCormick, K.K., "The Results of Using a Structured Methodology, Software Inspections, and a New Hardware/Software Configuration on Application Systems," *Proc. 2nd National Symp. EDP Quality Assurance*, 1981, DPMA Education Foundation, produced by US Professional Development Institute, Inc., 12611 Davan Drive, Silver Spring, MD 20904.

[MRS79] Myers, G.J., *The Art of Software Testing*, John Wiley & Sons, New York, N.Y., 1979.

[PEL81] Peele, R., "Design Code Inspection Pilot Project Evaluation," *Proc. 2nd Nat'l Symp. EDP Quality Assurance*, DPMA Education Foundation, produced by US Professional Development Institute, Inc. 12611 Davan Drive, Silver Spring, MD 20904.

[PEL82] Peele, R., "Code Inspections at First Union Corporation," *Proc. COMPSAC 82*, IEEE Computer Society Press, Los Alamitos, Calif., 1982, pp. 445–446.

[YRD78] Yourdon, E., *Structured Walkthroughs*, Yourdon, Inc., 1978.

INSPECTION PROFILE

System: _____ Release: _____ Increment: _____ Date: _____

Unit:_____

Inspection type:

☐ Internal Requirements ☐ Detail Design ☐ Test Plan

☐ High Level Design ☐ Code ☐ Test Cases

Size of material:_____ (unit) _____

Is this a re-inspection: ☐ No ☐ Yes

Summary of open items:_____

_____

_____

_____

Other comments:_____

_____

_____

_____

Prepared by:_____

Form 1: Sample software inspection profile form

INSPECTION PREPARATION LOG

System:_____ Release:_____ Increment:_____ Date:_____

Unit:_____

Inspector:_____ Room:_____ Phone:_____

Role: ☐ Author ☐ Moderator ☐ Peer Inspector

Overview attendance: ☐ No ☐ Yes

Date received Inspection Package: _____

                              date: time:

Preparation Log:_____ _____

                            _____ _____

                            _____ _____

                            _____ _____

Total Preparation: _____

                                                    hours

CONCERNS

Location   Description

_____   _____

                        _____

                        _____

_____   _____

                        _____

                        _____

_____   _____

                        _____

                        _____

_____   _____

                        _____

Form 2: Sample inspection preparation log

INSPECTION MANAGEMENT REPORT

System:_____ Release: _____ Increment:___ Inspection date: _____

Unit:_____

Moderator:_____ Room:_____ Phone:_____

Inspection type:

☐ Internal Requirements ☐ Detail Design ☐ Test Plan

☐ High Level Design ☐ Code ☐ Test Cases

Overview held: ☐ No ☐ Yes Overview duration: _____

Number attending: _____

Number of inspection meetings:_____Total meeting duration:_____

Total number of inspectors:_____ Total preparation time:_____

Module disposition: ☐ meets ☐ follow-up ☐ re-inspect

Estimated rework effort:_____ (days)

Rework to be completed by:_____

Actual rework effort:_____

Re-inspection scheduled for:_____

Other inspectors:

_____   _____

_____   _____

_____   _____

_____   _____

Moderator certification:_____ Date: _____

Additional comments:_____

_____

_____

_____

_____

Form 3: Sample software inspection management report

INSPECTION DEFECT LIST

System: _____ Release: _____ Increment: _____ Date: _____

Unit: _____

Moderator: _____ Room: _____ Phone: _____

Inspection type:

☐ Internal Requirements ☐ Detail Design ☐ Test Plan
☐ High Level Design ☐ Code ☐ Test Cases

Document:	Location:	Defect Description:	Defect Type:	Class:
_____	_____	_____	____	____
_____	_____	_____	____	____
_____	_____	_____	____	____
_____	_____	_____	____	____
_____	_____	_____	____	____
_____	_____	_____	____	____
_____	_____	_____	____	____
_____	_____	_____	____	____
_____	_____	_____	____	____
_____	_____	_____	____	____
_____	_____	_____	____	____
_____	_____	_____	____	____
_____	_____	_____	____	____
_____	_____	_____	____	____
_____	_____	_____	____	____
_____	_____	_____	____	____
_____	_____	_____	____	____
_____	_____	_____	____	____
_____	_____	_____	____	____

Error type: IF=Interface DA=Data LO=Logic IO=Input/Output PF=Performanc HF=Human factors ST=Standards
     DC=Documentation SN=Syntax OT=Other
Error class: M=Missing W=Wrong E=Extra
Error stage: RQ=Requirements HL=High Level Design DD=Detail Design CD=Code TP=Test Plan TC=Test Case

Form 4: Sample software inspection defect list

Page____of____

INSPECTION SUMMARY

System: _____ Release: _____ Increment: _____ Inspection Date: _____

Unit: _____

Moderator: _____ Room: _____ Phone: _____

Inspection type:

☐ Internal Requirements ☐ Detail Design ☐ Test Plan
☐ High Level Design ☐ Code ☐ Test Cases

Error		DEFECTS THIS OPERATION			
		M	W	E	Total
IF:	Interface				
DA:	Data				
LO:	Logic				
IO:	Input/Output				
PF:	Performanc				
HF:	Human factors				
ST:	Standards				
DC:	Documentation				
SN:	Syntax				
TE:	Test Environment				
TC:	Test Coverage				
OT:	Other				
				Total	

DEFECT IN PRIOR OPERATIONS			
Defect Stage	Defect Type	Defect Class	MR Number

Major Errors This Stage:
Requirement=IF+PF+HF
High Level Design=IF+DA+LO+IO+PF+HF
Detail Design=IF+DA+LO+IO+PF
Code=IF+DA+LO+IO+PF
Test Plan=TE+TC
Test Case=TE+TC

MAJOR DEFECT THIS OPERATION	
Defect Type	Total
Total	

Form 5: Sample software inspections summary form

IEEE Standard 1028-1997
Software Reviews

Abstract: This standard defines five types of software reviews, together with procedures required for the execution of each review type. This standard is concerned only with the reviews; it does not define procedures for determining the necessity of a review, nor does it specify the disposition of the results of the review. Review types include management reviews, technical reviews, inspections, walk-throughs, and audits.

At the time this standard was completed, the Software Engineering Review Working Group had the following membership:

J. Dennis Lawrence, *Chair*
Patricia A. Trellue, *Technical Editor*

Frank Ackerman	Leo Beltracchi	Ron Berlack
Antonio Bertolino	Richard J. Blauw	Audrey Brewer
James E. Cardow	Hu Cheng	Pat Daggett
Ronald Dean†	Janet Deeney*†	Claude G. Diderich
Leo G. Egan	Martin Elliot	Jon Fairclough*
Karol Fruehauf	Andrew Gabb	Tom Gilb
Jon Hagar	John Harauz	Hans-Ludwig Hausen
Michael Haux	Herb Hecht	Chuck Howell
Laura Ippolito	Rikkila Juha	George X. Kambic
Myron S. Karasik	Stanley H. Levinson	Michael S. Lines
Jordan Matejceck	Archibald McKinlay	Warren L. Persons†
Peter T. Poon	Christian Reiser	Helmut Sandmayr
Hans Schaefer*	Katsu Shintani	Mel E. Smyre
Julia Stesney	Gina To†	André Villas-Boas
Dolores Wallace	David A. Wheeler	Ron Yun
Tony Zawilski		

* Principal writers † Ballot resolution

Sponsored by

Software Engineering Standards Committee
of the IEEE Computer Society

The Institute of Electrical and Electronic Engineering, Inc.
345 East 47th Street, New York, NY 10017-2394, USA

December 9, 1997

Table of Contents

IEEE Standard 1028-1997
Software Reviews

IEEE Standard for
Software Reviews

1. Overview

1.1 Purpose

The purpose of this standard is to define systematic reviews applicable to software acquisition, supply, development, operation, and maintenance. This standard describes how to carry out a review. Other standards or local management define the context within which a review is performed, and the use made of the results of the review. Software reviews can be used in support of the objectives of project management, system engineering (for example, functional allocation between hardware and software), verification and validation, configuration management, and quality assurance. Different types of reviews reflect differences in the goals of each review type. Systematic reviews are described by their defined procedures, scope, and objectives.

1.2 Scope

This standard provides minimum acceptable requirements for systematic software reviews, where "systematic" includes the following attributes:

a) Team participation;

b) Documented results of the review; and

c) Documented procedures for conducting the review.

Reviews that do not meet the requirements of this standard are considered to be nonsystematic reviews. This standard is not intended to discourage or prohibit the use of nonsystematic reviews.

The definitions, requirements, and procedures for the following five types of reviews are included within this standard:

a) Management reviews;

b) Technical reviews;

c) Inspections;

d) Walk-throughs; and

e) Audits.

This standard does not establish the need to conduct specific reviews; that need is defined by other software engineering standards or by local procedures. This standard provides definitions, requirements, and procedures that are applicable to the reviews of software development products throughout the software life cycle. Users of this standard shall specify where and when this standard applies and any intended deviations from this standard.

It is intended that this standard be used with other software engineering standards that determine the products to be reviewed, the timing of reviews, and the necessity for reviews. This standard is closely aligned with IEEE Std 1012-1986, but can also be used with IEEE Std 1074-1995, IEEE Std 730-1989, ISO/IEC 12207:1995, and other standards. A useful model is to consider IEEE Std 1028-1997 as a subroutine to the other standards. Thus, if IEEE Std 1012-1986 were used to carry out the verification and validation process, the procedure in IEEE Std 1012-1986 could be followed until such time as instructions to carry out a specific review are encountered. At that point, IEEE Std 1028-1997 would be "called" to carry out the review, using the specific review type described herein. Once the review has been completed, IEEE Std 1012-1986 would be returned to for disposition of the results of the review and any additional action required by IEEE Std 1012-1986.

In this model, requirements and quality attributes for the software product are "parameter inputs" to the review and are imposed by the "caller." When the review is finished, the review outputs are "returned" to the "caller" for action. Review outputs typically include anomaly lists and action item lists; the resolution of the anomalies and action items are the responsibility of the "caller."

1.3 Conformance

Conformance to this standard for a specific review type can be claimed when all mandatory actions (indicated by "shall") are carried out as defined in this standard for the review type used. Claims for conformance should be phrased to indicate the review types used; for example, "conforming to IEEE Std 1028-1997 for inspections." The word "shall" is used to express a requirement, "should" to express a recommendation, and "may" to express alternative or optional methods of satisfying a requirement.

1.4 Organization of standard

Paragraphs 4–8 of this standard provide guidance and descriptions for the five types of systematic reviews addressed by this standard. Each of these paragraphs contain the following information:

a) *Introduction.* Describes the objectives of the systematic review and provides an overview of the systematic review procedures.

b) *Responsibilities.* Defines the roles and responsibilities needed for the systematic review.

c) *Input.* Describes the requirements for input needed by the systematic review.

d) *Entry criteria.* Describes the criteria to be met before the systematic review can begin, including:

　1) Authorization; and

　2) Initiating event.

e) *Procedures.* Details the procedures for the systematic review, including:

　1) Planning the review;

　2) Overview of procedures;

　3) Preparation;

　4) Examination/evaluation/recording of results; and

　5) Rework/follow-up.

f) *Exit criteria.* Describes the criteria to be met before the systematic review can be considered complete.

g) *Output.* Describes the minimum set of deliverables to be produced by the systematic review.

1.5 Application of standard

The procedures and terminology defined in this standard apply to software acquisition, supply, development, operation, and maintenance processes requiring systematic reviews. Systematic reviews are performed on a software product as required by other standards or local procedures.

The term "software product" is used in this standard in a very broad sense. Examples of software products include, but are not limited to, the following:

a) Anomaly reports;

b) Audit reports;

c) Back-up and recovery plans;

d) Build procedures;

e) Contingency plans;

f) Contracts;

g) Customer or user representative complaints;

h) Disaster plans;

i) Hardware performance plans;

j) Inspection reports;

k) Installation plans;

l) Installation procedures;

m) Maintenance manuals;

n) Maintenance plans;

o) Management review reports;

p) Operations and user manuals;

q) Procurement and contracting methods;

r) Progress reports;

s) Release notes;

t) Reports and data (for example, review, audit, project status, anomaly reports, test data);

u) Request for proposal;

v) Risk management plans;

w) Software configuration management plans (see IEEE Std 828-1990);

x) Software design descriptions (see IEEE Std 1016-1987);

y) Software project management plans (see IEEE Std 1058-1987);

z) Software quality assurance plans (see IEEE Std 730-1989);

aa) Software requirements specifications (see IEEE Std 830-1993);

ab) Software safety plans (see IEEE 1228-1994);

ac) Software test documentation (see IEEE Std 829-1983);

ad) Software user documentation (see IEEE Std 1063-1987);

ae) Software verification and validation plans (see IEEE Std 1012-1986);

af) Source code;

ag) Standards, regulations, guidelines, and procedures;

ah) System build procedures;

ai) Technical review reports;

aj) Vendor documents; and

ak) Walk-through reports.

This standard permits reviews that are held by means other than physically meeting in a single location. Examples include telephone conferences, videoconferences, and other means of group electronic communication. In such cases, the communication means should be defined in addition to the meeting places, and all other review requirements remain applicable.

In order to make use of this standard to carry out a software review, first decide the objective of the review. Next, select an appropriate review type. Then follow the procedure described in the appropriate paragraph (4–8) of this standard.

2. References

The supporting references and citations pertaining to this standard can be found in the *Centralized IEEE Software Engineering Standards References* contained in this tutorial. These references provide additional information on software reviews to assist in understanding and applying this standard.

3. Definitions

The definitions and acronyms pertaining to this standard can be found in the *Centralized IEEE Software Engineering Standards Glossary* contained in this tutorial. These are contextual definitions serving to augment the understanding of software review activities as described within this standard.

4. Management reviews

4.1 Introduction

The purpose of a management review is to monitor progress, determine the status of plans and schedules, confirm requirements and their system allocation, or evaluate the effectiveness of management approaches used to achieve fitness for purpose. Management reviews support decisions about corrective actions, changes in the allocation of resources, or changes to the scope of the project.

Management reviews are carried out by, or on behalf of, the management personnel having direct responsibility for the system. Management reviews identify consistency with and deviations from plans, or adequacies and inadequacies of management procedures. This examination may require more than one meeting. The examination need not address all aspects of the product.

Examples of software products subject to management review include, but are not limited to, the following:

a) Anomaly reports;

b) Audit reports;

c) Back-up and recovery plans;

d) Contingency plans;

e) Customer or user representative complaints;

f) Disaster plans;

g) Hardware performance plans;

h) Installation plans;

i) Maintenance plans;

j) Procurement and contracting methods;

k) Progress reports;

l) Risk management plans;

m) Software configuration management plans;

n) Software project management plans;

o) Software quality assurance plans;

p) Software safety plans;

q) Software verification and validation plans;

r) Technical review reports;

s) Software product analyses; and

t) Verification and validation reports.

4.2 Responsibilities

Management reviews are carried out by, or on behalf of, the management personnel having direct responsibility for the system. Technical knowledge may be necessary to conduct a successful management review. Management reviews shall be performed by the available personnel who are best qualified to evaluate the software product.

The following roles shall be established for the management review:

a) Decision maker;

b) Review leader;

c) Recorder;

d) Management staff;

e) Technical staff;

The following roles may also be established for the management review:

f) Other team members;

g) Customer or user representative; and

h) Individual participants may act in more than one role.

4.2.1 Decision maker

The decision maker is the person for whom the management review is conducted. The decision maker shall determine if the review objectives have been met.

4.2.2 Review leader

The review leader shall be responsible for administrative tasks pertaining to the review, shall be responsible for planning and preparation as described in Paragraph 4.5.2 and Paragraph 4.5.4, shall ensure that the review is conducted in an orderly manner and meets its objectives, and shall issue the review outputs as described in Paragraph 4.7.

4.2.3 Recorder

The recorder shall document anomalies, action items, decisions, and recommendations made by the review team.

4.2.4 Management staff

Management staff assigned to carry out management reviews is responsible for active participation in the review. Managers responsible for the system as a whole have additional responsibilities as defined in Paragraph 4.5.1.

4.2.5 Technical staff

The technical staff shall provide the information necessary for the management staff to fulfill its responsibilities.

4.2.6 Customer or user representative

The role of the customer or user representative should be determined by the review leader prior to the review.

4.3 Input

Input to the management review shall include the following:

a) A statement of objectives for the management review;

b) The software product being evaluated;

c) Software project management plan;

d) Status, relative to plan, of the software product completed or in progress;

e) Current anomalies or issues list;

f) Documented review procedures;

Input to the management review should also include the following:

g) Status of resources, including finance, as appropriate;

h) Relevant review reports;

i) Any regulations, standards, guidelines, plans, or procedures against which the software product should be evaluated; and

j) Anomaly categories (See IEEE Std 1044-1993).

Additional reference material may be made available by the individuals responsible for the software product when requested by the review leader.

4.4 Entry criteria

4.4.1 Authorization

The need for conducting management reviews should initially be established in the appropriate project planning documents, as listed in Paragraph 4.1. Under these plans, completion of a specific software product or completion of an activity may initiate a management review. In addition to those management reviews required by a specific plan, other management reviews may be announced and held at the request of software quality management, functional management, project management, or the customer or user representative, according to local procedures.

4.4.2 Preconditions

A management review shall be conducted only when both of the following conditions have been met:

a) A statement of objectives for the review is established by the management personnel for whom the review is being carried out; and

b) The required review inputs are available.

4.5 Procedures

4.5.1 Management preparation

Managers shall ensure that the review is performed as required by applicable standards and procedures and by requirements mandated by law, contract, or other policy. To this end, managers shall:

a) Plan time and resources required for reviews, including support functions, as required in IEEE Std 1058-1998 or other appropriate standards.

b) Provide funding and facilities required to plan, define, execute, and manage the reviews.

c) Provide training and orientation on review procedures applicable to a given project.

d) Ensure management review team members possess appropriate levels of expertise and knowledge sufficient to comprehend the software product under review.

e) Ensure that planned reviews are conducted.

f) Act on review team recommendations in a timely manner.

4.5.2 Planning the review

The review leader shall be responsible for the following activities:

a) Identify, with appropriate management support, the review team;

b) Assign specific responsibilities to the review team members;

c) Schedule and announce the meeting;

d) Distribute review materials to participants, allowing adequate time for their preparation; and

e) Set a timetable for distribution of review material, the return of comments, and forwarding of comments to the author for disposition.

4.5.3 Overview of review procedures

A qualified person should present an overview session for the review team when requested by the review leader. This overview may occur as part of the review meeting (see Paragraph 4.5.6) or as a separate meeting.

146

4.5.4 Preparation

Each review team member shall examine the software product and other review inputs prior to the review meeting. Anomalies detected during this examination should be documented and sent to the review leader. The review leader should classify anomalies to ensure that review-meeting time is used most effectively. The review leader should forward the anomalies to the author of the software product for disposition.

4.5.5 Examination

The management review shall consist of one or more meetings of the review team. The meetings shall accomplish the following goals:

a) Review the objectives of the management review;

b) Evaluate the software product under review against the review objectives;

c) Evaluate project status, including the status of plans and schedules;

d) Review anomalies identified by the review team prior to the review;

e) Generate a list of action items, emphasizing risks;

f) Document the meeting;

The meetings should accomplish the following goals as appropriate:

g) Evaluate the risk issues that may jeopardize the success of the project;

h) Confirm software requirements and their system allocation;

i) Decide the course of action to be taken or recommendations for action; and

j) Identify other issues that should be addressed.

4.5.6 Rework/follow-up

The review leader shall verify that the action items assigned in the meeting are closed.

4.6 Exit criteria

The management review shall be considered complete when the activities listed in Paragraph 4.5.5 have been accomplished and the output described in Paragraph 4.7 exists.

4.7 Output

The output from the management review shall be documented evidence that identifies:

a) The project being reviewed;

b) The review team members;

c) Review objectives;

d) Software product reviewed;

e) Specific inputs to the review;

f) Action item status (open, closed), ownership and target date (if open) or completion date (if closed); and

g) A list of anomalies identified by the review team that must be addressed for the project to meet its goals.

Although this standard sets minimum requirements for the content of the documented evidence, it is left to local procedures to prescribe additional content, format requirements, and media.

5. Technical reviews

5.1 Introduction

The purpose of a technical review is to evaluate a software product by a team of qualified personnel to determine its suitability for its intended use and identify discrepancies from specifications and standards. It provides management with evidence to confirm whether:

a) The software product conforms to its specifications;

b) The software product adheres to regulations, standards, guidelines, plans, and procedures applicable to the project; and

c) Changes to the software product are properly implemented and affect only those system areas identified by the change specification.

Technical reviews may also provide the recommendation and examination of various alternatives, which may require more than one meeting. The examination need not address all aspects of the product.

Examples of software products subject to technical review include, but are not limited to, the following:

a) Software requirements specification;

b) Software design description;

c) Software test documentation;

d) Software user documentation;

e) Maintenance manual;

f) System build procedures;

g) Installation procedures; and

h) Release notes.

5.2 Responsibilities

The following roles shall be established for the technical review:

a) Decision maker;

b) Review leader;

c) Recorder;

d) Technical staff;

The following roles may also be established for the technical review:

e) Management staff;

f) Other team members; and

g) Customer or user representative.

Individual participants may act in more than one role.

5.2.1 Decision maker

The decision maker is the person for whom the technical review is conducted. The decision maker shall determine if the review objectives have been met.

5.2.2 Review leader

The review leader shall be responsible for the review. This responsibility includes performing administrative tasks pertaining to the review, ensuring that the review is conducted in an orderly manner, and ensuring that the review meets its objectives. The review leader shall issue the review outputs as described in Paragraph 5.7.

5.2.3 Recorder

The recorder shall document anomalies, action items, decisions, and recommendations made by the review team.

5.2.4 Technical staff

The technical staff shall actively participate in the review and evaluation of the software product.

5.2.5 Management staff

The management staff may participate in the technical review for the purpose of identifying issues that require management resolution.

5.2.6 Customer or user representative

The role of the customer or user representative should be determined by the review leader prior to the review.

5.3 Input

Input to the technical review shall include the following:

a) A statement of objectives for the technical review;

b) The software product being examined;

c) Software project management plan;

d) Current anomalies or issues list for the software product;

e) Documented review procedures;

Input to the technical review should also include the following:

f) Relevant review reports;

g) Any regulations, standards, guidelines, plans, and procedures against which the software product is to be examined; and

h) Anomaly categories (See IEEE Std 1044-1993).

Additional reference material may be made available by the individuals responsible for the software product when requested by the review leader.

5.4 Entry criteria

5.4.1 Authorization

The need for conducting technical reviews of a software product shall be defined by project planning documents. In addition to those technical reviews required by a specific plan, other technical reviews may be announced and held at the request of functional management, project management, software quality management, systems engineering, or software engineering according to local procedures. Technical reviews may be required to evaluate impacts of hardware anomalies or deficiencies on the software product.

5.4.2 Preconditions

A technical review shall be conducted only when both of the following conditions have been met:

a) A statement of objectives for the review is established; and

b) The required review inputs are available.

5.5 Procedures

5.5.1 Management preparation

Managers shall ensure that the review is performed as required by applicable standards and procedures and by requirements mandated by law, contract, or other policy. To this end, managers shall:

a) Plan time and resources required for reviews, including support functions, as required in IEEE Std 1058-1998 or other appropriate standards;

b) Provide funding and facilities required to plan, define, execute, and manage the reviews;

c) Provide training and orientation on review procedures applicable to a given project;

d) Ensure that review team members possess appropriate levels of expertise and knowledge sufficient to comprehend the software product under review;

e) Ensure that planned reviews are conducted; and

f) Act on review team recommendations in a timely manner.

5.5.2 Planning the review

The review leader shall be responsible for the following activities:

a) Identify, with appropriate management support, the review team;

b) Assign specific responsibilities to the review team members;

c) Schedule and announce the meeting place;

d) Distribute review materials to participants, allowing adequate time for their preparation; and

e) Set a timetable for distribution of review material, the return of comments and forwarding of comments to the author for disposition.

As a part of the planning procedure, the review team shall determine if alternatives are to be discussed at the review meeting. Alternatives may be discussed at the review meeting, afterwards in a separate meeting, or left to the author of the software product to resolve.

5.5.3 Overview of review procedures

A qualified person should present an overview of the review procedures for the review team when requested by the review leader. This overview may occur as a part of the review meeting (see Paragraph 5.5.6) or as a separate meeting.

5.5.4 Overview of the software product

A technically qualified person should present an overview of the software product for the review team when requested by the review leader. This overview may occur either as a part of the review meeting (see Paragraph 5.5.6) or as a separate meeting.

5.5.5 Preparation

Each review team member shall examine the software product and other review inputs prior to the review meeting. Anomalies detected during this examination should be documented and sent to the review leader. The review leader should classify anomalies to ensure that review-meeting time is used most effectively. The review leader should forward the anomalies to the author of the software product for disposition.

The review leader shall verify that team members are prepared for the technical review. The review leader should gather individual preparation times and record the total. The review leader shall reschedule the meeting if the team members are not adequately prepared.

5.5.6 Examination

During the technical review, the review team shall hold one or more meetings. The meetings shall accomplish the following goals:

a) Decide on the agenda for evaluating the software product and anomalies;

b) Evaluate the software product;

c) Determine if:

1) The software product is complete;

2) The software product conforms to the regulations, standards, guidelines, plans and procedures applicable to the project;

3) Changes to the software product are properly implemented and affect only the specified areas;

4) The software product is suitable for its intended use;

5) The software product is ready for the next activity; and

6) Hardware anomalies or specification discrepancies exist.

d) Identify anomalies;

e) Generate a list of action items, emphasizing risks; and

f) Document the meeting.

After the software product has been reviewed, documentation shall be generated to document the meeting, list anomalies found in the software product, and describe any recommendations to management.

When anomalies are sufficiently critical or numerous, the review leader should recommend that an additional review be applied to the modified software product. This, at a minimum, should cover product areas changed to resolve anomalies, as well as side effects of those changes.

5.5.7 Rework/follow-up

The review leader shall verify that the action items assigned in the meeting are closed.

5.6 Exit criteria

A technical review shall be considered complete when the activities listed in Paragraph 5.5.6 have been accomplished, and the output described in Paragraph 5.7 exists.

5.7 Output

The output from the technical review shall consist of documented evidence that identifies:

a) The project being reviewed;

b) The review team members;

c) The software product reviewed;

d) Specific inputs to the review;

e) Review objectives and whether they were met;

f) A list of resolved and unresolved software product anomalies;

g) A list of unresolved system or hardware anomalies or specification action items;

h) A list of management issues;

i) Action item status (open, closed), ownership and target date (if open), or completion date (if closed);

j) Any recommendations made by the review team on how to dispose of unresolved issues and anomalies; and

k) Whether the software product meets the applicable regulations, standards, guidelines, plans, and procedures without deviations.

Although this standard sets minimum requirements for the content of the documented evidence, it is left to local procedures to prescribe additional content, format requirements, and media.

6. Inspections

6.1 Introduction

The purpose of an inspection is to detect and identify software product anomalies. This is a systematic peer examination that:

a) Verifies that the software product satisfies its specifications;

b) Verifies that the software product satisfies specified quality attributes;

c) Verifies that the software product conforms to applicable regulations, standards, guidelines, plans, and procedures;

d) Identifies deviations from standards and specifications;

e) Collects software engineering data (for example, anomaly and effort data) (optional); and

f) Uses the collected software engineering data to improve the inspection process itself and its supporting documentation (for example, checklists) (optional).

Inspections consist of three to six participants. An inspection is led by an impartial facilitator who is trained in inspection techniques. Determination of remedial or investigative action for an anomaly is a mandatory element of a software inspection, although the resolution should not occur in the inspection meeting. Collection of data for the purpose of analysis and improvement of software engineering procedures (including all review procedures) is strongly recommended but is not a mandatory element of software inspections.

Examples of software products subject to inspections include, but are not limited to, the following:

a) Software requirements specification;

b) Software design description;

c) Source code;

d) Software test documentation;

e) Software user documentation;

f) Maintenance manual;

g) System build procedures;

h) Installation procedures; and

i) Release notes.

6.2 Responsibilities

The following roles shall be established for the inspection:

a) Inspection leader;

b) Recorder;

c) Reader;

d) Author; and

e) Inspector.

All participants in the review are inspectors. The author shall not act as inspection leader and should not act as reader or recorder. Other roles may be shared among the team members. Individual participants may act in more than one role.

Individuals holding management positions over any member of the inspection team shall not participate in the inspection.

6.2.1 Inspection leader

The inspection leader shall be responsible for administrative tasks pertaining to the inspection, shall be responsible for planning and preparation as described in Paragraph 6.5.2 and Paragraph 6.5.4, shall ensure that the inspection is conducted in an orderly manner and meets its objectives, should be responsible for collecting inspection data (if appropriate), and shall issue the inspection output as described in Paragraph 6.7.

6.2.2 Recorder

The recorder shall document anomalies, action items, decisions, and recommendations made by the inspection team. The recorder should record inspection data required for process analysis. The inspection leader may be the recorder.

6.2.3 Reader

The reader shall lead the inspection team through the software product in a comprehensive and logical fashion, interpreting sections of the work (for example, generally paraphrasing groups of 1–3 lines), and highlighting important aspects.

6.2.4 Author

The author shall be responsible for the software product meeting its inspection entry criteria, for contributing to the inspection based on special understanding of the software product, and for performing any rework required to make the software product meet its inspection exit criteria.

6.2.5 Inspector

Inspectors shall identify and describe anomalies in the software product. Inspectors shall be chosen to represent different viewpoints at the meeting (for example, sponsor, requirements, design, code, safety, test, independent test, project management, quality management, and hardware engineering). Only those viewpoints pertinent to the inspection of the product should be present.

Some inspectors should be assigned specific review topics to ensure effective coverage. For example, one inspector may focus on conformance with a specific standard or standards, another on syntax, another for overall coherence. These roles should be assigned by the inspection leader when planning the inspection, as provided in Paragraph 6.5.2 (b).

6.3 Input

Input to the inspection shall include the following:

a) A statement of objectives for the inspection;

b) The software product to be inspected;

c) Documented inspection procedure;

d) Inspection reporting forms;

e) Current anomalies or issues list;

Input to the inspection may also include the following:

f) Inspection checklists;

g) Any regulations, standards, guidelines, plans, and procedures against which the software product is to be inspected;

h) Hardware product specifications;

i) Hardware performance data; and

j) Anomaly categories (see IEEE Std 1044-1993).

Additional reference material may be made available by the individuals responsible for the software product when requested by the inspection leader.

6.4 Entry criteria

6.4.1 Authorization

Inspections shall be planned and documented in the appropriate project planning documents (for example, the overall project plan, or software verification and validation plan).

Additional inspections may be conducted during acquisition, supply, development, operation, and maintenance of the software product at the request of project management, quality management, or the author, according to local procedures.

6.4.2 Preconditions

An inspection shall be conducted only when both of the following conditions have been met:

a) A statement of objectives for the inspection is established; and

b) The required inspection inputs are available.

6.4.3 Minimum entry criteria

An inspection shall not be conducted until all of the following events have occurred, unless there is a documented rationale, accepted by management, for exception from these provisions:

a) The software product that is to be inspected is complete and conforms to project standards for content and format.

b) Any automated error-detecting tools (such as spell-checkers and compilers) required for the inspection are available.

c) Prior milestones are satisfied as identified in the appropriate planning documents.

d) Required supporting documentation is available.

e) For a re-inspection, all items noted on the anomaly list that affect the software product under inspection are resolved.

6.5 Procedures

6.5.1 Management preparation

Managers shall ensure that the inspection is performed as required by applicable standards and procedures and by requirements mandated by law, contract, or other policy. To this end, managers shall:

a) Plan time and resources required for inspection, including support functions, as required in IEEE Std 1058-1998 or other appropriate standards;

b) Provide funding and facilities required to plan, define, execute, and manage the inspection;

c) Provide training and orientation on inspection procedures applicable to a given project;

d) Ensure that review team members possess appropriate levels of expertise and knowledge sufficient to comprehend the software product under inspection;

e) Ensure that planned inspections are conducted; and

f) Act on inspection team recommendations in a timely manner.

6.5.2 Planning the inspection

The author shall assemble the inspection materials for the inspection leader.

The inspection leader shall be responsible for the following activities:

a) Identifying, with appropriate management support, the inspection team;

b) Assigning specific responsibilities to the inspection team members;

c) Scheduling the meeting and selecting the meeting place;

d) Distributing inspection materials to participants, and allowing adequate time for their preparation; and

e) Setting a timetable for distribution of inspection material and for the return of comments and forwarding of comments to the author for disposition.

As a part of the planning procedure, the inspection team shall determine if alternatives are to be discussed at the inspection meeting. Alternatives may be discussed at the inspection meeting, afterwards in a separate meeting, or left to the authors of the software product to resolve.

6.5.3 Overview of inspection procedures

The author should present an overview of the software product to be inspected. This overview should be used to introduce the inspectors to the software product. The overview may be attended by other project personnel who could profit from the presentation.

Roles shall be assigned by the inspection leader. The inspection leader shall answer questions about any checklists and the role assignments and should present inspection data, such as minimal preparation times and the typical number of anomalies found in past similar products.

6.5.4 Preparation

Each inspection team member shall examine the software product and other review inputs prior to the review meeting. Anomalies detected during this examination shall be documented and sent to the inspection leader. The inspection leader should classify anomalies to ensure that inspection-meeting time is used effectively. The inspection leader should forward the anomalies to the author of the software product for disposition.

The inspection leader or reader shall specify a suitable order in which the software product will be inspected (such as sequential, hierarchical, data flow, control flow, bottom up, or top down). The reader shall ensure that he or she is able to present the software product at the inspection meeting.

6.5.5 Examination

The inspection meeting shall follow this agenda:

6.5.5.1 Introduce meeting

The inspection leader shall introduce the participants and describe their roles. The inspection leader shall state the purpose of the inspection and should remind the inspectors to focus their efforts toward anomaly detection, not resolution. The inspection leader should remind the inspectors to direct their remarks to the reader and to comment only on the software product, not their author. Inspectors may pose questions to the author regarding the software product. The inspection leader shall resolve any special procedural questions raised by the inspectors.

6.5.5.2 Establish preparedness

The inspection leader shall verify that inspectors are prepared for the inspection. The inspection leader shall reschedule the meeting if the inspectors are not adequately prepared. The inspection leader should gather individual preparation times and record the total in the inspection documentation.

6.5.5.3 Review general items

Anomalies referring to the software product in general (and thus not attributable to a specific instance or location) shall be presented to the inspectors and recorded.

6.5.5.4 Review software product and record anomalies

The reader shall present the software product to the inspection team. The inspection team shall examine the software product objectively and thoroughly, and the inspection leader shall focus this part of the meeting on creating the anomaly list. The recorder shall enter each anomaly, location, description, and classification on the anomaly list. IEEE Std 1044-1993 may be used to classify anomalies. During this time, the author shall answer specific questions and contribute to anomaly detection based on the author's special understanding of the software product. If there is disagreement about an anomaly, the potential anomaly shall be logged and marked for resolution at the end of the meeting.

6.5.5.5 Review the anomaly list

At the end of the inspection meeting, the inspection leader should have the anomaly list reviewed with the team to ensure its completeness and accuracy. The inspection leader should allow time to discuss every anomaly where disagreement occurred. The inspection leader should not allow the discussion to focus on resolving the anomaly but on clarifying what constitutes the anomaly.

6.5.5.6 Make exit decision

The purpose of the exit decision is to bring an unambiguous closure to the inspection meeting. The exit decision shall determine if the software product meets the inspection exit criteria and shall prescribe any appropriate rework and verification. Specifically, the inspection team shall identify the software product disposition as one of the following:

a) *Accept with no or minor rework.* The software product is accepted as is or with only minor rework (for example, that would require no further verification).

b) *Accept with rework verification.* The software product is to be accepted after the inspection leader or a designated member of the inspection team (other than the author) verifies rework.

c) *Re-inspect.* Schedule a re-inspection to verify rework. At a minimum, a re-inspection shall examine the software product areas changed to resolve anomalies identified in the last inspection, as well as side effects of those changes.

6.5.6 Rework/follow-up

The inspection leader shall verify that the action items assigned in the meeting are closed.

6.6 Exit criteria

An inspection shall be considered complete when the activities listed in Paragraph 6.5.5 have been accomplished, and the output described in Paragraph 6.7 exists.

6.7 Output

The output of the inspection shall be documented evidence that identifies:

a) The project being inspected;

b) The inspection team members;

c) The inspection meeting duration;

d) The software product inspected;

e) The size of the materials inspected (for example, the number of text pages);

f) Specific inputs to the inspection;

g) Inspection objectives and whether they were met;

h) The anomaly list, containing each anomaly location, description, and classification;

i) The inspection anomaly summary listing the number of anomalies identified by each anomaly category;

j) The disposition of the software product;

k) An estimate of the rework effort and rework completion date; and

The output of the inspection should include the following documentation:

l) The total preparation time of the inspection team.

Although this standard sets minimum requirements for the content of the documented evidence, it is left to local procedures to prescribe additional content, format requirements, and media.

6.8 Data collection recommendations

Inspections should provide data for the analysis of the quality of the software product, the effectiveness of the acquisition, supply, development, operation and maintenance processes, and the efficiency of the inspection itself. In order to maintain the effectiveness of inspections, data should not be used to evaluate the performance of individuals. To enable these analyses, anomalies that are identified at an inspection meeting should be classified in accordance with Paragraphs 6.8.1 through 6.8.3.

Inspection data should contain the identification of the software product, the date and time of the inspection, the inspection leader, the preparation and inspection times, the volume of the materials inspected, and the disposition of the inspected software product. The capture of this information can be used to optimize local guidance for inspections.

The management of inspection data requires a capability to store, enter, access, update, summarize, and report categorized anomalies. The frequency and types of the inspection analysis reports, and their distribution, are left to local standards and procedures.

6.8.1 Anomaly classification

Anomalies may be classified by technical type according to, for example, IEEE Std 1044-1993.

6.8.2 Anomaly classes

Anomaly classes provide evidence of non-conformance and may be categorized, for example, as:

a) Missing;

b) Extra (superfluous);

c) Ambiguous;

d) Inconsistent;

e) Improvement desirable;

f) Not conforming to standards;

g) Risk-prone, e.g., the review finds that, although an item was not shown to be "wrong," the approach taken involves risks (and there are known safer alternative methods);

h) Factually incorrect;

i) Not implementable (e.g., because of system constraints or time constraints); and

j) Editorial.

6.8.3 Anomaly ranking

Anomalies may be ranked by potential impact on the software product, for example, as:

a) *Major*. Anomalies that would result in failure of the software product or an observable departure from specification.

b) *Minor*. Anomalies that deviate from relevant specifications but will not cause failure of the software product or an observable departure in performance.

6.9 Improvement

Inspection data should be analyzed regularly in order to improve the inspection itself, and the software activities used to produce software products. Frequently occurring anomalies may be included in the inspection checklists or role assignments. The checklists themselves should also be inspected regularly for superfluous or misleading questions. The preparation times, meeting times, and number of participants should be analyzed to determine connections between preparation rate, meeting rate, and number and severity of anomalies found.

A "chief inspector" role should exist. The chief inspector acts as the inspection owner, and collects and feeds back data about the inspection. This chief inspector should be responsible for the proposed follow-up on the inspection itself.

7. Walk-throughs

7.1 Introduction

The purpose of a systematic walk-through is to evaluate a software product. A walk-through may be held for the purpose of educating an audience regarding a software product. The major objectives are to:

a) Find anomalies;

b) Improve the software product;

c) Consider alternative implementations; and

d) Evaluate conformance to standards and specifications.

Other important objectives of the walk-through include exchange of techniques and style variations and training of the participants. A walk-through may point out several deficiencies (for example, efficiency and readability problems in the software product, modularity problems in design or code, or untestable specifications).

Examples of software products subject to walk-throughs include, but are not limited to, the following:

a) Software requirements specification;

b) Software design description;

c) Source code;

d) Software test documentation;

e) Software user documentation;

f) Maintenance manual;

g) System build procedures;

h) Installation procedures; and

i) Release notes.

7.2 Responsibilities

The following roles shall be established for the walk-through:

a) Walk-through leader;

b) Recorder;

c) Author; and

d) Team member.

For a review to be considered a systematic walk-through, a team of at least two members shall be assembled. Roles may be shared among the team members. The walk-through leader or the author may serve as the recorder. The walk-through leader may be the author.

Individuals holding management positions over any member of the walk-through team shall not participate in the walk-through.

7.2.1 Walk-through leader

The walk-through leader shall conduct the walk-through, shall handle the administrative tasks pertaining to the walk-through (such as distributing documents and arranging the meeting), and shall ensure that the walk-through is conducted in an orderly manner. The walk-through leader shall prepare the statement of objectives to guide the team through the walk-through. The walk-through leader shall ensure that the team arrives at a decision or identified action for each discussion item, and shall issue the walk-through output as described in Paragraph 7.7.

7.2.2 Recorder

The recorder shall note all decisions and identified actions arising during the walk-through meeting. In addition, the recorder should note all comments made during the walk-through that pertain to anomalies found, questions of style, omissions, contradictions, suggestions for improvement, or alternative approaches.

7.2.3 Author

The author should present the software product in the walk-through.

7.3 Input

Input to the walk-through shall include the following:

a) A statement of objectives for the walk-through;

b) The software product being examined;

c) Standards that are in effect for the acquisition, supply, development, operation, and/or maintenance of the software product;

Input to the walk-through may also include the following:

d) Any regulations, standards, guidelines, plans, and procedures against which the software product is to be inspected; and

e) Anomaly categories (see IEEE Std 1044-1993).

7.4 Entry criteria

7.4.1 Authorization

The need for conducting walk-throughs shall be established in the appropriate project planning documents. Additional walk-throughs may be conducted during acquisition, supply, development, operation, and maintenance of the software product at the request of project management, quality management, or the author, according to local procedures.

7.4.2 Preconditions

A walk-through shall be conducted only when both of the following conditions have been met:

a) A statement of objectives for the review is established by the management personnel for whom the review is being carried out; and

b) The required review inputs are available.

7.5 Procedures

7.5.1 Management preparation

Managers shall ensure that the walk-through is performed as required by applicable standards and procedures and by requirements mandated by law, contract, or other policy. To this end, managers shall:

a) Plan time and resources required for walk-throughs, including support functions, as required in IEEE Std 1058-1998 or other appropriate standards;

b) Provide funding and facilities required to plan, define, execute, and manage the walk-through;

c) Provide training and orientation on walk-through procedures applicable to a given project;

d) Ensure that walk-through team members possess appropriate levels of expertise and knowledge sufficient to comprehend the software product;

e) Ensure that planned walk-throughs are conducted; and

f) Act on walk-through team recommendations in a timely manner.

7.5.2 Planning the walk-through

The walk-through leader shall be responsible for the following activities:

a) Identifying the walk-through team;

b) Scheduling the meeting and selecting the meeting place; and

159

c) Distributing necessary input materials to participants, and allowing adequate time for their preparation.

7.5.3 Overview

An overview presentation should be made by the author as part of the walk-through meeting.

7.5.4 Preparation

The walk-through leader shall distribute the software product and convene a walk-through meeting. Team members shall prepare for the meeting by examining the software product and preparing a list of items for discussion in the meeting. These items should be divided into two categories: general and specific. General items apply to the whole product; specific items apply to a part of it.

Each walk-through team member shall examine the software product and other review inputs prior to the review meeting. Anomalies detected during this examination shall be documented and sent to the walk-through leader. The walk-through leader should classify anomalies to ensure that walk-through meeting time is used effectively. The walk-through leader should forward the anomalies to the author of the software product for disposition.

The author or walk-through leader shall specify a suitable order in which the software product will be inspected (such as sequential, hierarchical, data flow, control flow, bottom up, or top down).

7.5.5 Examination

The walk-through leader shall introduce the participants and describe their roles. The walk-through leader shall state the purpose of the walk-through and should remind the team members to focus their efforts toward anomaly detection, not resolution. The walk-through leader should remind the team members to comment only on the software product, not its author. Team members may pose questions to the author regarding the software product. The walk-through leader shall resolve any special procedural questions raised by the team members.

The author shall present an overview of the software product under review. This is followed by a general discussion during which team members raise their general items. After the general discussion, the author serially presents the software product in detail (hence the name "walk-through"). Team members raise their specific items when the author reaches them in the presentation. New items may be raised during the meeting. The walk-through leader coordinates discussion and guides the meeting to a decision or identified action on each item. The recorder notes all recommendations and required actions.

During the walk-through meeting:

a) The author or walk-through leader should make an overview presentation of the software product under examination;

b) The walk-through leader shall coordinate a discussion of the general anomalies of concern;

c) The author or walk-through leader shall present the software product, describing every portion of it;

d) Team members shall raise specific anomalies as the author reaches the part of the software product to which the anomalies relate; and

e) The recorder shall note recommendations and actions arising out of the discussion upon each anomaly.

After the walk-through meeting, the walk-through leader shall issue the walk-through output detailing anomalies, decisions, actions, and other information of interest. Minimum content requirements for the walk-through output are provided in Paragraph 7.7.

7.5.6 Rework/follow-up

The walk-through leader shall verify that the action items assigned in the meeting are closed.

7.6 Exit criteria

The walk-through shall be considered complete when:

a) The entire software product has been examined;

b) Recommendations and required actions have been recorded; and

c) The walk-through output has been completed.

7.7 Output

The output of the walk-through shall be documented evidence that identifies:

a) The walk-through team members;

b) The software product being examined;

c) The statement of objectives that were to be accomplished during this walk-through meeting and whether they were met;

d) A list of the recommendations made regarding each anomaly;

e) A list of actions, due dates, and responsible people;

f) Any recommendations made by the walk-through team on how to dispose of deficiencies and unresolved anomalies; and

g) Any proposals made by the walk-through team for follow-up walk-throughs.

Although this standard sets minimum requirements for the content of the documented evidence, it is left to local procedures to prescribe additional content, format requirements, and media.

7.8 Data collection recommendations

Walk-throughs should provide data for the analysis of the quality of the software product, the effectiveness of the acquisition, supply, development, operation, and maintenance processes, and the efficiency of the walk-through itself. In order to maintain the effectiveness of walk-throughs, data should not be used to evaluate the performance of individuals. To enable these analyses, anomalies that are identified at a walk-through meeting should be classified in accordance with Paragraphs 7.8.1 through 7.8.3.

Walk-through data should contain the identification of the software product, the date and time of the walk-through, the walk-through leader, the preparation and walk-through times, the volume of the materials walked through, and the disposition of the software product. The capture of this information can be used to optimize local guidance for walk-throughs.

The management of walk-through data requires a capability to store, enter, access, update, summarize, and report categorized anomalies. The frequency and types of the walk-through analysis reports, and their distribution, are left to local standards and procedures.

7.8.1 Anomaly classification

Anomalies may be classified by technical type according to, for example, IEEE Std 1044-1993.

7.8.2 Anomaly classes

Anomaly classes provide evidence of non-conformance, and may be categorized, for example, as:

a) Missing;

b) Extra (superfluous);

c) Ambiguous;

d) Inconsistent;

e) Improvement desirable;

f) Not conforming to standards;

g) Risk-prone, e.g., the review finds that although an item was not shown to be "wrong," the approach taken involves risks (and there are known safer alternative methods);

h) Factually incorrect;

i) Not implementable (e.g., because of system constraints or time constraints); and

j)   Editorial.

7.8.3 Anomaly ranking

Anomalies may be ranked by potential impact on the software product, for example, as:

a)   *Major.*   Anomalies that would result in failure of the software product or an observable departure from specification.

b)   *Minor.*   Anomalies that deviate from relevant specifications but will not cause failure of the software product or an observable departure in performance.

7.9 Improvement

Walk-through data should be analyzed regularly in order to improve the walk-through itself and to improve the software activities used to produce the software product.   Frequently occurring anomalies may be included in the walk-through checklists or role assignments.   The checklists themselves should also be inspected regularly for superfluous or misleading questions.   The preparation times, meeting times, and number of participants should be analyzed to determine connections between preparation rate, meeting rate, and number and severity of anomalies found.

8. Audits

8.1 Introduction

The purpose of a software audit is to provide an independent evaluation of conformance of software products and processes to applicable regulations, standards, guidelines, plans, and procedures.

Examples of software products subject to audit include, but are not limited to, the following:

a)   Back-up and recovery plans;

b)   Contingency plans;

c)   Contracts;

d)   Customer or user representative complaints;

e)   Disaster plans;

f)   Hardware performance plans;

g)   Installation plans;

h)   Installation procedures;

i)   Maintenance plans;

j)   Management review reports;

k)   Operations and user manuals;

l)   Procurement and contracting methods;

m)   Reports and data (for example, review, audit, project status, anomaly reports, test data);

n)   Request for proposal;

o)   Risk management plans;

p)   Software configuration management plans (see IEEE Std 828-1990);

q)   Software design descriptions (see IEEE Std 1016-1987);

r)   Source code;

s)   Unit development folders;

t)   Software project management plans (see IEEE Std. 1058-1987);

u) Software quality assurance plans (see IEEE Std 730-1989);

v) Software requirements specifications (see IEEE Std 830-1993);

w) Software safety plans (see IEEE Std 1228-1994);

x) Software test documentation (see IEEE Std 829-1983);

y) Software user documentation (see IEEE Std 1063-1987);

z) Software verification and validation plans (see IEEE Std 1012-1986);

aa) Standards, regulations, guidelines, and procedures;

ab) System build procedures;

ac) Technical review reports;

ad) Vendor documents;

ae) Walk-through reports; and

af) Deliverable media (such as tapes and diskettes).

The examination should begin with an overview meeting during which the auditors and audited organization examine and agree upon the arrangements for the audit.

When stipulated in the audit plan, the auditors may make recommendations. These should be reported separately.

8.2 Responsibilities

The following roles shall be established for an audit:

a) Lead auditor;

b) Recorder;

c) Auditor(s);

d) Initiator; and

e) Audited organization.

The lead auditor may act as recorder. The initiator may act as lead auditor. Additional auditors should be included in the audit team; however, audits by a single person are permitted.

8.2.1 Lead auditor

The lead auditor shall be responsible for the audit. This responsibility includes administrative tasks pertaining to the audit, ensuring that the audit is conducted in an orderly manner, and ensuring that the audit meets its objectives:

a) Preparing the audit plan (see Paragraph 8.5.2);

b) Assembling the audit team;

c) Managing the audit team;

d) Making decisions regarding the conduct of the audit;

e) Making decisions regarding any audit observations;

f) Preparing the audit report (see Paragraph 8.7);

g) Reporting on the inability, or apparent inability, of any of individuals involved in the audit to fulfill their responsibilities;

h) Negotiating any discrepancies or inconsistencies with the initiator which could impair the ability to satisfy the exit criteria (see Paragraph 8.6); and

i) Recommending corrective actions.

The lead auditor shall be free from bias and influence that could reduce his or her ability to make independent, objective evaluations.

8.2.2 Recorder

The recorder shall document anomalies, action items, decisions, and recommendations made by the audit team.

8.2.3 Auditor

The auditors shall examine products, as defined in the audit plan. They shall document their observations and recommend corrective actions. All auditors shall be free from bias and influences that could reduce their ability to make independent, objective evaluations, or shall identify their bias and proceed with acceptance from the initiator.

8.2.4 Initiator

The initiator shall be responsible for the following activities:

a) Decide upon the need for an audit;

b) Decide upon the purpose and scope of the audit;

c) Decide the software products to be audited;

d) Decide the evaluation criteria, including the regulations, standards, guidelines, plans, and procedures to be used for evaluation;

e) Decide upon who will carry out the audit;

f) Review the audit report;

g) Decide what follow-up action will be required; and

h) Distribute the audit report.

The initiator may be a manager in the audited organization, a customer, or user representative of the audited organization, or a third party.

8.2.5 Audited organization

The audited organization shall provide a liaison to the auditors and shall provide all information requested by the auditors. When the audit is completed, the audited organization should implement corrective actions and recommendations.

8.3 Input

Inputs to the audit shall be listed in the audit plan and shall include the following:

a) Purpose and scope of the audit;

b) Background information about the audited organization;

c) Software products to be audited;

d) Evaluation criteria, including applicable regulations, standards, guidelines, plans, and procedures to be used for evaluation;

e) Evaluation criteria: for example, "acceptable," "needs improvement," "unacceptable," "not rated; and

Inputs to the audit should also include the following:

f) Records of previous similar audits.

8.4 Entry criteria

8.4.1 Authorization

An initiator decides upon the need for an audit. This decision may be prompted by a routine event, such as the arrival at a project milestone, or a non-routine event, such as the suspicion or discovery of a major non-conformance.

The initiator selects an auditing organization that can perform an independent evaluation. The initiator provides the auditors with information that defines the purpose of the audit, the software products to be audited, and the evaluation criteria. The initiator should request the auditors to make recommendations. The lead auditor produces an audit plan and the auditors prepare for the audit.

The need for an audit may be established by one or more of the following events:

a) The supplier organization decides to verify compliance with the applicable regulations, standards, guidelines, plans, and procedures (this decision may have been made when planning the project).

b) The customer organization decides to verify compliance with applicable regulations, standards, guidelines, plans, and procedures.

c) A third party, such as a regulatory agency or assessment body, decides upon the need to audit the supplier organization to verify compliance with applicable regulations, standards, guidelines, plans, and procedures.

In every case, the initiator shall authorize the audit.

8.4.2 Preconditions

An audit shall be conducted only when all of the following conditions have been met:

a) The audit has been authorized by an appropriate authority;

b) A statement of objectives of the audit is established; and

c) The required audit inputs are available.

8.5 Procedures

8.5.1 Management preparation

Managers shall ensure that the audit is performed as required by applicable standards and procedures and by requirements mandated by law, contract, or other policy. To this end, managers shall:

a) Plan time and resources required for audits, including support functions, as required in IEEE Std 1058-1998, legal or regulatory documents, or other appropriate standards;

b) Provide funding and facilities required to plan, define, execute, and manage the audits;

c) Provide training and orientation on the audit procedures applicable to a given project;

d) Ensure that audit team members possess appropriate levels of expertise and knowledge sufficient to comprehend the software product being audited;

e) Ensure that planned audits are conducted; and

f) Act on audit team recommendations in a timely manner.

8.5.2 Planning the audit

The audit plan shall describe the:

a) Purpose and scope of the audit;

b) Audited organization, including location and management;

c) Software products to be audited;

d) Evaluation criteria, including applicable regulations, standards, guidelines, plans, and procedures to be used for evaluation;

e) Auditor's responsibilities;

f) Examination activities (for example, interview staff, read and evaluate documents, observe tests);

g) Audit activity resource requirements;

h) Audit activity schedule;

i) Requirements for confidentiality (for example, company confidential, restricted information, classified information);

j) Checklists;

k) Report formats;

l) Report distribution; and

m) Required follow-up activities.

Where sampling is used, a statistically valid sampling method shall be used to establish selection criteria and sample size.

The audit plan shall be approved by the initiator. The audit plan should allow for changes based on information gathered during the audit, subject to approval by the initiator.

8.5.3 Opening meeting

An opening meeting between the audit team and audited organization shall occur at the beginning of the examination phase of the audit. The overview meeting agenda shall include:

a) Purpose and scope of the audit;

b) Software products being audited;

c) Audit procedures and outputs;

d) Expected contributions of the audited organization to the audit (for example, the number of people to be interviewed, meeting facilities);

e) Audit schedule; and

f) Access to facilities, information, and documents required.

8.5.4 Preparation

The initiator shall notify the audited organization's management in writing before the audit is performed, except for unannounced audits. The notification shall define the purpose and scope of the audit, identify what will be audited, identify the auditors, and identify the audit schedule. The purpose of notification is to enable the audited organization to ensure that the people and material to be examined in the audit are available.

Auditors shall prepare for the audit by studying the:

a) Audit plan;

b) Audited organization;

c) Software products to be audited;

d) Applicable regulations, standards, guidelines, plans, and procedures to be used for evaluation;

e) Evaluation criteria;

In addition, the lead auditor shall make the necessary arrangements for:

f) Team orientation and training;

g) Facilities for audit interviews;

h) Materials, documents, and tools required by the audit procedures; and

i) Examination activities.

8.5.5 Examination

Examination shall consist of evidence collection and analysis with respect to the audit criteria, a closing meeting between the auditors and audited organization, and preparing an audit report.

8.5.5.1 Evidence collection

The auditors shall collect evidence of conformance and non-conformance by interviewing audited organization staff, examining documents, and witnessing processes. The auditors should attempt all the examination activities defined in the audit plan. They shall undertake additional investigative activities if they consider such activities required to define the full extent of conformance or non-conformance.

Auditors shall document all observations of non-conformance and exemplary conformance. An observation is a statement of fact made during an audit that is substantiated by objective evidence. Examples of non-conformance are:

a) Applicable regulations, standards, guidelines, plans, and procedures not used at all; and

b) Applicable regulations, standards, guidelines, plans, and procedures not used correctly.

Observations should be categorized as major or minor. An observation should be classified as major if the non-conformity will likely have a significant effect on product quality, project cost, or project schedule.

All observations shall be verified by discussing them with the audited organization before the closing audit meeting.

8.5.5.2 Closing meeting

The lead auditor shall convene a closing meeting with the audited organization's management. The closing meeting should review:

a) Actual extent of implementation of the audit plan;

b) Problems experienced in implementing the audit plan, if any;

c) Observations made by the auditors;

d) Preliminary conclusions of the auditors;

e) Preliminary recommendations of the auditors; and

f) Overall audit assessment (for example, whether the audited organization successfully passed the audit criteria).

Comments and issues raised by the audited organization should be resolved. Agreements should be reached during the closing audit meeting and must be completed before the audit report is finalized.

8.5.5.3 Reporting

The lead auditor shall prepare the audit report, as described in Paragraph 8.7. The audit report should be prepared as soon as possible after the audit. Any communication between auditors and the audited organization made between the closing meeting and the issue of the report should pass through the lead auditor.

The lead auditor shall send the audit report to the initiator. The initiator should distribute the audit report within the audited organization.

8.5.6 Follow-up

Rework, if any, shall be the responsibility of the initiator and audited organization and shall include:

a) Determining what corrective action is required to remove or prevent a non-conformity; and

b) Initiating the corrective action.

8.6 Exit criteria

An audit shall be considered complete when:

a) The audit report has been submitted to the initiator; and

b) All of the auditing organization's follow-up actions included in the scope of the audit have been performed, reviewed, and approved.

8.7 Output

The output of the audit is the audit report. The audit report shall contain the:

a) Purpose and scope of the audit;

b) Audited organization, including location, liaison staff, and management;

c) Identification of the software products audited;

d) Applicable regulations, standards, guidelines, plans, and procedures used for evaluation;

e) Evaluation criteria;

f) Summary of auditor's organization;

g) Summary of examination activities;

h) Summary of the planned examination activities not performed;

i) Observation list, classified as major or minor;

j) A summary and interpretation of the audit findings, including the key items of non-conformance; and

k) The type and timing of audit follow-up activities.

Additionally, when stipulated by the audit plan, recommendations shall be provided to the audited organization or the initiator. Recommendations may be reported separately from results.

Although this standard sets minimum requirements for report content, it is left to local standards to prescribe additional content, report format requirements, and media.

Chapter 6

Software Documentation Process

1. Introduction to Chapter

This chapter describes the software documentation processes. Portions of this text are paraphrased from IEEE/EIA Standard 12207.0-1996, Paragraphs 6.1. Paragraph 2 provides an overview and introduction to the papers contained in this chapter.

1.1 Documentation process

The *documentation process* is a process for recording information produced by a life cycle process or activity. The process contains the set of activities which plan, design, develop, produce, edit, distribute, and maintain those documents needed by all concerned such as managers, engineers, and users of the system or software product. This process consists of the following activities:

1. Documentation plan

2. Design and development

3. Production

4. Maintenance.

1.2 Documentation plan

A plan, identifying the documents to be produced during the life cycle of the software product, is developed, documented, and implemented. The following are addressed for each identified document:

- Title or name

- Purpose

- Intended audience

- Procedures and responsibilities for inputs, development, review, modification, approval, production, storage, distribution, maintenance, and configuration management

- Schedule for intermediate and final versions.

1.3 Design and development

- Each identified document is designed in accordance with applicable documentation standards for format, content description, page numbering, figure/table placement, proprietary/security marking, packaging, and other presentation items.

- The source and appropriateness of input data for the documents is then confirmed. Automated documentation tools may be used.

- The prepared documents are reviewed and edited for format, technical content, and presentation style against their documentation standards. They are then approved for adequacy by authorized personnel prior to issue.

1.4 Production

- The documents are produced and provided in accordance with the plan. Production and distribution of documents may use paper, electronic, or other media. Master materials are stored in accordance with requirements for record retention, security, maintenance, and backup.

- Controls are established in accordance with the *configuration management process.*

1.5 Maintenance

The tasks required for performance when documentation is to be modified, are executed in accordance with the *maintenance process.* For those documents under configuration management, modifications are managed in accordance with the *configuration management process.*

2. Overview of Papers

The first paper titled "Documentations" was written specifically for the *Tutorial* by the well-known author Ian Sommerville. Sommerville is the author of *Software Engineering,* 6th edition, Addison-Wesley, Reading, MA, 2000.

The objectives of this paper are to describe the documentation that must be produced during the software process, to discuss document quality, and documentation preparation.

Documentation may be either product or process documentation. Product documentation includes both user and system documents. High-quality documents are increasingly important and factors affecting document quality include documentation standards, a document quality assurance process, and effective writing style. In the final part of the chapter, tools used in the document preparation process are described including word-processors, desktop publishing systems, and document management systems.

The second paper in this chapter is extracted from IEEE Standard 1063-1998, *Standard for Software Users Manual,* IEEE, Inc., New York, 1998. It provides a template for developing a software users' manual (UM). The standard provides the minimum required contents of a user manual, in conjunction with a quality guide.

The reader is reminded again that this copy of the standard is incomplete and cannot be used to cite compliance with the standard in a contractual situation. It is intended to provide the reader and CSDP test taker with a basic understanding of the contents of the user manual standards and an outline of a user manual.

Software Documentation

Ian Sommerville
Lancaster University, UK

Introduction

All large software development projects, irrespective of application, generate a large amount of associated documentation. For moderately sized systems, the documentation will probably fill several filing cabinets; for large systems, it may fill several rooms. A high proportion of software process costs is incurred in producing this documentation. Furthermore, documentation errors and omissions can lead to errors by end users and consequent system failures with their associated costs and disruption. Therefore, managers and software engineers should pay as much attention to documentation and its associated costs as to the development of the software itself.

The documents associated with a software project and the system being developed have a number of associated requirements:

1. They should act as a communication medium between members of the development team.

2. There should be a system information repository to be used by maintenance engineers.

3. They should provide information for management to help them plan, budget, and schedule the software development process.

4. Some of the documents should tell users how to use and administer the system.

Satisfying these requirements requires different types of documents ranging from informal working documents to professionally produced user manuals. Software engineers are usually responsible for producing most of this documentation although professional technical writers may assist with the final polishing of externally released information.

The goals of this paper are to describe the documentation that may be produced during the software development process, to provide hints of ways to write effective documents, and to describe processes involved in producing these documents. I begin by discussing different types of documentation that may be produced in a software project. I then cover the important topic of document quality and discuss document structure, documentation standards, and effective writing style. Finally, the processes of preparing, producing, and managing documents are discussed.

The focus of this paper is on documentation that is intended to be printed, hence delivered on paper or in a format such as Adobe Portable Document Format (PDF), which may be viewed on a screen or printed locally. Many systems are now equipped with associated hypertext help systems. Producing these systems requires a different set of skills from those required to produce paper documentation. These skills are discussed briefly here.

Process and product documentation

Documentation for large software projects usually begins to be generated well before the development process begins. A proposal to develop the system may be produced in response to a request for proposal (called "request for tender" in the United Kingdom) by an external client or in response to other business strategy documents. For some types of systems, a comprehensive requirements document, which defines the required features and expected system behavior, may be produced. During the development process itself, all sorts of different documents may be produced: project plans, design specifications, test plans, and so on.

It is not possible to define a specific required document set. This depends on the contract with the client for the system, the type of system being developed and its expected lifetime, the culture and size of the company developing the system, and the expected development schedule. However, we can generally say that the documentation produced falls into two classes:

1. *Process documentation.* These documents record the process of development and maintenance. Plans, schedules, process-quality documents, and organizational and project standards are included in this documentation.

2. *Product documentation.* This documentation describes the product being developed. System documentation describes the product from the point of view of the engineers developing and maintaining the system. User documentation provides a product description that is oriented toward system users.

Process documentation is produced to manage system development. Product documentation is used after the system is operational, but is also essential for managing system development. The creation of a document, such as a system specification, may represent an important milestone in the software development process.

Process documentation

[handwritten: Documentation Inspection.]

Effective management requires that the process being managed is (visible). Because software is intangible and the software process involves apparently similar cognitive tasks rather than obviously different physical tasks, the only way this visibility can be achieved is through the use of process documentation.

Process documentation falls into a number of categories:

1. *Plans, estimates, and schedules.* These documents are produced by managers and are used to predict and control the software process.

2. *Reports.* These documents report how resources are used during the development process.

3. *Standards.* These documents set out how the process is to be implemented. They may be developed from organizational, national, or international standards.

4. *Working papers.* These are often the principal technical communication documents in a project. They record the ideas and thoughts of the engineers working on the project, serve as interim versions of product documentation, describe implementation strategies, and set out problems that have been identified. They often implicitly record the rationale for design decisions.

5. *Memos and electronic mail messages.* These record the details of everyday communications between managers and development engineers.

The major characteristic of process documentation is that most of it becomes outdated. Plans may be drawn up on a weekly, biweekly, or monthly basis. Progress will normally be reported weekly. Memos record thoughts, ideas, and intentions, all of which change.

Although of interest to software historians, much of this process information is of little real use after it has gone out of date. There is normally no need to preserve it after the system has been delivered. However, there are some process documents that can be useful as the software evolves in response to new requirements.

For example, test schedules are of value during software evolution since they act as a basis for replanning the validation of system changes. Working papers that explain the reasons behind design decisions (design rationale) are also potentially valuable as they discuss design options and choices made. Access to this information helps avoid making changes that conflict with these original decisions. Ideally, of course, the design rationale should be extracted from the working papers and separately maintained. Unfortunately, this hardly ever happens.

172

Product documentation

Product documentation is concerned with describing the delivered software product. Unlike most process documentation, it has a relatively long life. It must evolve in step with the product it describes. Product documentation includes user documentation, which tells users how to use the software product, and system documentation, which is principally intended for maintenance engineers.

User documentation

Users of a system are not all the same. The producer of documentation must structure it to cater to different user tasks and different levels of expertise and experience. It is particularly important to distinguish between end users and system administrators.

1. End users use the software to assist with some task. This may be flying an aircraft, managing insurance policies, or writing a book. Users want to know how the software can help them. They are not interested in computer or administration details.

2. System administrators are responsible for managing the software used by end users. This may involve acting as an operator for a large mainframe system, as a network manager if the system involves a network of workstations, or as a technical guru who fixes end-user software problems and who liaises between users and the software supplier.

To cater to these different classes of users and different levels of user expertise, there are at least five documents (or perhaps chapters in a single document) that should be delivered with the software system (See Figure 1).

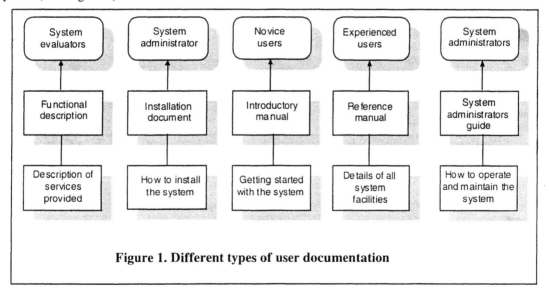

Figure 1. Different types of user documentation

The *functional description* of the system outlines the system requirements and briefly describes the services provided. This document should provide a system overview. Users should be able to read this document with an introductory manual and decide if the system is what they need.

The *system installation document* is intended for system administrators. It should explain how to install the system in a particular environment. It should describe the files making up the system and the minimal hardware configuration required. How to start the system, the permanent files that must be established, and the configuration-dependent files that must be changed to tailor the system to a particular host system should also be described. The use of automated installers for PC software has meant that some suppliers see this document as unnecessary. In fact, it is still required to help system managers discover and fix problems with the installation.

The *introductory manual* should present an informal introduction to the system, describing its "normal" usage. It should describe how to get started and how end users might make use of the common system facilities. It should be liberally illustrated with examples. Inevitably, beginners, whatever their background and experience, will make mistakes. Easily discovered information on how to recover from these mistakes and restart useful work should be an integral part of this document.

The *system reference manual* should describe the system facilities and their use, provide a complete listing of error messages, and describe how to recover from detected errors. It should be complete. Formal descriptive techniques may be used. The style of the reference manual should not be unnecessarily pedantic and turgid, but completeness is more important than readability.

A more general *system administrator's guide* should be provided for some types of systems such as command and control systems. This should describe the messages generated when the system interacts with other systems, and how to react to these messages. If system hardware is involved, it might also explain the operator's task in maintaining that hardware. For example, it might describe how to clear faults in the system console or how to connect new peripherals.

Other, easy-to-use documentation might be provided in addition to manuals. A quick reference card listing available system facilities and how to use them is particularly convenient for experienced system users. Online help systems, which contain brief information about the system, can save the user from spending time consulting manuals, although this should not be seen as a replacement for more comprehensive documentation. A later section of this paper briefly discusses online documentation.

System documentation

System documentation includes all of the documents describing the system, from the requirements specification to the final acceptance test plan. Documents describing the design, implementation, and testing of a system are essential if the program is to be understood and maintained. Like user documentation, it is important that system documentation is structured, with overviews leading the reader into more formal and detailed descriptions of each aspect of the system.

For large systems that are developed to a customer's specification, the system documentation should include

1. The requirements document and an associated rationale.

2. A document describing the system architecture.

3. A description of the architecture of each program in the system.

4. A description of the functionality and interfaces of each system component.

5. Program source code listings. These should explain complex sections of code and provide a rationale for the coding method used. If meaningful names are used along with a good, structured programming style, much of the code will be self-documenting and not need additional comments. This information is now normally maintained electronically rather than on paper, with selected information printed on demand from readers.

6. Validation documents describing how each program is validated and how the validation information relates to the requirements.

7. A system maintenance guide that describes known problems with the system, describes which parts of the system are hardware and software dependent, and describes how evolution of the system has been taken into account in its design.

A common system maintenance problem is ensuring that all representations are kept in step when the system is changed. To help with this, the relationships and dependencies between documents and parts of documents should be recorded in a document management system as discussed in the final part of this paper.

For smaller systems and systems that are developed as software products, system documentation is usually less comprehensive. This is not necessarily a good thing, but schedule pressures on developers mean that documents are simply never written or, if written, are not kept up-to-date. Although these pressures are sometimes inevitable, at the very least you should always try to maintain a specification of the system, an architectural design document, and the program source code.

Unfortunately, documentation maintenance is often neglected. Documentation may fall out of step with its associated software, causing problems for both users and maintainers of the system. The natural tendency is to meet a deadline by modifying code with the intention of modifying other documents later.

Pressure of work often means that this modification is continually set aside until finding what is to be changed becomes very difficult. The best solution to this problem is to support document maintenance with software tools that record document relationships, remind software engineers when changes to one document affect another, and record possible inconsistencies in the documentation. Such a system is described by Garg and Scacchi (1990).

Document quality

Unfortunately, a large portion of computer system documentation is badly written, difficult to understand, out-of-date, or incomplete. Although the situation is improving, many organizations still do not pay enough attention to producing system documents that are well-written pieces of technical prose.

Document quality is as important as program quality. Without information on how to use a system or how to understand it, the utility of that system is degraded. Achieving document quality requires management commitment to document design, standards, and quality assurance processes. Producing good documents is neither easy nor cheap and many software engineers find it more difficult that producing good quality programs.

Document Structure

The document structure is the way in which the material in the document is organized into chapters, sections, and subsections. Document structure has a major impact on readability and usability, and it is important to design this carefully so that the different parts are as independent as possible. This allows each part to be read as a single item and reduces cross-referencing problems when changes are required.

Structuring a document properly also allows readers to find information more easily. As with document components, content lists, and indexes, well-structured documents can be skimmed, permitting readers to quickly locate the sections or subsections that are of most interest to them.

The IEEE standard for user documentation (IEEE, 2001) proposes that the structure of a document include the components shown in Table 1. The standard makes clear that these are desirable or essential features of a document, but also makes clear that how these components are provided depends on the documentation designers. Some (such as a table of contents) are clearly separate sections; other components, such as navigational features, will be found throughout the document.

As discussed in the next section, this IEEE standard is a generic standard. If use of this standard is mandated, all of these components must be included. However, many organizations will use the standard as a guide and will not necessarily include all of the components shown in Table 1.

Table 1. Suggested components in a software user document

Component	Description
Identification data	Data, such as a title and identifier, that uniquely identifies the document.
Table of contents	Chapter/section names and page numbers.
List of illustrations	Figure numbers and titles.
Introduction	The purpose of the document and a brief summary of the contents.
Information for use of the documentation	Suggestions for different readers on how to use the documentation effectively.
Concept of operations	An explanation of the software's conceptual background.
Procedures	Directions on how to use the software to complete the tasks it is designed to support.
Information on software commands	A description of each command supported by the software.
Error messages and problem resolution	A description of the errors that can be reported and recovery from these errors.
Glossary	Definitions of specialized terms used.
Related information sources	References or links to other documents that provide additional information.
Navigational features	Features that allow readers to find their current location and move around the document.
Index	A list of key terms and the pages where these terms are referenced.
Search capability	In electronic documentation, a way of finding specific terms in the document.

In such circumstances, there are some minimal structuring guidelines that should always be followed.

1. All documents, however short, should have a cover page that identifies the project, the document, the author, the date of production, the type of document, configuration management and quality assurance information, the intended recipients of the document, and the confidentiality class of the document. It should also include information for document retrieval (an abstract or keywords) and a copyright notice. Figure 2 is an example of a possible front cover format.

2. Documents that are more than a few pages long should be divided into chapters, with each chapter structured into sections and subsections. A content page listing these chapters, sections, and subsections should be produced. A consistent numbering scheme for chapters, sections, and subsections should be defined, and chapters should be individually page-numbered (the page number should be *chapter-page*). This simplifies document changes as individual chapters may be replaced without reprinting the whole document.

3. If a document contains a lot of detailed reference information, it should have an index. A comprehensive index allows information to be discovered easily and can make a badly written document usable. Without an index, reference documents are virtually useless.

4. If a document is intended for a wide spectrum of readers who may have differing vocabularies, a glossary that defines the technical terms and acronyms used in the document should be provided.

Document structures are often defined in advance and set out in documentation standards. This has the advantage of consistency although it can cause problems. Standards may not be appropriate in all cases and an unnatural structure may have to be used if standards are thoughtlessly imposed.

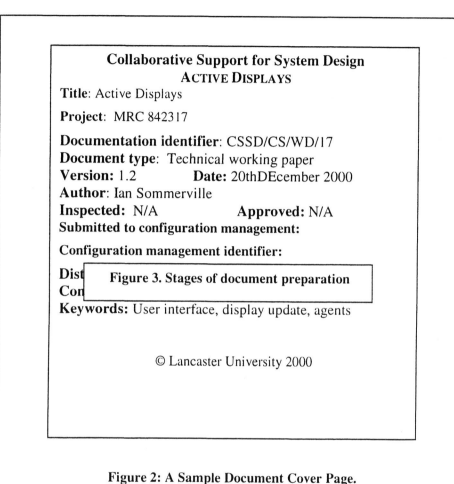

Collaborative Support for System Design
ACTIVE DISPLAYS

Title: Active Displays

Project: MRC 842317

Documentation identifier: CSSD/CS/WD/17
Document type: Technical working paper
Version: 1.2   **Date:** 20thDEcember 2000
Author: Ian Sommerville
Inspected: N/A   **Approved:** N/A
Submitted to configuration management:

Configuration management identifier:

Dist   **Figure 3. Stages of document preparation**
Con

Keywords: User interface, display update, agents

© Lancaster University 2000

Figure 2: A Sample Document Cover Page.

Documentation standards

Documentation standards act as a basis for document quality assurance. Documents produced according to appropriate standards have a consistent appearance, structure, and quality. I have already introduced the IEEE standard for user documentation in focus on documentations that are relevant. Other standards that may be used in the documentation process are

1. *Process standards.* These standards define the process that should be followed for high-quality document production.

2. *Product standards.* These are standards that govern the documents themselves.

3. *Interchange standards.* It is increasingly important to exchange copies of documents via electronic mail and to store documents in databases. Interchange standards ensure that all electronic copies of documents are compatible.

Standards are, by their nature, designed to cover all cases and, consequently, can sometimes seem unnecessarily restrictive. It is therefore important that for each project, the appropriate standards are chosen and modified to suit that particular project. Small projects developing systems with relatively short expected lifetimes require different standards from large software projects, where the software may have to be maintained for 10 years or more.

Process standards

Process standards define the approach to be taken in producing documents. This generally means defining the software tools that should be used for document production and defining the quality assurance procedures that ensure that high-quality documents are produced.

Document process quality assurance standards must be flexible and must be able to cope with all types of documents. If documents are simply working papers or memos, no explicit quality check is required. However, where documents are formal documents, that is, when their evolution is to be controlled by configuration-management procedures, a formal quality process should be adopted. Figure 3 illustrates one possible process.

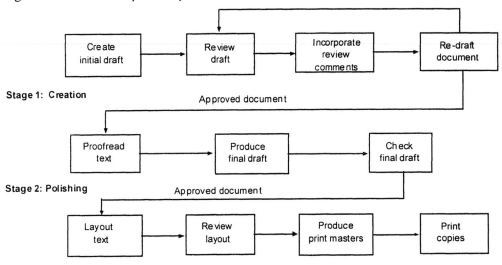

Figure 3. Stages of document preparation

Drafting, checking, revising, and redrafting are iterative processes that should be continued until a document of acceptable quality is produced. The acceptable quality level will depend on the document type and the document's potential readers.

Product standards

Product standards apply to all documents produced in the course of software development. Documents should have a consistent appearance and documents of the same class should have a consistent structure. Document standards are frequently project specific, but should be based instead on more general organizational standards.

Examples of product standards that should be developed are

1. *Document identification standards.* Since large projects typically produce thousands of documents, each document must be uniquely identified. For formal documents, this identifier

178

may be the formal identifier defined by the configuration manager. For informal documents, the style of the document identifier should be defined by the project manager.

2. *Document structure standard.* As discussed in the previous section, there is an appropriate structure for each class of document produced during a software project. Structure standards should define this organization. They should also specify the conventions used for page numbering, page header and footer information, and section and subsection numbering.

3. *Document presentation standards.* Document presentation standards define a "house style" for documents and contribute significantly to document consistency. They include the definition of fonts and styles used in the document, the use of logos and company names, and the use of color to highlight document structure.

4. *Document update standards.* As a document is changed to reflect changes in the system, a consistent way of indicating these changes should be used. This might include the use of different colored covers to indicate a new document version and the use of change bars to indicate modified or deleted paragraphs.

Document standards should apply to all project documents and to the initial drafts of user documentation. In many cases, however, user documentation has to be presented in a form appropriate to the user rather than the project, and it should be recast into that form during the production process.

Interchange standards

Document interchange standards are important as more and more documents are produced in electronic format as well as or instead of on paper. For documentation that is delivered with a software system, the Adobe Portable Document Format (PDF) is the most commonly used document delivery software system. However, when documents are exchanged by the development team and drafts are circulated within an organization, these are often in the format of the preferred word processing program (often Microsoft Word).

Assuming that the use of a standard word processor and graphical editing system is mandated in the process standards, interchange standards define the conventions for using these tools. The use of interchange standards allows documents to be transferred electronically and recreated in their original form.

Interchange standards are more than simply an agreement to use a common version of a system for document production. Examples of interchange standards include the use of an agreed-on standard macro set if a text-formatting system is used for document production, or the use of a standard style sheet for a word processor. Interchange standards may also limit the fonts and text styles used because of differing printer and display capabilities.

The IEEE standard for user documentation

The first IEEE standard for user documentation (IEEE, 1987) was produced in 1987 and, at the time of this writing, a new draft of the standard is being prepared for publication (IEEE, 2001).

Like all standards, this standard encapsulates wisdom and experience about software documentation and proposes a structure for user documentation. Using this structure as a basis, the standard discusses the content of software user documentation and proposes formatting standards for these documents.

The documentation structure proposed by the latest version of the standard has been covered. Following are some quotations from the current draft standard of good practice to illustrate the formatting advice in the standard:

The documentation should be provided in media and formats that allow its use by those with vision, hearing, or other physical limitations.

A description of how to print the electronic documentation should be included in both the electronic and the printed documentation.

179

Because some users cannot distinguish between colors, documentation should provide text cues rather than using colors such as red and green as the only way to convey meaning.

Warnings, cautions, and notes shall be displayed in a consistent format that is readily distinguishable from ordinary text or instructional steps.

Documentation formats for user-entered commands or codes shall clearly distinguish between literals (to be input exactly as shown) and variables (to be selected by the user).

Illustrations that accompany text should appear adjacent to their first reference in the text so that the associated text and illustration can be viewed simultaneously.

You can see from these quotations that the standard is helpful without being proscriptive and therefore, different conventions used by different companies and organizations can be accommodated.

Like all standards, this documentation standard has to be adapted to the situation in which it is used. These should instantiate the advice in the standard to the local situation and define the specific structures and formats that should be used.

Writing style

Standards and quality assessment are essential if good documentation is to be produced, but document quality is fundamentally dependent on the writer's ability to construct clear and concise technical prose. In short, good documentation requires good writing.

Writing documents well is neither easy nor is it a single stage process. Written work must be written, read, criticized, and then rewritten until a satisfactory document is produced. Technical writing is a craft rather than a science. Listed below are some broad guidelines about how to write well.

1. *Use active rather than passive tenses.* It is better to say, "You should see a flashing cursor at the top left of the screen," than, "A flashing cursor should appear at the top left of the screen".

2. *Use grammatically correct constructs and correct spelling.* To boldly go on splitting infinitives (like this) and misspell words (like mispell) irritates many readers and reduces the credibility of the writer in their eyes. Unfortunately, English spelling is not standardized and both British and American readers are sometimes irrational in their dislike of alternative spellings.

3. *Do not use long sentences that present several different facts.* It is better to use a number of shorter sentences. Each sentence can then be assimilated on its own. The reader does not need to maintain several pieces of information at one time to understand the complete sentence.

4. *Keep paragraphs short.* As a general rule, no paragraph should consist of more than seven sentences. Our capacity for holding immediate information is limited. In short paragraphs, each concept can be maintained in our short-term memories, which can hold about 7 chunks of information.

5. *Don't be verbose.* If you can say something in a few words, do so. A lengthy description is not necessarily more profound. Quality is more important then quantity.

6. *Be precise and define the terms that you use.* Computing terminology is fluid and many terms have more than one meaning. If you use terms like *module* or *process*, make sure that your definition is clear. Collect definitions in a glossary.

7. *If a description is complex, repeat yourself.* It is often a good idea to present two or more differently phrased descriptions of the same thing. If readers fail to completely understand one description, they may benefit from having the same thing said in a different way.

8. *Make use of headings and subheadings.* These break a chapter into parts, which may be read separately. Always use a consistent numbering convention.

9. *Itemize facts wherever possible.* It is usually clearer to present facts in a list than in a sentence. Use textual highlighting (italics or underlining) for emphasis.

10. *Do not refer to information by reference number alone.* Give the reference number and remind the reader what that reference covered. For example, rather than say, "In section 1.3 ..." you should say, "In section 1.3, which described management process models, ..."

Documents should be inspected (sometimes called *peer reviewed*) in the same way as programs. During a document inspection, the text is criticized, omissions are pointed out, and suggestions made on how to improve the document. In the latter respect, document inspection differs from code inspection, which is an error-finding rather than an error-correction mechanism.

As well as personal criticism, you can also use grammar checkers, which are incorporated in word processors. These checkers find ungrammatical or clumsy uses of words. They identify long sentences and paragraphs and the use of passive rather than active tenses. These checkers are not perfect and sometimes they use outmoded style rules or rules that are specific to one country. Nevertheless, because they often check style as you are typing, they can help identify phrases that could be improved.

On-line documentation

It is now normal to provide some online documentation with delivered software systems. This can range from simple "read me" files that provide very limited information about the software through interactive hypertext-based help systems, to a complete online suite of system documentation. Most commonly, however, hypertext-based help systems are provided. These may be based on a specialized hypertext system or may be HTML based and rely on Web browsers for access.

The main advantage with online documentation is, of course, its accessibility. It is not necessary for users to find manuals, there is no possibility of picking up out-of-date documentation, and built-in search facilities can be used to locate information quickly.

However, online hypertext systems have several disadvantages (listed below), which mean that they should be used to supplement rather than replace paper based documentation.

- They lack "browsability," so readers cannot easily skim through them to find the information they need. We often find it difficult to characterize the information we want from documentation, although we can recognize it when we find it. Browsing is the key mechanism we use when searching in this way. Browsing also offers opportunities for serendipitous discovery of unknown system facilities.

- Screens, at least with monitors normally used in 2001, have a much lower resolution than paper, and hence it is more difficult and tiring to read a document on the screen rather than on paper.

- It is very easy for users to get lost in hypertext-based help systems and they consequently find it difficult to navigate to where they want to go.

When designing screen-based documentation, you should always bear these problems in mind. Consequently, although both screen-based and paper-based documents should be well written, different designs are needed for electronic and paper documentation. Because of the differences between screens and paper, simply converting a word-processing document to HTML (say) rarely produces high-quality online documentation.

The design of screen-based documents is a major topic in its own right, and I don't have space to discuss it here. Interested readers can find a brief introduction to this topic in Chapter 15 of my book on software engineering (Sommerville, 2001), and a much more comprehensive account in the book on HCI design by Dix et al (1998).

Document preparation

Document preparation is the process of creating a document and formatting it for publication. Figure 3 shows the document-preparation process as being split into three stages, namely, document creation, polishing, and production. Modern word-processing systems are now integrated packages of software tools that support all parts of this process. However, it is still the case that for the highest quality documents, it is best to use separate tools for some preparation processes rather than the built-in word processor functions.

The three phases of preparation and associated support facilities are

1. *Document creation.* The initial input of the information in the document. This is supported by word processors and text formatters, table and equation processors, and drawing and art packages.

2. *Document polishing.* This process involves improving the writing and presentation of the document to make it more understandable and readable. This involves finding and removing spelling, punctuation, and grammatical errors, detecting clumsy phrases, and removing redundancy in the text. The process may be supported by tools such as online dictionaries, spelling checkers, and grammar and style checkers.

3. *Document production.* This is the process of preparing the document for professional printing. It is supported by desktop-publishing (DTP) packages, artwork packages, and type-styling programs.

In addition to these tools to support the document production process, configuration-management systems, information-retrieval systems, and hypertext systems may also be used to support document maintenance, retrieval, and management.

Modern word-processing systems are screen based and combine text editing and formatting. The image of the document on the user's terminal is, more or less, the same as the final form of the printed document. The finished layout is immediately obvious. Errors can be corrected and layout improved before printing the document. However, programmers who already use an editor for program preparation may sometimes prefer to use a separate editor and text-formatting system.

Text-formatting systems, such as Latex, interpret a layout program specified by the document writer. Layout commands (often chosen from a standard, definable command set) are interspersed with the text of the document. The text formatter processes these commands and the associated text, and lays the document out according to the programmer's instructions. The distinction between these systems and word processors is illustrated in Figure 4.

Text-formatting systems can look ahead at the text to be laid out to make better layout decisions than word-processing systems. whose working context is more restricted. Because the commands are really a programming language, programmers often prefer them to word processors, but other, nontechnical users usually find them more difficult to use.

The major disadvantage of text processors, once their programming has been mastered, is that they do not provide an immediate display of the output they produce. The user must process the text (this may take several minutes), then display the output using a preview package. If an error is discovered, it cannot be fixed immediately. The original source must be modified and the preview process repeated. Thus, although they can result in higher-quality documents, most users find text formatters more inconvenient than word processors.

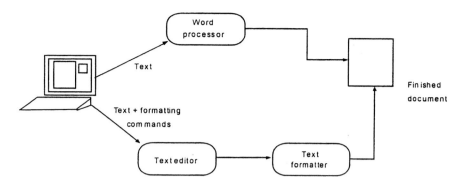

Figure 4. Word processors and text formatters

The final stage of document production is a skilled task that, for documents with large print runs, should be left to professional printers. However, DTP systems and graphics systems that support scanning, photograph processing, and artwork are now widely available. These have revolutionized document production. DTP systems partially automate the layout of text and graphics. They allow a fine-grained control over the layout and look of a document, and can be used by engineers to produce finished system documentation.

The advantage of using a DTP system is that the cost of producing high-quality documents is reduced because some of the steps in the production process are eliminated. Even documents that are produced in small numbers can be produced to a high standard. The disadvantage of using DTP systems is that they do not automate the skills of the graphic designer. Their seductive ease of use means that they are accessible to unskilled users who may produce unattractive and badly designed documents.

An enormous number of documents are produced in the course of a project and these need to be managed so that the right version of the document is available when required. If a project is distributed, copies of documents will be produced and stored at different locations, and it is very important to maintain a "master file," which contains the definitive versions of each document. This helps minimize a very common problem that arises when document users make mistakes because they are not working from the current version.

Each document should have a unique record, and this can be used as a key in a document database record. However, retrieval by other fields such as the title and author should also be supported.

The basic problem with using a file system to store the documents and a database-management system to maintain document information is that users have to be disciplined in the way the system is used. They must ensure that they check out a copy of the document from the system each time they need it rather than use a local copy or the copy they have printed. In practice, achieving this level of discipline is difficult and errors are likely to arise.

In very large projects, specialized document-management systems may be used to integrate document storage and the maintenance of document information (see Figure 5).

Document management software allows related documents to be linked, maintains records of who has checked out documents, provides indexing and information-retrieval facilities so documents can be found, and may support the compression and decompression of document text,. Document-management systems may also include version-management facilities to maintain different document versions.

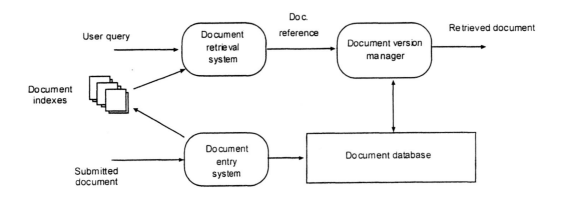

Figure 5. Document management

References

A. Dix, J. Finley, G. Abowd, and R. Beale, *Human-Computer Interaction,* 2nd edition, Prentice-Hall, London, 1998.

P. K. Garg and W. Scacchi, "A Hypertext System to Maintain a Software Life-Cycle Document," *IEEE Software*, vol. 7, no. 3, 1990, pp. 90-98.

IEEE Standard for Software User Documentation, IEEE-Std1063-1987, Inst. of Electrical and Electronics Engineers, New York, 1987.

Draft Standard for Software User Documentation, IEEE-Std1063/D5.1. 2001, IEEE, New York, 2001.

I. Sommerville, *Software Engineering,* 6th edition, Harlow, UK, Pearson Education Ltd., London, 2001.

Further reading

The Art of Technical Documentation, 2nd edition, K. Haramundanis, Butterworth-Heinemann, Woburn, MA, 1998.

This book is primarily aimed at technical writers and prospective technical writers and is not specific to software documentation. However, it includes good general advice on document presentation and style.

Writing for Science and Engineering: Papers, Presentations, and Reports, H. Silyn-Roberts, Butterworth-Heinemann, Woburn, MA., 2000.

Again, this is a general book on documentation. It is more detailed than Haramundanis's book and includes very specific advice and checklists on structure and style.

A Style Guide for the Computer Industry, Sun Microsystems, Mountain View, CA., 1996.

This book includes specific information and advice on writing styles for software and hardware documents. Includes information on writing for international audiences. It was originally developed for people involved in writing documentation for Sun software and hardware systems.

Designing and Writing Online Documentation, 2nd edition, W. Horton, Wiley Publishers, New York.

This is based on a hypermedia model of online documentation as discussed in this paper. It includes good general advice but is rather outdated as it predates the general use of the WWW, and therefore does not mention HTML-based systems.

Acknowledgements

This paper is a revised version of Chapter 30 of my book *Software Engineering,* 4th edition, published by Addison Wesley in 1992. Thanks to the publishers (now Pearson Education, Ltd.) for permission to republish this material.

IEEE Standard 1063-2001
Software User Documentation

At the time of completion, the Working Group on Software User Manual documentation, which prepared this standard, had the following membership:

Annette D. Reilly, *Chair*
Philip Bernick, *Secretary*

Jill Boogaard	Ingar Brauti	Fletcher Buckley
Lorie J. Call	Francois Coallier	Elizabeth Connolly
Margaret Daniel	J. T. Deignan	Claudia Dencker
Mary Jane Dodgen	Henry H. Fong	Yair Gershkovitch
John W. Horch	Ed Humphries	Tim Kalisz
Tom Kurihara	Joel Lang	Richard Alan Lee
F. C. Lim	William Lyon	Borut Maricic
Phillip C. Marriott	Roger J. Martin	Alicia McCurdy
Sandra L. Merscher	Carolyn J. Mullins	Sarah H. Nash
Frank Nellis	Francoise Perrodeau	William E. Perry
Polly Perryman	Sherwood F. Prescott, Jr	Ian C. Pyle
Annette D. Reilly	Luke J. Rheaume	Horst P. Richter
Richard A. Ries	Lois K. Rosstedt	Julio Gonzalez Sanz
Hans Schaefer	Mitzi Sokol	Peter Stein
William Sutcliffe	Jan Tanzer	Peter Thorp
William S. Turner III	Clifford Way	Andrew H. Weigel
Edmond H. Weiss	Timothy Whalen	

Sponsored by

Software Engineering Standards Committee
of the IEEE Computer Society

The Institute of Electrical and Electronic Engineering, Inc.
345 East 47th Street, New York, NY 10017-2394, USA
February 12, 2001

Table of Contents
IEEE Standard 1063-2001
Software User Documentation

Subject	Paragraph Number

IEEE Standard for Software User Documentation

1. Overview

This paragraph presents the scope, purpose, organization, and candidate uses of this standard.

1.1 Scope

This standard provides minimum requirements for the structure, information content, and format of user documentation, including both printed and electronic documents used in the work environment by users of systems containing software. The standard is limited to the software documentation product and does not include the processes of developing or managing software user documentation. The standard includes printed user manuals, online help, and user reference documentation. It does not apply to specialized course materials intended primarily for use in formal training programs.

This standard is not intended to specify or discourage the use of either printed or electronic (online) media for documentation, or of any particular documentation development or management tools or methodologies. Users of this standard may want to develop a style manual for use within their own organizations to complement the guidance provided in the standard, or to adopt an industry-recognized style guide. Users of this standard may also want to perform usability testing on the software user documentation.

1.2 Purpose

This revision of IEEE Std. 1063 updates the previous standard, which addressed the structure and information content of printed documentation only. It provides requirements for the structure, information content, and format of both printed and electronic documentation. It addresses the interests of software acquirers, producers, and users in standards for consistent, complete, accurate, and usable documentation.

1.3 Organization of the standard

After the references (Paragraph 2) and definitions (Paragraph 3), this standard is organized according to the different aspects of user documentation: information content (Paragraph 4) and format (Paragraph 5). In each paragraph, the requirements are media-independent, as far as possible. Requirements specific to either print or electronic media are identified as such, particularly in Paragraph 5. The order of paragraphs in this standard does not imply that the software user documentation should be developed in this order or presented to the user in this order.

1.4 Candidate uses

The wording of each paragraph in this standard assists those intending to claim conformance with the standard. The word *shall* identifies mandatory requirements to claim conformance with this standard. The word *should* identifies an approach that is recommended, but not required, to claim conformance with this standard. The word *may* identifies an approach that is permitted within the limits of the standard, but not required to claim conformance with this standard.

This standard may be included or referenced in contracts or similar agreements when the parties (called the acquirer and the producer) agree that the producer will deliver documentation in accordance with the standard. This standard may also be adopted as an in-house standard by a project or organization that decides to produce documentation in accordance with the standard. Although this standard is intended for software documentation for end users, it may be applied to documentation produced for computer operators or system administrators who are not end users.

This standard is meant to be tailored so that only necessary and cost-effective requirements are applied. Tailoring may take the form of specifying approaches to comply with its mandatory requirements, or altering its non-mandatory recommendations and approaches to reflect the particular software and documentation product more explicitly. Tailoring decisions made by the acquirer should be specified in the contract.

2. References

The supporting references and citations pertaining to this standard can be found in the *Centralized IEEE Software Engineering Standards References* contained in this tutorial. These references provide additional information on software user documentation to assist in understanding and applying this standard.

3. Definitions

The definitions and acronyms pertaining to this standard can be found in the *Centralized IEEE Software Engineering Standards Glossary* contained in this tutorial. These are contextual definitions serving to augment the understanding of software user documentation activities as described within this standard.

4. Information content of software user documentation

This paragraph specifies characteristics of information contained in user documentation (see Paragraph 4.1 and Paragraph 4.2), including completeness and accuracy. This paragraph also defines the required information for inclusion in user documentation (see Paragraphs 4.3 through 4.11). The information required in this paragraph shall be included in software user documentation, unless the information does not exist or is not applicable for a specific document.

The content of documentation is related to its usage mode. Users of software need documents either to learn about the software (*instructional mode*) or to refresh their memory about it (*reference mode*). Instructional mode documents may be either information- or task-oriented. Information-oriented documents instruct the user on the concepts and technical information needed to use the software properly (see Paragraph 4.5). Task-oriented documents show the user how to complete procedures to reach a goal (see Paragraph 4.6). Reference mode documentation may be context-sensitive and integrated in the software; for example, pop-up or drop-down lists of acceptable data values or commands. In either instructional or reference documentation, the content of documentation can be improved by the inclusion of examples and illustrations.

Table 1 – Components of Software User Document

Component	Required?
Identification data (package label/title page)	Yes
Table of contents	Yes, in documents of more than eight pages after the identification data
List of illustrations	Optional
Introduction	Yes
Information for use of the documentation	Yes
Concept of operations	Yes
Procedures	Yes (instructional mode)
Information on software commands	Yes (reference mode)
Error messages and problem resolution	Yes
Glossary	Yes, if documentation contains unfamiliar terms
Related information sources	Optional
Navigational features	Yes
Index	Yes, in documents of more than 40 pages
Search capability	Yes, in electronic documents

4.1 Completeness of information

Documentation shall provide complete instructional and reference information for all critical software functions (software whose failure could have an impact on safety, or could cause large financial or social loss). Instructional mode documentation shall include complete information to enable performance of selected tasks using the software functions by the least experienced members of the audience. Reference mode documentation shall include all instances of the selected elements being documented. For example, if reference mode documentation covers a subset of software commands, it shall include all user-entered and system-displayed commands and error messages in that subset.

4.2 Accuracy of information

Documentation shall accurately reflect the functions and results of the applicable software version. If the previous documentation version is no longer accurate, new documentation shall be available with software updates or upgrades. Documentation corrections and updates may be provided via a new manual, a read-me file or errata sheet, or a downloaded file from a Web site.

4.3 Content of identification data

Documentation shall contain unique identification data. The identification data shall include the (1) documentation title, (2) documentation version and date published, (3) software product and version, and (4) issuing organization. Identification data shall appear on a package label, legible without opening the package, and on a title page. A package label is not required if the title page is legible without opening the package. Each document in a document set shall have a unique title page. For single-page documents, such as quick reference cards, the identification data may appear on the same page as the rest of the document.

The title of the document should indicate its nature and scope and should not include abbreviations or acronyms unless they are familiar to the intended audience. If different versions of the software are available for different operating environments, the title page should specify the applicable operating environment(s), including version(s) of hardware, communications, and operating system(s). Other information, including document or software product part numbers, serial numbers, and restrictions on use, may be included on the package label and on the title page or following pages. The package label and pages immediately following the title page should include copyright and trademark notices, restrictions on copying or distributing the documentation, information for contacting the issuing organization (reader's comments), warranties, contractual obligations or disclaimers, and general warnings and cautions.

The identification of the document and the software shall be consistent with the configuration management practices of the issuing organization or the acquiring organization. Information (change history) shall be provided in the document set to document the date of issue and version number of the current version and each previous version of the documentation.

4.4 Information for use of the documentation

The documentation shall include information on how it is to be used (for example, help on help), and an explanation of the notation (a description of formats and conventions--see Paragraph 5.8). At least one document in a document set shall identify all documents in the set by title and intended use, including recommendations on which members of the audience should consult which sections of the documentation. In document sets comprising many volumes or products, this information may be provided in a separate "road map" or guide to the document set. Documentation may include identification and discussion of notable changes from the previous version of the document set and the software.

4.5 Concept of operations

Documentation shall explain the conceptual background for use of the software, using such methods as a visual or verbal overview of the process or workflow; or the theory, rationale, algorithms, or general concept of operation. Explanations of the concept of operation should be adapted to the expected familiarity of the users with any specialized terminology for user tasks and software functions. Documentation shall relate each documented function to the overall process or tasks. Conceptual information may be presented in one section or immediately preceding each applicable procedure.

4.6 Information for general use of the software

Task-oriented instructional mode documentation shall include instructions for routine activities that are applied to several functions, including the following:

a) Software installation and de-installation, if performed by the user;

b) Orientation to use of the features of the graphical user interface (see Paragraph 5.6);

c) Access, or log-on and sign-off the software;

d) Navigation through the software to access and to exit from functions;

e) Data operations (enter, save, read, print, update, and delete); and

f) Methods of canceling, interrupting, and restarting operations.

These common procedures should be presented once to avoid redundancy when they are used in more complex functions.

4.7 Information for procedures and tutorials

Instructional mode documentation provides directions for performing procedures. Instructions shall include preliminary information, instructional steps, and completion information.

Preliminary information common to several procedures may be grouped and presented once to avoid redundancy. Preliminary information for instructions shall include the following:

a) A brief overview of the purpose of the procedure and definitions or explanations of necessary concepts not elsewhere included;

b) Any technical or administrative activities that must be done before starting the task;

c) Any materials the user will need to complete the task, which may include data, documents, passwords, additional software, and identification of drivers, interfaces, or protocols; and

d) Relevant warnings, cautions, and notes that apply to the entire procedure.

Relevant warnings, cautions, and notes shall immediately precede each applicable instructional step or group of steps. Instructional steps shall use the imperative mood for the user's action. Instructional steps shall indicate the expected result or system response. Instructional steps shall include or provide references to documentation of the acceptable range, maximum length and applicable format, and unit of measurement of data fields for user-supplied data. Acceptable data formats and values are commonly documented through pop-up lists. Instructional steps shall include or provide references to explanations of error messages and recovery procedures.

Instructional steps shall be presented in the order of performance. Alternative or repeated procedures should be clearly indicated, so the user can determine which alternate or repeated steps to perform or skip and where to rejoin the main procedure.

Completion information for instructions shall indicate which is the last step in the procedure, how the user can determine whether the procedure has successfully completed, and how the user should exit from the procedure.

4.8 Information on software commands

Documentation shall explain the formats and procedures for user-entered software commands, including required parameters, optional parameters, default options, order of commands, and syntax. Documentation may be provided on the development and maintenance of macros and scripts. Reference mode documentation shall contain a reference listing of all reserved words or commands. Examples should illustrate the use of commands. Documentation shall explain how to interrupt and undo operation during execution of a command and how to restart it, if possible. Documentation shall describe how to recognize that the command has successfully executed or abnormally terminated.

4.9 Information on error messages and problem resolution

Documentation should address all known problems in using the software in sufficient detail that the users can either recover from the problems themselves or clearly report the problem to technical support personnel. Reference mode documentation shall include each error message with an identification of the problem, probable cause, and corrective actions that the user should take. A quick reference card may address error messages by referring the user to more detailed reference documentation. The documentation on resolving problems shall also include contact information for reporting problems with software or its documentation and suggesting improvements.

4.10 Information on terminology

Documentation shall include a glossary, if terms or their specific uses in the software user interface or documentation are likely to be unfamiliar to the audience. The glossary shall include an alphabetical list of terms and definitions. Documentation using abbreviations and acronyms unfamiliar to the audience shall include a list with definitions, which may be integrated with the glossary. Terms included in the glossary should also be defined on their first appearance in printed documentation. Electronic documentation may include links from terms to glossaries or explanations in secondary windows.

4.11 Information on related information sources

Documentation may contain information on accessing related information sources, such as a bibliography, list of references, or links to related Web pages. Related information sources and references may include the following:

a) Requirement specifications, design specifications, and applicable standards for the software and the documentation;

b) Test plans and procedures for the software and the documentation;

c) Configuration management policies and procedures for the software and the documentation;

d) Documentation for the hardware and software environment; and

e) Explanations of the concept of operations or scientific, technical, or business processes embodied in the software.

The documentation should indicate whether the references contain mandatory requirements or informative background material.

5. Format of software user documentation

The documentation format includes the selected electronic or print media and presentation conventions for stylistic, typographic, and graphic elements. This paragraph specifies formats for various documentation components. The format for reference mode documentation should be accessible and usable in the expected users' work environment. The size of printed and bound reference documentation, or required equipment, electronic storage space, operating system software, and browsers to access online reference documentation, shall be consistent with the capacity of the expected users' work environment.

The documentation should be provided in media and formats that allow its use by those with vision, hearing, or other physical limitation, if they are able to use the software and to perform the tasks supported by the software. Alternative documentation media and formats for users with physical limitations may require special adaptive software and equipment not provided with the user software or the user software documentation.

5.1 Consistency of terminology and formats

Documentation shall use consistent terminology throughout a document set for elements of the user interface, data elements, field names, functions, pages, topics, and processes. Formatting conventions for highlighting information of special importance, such as warnings, cautions and notes, shall be applied consistently throughout the document set. The documentation may use special formatting to identify new or changed content. Formatting conventions may include colors, borders, indenting, spacing, and font variations. Similar material, such as sets of instructions, shall be presented in a consistent format.

If documentation is adapted for use in another operating environment, language, or culture, a common glossary and style guides for text and illustrations should be used to assist documentation developers and translators in maintaining consistency. Consideration should be given to selecting terminology, examples, graphics, and colors that are not culture-specific, so documentation can be more easily adapted, localized, or translated while preserving the intended meaning of the original.

5.2 Use of printed or electronic formats

Whether or not electronic documentation is provided, the following documentation shall be presented in printed form:

a) Hardware, operating system, and browser software requirements for the software and the documentation;

b) Installation information, including recovery and troubleshooting information for installation instructions;

c) Instructions for starting the software;

d) Instructions for access to any electronic documentation; and

e) Information for contacting technical support or performing recovery actions available to users.

A description of how to print the electronic documentation should be included in both the electronic and the printed documentation. A means shall be provided for printing online documentation for those software systems designed for use when attached to a printer. The system should include software features designed to enable printing of electronic documentation.

Online documentation shall be available for display at any time when user input to the software is possible. The user should be able to perform a function and read the relevant function-specific online documentation simultaneously. The user should be able to view the online documentation and navigate to related software functions during system operations.

5.3 Legibility

Printed and electronic documentation shall be legible to the user, considering the distance between the user and the documentation in the expected work environment. Documentation shall use a font style and color that is legible against the expected background (paper color or screen background color). Online documentation shall remain legible if the user is able to enlarge, shrink, or reshape the screen or window. Uppercase (all capital letters) shall not be used for continuous text of more than 25 words. Text, including text in illustrations, shall be no smaller than 3 mm (approximately 7.5 points).

Online documentation should be legible in the users' expected work environment, which includes the anticipated combination of computer monitor or display and software graphics drivers. Legibility may be affected by output devices (monitors and printers) that are monochrome, have limited resolution, render colors differently, or support a limited range of colors. Some output devices may apply substitute fonts or special characters if the specified font is not available. Distinctions that depend upon more than two gradations of colors or shades of gray may not be visible. Because some users cannot distinguish between colors, documentation should provide text cues rather than using colors such as red and green as the only way to convey meaning.

5.4 Formats for warnings, cautions, and notes

Warnings, cautions, and notes shall be displayed in a consistent format that is readily distinguishable from ordinary text or instructional steps. The flag word (for example, *warning, caution,* or *note*) shall precede the accompanying text. The word *Note* shall not be used to identify hazards. Warnings and cautions shall be identified by consistent and distinct graphic symbols, for example, an exclamation point or lightning bolt inside a triangle. A warning or caution shall include the following parts:

a) Flag word;

b) Graphic symbol;

c) Brief description of the hazard;

d) Instructional text on avoiding the hazard;

e) Consequences of incurring the hazard; and

f) User's remedies for the adverse consequences, if any.

5.5 Format for instructions

Instructional steps shall be consecutively numbered. A consistent numbering or lettering convention should be established for sub-steps or actions, alternative steps, and repeated procedures.

5.6 Formats for representing user interface elements

Graphical user interface (GUI) elements of the software, such as buttons, icons, variable cursors and pointers; special uses of keyboard keys or combinations of keys; and system responses shall be represented in documentation by consistent graphic or typographical formats so that the various elements are each distinguished from the text. Documentation should include a representation of the element, its purpose, and an explanation of its action (functional consequence), with examples of actual operational instances. Online documentation may include pop-up text labels for GUI elements.

Documentation formats for user-entered commands or codes shall clearly distinguish between literals (to be input exactly as shown) and variables (to be selected by the user). Quotation marks should not be used in command representations unless the user should input them literally. Documentation should address variations in keyboards or data entry devices in the expected users' work environment.

194

5.7 Formats for documentation features for accessing information

Documentation shall contain features to provide access to information, including a table of contents; a list of figures, tables, or illustrations; an index; and electronic search capabilities.

5.7.1 Table of contents

A table of contents shall immediately follow the identification data (Paragraph 4.3). The table of contents shall list the headings of the chapters or topics of a document with an access point for each (its initial page number or an electronic link). Documents with fewer than eight pages after the identification data may omit the table of contents.

The table of contents may be comprehensive or simple. A comprehensive table of contents lists all chapter or topic titles (headings) down to the third level. A simple table of contents includes only the first-level headings. Documents with a simple table of contents may include secondary comprehensive tables of contents appearing at the beginning of each chapter or topic or accessible through pop-ups, expandable lists, or secondary windows. Electronic documentation may display tables of contents in expandable and collapsible formats to provide top-level and detailed access to headings without excessive scrolling. At least one volume of a document set shall include a simple table of contents for all volumes in the set.

The table of contents shall include all portions of the documentation, including front matter that follows the table of contents and back matter (for example, appendixes, glossary, and index). The headings in the table of contents shall be identical in wording to those in the document, including chapter or topic numbers. The format of the table of contents shall distinguish the hierarchy of headings by consistent typography or indentation. In printed documentation, the table of contents shall list the headings in the same order as in the text. For electronic documentation, the table of contents should order the headings according to browse sequence, task, topic type, or other logical criteria.

5.7.2 List of illustrations

Documentation should contain a list of tables, a list of figures, or a list of illustrations (including both tables and figures) if the document contains more than five numbered illustrations and the illustrations are not visible at the same time as text references to them. The list of illustrations shall list the illustration numbers and titles with an access point for each (such as its initial page number or an electronic link). The titles in the list of tables, figures, or illustrations shall be identical in wording to those in the document, including table, figure, or illustration numbers.

5.7.3 Index

An index is an alphabetical listing of keywords, graphics, or concepts with an access point for each. Printed documents over 40 pages shall include an index, whose access points may be page numbers, topic numbers, illustration numbers, or references to another index entry. Electronic documents over 40 topics shall include either a search tool (see Paragraph 5.7.4) or an index whose access points are electronic links. An index entry may cross-reference another index entry; however, the referenced entry shall give an access point to the documentation and shall not point to a third index entry.

5.7.4 Search capability

Electronic documentation shall provide a method of locating words in the text. Electronic search capabilities may include full text search of the document or document set; search for words in illustrations; keyword search; finding a text string in the current topic; a Boolean search; and the restriction of a search to specific chapters, topics, or pages.

5.8 Formats for features for navigation

Features for navigation include chapter and topic headings; page or screen titles; chapter, title, page, and screen numbers; tabs; page headers and footers; bookmarks; jumps (links); cross references; navigational icons; and buttons. Features for navigation shall be provided such that users can determine their location within the printed or electronic document and all of the locations to which they can move from their current location. Documentation shall include explanations of system- and document-specific navigational features. In printed documentation, each page shall have a unique page number. In electronic documentation, each page or screen shall have a unique identifier (alphanumeric and/or caption) accessible to the user. Navigation features shall allow documentation users to go to the following locations:

a) Back, to return to the section/page most recently jumped from (linked);

b) Next, next logical topic/page in the sequence of topics (if any);

c) Previous, logical topic/page just prior to the one being viewed (if any);

d) Table of contents (if any); and

e) Index (if any).

Navigational features shall use consistent formats for typography such as underscored links, color, or graphics to distinguish them from plain text. Navigation features should remain accessible in a static location if electronic documentation allows scrolling through the text.

Jumps (links) shall provide a clear indication of the destination of the link. For example, use "More troubleshooting tips" rather than "Click here." Links should provide information that the user expects in one jump, rather than requiring a link to another link that has the sought information. If the destination is outside the documentation, the documentation should provide users with an alternate way of locating the information, in case the link has been broken or the destination removed. Links between related topics shall be bi-directional, so that whichever topic the users access first, they can jump to the related information on the other topic.

Electronic reference mode documentation shall be accessible from the software it documents, and shall provide a clear means of exiting the documentation and returning to the software. Software may be linked to online help, tutorials, or reference mode documentation in various ways, such as the following:

a) Through a help menu linked to a listing of topics or a point of entry to the help system;

b) Through help buttons on the software screens providing information on a particular topic (dialog box and field level help); and

c) Through context-sensitive help and pop-up text (tool tips).

5.9 Formats for illustrations

Illustrations that accompany text should appear adjacent to their first reference in the text, so the associated text and illustration can be viewed simultaneously. In documentation with more than five illustrations, each illustration should have a unique number and title (see Paragraph 5.7.2). Informal illustrations, referred to only once in the text or having no text, may be untitled and unnumbered.

The format of illustrations of similar content shall be consistent for scale, screen size, fonts, line thickness, and use of color. In electronic documentation, illustrations should be sized so they are legible and viewable in their entirety, without scrolling, on the expected viewing device. Consider simplifying or showing only salient features of a large graphic so it is visible at one time without scrolling. Long tables that cannot fit on a single page shall repeat the table title and column or row headings on each page or two-page spread. Long tables that span multiple pages should also be identified with a sheet number, for example, "Table 15. Metric units (sheet 2 of 4)."

Documentation that is intended for both print and electronic distribution should be logically complete, including illustrations and references to illustrations, in both media. Fewer illustrations may be needed in electronic documentation that allows links to the actual software screens. Representations of GUI elements in documentation should be consistent with the version of the software being documented.

Chapter 7

Management Process

1. Introduction to Chapter

This chapter describes the software management process. Paragraph 2 describes the management process. Portions of this text are paraphrased from IEEE/EIA Standard 12207.0-1996, Paragraph 7.1. Paragraph 3 lists the applicable IEEE Software Engineering standards that are contained in other IEEE Computer Society Press publications. Paragraph 4 provides an overview and introduction to the papers contained in this chapter.

2. Management process

The *management process* contains the generic activities and tasks that may be employed by any party having to manage its respective process(es). The manager is responsible for product management, project management, and task management of the applicable process(es), such as the *acquisition, supply, development, operation, maintenance,* or *supporting process.* This process consists of the following activities:

1. Initiation and scope definition

2. Planning

3. Execution and control

4. Review and evaluation

5. Closure.

2.1 Initiations and scope definition

- The management process is initiated by establishing the requirements of the process to be undertaken.

- Once the requirements are established, the manager establishes the feasibility of the process by checking that the resources (personnel, materials, technology, and environment) required executing and managing the process is available, adequate, and appropriate and that the time-scales to completion are achievable.

- As necessary, and by agreement of all parties concerned, the requirements of the process may be modified at this point to achieve the completion criteria.

2.2 Planning

- The manager then prepares the plans for execution of the process. The plans associated with the process execution contain descriptions of the associated activities, tasks and identification of the software products that will be provided. These plans include, but are not limited to, the following:

- Schedules for the timely completion of tasks

- Estimation of effort

- Adequate resources needed to execute the tasks

- Allocation of tasks

- Assignment of responsibilities

- Quantification of risks associated with the tasks or the process itself

- Quality control measures to be employed throughout the process

- Costs associated with the process execution

- Provision of environment and infrastructure.

2.3 Execution and control

- The manager initiates the implementation of the plan to satisfy the objectives and criteria set, exercising control over the process.

- The manager monitors the execution of the process, providing both internal reporting of the process progress and external reporting to the acquirer as defined in the contract.

- The manager shall investigate, analyze, and resolve the problems discovered during the execution of the process. The resolution of problems may result in changes to plans. It is the manager's responsibility to ensure that the impact of any changes is determined, controlled, and monitored. Problems and their resolutions are documented.

- The manager reports, at agreed points, the progress of the process, declaring adherence to the plans and resolving instances of the lack of progress. These include internal and external reporting as required by the organizational procedures and the contract.

2.4 Review and evaluation

- The manager ensures that the software products and plans are evaluated for satisfaction of requirements.

- The manager assesses the evaluation results of the software products, activities, and tasks completed during the execution of the process for achievement of the objectives and completion of the plans.

2.5 Closure

- Once all software products, activities and tasks are completed, the manager determines whether the process is complete, taking into account the criteria as specified in the contract or as part of the organization's procedure.

- The manager checks the results and records of the software products, activities, and tasks employed for completeness. These results and records are archived in a suitable environment as specified in the contract.

- 3. Software Engineering Standards

- The software engineering standards that apply to this subject can be found in a separate Computer Society Press tutorial, Software Engineering Project Management, 2nd edition, 1997. The standards included are:

- IEEE Standard 1058-1998, Standard for Software Project Management Plans (paper by Fairley and Thayer)

- IEEE Standard 1062-1998, Recommended Practice for Software Acquisition

- IEEE Standard 1540-2001, Standard for Software Life Cycle Processes — Risk Management.

3. Overview of Papers

The first article in this chapter was written by Richard Thayer, an editor of this Tutorial. This paper describes the management processes and tasks in managing the various modes of software management. The modes of software management operations to be discussed are organizational management, senior-level management, software acquisition management, user/operator management, supplier management, project management, maintenance management and risk management. This article also defines and applies the universality of management concept to the application of software management. Also described are those management processes that are necessary to successfully manage any of these software engineering efforts.

Management can be defined as all activities and tasks undertaken by one or more persons for the purpose of planning and controlling the activities of others in order to achieve an objective or to complete an activity that could not be achieved by the others acting independently [1]. The classic management model as portrayed by well-known authors in the field of management [2, 3, 4, 5, 6] contains the following components:

- Planning

- Organizing

- Staffing

- Directing

- Controlling.

The second paper, also authored by Richard Thayer, discusses Software Engineering Project Management (a subject briefly discussed in the first paper). *Project management* is defined as a system of procedures, practices, technologies, and know-how that provide the planning, organizing, staffing, directing, and controlling necessary to successfully manage an engineering project. *Know-how* in this case means the skill, background, and wisdom necessary to apply knowledge effectively in practice.

A project is a temporary organizational structure with an established beginning and end date, established goals and objectives, defined responsibilities, and a defined budget and schedule.

The third paper, written by F.J. Heemstra, presents a thorough overview of the state of the art in software cost estimation. Heemstra points out that it is very easy to ask the question, "Why are software overruns on budget and schedule so prevalent?" However, the answer is not so simple.

The author thoroughly discusses why software cost estimation is so difficult. The primary reason given is that a lack of data exists for completed software projects. Without this data, it becomes very difficult to make project management estimates on future software costs.

The many factors that influence software development effort and duration are discussed. Heemstra asserts that the estimator must know, among other things, the size of the software project, required quality, requirements volatility (that is, the amount and rate of requirements change), software complexity, the level of software reuse, the amount of documentation required, and the type of application required.

The varying types of software cost-estimation techniques and tools are also discussed. Two main approaches can be distinguished from each other -- the top-down and the bottom-up approaches.

Lastly, Heemstra discusses several cost estimation models, beginning with the principles of these models. He then presents an overview of COCOMO, function point analysis, the Putnam model, and others. He manages to pinpoint most of the major software cost-estimation techniques available today.

The third paper, written by Ronald Nusenoff and Dennis Bunde of Loral Corporation (now part of Lockheed Martin), describes Loral's Software Productivity Laboratory's (SPL) use of metrics to improve its software engineering process maturity. The SPL has developed a metrics guidebook to define a set of standards for software metrics and to specify procedures for collecting and analyzing metrics data. The SPL also developed a spreadsheet tool to provide automated support for metrics generation, collection, graphical representation, and analysis.

These Loral corporate metrics were defined to map to the corporate development methodology. Both were part of the program being developed to advance Loral Corporation to Levels 4 and 5 on the SEI's process maturity scale. This paper demonstrates Loral's commitment to process improvement, as defined by the SEI, and Loral's belief in the close relationship of process and metrics.

The Loral metrics were based on MITRE software management metrics [7]. This paper compares the MITRE and Loral metrics to those defined in the SEI's 1987 software maturity questionnaire [8], the precursor to the CMM. Loral used the 1987 document as the basis for its process improvement efforts since most of the work was finished prior to the 1993 publication of the CMM.

The fourth paper in this section is an original article titled "Risk Management for Software Development," written by the late Paul Rook of the Center for Software Reliability in London, and completed after Rook's death by Dr. Richard Fairley. The paper defines the many aspects of risk management such as risk, risk impact, risk exposure, and risk reduction or elimination. The classic definition of risk as the "potential for realization of unwanted, negative consequences of an event" is restated. It concentrates on describing the importance of the relationship between risk management and project control, while illustrating the sources of risk, how risk can be tackled, and how to carry out risk assessment, risk identification, and risk analysis. Risk management planning and risk resolution are also covered.

1. Koontz, H., C. O'Donnell, and H. Weihrich, *Management*, 7th ed., McGraw-Hill Book Co., NY, 1980.

2. Koontz, H., C. O'Donnell, and H. Weihrich, *Management*, 7th ed., McGraw-Hill Book Co., NY, 1980.

3. Cleland, D.I., and W.R. King, *Management: A Systems Approach,* McGraw-Hill Book Company, NY, 1972.

4. MacKenzie, R.A., "The Management Process in 3-D," *Harvard Business Review,* November-December 1969, pp. 80-87.

5. Blanchard, Benjamin S. and Walter J. Fabrycky, *System Engineering and Analysis*, Prentice Hall, Inc., Englewood Cliffs, NJ, Second Edition, 1990.

6. Kerzner, Harold, *Project Management: A Systems Approach to Planning, Scheduling, and Controlling*, 3rd ed., Van Nostrand Reinhold, New York, 1989.

7. Schultz, H.P., *Software Management Metrics*, ESD TR-88-001, prepared by The MITRE Corporation for the U.S. Air Force, Electronic Systems Division, Hanscom AFB, MA, 1988.

8. Humphrey, W. S., and W. L. Sweet, *A Method for Assessing the Software Engineering Capability of Contractors,* Software Engineering Institute Technical Report CMU/SEI-87-TR-23, 1987.

Software Engineering Management

Richard H. Thayer
Emeritus Professor in Software Engineering
California State University, Sacramento
Sacramento, CA 95819

Abstract — This article describes the management processes and tasks necessary to manage the various modes of software management. The modes of software management operations to be discussed are *organizational management, senior-level management, software acquisition management, user/operator management, supplier management, project management, maintenance management, and risk management.*

This article also defines and applies the universality of management concept to the application of software management. Management processes that are necessary to successfully manage any of these software engineering efforts are also discussed.

1. The universality of management

Management, the universality of management concepts, and the activities and tasks of software engineering management are identified, defined, and discussed in this article.

Management involves the activities and tasks undertaken by one or more persons for the purpose of planning and controlling the activities of others to achieve objectives that could not be achieved by the others acting alone. *Management functions* can be categorized as planning, organizing, staffing, directing, and controlling.

There are two types of software organizations. One is called a "permanent organization" and the other is called a "temporary organization." A *permanent organization* exists to perform a continuous function such as system engineering, computer operations, building security, information technology maintenance, and any other component of an organization that exists to operate or manage a continuous product. A *temporary organization* typically exists to accomplish a specific task or deliver a specific product, such as a software engineering project, an acquisition project, a special task force, an ad hoc committee, or any task in which the organization has no purpose once the activity or product is complete.

Software engineering projects are frequently part of larger, more comprehensive projects that include equipment (hardware), facilities, personnel, procedures, and software. Examples include aircraft, accounting, radar, inventory-control, and railroad-switching systems. These *systems engineering projects* are typically managed by one or more system project managers (also called *program managers*) who manage projects composed of engineers, domain experts, scientific specialists, programmers, support personnel, and others. If the software to be delivered is a "stand-alone" software system (a system that does not involve development of other nonsoftware components), the software engineering project manager may be called the system project manager.

Other software engineering management efforts involve managing larger organizational entities that contain software functions as part of their responsibility. Examples might be software maintenance, production of software-generated reports (frequently call *operations*), software acquisition, and software development.

Universality of management is a concept defined in management science [Koontz and O'Donnell, 1972], [Fayol, 1949] and means:

- Management performs the same functions (planning, organizing, staffing, directing, and controlling) regardless of position in the organization or the enterprise managed.

- Management functions are characteristic duties of managers; management practices, methods, activities, and tasks are specific to the enterprise or job managed.

The universality of management concepts allows us to apply general management concepts to software engineering project management.

The management functions necessary to plan, organize, staff, direct, and control an activity or enterprise are discussed in this article. The universality of these concepts provides a management framework for adapting traditional management functions to software engineering management.

This article also provides a broad background in software management to provide study material for the Certified Software Development Professional (CSDP) exam.

Section 2 lists some of the major issues in software engineering that pertain to project management. Section 3 partitions management functions into a detailed list of management activities. Section 4 describes a general management process, and Section 5 describes some of the various management processes in existence.

2. Major issues in software engineering

Over 70 percent of software development organizations develop their software through ad hoc and unpredictable methods [Zubrow, et al., 1995]. These organizations (considered "immature" according to the Software Engineering Institute Capability Maturity Model) do not have an objective basis for determining software cost or schedule, or for judging software quality. Software development processes are generally improvised by practitioners and their managers during the course of the project. Such organizations do not have any standard practices or if they do, they do not follow them. Managers use what worked best in their last project. Proven software engineering techniques such as in-depth requirements analysis, inspections, reviews, testing, and documentation are reduced or eliminated when the project falls behind in cost, schedule and/or the customer demands more functionality without an increase in budget [Paulk et al., 1996]. All of the above are frequently called the "software crisis" [Gibbs, 1994].

The importance of software engineering management is best illustrated in the following paragraphs, which are extracted from the Department of Defense (DoD) reports indicated.

- A report from the STARS initiative (STARS: Software Technology for Adaptable, Reliable Systems) states, "The manager plays a major role in software and systems development and support. The difference between success or failure—between a project being on schedule and on budget or late and over budget—is often a function of the manager's effectiveness." [DoD Software Initiative, 1983]

- A *Report to the Defense Science Board Task Force on Military Software*, states that "today's major problems with software development are not technical problems, but management problems." [Brooks, 1987]

- A General Accounting Office (GAO) report that investigated the cost and schedule overrun of the C-17 reinforces the above statement, "... software development has clearly been a major problem during the first six years of the program. In fact, the C-17 is a good example of how not to manage software development...." [GAO/IMTEC-92-48 C-17 Aircraft Software]

3. Functions and activities of management

This article presents a top-down overview of the software engineering management responsibilities, activities, and tasks that should be undertaken by any manager responsible for a software engineering project or effort. A top-down approach is used to partition and allocate top-level functions to lower-level activities and tasks.

Figure 1 depicts the classic management model as portrayed by well-known authors in the field of management, such as Koontz and O'Donnell [1972], [Rue and Byars, 1983], [Cleland and King, 1972], [MacKenzie, 1969].

According to this model, management is partitioned into five separate functions or components: *planning, organizing, staffing, directing, and controlling* (see Table 1 for definitions or explanations of these functions). All the activities of management, such as budgeting, scheduling, establishing authority and responsibility relationships, training, communicating, and allocating responsibility fall under one of these five headings.

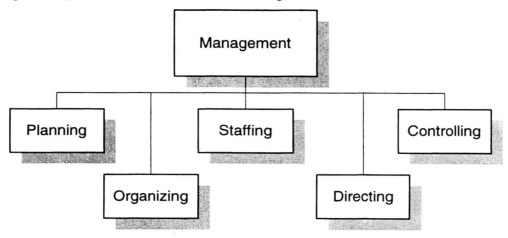

Figure 1. Classic management model

In a later edition of Koontz and O'Donnell's classic reference [Koontz, O'Donnell, and Weihrich 1980], the function "directing" is called "leading." However, the original term will be kept in this article.

Each of the five principal *functions* of management can be further partitioned into a set of more detailed management *activities*. These activities can then be further divided into more detailed tasks. These activities are the characteristic duties of managers and can be applied to the management of any organization or project.

Table 1. Major functions of management

Activity	Definition or explanation
Planning	Predetermining a course of action for accomplishing organizational objectives.
Organizing	Arranging the relationships among work units for accomplishment of objectives, and the granting of responsibility and authority to obtain those objectives.
Staffing	Selecting and training people for positions in the organization.
Directing	Creating an atmosphere that will assist and motivate people to achieve desired end results.
Controlling	Establishing, measuring, and evaluating performance of activities toward planned objectives.

4. Software management

The text in this paragraph is paraphrased from IEEE/EIA Standard 12207.0-1996, Paragraph 7.1. The management of a software activity such as acquisition, supply, development, operation, or maintenance requires a management process that is frequently independent of what is being managed (note the discussion in Paragraph 3 above). The software *management process* contains generic activities and tasks, which may be employed by any party who has to manage their respective functions. The software manager is responsible for product management, project management, and task management of the applicable area of responsibility.

- Initiation and scope definition
- Planning
- Execution and control (enactment)
- Review and evaluation
- Closure
- Post-closure activities

4.1 Initiation and scope definition

- The management process shall be initiated by establishing the requirements of the process to be undertaken.

- Once the requirements are established, the manager shall establish the feasibility of the process by checking that the resources (personnel, materials, technology, and environment) required to execute and manage the process are available, adequate, and appropriate and that the time scales to completion are achievable.

- As necessary, and by agreement of all parties concerned, the process requirements may be modified at this point to achieve the completion criteria.

4.2. Planning

- The manager shall prepare the plans for process execution. The plans associated with process execution shall describe the associated activities and tasks and identify the software products that will be provided. These plans shall include, but are not limited to,

  — schedules for the timely completion of tasks

  — estimation of effort

  — adequate resources to execute the tasks

  — allocation of tasks

  — assignment of responsibilities

  — quantification of risks associated with the tasks or the process itself

  — quality control measures to be employed throughout the process

  — costs associated with the process execution

  — provision of environment and infrastructure

4.4. Execution and control (enactment)

- The manager initiates the plan's implementation to satisfy the objectives and criteria set, exercising control over the process.

- The manager monitors process execution, reporting the progress of the process both internally and externally to the acquirer, as defined in the contract.

- The manager investigates, analyzes, and resolves the problems discovered during process execution. Resolving the problems may result in changes to plans. It is the manager's responsibility to ensure the impact of any changes is determined, controlled, and monitored. Problems and their resolutions shall be documented.

- The manager reports, at agreed points, the progress of the process, declaring adherence to the plans and resolving instances of the lack of progress. Reports are both internal and external, as required by the organizational procedures and the contract.

4.5. Review and evaluation

- The manager ensures that the software products and plans are evaluated for satisfaction of requirements.

- The manager assesses the evaluation results of the software products, activities, and tasks completed during process execution for achievement of the objectives and completion of the plans.

4.6. Closure

- When all software products, activities, and tasks are completed, the manager determines whether the process is complete by taking into account the criteria specified in the contract or included in the organization's procedure.

4.7. Post-closure activities

- The manager checks the results and records of the software products, activities, and tasks employed for completeness. These results and records are then archived in a suitable environment as specified in the contract.

5. Modes of engineering management

As indicted in the earlier paragraphs, management performs the same functions regardless of its position in the organization or the enterprise managed. There are a number of organizational modes involved in software management. Roughly, these organizational levels can be partitioned into *organizational management, senior-level management, software acquisition management, user/operator management, supplier management, project management, maintenance management,* and *risk management.* Each of these areas is covered in the paragraphs below.

5.1. Software engineering management organizations

- *Organizational management* includes all management activities that result in the design of a formal structure of tasks and authority relationships within an organization or enterprise. *Organizing* involves determining and enumerating the activities required to achieve the organization's objectives, grouping these activities, assigning the groups of activities to an organizational entity or group identifiers, delegating responsibilities and authority to carry them out, and coordinating authoritative relationships.

- *Senior-level management* is a term that is used to identify the highest level in the formal organizational structure that has responsibility for the software development and/or operation of the software systems. Senior-level management titles include vice president (VP) of engineering, chief information officer (CIO), chief executive officer (CEO), director of software development, and chief, computer operations. Upper-level management can be the software engineering manager's direct supervisor or it can be several levels above the manager. In any case, upper-level management is responsible for establishing general management and development policy and is ultimately responsible for delivering the software system to or operating the software system for the customer. The position may also include such activities as managing personnel, establishing lines of authority and communications, overseeing the enterprise's customer relationships, and protecting assets.

- *Software acquisition management* (SAM) is an agency directly responsible to the software system user or software operator for overseeing the development of the software system. SAM is the interface between the developer and the eventual system user or operator. For example, if a developer (sometimes called a supplier) is a separate organization from the user, the acquirer is responsible for helping the user to define system needs by preparing and issuing an RFP, selecting a supplier, and managing the acquisition process from the beginning to the acceptance of the final system, software product, or software service. The organization needing the software may be called the *owner.* The acquirer is frequently called (by the contractor) the *customer,* and the supplier is frequently called the *developer.*

- The *user or operator management* is the agency responsible for supporting some enterprise function it is associated with through the application of software. Examples include personnel management, communications systems, finance accounting and reporting, and shipping and receiving. The developer of process software for a chemical plant, a guidance system for a commercial aircraft, or a student-records system for a university are additional examples. These latter applications are called *embedded systems.* User or operator management is concerned with obtaining a software system that will make their jobs easier, more accurate, less costly, and more effective.

- *Supplier management* is the agency responsible for the activities and tasks of the software system supplier, such as a decision to prepare a proposal to answer an acquirer's RFP, or to sign and enter into a contract with the acquirer to provide the system, software product, or software service. Supplier management might continue to determine procedures and resources needed to manage and assure the project, including development of project plans and execution of the plans, through delivery of the system, software product, or software service to the acquirer. The actual day-to-day management of the development of a software system is left to *project management.*

- *Project management* is the "hands-on" management of personnel, material, and monetary funds for the purpose of successfully delivering a software system. Project management is a system of management procedures, practices, technologies, skill, and experience necessary to successfully manage an engineering project. If the product of a project is software, the act of managing the project is called *software engineering project management.* The *manager* of a software engineering project is called a *software engineering project manager*, a *software project manager*, or in many cases simply a project manager.

- *Maintenance management* is the agency responsible for the activities and tasks of the maintainer. The maintenance activity is initiated toward the end of a software development project or when the software system is turned over to the user/operator. Maintenance management begins when the software product undergoes modifications to code an associated documentation due to a problem with the software system, the need for improvements in the system, or the adaptation of the software to a changing environment. The objective of maintenance is to modify existing software products while preserving their integrity. The maintenance process ends with the retirement of the software product.

- *Risk management* is an organized means of identifying risk factors (called *risk identification*), developing and selecting risk-handling options (called *risk analysis*), and mitigating risk once problems are posed (called *risk handling*). The primary goal of risk management is to identify and respond to potential problems with sufficient lead-time to avoid a crisis. It is important to establish a risk-management strategy early in a software project and to continually address the risk throughout the system life-cycle.

6. Senior-level management

Many of the activities and tasks associated with managing a multilevel organization can only be done effectively by what we call "senior-level management." The next several paragraphs provide examples of senior-level activities.

- *Policies* are concerned with predetermined management decisions. They are general statements or understandings that guide decision-making activities. Policies limit freedom in making decisions but allow for some discretion. Senior management is responsible for establishing senior-level policies for administrating the organization and technical policies for planning and controlling the operation, use, and development of software systems.

- *Personnel management* is the management of activities involving the hiring, retaining, promoting, training, and terminating of personnel. Personnel are all the members of an enterprise or organization, ranging from senior vice president to mailroom clerk. Senior management manages personnel through policies. Examples include policies regarding who to hire, starting salaries, amount of education, pay raises, and periodic evaluations.

- *Communications* is the process of transferring information from one person or group to another person or group with the understanding that the message being transmitted is understood by both groups or individuals. Communication channels can be electronic, manual, or word-of-mouth. Communication channels should be established by higher-management and are independent from management lines of authority.

- *Customer relations* are the agreements, interactions, and contacts between the developer or operator of a software system and the organization employing them. It is usually a set of agreements, both formal and informal, regarding how the customer will be treated by the developer. Good customer relations can be extremely important to many corporations and frequently will make the difference between success and failure in their business.

- *Asset protection* can generally only be applied at an enterprise-wide level. A company's assets can be tangible (computer center, buildings, employees, and equipment) or intangible (reputation, good will, and honor). To protect these tangible assets from being harmed or damaged normally requires a set of policies (for example, no strangers in the buildings without escort), physical barriers (locked doors), and motivated people (security personnel). Intangible assets require policies on how the enterprise will deal with its customers and the outside world, as well as the attitude it instills in its employees.

7. Software acquisition management

This paragraph is paraphrased from IEEE/EIA Standard 12207.0-1996, Paragraph 5.1. The acquisition management process directs the activities and tasks of the acquirer. The process begins with the definition of the need to acquire a system, software product, or software service. The process continues with the preparation and issue of an RFP, selection of a supplier, and management of the acquisition process to the acceptance of the system, software product, or software service.

The organization having the need may be called the *owner*. The owner may contract any or all of the acquisition activities to an *agent*, who will conduct these activities according to the organization's acquisition process. The acquirer in this subclause may be the owner or the agent.

The acquirer manages the acquisition process at the project level, following the management process described in Paragraph 4.

The *acquisition management process* consists of the following activities:

- initiation
- request-for-proposal preparation (called request-for-tender in the United Kingdom)
- contract preparation and update
- supplier monitoring
- acceptance and completion

7.1. Initiation

7.1.1. The acquirer begins the acquisition process by describing a concept or a need to acquire, develop, or enhance a system, software product, or software service.

7.1.2. The acquirer defines and analyzes the system requirements. The system requirements should include business, organizational, and user requirements as well as safety, security, and other critical requirements along with related design, testing, and compliance standards and procedures.

7.1.3. The acquirer may perform the definition and analysis of software requirements itself, or it may retain a supplier to perform this task. However, if the acquirer retains a *supplier* to perform system requirements analysis, the acquirer will approve the analyzed requirements.

7.1.4. The acquirer considers options for acquisition against analysis of appropriate criteria to include risk, cost, and benefits for each option. Options include

- purchase an off-the-shelf software product that satisfies the requirements,

- develop the software product or obtain the software service internally,

- develop the software product or obtain the software service through contract,

- enhance an existing software product or service,

- any combination of the above.

7.1.5. When an off-the-shelf software product is to be acquired, the acquirer will ensure that the following conditions are satisfied:

- The requirements for the software product are satisfied.

- The documentation is available.

- Proprietary, usage, ownership, warranty, and licensing rights are satisfied.

- Future support for the software product is planned.

7.1.6. The acquirer prepares, documents, and executes an acquisition plan. The plan should contain

- requirements for the system,

- planned employment of the system,

- type of contract to be employed,

- responsibilities of the organizations involved,

- support concept to be used,

- risks considered as well as methods to manage the risks.

7.1.7. the acquirer should define and document the acceptance strategy and conditions (criteria).

7.2. Request-for-proposal (a.k.a. *tender* in the U.K.) preparation

7.2.1. The acquirer documents the acquisition requirements (for example, an RFP), the content of which depends upon the acquisition option selected in Paragraph 7.1. The acquisition documentation should include, as appropriate,

- system requirements

- scope statement

- instructions for bidders

- list of software products

- terms and conditions

- control of subcontracts

- technical constraints (such as target environment).

7.2.2. The acquirer determines which processes, activities, and tasks of any organizational standards are appropriate for the project and tailors them accordingly. The acquirer should specify the applicable *supporting processes* and their performing organizations, including responsibilities (if other than supplier), so the suppliers may, in their proposals, define the approach to each of the specified supporting processes. The acquirer defines the scope of the tasks that reference the contract.

7.2.3. The acquisition documentation also defines the contract milestones at which the supplier's progress will be reviewed and audited as part of monitoring the acquisition.

7.2.4. The acquisition requirements should be given to the organization selected for performing the acquisition activities.

7.3. Contract preparation and update

7.3.1. The acquirer establishes a procedure for supplier selection, including proposal evaluation criteria and requirements compliance weighting.

7.3.2. The acquirer selects a supplier based on an evaluation of the suppliers' proposals, capabilities, and other factors.

7.3.3. The acquirer prepares and negotiates a contract with the supplier that addresses the acquisition requirements, including the cost and schedule of the software product or service to be delivered. The contract will address proprietary, usage, ownership, warranty, and licensing rights associated with reusable off-the-shelf software products.

7.3.4. Once the contract is under way, the acquirer controls changes to the contract through negotiation with the supplier as part of a change-control mechanism. Changes to the contract should be investigated for impact on project plans, costs, benefits, quality, and schedule.

7.4. Supplier monitoring

7.4.1. The acquirer monitors the supplier's activities in accordance with the *joint review process* and *audit process*. The acquirer should supplement the monitoring with the *verification* and *validation (V&V) process* as needed.

7.4.2. The acquirer cooperates with the supplier to provide all necessary information in a timely manner and resolve all pending items.

7.5. Acceptance and completion

7.5.1. The acquirer prepares for acceptance based on the defined acceptance strategy and criteria. The preparation of test cases, test data, test procedures, and test environment should be included. The extent of supplier involvement should also be defined.

7.5.2. The acquirer conducts acceptance reviews and acceptance testing of the deliverable software product or service and accept its from the supplier when all acceptance conditions are satisfied. The acceptance procedure should comply with the provisions of Paragraph 7.1.8.

7.5.3. After acceptance, the acquirer should take responsibility for the *configuration management* of the delivered software product. Note: the acquirer may install the software product or perform the software service in accordance with instructions defined by the supplier.

8. User or operator management

This paragraph is paraphrased from IEEE/EIA Standard 12207.0-1996, Paragraph 5.4. The user and operator management process directs the activities and tasks of the system user and/or operator. The process covers the use of the software to support some enterprise function and/or the operation of the software product and operational support to users. Because operation of a software product is integrated into the system operation, the activities and tasks of this process refer to the larger system that includes software. The user and/or operator management uses a *management process* like that in Paragraph 4. When the operator/user is the supplier of the operation service, the operator/user performs the *supply process*. This management process consists of the following activities:

- process implementation
- operational testing
- system operation
- user support

8.1. Process implementation

8.1.1. The operator and/or user develops a plan and sets operational standards for performing the activities and tasks of this process. The plan should be documented and executed.

8.1.2. The operator establishes procedures for receiving, recording, resolving, tracking problems, and providing feedback to the *maintenance process*. Whenever problems are encountered, they should be recorded and entered into the problem-resolution process.

8.1.3. The operator and/or user establishes procedures for testing the software product in its environment, for entering problem reports and modification requests to the *maintenance process*, and for releasing the software product for operational use.

8.2. Operational (a.k.a. acceptance) testing

8.2.1. For each software product release, the operator and/or user performs operational testing, and, on satisfying the specified criteria, releases the software product for operational use.

8.2.2. The operator and/or user ensures that the software code and databases initialize, execute, and terminate as described in the plan.

8.3. System operation

8.3.1. The system is operated in its intended environment according to the user documentation.

8.4. Operator-user relationships

8.4.1. The operator provides assistance and consultation to the users as requested. These requests and subsequent actions are recorded and monitored.

8.4.2. The operator forwards user requests, as necessary, to the *maintenance process* for resolution. These requests are addressed and the actions that are planned and taken are reported to the request originators. All resolutions are monitored to conclusion.

8.4.3. If a reported problem has a temporary work-around before a permanent solution can be released, the originator of the problem report is given the option to use it. Permanent corrections, releases that include previously omitted functions or features, and system improvements are applied to the operational software product using the maintenance process.

9. Supplier management

This paragraph is paraphrased from IEEE/EIA Standard 12207.0-1996, Paragraph 5.2. The *supply process* includes the activities and tasks of the supplier (sometimes called developer). The process may be initiated either by a decision to prepare a proposal to answer an acquirer's RFP or by signing and entering into a contract with the acquirer to provide the system, software product, or software service. The process continues with the determination of procedures and resources needed to manage and assure the project, including development of project plans and execution of plans through delivery of the system, software product, or software service to the acquirer.

The supplier manages the *supply (development) process* at the project level following the *management process* (see Paragraph 4), which is instantiated in this process; establishes an infrastructure under the process following the *infrastructure process* (see Volume 2, Chapter 5); tailors the process for the project, and manages the process at the organizational level following the *improvement process* (see Volume 2, Chapter 9) and the *training process* (see Volume 2, Chapter 9). The supply process consists of the following activities:

- initiation
- preparation of response
- contract
- planning
- execution and control
- review and evaluation
- delivery and completion

9.1. Initiation

9.1.1. The supplier conducts a review of requirements in the RFP, taking into account organizational policies and other regulations.

9.1.2. The supplier decides to bid or accept the contract.

9.2. Preparation of response

9.2.1. The supplier defines and prepares a proposal in response to the RFP.

9.3. Contract

9.3.1. The supplier negotiates and enters into a contract with the acquirer organization to provide the software product or service.

9.3.2. The supplier may request modification to the contract as part of the change-control mechanism.

9.4. Planning

9.4.1. The supplier conducts a review of the acquisition requirements to define the framework for managing and assuring the project and for assuring the quality of the deliverable software product or service.

9.4.2. If not stipulated in the contract, the supplier should define or select a software life-cycle model appropriate to the project's scope, magnitude, and complexity.

9.4.3. The supplier establishes requirements for managing plans, assuring the project, and assuring the quality of the deliverable software product or service. Requirements for the plans should include resource needs and acquirer involvement.

9.4.4. Once the planning requirements are established, the supplier considers the options for developing the software product or providing the software service against an analysis of risks associated with each option. Options include:

- developing the software product or providing the software service using internal resources,

- developing the software product or providing the software service by subcontracting,

- obtaining off-the-shelf software products from internal or external sources,

- a combination of the three above.

9.4.5. The supplier develops and documents project management plans based on the planning requirements and options selected in Paragraph 9.4.4. Items to be considered in the plan include but are not limited to

- project organizational structure, authority, and responsibility of each organizational unit, including external organizations;

- engineering environment (for development, operation, or maintenance, as applicable), including test environment, library, equipment, facilities, standards, procedures, and tools;

- work breakdown structure of the life-cycle processes and activities, including the software products, software services, and nondeliverable items to be performed together with budgets, staffing, physical resources, software size, and schedules associated with the tasks;

- management of the quality characteristics of the software products or services (separate plans for quality may be developed);

- management of the safety, security, and other critical requirements of the software products or services (separate plans for safety and security may be developed);

- subcontractor management, including subcontractor selection and relationship between the subcontractor and the acquirer, if any;

- quality assurance (see Volume 2, Chapter 4);

- verification and validation (see Volume 2, Chapter 3), including the approach for interfacing with the verification and validation agent, if specified;

- acquirer involvement by such means as joint reviews and audits (see Volume 2, Chapter 5), informal meetings, reporting, modification and change, implementation, approval, acceptance, and access to facilities;

- user involvement, by such means as requirements-setting exercises, prototype demonstrations, and evaluations;

- risk management, including management of the project areas that involve potential technical, cost, and schedule risks;

- security policy, such as need-to-know and access-to-information rules at each project organization level;

- approval required by such means as regulations, required certifications, proprietary, usage, ownership, warranty, and licensing rights;

- means for scheduling, tracking, and reporting;

- training of personnel (see Volume 2, Chapter 9).

9.5. Execution and control

9.5.1. The supplier implements and executes the project management plan(s) developed in Paragraph 9.4. The supplier shall

- develop the software product in accordance with the *development process* (see Paragraph 10);

- operate the software product in accordance with the *operation process* (see Paragraph 8);

- maintain the software product in accordance with the *maintenance process* (see Paragraph 11).

9.5.2. The supplier monitors and controls the progress and quality of the project's software products or services throughout the contracted life-cycle. This is an ongoing, iterative task, which provides for

- monitoring progress of technical performance, costs and schedules, and reporting of project status;

- problem identification, recording, analysis, and resolution.

9.5.3. The supplier manages and controls the subcontractors in accordance with the acquisition process (see Paragraph 7). The supplier passes down all contractual requirements necessary to ensure that the software product or service delivered to the acquirer is developed or performed in accordance with the prime contract requirements.

9.5.4. The supplier interfaces with the independent verification, validation, or test agent and other parties as specified in the contract and project plans.

9.6. Review and evaluation

9.6.1. The supplier coordinates contract review activities, interfaces, and communication with the acquirer's organization.

9.6.2. The supplier conducts or supports the informal meetings, acceptance review, acceptance testing, joint reviews, and audits with the acquirer as specified in the contract and project plans.

9.6.3. The supplier performs verification and validation to demonstrate that the software products or services and processes fully satisfy their respective requirements.

9.6.4. The supplier makes available to the acquirer the evaluation reports, reviews, audits, testing, and problem resolutions as specified in the contract.

9.6.5. The supplier gives the acquirer access to the supplier's and subcontractors' facilities for review of software products or services as specified in the contract and project plans.

9.6.6. The supplier performs quality assurance activities.

9.7. Delivery and completion

9.7.1. The supplier delivers the software product or service as specified in the contract.

9.7.2. The supplier provides support of the delivered software product or service as specified in the contract.

10. Software engineering project management

The *software engineering project process* contains the activities and tasks of the software engineering project manager (PM). The process contains the requirements analysis, design, coding, integration, testing, and installation activities and acceptance related to software products.

It may contain system-related activities if stipulated in the contract. The PM performs or supports the activities in this process in accordance with the contract.

Details of software engineering project management can be found in R.H. Thayer, "Software Engineering Project Management," in *Software Engineering: Volume 2: The Supporting Processes*, R.H. Thayer and M. J. Christensen, eds., IEEE Computer Society Press, Los Alamitos, CA, 2002.

10.1. Planning the software engineering project

Planning a software engineering project consists of the management activities leading to selection of future courses of action for the project and a program for completing those actions.

The PM's responsibilities for planning the software engineering project include

- determining the desired project outcome;

- deciding major organizational goals and developing a general program of action for reaching those goals;

- making standing decisions on important recurring matters to guide decision making;

- anticipating events or making assumptions about the future, predicting future results or expectations from courses of action;

- anticipating possible adverse events and problem areas, stating assumptions, developing contingency plans, and predicting results of possible courses of action;

- developing, analyzing, and/or evaluating different ways to conduct the project;

- evaluating and selecting a course of action;

- establishing methods, guides, and limits for accomplishing the project activity;

- establishing the policies, procedures, rules, tasks, schedules, and resources necessary to complete the project;

- allocating estimated costs to project functions, activities, and tasks;

- recording policy decisions, courses of action, budget, program plans, and contingency plans.

10.2 Organizing the software engineering project

Organizing a software engineering project involves developing an effective and efficient organizational structure for assigning and completing project tasks and establishing the authority and responsibility relationships among the tasks.

Organizing involves itemizing the project activities required to achieve the project objectives and arranging these activities into logical clusters. It also involves assigning groups of activities to various organizational entities and delegating responsibility and authority needed to carry out the activities. Organizing includes planning the organizational interfaces between the project and other stakeholders (for example, customer, hardware, users, and contracts).

An organizational structure's purpose is to "focus the efforts of many on a selected goal." [Donnelly, Gibson, and Ivancevich, 1975].

Responsibilities for organizing the software engineering project include

- defining, sizing, and categorizing the project work;

- selecting appropriate structures to accomplish the project and to monitor, control, communicate, and coordinate;

- establishing titles, job descriptions, and job relationships for all project roles;

- defining responsibilities for each organizational position and the authority to be granted to fulfill those responsibilities;

- defining position qualifications;

- documenting titles, positions, job, descriptions, responsibilities, authorities, relationships, and position qualifications.

Note that organizing does not involve people. Placing people in the organization is a function of staffing (see Paragraph 10.3).

10.3. Staffing the software engineering project

Staffing a software engineering project consists of all management activities that involve filling (and keeping filled) the positions that were established in the project organizational structure. This includes selecting candidates for the positions and training or otherwise developing them to accomplish their tasks effectively. Staffing also involves terminating project personnel when necessary.

Staffing is different from organizing: staffing involves filling the roles created in the project organizational structure through selection, training, and personnel development. The objective of staffing is to ensure that project roles are filled by personnel who are qualified (both technically and temperamentally) to occupy them.

Responsibilities for staffing the software engineering project include

- selecting, recruiting, or promoting qualified people for each project position;

- orienting and familiarizing new people with the organization, facilities, and project tasks;

- making up deficiencies in position qualifications through training and education;

- improving knowledge, attitudes, and skills of project personnel;

- recording and analyzing the quantity and quality of project work as the basis for personnel evaluations, setting performance goals and appraising personnel periodically;

- providing wages, bonuses, benefits, or other financial remuneration commensurate with project responsibilities and performance;

- transferring or separating project personnel as necessary;

- recording staffing plans, training and training plans, appraisal records, and compensation recommendations.

10.4. Directing the software engineering project

The PM is responsible for directing (sometimes called leading) the software engineering project. *Directing* a software engineering project consists of the management activities that involve motivational and interpersonal aspects by which project personnel come to understand and contribute to the achievement of project goals. Once subordinates are trained and oriented, the project manager has a continuing responsibility to clarify their assignments, guide them toward improved performance, and motivate them to work with enthusiasm and confidence toward project goals.

Directing, like staffing, involves people. Directing is sometimes considered synonymous with leading (compare reference [Koontz and O'Donnell, 1972] with reference [Koontz, O'Donnell, and Weihrich, 1984]). Directing a project involves providing leadership, supervising personnel, delegating authority, coordinating activities, facilitating communications, resolving conflicts, managing change, and documenting important decisions.

Responsibilities for directing the software engineering project include

- selecting, recruiting, or promoting qualified people for each project position;

- orienting and familiarizing new people with the organization, facilities, and project tasks;

- making up deficiencies in position qualifications through training and education;

- improving knowledge, attitudes, and skills of project personnel;

- recording and analyzing the quantity and quality of project work as the basis for personnel evaluations, setting performance goals and appraising personnel periodically;

- providing wages, bonuses, benefits, or other financial remuneration commensurate with project responsibilities and performance;

- transferring or separating project personnel as necessary;

- recording staffing plans, training and training plans, appraisal records, and compensation recommendations.

10.5. Controlling the software engineering project

Controlling is the collection of management activities used to ensure that the project goes according to plan. Performance and results are measured against plans, deviations are noted, and corrective actions are taken to ensure conformance to plans.

Control is a feedback system that provides information on how well the project is going. Control asks the questions: Is the project on schedule? Is it within cost? Are there any potential problems that will cause delays in meeting the requirement within the budget and schedule? Controls also provide plans and approaches for eliminating the difference between the plans and/or standards and the actual results.

The control process also requires organizational structure, communication, and coordination. For example, who is responsible for assessing progress? Who will take action on reported problems?

Controlling methods and tools must be objective. Information must be quantified. The methods and tools must point out deviations from plans without regard to the particular people or positions involved. Control methods must be tailored to individual environments and managers. The methods must be flexible and adaptable to deal with the changing environment of the organization. Control also must be economical; the cost of control should not outweigh its benefits.

Control must lead to corrective action—either to bring the actual status back to plan, to change the plan, or to terminate the project.

The PM's responsibilities for staffing the software engineering project include

- setting goals that will be achieved when tasks are correctly accomplished;

- determining necessary data, who will receive it, when they will receive it, and what they will do with it to control the project;

- comparing achievements with standards, goals, and plans;

- bringing requirements, plans, and actual project status into conformance;

- praising, remunerating, and disciplining project personnel as appropriate;

- documenting the standards of performance, monitoring and controlling systems, and rewarding and disciplining personnel.

11. Maintenance management

This paragraph is paraphrased from IEEE/EIA Standard 12207.0-1996, Paragraph 8. The *maintenance process* contains the activities and tasks of the maintainer. This process is activated when the software product undergoes modifications to code and associated documentation due to a problem or the need for improvement or adaptation. The objective is to modify an existing software product while preserving its integrity. This process includes the migration and retirement of the software product. It ends with the retirement of the software product.

The activities provided in this clause are specific to the maintenance process; however, the process may utilize other processes used by the supplier. In this case, the developer or project manager is interpreted as a maintainer. The maintenance process consists of the following activities:

- process implementation

- problem and modification analysis

- modification implementation

- maintenance review/acceptance

- migration

- software retirement.

11.1. Process implementation

11.1.1. The maintainer develops, documents, and executes plans and procedures for conducting the activities and tasks of the maintenance process.

11.1.2. The maintainer establishes procedures for receiving, recording, and tracking problem reports and modification requests from the users and providing feedback to the users. Whenever problems are encountered, they are recorded and entered into the *problem resolution process*.

11.1.3. The maintainer implements (or establishes organizational interfaces with) the *configuration management process* for managing modifications to the existing system.

11.2. Problem and modification analysis

11.2.1. The maintainer analyzes the problem report or modification request for its impact on the organization, the existing system, and the interfacing systems for the following:

- *type*—for example, corrective, improvement, preventive, or adaptive to new environment

- *scope*—for example, size of modification, cost involved, time to modify

- *criticality*—for example, impact on performance, safety, or security.

11.2.2. The maintainer replicates or verifies the problem.

11.2.3. Based on the analysis, the maintainer considers options for implementing the modification.

11.2.4.The maintainer documents the problem/modification request, the analysis results, and implementation options.

11.2.5. The maintainer obtains approval for the selected modification option as specified in the contract.

11.3. Modification implementation

11.3.1. The maintainer conducts analyses and determines which documentation, software units, and versions need to be modified. These should be documented.

11.3.2. The maintainer enters the *development process* to implement the modifications. The requirements of the development process are supplemented as follows:

- Criteria for testing and evaluating the modified and the unmodified parts (software units, components, and configuration items) of the system are defined and documented.

- The complete and correct implementation of the new and modified requirements are verified. Also, ensure that the original, unmodified requirements were not affected. The test results are then documented.

11.4. Maintenance review/acceptance

11.4.1. The maintainer conducts a review with the organization authorizing the modification to determine the integrity of the modified system.

11.4.2. The maintainer obtains approval for the satisfactory completion of the modification as specified in the contract.

11.5. Migration

11.5.1. If a system or software product (including data) is migrated from an old to a new operational environment, any software product or data produced or modified during migration will be in accordance with the migration process.

11.5.2. A migration plan is developed, documented, and executed. The planning activities involve users. Items included in the plan are

- requirements analysis and migration definition

- development of migration tools

- conversion of software product and data

- migration execution

- migration verification

- support for the old environment in the future

11.5.3. Users are notified of the migration plans and activities. Notifications include

- statement of why the old environment will no longer be supported

- description of the new environment with its availability date

- description of other support options available, if any, once support for the old environment has been removed

11.5.4. Parallel operations of the old and new environments may be conducted for a smooth transition. During this period, necessary training is provided as specified in the contract.

11.5.5. When the scheduled migration arrives, notification is sent to all concerned. All associated old environment documentation, logs, and code should be archived.

11.5.6. A post-operation review is performed to assess the impact of changing to the new environment. The results of the review are sent to the appropriate authorities for information, guidance, and action.

11.5.7. Data used by or associated with the old environment are accessible in accordance with the contract requirements for data protection and audit applicable to the data.

11.6. Software retirement (Note: the software product will be retired on the request of the owner.)

11.6.1. A retirement plan is developed and documented by the operation and maintenance organizations. The planning activities involve users. Plan activities include

- cessation of full or partial support after a certain period of time
- archiving of the software product and its associated documentation
- responsibility for any future residual support issues
- transition to new software products, if applicable
- accessibility of archive copies of data

After these items are addressed, the retirement plan is executed.

11.6.2. Users are notified of the retirement plans and activities. Notifications include

- description of the replacement or upgrade with its date of availability
- statement of why the software product is no longer to be supported
- description of other support options available, once support has been removed

11.6.3. Parallel operations of the retiring and new software products ease transition to the new system. During the transition period, user training is provided as specified in the contract.

11.6.4. When the scheduled retirement arrives, notification is sent to all concerned. All associated development documentation, logs, and code are archived, when appropriate.

11.6.5. Data used or associated with the retired software product is accessible in accordance with the contract requirements for data protection and audit applicable to the data.

12. Risk management

A *project risk* is a potential problem that would be detrimental to a project's success should it materialize. Risk management is an organized means of identifying risk factors (*risk identification*), developing and selecting risk handling options (*risk analysis*), and mitigating risk when it becomes problematic (*risk handling*). The primary goal of risk management is to identify and respond to potential problems with sufficient lead time to avoid a crisis. It is important that a risk management strategy is established early in a software project and that risk is addressed throughout the system life cycle. This paragraph defines and explains the various elements of risk management.

Project risk is characterized by

- uncertainty is involved ($0 <$ probability < 1)
- an associated loss (life, money, property, reputation, and so on)

- manageability, in the sense that human action can be applied to change its form and degree

The risk management process consists of

- risk identification
- risk analysis
- risk handling
- determining cost-effectiveness for risk handling
- risk monitoring

12.1. Risk identification

12.1.1 Risk identification is the initial effort in risk management, and involves identifying the risks for a particular project.

12.2. Risk analysis

12.2.1. *Risk analysis* is the examination of identified risks to determine the probabilities of undesired events and the consequences associated with those events.

12.2.2. R*isk exposure* is the product of probability of occurrence and financial loss if a problem arises.

12.2.3. Prioritize risks according to the level of risk exposure. This is a "watch list" of a reasonable number of project risks (say 10), and includes prioritized risk factors, consequences of those risks, and the indicators that signal the onset of a problem (called a "risk trigger")—the event that indicates a potential problem has become a real problem.

12.2.4. The watch list is periodically re-evaluated (weekly at the working level, monthly at the management and customer levels), items are added, modified, or deleted as appropriate.

12.3. Risk handling

12.3.1. Risk handling (also called risk mitigation) includes techniques and methods developed to reduce and/or control risk. Techniques for handling risk fall into five categories:

- risk avoidance
- risk assumption
- problem control (risk reduction)
- risk transfer
- knowledge acquisition

12.3.1. *Risk avoidance* involves avoiding a high-risk approach to software development by selecting a lower-risk approach. To avoid risk means to avoid the probability and/or consequences of an undesired event occurring.

12.3.2. *Risk assumption* involves a conscious decision to accept the consequences should an undesired event occur. Risk assumption acknowledges the existence of risk and a decision to accept the consequences if problems occur. Some amount of risk assumption is always present in software development programs.

12.3.3. *Risk control* involves the continuous monitoring of project status and the development of other solutions if the risk becomes a problem. Risk control includes

- developing a risk reduction plan and tracking to that plan

- determining the "risk trigger"—the metric that will indicate that the risk has become a problem—and the risk reduction plan that will need to be implemented

- continually measuring project status and developing options and fallback positions

12.3.4. *Risk transfer* involves transferring potential problems to other areas of responsibility. It also may include the transfer of responsibility for a successful outcome.

12.3.5. *Knowledge acquisition* is the gathering of additional information to further assess risk and to develop new contingency plans.

12.4. Determining cost-effectiveness of risk handling

12.4.1. Determine the cost-effectiveness of risk management by

- determining the probability of an undesired event

- determining the loss if the risk becomes a problem

- determining the maximum amount that should be spent on risk management, multiplying the amount of maximum loss (in dollars) times the probability of loss

12.5. Risk monitoring

12.5.1. Risk monitoring involves

- tracking the risks that have been identified in the risk identification action

- paying particular attention to the "risk triggers," which are values of indicator metrics that have been identified to "sound the alarm" when a potential problem is likely to become a real problem.

- avoiding one of the major traps of risk management, which is refusal to acknowledge that a risk has become a problem, and the resulting need to implement a risk-handling plan

13. Summary and conclusions

Management is invariable regardless of the organization managed or the level of management. All managers must *plan, organize, staff, direct,* and *control* their organization and activities to be performed.

References

[Brooks 1987] "Report on the Defense Science Board Task Force on Military Software," Office of the Undersecretary of Defense for Acquisition, Department of Defense, Washington, D.C., Sept. 1987.

[Cleland and King, 1972] D.I. Cleland and W.R. King, *Management: A Systems Approach,* See Table 5-1: Major Management Functions as Seen by Various Authors, McGraw-Hill, New York, 1972.

[DoD Software Initiative 1983] *Strategy for a DoD Software Initiative*, Department of Defense Report, 1 Oct. 1982. (An edited public version was published in *Computer*, Nov. 1983.)

[Donnelly, Gibson, and Ivancevich 1975] J.H. Donnelly Jr., J.L. Gibson, and J.M. Ivancevich, *Fundamentals of Management: Functions, Behavior, Models*, rev. ed., Business Publications, Dallas, Tex., 1975.

[Fayol 1949] H. Fayol, *General and Industrial Administration*, Sir Isaac Pitman & Sons, Ltd., London, 1949.

[GAO/IMTEC-92-48 C-17 Aircraft Software] "Embedded Computer Systems: Significant Software Problems on C-17 Must be Addressed." General Accounting Office GAO/IMTEC-92-48, Gaithersburg, Md, May 1992.

[Koontz and O'Donnell, 1972] H. Koontz and C. O'Donnell, *Principles of Management: An Analysis of Managerial Functions,* 5th ed., McGraw-Hill, New York, 1972.

[Koontz, O'Donnell, and Weihrich 1980] H. Koontz, C. O'Donnell, and H. Weihrich, *Management*, 7th ed., McGraw-Hill, New York, 1980.

[Koontz, O'Donnell, and Weihrich 1984] H. Koontz, C. O'Donnell and H. Weihrich, *Management*, 8th ed., McGraw-Hill, New York, 1984.

[MacKenzie, 1969] R.A. MacKenzie, "The Management Process in 3-D," *Harvard Business Review*, vol. 47, no. 6, Nov./Dec. 1969, pp. 80-87. Reprinted in *Tutorial: Software Engineering Project Management*, R.H. Thayer, ed., IEEE Computer Society Press, Los Alamitos, Calif,, 1988.

[Paulk, et al. 1996] M.C. Paulk, B. Curtis, M.B. Chrissis, and C.V. Weber, "The Capability Maturity Model for Software," in *Software Engineering,* M. Dorfman and R.H. Thayer, eds., IEEE Computer Society Press, Los Alamitos, Calif., 1996.

[Rue and Byars, 1983] L.W. Rue and L.L. Byars, *Management: Theory and Application*, Richard D. Irwin, Homewood, Ill., 1983.

[Zubrow, et al. 1995] D. Zubrow, J. Herbsleb, W. Hayes, D. Goldenson, "Process Maturity Profile of the Software Community 1995 Update," Nov. 1995, based on data up to Sept. 1995 for most recent assessment of 440 organizations: ML1 - 70.2 percent; ML2 - 18.4 percent; ML3 - 10.2 percent; ML4 - 1 percent; ML5 - 0.2 percent; Source: e-mail, Mark Paulk, Software Engineering Institution, 14 Feb. 1996.

Software Engineering Project Management

Richard H. Thayer, Fellow IEEE
California State University, Sacramento
Sacramento, CA 95819

Abstract. This article describes the management functions and tasks necessary to manage a software engineering project. The universality of these concepts provides a framework for adapting traditional management functions to project management. From these management functions, this article derives the activities and tasks that should be undertaken by any manager assigned to a software engineering project.

This article describes the management procedures, practices, technologies, and skill necessary to successfully manage a software engineering project.

1. Introduction

This article is about management, the universality of management concepts, and the activities and tasks of software engineering management.

Management involves the activities and tasks undertaken by one or more persons for the purpose of planning and controlling the activities of others in order to achieve objectives that could not be achieved by the others acting alone. Management functions can be categorized as planning, organizing, staffing, directing, and controlling [Koontz and O'Donnell, 1972].

Project management is a system of management procedures, practices, technologies, skill, and experience necessary to successfully manage an engineering project. If a project's product is software, then the act of managing the project is called *software engineering project management* or *software engineering management*. The manager of a software engineering project is called a *software engineering project manager*, a *software project manager*, or in many cases, just *project manager*.

Software engineering projects are frequently part of larger, more comprehensive projects that include equipment (hardware), facilities, personnel, and procedures, as well as software. Examples include aircraft, accounting, radar, inventory control, and railroad switching systems. These *systems engineering projects* are typically managed by one or more system project managers (sometimes called *program managers*) who manage projects composed of engineers, domain experts, scientific specialists, programmers, support personnel, and others. If the software to be delivered is a "stand-alone" software system (a system that does not involve development of other nonsoftware components), the software project manager may be called the *system project manager*.

Universality of management is a concept that comes from management science [Koontz and O'Donnell 1972], [Fayol 1949] and means:

- Management performs the same functions (planning, organizing, staffing, directing, and controlling) regardless of position in the organization or the enterprise managed.

- Management functions are characteristic duties of managers; management practices, methods, activities, and tasks are specific to the enterprise or job managed.

The universality of management concepts allows us to apply them to software engineering project management [Thayer and Pyster 1984].

This article describes the management functions that are necessary to plan, organize, staff, direct, and control an activity or enterprise. The universality of these concepts provides a management framework for adapting traditional management functions to project management. From these management functions, this article derives the detailed activities and tasks that should be undertaken by a manager assigned to a software engineering project.

Section 2 lists some of the major software engineering issues that pertain to project management. Section 3 partitions the functions of management into a detailed list of management activities. Sections 4 through 8 partition these management activities into the detailed activities and tasks of a software engineering project manager. Section 9 summarizes the article.

2. Project management vs. acquisition management

There are two types of software development projects and two types of project managers:

- development projects and acquisition projects

- software project managers and software acquisition managers

Software development is: (1) the process of developing or modifying a software-intensive system to successfully deliver a product that satisfies the acquirer's contractual requirements, and (2) the process of developing or modifying a software-intensive system to deliver on-time and within budget a product that satisfies user needs and customer expectations.

Software acquisition is the process of contractually obtaining, from one group or organization (the supplier), a software-intensive system for use by another group or organization (the users). The contract is managed by a customer (acquisition) organization. Table 1 delineates the differences between project management and acquisition management.

Project managers must be able to do project management and understand acquisition management. Acquisition managers must be able to do acquisition management and understand **project** management.

3. Major issues of software engineering

Over 70 percent of software development organizations develop their software through ad hoc and unpredictable methods [Zubrow, et al. 1995]. These organizations (considered to be "immature" according to the Software Engineering Institute Capability Maturity Model) do not have an objective basis for determining software cost or schedule, or for judging software quality. Software development processes are generally improvised by practitioners and their management over the course of the project. The company does not have any standard practices or, if they do, the practices are not followed. Managers use what worked best on their last project. Proven software engineering techniques such as in-depth requirements analysis, inspections, reviews, testing, and documentation are reduced or eliminated when the project falls behind in cost, schedule, and/or the customer demands more functionality without a budget increase [Paulk et al. 1996].

The "software crisis" is identified by software that is late, over budget, and fails to meet the customer's system requirements [Gibbs 1994]. Many, if not most, of these problems have been blamed on inadequate or inferior software project management.

The importance of software project management is best illustrated in the following paragraphs, extracted from Department of Defense (DoD) reports.

- A report from the STARS initiative (STARS: Software Technology for Adaptable, Reliable Systems) states, "The manager plays a major role in software and systems development and support. The difference between success or failure—between a project being on schedule and on budget or late and over budget—is often a function of the manager's effectiveness." [DoD Software Initiative 1983]

**Table 1. Differences between project management
and acquisition management**

Management functions	Acquisition management	Project management
Planning	Macro-level	Micro-level
Organizing	Same	Same
Staffing	Same	Same
Directing	Same	Same
Control	Macro-level, simple	Micro-level, complex
Costing	Macro-level	Micro-level
Scheduling	Milestones	Detailed-level
Risk management	Macro-level	Micro-level
Metrics	Requires	Does
Subcontractor management	Requires	Does
Configuration management	External	Internal
Quality assurance	Requires	Does
Verification and Validation	Requires	Does
Documentation	Top-level	Bottom-level
Joint reviews	Receives	Gives
Audits	Directs	Does
Problem resolution	Same	Same

- A Report to the Defense Science Board Task Force on Military Software states, "today's major problems with software development are not technical problems, but management problems." [Brooks 1987]

- The *above statement* was reinforced by a General Accounting Office (GAO) report that investigated the cost and schedule overrun of the C-17 and said, "software development has clearly been a major problem during the first six years of the program. In fact, the C-17 is a good example of how *not* to manage software development." [GAO/IMTEC-92-48 C-17 Aircraft Software]

4. Functions and activities of management

This article presents a top-down overview of the software engineering project management responsibilities, activities, and tasks that should be undertaken by any manager responsible for a software engineering project. A top-down approach partitions and allocates top-level functions to lower-level activities and tasks.

Figure 4.1 depicts the classic management model as portrayed by such well-known authors in the management field as Koontz and O'Donnell [1972], Rue and Byars [1983], Cleland and King [1972], and MacKenzie [1969].

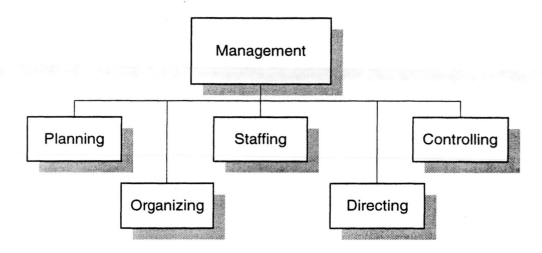

Figure 4-1. Classic management model

According to this model, management is partitioned into five separate functions or components: *planning, organizing, staffing, directing, and controlling* (see Table 4.1 for definitions or explanations of these functions). All management activities, such as budgeting, scheduling, establishing authority and responsibility relationships, training, communicating, and allocating responsibility fall under one of these five functions.

In a later edition of Koontz and O'Donnell's classic reference [Koontz, O'Donnell, and Weihrich 1980], the directing function is called "leading." The original term will be kept in this article.

Each of the five principal management *functions* can be further partitioned into a set of more detailed management *activities*. These activities can then be further divided into tasks that are more detailed. These activities are the characteristic duties of managers and can be applied to the management of any organization or project. (The definitions or explanations of these activities can be found in Tables 5.1, 6.1, 7.1, 8.1, and 9.1.)

The detailed activities and tasks particular to a software engineering project are defined and discussed in Sections 5 through 9. Each of these sections defines and discusses one of the five management functions along with some of the major issues related to that function. The management activities from Table 4.1 are partitioned into one or more levels of detailed tasks, which are then discussed and/or illustrated in the appropriate section.

5. Planning a software engineering project

5.1. Introduction and definitions

Planning a software engineering project consists of the management activities that lead to selecting, among alternatives, future courses of action for the project and a program for completing those actions.

Table 4.1. Major functions of management

Activity	Definition or explanation
Planning	Predetermining a course of action for accomplishing an objective.
Organizing	Arranging the relationships among work units for accomplishment of objectives and the granting of responsibility and authority to obtain those objectives.
Staffing	Selecting and training people for positions in the organization.
Directing	Creating an atmosphere that will assist and motivate people to achieve desired end results.
Controlling	Establishing, measuring, and evaluating performance of activities toward planned objectives.

5.2. Major issues in planning a software project

Planning thus involves specifying the *goals* and *objectives* for a project and the *strategies, policies, plans*, and *procedures* for achieving them. "Planning is deciding in advance what to do, how to do it, when to do it, and who is to do it" [Koontz and O'Donnell 1972].

Every software engineering project should start with a good plan. Uncertainties and unknowns, both within the software project environment and from external sources, make planning necessary. Planning focuses attention on project goals, actions necessary to reach those goals, and potential risks and problems that might interfere with obtaining those goals.

It is difficult to prepare software requirements that are correct, complete, and clear [Davis 1990][Faulk 1997]. As a result, the project may have incorrect or incomplete objectives. This vagueness can result in poor cost and schedule estimates, which are essential elements of a management plan.

In addition, when requirements often change drastically, cost and schedule estimates remain unchanged. This is caused by the reluctance of project managers to ask their supervisors or the customer for more resources. The failure to recognize even a minor change can have a drastic effect on cost and schedule.

More importantly, planning is often not done or is poorly done. Plans are often neglected and not updated as conditions change. Project plans are usually not deliverable items. To some managers, planning appears to be an unnecessary activity that can be discarded to save money for programming and testing. Even in Department of Defense (DoD) projects, where a planning document is usually required 30 days after award of contract, the project plan may receive only a superficial review. In many cases, it is allowed "to gather dust on a shelf" after it is produced.

Accurate budgets and schedules are hard to prepare. Most realistic cost estimates are based on past histories of cost and schedule for similar projects modified by the expected size and complexity of the proposed project. Accurate size

231

estimates are extremely difficult to obtain in the planning stage of a project. The real culprit for inaccurate estimates is lack of relevant historical data on which to base the estimates.

Many project managers do not get a chance to make a realistic attempt to create an accurate cost and schedule estimate. Outside forces, such as marketing or software contracts that have been bid too low, can establish a cost and schedule ceiling. This can be far from the probable cost of the software system. Many senior managers do not realize that forcing a low estimate will drive the cost of a software system up. This causes software developers to make many false starts trying to deliver within unrealistic low-cost goals. As a result, they lose good software engineers, who quit in frustration.

It is all right to take risks as long as the possible effect of the risks on the project, and the effect on the project if the risk becomes a problem are known. Project requirements and plans are frequently based on assumptions that are not documented or known by the responsible managers. Then, when a risk becomes a problem, it catches the development staff and management completely by surprise.

Policies are the tools of upper management. Many major corporations operate without adequate policies for developing and managing software systems. This results in a lack of control between and among project environments. For an exception, see TRW's policies in [Goldberg 1978].

5.3. Planning activities for a software project

Table 5.1 gives an outline of the planning activities that must be accomplished by software project managers. The project manager is responsible for developing numerous types of plans. Table 5.2 contains a list of general management plans that can be applicable to any software engineering project.

The balance of this section discusses and provides greater detail on the activities outlined in Table 5.1.

5.3.1. Set project objectives and goals. The first planning step for a software engineering project is determining the overall software mission, goal, objectives, and principles. There is a need to understand what the project must accomplish, when it must be accomplished, and what resources are needed.

This involves analyzing and documenting the system and software requirements. The management requirements and constraints must be determined. Management constraints are often expressed as resource and schedule limitations. Set project objectives and goals based on an understanding of desired project outcomes, such as schedule, quality, performance, and cost.

Success criteria must also be specified. Success criteria normally include delivery of a software system that satisfies the requirements, on time and within cost. However, there may be other criteria. For instance, success could include winning a follow-on contract. Other criteria might include increasing the size and scope of the present contract, or increasing the profit margin by winning an incentive award.

Success criteria might also be placed in a relative hierarchy of importance. For example, being on time might be more important than being within budget.

5.3.2. Develop project strategies. Another planning activity is to develop and document a set of management strategies (sometime called strategic policies) for a project. Strategies are defined as long-range goals and the methods to obtain those goals. These long-range goals are usually developed at a corporate level. The project manager can also have strategic plans within an individual project. This is particularly true for large projects. An example of a strategic plan might be to develop a new area of expertise or business for the organization by conducting a project in that area.

5.3.3. Develop project policies. *Policies* are predetermined management decisions. The project manager may establish policies for the project to provide guidance to supervisors and individual team members in making routine decisions. For example, a project policy might be that team leader status reports are due in the project manager's office by close of business each Thursday. Policies can reduce the need for interaction on every decision and provide a sense of direction for team members. In many cases, the project manager does not develop new policies for the project, but follows policies established at the corporate level.

Table 5.1. Planning activities for software projects

Activity	Definition or explanation
Set objectives and goals	— Determine the desired outcome for the project.
Develop strategies	— Decide major organizational goals and develop a general program of action for reaching those goals.
Develop policies	— Make standing decisions on important recurring matters to provide a guide for decision-making.
Forecast future situations	— Anticipate future events or make assumption about the future; predict future results or expectations from courses of action.
Conduct a risk assessment	— Anticipate possible adverse events and problem areas; state assumptions; develop contingency plans; predict results of possible courses of action.
Determine possible courses of action	— Develop, analyze, and/or evaluate different ways to conduct the project.
Make planning decisions	— Evaluate and select a course of action from among alternatives.
Set procedures and rules	— Establish methods, guides, and limits for accomplishing the project activity.
Develop project plans	— Establish policies, procedures, rules, tasks, schedules, and resources needed to complete the project.
Prepare budgets	— Allocate estimated costs to project functions, activities, and tasks.
Document project plans	— Record policy decisions, courses of action, budget, program plans, and contingency plans.

5.3.4. Forecast future situations. Determining future courses of action will be based on the current status and environment as well as the project manager's vision of the future. The project manager is responsible for forecasting situations that might impact the software project.

Forecasting is addressed in two steps. The first step is predicting the future environment of the project: the second involves the project's response to that prediction. Step one involves the prediction of future events such as availability of personnel, inflation rate, availability of new computer hardware, and the impact these events will have on the project.

The second step involves predicting the results of a project, such as the specification of future expenditures of project resources and funds on the future environment. The project manager is also responsible for estimating risks and developing contingency plans for countering those risks.

Table 5.2. Types of plans for software projects

Types of plans	Definition or explanation
Objectives	— The project goals toward which activities are directed.
Strategic	— The overall approach to a project that provides guidance for placing emphasis and using resources to achieve the project objectives.
Policies	— Directives that guide decision-making and project activities. Policies limit the freedom in making decisions but allow for some discretion.
Procedures	— Directives that specify customary methods of handling activities; guides to actions rather than decision-making. Procedures detail the exact manner in which a project activity must be accomplished and allow very little discretion.
Rules	— Requirements for specific and definite actions to be taken or not taken with respect to particular project situations. No discretion is allowed.
Plans	— An interrelated set of goals, objectives, policies, procedures, rules, work assignments, resources to be used, and other elements necessary to conduct a software project.
Budget	— A statement of constraints on resources, expressed in quantitative terms such as dollars or staff hours.

5.3.5. Conduct a project risk assessment. *Risk* is the likelihood of a specified hazardous or undesirable event occurring within a specified period or circumstance. The concept of risk has two elements: the frequency or probability that a specified hazard might occur and the consequences of it occurring. Risk factors must be identified and forecasts of situations that might adversely impact the software project must be prepared [Fairley and Rook 1997]. For example, if, for a particular project, the software cannot be developed for the amount specified in the contract, the development company would lose profit.

Contingency plans specify the actions to be taken should a risk (a potential problem) become a real problem. The risk becomes a problem when a predetermined risk-indicator metric crosses a predetermined threshold. For example, the budget has been overrun by 12 percent at software specifications review (SSR). The preset threshold metric was 10 percent; therefore, the appropriate contingency plan must be put in effect [Boehm 1987].

5.3.6. Determine possible courses of action. In most projects, there is more than one way to conduct the project—but not with equal cost, equal schedule, or equal risk. It is the project manager's responsibility to examine various approaches that could achieve the project objectives and satisfy the success criteria. For example, should you build the software system in-house, contract to build it, or buy an off-the-shelf copy? Can you reuse existing parts of another system? What is the "go/no go" point?

If this is an acquisition project, the acquisition manager will identify and select vendors and subcontractors.

One approach might be very costly in terms of personnel and machines yet reduce the schedule dramatically. Another approach might reduce both schedule and cost but take a severe risk of being unable to deliver a satisfactory system. A third approach might be to stretch the schedule, thereby reducing the cost of the project. The manager must examine each course of action to determine advantages, disadvantages, risks, and benefits. (See paper by Boehm [1987] for a description of a software development life-cycle model that incorporates risk-analysis and decision making.)

5.3.7. Make project planning decisions. The project manager, in consultation with higher-level management, the customer, and other appropriate parties is responsible for selecting the best course of action for meeting project goals and objectives. The project manager is responsible for making trade-off decisions involving cost, schedule, design strategies, and risks [Bunyard and Coward 1982].

The project manager contributes to product plan development (for example, schedule, market segment, market growth, launch, competitive analysis, funding success criteria, organizations, and pricing).

The project manager is also responsible for approving the methods and tools, both technical and managerial, with which the project will be managed and the product developed. For example, will the requirements be documented using "structured analysis" methods or Coad's "Object-Oriented Analysis" charts? Will testing be done top-down, bottom-up, or both? Which tools, techniques, and procedures will be used in planning the development schedule: PERT, CPM, workload chart, work breakdown chart (WBS), or Gantt chart? [Cori 1985]

5.3.8. Set project procedures and rules. The project manager establishes procedures and rules for the project. Unlike policies, *procedures* establish customary methods and provide detailed guidance for project activities. Procedures detail the exact manner in which to accomplish an activity. For example, there may be a procedure for conducting design reviews.

In another contrast, a *rule* establishes specific and definite actions to be taken or not taken with respect to a given situation. A rule allows no discretion. For example, a rule might require two people to be on duty in the machine room at all times.

Process standards (in contrast to *product standards*) can be used to establish procedures. Process standards may be adopted from the corporate standards or written for a particular project. Process standards might cover topics such as reporting methods, reviews, and documentation preparation requirements.

5.3.9. Develop a software project plan. A project plan specifies all of the actions necessary to successfully deliver a software product.

Typically, the plan specifies

- the *tasks* to be performed by the software development staff in order to deliver the final software product. This usually requires partitioning the project activities into small, well-specified tasks. A useful tool for representing the partitioned project is the work breakdown structure (WBS).

- the *cost* and resources necessary to accomplish each project task [Boehm 1984].

- the project *schedule* that specifies dependencies among tasks and establishes project milestones.

Other plans are

- retirement plan (for example, criteria, notifications, archiving, residual support, transition to a new product, disposal, and accessibility to archived data)

- disaster recovery plan (for example, backups, replications, or mirror sites)

For further discussion on project planning, see [Miller 1978].

5.3.10. Prepare project budgets. *Budgeting* is the process of placing cost figures on the project plan. The project manager is responsible for determining the cost of the project and allocating the budget to project tasks. Cost is the common denominator for all project plan elements. Requirements for personnel, computers, travel, office space, equipment, and so forth can only be compared and cost tradeoffs made when these requirements are measured in terms of their monetary value.

5.3.11. Document project plans. Document and maintain project plans (for example, schedule, budget, work activities, allocations, policy decisions, contingency plans, start up, and closeout). The project manager is responsible for documenting the project plan [Fairley 1987] and for preparing other plans such as the software quality assurance plan, software configuration management plan, staffing plan, and test plan. The project plan is the primary means of communicating with other entities that interface with the project.

6. Organizing a software engineering project

6.1. Introduction and definitions

Organizing a software engineering project involves developing an effective and efficient organizational structure for assigning and completing project tasks and establishing authority and responsibility relationships among tasks.

Organizing involves itemizing the project activities required to achieve project objectives and arranging these activities into logical clusters. It also involves assigning groups of activities to various organizational entities and delegating responsibility and authority needed to carry out the activities. Organizing also involves planning the organizational interfaces between the project and other stakeholders (such as the customer, hardware, users, and contracts).

The purpose of an organizational structure is to "focus the efforts of many on a selected goal." [Donnelly, Gibson, and Ivancevich 1975]

6.2. Major issues in organizing

It is difficult to determine the best organizational structure for a project and for the organization conducting the project. According to Youker [1977], there is a spectrum of organizational techniques for software projects, ranging from the functional format, to the matrix format, to the project format. The project format creates centralized control and makes the project manager responsible for all aspects of the project. Conversely, the functional organization distributes authority and control of a project among the functional elements involved.

The matrix organization incorporates elements of the project and functional formats. Project managers are given authority over the project, and project members are drawn from their functional "homes" and assigned to the project for its duration. In a matrix structure, conflicts can arise between the project manager, who is responsible for the project, and the functional managers, who provide the software engineers. Matrix structures require special attention to overcome this "two-boss" phenomenon.

Software developers and many managers are frequently unsupportive of the matrix organizational structure. Software developers are not enthusiastic about the matrix because they are always being treated as "temporary" help and are rarely given responsibility for system delivery. Functional managers, especial long-time employees, view the new matrix organizations as usurping the power and authority they had under the functional project structure.

Papers by Stuckenbruck [1982], Youker [1977], and Mantei [1981] provide criteria for selecting the appropriate organizational structure for a software project. Both Stuckenbruck and Youker indicate the need for top management to provide a clear charter for the matrix organization. This charter must define the responsibilities and authority of the project manager and the functional departments.

The last issue is over the role of the team leader. A team is a group of 5 to 15 software engineers working together toward a common goal. The team is headed by a team leader. Team leaders are generally senior project personnel with responsibility and authority for developing an assigned part of the overall software product. Unfortunately, top-level managers sometimes expect team leaders to do "their share" of the technical effort in addition to managing the team. This, of course, has a major impact on team leaders' management functions.

6.3. Organizing a software project

Table 6.1 outlines the activities a project manager must accomplish when organizing a project. The remainder of this section gives greater detail about these activities.

6.3.1. Identify and group project tasks. The manager is responsible for reviewing the project requirements, defining the various tasks to be accomplished, and sizing and grouping those tasks into logical entities. Titles and organizational entities are assigned to the task groups (for example, analysis tasks, design tasks, coding tasks, and testing tasks), enabling the project manager to select an organizational structure to control these groups. See Table 6.2 for an example of task identification and grouping.

The project manager must also identify the supporting tasks needed, both internal and external to the project. Examples of internal tasks are secretarial or word processing support, financial monitoring, project administration, and project control. External to the project, there may be tasks associated with travel requirements, motor pools, security guards, computer operation support, and so on.

6.3.2. Select an organizational structure for the project. After identifying and grouping project tasks, the project manager must select an organizational structure. A software development project can be organized using one of several overlapping organizational types. For example,

- *conventional organization structure*—line or staff organization,

- *project organization structure*—functional, project, or matrix,

- *team structure*—egoless, chief programmer, or hierarchical.

Table 6.1. Organizing activities for software project

Activity	Definition or explanation
Identify and group project function, activities, and tasks	— Define, size, and categorize the project work.
Select organizational structures	— Select appropriate structures to accomplish the project and to monitor, control, communicate, and coordinate.
Create organizational positions	— Establish title, job description, and job relationships for each project role.
Define responsibilities and authority	— Define responsibilities for each organizational position and the authority to be granted for fulfillment of those responsibilities.
Establish position qualifications	— Define qualifications for each position.
Document organizational decisions	— Document titles, positions, job descriptions, responsibilities, authorities, relationships, and position qualifications.

The project manager may not have the luxury of selecting the best project organizational type, because this may be determined by corporate policy. Regardless of who selects the organizational structure, it should match the needs and goals of the project, and the project environment should facilitate communication among organizational entities.

The following paragraphs describe these organizational considerations.

6.3.2.1. Conventional organizational structures. A *line* organization has the responsibility and authority to perform the work that represents the primary mission of the larger organizational unit. In contrast, a *staff* organization is a group of functional experts that has responsibility and authority to perform special activities that help the line organization do its work. All organizations in a company are either line or staff. Figure 6.1 illustrates a line organization, and is the organizational structure for the example in Table 6.2. (This could just as well be a staff organization depending on the major activities and mission of the general management structure.)

Table 6.2. Software engineering project tasks that have been grouped and assigned an organizational entity

Project tasks	Organizational entity
Determine software system requirements.	*Software system engineering*
Partition and allocate software requirements to software components.	
Develop software architectural design.	
Identify and schedule tasks to be done.	
Establish and maintain external and internal interfaces.	
Control the software development process.	
Verify and validate the software process and product.	
Analyze software components for product 1 requirements.	*Software engineering applications group 1*
Design components of product 1.	
Implement product 1 software components.	
Prepare documents.	
Support verification and validation.	
Same tasks and activities as defined for product 1.	*Software engineering applications group 2*
Prepare software verification and validation plan.	*Software verification and validation*
Conduct verification and validation activities.	
Prepare and support software testing.	
Establish software quality assurance plan.	*Software quality assurance*
Conduct software quality activities.	
Document results of software quality activities.	

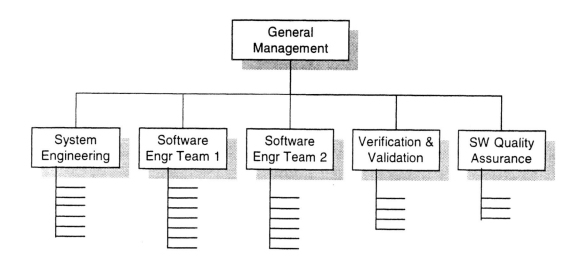

Figure 6.1. A line organization in a software development organization

6.3.2.2. Software project structures. A project structure is a temporary organizational form established to develop and build a system that is too big to be done by one person or, at most, a few people. In a software engineering project, the system to be built is a software system. A project structure can be superimposed on a line or staff organization.

Functional project organization. A functional organization is a project structure built around a software engineering function or group of similar functions. A project is accomplished either within a functional unit or, if multifunctional, by two or more functional units. The project is accomplished by passing the work products from function to function as the project passes through the life-cycle phases. Figure 6.2 illustrates the tasks and lines of authority of a functional organization used to develop a software product.

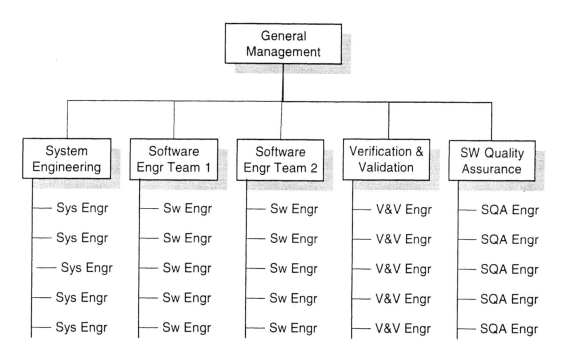

Figure 6.2. Functional project organization

239

In Figure 6.2, the software requirements specifications are prepared by the *software systems engineering group* under the supervision of the group leader. When finished, the system engineering group transfers the requirement specifications to the *software engineering applications group* that is most familiar with the application. The software engineering applications group, using the requirement specifications, designs the software system under the supervision of their group leader. In Figure 6.2, the applications group also programs the software system and then passes the finished code to the *software verification and validation (V&V) engineering group* for testing. Software quality assurance (SQA) is provided as an oversight by the *software quality assurance group*. There is no single supervisor over the whole project, but there is generally a project coordinator or customer and/or user liaison.

The customer and/or user liaison does not supervise the staff or control the project. The project coordinator does not usually have the responsibility for hiring, discharging, training, or promoting people within the project. The user liaison coordinates the project, monitors the progress (reporting to top management when things do not go according to plan), and acts as a common interface with the user.

Project organization. Another type of project organization is built around specific projects, and project managers are given the responsibility, authority, and resources for conducting the projects [Middleton, 1967]. (Project organization is sometimes called a *projected* organization to get away from the term "project project organization."). The manager must meet project goals within the resources of the organization. The project manager usually has the responsibility for hiring, discharging, training, and promoting people within the project. Figure 6.3 illustrates the tasks and lines of authority of a project organization. Note that the software project manager has total control over the project and the assigned software personnel.

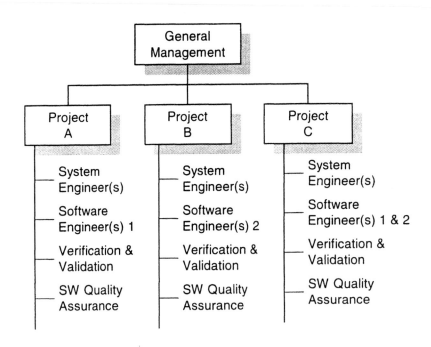

Figure 6.3. Project organization

Matrix project organization. The matrix organization (sometimes called matrix project organization) is a composite of the functional organization and the project organization [Stuckenbruck 1981]. The project manager is given responsibility and authority for completing the project, and the functional managers provide the resources needed to conduct the project. In a matrix organization, the project manager usually does not have the authority to hire, discharge, train, or promote personnel within the project. Figure 6.4 illustrates the tasks and lines of authority in a matrix organization. Engineers labeled "A" are temporarily assigned to Project A, engineers labeled "B" are temporarily assigned to Project B, and engineers labeled "C" are temporarily assigned to Project C.

In Figure 6.4, a project manager supervises each project and its functional workers. Typically, the software project manager is responsible for the day-to-day supervision of the software project members and the functional manager is responsible for the career, training, and well being of those people.

Since each individual worker is "supervised" by two separate managers, the system is sometimes called the "two-boss" system.

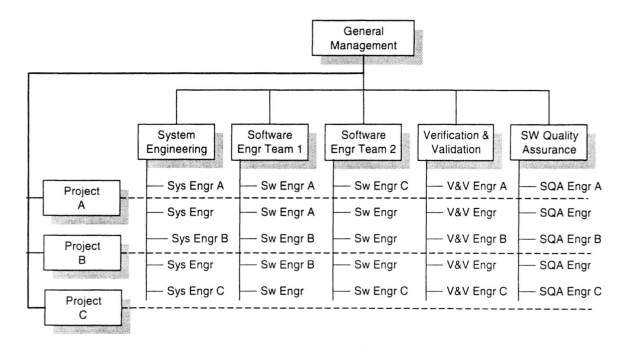

Figure 6.4. Matrix project organization

6.3.2.3. Software project teams. Within the larger organizational structures discussed above, a software development project is typically organized around a number of software engineering teams. These teams usually consist of five to seven members. Examples of structures for these teams include *egoless programming teams, chief programmer teams,* and *hierarchical teams* [Mantei 1981].

Egoless programming team. The egoless team (also know as the democratic team) structure was introduced by Gerald Weinberg [Weinberg 1971]. An egoless team typically consists of 10 or 12 members. Decisions are made by consensus. Group leadership responsibility rotates; there is no permanent central authority.

Chief programmer team. The chief programmer team was first used by IBM in the now-famous New York Times Morgue Project [Baker 1972]. The team consists of three or four permanently assigned team members—chief programmer, backup programmer, and program librarian—plus other auxiliary programmers and/or analysts who are added as needed. The chief programmer manages all technical aspects and makes all managerial and technical decisions. The librarian maintains all documents, code, and data, and performs all administrative work [Cooke 1976].

Hierarchical team. A hierarchical structure (also know as controlled decentralized) team is a structured organization in which the project leaders manage senior engineers (programmers) and senior engineers (programmers) manage junior engineers (programmers). The project team is called a hierarchical structure team because of its top-down flow of authority.

In today's environment, egoless and chief programming teams are seldom used. Egoless teams can sometimes be found in research organizations. Chief programmer teams, after a flurry of use in the 1970s, are seldom found because of the difficulties in recruiting and training "chief programmers." Therefore, the most used method is the hierarchical team (usually called a project team).

One of the cardinal rules of project management is that on any team of five or more individuals, the team leader (manager) is a full-time job; thus, the team leader should not be expected to carry any share of the "technical" work.

6.3.2.4. Strengths and weaknesses of the project organization types. In selecting an organizational structure, it is important that the needs of the project be matched to the various strengths and weaknesses of the organization type. Table 6.3 displays the advantages and disadvantages of the six organizational types.

The software engineering project is either a *line* or *staff* organization. The project manager must decide whether the project will operate as a functional, project, or matrix organization and whether the project will use egoless, chief programmer, or project team types. The chief programmer and egoless teams are seldom used, but the librarian concept from the chief programmer team and the egoless technical reviews (walk-throughs) are frequently used by software engineering project teams.

Most software engineering projects in the aerospace industry use the matrix organization with project teams.

6.3.3. Create organizational position for the software project. Once the tasks are identified, sized, and grouped, and the organizational structure has been specified, the project manager must create job titles and position descriptions, with which to recruit personnel for the project. Some short examples of typical software engineering titles and position descriptions are listed below [High Technology Career Magazine 1996]:

- *Project managers.* Responsible for system development and implementation within major functional areas. Direct the efforts of software engineers, analysts, programmers, and other project personnel.

- *Software system engineers.* Design and develop software to drive computer systems. Develop firmware, drivers, and specialized software such as graphics, communications controllers, operating systems, and user-friendly interfaces. Work closely with hardware engineers and applications and systems programmers. Requires understanding of all aspects of the product.

- *Scientific/engineering programmers, programmer-analysts.* Perform detailed program design, coding, testing, debugging, and documentation of scientific/engineering computer applications and other applications that are mathematical in nature. May assist in overall system specification and design.

- *Software verification and validation engineers.* Able to develop independent V&V plans, procedures, and tools. Able to develop test procedures and develop test cases for real-time and non-real-time software systems.

- *Software quality assurance engineers.* Able to develop software development procedures and standards. Conducts audits of software systems and overview tests. Will work closely with independent V&V teams.

6.3.4. Define responsibilities and authority. *Responsibility* is the obligation to fulfill commitments. *Authority* is the right to make decisions and exert power. It is often stated that authority can be delegated, but responsibility cannot. Koontz and O'Donnell [1976] support this view by defining responsibility as "the obligation owed by subordinates to their supervisors for exercising authority delegated to them in a way to accomplish results expected." Responsibility and authority for organizational activities or tasks should be assigned to the organizational position at the time it is created or modified. The project manager is assigned and in turn assigns responsibilities and the corresponding authorities to the various organizational positions within the project.

242

Table 6.3. Strengths and weaknesses of organizational models for software projects

Functional project organization	
Strengths	**Weaknesses**
• Organization already exists (quick start-up and phase-down).	• No central position of responsibility or authority for the project.
• Recruiting, training, and retention of functional specialists are easier.	• Interface problems are difficult to solve.
• Policies, procedures, standards, methods, tools, and techniques are already established.	• Projects are difficult to monitor and control.
Project organization	
Strengths	**Weaknesses**
• A central position of responsibility and authority for the project.	• Organization must be formed for each new project.
• Central control over all system interfaces.	• Recruiting, training, and retention of functional specialists may be more difficult than for functional format.
• Decisions can be made quickly.	• Policies, procedures, standards, methods, tools, and techniques must be developed for each project.
• Staff motivation is typically high.	

6.3.5. Establish position qualifications. Position qualifications must be identified for each position in the project. Position qualifications are established by considering such issues as the types of individuals you need for your project; the amount of experience necessary in the application area; the level of education required (for example, a BS in computer science and an MS in artificial intelligence); the amount of training required, either before or after the project is initiated; and the programming languages the applicant should know (such as Fortran or Lisp). Proper and accurate position qualifications will allow the manager to correctly staff the project.

Some short examples of typical position qualifications for software engineering titles and positions are illustrated below.

- *Project managers.* Background in successful systems implementation, advanced industrial knowledge, awareness of current computer technology, intimate understanding of user operations and problems, and proven management ability. Minimum requirements are four years of significant system development and project management experience.

- *Software system engineers.* Seven years experience in aerospace applications designing real-time control systems for embedded computers. Experience with Ada preferred. BS in computer science, engineering, or related discipline.

- *Scientific/engineering programmers, programmer-analysts.* Three years experience in programming aerospace applications, control systems, and/or graphics. One-year minimum with FORTRAN,

- assembly, or C programming languages. Large-scale or mini/micro hardware exposure and system software programming experience desired. Minimum requirements include undergraduate engineering or math degree.

- *Verification and validation engineer.* Minimum of three years experiences in one or more aspects of V&V for real-time systems. Must be able to work independently of the development teams. MS in software engineering preferred. Salary commensurate with experience.

- *Software quality assurance engineer.* Minimum of three years experiences working in a software QA environment. Some CM experience desirable. BS or MS in computer science with specialty in software engineering. Travel required.

**Table 6.3. Strengths and weaknesses of organizational
models for software projects (continued)**

Matrix project organization	
Strengths	**Weaknesses**
• Improved central position of responsibility and authority compared to functional format.	• Responsibility for and authority over individual project members is shared between two or more managers, unlike project or functional formats.
• Interfaces between functions can be controlled more easily than in functional format.	• Too easy to move people from one project to another, unlike project or functional formats.
• Recruiting, training, and retention may be easier than in project format.	• More organizational coordination is required than in project or functional formats.
• Easier to start and end a project than in project format.	• Greater competition for resources among projects than in project or functional formats.
• Policies, procedures, standards, methods, tools, and techniques are already established, unlike project organization.	
• More flexible use of people than in project or functional formats.	

6.3.6. Document organizational structures. Lines of authority, tasks, and responsibilities should be documented in the project plan. Justifications for decisions must be well documented and made available to guide project staffing.

7. Staffing a software engineering project

7.1. Introduction and definitions

Staffing a software engineering project consists of all the management activities that involve filling (and keeping filled) the positions that were established in the project organizational structure. This includes selecting candidates for the positions and training or otherwise developing them to accomplish their tasks effectively. Staffing also involves terminating project personnel when necessary.

Staffing is not the same as organizing. Staffing involves filling the roles created in the project organizational structure through selection, training, and development of personnel. The objective of staffing is to ensure that project roles are filled by personnel who are qualified (both technically and temperamentally) to occupy them.

7.2. Major issues in staffing

It is common practice today to use programmers and software engineers who have excelled at their technical activities as project managers. Unfortunately, success as a software developer (for example, a software engineer, programmer, or tester) does not always indicate a potential as a project manager. Compounding this problem is the lack of training in project management techniques and procedures that can be made available to these budding project managers.

A major issue in staffing a project with capable people is that programming and software engineering skills vary greatly from individual to individual. Sackman and others proved that the difference in productivity among programmers was as high as 26 to 1 [H. Sackman et al. 1968]. In his book, *Software Engineering Economics*, Boehm [1981] reports differences as high as 4 to 1 in productivity due to personnel and/or team capability. This inability to accurately predict the productivity of individuals in a project undermines our ability to accurately estimate the cost and schedule of software projects.

Experience is a valuable commodity in a software development activity. Unfortunately, obtaining this experience is hampered by the constant turnover of project personnel. When there are people shortages, companies raid their rivals' personnel, resulting in the movement of people from one company to another and from one project to another. The use of the matrix organizational project format, discussed in the previous section, encourages the movement of software people from one project to another as priorities change within a company. In addition, many software people recognize that the only way to get a raise is to look for and accept a position in a different company (always good for a 10-percent raise). All this turnover makes a major impact on the ability of software projects to deliver the system on time, within cost, and within the system requirements.

Training in the techniques and sciences to be applied to an assigned job is a necessary element of staffing. To ensure that training is properly applied to meet the short- and long-term needs of the individual and the organization, individual training plans are needed. Training plans are agreements between individuals and their managers as to what training (courses, seminars, study groups, tuition support) the organization will provide. In many, if not most organizations, these plans are not realized, leaving the pairing of individuals and appropriate courses to a rather ad hoc approach.

Universities are not producing sufficient numbers of software engineers. Most of the computer science programs in the United States are turning out theoretical computer scientists at best, or merely programmers (coders) at worst. Most industry personnel and others involved in hiring new college graduates seek graduates of computer science programs who have education and experience in developing software systems—that is, software engineering skills [McGill 1984].

7.3. Staffing a software project

Table 7.1 outlines the activities and tasks that must be accomplished by project managers to staff their projects. The remainder of this section provides greater detail on the activities and tasks outlined in Table 7.1.

Table 7.1. Staffing activities for software projects

Activity	Definition or explanation
Fill organizational positions	— Select, recruit, or promote qualified people for each project position.
Assimilate newly assigned personnel	— Orient and familiarize new people with the organization, facilities, and tasks to be done on the project.
Educate or train personnel	— Make up deficiencies in position qualifications through training and education.
Provide for general development	— Improve knowledge, attitudes, and skills of project personnel.
Evaluate and appraise personnel	— Record and analyze the quantity and quality of project work as the basis for personnel evaluations. Set performance goals and appraise personnel periodically.
Compensate	— Provide wages, bonuses, benefits, or other financial remuneration commensurate with project responsibilities and performance.
Terminate assignments	— Transfer or separate project personnel as necessary.
Document staffing decisions	— Record staffing plans, training and training plans, appraisal records, and compensations recommendations.

7.3.1. Fill organizational positions in a software project. The project manager is responsible for filling the positions that were established during organizational planning for the project. In staffing any software project, the following factors should be considered.

- *Education.* Does the candidate have the minimum level of education for the job? Does the candidate have the proper education for future growth in the company?

- *Experience.* Does the candidate have an acceptable level of experience? Is it the right type and variety of experience?

- *Training.* Is the candidate trained in the language, methodology, and equipment to be used, and in the application area of the software system?

- *Motivation.* Is the candidate motivated to do the job, work for the project, work for the company, and take on the assignment?

- *Commitment.* Will the candidate demonstrate loyalty to the project, the company, and to the decisions made? [Powell and Posner 1984]

- *Self-motivation.* Is the candidate a self-starter, willing to carry a task through to the end without excessive direction?

- *Group affinity.* Does the candidate fit in with the current staff? Are there potential conflicts that need to be solved?

- *Intelligence.* Does the candidate have the capability to learn, to take difficult assignments, and to adapt to changing environments?

Deficiencies in any of these factors can be offset by strengths in other factors. For example, deficiencies in education can be offset by better experience, a particular type of training, or enthusiasm for the job. Serious deficiencies should be cause for corrective action.

7.3.1.1. Sources of qualified project individuals. One source of qualified individuals is the project itself. It is the project manager's prerogative to move people from one task to another within a project. Another source is other projects within the organization. Transfers can be done anytime but they often occur when another software engineering project is either phasing down or is canceled.

Other sources of qualified personnel are new hires from other companies through such methods as job fairs, referrals, headhunters, want ads, and unsolicited resumes. New college graduates can be recruited either through on-campus interviews or through referrals from recent graduates who are now company employees.

If the project manager is unable to obtain qualified individuals to fill positions, one option is to hire unqualified but motivated individuals and train them for those vacancies.

7.3.1.2. Selecting a productive software staff. Two metrics may indicate a productive software staff:

- *Amount of experience.* An experienced staff is more productive than an inexperienced staff [Boehm 1984]. Some of the best experience comes from having worked on software projects similar to the project being staffed.

- *Diversity of experience.* Diversity of experience is a reasonable predictor of productivity [Kruesi 1982]. It is better that the individuals under consideration have done well in several jobs over a period of time than one job for the same time period.

Other qualities indicative of a highly productive individual are communications skills (both oral and written), a college degree (usually in a technical field), self-motivation, and experience in the project's application area.

7.3.2. Assimilate newly assigned software personnel. The manager is responsible not only for hiring the people but also for familiarizing them with any project procedures, facilities, and plans necessary to assure their effective integration into the project. In short, the project manager is responsible for introducing new employees to the company and the company to the employees.

Many large companies have formal orientation programs, with many lasting several days. Orientation programs include the features and history of the company, the products or services that are the main sources of revenue for the company, general policies and procedures, organizational structure, company benefits, and the availability of in-company service organizations.

7.3.3. Educate or train personnel as necessary. It is not always possible to recruit or transfer employees with exactly those skills needed for a particular project. Therefore, the manager is responsible for educating and training the personnel to ensure that they can meet the project requirements.

Education differs from training. *Education* involves teaching the basics, theory, and underlying concepts of a discipline with a view toward a long-term payoff. *Training* means teaching a skill, such as how to use, operate, or make something. The skill is typically needed in the near future and has a short-term payoff.

For example, managers should be educated in the management sciences and business techniques. They should be trained in management techniques and administrative duties. Engineers, on the other hand, are educated in science, physics, and mathematics, but must be trained in the application domain. Everyone must be familiar with the procedures, tools, techniques, and equipment they operate and use.

Training methods include on-the-job training, formal company courses, courses through local universities and schools [Mills 1980], self-study, and in-house lectures.

Each individual within an organization must have a *training plan* that specifies career education and training goals and the steps the individual will take to achieve those goals. To be successful, top management must actively support training programs.

Another technique is retraining into software engineering (sometimes called "retreading") of long-time, valuable employees with somewhat obsolete skills. Two organizations that have used this technique are the Israel Aircraft Industry [Ben-David, et al. 1984] and Lockheed Missiles & Space Company [McGill 1984].

7.3.4. Provide for general development of the project staff. In addition to education and training, the project manager must ensure that the project staff grows with the project and company. The manager must ensure that their professional knowledge will increase and that they maintain a positive attitude toward the project, the company, and the customers.

One of the purposes of providing general development for the employee is to improve organizational effectiveness. For example, local university courses and degree programs in any worthwhile skill, funded by the company, will improve employee morale, aid in employee retention, and broaden the skill base available to the company. Even indirect skills such as typing and communication should be enhanced.

7.3.5. Evaluate and appraise project personnel. The project manager is also responsible for periodically evaluating and appraising personnel. An appraisal provides feedback to staff members concerning the positive and negative aspects of their performance. This feedback allows the staff member to strengthen good qualities and improve those that are negative. Appraisals should be done at regular intervals and should concentrate on the individual's performance and not on personality, unless personality issues interfere with performance [Moneysmith 1984].

One well-known evaluation technique that is applicable to project management is "management by objectives" [Maslow 1954]. At the beginning of the appraisal period, the individual and the project manager establish a set of verifiable objectives that the individual believes he or she can meet over the next reporting period. These measurable objectives are a verifiable goal that will form the basis of the next appraisal. This approach is superior to evaluation by personal traits and work characteristics, such as promptness, neatness, punctuality, and golf scores.

7.3.6. Compensate the project personnel. The manager (sometimes directly, sometimes indirectly) is responsible for determining the salary scale and benefits of project personnel. Benefits take on many forms. Most benefits are monetary or can be equated to money. These include stock options, a company car, first-class tickets for all company trips, or a year-end bonus. Some benefits are nonmonetary but appeal to the individual's self-esteem. Examples are military combat medals, a reserved parking place at the company plant, or an impressive title on the door.

7.3.7. Terminate project assignments. The project manager is not only responsible for hiring people, but must also terminate assignments as necessary. "Terminate" includes reassignment of personnel at the end of a successful project (a pleasant termination) and dismissal of personnel due to project cancellation (an unpleasant termination). Termination also includes firing an employee if that person is determined to be unsatisfactory [Davis 1997].

Termination is important. Poor performers are not just failing to pull their weight, they frequently hurt the morale of others on the project. Management may be seen as ineffective if poor performers are not dealt with. Other people resent it when another team member regularly shows up late or misses deadlines.

7.3.8. Document project staffing decisions. Project managers should document their staffing plan and evaluation and training policies for all to read. Each individual within an organization should have a personal training plan reflecting course work needed and progress made. Other staffing documents that might be produced include orientation plans and schedules, salary schedules, and promotion policies. The project manager and each employee should have a copy of the employee's annual performance objectives signed by both individuals.

8. Directing a software engineering project

8.1. Introduction and definitions

Directing a software engineering project consists of the management activities that involve motivational and interpersonal aspects by which project personnel come to understand and contribute to the achievement of project goals. Once subordinates are trained and oriented, the project manager has a continuing responsibility to clarify their assignments, guiding them toward improved performance, and motivating them to work with enthusiasm and confidence toward project goals.

Directing, like staffing, involves people. Directing is sometimes considered synonymous with leading (compare reference [Koontz and O'Donnell 1972] with reference [Koontz, O'Donnell, and Weihrich 1984]). Directing a project involves providing leadership and day-to-day supervision of personnel, delegating authority, coordinating activities, facilitating communications, resolving conflicts, managing change, and documenting important decisions.

8.2. Major issues in directing a software project

One of the major goals of software engineering is to improve communication among the many organizations that are involved in developing a software system. Most software engineering documents are written in English, which is notoriously imprecise and ambiguous. Research in software engineering is concerned with developing tools and techniques that will ease communication of requirements specifications, design documents, and other software engineering documents.

Most software engineers are well paid, work in pleasant surroundings, and are reasonably satisfied with their position in life. According to Maslow's hierarchy of unfulfilled needs, the average software engineer is high on the ladder of satisfied needs [Maslow 1954]. Most software engineers are at the "esteem and recognition" level and occasionally reach the "self-actualization" level. At this level, money alone is not a strong motivator. As a result, management is faced with the issue of how to motivate software engineers to produce more and better software (called *software psychology* in some circles), since money cannot do it alone.

The opportunity to use modern tools and techniques is a strong motivator for many software engineers. *Technology transfer* is defined as the time interval between the development of a new product, tool or technique and its use by consumers. In their paper, Redwine and Riddle [1985] estimated that this time could be on the order of 15 to 18 years. The cause of this technology transfer gap can be seen from two viewpoints:

- The leadership team may be reluctant to introduce unfamiliar methods and tools because it may increase the risks to their projects.

- The use of unfamiliar methods and tools may make it more difficult for the leadership team to estimate project cost and schedule.

A plan for improving technology transfer is discussed in paragraph 8.3.8, *Manage change.*

Software developers are discouraged by the seeming lack of understanding on the part of managers and customers of the software development process. Software engineering is one of the most difficult jobs in the world today. There are no small or easy software jobs or changes. Software engineers under pressure to hurry up and finish that "simple change" become discouraged and may eventually "burn out" [Cherlin 1981].

8.3. Directing the project team. Table 8.1 provides an outline of leadership activities and tasks that must be accomplished by project managers and team leaders. The remainder of this section discusses and provides greater detail on the activities outlined in Table 8.1.

8.3.1. Provide leadership to the project team. The project manager provides leadership to the project team by interpreting plans and requirements to ensure that everybody on the project team is working toward common goals.

Leadership results from the power of the leader and his or her ability to guide and influence individuals. The project manager's power can be derived from his or her leadership position. This is called *positional power*. The project manager's power can also be derived from his or her own "charm," sometimes called *charisma*. This is called *personal power*.

A good leader can align the personal goals of subordinates with the project's organizational goals. Problems can arise when a project manager who has only positional power comes into conflict with a subordinate who has personal power over project members. For a discussion of different uses of power by managers, see [Boyatzis 1971].

8.3.2. Supervise project personnel. The project manager is responsible for overseeing the project members' work and providing day-to-day supervision of the personnel assigned to the project. It is the project manager's responsibility to provide guidance and, when necessary, discipline project members to ensure that they fulfill their assigned duties.

Supervisory responsibilities can involve such mundane tasks as "clocking in" the employees at the beginning of the work day, approving vacation time, reprimanding an individual for a missed appointment, or approving a deviation from company policy. At other times, the project manager can provide a crucial decision on a software design approach, make a well-reasoned argument to top management that results in procurement of better tools and work space, or be a sympathetic listener to a project member's personal problems.

8.3.3. Delegate authority to the appropriate project members. The software engineering project manager is also responsible for delegating authority to the project staff. Tasks are assigned to subgroups, teams, and individuals, and authority is delegated to these teams so that they can accomplish their tasks in an efficient and effective manner. Typically, a good project manager will always delegate authority down through the lowest possible level of the project [Raudsepp 1981].

The proper delegation of the right kind of authority can free managers from time-consuming, routine supervision and decisions, thus enabling them to concentrate on the important aspects of the project. The project manager should ensure that individual project members understand what authority is delegated for what responsibility. Project members should also clearly understand the scope, limitations, and purpose of the delegation.

8.3.4. Motivate project personnel. The project manager is responsible for motivating and inspiring personnel to do their best. Several motivational techniques from mainstream management are applicable to software engineering projects, such as management by objective, Maslow's hierarchy of needs [Maslow 1954], Herzberg's hygiene factors [Herzberg, Mausner, and Snyderman 1959], and sometimes just the manager's charisma. The project manager should always acknowledge the special needs of the highly qualified, technically trained engineers and scientists who staff the project. Dollars will attract good software engineers to a company; dollars will not keep them. For more discussion of motivating software development personnel, see [Fitz-enz 1978]. For another paper with a unique method of motivating software people, see [Powell and Posner 1984].

The motivational models and techniques from Table 8.2 have been developed over the past 50 years and should be familiar to project managers. The following paragraphs describe several of these motivation techniques:

8.3.4.1. McGregor's Theories X and Y. McGregor presented two theories concerning human nature called Theory X and Theory Y [McGregor 1960]. It should be noted that contrary to popular belief, McGregor did not favor one view over the other. He did not say that Theory Y was a better view than Theory X, only that there were two theories.

Theory X assumptions:

- Human beings have an inherent dislike for work and will avoid it if they can.

- Because of this dislike for work, most people must be coerced, controlled, directed, and threatened with punishment to get them to put adequate effort toward the achievement of organizational objectives.

- Human beings prefer to be directed, wish to avoid responsibility, have relatively little ambition, and want security above all.

Theory Y assumptions:

- The expenditure of physical and mental effort in work is as natural as in play or rest.

- External control and the threat of punishment are not the only means of achieving organizational objectives. People will exercise self-direction and self-control in the attainment of objectives to which they are committed.

- Commitment to objectives is a function of the rewards associated with their achievement.

- Motivated human beings not only accept responsibility but will also seek it.

Table 8.1. Directing activities for software projects

Activity	Definition or explanation
Provide leadership	— Create an environment in which project members can accomplish their assignments with enthusiasm and confidence.
Supervise personnel	— Provide day-to-day instruction, guidance, and discipline to help project members fulfill their assigned duties.
Delegate authority	— Allow project personnel to make decisions and expend resources within the limitations and constraints of their roles.
Motivate personnel	— Provide a work environment in which project personnel can satisfy their psychological needs.
Build teams	— Provide a work environment in which project personnel can work together toward common project goals. Set performance goals for teams as well as for individuals.
Coordinate activities	— Combine project activities into effective and efficient arrangements.
Facilitate communication	— Ensure a free flow of correct information among project members.
Resolve conflicts	— Encourage constructive differences of opinion and help resolve the resulting conflicts.
Manage changes	— Stimulate creativity and innovation in achieving project goals.
Document directing decisions	— Document decisions involving delegation of authority, communication and coordination, conflict resolution, and change management.

Table 8.2. Motivation models and techniques

Motivation model	Definition or explanation
Frederick Taylor	Workers will respond to an *incentive wage*.
Elton Mayo	*Interpersonal (group) values* override *individual values*. Personnel will respond to group pressure.
Kurt Lewin	*Group forces* can overcome the interests of an *individual*.
Douglas McGregor	Managers must understand human nature in order to motivate them.
Maslow	Human needs can be categorized in a hierarchy. Satisfied needs are *not* motivators.
Frederick Herzberg	A decrease in *environmental factors* is dissatisfying; an increase in environmental factors is NOT satisfying. A decrease in *job content factors* is NOT dissatisfying; an increase in job content factors is satisfying.
Chris Argyris	The greater the disparity between *company needs* and *individual needs*, the greater the employee's dissatisfaction.
Rensis Likert	*Participative management* is essential to personal motivation.
Arch Patton	Executives are *motivated* by the challenge of work, status, the urge to achieve leadership, the lash of competition, fear, and money.
Theory Z	A combination of American and Japanese management style. People need goals and objectives; otherwise, they can easily impede their own progress and the progress of their company.
Total quality management (TQM)	A strategy for continually improving performance at each level and area of responsibility.

8.3.4.2. Theory Z. Theory Z is a combination of American and Japanese management styles [Ouchi 1981]. The basic principles of Theory Z are [Arthur 1983]

- People need goals and objectives. Goals help to keep one on a forward track while minimizing the time lost to nonproductivity.

- Motivation is essential for good performance and must be both positively and negatively reinforced by management. Optimal motivation is derived from both peer and managerial recognition and, to a lesser extent, from promotion and monetary reward.

- Merely having goals and motivation will not prevent people from making mistakes. Managers must correct their movement along paths that are in the best interests of the company.

- The best interests of any given company are achieved when each individual's work is standardized to ensure that similar goals are attained by similar means. In turn, any suggested improvement in one particular area of work automatically is incorporated into related areas.

- Goals must change as working conditions and corporate needs change. In anticipation of such change, Theory Z provides the mechanism for gradual change.

8.3.4.3. Hierarchy of needs (Maslow). Satisfied needs are not motivators. For example, an individual who has adequate job security cannot be motivated by increased job security. Maslow's hierarchy of human needs, in order of importance, is listed below and in Figure 8.1 [Maslow 1954]:

Figure 7.1: Maslow's Hierarchy of Human Needs

- *Biological survival needs*—basic needs to sustain human life, such as food, water, and shelter.

- *Security and safety needs*—freedom from physical danger.

- *Social needs*—the need to belong, to be accepted by others.

- *Esteem and recognition needs*—the need to be held in esteem by themselves and others.

- *Self-actualization needs*—the need to maximize one's potential and to accomplish something significant.

8.3.4.4. Total quality management (TQM). TQM can be thought of as a motivation technique for an organization or enterprise. TQM is a strategy for continually improving performance at each level and area of responsibility. Increasing user satisfaction is the overriding objective. TQM focuses on processes that create products. By delegating the authority to make decisions and improve quality to the lowest level, the TQM process provides a degree of motivation to the personnel implementing it. TQM is based on the work by Deming [1986].

8.3.4.5. Job factors for computer personnel. Table 8.3 provides a list of factors, in order of declining importance, that motivate computer personnel toward taking a job (left-hand column) and a list of factors that make a job dissatisfying to the job holder (right-hand column).

8.3.5. Build software project teams. As discussed in Section 5, software is built by project teams. *Team building* is the process of improving the interrelationship between team members to improve the efficiency and effectiveness of the team as a whole. Techniques such as team building exercises, "off-site" meetings, and group dynamics improve the capabilities of the team so they can be more productive as a group.

8.3.6. Coordinate project activities. *Coordination* is the arrangement of project entities to work together toward common goals with minimal friction. Documents, policies, procedures, and so forth are viewed differently by various people. The task of the project manager is to reconcile differences in approaches, effort, and schedules for the benefit of the project.

The project manager is responsible for coordinating the activities of the project to ensure that people understand and communicate with one another. The manager wants to ensure that other personnel in contact with the project are aware of the organizational structure, the task being done, and the expectations of other organizations.

8.3.7. Facilitate communication. Along with coordination, the project manager is responsible for facilitating communication both within the project and between the project and other organizations. *Facilitate* means to expedite, ease, and to assist the progress of communication. *Communication* is the exchange of information among entities working toward common goals.

For example, the project manager should disseminate the staffing plans and project schedule throughout the organization when practical. Nothing can destroy the morale of an organization faster than false and misleading rumors. A good project manager will ensure that the project staff is kept well informed so that rumors are quickly dispelled.

Table 8.3. Job factors for software personnel

Job attractors	Job dissatisfiers
Salary	Company mismanagement
Chance to advance	Poor work environment
Work environment	Little feeling of accomplishment
Location	Poor recognition
Benefits	Inadequate salary
Facilities/equipment	Little chance to advance
Job satisfaction	Poor facilities/equipment
Company management	Poor benefits
Job responsibility	Poor career path definition

8.3.8. Resolve conflicts. It is the project manager's responsibility to resolve conflicts among project staff members and between the staff and outside agencies in both technical and managerial matters. The project manager is not expected to be an expert in all aspects of the project, but should possess good judgment and problem-solving skills.

The project manager should reduce the opportunity for future conflict by removing potential sources of disagreement whenever possible, for example, team members with somewhat equal positions should have equal benefits, access to the manager, parking places, and so forth.

Another type of conflict the project manager should watch for is the conflict between the employee's work activities and his or her personal life. When this conflict reaches epic proportions, it is called "burnout" [Cherlin 1981].

8.3.9. Manage change that impacts the software project. The project manager is responsible for encouraging independent thought and innovation in achieving project goals. A good manager must always accommodate change, when that change is cost effective and beneficial to the project [Kirchof and Adams 1986].

It is important that the project manager control change so as not to discourage cost-effective changes. Clearly, requirements, design, and the application area for which the software system is built will change. There will be social changes. What is acceptable to build at one time will not necessarily be acceptable at another time. People change. Newly graduated engineers will have new ideas, as they have been taught new ways to develop software systems. The bottom line is not to eliminate change, but to control it. Yourdon [1987] presents a simple step-by-step plan for transferring a new software technology (a change) into a software development organization:

- Explain the risks and benefits of the new method, tool, or technique.

- Provide training for the project team.

- Prototype the technique before it is used.

- Provide technical support throughout the project.

- Listen to users' concerns and problems.

- Avoid concentrating on the technology at the expense of the project.

As another example of controlling (taking advantage of) change, staff turnover is usually considered a problem in most software development organizations. The paper by Bartol and Martin [1983] discusses how to make positive use of staff turnover.

8.3.10. Document directing decisions. The project manager must document all tasks, assignments of authority and responsibility, and outcomes of conflict resolution. In addition, all decisions concerning lines of communication and coordination must be documented.

9. Controlling a software engineering project

9.1. Introduction and definitions

Controlling is the collection of management activities used to ensure that the project goes according to plan. Performance and results are measured against plans, deviations are noted, and corrective actions are taken to ensure conformance of plans and actuals.

Control is a feedback system that provides information on how well the project is going. Control asks the questions: Is the project on schedule? Is it within cost? Are there any potential problems that will cause delays in meeting the requirement within the budget and schedule? Control also provides plans and approaches for eliminating the difference between the plans and/or standards and the actuals or results.

The control process also requires organizational structure, communication, and coordination. For example, who is responsible for assessing progress? who will take action on reported problems?

Controlling methods and tools must be objective. Information must be quantified. The methods and tools must point out deviations from plans without regard for the particular people or positions involved. Control methods must be tailored to individual environments and managers. The methods must be flexible and adaptable to deal with the changing environment of the organization. Control must also be economical; its cost should not outweigh its benefits.

Control must lead to corrective action—by either bringing the actual status back to plan, changing the plan, or terminating the project.

9.2. Major issues in controlling

A major issue in controlling a software project involves reliance on budget expenditures for the management of progress. For example, when a project manager is asked for the status of a software project, he or she will typically look at the resources expended. If three-quarters of project funds have been expended, the project manager will report that the project is three-quarters completed. The obvious problem is that the relationship between resources consumed and work actually accomplished is only a rough measure at best and completely incorrect at worst.

Other methods of determining progress are not yet accurate or easy to use. Progress metrics such as the "earned-value method" and "binary tracking system" of monitoring software projects are two of the most accurate methods, but are time consuming and costly to implement.

Standard methods that can be used to measure progress and products are either not written or, if written, not enforced. Standards are sometimes considered detrimental to software projects because they "stifle creativity." Therefore, it is not unusual for entire project staffs, including the project manager, to ignore the company standards in favor of local, ad hoc, and frequently inadequate project control systems.

Users and buyers of software systems do not specify quality in their software system or in their request for proposals (RFP). Project managers do not feel obligated to build a quality product if the customer has not requested it, enforced it, or funded it specifically.

This is primarily because the body of knowledge known as "software metrics" is not fully developed. For example, software quality metrics are used to measure the reliability, maintainability, usability, safety, and security of a software product. However, we do not know how to do *a priori* design of software systems that, when implemented, will have the desired quality attributes. This has resulted in emphasis being placed on the software engineering processes in the belief that sound development processes will result in high-quality products. Budget expenditure is still the primary metric of progress in a software engineering project.

9.3. Controlling the software project

Table 9.1 outlines the project management activities that project managers must accomplish to control their projects. The remainder of this section discusses the activities outlined in Table 9.1. Figure 9.1 reflects the activities and sequence of activities that take place when applying a control process to a software engineering project.

9.3.1. Develop standards of performance. The project manager is responsible for developing and specifying standards of performance for the project. The project manager either develops standards and procedures for the project, adopts and uses standards developed by the parent organization, or uses standards developed by the customer or a professional society (see, for example, [IEEE Software Engineering Standards 1993]).

9.3.1.1. Standards. A *standard* is a documented set of criteria used to specify and determine the adequacy of an action or object. A *software engineering standard* is a set of procedures that defines the process for developing a software product and/or specifies the quality of a software product. See [Buckley 1987] for a discussion of implementing software engineering standards in a company.

Table 9.1. Controlling activities for software projects

Activity	Definition or explanation
Develop standards of performance	— Set goals that will be achieved when tasks are correctly accomplished.
Establish monitoring and reporting systems	— Determine necessary data, who will receive it, when they will receive it, and what they will do with it to control the project.
Measure and analyze results	— Compare achievements with standards, goals, and plans.
Initiate corrective actions	— Bring requirements, plans, and actual project status into conformance.
Reward and discipline	— Praise, remunerate, and discipline project personnel as appropriate.
Document controlling methods	— Document the standards of performance, monitoring and control systems, and reward and discipline mechanisms.

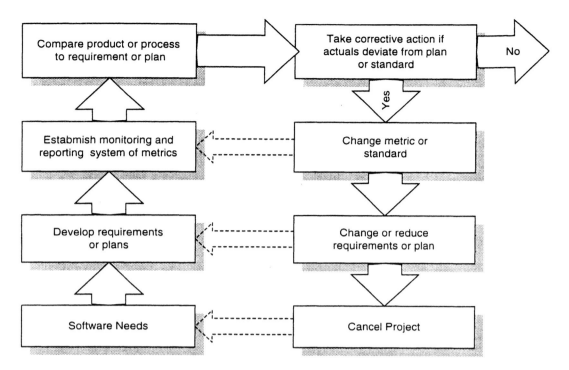

Figure 9.1: Project Control

Process and product standards are both important in developing high-quality software. Software engineering is primarily concerned with the *process* of developing software rather than the measurement of the product. This is because software quality metrics (measuring such quality attributes as software reliability, maintainability, portability, and other "-ilities") is not a well-developed science. Tools and techniques that effectively measure the quality of a software product are generally not available. Most software engineering standards are concerned with the process of developing software.

9.3.1.2. Software quality assurance. Software quality assurance (SQA) is "a planned and systematic pattern of all actions necessary to provide adequate confidence that the item or product conforms to established technical requirements" [IEEE-STD 729-1983]. SQA includes the development process and management methods (requirements and design), standards, configuration management methods, review procedures, documentation standards, verification and validation, and testing specifications and procedures. SQA is one of the major control techniques available to the project manager.

9.3.1.3. Software configuration management. Software configuration management (SCM) is a method for controlling and reporting on software status. SCM is the discipline of identifying the configuration of a system at discrete points in time. This is done for the purpose of systematically controlling changes to the configuration and maintaining its integrity and traceability throughout the system life cycle [Bersoff 1984].

9.3.1.4. Process and product metrics. A *metric* is a measure of the degree to which a process or product possesses a given attribute. Besides process and product metrics, there are other definitions of metric types (adapted from [IEEE Std 610.12-1990]):

- *Software quality metric*—a quantitative measure of the degree to which software possesses a given attribute that affects its quality. Examples are reliability, maintainability, and portability.

- *Software quantity metric*—a quantitative measure of some physical software attribute. Examples are lines of code, function points, and pages of documentation.

- *Management metric*—a management indicator that can be used to measure management activities such as budget spent, value earned, costs overrun, and schedule delays.

In the early 1980s, the U.S. Air Force's Rome Air Development Center (also known as Rome Laboratories) developed a set of software metrics called quality factors, which represent the product attributes most desired by customers [RADC-TR-175]. These metrics have become part of our metrics environment and are used in the development of many software systems. These metrics are

- correctness
- efficiency
- usability
- maintainability
- flexibility

- reliability
- integrity
- survivability
- verifiability

- reusability
- expandability
- portability
- interoperability

Perhaps the most important software quality attribute is software reliability. Software reliability measures the extent to which the software will perform without failures within a specified time period [RADC TR-85-37].

Other important attributes not on the RADC list include safety, security, complexity, and user friendliness.

An important set of metrics for software management was developed by the MITRE Corporation for the U.S. Air Force Electronic System Division (now Electronic Systems Center)[Schultz 1988]. These 10 metrics (listed below) are considered by many to be the best set of management metrics available today.

- software size metric
- software volatility metric
- design complexity metric
- design progress metric
- testing progress metric

- software personnel metric
- computer resources utilization metric
- schedule progress metric
- computer software unit (CSU) development progress metric
- incremental release content metric

Another set of management metrics was published by the U.S. Air Force Systems Command (now part of the Air Force Material Command) in 1986 [AFSC Pamphlet 800-43 1986].

This set includes

- computer resource utilization

- software development manpower

- requirements definition and stability

- software progress (development and test)

- cost and schedule deviations

- software development tools

Measurement has been an integral part of the Software Engineering Institute's process improvement project. The first set of guidelines published by this project [Humphrey and Sweet 1987] included 10 metrics at process maturity level 2:

- planned versus actual staffing profiles

- software size versus time

- statistics on software code and test errors

- actual versus planned units designed

- actual versus planned units completing unit testing

- actual versus planned units integrated

- target computer memory utilization

- target computer throughput utilization

- target computer I/O channel utilization

- software build/release content

With the 1993 publication of the Software Engineering Institute's Capability Maturity Model for Software [Paulk 1993] measurements became one of the "common features" that are part of every key process area.

9.3.2. Establish monitoring and reporting systems. The project manager is responsible for establishing the methods of monitoring the software project and reporting project status. Monitoring and reporting systems must be specified in order to determine project status. The project manager needs feedback on the progress of the project and quality of the product to ensure that everything is going according to plan. The type, frequency, originator, and recipient of project reports must be specified. Status-reporting tools must be implemented to provide visibility of progress, not just resources used or time passed.

Software methods, procedures, tools, and techniques must also be specified. Table 9.2 lists typical monitoring and reporting systems. PERT and CPM, workload charts, and Gantt charts are tools that help control a software engineering project [Cori 1985]. The paper by Howes [1984] presents the earned-value method of tracking a software engineering project.

9.3.2.1. Baseline management system. The baseline management system is a management and software life-cycle development strategy that integrates a series of life-cycle phases, reviews, and baseline documents into a system for managing a software engineering project. Specifically, it uses the waterfall life-cycle model to partition the project into manageable phases: requirements, design, implementation, and testing. It also establishes milestones, documents, and reviews at the end of each phase.

Milestones. Milestones and milestone charts play a major part in the controlling process. A *milestone* is a discrete event. Achievement of a milestone must be based on completion of one or more tangible work products.

259

Table 9.2. Methods of monitoring software projects

Method	Definition or explanation
Formal (milestone) reviews	— Periodic, planned reviews of work products by developers, customers, users, and management to assess progress.
Budget reviews	— A comparison of estimated budget with actual expenditures to determine compliance with or deviations from plan.
Independent auditing	— An independent examination of a software project to determine compliance with plans, specifications, and standards.
Binary tracking system	— A method of measuring progress on a work package by accepting only 0- or 100-percent completion
Software quality assurance (SQA)	— A planned and systematic pattern of actions necessary to provide adequate confidence that the development process and work products of a software project conform to established standards.
Unit development folder (UDF)	— A specific form of development notebook that provides an orderly approach to the development process and the work products of a software project conforming to established standards
Configuration management (CM)	— A method for controlling and reporting on the status of work products generated by a software project.
Testing	— The controlled exercise of the program code to expose errors.
Verification and validation	— The process of assuring that each phase of the development life cycle correctly implements the specifications from the previous phase and that each software work product satisfies its requirements.
Walk-throughs and inspections	— Systematic examination of software work products by the producer's peers, conducted for the purpose of finding errors.

Milestones allow the project manager to partition a project into measurable units, each of which can be demonstrated to be complete. Examples of milestones are the completion of a software requirements specification, a software design, code, and of course the major milestone, the completion of the project.

Milestone Reviews. Reviews are analyses of project processes and products by customers, users, and management to assess progress. A milestone review is held at the end of each life-cycle phase of the project. For example, a preliminary design review (PDR) (sometimes called architectural design review) is held at the completion of the preliminary design phase.

Milestone reviews are usually chaired by the customer or higher-level management. The project manager presents the current status and progress, the work to date, the money expended, the current schedule, and any management and technical problems that may have surfaced since the last review. The review is a success when the customer or top management gives permission for the project manager to proceed to the next phase.

Baseline. A baseline is an agreed-on technical configuration at some point in the software project. Baselines are typically agreed on among developers, customers, and managers and are controlled and maintained by a software configuration management board. Baselines are normally established at the end of a successful milestone review. Baselines commonly used by the Department of Defense are functional, allocated, and product baselines [Mil-Std-498 1995].

9.3.3. Measure and analyze results. The project manager is responsible for measuring the results of the project both during and at the end of the project. For instance, actual phase deliverables should be measured against planned phase deliverables. The measured results can be management (process) results and/or technical (product) results. An example of a process result is the status of the project schedule. An example of a product result is the degree to which the design specifications correctly interpreted the requirement specifications. Some of the tools and methods for measuring results are described in the following paragraphs.

9.3.3.1. Binary tracking and work product specifications. These documents specify the work to be accomplished in completing a function, activity, or task. A work package specifies the objectives of the work, staffing, the expected duration, the resources, the results, and any other special considerations. Work packages are normally small tasks that can be assigned to two to three individuals to be completed in two to three weeks. A series of work packages makes up a software project.

The "98-percent completion syndrome" is a cynical view of the method of determining project status by looking at the project as a whole and trying to determine what percentage is complete. For example, given a six-week project, an immature project team will report that the project is 98 percent complete in the final week of the project with only "one or two bugs to find and fix." The project manager continues to report 98-percent completion for the next six or more weeks until the project is finally complete, long after its estimated due date. The real issue is that no one knew the project's real status.

Binary tracking is the concept that a work pack is either done or not done (that is, assigned a "1" or "0"). Binary tracking of work packages is a reasonably accurate means of tracking the completion of a software project. For example, if a project has 880 work packages and 440 are complete at the end of the fifth week, the project is 50 percent complete, not 98 percent complete.

Binary tracking is also a major support tool to the earned value concept (see Howes [1984] for a good description of the earned value concept).

9.3.3.2. Unit development folders. The unit development folder (UDF) (sometime called software development folder) is a specific form of development notebook that has proven to be useful and effective in collecting and organizing software products as they are produced. The purpose of the UDF is to provide an orderly approach to the development of a program unit and to provide management visibility and control over the development process [Ingrassia 1987].

9.3.3.3. Walk-throughs and inspections. Walk-throughs and inspections are reviews of a software product (design specifications, code, test procedures, and so on) conducted by the peers of the group being reviewed [Ackerman 1997]. Walk-throughs are a software product critique by the producer's peers for the sole purpose of finding errors. The inspection system is another peer review developed by Michael Fagan [Fagan 1976] [Fagan 1986] of IBM in 1976. Inspections are typically more structured than walk-throughs.

9.3.3.4. Independent auditing. The software project audit is an independent review of a software project to determine compliance with software requirements, specifications, baselines, standards, policies, and software quality assurance plans.

An independent audit is an audit done by an outside organization not associated with the project [Bernstein 1981]. On the positive side, an independent team can provide a totally unbiased opinion. When there is a need for expert knowledge, the independent team can supplement existing talent.

The negative side of the independent audit is that the audit team needs to be brought up to speed on the project. An audit team requires ongoing involvement to be effective.

9.3.3.5. Verification and validation. One of the best methods of determining whether the product is correct is verification and validation. *Verification* is assuring that each phase of the life cycle correctly interprets the specification from the previous phase. *Validation* is assuring that each completed software product satisfies its requirements [Fujii and Wallace 1997].

9.3.3.6. Testing. *Testing* is the controlled exercise of the program code in order to expose errors. *Unit testing* is the testing of one unit of code (usually a module) by the programmer who programmed the unit. *Integration testing* is the testing of each unit or element in combination with other elements to show the existence of errors between the units or elements. *System testing* is the controlled exercise of the completed system. In each case, it is important to develop test plans, test procedures, test cases, and test results [ANSI/IEEE-STD 829-1983].

9.3.3.7. Software configuration audit. Software configuration audits provide the mechanism for determining the degree to which the current software system mirrors the software system contained in the baseline and the requirements document [Bersoff 1984].

9.3.4 Initiate corrective actions for the project. If standards and requirements are not being met, the project manager must initiate corrective action. For instance, the project manager can change the plan or standard, use overtime or other procedures to get back on plan, or change the requirements (for example, deliver less).

The project manager might change the plans or standards if it seems the original plans or standards cannot be met. This might involve requiring a larger budget, more people, or more checkout time on the development computer. It also might require reducing the standards (and indirectly the quality) by decreasing the number of walk-throughs or by reviewing only the critical software modules.

It is sometimes possible to get back on schedule by increasing the resources, which increases the resources requirements plan. It is also sometime possible to keep the original cost by stretching the schedule or reducing the software system's functionality.

An example of changing the requirements is delivering software that does not completely meet all the functional requirements laid out in the original software requirements specifications.

9.3.5. Reward and discipline the project members. The project manager should reward people for meeting their standards and plans, and discipline those who without good reason do not. This should not be confused with rewarding and disciplining workers who perform, or do not perform, their assigned duties—that is a staffing function. The system of rewards and discipline discussed here is a mechanism for controlling ability to meet a plan or standard.

9.3.6. Document controlling methods. The project manager must document all standards, software quality procedures, metrics, and other means of measuring production and products. In addition, the project manager must establish metrics for determining when corrective action must be initiated and determine in advance possible corrective action to be taken.

10. Summary

Software engineering procedures and techniques do not alone guarantee a successful project. A good project manager can sometimes overcome or work around deficiencies in organization, staffing, budgets, standards, and so on. A poor manager stumbles over every problem, real or imaginary—no number of rules, policies, standards, or techniques will help. In the hands of a competent project manager, the methods and techniques discussed in this article can significantly improve the probability of a successful project.

In this article and in many other documents, the terms "project management" and "software engineering project management" are used interchangeably. This is because the management of a software engineering project and other types of projects require many of the same tools, techniques, approaches, and methods of mainstream management. The functions and general activities of management are the same at all levels; only the detailed activities and tasks are different.

References

[Ackerman 1997] F.A. Ackerman, "Software Inspections and the Cost-Effective Production of Reliable Software," in *Software Engineering,* M. Dorfman and R.H. Thayer, eds., IEEE Computer Society Press, Los Alamitos, CA, 1997.

[AFSC Pamphlet 800-43 1986] "Air Force Systems Command Software Management Indicators: Management Insight," AFSC Pamphlet 800-43, HQ AFSC, Andrews AFB, DC, 31 Jan. 1986.

[ANSI/IEEE-STD 829-1983] ANSI/IEEE Standard 829-1983, *IEEE Standard for Software Test Documents,* Institute of Electrical and Electronics Engineers, Inc., New York, 1987, approved by American National Standards Inst., 19 Aug. 1983.

[Arthur 1983] L.J. Arthur, *Programmer Productivity: Myths, Methods, and Murphology,* John Wiley & Sons, New York, 1983.

[Baker 1972] F.T. Baker, "Chief Programmer Team Management of Production Programming," *IBM System J.,* vol. 11, 1972, p. 56-73.

[Bartol and Martin 1983] K.M. Bartol and D.C. Martin, "Managing the Consequences of DP Turnover: A Human Resources Planning Perspective," *Proc. 20th ACM Computer Resources Planning Perspective,* ACM Press, New York, 1983, pp. 79-86. Reprinted in *Tutorial: Software Engineering Project Management,* R.H. Thayer, ed., IEEE Computer Society Press, Los Alamitos, CA, 1988.

[Ben-David, Et al. 1984] A. Ben-David, M. Ben-Porath, J. Loeb, and M. Rich, "An Industrial Software Engineering Retraining Course: Development Considerations and Lessons Learned," *IEEE Trans. Software Eng.,* vol. 10, no. 1, Nov. 1984, pp. 748-755.

[Bernstein 1981] L. Bernstein, "Software Project Management Audits," *J. Systems and Software,* Elsevier North Holland, 1982, pp. 281-287.

[Bersoff 1984] E.H. Bersoff, "Elements of Software Configuration Management," *IEEE Trans. Software Engineering,* vol. SE-10, no. 1, Jan. 1984, pp. 79-87. Reprinted in *Tutorial: Software Engineering Project Management,* R.H. Thayer, ed., IEEE Computer Society Press, Los Alamitos, CA, 1988.

[Boehm 1981] B.W. Boehm, *Software Engineering Economics,* Prentice-Hall, Englewood Cliffs, NJ, 1981.

[Boehm 1984] B.W. Boehm, "Software Engineering Economics," *IEEE Trans. Software Eng.,* vol. 10, no. 1, Jan./Feb. 1984, pp. 4-21.

[Boehm 1987] B.W. Boehm, *Tutorial: Software Risk Management,* IEEE Computer Society Press, Los Alamitos, CA, 1989.

[Boehm 1988] B.W. Boehm, "A Spiral Model of Software Development and Enhancement," *Tutorial: Software Engineering Project Management,* IEEE Computer Society Press, Los Alamitos, CA, 1988.

[Boyatzis 1971] R.E. Boyatzis, "Leadership: The Effective Use of Power," *Management of Personnel Quarterly*, Bureau of Industrial Relations, 1971, pp. 1-8. Reprinted in *Tutorial: Software Engineering Project Management*, R.H. Thayer, ed., IEEE Computer Society Press, Los Alamitos, CA, 1988.

[Brooks 1987] "Report on the Defense Science Board Task Force on Military Software," Office of the Undersecretary of Defense for Acquisition, U.S. Department of Defense, Washington, D.C., Sept. 1987.

[Buckley 1987] F.J. Buckley, "Establishing Software Engineering Standards in an Industrial Organization," in *Tutorial: Software Engineering Project Management*, R.H. Thayer, ed., IEEE Computer Society Press, Los Alamitos, CA, 1988.

[Cherlin 1981] M. Cherlin, "Burnout: Victims and Avoidance's," *Datamation*, July 1981, pp. 92-99.

[Cooke 1976] L.H. Cooke, Jr., "The Chief Programmer Team Administrator," *Datamation*, June 1976, pp. 85-86.

[Cori 1985] K.A. Cori, "Fundamentals of Master Scheduling for the Project Manager," *Project Management J.*, June 1985, pp. 78-89. Reprinted in *Tutorial: Software Engineering Project Management*, R.H. Thayer, ed., IEEE Computer Society Press, Los Alamitos, CA, 1988.

[Davis 1990] A.M. Davis, "The Analysis and Specification of System and Software Requirements," in *System and Software Requirements Engineering*, R.H. Thayer and M. Dorfman, eds., IEEE Computer Society Press, Los Alamitos, CA 1990.

[Davis 1997] A. Davis, "Trial by Firing: Saga of a Rookie Manager," in *Software Engineering Project Management*, R.H. Thayer, ed., IEEE Computer Society Press, Los Alamitos, CA, 1997.

[Deming 1986] W. Edward Deming, *Out of the Crisis*, MIT Center for Advanced Engineering Study, Cambridge, MA, 1986.

[DoD Software Initiative 1983] *Strategy for a DoD Software Initiative*, U.S. Department of Defense Report, 1 Oct. 1982 (an edited public version was published in *Computer*, Nov. 1983.)

[Donnelly, Gibson, and Ivancevich 1975] J.H. Donnelly Jr., J.L. Gibson, and J.M. Ivancevich, *Fundamentals of Management: Functions, Behavior, Models*, revised edition, Business Publications, Dallas, TX, 1975.

[Fagan 1976] M.E. Fagan, "Design and Code Inspections to Reduce Errors in Program Development," *IBM Systems J.*, vol. 15, no. 3, 1976, pp. 182-211.

[Fagan 1986] M.E. Fagan, "Advances in Software Inspections," *IEEE Trans. Software Engineering*, vol. SE-12, no. 7, July 1986, pp. 744-751. Reprinted in *Tutorial: Software Engineering Project Management*, R.H. Thayer, ed., IEEE Computer Society Press, Los Alamitos, CA, 1988.

[Fairley 1987] R.E. Fairley, "A Guide for Preparing Software Project Management Plans," in *Tutorial: Software Engineering Project Management*, R.H. Thayer, ed., IEEE Computer Society Press, Los Alamitos, CA, 1988.

[Fairley and Rook 1997] R.E. Fairley and P. Rook, "Risk Management for Software Development," in *Software Engineering*, M. Dorfman and R.H. Thayer, eds., IEEE Computer Society Press, Los Alamitos, CA, 1997.

[Faulk 1997] S. Faulk, "Software Requirements Engineering," in *Software Engineering*, M. Dorfman and R.H. Thayer, eds., IEEE Computer Society Press, Los Alamitos, CA, 1997.

[Fayol 1949] H. Fayol, *General and Industrial Administration*, Sir Isaac Pitman & Sons Ltd., London, 1949.

[Fitz-enz 1978] J. Fitz-enz, "Who is the DP Professional?" *Datamation*, Sept. 1978, pp. 125-128. Reprinted in *Tutorial: Software Engineering Project Management*, R.H. Thayer, ed., IEEE Computer Society Press, Los Alamitos, CA, 1988.

[Fujii and Wallace 1997] R. Fujii and D.R. Wallace, "Software Verification and Validation," in *Software Engineering*, M. Dorfman and R.H. Thayer, eds., IEEE Computer Society Press, Los Alamitos, CA, 1997.

[GAO/IMTEC-92-48 C-17 Aircraft Software] "Embedded Computer Systems: Significant Software Problems on C-17 Must be Addressed," General Accounting Office GAO/IMTEC-92-48, Gaithersburg, MD 20877, May 1992.

[Goldberg 1978] E.A. Goldberg, "Applying Corporate Software Development Policies," TRW, Defense and Space Systems Group, Jan. 1978. Reprinted in *Tutorial: Software Engineering Project Management*, R.H. Thayer, ed., IEEE Computer Society Press, Los Alamitos, CA, 1988.

[Herzberg, Mausner, and Snyderman 1959] F. Herzberg, B. Mausner, and B.B. Snyderman, *The Motivation to Work*, John Wiley & Son, New York, 1959.

[High Technology Careers Magazine 1996] *High Technology Careers Magazine,* vol. 13, no. 1, Feb./Mar. 1996.

[Howes 1984] N.R. Howes, "Managing Software Development Projects for Maximum Productivity," *IEEE Trans. Software Engineering*, vol. SE-10, no. 1, Jan. 1984, pp. 27-35. Reprinted in *Tutorial: Software Engineering Project Management*, R.H. Thayer, ed., IEEE Computer Society Press, Los Alamitos, CA, 1988.

[Humphrey and Sweet 1987] W.S. Humphrey and W.L. Sweet, "A Method for Assessing the Software Development Capability of Contractors," CMU/SEI-87-TR-23, Sept. 1987.

[IEEE Software Engineering Standards 1993] Hardbound edition of Software Engineering Standards, IEEE, New York, 1993.

[IEEE Std 610.12-1990] IEEE Standard 610.12-1990, *Glossary of Software Engineering Terminology*, Inst. of Electrical and Electronic Engineers, Piscataway, NJ, 1990

[IEEE-STD 729-1983] ANSI/IEEE Std. 729-1983, *IEEE Standard Glossary of Software Engineering Terminology*, IEEE, New York, 1983.

[Ingrassia 1987] F.S. Ingrassia, "The Unit Development Folder (UDF): A Ten-Year Perspective," *Tutorial: Software Engineering Project Management*, R.H. Thayer, ed., IEEE Computer Society Press, Los Alamitos, CA, 1988.

[Kirchof and Adams 1986] N.S. Kirchof and J.R. Adams, "Conflict Management for Project Managers: An Overview," extracted from *Conflict Management for Project Managers*, Project Management Inst., Feb. 1986, pages 1-13. Reprinted in *Tutorial: Software Engineering Project Management*, R.H. Thayer, ed., IEEE Computer Society Press, Los Alamitos, CA, 1988.

[Koontz and O'Donnell 1972] H. Koontz and C. O'Donnell, *Principles of Management: An Analysis of Managerial Functions*, 5th ed., McGraw-Hill, New York, 1972.

[Koontz, O'Donnell, and Weihrich 1980] H. Koontz, C. O'Donnell, and H. Weihrich, *Management*, 7th ed., McGraw-Hill, New York, 1980.

[Koontz, O'Donnell, and Weihrich 1984] H. Koontz, C. O'Donnell and H. Weihrich, *Management*, 8th ed., McGraw-Hill, New York, 1984.

[Kruesi 1982] B. Kruesi, seminar on "Software Psychology," California State University, Sacramento, Fall 1982.

[Mantei 1981] M. Mantei. "The Effect of Programming Team Structures on Programming Tasks," *Comm. ACM*, vol. 24, no. 3, Mar. 1981, pp. 106-113. Reprinted in *Tutorial: Software Engineering Project Management*, R.H. Thayer, ed., IEEE Computer Society Press, Los Alamitos, CA, 1988.

[Maslow 1954] A.H. Maslow, *Motivation and Personality*, Harper & Brothers, New York, 1954.

[McGill 1984] J.P. McGill, "The Software Engineering Shortage: A Third Choice," *IEEE Trans. Software Eng.*, vol. 10, no. 1, Jan. 1984, pp. 42-48. Reprinted in *Tutorial: Software Engineering Project Management*, R.H. Thayer, ed., IEEE Computer Society Press, Los Alamitos, CA, 1988.

[McGregor 1960] D. McGregor, *The Human Side of Enterprise*, McGraw-Hill, New York, 1960.

[Middleton, 1967] C.J. Middleton, "How to Set Up a Project Organization," *Harvard Business Rev.*, Nov./Dec. 1967, pp. 73-82.

[Miller 1978] W.B. Miller, "Fundamentals of Project Management," *J. Systems Management*, vol. 29, no. 11, issue 211, Nov. 1978, pp. 22-29.

[Mills 1980] H.D. Mills, "Software Engineering Education," *Proc. IEEE*, vol. 68, no. 9, Sept. 1980, pp. 1158-1162.

[Mil-Std-498 1995] *Software Development and Documentation*, U.S. Department of Defense, 5 Dec. 1995.

[Moneysmith 1984] M. Moneysmith, "I'm OK—and You're Not," *Savvy*, Apr. 1984, pp. 37-38. Reprinted in *Tutorial: Software Engineering Project Management*, R.H. Thayer, ed., IEEE Computer Society Press, Los Alamitos, CA, 1988.

[Ouchi 1981] W. Ouchi, *Theory Z: How American Business Can Meet the Japanese Challenge*, Addison-Wesley, Reading, MA 1981.

[Paulk 1993] M.C. Paulk, B. Curtis, M.B. Chrissis, and C.V. Weber, "Key Practices of the Capability Maturity Model, Version 1.1," CMU/SEI-93-TR-25, Feb. 1993.

[Paulk, et al. 1997] M.C. Paulk, B. Curtis, M.B. Chrissis, and C.V. Weber, "The Capability Maturity Model for Software," in *Software Engineering*, M. Dorfman and R.H. Thayer, eds., IEEE Computer Society Press, Los Alamitos, CA, 1997.

[Powell and Posner 1984] G.N. Powell and B.Z. Posner, "Excitement and Commitment: Keys to Project Success," *Project Management J.*, Dec. 1984, pp. 39-46. Reprinted in *Tutorial: Software Engineering Project Management*, R.H. Thayer, ed., IEEE Computer Society Press, Los Alamitos, CA, 1988.

[RADC TR-85-37] T.P. Bowen, G.B. Wigle, and J.T. Tsai, *Specification of Software Quality Attributes: vol. 1, Final Technical Report; vol. 2, Software Quality Specifications Guidebook; vol. 3, Software Quality Evaluation Guidebook*; RADC TR-85-37, prepared by Boeing Aerospace Company for Rome Air Development Center, Griffiss AFB, NY, February Feb. 1985.

[RADC-TR-175] *Software Quality Measures for Distributed Systems (vol. I), Software Quality Measures for Distributed Systems: Guide Book for Software Quality Measurements (vol. II), and Software Quality Measures for Distributed Systems: Impact on Software Quality (vol. III)*, TR RADC-TR-175, Rome Air Development Center, Griffiss Air Force Base, NY, 1983.

[Raudsepp 1981] E. Raudsepp, "Delegate Your Way to Success," *Computer Decisions*, Mar. 1981, pp. 157-164. Reprinted in *Tutorial: Software Engineering Project Management*, R.H. Thayer, ed., Computer Society , Los Alamitos, CA, 1988.

[Sackman, H. et al 1968] H. Sackman, W.J. Erikson, and E.E. Grant, "Exploratory Experimental Studies Comparing On-Line and Off-Line Programming Performance," *Comm. ACM*, vol. 11, no. 1, Jan. 1968, pp. 3-11. Reprinted in *Tutorial: Software Engineering Project Management*, R.H. Thayer, ed., IEEE Computer Society Press, Los Alamitos, CA, 1988.

[Schultz 1988] H.P. Schultz, *Software Management Metrics*, ESD TR-88-001, prepared by the MITRE Corporation for the U.S. Air Force, Electronic Systems Division, Hanscom Air Force Base, MA, 1988.

[Stuckenbruck 1981] L.C. Stuckenbruck, "The Matrix Organization," *A Decade of Project Management*, Project Management Inst., 1981, pp. 157-169. Reprinted in *Tutorial: Software Engineering Project Management*, R.H. Thayer, ed., IEEE Computer Society Press, Los Alamitos, CA, 1988.

[Thayer and Pyster 1984] R.H. Thayer and A.B. Pyster, "Guest Editorial: Software Engineering Project Management," *IEEE Trans. Software Eng.*, vol. SE-10, no. 1, Jan. 1984.

[Weinberg 1971] G. Weinberg, *The Psychology of Computer Programming*, Van Nostrand Reinhold, New York, 1971.

[Youker 1977] R. Youker, "Organizational Alternatives for Project Management," *Project Management Quarterly*, vol. VIII, no. 1, Mar. 1977, pp. 18-24.

[Yourdon 1987] E. Yourdon, "A Game Plan for Technology Transfer," *Tutorial: Software Engineering Project Management*, R.H. Thayer, ed., IEEE Computer Society Press, Los Alamitos, CA, 1988.

[Zubrow, et al. 1995] D. Zubrow, J. Herbsleb, W. Hayes, and D Goldenson, "Process Maturity Profile of the Software Community 1995 Update," presentation, Nov. 1995; based on data up to September 1995 for most recent assessment of 440 organizations: ML1 - 70.2 percent; ML2 - 18.4 percent; ML3 - 10.2 percent; ML4 - 1 percent; ML5 - 0.2 percent -- Source: e-mail, M. Paulk, Software Eng. Institution, 14 Feb. 1997.

Software cost estimation

F J Heemstra

The paper gives an overview of the state of the art of software cost estimation (SCE). The main questions to be answered in the paper are: (1) What are the reasons for overruns of budgets and planned durations? (2) What are the prerequisites for estimating? (3) How can software development effort be estimated? (4) What can software project management expect from SCE models, how accurate are estimations which are made using these kind of models, and what are the pros and cons of cost estimation models?

software, cost estimation, project control, software cost estimation model

SIMPLE QUESTIONS, DIFFICULT ANSWERS

Judging by reports from everyday practice and findings in the literature, software projects regularly get out of hand and invariably the effort expended on development exceeds the estimated effort, resulting in the software being delivered after the planned date. There is no doubt that SCE is a serious problem for software project management. At first glance the questions to be answered are simple: How much time and effort will it cost to develop the software? What are the dominating cost factors? What are the important risk factors? Unfortunately, however, the answers are neither simple nor easy.

The article gives an overview of the field of software cost estimation (SCE). Special attention is paid to the use of SCE models. These models are one of the techniques project management can use to estimate and control the effort and duration of software development. The paper starts with a description of the importance of accurate cost estimates. From this it will be clear that SCE is not easy, and management is confronted with many problems. In the following section some reasons for the problems will be highlighted, the paper going on to explain which prerequisites are necessary for an estimate to be possible. It is important to have knowledge about the product that must be developed, the development process, the development means, the development personnel, and the user organization. Also it is necessary to have available a set of estimation methods and techniques. An overview of the existing

Faculty of Public Administration and Public Policy, Twente University, POB 217, Enschede, The Netherlands

techniques for cost estimation is given in the fifth section, and the sixth section describes the principles of cost estimation models with an overview of models available nowadays. The rest of the paper deals with one of these techniques, that is to say parametric models. The penultimate section offers a comparison of SCE models, focusing mainly on the question 'How accurate are estimates made as a result of using models?' Despite the fact that software cost estimation is in its infancy plus the shortcomings of the current SCE models, the use of models has several advantages. The last section deals with the pros and cons and gives a critical evaluation of the state of the art of the use of these models.

OVERSHOOTS OF SOFTWARE DEVELOPMENT COSTS

Estimation of effort and duration of software development has become a topic of growing importance. This is not surprising. It often happens that software is more expensive than estimated and completion is later than planned. Moreover it turns out that much software does not meet the demands of the customer. There are a number of examples of such automation projects. The development costs of the automation of the education funding in The Netherlands proved to be three times as much as expected. Delays and wrong payments are a daily occurrence (*Volkskrant*, 24 June 1987). The development of the software for the purpose of the house-rent subsidies, produced to government order, proved to be twice as much as planned (NRC *Handelsblad*, 28 February 1989). In September 1989 the Dutch media announced as front page news the results of a governmental audit concerning the automation for the police. It proved to be an expensive disaster. The development costs of a computerized identifying system were US$43 million instead of the estimated US$21 million. Furthermore the system did not answer the formulated goals. The findings of a well-known Dutch consultancy organization (Berenschot) were that the costs of the automation of the registration of the Dutch population at the municipal offices were more than twice as much as were estimated (*Volkskrant*, 5 January 1990). A few years ago the estimates of the costs were about US$25 million. New calculations show that there is a deficit of more than US$30 million.

A field study by the Eindhoven University of Technology[1] gives an overview of the present state of the art of

Reprinted from *Information and Software Technology*, Vol. 34, No. 10, Oct. 1992, F.J. Heemstra, "Software Cost Estimation," pp. 627–639, 1992, with kind permission from Elsevier Science–NL, Sara Burgerhartstraat 25; 1055 KV Amsterdam, The Netherlands.

the estimation and control of software development projects in 598 Dutch organizations. The most remarkable conclusions are:

- 35% of the participating organizations do not make an estimate
- 50% of the responding organizations record no data on an ongoing project
- 57% do not use cost-accounting
- 80% of the projects executed by the participating organizations have overruns of budgets and duration
- the mean overruns of budgets and duration are 50%

Van Lierop et al.[2] measured extensively whether development activities were executed according to plan. They investigated the reasons for the differences between plan and reality, and overall 80 development activities were measured. For all these activities 3203 hours were planned but 3838 hours were used, which means an overshoot of 20% on average of the planned number of hours. The duration of the activities (in days) proved to be 28% longer on average than planned. For all the activities 406 days of duration were planned, while the actual number of days proved to be 526.

In the literature the impression is given, mistakenly, that software development without overshoots of plans and budgets is not possible. This impression is inaccurate, and other measurements confirm this[3]. These show that 6% of all the activities had a shorter duration than planned and 58% were executed according to plan and were ready exactly on time. With regard to the development effort, it appeared that 25% of the activities needed less effort than estimated and 30% needed precisely the estimated effort. The reasons for the differences between plan and reality prove to be very specific for the development situation. In the organization where the measurements were taken the reasons were mainly related to things underestimation of the quantity of work, underestimation of the complexity of the application, and specifications which proved to be unrealistic from a technical point of view. In other organizations, where similar measurements were taken, other reasons were discovered. As a result, other control actions are, of course, necessary. This conclusion fits well with the results of research carried out by Beers[4]. Thirty experienced software developers, project managers, and others, were asked to give the reasons for unsuccessful software projects. The answers can be summarized briefly as 'many minds, many thoughts'. It was not possible to indicate just one reason. A long list of all kinds of reasons were given.

It is alarming that it is so difficult for organizations to control the development of software. This is sufficient reason to emphasize that software development cost estimation and control should take its place as a fully fledged branch within discipline of software development.

WHAT MAKES SOFTWARE COST ESTIMATION SO DIFFICULT?

The main question, when confronting the above-mentioned problems, is what it is that makes software cost estimation so difficult. There are many reasons and, without going into detail, some can be listed as follows:

(1) There is a lack of data on completed software projects. This kind of data can support project management in making estimates.
(2) Estimates are often done hurriedly, without an appreciation for the effort required to do a credible job. In addition, too often it is the case that an estimate is needed before clear specifications of the system requirements have been produced. Therefore, a typical situation is that estimators are being pressured to write an estimate too quickly for a system that they do not fully understand.
(3) Clear, complete and reliable specifications are difficult to formulate, especially at the start of a project. Changes, adaptations and additions are more the rule than the exception: as a consequence plans and budgets must be adapted too.
(4) Characteristics of software and software development make estimating difficult. For example, the level of abstraction, complexity, measurability of product and process, innovative aspects, etc.
(5) A great number of factors have an influence on the effort and time to develop software. These factors are called 'cost drivers'. Examples are size and complexity of the software, commitment and participation of the user organization, experience of the development team. In general these cost drivers are difficult to determine in operation.
(6) Rapid changes in information technology (IT) and the methodology of software development are a problem for a stabilization of the estimation process. For example, it is difficult to predict the influence of new workbenches, fourth and fifth generation languages, prototyping strategies, and so on.
(7) An estimator (mostly the project manager) cannot have much experience in developing estimates, especially for large projects. How many 'large' projects can someone manage in, for example, 10 years?
(8) An apparent bias of software developers towards underestimation. An estimator is likely to consider how long a certain portion of the software would take and then to extrapolate this estimate to the rest of the system, ignoring the non-linear aspects of software development, for example co-ordination and management.
(9) The estimator estimates the time it would take to perform the task personally, ignoring the fact that a lot of work will be done by less experienced people, and junior staff with a lower productivity rate.

(10) There exists a serious mis-assumption of a linear relation between the required capacity per unit of time and the available time. This would mean that software developed by 25 people in two years could be accomplished by 50 people in one year. The assumption is seriously wrong. According to Brooks[5] the crucial corollary is: 'Adding people to a late project only makes it later'.

(11) The estimator tends to reduce the estimates to some degree, in order to make the bid more acceptable.

PREREQUISITES FOR SOFTWARE COST ESTIMATION

There are many ways to get to grips with the SCE problems. From an organizational perspective there are numerous ways to improve software project management: allocation of responsibilities; decision-making; organizing project work; monitoring and auditing of development tasks. Also software cost estimation can be looked at from a sociological and psychological point of view. This refers, for example, to commitment, organizing group cohesion, style of leadership, and so on. The technical side of the job is also an important issue to take into consideration. For example, the availability of good equipment such as design, programming, test and documentation tools, hardware facilities, etc.

There are many factors that have an influence on the effort and duration of software development. Several prerequisites must be fulfilled to address the problems listed above and to guarantee a sound basis for predicting effort, duration and the capacity to develop the software. These prerequisites are:

Insight in the characteristics of:

- the product (software) that has to   WHAT
  be developed
- the production means   WITH WHAT
- the production personnel   WHO
- the organization of the production   HOW
- the user/user organization   FOR WHOM

Availability of:

- Techniques and tools for software cost estimation.

In this section the attention will be focused on the WHAT, WITH WHAT, WHO, HOW and FOR WHOM factors, referred to as cost drivers in the literature. In the next section, SCE techniques and tools will be discussed.

There are many cost drivers. A study by Noth and Kretzschmar[6] found that more than 1200 different drivers were mentioned. Although there was considerable overlap in meaning, it is impossible to take them all into consideration during SCE. It is important for an organization to consider what are the most dominant cost factors. Within the context of this paper it is impossible to give an extended overview of the overwhelming number of drivers, so concentration will be on:

- a way of structuring the cost drivers
- listing the drivers which are commonly regarded as important
- some general considerations

Table 1 presents a structure of cost drivers in five categories. For each category the most important drivers are listed. From the literature and practice it is known that it is not easy to handle the cost drivers. When making an estimate one has to know which cost drivers are the most important in the specific situation, what the values are of the drivers, and what the influences are on effort and duration. In answering these questions it is important to pay attention to several issues:

Definition   There is a lack of clear and accepted definitions for drivers, such as size, quality, complexity, experience, etc.

Quantification   The majority of the cost drivers are hard to quantify. Often one has to use measures such as many, moderate, few, etc.

Table 1. A structure of important cost drivers[7]

WHAT (product)	WITH WHAT (means)	WHO (personnel)	HOW (project)	FOR WHOM (user)
Size of the software	Computer constraints —execution time	Quality of personnel	Requirements project duration —stretch out	Participation
Required quality	—response time —memory capacity	Experience of personnel	—compression	Number of users
Requirements volatility	User of tools		Basis for	Stability of user organization, procedures, way of working
Software complexity	Use of modern	Quality management	project control —matrix org.	
Level of reuse	programming techniques —information hiding	Availability for project	—project org. —prototyping —incremental	Experience of user with automation,
Amount of documentation	—chief prog. team —structured program		—linear devel.	level of education in automation
Type of application	—top-down design		—software devel.	

Objectivity Subjectivity is a potential risk factor. What may be complex for developer A is not complex for developer B.

Correlation It is difficult to consider one driver by itself. A change in the value of driver A may have consequences in the values of several other cost drivers. This is a difficulty from the viewpoint of measurability.

Relation between driver and effort For estimation it is important to predict the relation between, for example, software size and the required effort, a specified quality level and required effort, etc. From the literature we know that there is little clarity about these relations.

Calibration It is impossible to talk about 'the most important' cost drivers in isolation. It differs from situation to situation.

Effectivity and efficiency There is conflict between effectivity and efficiency. From an effectivity perspective it is worthwhile to pay a lot of attention to, for example, user participation. For the efficiency of a project it is justifiable to avoid user involvement.

Human factors Almost all research agrees on the dominating influence of cost drivers, such as experience and quality of the personnel. This means that investment in 'good' developers is important.

Reuse In many studies reuse is regarded as (one of) the most important factors to increase productivity[8-10].

SOFTWARE COST ESTIMATION: TECHNIQUES AND TOOLS

In the literature you can find a great number of techniques for estimating software development costs. Most of them are a combination of the following primary techniques[11]:

(1) Estimates made by an expert.
(2) Estimates based on reasoning by analogy.
(3) Estimates based on Price-to-Win.
(4) Estimates based on available capacity.
(5) Estimates based on the use of parametric models.

Furthermore two main approaches can be distinguished:

(1) Top-down
   In the top-down approach the estimation of the overall project is derived from the global characteristics of the product. The total estimated cost is then split up among the various components.
(2) Bottom-up
   In the bottom-up approach the cost of each individual component is estimated by the person who will be responsible for developing the component. The individual estimated costs are summed to get the overall cost estimate of the project.

The reliability of estimates based on expert judgement (1) depends a great deal to the degree in which a new project conforms with the experience and the ability of the expert to remember facts of historical projects. Mostly the estimates are qualitative and not objective. An important problem in using this method is that it is difficult for someone else to reproduce and use the knowledge and experience of an expert. This can lead to misleading situations where the rules of thumb of an expert are becoming general rules and used in inapplicable situations. Despite the disadvantages, this technique is usually used in situations where a first indication of effort and time is needed, especially in the first phases of software development in which the specifications of the product are vague and continually adapted.

The foundation of a cost estimation technique based on reasoning by analogy (2) is an analysed database of similar historical projects or similar project parts or modules. To find a similarity between a new project and one or more completed projects it is necessary to collect and record data and characteristics of old projects.

The Price-to-Win (3) technique can hardly be called an SCE technique. Primarily commercial motives play an important part in using this approach. It is remarkable that the estimates of organizations which use Price-to-Win are no less accurate than organizations which use other methods[7].

The basis of the estimation method which regards SCE as a capacity (4) problem is the availability of means, especially of personnel. An example is: 'Regarding our capacity planning, three men are available for the new project over the next four months. So the planned effort will be 12 man months'. If the specifications of the software are not clear, this method can be successful. An unfavourable side-effect is that in situations of overestimation the planned effort will be used completely. This effect is based on Parkinson's law that 'Work expands to fill the available volume'.

In parametric models (5) the development time and effort is estimated as a function of a number of variables. These variables represent the most important cost drivers. The nucleus of an estimation model is a number of algorithms and parameters. The values of the parameters and the kind of algorithms are, to a significant extent, based on the contents of a database of completed projects. In the next section a more comprehensive explanation of estimation models is given.

As mentioned earlier only 65% of the organizations which participated on the field study estimate a software project. Table 2 shows the frequency of use of the different techniques. The figures show that most organizations make use of data from past projects in some way. Obviously this works on an informal basis, because only 50% of the participating organizations record data from completed projects. Estimates based on expert judgement and the capacity method prove to be quite popular despite the disadvantages of these methods.

Table 2. Use of cost estimation techniques (an organization can use more than one technique)

	Use (%)
Expert judgement	25.5
Analogy method	60.8
Price-to-Win	8.9
Capacity problem	20.8
Parametric models	13.7

The next sections of this paper focus on the use of SCE models. There was a rapid growth of models in the 1970s. In the 1980s and the 1990s, however, few new models have been developed despite the increasing importance of controlling and estimating software development. Most of the 1970 models are of no interest to present industrial practitioners. There is a tendency towards automated versions (tools) of (combinations or refinements) existing models. An important question is whether this kind of model can solve all of the problems discussed above.

SOFTWARE COST ESTIMATION MODELS

In this section, one estimation technique, namely SCE models, will be discussed and the principles of SCE models described, making a distinction between sizing and productivity models. The characteristics of some well-known models will also be given.

The principles of SCE models

Most models found nowadays are two-stage models[7]. The first stage is a sizer and the second stage provides a productivity adjustment factor.

In the first stage an estimate regarding the size of the product to be developed is obtained. In practice several sizing techniques are used. The most well-known sizers nowadays are function points[12] and lines of code[11]. But other sizing techniques like 'software science'[13] and DeMarco's Bang method[14,15], have been defined. The result of a sizing model is the size/volume of the software to be developed, expressed as the number of lines of source code, number of statements, or the number of functions points.

In the second stage it is estimated how much time and effort it will cost to develop the software of the estimated size. First, the estimate of the size is converted into an estimate in nominal man-months of effort. As this nominal effort takes no advantage of knowledge con-

cerning the specific characteristics of the software-product, the way the software-product will be developed and the production means, a number of cost influencing factors (cost drivers) are added to the model. The effect of these cost drivers must be estimated. This effect is often called a productivity adjustment factor. Application of this correction factor to the nominal estimation of effort provides a more realistic estimate.

Some models, like FPA[16], are focused more on the sizing stage. Others, like the well-known COCOMO model[11] on the productivity stage and some tools, such as Before You Leap[17] combine two models to cover both stages. Figure 1 shows the two stages in SCE models.

Figure 2 shows the sizing and the productivity stages in the context of general cost estimation. In Figure 2 five components of the general cost estimation structure are shown. Besides the sizing and productivity components, a phase distribution and sensitivity/risk analysis component are distinguished. In the phase distribution component the total effort and duration is split up over the phases and activities of a project. This division has to be based on empirical data of past projects. The sensitivity and risk analysis phase supports project management — especially at the start of a project when the uncertainty is great — in determining the risk factors of a project and the sensitivity of the estimates to the cost drivers settings. Again data on past projects provide an important input for this component. Before using a model for the first time validation is necessary, and it may also be necessary to calibrate the model. Mostly the environment in which the SCE model has been developed and the database of completed projects on which the model is based will differ from the project characteristics of the environment(s) in which the model is to be used. To make validation and calibration possible, data on historical projects have to be available in an organization. As already mentioned, this information is often lacking.

Most of the tools implementing SCE models do not support project management in all of these steps. The seven steps are:

(1) Creation of database of completed projects.
(2) Size estimation.
(3) Productivity estimation.
(4) Phase distribution.
(5) Sensitivity and risk analysis.
(6) Validation.
(7) Calibration.

Calibration and risk and sensitivity analysis are especially lacking.

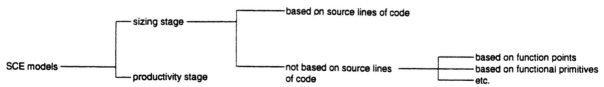

Figure 1. Structuring of SCE models

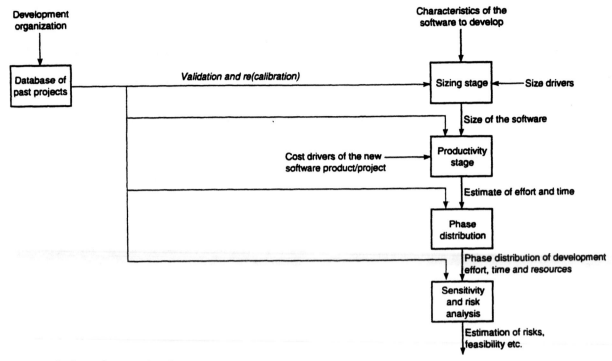

Figure 2. General cost estimation structure

An overview of SCE models

In the past 10 years a number of SCE models have been developed. This section does not give an exhaustive treatment of all the models: the overview is limited to one example of a sizing model, one productivity model, some models which are relevant from an historical point of view, well documented and within the experience of the author, and some models which introduce new ideas.

The COnstructive COst MOdel (COCOMO)

COCOMO[11,18] is the best documented and most transparent model currently available. The main focus in COCOMO is upon estimating the influence of 15 cost drivers on the development effort. Before this can be done, an estimate of the software size must be available. COCOMO does not support the sizing estimation stage: it only gives several equations based on 63 completed projects at TRW. The equations represent the relations between size and effort and between effort and development time. The equations are shown in Table 3. A distinction is made between three development modes: the organic mode (stable development environment, less innovative, relatively small size); the embedded mode (developing within tight constraints, innovative, complex, high volatility of requirements); and the semi-detached mode (between organic and embedded mode).

The nominal effort is adjusted by the influence of 15 cost drivers. In Table 4 the 15 COCOMO cost drivers are listed with the adjustment for each driver value. For example: where the required reliability of the software is

determined to be very high, the nominal effort has to be multiplied by 1.40. Furthermore COCOMO provides tables to apportion the adjusted estimated effort and development over the project phases and, in the detailed version of the model, to refine the adjustment for each phase. For example: the quality of the programmer has less influence in the feasibility phase than in the design phase. Thus phase dependent adjustment factors are used in the detailed model.

Function point analysis (FPA)

FPA has been developed by Albrecht[16] of IBM, and made widely available through the user groups *Guide and Share*. Albrecht was looking for a method to measure productivity in software development. For that purpose he developed FPA as an alternative measure to the number of lines of code. The method is programming language or fourth generation tool independent. The method has been refined several times by Rudolph[19,20], Albrecht and Gaffney[12], and Symons[21,22]. The principle of FPA is simple and is based on the number of 'functions' the software has to fulfil. These functions are

Table 3. The relation between the nominal effort and size and between development time and effort. KDSI = number of delivered source instructions/1000

Development mode	Man-month (nominal)	Development time (nominal)
Organic	$3.2 * KDSI^{1.05}$	$2.5 * MM (nom)^{0.38}$
Semi-detached	$3.0 * KDSI^{1.12}$	$2.5 * MM (nom)^{0.35}$
Embedded	$2.8 * KDSI^{1.20}$	$2.5 * MM (nom)^{0.32}$

Table 4. The COCOMO cost drivers and their influence on the nominal effort

Cost drivers	Value of the cost drivers					
	Very low	Low	Average	High	Very high	Extra high
Required reliability	0.75	0.88	1.00	1.15	1.40	
Database size		0.94	1.00	1.08	1.16	
Complexity software	0.70	0.85	1.00	1.15	1.30	1.65
Constraints execution time			1.00	1.11	1.30	1.66
Memory constraints			1.00	1.06	1.21	1.56
Hardware volatility		0.87	1.00	1.15	1.30	
Response time constraints		0.87	1.00	1.07	1.15	
Quality analysts	1.46	1.19	1.00	0.86	0.71	
Experience with application	1.29	1.13	1.00	0.91	0.82	
Quality programmers	1.42	1.17	1.00	0.86	0.70	
Hardware experience	1.21	1.10	1.00	0.90		
Programming language experience	1.14	1.07	1.00	0.95		
Use modern programming techniques	1.24	1.10	1.00	0.91	0.82	
Use software tools	1.24	1.10	1.00	0.91	0.83	
Project duration constraints	1.23	1.08	1.00	1.04	1.10	

related to the types of data the software uses and generates. Within FPA the software is characterized by the five functions:

- the external input type
- the external output type
- the external inquiry type
- the logical internal file type
- the external interface file type

For each of these five types the number of simple, average and complex occurrences that are expected in the software is estimated. By weighting each number with an appropriate weight a number is obtained, the unadjusted number of function points. This indication for nominal size is then adjusted, using 14 technical characteristics. Figure 3 gives an overview of function point analysis.

PRICE-S

The PRICE-S model (Programming Review of Information Costing and Evaluation — Software) is developed and supported by RCA PRICE Systems. An important disadvantage with regard to COCOMO and FPA is that the underlying concepts and ideas are not publicly defined and the users are presented with the model as a black box. The user of PRICE sends the input to a time-sharing computer in the USA, UK, or France and gets back his estimates immediately. Despite this disadvantage and the high rental price, there are many users, especially in America. There is, however, an important motivation for American companies to use the model. The US Department of Defense demands a PRICE estimate for all quotations for a software project. PRICE has separate sizer and productivity function.

The PUTNAM model

This SCE model was developed by Putnam in 1974[23]. He based his model on the work of Norden[34]. For many projects at IBM, Norden plotted frequency distributions, in which he showed how many people were allocated to the development and maintenance of a software product during the life-cycle. The curves he made fitted very well with the Rayleigh curves. His findings were merely empirical. He found no explanations for the shape of the effort curve. On the assumptions of Norden, Putnam formulated his model. There is not enough space in this paper to explain the principles of the model and the reader is referred to Putnam[23,24], Putnam and Fitzsimmons[25] and Londeix[26].

Before You Leap (BYL)

BYL is a commercial package based on a link-up between FPA and COCOMO[17]. BYL starts with a calculation of the amount of net function points. This amount is then translated into source lines of code, taking in account the language used. For Cobol, for instance, one function point is equal to 105 SLOC, for LISP 64, etc. This estimate of the size in SLOC is precisely the necessary input for COCOMO and the COCOMO part of BYL, taking into account the influence on effort of the 15 COCOMO cost drivers, calculates the estimates of costs and timescale.

Estimacs

Estimacs has been developed by H. Rubin[27-29] and Computer Associates[30], and is available as a software package. The model consists of nine modules: a function point module; a risk module; an effort module (to estimate development and maintenance effort), etc. The most important and extensive module is Effort. The user has to answer 25 input questions. These questions are partly related to the complexity of the user-organization and partly to the complexity and size of the software to be developed. The way Estimacs translates the input to an estimation of effort is not clear. Like many other models, Estimacs is a 'closed model'.

Function count		←	Max range: Factor * 2	→	
			Level of information processing function		
Type ID	**Description**	**Simple**	**Average**	**Complex**	**Total**
IT	External input	--*3 = --	--*4 = ---	--*6 = ---	-----
OT	External output	--*4 = --	--*5 = ---	--*7 = ---	-----
FT	Logical internal file	--*7 = --	--*10 = --	--*15 = --	-----
EI	External interface file	--*5 = --	--*7 = ---	--*10 = --	-----
QT	External inquiry	--*3 = --	--*4 = ---	--*6 = ---	-----
FC			Total unadjusted function points		

↑ Maximum range factor 2.5 ↓

General information processing characteristics

	Characteristics	DI		Characteristics	DI
C1	Data communications	---	C8	On-line update	---
C2	Distributed functions	---	C9	Complex processing	---
C3	Performance	---	C10	Re-usability	---
C4	Heavily used configuration	---	C11	Installation ease	---
C5	Transaction rate	---	C12	Operational ease	---
C6	On-line data entry	---	C13	Multiple sites	---
C7	End-user efficiency	---	C14	Facilitate change	---
PC			Total degree of influence		---

DI Values

Not present or no influence	= 0	Average influence = 3
Insignificant influence	= 1	Significant influence = 4
Moderate influence	= 2	Strong influence, throughout = 5

FC	(Function count)	≡	Total unadjusted function points
PC	(Process complexity)	≡	Total degree of influence
PCA	(Process complexity adjustment)	=	$0.65 + 0.01 * PC$
FP	(Function point measure)	=	$FC * PCA$

Figure 3. Overview of function point analysis

SPQR-20

SPQR stands for Software Productivity, Quality and Reliability. The model has been developed by C. Jones[31]. SPQR claims to be applicable for all kinds of software projects as well as an estimate of duration, costs and effort to develop software; the model also gives an estimate of maintenance costs. SPQR uses FPA to size the volume of a program. The model is based on an extensive database of past projects. There are four versions of model, SPQR 10, 20, 50 and 100 (the numbers stand for the number of questions the model user has to answer and gives an indication of the degree of refinement of the versions). SPQR-20 is the only commercially available version at the moment, not marketed by C. Jones any more but overtaken by his Checkmark product.

BIS-Estimator

BIS-Estimator is completely different from the previously described models. According to the documentation[32] the model claims to be a 'knowledge-based tool'. This cannot be fully confirmed, because the principles of the model are secret for the most part. The model starts with a 'soft' estimate. This is a rough estimate of duration and effort based on (far too few) input questions. Next a 'hard' estimate is made for each phase. Based on the estimates by phase, by means of extrapolation, an estimate of the complete project is made. The 'hard' estimate has to be made at the start of and/or during each phase. The model has facilities to base the estimate upon a comparison with a number of projects, selected by the model user. A positive feature of the model is the evolutionary approach. This means that the estimation process changes during software development. As a result of the kind of questions, data and considerations, an estimate is based on the model changes for each phase.

Several models and computerized versions (tools) are available, but just a few of these have been described briefly above. Without going into detail, Table 5 gives a more extensive list of models and tools. The reader is referred to publications in the literature for a more comprehensive description of each. The models in the list are in chronological order (year of publication). The first 11 are ancient models and of no current interest to practitioners.

COMPARISON OF SCE MODELS

During the past few years several empirical studies have been carried out to validate the various SCE models. Validation is important but difficult to do, because of the demand to capture large amounts of data about completed software projects. As mentioned before, data collection is not common in the software community. It is labour and time-intensive and requires an attitude not only focused on the constructive part but also on the analytical part of software engineering. Furthermore data collection, usable for validating SCE, is limited to a relative small number of software development organizations. Only a few organizations realize large software projects each year. Nevertheless, a number of validation research investigations have been carried out. In this section some of them will be discussed.

The models discussed earlier differ considerably. Experiments show that estimates made by the different models for the same project vary strongly. Furthermore the estimates differ very much from the real development cost and duration. To give an opinion upon the quality of SCE models, it must be known what kind of demands have to be made upon these models. In Table 6 an overview of these demands/requirements is presented. These requirements are a part of an evaluation method for SCE models. This method has been developed by Heemstra, Kusters and van Genuchten[1] and used to

Table 5. SCE models and tools with references

Model	Source
SDC	Nelson, E A *Management handbook for the estimation of computer programming costs*, AD-A648750, Systems Development Corporation (1966)
TRW Wolverton	Wolverton, R W 'The cost of development large-scale software' *IEEE Trans. on computers*, Vol c-23, No 6 (June 1974)
TELECOTE	Frederic, B C *A professional model for estimating computer program development costs*. Telecote Research Inc. (1974)
BOEING	Black, R K D, Curnow, R P, Katz, R and Gray, M D 'BCS software production data' *Final technical report*, *RADC-TR-77-116*, Boeing Computer Services Inc. (March 1977)
IBM/FSD	Walston, C E and Felix, C P 'A method of programming measurement and estimating' *IBM System J.* Vol 16 (1977)
DOTY	Herd, J R, Postak, J N, Russell, W E and Stewart, K R 'Software cost estimation — study results. *Final technical report*, *RA-DC-TR-77-220*, Vol 1, DOTY Associates, Inc., Rockville, MD (1977)
ESD1	Duquette, J A and Bourbon, G A 'ESD, A computerized model for estimating software life cycle costs' *FSD-TR-235* Vol 1 (April 1978)
SLIM	Putnam, L H 'A general empirical solution to the macro software sizing and estimating problem' *IEEE Trans. Soft. Eng.* SE-4, 4 (1978)
Surbock	Surbock, E K *Management software development* Projekten Berlin (1978) (In German)
GRC	Carriere, W M and Thibodeau, R 'Development of a logistic software cost estimating technique for foreign military sales' *GRC Report CR-3-839* (1979)
Grumman	Sandler, G and Bachowitz, B 'Software cost models — Grumman experience' *IEEE, quantitative software model conference* (1979)
PRICE-S	Freiman, F R and Park, R E 'The Price software cost model: RCA government systems division' *IEEE* (1979)
FPA	Albrecht, A J 'Measuring application development productivity' *Proc. of Joint SHARE/GUIDE/IBM application development symp.* (October 1979)
SLICE	Kustanowitz, A L 'System life cycle estimation (SLICE): a new approach to estimating resources for application program development' *IEEE first international computer software and application conference, Chicago* (1980)
FAST	Freiman, F R 'The FAST methodology' *J. of parametrics*, Vol 1 No 2 (1981)
Baily/Basili	Bailey, J W and Basili V R 'A meta-model for software development resource expenditures' *Proc. 5th Int. Conf. Soft. Engin., IEEE* (1981)
COCOMO	Boehm, B W *Software engineering economics* Prentice-Hall (1981)
SOFTCOST	Tausworthe, R C 'Deep space network software cost estimation model' Publication 81-7, *Jet Propulsion Laboratory*, Pasadena, CA (1981)
BANG	DeMarco, T *Controlling software projects: management, measurement and estimation* Yourdon Press, New York (1982)
JS 3/System-4/Seer	Jensen, R W 'An improved macrolevel software development resource estimation model' *Proc. 5th ISPA Conf.* St Louis MO (1983)
COPMO	Thebaut, S M and Shen, V Y 'An analytic resource model for large-scale software development' *Inf. Proc. Management*, Vol 20 No 1-2 (1984)
GECOMO	Gecomo 'Software tools for professionals' *GEC Software Documentation*, G & C Company, London (1985)
ESTIMACS	Computer Associates. CA-Estimacs *User Guide*, Release 5.0 (July 1986)
BYL	Before You Leap. *User's Guide*, Gordon Group (1986)
SPQR/Checkmark	Jones, C *Programming productivity* McGraw-Hill (1986)
Jeffery	Jeffery, D R 'A software development productivity model for MIS environments' *J. of Systems and Software* 7 (1987)
ESTIMATE/1	Estimate/1. Documentative Method/1: Automated Project Estimating Aid. Arthur Anderson (1987)
BIS	BIS/Estimator. User Manual, version 4.4, BIS Applied System Ltd (1987)
SECOMO	Goethert, W B 'SECOMO' in Boehm, B W *Documentation of the seminar: software cost estimation using COCOMO and ADA COCOMO*, SAL, London. 1988' ITT Research Institute, Data & Analysis Center for Software.

Table 6. Requirements for SCE models

Model requirements	Application requirements	Implementation requirements
Linked to software control method	Possibilities for calibration	User-friendliness of the tool
Applicability at the start of a project	Accuracy of the estimations	Possibilities for sensitivity analyses
Fit with the data that is available during development		Possibilities for risk analysis
Possible to adjust estimate due to changing objectives		Open model, is it possible to see how the results were obtained
Definition of domain model is suitable for		Clarity of input definition
		Completeness and detail of output

evaluate the eight models described above. The results of that evaluation are presented in Table 7 and described in more detail in Heemstra[7]. From the table it can be seen that there are only few plusses. The conclusion is that the quality of the models is poor and much improvement is necessary. The accuracy of the estimations were evaluated by several tests. The way the tests were executed and the results obtained will be described. The objectives of the tests were:

- to determine the accuracy of the estimate using SCE models in a semi-realistic situation
- to determine whether these models will be accepted by project management

After a severe selection procedure only two SCE models remained. These were the BYL and Estimacs models. During the tests 14 experienced project leaders were asked to make a number of estimates for a project that had actually been carried out. The project was described as if it was at the start of the project. The project leaders had to make three estimates. The first estimate of effort and duration (the 'manual' estimate) was made on the basis of the project leaders' knowledge and experience. Next, two estimates were made using the models selected. In conclusion, a final estimate was made on the basis of the project leaders' knowledge and experience together with the model estimates. Each estimate was

evaluated directly using a questionnaire, and the tests ended with a discussion session. The results are presented in Table 8.

The real effort and duration were eight man-months and six months. The main conclusions of the experiment were that on the basis of the differences found between the estimates and reality, it has not been shown that the selected models can be used for a reliable estimation tool at an early stage of software development. All in all, the project leaders were not wildly enthusiastic about these tools, but they were, nevertheless, felt to be acceptable as a check-list and as a means of communication. It should be mentioned that the selected project is small. Most models are calibrated on data from medium/large projects.

Kemerer[33] shows that estimates of different models can differ considerably. For each model he investigated the difference between actual and estimated number of man-months. He used COCOMO, Estimacs, FPA and Putnam's model to estimate the required effort of 15 already realized projects. From Table 9 it can be seen that for both COCOMO and Putnam's model there were sharp overestimations. FPA and Estimacs gave distinctly better results with overshoots of 100% and 85%, respectively. A similar study was carried out by Rubin[29]. A project description was sent to Jensen (Jensen's model), Greene (Putnam's model SLIM) and Rook (GECOMO) and to himself (Rubin's model Estimacs).

Table 7. Evaluation of models

Requirements	Models							
	COCOMO	PRICE	PUTNAM	FPA	BYL	ESTIMACS	SPQR	BIS
Model requirements								
Linked to software control method	– –	– –	– –	– –	– –	+ +	– –	– –
Applicable at an early stage	– –	– –	– –	+	+	+ +	+	–
Using available data	+	– –	– –	– –	– –	– –	– –	+ +
Adjustment to objectives	+	+	+	– –	– –	+	+ +	– –
Definition of scope/domain	+	–	–	+ +	–	–	–	+ +
Application requirements								
Calibration	–	– –	– –	–	+	+	–	–
Accuracy	nt	nt	nt	nt	t	t	nt	nt
Implementation requirements								
User friendliness	+ +	–	+	+	+ +	+	+	+
Sensitivity analysis	– –	+	– –	– –	+ +	+ +	–	–
Risk analysis	– –	– –	– –	– –	– –	+ +	+	– –
Open model/traceability	+ +	– –	+ +	+ +	+ +	–	–	+
Definition input	+ +	–	+ +	–	+	+	+	+
Completeness and detail output	+	+ +	–	–	+ +	+ +	+ +	+ +

+ + = satisfies the requirement; + = sufficient; – = insufficient; – – = the model does not satisfy the requirement; nt = the model was not tested on accuracy; t = the models were tested

Table 8. Some results of the tests. Duration is given in months, effort in man-months

Variable	μ	σ
Effort		
Manual estimate	28.4	18.3
BYL estimate	27.7	14.0
Estimacs estimate	48.5	13.9
Final estimate	27.7	12.8
Duration		
Manual estimate	11.2	3.7
BYL estimate	8.5	2.4
Final estimate	12.1	3.4

Table 9. Estimates of the actual and estimated number of man-months using four different models

| Models | Averages for all projects | | |
	Actual number of MM	Estimated number of MM	(Estimated divided by actual) * 100%
GECOMO	219.25	1291.75	607.85
Putnam	219.25	2060.17	771.87
FPA	260.30	533.23	167.29
Estimacs	287.97	354.77	85.48

The main purpose was to compare and contrast the different sort of information required by the four models. Also a comparison was made between the estimates obtained using the models, that is to say the number of man-months and the duration for the development of the selected project. From Table 10 it can be seen that the estimates vary significantly. Also Rubin's explanation is that the models are based on different databases of completed projects and have not been calibrated and the four participants made different assumptions in choosing the settings of the cost drivers.

THE IMPORTANCE OF SCE MODELS

The field study, mentioned earlier in the paper, shows that SCE models are currently not generally accepted in organizations surveyed. Only 51 of the 364 organizations that estimate software development use models. An analysis showed that these 51 model-users make no better estimates than the non-model-users. These results are disappointing at first glance. It does not mean, however, that it makes no sense to spend further research effort on models. All the investigations mentioned before agree that the poor quality is primarily due to using the models wrongly. For example: use of models requires organizational bounded data of past projects. Most of the time models are used without calibration. If models cannot be adapted the result will be less accurate estimates. The majority of the models do not support calibration.

It is worth while to promote the development of better estimation tools, despite the shortcomings of the existing models. In this section some arguments are put forward that underline the necessity to invest more effort and time in the development of SCE models.

In making an estimate, especially at an early stage of development, a lot of uncertainty and fuzziness exists. It is not known which cost drivers play a part in the estimation and what the influence of the cost drivers will be. There are many participants involved in the project (project manager, customer, developer, user, etc.). Often they all have their own hidden agendas and goals conflicting with each other (minimalization of the costs, maximalization of the quality, minimalization of the duration, optimal use of

employees, etc.). For project management it is difficult to predict the progress of a project in such fuzzy situations. To make point estimations like 'duration will be 321 man-months of which 110 for analysis, 70 for design, etc.', will be of less importance. Such exact figures do not fit in with the nature of the problem. Project management will be more interested in a number of scenarios from which alternatives can be chosen and in the sensitiveness of an estimation to specific cost drivers. For example: what will be the result on the duration of the addition of two more analysts to the project: what will be the influence on effort if the available development time will be decreased sharply; what will be the result on effort and duration if the complexity of the software to be developed has been estimated too high or too low, etc. An approach of the estimation problem like this gives project management more insight and feeling for alternative solutions. Furthermore this approach offers a proper basis for project control. If an estimate proves to be sensible for changes of a specific cost driver, this provides a warning for project management to pay full attention to this cost driver during development.

Often project management will be confronted with little tolerance in defined duration, price and quality. In such cases project management wants support in choosing the values of the decision variables. What are the available possible choices to meet the given objectives. Which personnel in combination with which tools and by means of which kind of project organization are suitable as possible solutions. The conclusion is that there is no need for a rigid 'calculation tool'. This does not fit with the characteristics of the estimation problem, namely uncertainty, fuzziness, little structuring, and unclear and incomplete specifications.

An important prerequisite for successful estimation is the development, acceptance and use of a uniform set of

Table 10. Comparison of SCE models by Rubin[29]

		Effort	Duration
Mode	Jensen	940 MM	31 m
	Putnam	200 MM	17 m
	GECOMO	363 MM	23 m
	Estimacs	17 100 hrs	16 m

MM = man-months; m = months

definitions and standards. This results in agreements such as:

- How many times an estimate is made for a project. For example: five times for each project that costs more than 12 man-months.
- In what phases during execution an estimate is made. For example: during the feasibility study, during the specification phase and after finishing the design.
- Which employees are involved in the estimation process. For example: project management, customers, developers.
- What will be estimated. For example: all development activities with regard to the phases feasibility, specification, design, etc. or all activities including training, documentation, etc.
- The output of an estimate. For example: costs in dollars, effort in man-months, duration in months.
- The factors which can be regarded as the most important cost drivers and have to be recorded. For example: size, reliability, type of application, quality of personnel, etc.
- A set of definitions. For example: volume will be expressed in function points, documentation contains of ..., high complexity means ..., etc.

The result will be a comprehensive list of standardized agreements. It is important that these are really applied in the subsequent project. An SCE model that meets requirements such as a set of clear definitions, measurable and relevant cost drivers, flexibility with regards to other control methods, etc. will result in a more structural approach to software cost estimation and control.

CONCLUSIONS AND RECOMMENDATIONS

In this final section some concrete guidelines for controlling and estimating software development will be offered. Most of these guidelines have been discussed at different levels of detail in the previous sections.

Determine the level of uncertainty

High uncertainty needs another approach of cost estimation and control than does low uncertainty. High uncertainty corresponds with risk analysis, estimating and margins, exploration oriented problem-solving, expert-oriented estimating techniques, etc. Low uncertainty corresponds with cost estimation models (calculation tools), experiences from past projects, realization oriented problem-solving, the estimate is regarded as a norm, etc.

Cost estimation and data collection

Collection of data of completed projects is necessary for successful cost estimation. Cost models, estimation by analogy and experts require such data. It is no solution to use data collected from other organizations. The relevant data are different for each organization.

Use more than one estimation technique

A lot of research shows that the quality of the current estimation techniques is poor. The lack of accurate and reliable estimation techniques combined with the financial, technical, organizational and social risks of software projects, require a frequent estimation during the development of an application and the use of more than one estimation technique. More and different techniques are required, especially at the milestones of the development phases. The level of knowledge of the software whose cost we are trying to estimate is growing during a project. A possibility is to use another model during a project, because more information and more *accurate* information is available; a cascade of techniques — for example Wide Band Delphi, Estimacs, DeMarco, COCOMO — is a possible solution.

Cost estimation needs commitment

Software development has to be done by highly qualified professionals. For such people some characteristics are relevant, such as:

- individuality in work performance is important
- a good professional result of their work is important
- professionals want to be consulted in decisions, work planning, the desired result, etc.
- professionals do not want to be disturbed by management during the execution of their work

It is not wise to confront professional developers with a plan and estimate without any consultation. A hierarchical leadership is not suitable. In consulting the developers not only their expertise is used but also their involvement in the estimation process is increased. This results in a higher commitment than is necessary for the success of a project.

Cost estimation: a management problem

Software cost estimation is often wrongly regarded as a technical problem that can be solved with calculation models, a set of metrics and procedures. However, the opposite is true. The 'human aspects' are much more important. The quality, experience and composition of the project team, the degree in which the project leader can motivate, kindle enthusiasm and commit his developers, has more influence on delivering the software in time and within budget than the use of rigid calculations.

REFERENCES

1 Heemstra, F J, Kusters, R and van Genuchten, M 'Selections of software cost estimation models' *Report TUE/BDK* University of Technology Eindhoven (1989)

2 **Lierop van, F L G, Volkers, R S A, Genuchten, M van and Heemstra, F J** 'Has someone seen the software?' *Informatie* Vol 33 No 3 (1991) (In Dutch)

3 **Genuchten, van M I J M** 'Towards a software factory' *PhD Thesis,* University of Technology Eindhoven (1991)

4 **Beers** 'Problems, planning and knowledge, a study of the processes behind success and failure of an automation project' *PhD Series in general management. No 1* Faculty Industrial Engineering/Rotterdam School of Management, Erasmus University Rotterdam (1991) (In Dutch)

5 **Brooks, F B** *The mythical manmonth. Essays on software engineering* Addison-Wesley (1975)

6 **Noth, T and Kretzschmar, M** *Estimation of software development projects* Springer-Verlag (1984) (In German)

7 **Heemstra, F J** *How expensive is software? Estimation and control of software-development* Kluwer (1989) (In Dutch)

8 **Druffel, L E** 'Strategies for a DoD Software initiative' *CSS DUSD(RAT)* Washington, DC (1982)

9 **Conte, S D, Dunsmore, H F and Shen, V Y** *Software engineering metrics and models* Benjamin Cummins (1986)

10 **Reifer, D J** 'The economics of software reuse' *Proc. 14th Annual ISPA Conf.,* New Orleans (May 1991)

11 **Boehm, B W** *Software engineering economics* Prentice-Hall (1981)

12 **Albrecht, A J and Gaffney, J E** 'Software function, source lines of code, and development effort prediction: a software science validation' *IEEE Trans. Soft. Eng.* Vol SE-9 No 6 (1983)

13 **Halstead, M H** *Elements of software science* North-Holland (1977)

14 **DeMarco, T** *Controlling software projects: management, measurement and estimation* Yourdon Press, New York (1982)

15 **DeMarco, T** 'An algorithm for sizing software products' *Performance Evaluation Review* 12 pp 13–22 (1984)

16 **Albrecht, A J** 'Measuring application development productivity' *Proc. Joint SHARE/GUIDE/IBM application development symp.* (October 1979)

17 **Gordon** 'Before You Leap' *User's Guide* Gordon Group (1986)

18 **Boehm, B W** 'Software engineering economics' *IEEE Trans. Soft. Eng.* Vol 10 No 1 (January 1984)

19 **Rudolph, E E** 'Productivity in computer application development, Department of Management Studies' *Working paper No 9* University of Auckland (March 1983)

20 **Rudolph, E E** 'Function point analyses, cookbook' own edition from Rudolph (March 1983)

21 **Symons, C R** 'Function point analysis: difficulties and improvements' *IEEE Trans. Soft. Eng.* Vol 14 No 1 (January 1988)

22 **Symons, C R** *Software sizing and estimating—MARK II FPA* Wiley (1991)

23 **Putnam, L H** 'A general empirical solution to the macro software sizing and estimating problem' *IEEE Trans. Soft. Eng.* SE-4, 4 (1978)

24 **Putnam, L** 'Software costing estimating and life cycle control' *IEEE Computer Society Press* (1980)

25 **Putnam, L H and Fitzsimmons, A** 'Estimating software costs' *Datamation* (Sept. Oct. Nov. 1979)

26 **Londeix, B** *Cost estimation for software development* Addison-Wesley (1987)

27 **Rubin, H A** 'Interactive macro-estimation of software life cycle parameters via personal computer: a technique for improving customer/developer communication' *Proc. Symp. on application & assessment of automated tools for software development, IEEE,* San Francisco (1983)

28 **Rubin, H A** 'Macro and micro-estimation of maintenance effort: the estimacs maintenance models' *IEEE* (1984)

29 **Rubin, H A** 'A comparison of cost estimation tools' *Proc. 8th Int. Conf. Soft. Eng. IEEE* (1985)

30 **Computer Associates** CA-Estimacs *User Guide* Release 5.0 (July 1986)

31 **Jones, C** *Programming productivity* McGraw-Hill (1986)

32 **BIS/Estimator** *User manual version 4.4.* BIS Applied System Ltd. (1987)

33 **Kemerer, C F** 'An empirical validation of software cost estimation models' *Communications of the ACM* Vol 30 No 5 (May 1987)

34 **Norden, P V** *Useful tools for project management* (Operations research in research and development) Wiley (1963)

A Guidebook and a Spreadsheet Tool for a Corporate Metrics Program

Ronald E. Nusenoff and Dennis C. Bunde

Loral Software Productivity Laboratory, San Jose, California

A metrics guidebook and a spreadsheet tool have been developed at the Loral Software Productivity Laboratory as a start-up kit to enable Loral divisions and projects to implement the Loral corporate metrics program. The metrics guidebook defines a standard set of software metrics and specifies procedures for collection and analysis of metrics data. Guidelines are provided for revising schedules, resource allocations, and project procedures in light of the analysis of metrics data. The corporate-, division-, and project-level roles and responsibilities for metrics activities are discussed. The spreadsheet tool provides automated support for metrics generation, collection, graphical representation, and analysis.

This article explains the guidelines that were followed in constructing a guidebook and a spreadsheet tool that would both motivate and enable divisions and projects to implement the corporate metrics program. Metrics use is motivated at the division level as a means of developing a metrics database which will improve the organization's development and bidding capabilities, while motivating individual projects requires more emphasis on the role of metrics in monitoring and controlling project progress. Corporate metrics were tied to previous software metrics collection activities and to other data already collected and used within the organization and were mapped to Software Engineering Institute (SEI) level 2 and 3 maturity level requirements.

Guidelines for division and project tailoring of corporate metrics were provided. The corporate metrics were defined to map to the corporate development methodology, and so tailoring of that methodology by divisions or projects requires corresponding tailoring of the corporate metrics. Automated support for metrics collection and analysis, which also must be tailorable, was found to be a critical factor in enabling division and project implementation of corporate metrics. Feedback from divisions and projects that implemented the corporate metrics program is being used to improve the current program and extend it to cover SEI level 4 and 5 maturity level requirements.

1. INTRODUCTION

In a corporate software metrics program, a set of metrics, collection procedures, and analysis procedures are defined and then implemented throughout the company. A corporate metrics program presupposes a corporate standard software development methodology. A software development methodology consists of a process model which specifies all of the activities involved in software development, plus the individual methods, practices, and procedures which instantiate the steps of the process model. When a standard methodology has been specified, software development can be a defined, repeatable process rather than an ad hoc activity reinvented for each new project. Projects that follow the methodology can be planned, monitored, and controlled through the use of metrics which will have been defined in terms of the components of the methodology.

Projects that adopt a corporate metrics program need a guidebook (*Webster's Ninth New Collegiate Dictionary* defines a guidebook as a "handbook; esp: a book of information for travelers") that tells them how to implement this program. This guidebook should be a user-oriented handbook containing metrics definitions, collection and analysis procedures and tools, and guidelines for corrective actions. Projects also need automated support for metrics collection and analysis. This article explains guidelines we have found useful in constructing a metrics guidebook and a spreadsheet tool for the Loral Corporation corporate metrics program. Section 2 of this paper provides background on our metrics program. Section 3 covers the issues of enabling and motivating company divisions and projects to use metrics. Section 4 covers guidelines for

Address correspondence to *Ronald E. Nusenoff, Octel Communication Corporation, 1001 Murphy Ranch Road, Milpitas, CA 95035*

Reprinted from *J. Systems and Software*, Vol. 23, R.E. Nusenoff and D.C. Bunde, "A Guidebook and a Spreadsheet Tool for a Corporate Metrics Program," pp. 245–255, 1993, with kind permission from Elsevier Science–NL, Sara Burgerhartstraat 25; 1055 KV Amsterdam, The Netherlands.

defining a set of metrics. Section 5 covers guidelines about providing automated support for metrics collection and analysis. Section 6 discusses guidelines we are following in getting the guidebook and spreadsheet tool adopted on projects at Loral divisions. Section 7 describes the next steps planned in our metrics program.

2. BACKGROUND

The Loral Software Productivity Laboratory (SPL) is a central organization responsible for the formulation of a corporate standard software development methodology employing modern software engineering disciplines and techniques and meeting the software development requirements of Loral customers [1]. The SPL is also responsible for developing a corporate computer-aided software environment (CORCASE), which supports and enforces this methodology, and a software total quality management (TQM) program.

We have chosen the Software Engineering Institute (SEI) capability maturity model and associated assessment methodology as a framework for our software TQM program [2]. The levels within the SEI model provide the specific measurable goals which have been missing from previous TQM initiatives. The SEI maturity level hierarchy is shown in Figure 1. The three lower levels of the SEI capability maturity model are based on empirical observations about the best current software engineering and management practices. These practices are organized into levels 1–3 in a manner that provides a road map for increasing software development process capability maturity. The SEI has been conducting process assessments since 1987 and has found 81% of organizations assessed to be at level 1, 12% at level 2, and 7% at level 3. No level 4 or 5 organizations have been identified. Levels 4 and 5, therefore, represent a view of what software organizations beyond the current state of the practice might look like.

A central activity of the TQM program is the definition and implementation of a corporate software development metrics program. The goal of this metrics program is to improve contract bidding, software project management, and software engineering practices by enabling software project managers to measure, monitor, predict, and control project progress, costs, and quality. The SPL metrics program currently addresses the metrics required to achieve SEI levels 2 and 3. What characterizes the advance from a level 1 to a level 2 capability is the introduction and enforcement of formal engineering management controls and procedures, which are prerequisites to the availability and validity of schedule and effort metrics data. All software project managers must control projects using well-defined procedures for scheduling, effort and size estimation, collection of schedule and effort metrics, configuration management of baselines, and quality assurance monitoring. The advance from level 2 to level 3 is characterized by the introduction of a defined software development process in which all software engineers are formally trained in the process and its associated engineering methods. The advance to level 3 does not introduce substantial metrics collection requirements beyond those of level

Level	Characteristic	Key Challenges	Result
5 **Optimizing**	Improvement fed back into process	Still human intensive process Maintain organization at optimizing level	**Productivity & Quality**
4 **Managed**	(Quantitative) Measured process	Changing technology Problem analysis Problem prevention	
3 **Defined**	(Qualitative) Process defined and institutionalized	Process measurement Process analysis Quantitative quality plans	
2 **Repeatable**	(Intuitive) Process dependent on individuals	Training Technical practices • reviews, testing Process focus • standards, process groups	
1 **Initial**	(Ad hoc/chaotic)	Project management Project planning Configuration management Software quality assurance	**Risk**

Figure 1. SEI maturity level hierarchy.

2, but the defined process provides a stable baseline of technical activities which can be measured.

We divide these SEI level 2 and 3 metrics (which we call management metrics) into two types: schedule and effort, and quality. Schedule and effort metrics are used to detect variance between planned and actual progress and labor costs. A software schedule represents the planned progress of a project. Schedule metrics summarize project progress information so that the software manager can detect and compensate for unplanned schedule trends. Effort is the labor portion of software cost; it does not take into account overhead, travel, and capital expenses. Effort metrics summarize effort information so that the software manager can detect adverse trends and control software costs.

Schedule and cost variance are signals that future completion dates and the overall project budget are at risk. Further analysis is required to determine the causes of schedule and cost variances so management can adjust plans and take actions to maintain control of the project. Significant analysis of schedule and effort metrics requires plotting of collected values together with project estimates on a regular basis. This enables the identification of trends in both the measured data and its variance from estimates. These trends can be extrapolated to provide more reasonable revised estimates. Comparison with data and trends from previous projects can be used to predict where a current project is going. Where metrics are known to correlate, i.e., changes in one metric cause changes in others, comparisons of data are used to isolate problems and identify corrective actions.

Quality metrics are quantitative measures available during the software development process. They are indicators of final product quality (e.g., correctness, reliability, maintainability) and allow managers to predict and influence final product quality. The quality of the final product can be predicted by measuring the quality of the process used to produce it and of the products generated along the way. Measuring the quality of the process and its products provides early warning signs that there will be cost and schedule problems before they actually occur. Once a quality metrics data base has been established, quality data expectations can be established by reference to data and trends observed on previous projects.

Quality metrics include errors detected, the stability of requirements/design/code, and the complexity of requirements/design/code. Number of errors detected is a measure of intermediate product quality and of the quality of the error detec-tion process. Detected error data is a predictor of remaining errors, which is an indicator of system reliability and correctness. Design and code inspections, test reviews, and software problem/change reports are the primary sources of error data. Instability in intermediate products is measured by software problem/change reports. Large numbers of reports against a baselined intermediate product are a signal that subsequent products based on it could be delayed. The complexity of system components is an indicator of system maintainability. Increases in measured complexity across the development phases indicate that additional effort will be required later.

3. ENABLING AND MOTIVATING METRICS USE

Guideline 1: Produce and Publish a Metrics Guidebook

The first major step of the Loral metrics program has been the production of a metrics guidebook [3]. Individual projects have neither the time nor the resources to develop a metrics program. They need a start-up kit that enables them to implement a well-defined program. The metrics guidebook defines a standard set of software metrics and specifies procedures for collection and analysis of metrics data. Guidelines are provided for revising schedules, resource allocations, and project procedures in light of the analysis of metrics data. The corporate-, division-, and project-level roles and responsibilities for metrics activities are discussed. Automated support for metrics generation, collection, and analysis, which includes a spreadsheet tool for organizing and graphically representing metrics data, is explained.

Guideline 2: Provide Motivation for Implementing Metrics

Metrics are still neither well understood nor widely applied within the software industry, despite extensive literature which provides a good case for the use of software metrics in terms of increases in quality and productivity [4-8]. Fear and/or loathing is a typical reaction to metrics from upper management ("the only thing metrics adds to a project is cost"), project management ("we couldn't pass data on up even if we believed it"), and engineers ("they're going to measure *us*"). Such reactions made us realize that the guidebook must do more than describe how company divisions and projects can implement metrics collection and analysis; it also must provide motivation for doing so.

At the division level, a motivating goal for metrics use can be the development of a division metrics data base. The data base provides an empirical foundation for future project estimations, analysis, and predictions. Historical data is used to analyze measurements of current projects to predict subsequent progress and suggest adjustments to current plans and schedules. Data collected from projects is used to validate and refine the metrics data base. Project data is also used to measure how well the division's version of the corporate methodology is working and the effect of either changing it or introducing new methods or technology.

SEI maturity level has also become a significant motivating factor at the company division level. The Department of Defense and other government agencies are phasing in use of SEI capability maturity levels as a criteria for contract awards. Government agencies have been using the SEI model to evaluate contractors during the contract bidding stage. The government's rule of thumb may soon be, try to find a level 3 contractor and do not deal with a level 1 contractor. The improvement of SEI maturity level was selected as the incentive for implementing a software TQM program at Loral. The SEI model was used to derive requirements for capability improvement and actions to meet those requirements. The metrics involved in advancing to SEI levels 2 and 3 are minimum requirements for the Loral management metrics program. Our inter-

pretation of SEI level 2 and 3 metrics collection requirements is given in Figure 2. The SEI question numbers in parentheses are taken from the original SEI technical report [2].

Motivation at the project level is a different issue than motivation at the division level. Once a project has started, the main motivation for using metrics has to be that it will enable the project manager to monitor and control project progress, costs, and quality. In the early stages of the corporate metrics program, there will at best be disjoint historical data rather than a corporate metrics data base to use as an empirical basis for estimations and planning. The fact that a pioneer project's implementation of the corporate metrics plan will produce data to help future projects does nothing to help the pioneers in their current endeavors.

4. DEFINING A SET OF METRICS

Guideline 3: Align Metrics with External Requirements

Guideline 4: Relate Metrics Program to Previous Metrics Collection

The Loral management metrics were selected based on literature research and investigation into current metrics activities at Loral divisions. The 10 metrics presented in "Software Management Metrics" [9]

SEI Level 2 Metrics Collection Requirements

Plot planned and actual staffing over time. (2.2.1)

Plot computer software configuration item (CSCI) size versus time. (2.2.2)

Record number and type of code and test errors. (2.2.4)

Plot planned and actual number of software units for which design reviews have been completed, versus time. (2.2.7)

Plot planned and actual computer software units (CSUs) for which unit testing has been completed, versus time. (2.2.8)

Plot planned and actual CSUs for which integration testing has been completed, versus time. (2.2.9)

Plot estimated and actual target computer memory utilization versus time. (2.2.10)

Plot estimated and actual target computer central processing unit (CPU) utilization versus time. (2.2.11)

Plot actual target computer input/output (I/O) channel utilization versus time. (2.2.12)

Plot planned and actual CSCI test progress versus time. (2.2.18)

Plot software build size versus time. (2.2.19)

SEI Level 3 Metrics Collection Requirements

Record number and type of software design errors. (2.2.3)

Figure 2. SEI metrics collection requirements.

were selected as a primary model. The software management metrics were defined by The MITRE Corporation for the Electronic Systems Division of the Air Force Systems Command, based on three years of government and industry experiences in the collection and analysis of the 8 metrics presented in "Software Reporting Metrics" [10]. A comparison of the two sets of MITRE metrics is given in Figure 3. The MITRE metrics are collected and reported at monthly intervals. They are plotted in a format showing the past 12 months of planned and actual data and the next 5 months of planned data.

The MITRE metrics are a reasonable starting point for the Loral metrics program for several reasons. They cover all phases of the software development process as defined in Department of Defense standard 2167A, from which the Loral software development process model is derived. The SEI level 2 metrics were based on the first MITRE set of eight metrics. The only SEI level 2 and 3 metrics not covered by the MITRE metrics are the numbers and types of design, code, and test errors. These data are collected during design, code, and test case inspections. A metrics program which included all of the

Metric Name	Status	Description
Software complexity	deleted	initially plotted complexity of the 10 percent most complex CSUs. Complexity was estimated on a scale from 1 to 6, as found in Boehm [13]. This metric was replaced by design complexity.
Software Size	same	plots new, modified, and reused SLOCs for each CSCI as well as for the total system.
Software Personnel	same	plots total and experienced numbers of personnel, planned and actual, plus unplanned personnel losses.
Software Volatility	modified	plots total number of software requirements, cumulative number of requirements changes, and numbers of new and open software requirements action items. Initially was a plot of the number of lines of code affected by ECPs.
Computer Resource Utilization	same	plots planned spare and estimated/actual percentages of utilization for target computer CPU timing, memory, and I/O channels.
Design Complexity	new	plots the average design complexity of the 10 percent most complex CSUs, CSCs, and CSCIs. It is based on McCabe's measure of complexity.
Schedule Progress	new	plots estimated schedule to completion based on the delivery of software work packages defined in the Work Breakdown Structure.
Design Progress	new	plots planned and actual numbers of software requirements from system design documents which been completely documented in software requirements documents, and in software design documents.
CSU Development Progress	same	plots planned and actual numbers of CSUs designed, tested, and integrated.
Testing Progress	same	plots planned and actual numbers of CSCI and system tests completed, numbers of new and open SPRs, and number of SPRs per 1000 SLOC.
Incremental Release Content	same	plots planned and actual estimates of release date and number of CSUs included in each software release.

Figure 3. MITRE metrics comparison.

MITRE metrics, plus data from design, code, and test case inspections, would meet all of the SEI level 2 and 3 metrics collection requirements. Finally, the original MITRE metrics have been a model for much of the metrics collection currently practiced by Loral divisions and are required by several government customers.

Mapping of SEI metrics collection requirements and MITRE metrics to the Loral metrics is shown in Figure 4. Each of the SEI level 2 and 3 questions is mapped to a recommended Loral metric. Nine of the 10 MITRE software management metrics map at least partially to one or more Loral metrics.

Guideline 5: Tailor Metrics to Fit the Activities and Methods of the Methodology

Guideline 6: Specify Concrete Criteria for Applying Metrics

We needed to tailor several of the MITRE metrics to fit them to the Loral software development methodology. MITRE used software problem reports

as part of the testing progress metric and software action items as part of the software volatility metric. Loral methodology includes a software problem change report (SP/CR) system which is used for all configuration-controlled software and documents starting with the software requirements documents. It therefore seemed appropriate to define an SP/CR metric that corresponds to this system.

A corollary of guideline 5 is that defining metrics may suggest simple yet useful modifications to the corporate methodology. It would be useful to know when errors are introduced into the process, but the current SP/CR forms do not contain an entry for when a problem was introduced. This information is already determined when an SP/CR is assigned for resolution, but is not recorded in a readily collectable manner. It has therefore been suggested that a problem introduction entry, defined relative to the earliest document needing changes, be added to the SP/CR form.

A general rule we followed in defining management metrics to fit the corporate software development methodology was to establish concrete binary

Loral Metric	Mitre Metric	SEI Question
Schedule Progress	Schedule Progress	—
Software Cost	—	—
Software Size	Software Size (T)	2.2.2
Staffing Profile	Software Personnel	2.2.1
CSU Development Progress	CSU Development Progress (T) Incremental Release Content(T)	2.2.7, 2.2.8 2.2.9, 2.2.19
CSCI Test Progress	Testing Progress	2.2.18
Requirements Volatility	Software Volatility (T)	—
SP/CR	Testing Progress Software Volatility (T)	—
Computer Resource Utilization	Computer Resource Utilization	2.2.10, 2.2.11, 2.2.12
Inspection Defects/Hours	—	2.2.4, 2.2.3
Module Complexity	Design Complexity (T)	—
	(T) = significant tailoring	

Figure 4. Mapping of MITRE and SEI to Loral metrics.

criteria for applying metrics. For example, the completion criterion for the design of a computer software unit (CSU) had to be an all-or-nothing affair, with no partial (e.g., 90%) criterion accepted. The criterion we found within the methodology was that CSU design is finished if the detailed design inspection has been completed. This is the point at which the design is placed under configuration control. On the other hand, the MITRE design progress metric, which tracks the allocation of software requirements from system design documents to software requirements documents to design documents, was not adopted because its units are neither precisely defined nor readily collectable. Before baselining a document, it is not obvious how to count incrementally the number of individual requirements allocated within that document.

When projects have acquired experience using CORCASE analysis and design tools, we intend to introduce metrics based on discrete units which can be counted directly by these tools. These metrics should provide measures of the progress between the analysis and design phases and a means of tracking the evolution of system complexity. Detailed ongoing measurement of system complexity has long been advocated by DeMarco [4]. Streamlined versions of this approach have been advanced by Card [11] and by the Software Productivity Consortium [12].

Guideline 7: Relate Metrics to Other Data Already Collected and Used

The schedule progress metric calculates the estimated schedule to complete each month by multiplying the planned project schedule by the ratio of the budgeted cost of work scheduled (BCWS) to the budgeted cost of work performed (BCWP). BCWP and BCWS are based on an earned value assigned to each discrete task in a project, as described in Boehm's *Software Engineering Economics* [13]. The difference between BCWS and BWCP is the schedule variance for the entire project. What was needed to complement this overall schedule variance metric was an overall cost variance metric. We found that many Loral divisions use financial reporting systems that plot budget at completion (BAC), which is the budgeted cost to complete a project, along with a monthly estimate at completion (EAC). EAC is calculated by multiplying BAC by the ratio of the project's current expenditures to the earned value of the tasks actually completed (i.e., the ratio of actual cost of work performed (ACWP) to (BCWP). We

adopted this as our cost metric because it uses data already collected and used throughout the company.

The software size metric uses counting rules for added, modified, reused, and removed source statements presented in the IEEE *Standard for Software Productivity Metrics* [14]. These rules had already been adopted by metrics working groups at the SEI, the Software Productivity Consortium, and by at least one Loral division. This same division also develops some code for reuse, and we have adopted their suggestion that such code be tracked separately from other newly developed code.

Guideline 8: Provide Tailoring Guidelines for Metrics

No set of definitions will fit every project perfectly. Divisions and projects that tailor the corporate methodology according to customer requirements, division standards, or business area may also need to tailor their implementation of metrics. Where we were aware of established division procedures that implied changes to the metrics definitions or analysis guidelines, we included them in the guidebook as tailoring guidelines. One Loral division uses a series of quality point reviews during the development process rather than the corporate standard inspection process. Quality point reviews generate metrics which replace our inspection metric and supplement the SP/CR metric.

5. TOOL SUPPORT FOR A METRICS PROGRAM

Guideline 9: Make Collection Nonintrusive — Automate if Possible

Much of the current resistance to metrics use on projects is based on the concern that the benefits to be gained from the analysis of metrics data will not compensate for the effort required to collect the data. The key to overcoming this resistance is to point out that most of the data that need to be collected for metrics purposes are already collected for other purposes. Most of the metrics data items recommended for collection in the guidebook are either generated automatically within CORCASE or are already being entered manually into the system independent of their use for metrics.

A detailed table was prepared listing each primitive (i.e., noncalculated) metrics data item along with the tool or other source that generates it and its location within the CORCASE data base. Most data used in estimating, planning, and tracking schedules, cost, and personnel resources is either generated by or manually entered through a Loral proprietary project management software package. Although this package does not currently handle data on actual labor hours worked, those data are available from the time card accounting system. Software size and complexity data are generated using language-dependent source code processing tools and are already recorded in electronic module software development files. Data related to numbers of and changes to requirements are already recorded in a requirements data base. Resource spare capability requirements would also be stored in the requirements data base. Data related to SP/CRs are generated and managed within an automated software problem reporting system, which also contains some data on requirements changes. Inspection data are already entered by the inspection moderators into a spreadsheet which generates statistics and graphs based on the collected data.

Guideline 10: Provide Automated Analysis Templates and Tools

The problem with much metrics data collection is that the data are merely collected. Analysis of collected values, calculation of derived values, trend extrapolation, and graphical representation require a tool that can do the work and a template that provides a common format. A management metrics spreadsheet was developed which provides an organized format for recording collected metrics data together with automatic generation of metrics graphs. This spreadsheet was developed using Wingz, a commercial spreadsheet program which is included as a productivity tool in CORCASE. A spreadsheet template was set up to record and graph the metrics recommended in the guidebook. The spreadsheet template contains labels for all data to be entered, formulas that calculate derived values, and some explanatory text describing the contents of the data cells. When planned and actual data are entered in the appropriate cells, derived values are calculated and the accompanying graphs are automatically created and updated. An empty copy of this spreadsheet can be copied to create a spreadsheet for a project. A copy of the spreadsheet template with 18 months of data was also provided as part of a tutorial on how to use the spreadsheet. The layout of the spreadsheet template, along with brief descriptions of each labelled area, is given in Figure 5. A utility was added to the spreadsheet to provide printout of graphs without spreadsheet row and column headers. A sample of this printout is given in Figure 6.

Collection of metrics data for insertion into the metrics spreadsheet within CORCASE is presently a manual process performed by a project metrics coordinator. Metrics collection and insertion into the management metrics spreadsheet will be automated in later releases of CORCASE. A metrics collection utility will be written for use by the metrics coordinators which will collect all of the metrics data items, generate a report listing the collected items, and insert the collected data items into a specified spreadsheet upon request.

Guideline 11: Make the Tools and Templates Tailorable and Portable

As with the metrics definitions, the analysis tool may need to be adjusted to fit the needs of divisions or individual projects. We included instructions for adding metrics definitions, calculations, and graphs to the spreadsheet template. We have converted the spreadsheet template from the SUNView version of Wingz on which it was developed to an X Window version. We have also successfully converted a metrics spreadsheet file into Lotus and Excel formats (even the graphs converted over), which makes it accessible to those divisions and projects that are already committed to using those packages. In the interest of portability, we avoided using any unique special features of the Wingz program.

6. ONGOING GUIDELINES IN TECHNOLOGY TRANSFER

Guideline 12: Locate Metrics Technology Transfer Point Above the Project Level

The initial criterion of success for a corporate metrics program is that it be adopted by projects at different divisions of the company. (The second criterion is that it is subsequently adopted by other projects at those divisions.) Personnel in corporate-level organizations generally have limited access to personnel at the project level, and project personnel generally do not have the position and funding to sponsor the establishment of a metrics program (or generally, any new methods). We have so far found that implementation of the metrics program at the division level is best accomplished through a division software engineering process group (SEPG) [7]. As a corporate-level organization, the SPL tailors and integrates state-of-the-practice methods and tools into a corporate methodology. The division SEPG

INTRODUCTION
General comments which describe the spreadsheet.

RAW DATA
Rows for entry of project data. The first cell (column A) of each row contains the text string naming the data. The first row of this area contains the project calendar in text strings.

METRICS FORMULAS
Formulas for calculating values to be graphed. Column A contains the text string naming the value to be calculated. Copies of the formula are contained in all remaining cells of the row, up to the column for the last month of the project calendar.

GRAPH WINDOW DEFINITION
Rows for entry of current project month and software start month, and a formula to calculate which 18 months of data to store in the Graph Data area. Data is stored for the current month, the 11 previous months, and the 6 subsequent months.

GRAPH DATA
Rows of 19 columns each for storage of pointers used to create graphs. All rows for a given graph must be consecutive. Column A of the first row for each graph contains a pointer to the graph title. Column A of the subsequent data rows contains a pointer to the name of the data for that row. Columns B..S of the first rows use an INDEX function to access the required 18 columns of the project calendar. Columns B..S of the data rows use the INDEX function to access either raw data from the Raw Data area, or calculated values from the Metrics Formulas area.

GRAPH AXIS LABELS
Rows for storage of text strings to be used as labels for the graph axes. A new label can be added to any empty cell in this area.

GRAPHS
Area in which graphs using rows from Graph Data area are located.

Figure 5. Layout of the management metrics spreadsheet.

then tailors this methodology to meet the requirements of the division customers and business area. In the case of a metrics program, the SEPG would tailor the corporate metrics definitions, procedures, and tools to keep metrics in alignment with the division version of the corporate software development methodology. The SEPG is also responsible for using metrics data and analysis from projects for developing and maintaining a division metrics data base and a division cost model, for passing data base information back to the corporate data base, and for implementing enhancements to the corporate metrics program.

Each project should have a metrics coordinator who consolidates project metrics data and prepares reports and analysis for the project manager to review. The position of metrics coordinator may not be a full-time position, but requires an experienced engineer who is well versed in the corporate or division methodology. This position might best be filled by a person from the SEPG who is matrixed into several projects as metrics coordinator. This person from the SEPG could be someone who works on the division metrics data base. Using SEPG personnel as metrics coordinators would be an instance of the collaborative technology transfer method [15], in which end users are involved in developing the technology, rather than the more traditional transfer-and-feedback mechanism which most corporate–level organizations use.

Guideline 13: Find a Pilot Project

The best way to test a metrics guidebook and spreadsheet tool is to find a real development project on which to use them. Testing with a pilot

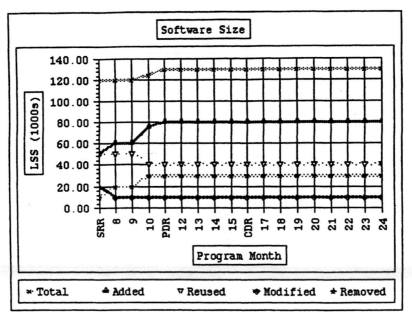

Figure 6. Sample spreadsheet graph printout.

project will uncover errors, omissions, and ambiguities more efficiently than one more review or simulation. It will also provide a practitioner's viewpoint as to what is useful, what is not, and what else is needed.

Guideline 14: Be Ready to Train and Consult

Even with the existence of a division SEPG, the corporate-level organization's job is not done. Some SEPGs may be as small as two people or may be staffed by project personnel devoting personal time to the effort. Even with a well-funded SEPG, comments and questions on the guidebook and on how to use the tool should come back. No metrics guidebook can anticipate all of the questions and even have all of the answers to the expected questions. Few (if any) tools can be used effectively without some expert guidance. No comments, questions, or corrections coming back is a bad sign: it means that users did not read the guidebook and did not try the tool.

7. NEXT STEPS

The program defined in our metrics guidebook has been implemented at four Loral divisions. The corporate metrics guidebook was used as the basis for division metrics standards, and the spreadsheet template has been modified to accommodate division tailoring of the corporate metrics definitions and procedures. Two divisions are using the Wingz spreadsheet and two divisions are using Excel versions. Several other divisions have requested soft copies of the spreadsheet. Up to this point, the availability of personnel and resources to experiment with the spreadsheet tool has been a critical factor in getting the corporate program implemented at the division level.

Loral software projects that use the metrics, procedures, and tools defined and explained in the management metrics guidebook will provide us with feedback in the form of spreadsheets and commentary on their use of analysis guidelines and corrective actions. We plan to develop a corporate management metrics data base using the spreadsheet format and will validate and refine the metrics and procedures contained in the guidebook. Changes in the corporate software development methodology will be reflected in the corporate metrics program as required.

We also plan to develop a process improvement metrics guidebook, based on SEI levels 4 and 5, which will provide methods, guidelines, and tools for stabilizing and improving the methodology. SEI level 4 metrics address improvement of the implementation of the defined process which was established in advancing to SEI level 3. Process performance variations are measured and their causes identified. The metrics required to advance to SEI level 5 address improvement of the defined process itself. The effects of planned changes to the process are measured and compared with the predicted values of the unchanged process.

REFERENCES

1. Loral Corporation Policy on the Development of Software, Policy Letter SW-01, San Jose, California, December 14, 1990.
2. W. S. Humphrey, and W. L. Sweet, A Method for Assessing the Software Engineering Capability of Contractors, Software Engineering Institute Technical Report CMU/SEI-87-TR-23, Pittsburgh, Pennsylvania, 1987.
3. D. Bunde and R. Nusenoff, Management Metrics Guidebook, Loral Software Productivity Laboratory Technical Report SPL_SEGB_9A-91008-M, San Jose, California, 1991.
4. T. DeMarco, *Controlling Software Projects*, Englewood Cliffs, New Jersey, Yourdon Press, 1982.
5. R. B. Grady and D. L. Caswell, *Software Metrics: Establishing a Company-Wide Program*, Prentice-Hall, Englewood Cliffs, New Jersey, 1987.
6. V. R. Basili and H. D. Rombach, The TAME Project: Towards Improvement-Oriented Software Environments, *IEEE Trans. Software Eng.* 14, 758–773 (1988).
7. W. S. Humphrey, *Managing the Software Process*, Addison-Wesley, Reading, Massachussetts, 1989.
8. F. McGarry et al., Experiences in the software engineering laboratory (SEL) applying software measurement, in *Proceedings of the Fourteenth Annual Software Engineering Workshop*, SEL-89-007, Goddard Space Flight Center, Greenbelt, Maryland, 1989.
9. H. P. Schultz, Software Management Metrics, MITRE Technical Report ESD-TR-88-001, Bedford, Massachusetts, 1988.
10. R. J. Coles et al., Software Reporting Metrics, MITRE Technical Report ESD-TR-85-145, Bedford, Massachusetts, 1985.
11. D. N. Card and R. L. Glass, *Measuring Software Design Quality*, Prentice-Hall, Englewood Cliffs, New Jersey, 1990.
12. J. E. Gaffney and R. Werling, Estimating Software Size from Counts of Externals, A Generalization of Function Points, Software Productivity Consortium Technical Report SPC_91094, Herndon, Virginia, 1991.
13. B. W. Boehm, *Software Engineering Economics*, Prentice-Hall, Englewood Cliffs, New Jersey, 1981.
14. Standard for Software Productivity Metrics, P1045/D4.0, Draft, IEEE, New York, New York, 1990.
15. J. D. Babcock, L. A. Belady, and N. C. Gore, The evolution of technology transfer at MCC's software technology program: From didactic to dialectic, *12th International Conference on Software Engineering*, IEEE Computer Society Press, Los Alamitos, California, 1990, pp. 290–299.

Risk Management for Software Development

Richard Fairley
Colorado Technical University
Colorado Springs, Colorado, USA

Paul Rook
The Centre for Software Reliability
City University, Northampton Square, London, UK

Keywords: Risk, Risk Management, Software Risk, Risk Exposure, Risk Factors

A risk is a potential problem; a problem is a risk that has materialized. By a problem, we mean an undesirable situation that will require time and resources to correct. In some cases the problem, should it occur, may be uncorrectable. A risk, being a potential problem, is characterized by:

- The probability that an undesired event might occur ($0 < P < 1$)
- A loss associated with occurrence of the undesired event

The loss associated with an undesired event is referred to as the *risk impact*. Sometimes, it is possible to quantify the loss in measurable terms, such as dollars or human lives. In other cases the loss is intangible; for example, loss of credibility or good will. In cases where loss can be quantified, the product of (probability * risk impact) is referred to as the *risk exposure*.

Probability and impact typically vary with time and circumstances. A small risk may become a large one, and conversely, a large risk may, with passing time, become a non-risk. For example, the probability of failing to achieve a desired result falls to zero upon attainment of the desired result. Furthermore, some risk factors may be interdependent so that reducing the probability and/or cost of one may increase the probability and/or cost of another. With hindsight, it will be determined that some potential problems occurred and others did not.

When we are dealing with risk in this general sense, it is not always easy to distinguish between single events, multiple events, continuous events, and interdependent events, or between cause and effect. In considering an undertaking, many risks may be identified. Systematic risk management requires that initial apprehensions be turned into specific root causes, and that the probabilities and potential losses be established. The specific outcome we wish to avoid must be explicitly stated in order to identify possible courses of action for risk reduction.

The first step in risk management for software development is to organize the development effort as a well-defined project having a schedule, a budget, a set of objectives to be achieved, and a set of skills needed to accomplish the work. Project objectives must be translated into a set of targets that cover, at least, cost (or effort), schedule, and product functionality, performance, and quality attributes.

In setting targets for a project, a subproject, or a development phase the following must be considered:

- *Constraints.* A constraint is an external condition imposed by forces over which project management has no control. There may be constraints on time, money, personnel, and other aspects of the work. There may also be design constraints imposed on the product. When a constraint is broken it may result in financial loss or cancellation of the project.

- *Estimates.* An estimate is a prediction of expected outcomes under certain circumstances. An estimate should be made for each of the project targets. Estimates should include ranges of values with associated probabilities, confidence levels, and most importantly, analyses of the assumptions underlying the estimates. Estimates must incorporate the process and product constraints placed on the project.

- *Types of targets.* Targets are set by the customer and by project management and specified in the project plan. Targets should include negotiated considerations of project constraints, and the estimate ranges and probabilities. These negotiations may involve the customer, management, and development staff.

- *Conditional minimax targets.* There may be a project attribute (cost, schedule, functionality, performance) that management and the customer desire to optimize. However, it may be that optimizing this target should only be achieved provided all other targets are achieved. Consequently, the optimization criteria must incorporate the full set of targets; otherwise, the desired attribute will be minimized or maximized at the expense of other attributes.

Risks are thus viewed as potential problems that, should they occur, will impact project targets. If there are no quantified targets, then there is no danger that the targets will not be achieved; risk management is meaningless unless targets are defined in measurable terms.

Identifying the risk factors for the various project targets allows risks to be traced through subsequent risk management plans, risk monitoring and reporting procedures, and corrective action.

Risk Management and Project Management

The goal of traditional project management is to control pervasive risks that might hinder the development of a satisfactory product on time and within budget. Traditional project management uses systematic procedures to estimate and plan the work, lead and direct the staff, monitor progress, and control the project by replanning and reassigning resources as necessary. This remains the fundamental basis for project management and is not invalidated by any consideration of risk management. However, on its own, traditional project management is a recipe for "problem management" in that difficult decisions are addressed and actions taken only when problems arise. In this sense, project management is reactive, whereas risk management is proactive.

Risk Management consists of Risk Assessment followed by Risk Control (see Figure 1). Risk assessment provides informed decisions based on systematic assessment of things that might go wrong, the associated probabilities, and the severities of the impacts. Risk control is concerned with developing strategies and plans to abate the major risk factors, to resolve

those risks that do become problems, and to continuously reassess risk. Real risk management occurs when significant decision making, planning, resources, money, and effort are expended to reduce the probabilities and/or impacts of identified risk factors. The extent to which time and effort are invested in these processes can be used as a test to determine whether risk management is being accomplished over and above traditional project management.

Risk management is not synonymous with project management, nor is it a replacement for project management, or something entirely separate. Rather, it is an explicit augmentation and extension of traditional project management, closely intertwined with the information gathering and decision making functions of project management. When a project is successful, it is not because there were no problems, but because the problems were overcome. Risk management does not guarantee success, but has the primary goal of identifying and responding to potential problems with sufficient lead time to avoid crisis situations, so that it becomes possible to conduct a project that meets its targets.

Types of Risks

Risks can be categorized as Contractual/Environmental, Management/Process, Resources/Personnel, and Technical/Operational. The introduction of systematic risk management requires managers to abandon the idea that all risks on a technically difficult project are technical in nature. While some risks should indeed be identified as technical risks, there are also risks in the use of resources (especially personnel), risks in the way of working the project (management/process) and, just as importantly, risks to the project which are beyond the control of project management (contractual/environmental).

Figure 2 lists these four types of risk with some examples of each. All identified risks must be correctly typed. If risks that come from other sources are misidentified as technical risks, there is a danger they will be passed down from the management level to become the responsibility of the technical staff, who may not be able to control them. The result may be that these risk factors are not explicitly managed until they have become significant problems. Ensuring that all risks are fully addressed by management, the customer, and the developers requires explicit identification of the processes, team structures, responsibilities and authorities, and environmental/contractual factors. This is properly the domain of good traditional project management in any case, and a necessary prerequisite for successful risk control.

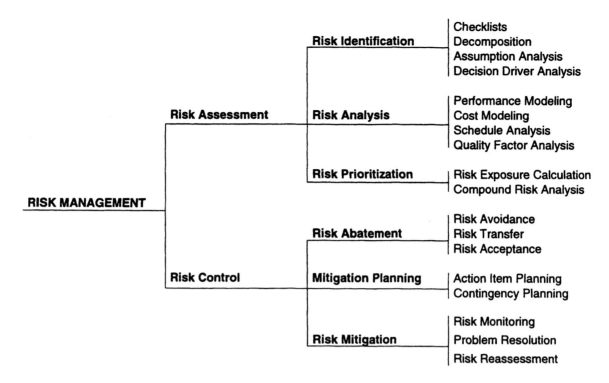

Figure 1. A Taxonomy for Risk Management (adapted from [Boehm89])

Contractual/Environmental	Management/Process	Personnel	Technical
"...to suffer the slings and arrows of outrageous fortune, or to take arms against a sea of troubles..."	"It is best to do things systematically since we are only human and disorder is our worst enemy"	"though all men be made of one metal, yet they be not cast all in one mold"	"The best laid plans..." Requirements changes
Unreasonable customers	Unclear responsibilities and authorities	Wrong people available –lack of skills –lack of training –lack of expertise	–customer changes mind –hidden implications emerge Failure to meet requirements
Nonperforming vendors and subcontractors	Ill-defined procedures	Lack of staff continuity	–cannot produce a feasible design –acceptance tests fail
Dependencies on and demands from other projects	Inadequate control of development process	Incorrect staffing	
Inappropriate corporate policies	Inadequate support facilities and services	–too many people for the current task –too few people for the current tasks	Problems or errors detected –inconsistent design
Change in management priorities	Lack of "visibility"		–missing components –inadequate time for testing

Figure 2. Sources of Risk

For purposes of risk control, risk factors fall into two categories:

- *Generic risks* are those risk factors common to all software projects. For example, costly late fixes (dealt with by early requirements and design verification), error-prone products (dealt with by verification, validation, and incremental testing throughout the life cycle), uncontrolled development processes (dealt with by planning and control based on well-defined processes), uncontrolled product (dealt with by configuration management and quality assurance), and poor communications (dealt with by documentation, reviews, and technical interchange meetings)

Over time, methods of reducing generic risks have become institutionalized in the tools and techniques used; for example, in project planning, configuration management, and verification and validation. In this sense, traditional software engineering and project management can be viewed as systematic approaches to controlling generic risk factors. Reduction of generic risk is evidenced in the choice of the overall development process (prototyping, incremental development, evolutionary development, design to cost, and so on) and the choice of methods, tools, and techniques used within that process.

Significant expenditures may be incurred in setting up a development process, acquiring tools, and training the managers and technical staff to cope with the generic risks inherent in a particular line of business. The outcomes of these risk reduction activities are the process(es), project plan(s), and work activities for each project. Generic risks for each phase of a software development project are controlled by explicitly designing the work processes of those phases.

- *Project-specific risks* are potential problems inherent to a particular project (for instance, insufficient personnel, key personnel not available when needed, unrealistic schedule and/or budget, inadequate requirements, shortfalls in externally supplied components or services, reliance on advances in the state of the art, and so on). Project-specific risks are dealt with in a Risk Management Plan which identifies the actions to be carried out should certain events occur. Risk management plans are especially useful when the customer, management, and developers agree that the project represents a risky undertaking.

A Risk Management Plan may contain both Action Plans and Contingency Plans. An action plan represents a decision to engage in a risk reduction activity that is to be conducted without further consideration; for example, acquiring training in a particular method or technique, acquiring work stations and software tools, or purchasing desks and work spaces. Like all plans, an action plan must specify a well-defined set of tasks, a schedule, a budget, and the responsibility and authority assigned to each involved person. A contingency plan is a risk reduction activity to be engaged in at some future time, should circumstances warrant; for example, rescoping the work or adding people should the schedule slip more than two weeks, or buying more memory or reducing functionality should the memory budget exceed its allocation by more than ten percent.

A contingency plan should contain the items illustrated by example in Figure 3. As illustrated in Figure 3, a contingency plan should describe the risk factor(s) dealt with by the plan, possible alternative courses of action to mitigate the risk factor(s) should it (they) become problem(s), the constraints on contingent actions, the risks created by the various possible alternatives, the risk indicator metric(s), the threshold value(s) of the indicator metric(s) that indicate the potential problem has become a real problem, the reset level for the indicator metric(s) that will signal resolution of the problem, the resources to be applied during the contingent action, the maximum duration of the contingency plan (after which the project goes into crisis mode), and the responsible party who will track the indicator metric(s) and implement the contingency plan. A project enters crisis mode when the maximum duration of a contingency plan is exceeded. A crisis is a "show-stopper;" all available resources are focused on solving the problem until the crisis is resolved or the project is rescoped or terminated.

Choosing the development process to be used is an essential risk reduction technique and is just as important as the risk reduction techniques identified in the risk management plan.

Various process models are summarized by Boehm [BOEHM89] as follows:

- *Buy COTS*: Buying a Commercial-Off-The-Shelf (COTS) product is a simple approach often overlooked in the enthusiasm to design and build something new, or because of the problems involved in administrative procedures required to buy rather than build. (Major risks for the COTS approach include failure to satisfy user needs, lack of compatibility with other system components, and the difficulties of integrating multiple COTS packages [Fairley94].)

- *Waterfall*: The sequential, single-pass requirements-design-code-test-maintain model.

- *Risk Reduction/Waterfall*: The waterfall model, preceded by one or more phases focused on reducing the risks of poorly understood requirements or architecture, technology uncertainties, potential performance shortfall, robustness issues, and so on.

```
1. Risk Factors:     Software Size (256K limit)
                     Processing Time (100 microsecond loop)
2. Alternatives:     Prototyping
                     Memory Overlays
                     Buy Memory
                     Faster Processor
                     Incremental Development plus Technical
                             Performance Measurement (ID + TPM)
3. Constraints:      Schedule and Budget
4. Risk Created:     Prototype: how to scale results?
                     Overlays: execution time penalty
                     Memory: hardware architectural constraints
                     Processor: customer constraint
                     ID + TPM:         reduced functionality
                                       unmaintainable product
5. Selected Approach:         Incremental Development plus TPM
                                       —partition design into a series of incremental builds
                                       —allocate 90% of memory and exection time to product functions
                                       —pursue incremental development based on partitioning
                                       —use TPM tracking on the memory and timing budgets
6. Risk Indicator Metrics:   Cost Performance Indices (CPI) for memory and timing budgets
7. Thresholds for Contingent Action: either CPI > 1.10
8. Reset Levels: CPI < 1.05
9. Resources to be Applied:           unlimited overtime for Sue Jones and Bill Williams
10. Maximum Duration: 2 weeks
11. Responsible Party: Sue Jones
```

Figure 3. A Contingency Plan

- *Capabilities-to-Requirements*: This model reverses the usual requirements-to-capabilities sequence inherent in the waterfall model. It begins with an assessment of the envelope of capabilities available from COTS or other reusable components, and then involves adjusting the requirements wherever possible to capitalize on the existing capabilities.

- *Transform*: This model relies on the availability of a generator that can automatically transform the specifications into code. If such a capability spans the system's growth envelope, the transform model may be most appropriate.

- *Evolutionary Development*: This approach involves developing an initial approximation to a desired software product, and evolving it into a final product based on feedback from users. This is a highly effective, low-risk approach if the system's growth envelope is covered by a 4GL, or if the system requirements are poorly understood but, the architecture of similar systems is well-understood, lowering the risk that the system will evolve into a configuration poorly supported by the architecture.

- *Evolutionary Prototyping*: This model is similar to evolutionary development, except that a prototype-quality system (low robustness) is acceptable.

- *Incremental Development*: This approach involves organizing a project into a series of builds that incrementally add increasing capabilities to the growing system. In contrast to the prototyping models, an incremental model requires that the requirements and architecture be (mostly) understood up-front and that the design be partitioned into a series of incremental builds. This is the preferred approach in many situations because, in contrast to the waterfall model, incremental integration and frequent demonstrations of progress are possible. Incremental development also lowers the risks of insufficient development personnel and failure to meet a fixed delivery date (with, perhaps, less than full capability).

- *Design-to-Cost and/or Design-to-Schedule*: This approach involves prioritizing the desired system capabilities, pruning the requirements to fit the time and money available, and organizing the architecture to facilitate dropping lower-priority capabilities if it is determined that those capabilities cannot be realized within the available budget and/or schedule.

These last two process models (incremental development and design-to-cost/schedule) can often be combined with other process model alternatives.

Boehm lists the following factors as critical decision drivers for choosing a process model:

- *Growth envelope*: This refers to the foreseeable limits of growth to a system's size and diversity over the course of its life cycle. A high-growth envelope implies high risk of using limited-domain implementation strategy such as commercial-off-the-shelf products or 4GLs.

- *Available technologies*: Alternatively, technologies such as commercial off-the-shelf products, application generators, or 4GL capabilities that do cover a system's growth envelope may determine the most attractive process model. (A related process model is the "capabilities-to-requirements" model, in which the availability of powerful, easy-to-adapt capabilities or reusable components strongly influences the system requirements.)

- *Knowledge of requirements*: Ill-defined requirements imply process models that incorporate the user-feedback loops of prototyping and evolutionary development, as opposed to the waterfall model which has a high risk of developing software that does not satisfy user requirements.

- *Architecture understanding*: The lower the level of understanding of system architecture, the higher the risk of a pure top-down waterfall approach. On the other hand, a high level of architecture understanding lowers one of the risks of evolutionary development: that the system will evolve in directions that the architecture cannot support.

- *Robustness*: Systems that must be highly robust and error-free encounter high risks from informal process models such as evolutionary prototyping. More rigorous process models such as the incremental model reduce these risks, although the incremental model may need to be preceded by less formal prototyping phases to address requirements understanding or architecture-understanding risks.

- *Budget and schedule limitations*: May require a design-to-cost or design-to-schedule approach.

- *High-risk system nucleus*: May dictate an evolutionary or incremental development approach.

Risk Management Procedures

The origins of risk management date from the 1800s when the concept of risk exposure (probability * cost) was used in the insurance industry to analyze data collected about fires and deaths. By the 1950s, decision theory and probabilistic modeling were being taught as academic subjects. Use of risk management in the petrochemical and construction industries dates from about 1980; recognition of risk management as an element of software engineering dates from about 1990. In the 1990s risk management is being applied to many diverse disciplines. In each discipline, the basic concepts of identifying, analyzing, planning, and controlling risks are used, although the terminology and procedures vary among disciplines. Figure 1 shows a suitable structure for risk management in a software development environment (adapted from [Boehm89]). As illustrated there, risk assessment is distinguished from risk control.

Risk Assessment (Risk Identification, Risk Analysis, and Risk Prioritization)

Risk Assessment deals with determining the threats to a project, with particular emphasis placed on identifying, analyzing, and prioritizing major risk factors that might become problems.

The three explicit steps of Risk Assessment involve (i) identifying risk factors so that they are brought to the attention and understanding of senior engineers, managers, and customers; (ii) analyzing the risk factors so that numerical values can be assigned to the risk impacts, probabilities, and cost and benefits of alternative courses of action; and (iii) determining which risk factors have the highest priority for the expenditure of time and effort (money) to reduce their probabilities and/or impacts.

Risk Identification

The techniques of risk identification rely on expertise and experience to identify specific risk factors for a project. Risk identification techniques include:

- risk-factor checklists
- cause-effect diagrams
- development process audits and capability assessments
- decomposition of plans to determine task dependencies
- decomposition of the design to find technical risk factors
- investigation of interface details
- examination of assumptions and decision drivers
- worst case scenarios
- group consensus techniques
- prototyping
- benchmarking
- simulation and modeling

Risk identification is improved by relying on past experience, often in the form of checklists (sometimes structured and quantified with weightings from historical data). The most useful checklists are those derived from local experience.

Customers and users, in addition to managers, lead engineers, and the development staff, need to be involved in the risk identification process. When a number of different organizations are involved in a development project, it is necessary to integrate the different perceptions—technical and organizational—of the different parties.

Risk Analysis

The primary issue in risk analysis is developing solid, numerical values for the probabilities and impacts of various risk factors. These numbers can be developed by examining historical data, by using cost estimation tools, and by converting expert judgment into numbers (for instance, Low -> 0<P<0.3; Medium -> 0.3<P<0.7; High -> 0.7<P<1.0).

Risk analysis techniques to be used depend on the types of risks being considered:

- *Risk of technical failure.* Techniques for analyzing technical risks include performance modeling, decision analysis, and cost-benefit analysis. Influence diagrams (fishbone or Ishikawa diagrams) can be used to identify areas of insufficient technical information. Various types of modeling, including simulation, benchmarking, and prototyping, can be used to analyze technical risk factors.

- *Risk of cost failure.* Techniques for analyzing cost risks include algorithmic cost models [Fairley93] and analysis of project assumptions. Monte Carlo simulation can be used to provide statistical ranges of cost based on probability distributions for the cost drivers [Fairley94].

- *Risk of schedule failure.* Techniques for analyzing schedule risks include algorithmic scheduling models, critical path methods, and PERT analysis. Probabilistic techniques, such as PERT and Monte Carlo simulation can provide ranges of probabilities for achieving various project milestones (including project completion) based on probabilistic values for the duration of the individual project tasks and the sequencing dependencies among those tasks.

- *Risk of operational failure.* Techniques for analyzing the risk of operational failure include performance modeling, reliability modeling, and quality factor analysis. By operational failure, we mean the risk that a project may produce a system that does not satisfy operational needs (that is, it does not possess the functional, performance, or other quality attributes the customer and users want and need). By operational risk, we do not mean the risk of hazard from a system in operation. Hazard is an intrinsic property or condition of a system that has the potential to cause an accident (hazard analysis constitutes a separate body of knowledge).

A risk factor may correspond to a single event, to a number of discrete events (any one of which may occur), or to a continuous distribution of possible events. Assessing the probabilities of discrete events and deriving probability distributions for continuous events is the most difficult part of risk analysis. Techniques available for determining these probabilities include expert judgment (especially expert group consensus techniques such as the Wideband Delphi technique), historical data, analogy, worst-case analysis, and what-if analysis. In many cases, these techniques provide a constructive framework for quantifying guesses (which is not all bad, provided the guesses are educated guesses). The best techniques are based on analysis of recorded data from past projects in the local environment.

Risk Prioritization

The purpose of risk prioritization is to choose,

from the list of identified risk factors, a prioritized subset of manageable proportions. The obvious choices for the most important risk factors are, theoretically, those with the largest risk exposures. In practice, however, the decision is more complex.

The following are some factors to consider in selecting the risk items to be included the prioritized list:

- Size of the risk exposure of the risk factor relative to the size of the target

- Size of the risk exposure of the risk factor relative to the largest risk exposure of any risk factor.

- Confidence level of the risk assessor in the reliability of the risk assessment carried out for the risk factor.

- Risk exposure range (ER), where:

  $RER = (RE_{maximum} - RE_{minimum})/RE_{nominal}$
  and $Re_{maximum}$, $Re_{minimum}$, and $RE_{nominal}$ are the largest, smallest, and nominal values of risk exposures among the identified risk factors. Projects having a wide risk exposure range require careful prioritization of the list. It is not necessary to perform a detailed risk analysis for a project having a small estimate range, provided the risk assessors have adequate confidence in their estimates.

- Compound risks—a risk factor that is conditioned on another risk factor that is of high priority should also be ranked high on the list.

- Maximum number of risk factors that can be interpreted and acted upon.

In selecting the risk factors to place on the prioritized list, we must not forget the objective, which is to choose those risk factors that are primary candidates for 1) immediate risk-abating actions (rather than waiting until they later become problems) or 2) are of such concern that contingency plans should be developed to trigger explicit actions should they become problems (that is, when a risk indicator metric crosses a predetermined threshold, such as a schedule delay of more than two weeks or a performance shortfall of more than 100 milliseconds).

The prioritized list is a dynamic subset of the total list of risk factors. Risk assessment should be a continuous, on-going activity, and both the total list and the prioritized, managed list will change as the project progresses. Risk factors will disappear as their threat vanishes, new risks will be identified, and risk exposures will change with the passage of time or as the result of reducing or eliminating the risks.

Risk Control (Risk Abatement Strategies, Risk Mitigation Planning, Risk Mitigation)

The conceptual basis of risk control, as in all control theory, is the feedback loop. Initial action plans are executed to reduce risk, and contingency plans are developed to trigger further risk-mitigating actions upon occurrence of certain events. As a project progresses, the operation is monitored to verify that risk factors are indeed being controlled and, if not, the project is redirected as appropriate, thus closing the control loop. The controller is the project manager who works with the project team to meet project targets by assessing risk and acting on the prioritized risk factors to protect against their possible consequences.

Risk control depends on the risk assessment procedures put in place at the beginning of a project. It is difficult to incorporate risk control into a project that has encountered problems as a result of the lack of risk assessment. The three explicit steps of risk control are (1) determining the best strategies for abating assessed risks, (2) producing risk mitigation plans, and (3) mitigating risks.

Risk Abatement Strategies

In choosing where to expend effort, time, and money on risk-reducing activities, we need to first consider areas where we do not know enough about the risks involved—or even do not know what we don't know—and proceed to gain information by prototyping, simulation, surveys, benchmarks, reference checks, examining local history, consulting experts, and so on.

In dealing with known, assessed risks there are three strategies for risk abatement:

- *Risk avoidance*, for example, by reducing functionality or performance requirements, or buying more hardware—thus eliminating the source of the risk.

- *Risk transfer*, for example, by reallocating functionality or performance requirements into hardware, moving complexity into the human element, subcontracting to specialists, or realigning authority and responsibility.

- *Risk acceptance*, by which a risk factor is acknowledged, and responsibility accepted by all affected parties, with the understanding that the accepted risk will be explicitly managed and that, in spite of our best efforts, the project might encounter significant difficulties.

Risk transfer can be a risky strategy. If, for example, there is significant risk that a specialty subcontractor may fail to deliver a satisfactory component, that problem (should it materialize) will affect the outcome of the project. We must take care to distinguish risk transfer situations from those where we retain responsibility for the outcome and those where the transfer of risk results in a transfer of responsibility as well.

Risk abatement strategies are often based on expert judgment and local experience. For example, Figure 4 illustrates the top-ten risk factors identified by Boehm in his work environment at TRW, along with risk management techniques for abating those risks [Boehm89]. Depending on your work environment, the relative priorities among the risk factors in Figure 4 (and others not on the list) may be different. For example, item 6 in Figure 4 might be the most difficult risk factor in your environment; lack of well defined development processes (not on the list in Figure 4) might be a significant risk factor in your environment.

The costs as well as the benefits of alternative courses of action must be considered; it is not sensible to spend more on risk reduction than the cost to fix the resulting problem, should it materialize. The cost incurred is the cost of the risk-reducing action and the benefit gained is the reduction of risk exposure that results from the action. Cost/benefit decisions can be based on calculations of risk reduction leverage, where:

Risk Reduction Leverage = $(RE_{Before} - RE_{After})$/Risk Reduction Cost

RE_{Before} is the risk exposure before initiating the risk reduction activity and RE_{After} is the risk exposure afterwards.

In addition to providing a rationale for choosing among alternative courses of action, risk reduction leverage can be used to decide "How much is enough?" when an activity is seen to be good (such as reviews and tests at every stage of product development) but very expensive when carried to extremes. It is clear that difficult decisions will only be made early enough and firmly enough when the risk reduction leverage calculations have sufficient credibility to support those decisions.

Risk Mitigation Planning

It is important to coordinate and reconcile the effects of various risk mitigation plans on the schedule and planned utilization of resources. This is typically done by developing the risk management plan and the risk abatement strategies and then comparing the initial risk exposure for the project to the adjusted risk exposure, taking into account the effect of the proposed risk reduction plans and their associated costs.

For example, on a project having a budget of $1M and a risk factor having an original risk exposure of $500K, implementing various risk mitigation strategies and plans, at a cost of $100K, might reduce the adjusted risk exposure to $50K. The project now has a budget/plan of, effectively, $900K with a risk exposure of $50K, which is a much less risky project. However, some other risk exposures may have increased due to the budget reduction for some of the tasks; they will have to be re-estimated or the lowest-priority requirements may have to be eliminated. Iterative reworking of all the action plans and contingency plans must be accomplished. Also note that real technical insight and real re-estimation is required, not just some playing around with risk exposure numbers.

RISK ITEM	RISK REDUCTION TECHNIQUE
1. Personnel shortfalls	Staffing with top talent; job matching; team building; training; prescheduling key people
2. Unrealistic schedules and budgets	Multisource estimates; design to cost; software reuse; requirements scrubbing
3. Wrong software functions	Mission analysis; Ops-Concept; user surveys; prototyping; early users' manual
4. Wrong user interface	Operational scenarios; prototyping; task analysis; user characterization
5. Gold plating	Requirements scrubbing; prototyping; cost/benefit analysis; design to cost
6. Continuing changes in requirements	High change threshold; information hiding; incremental development (defer changes to later)
7. Shortfalls in externally supplied components	Benchmarking; inspections; reference checking; compatibility analysis
8. Shortfalls in externally performed tasks	Reference checking; preaward audits; award-fee contracts; competitive design or prototyping; teambuilding
9. Real-time performance shortfalls	Simulation; benchmarking; modeling; prototyping; instrumentation; tuning
10. Straining computer science capabilities	Technical analysis; cost/benefit analysis; prototyping; reference checking

Figure 4. A Checklist of Software Risk Items and Risk Reduction Techniques

If systematic risk management is to be used to control risks to a project, then the estimates on which the project plan is based should not be padded for contingency. Estimates should be based on expected costs, with the assumptions clearly defined. This provides a baseline cost estimate for the project.

Each chance of an assumption being invalid is treated as a risk factor, with assessed probability and cost/schedule impact. For a high risk project, it is highly probable that the project cannot be completed within the baseline cost estimate; an extra budgetary reserve is necessary for successful project completion. The size of this reserve is usually more a matter for negotiation than true analysis based on risk exposure. Having been agreed to and allocated to the project manager's budget, this reserve is usually referred to as the "management reserve." The reserve is used by the project manager to support implementation of risk management plans and to cover unforeseen eventualities (the unknown unknowns) which require resource expenditure. A similar procedure can be applied for schedule contingency.

The management reserve can, in theory, be defined statistically to cover a reasonable percentage of the costs that would be required to deal with foreseeable project uncertainties—the 'known unknowns'. In practice, this reserve is usually negotiated downward, which creates an additional risk; that is, the risk of insufficient funds for the risk management plans. Also, having been allocated to the project, the reserve does not have the senior management's immediate attention. Major schedule delays may be introduced when the project manager has to finally go back and ask for more money or time.

An alternative approach is for the agreed-to reserve to be held outside the project (by the customer or senior management) even though inalienably committed to the project. When the project manager needs to call on the reserve, a case must be made that the perceived risk can be best mitigated by an action involving expenditure from the reserve. This encourages, in fact ensures, continuing communication between the project manager and the funding organization on the basis of management of risk.

In financial terms, the total unmitigated risk exposure for the project can be calculated from the sum of the risk exposures for all identified risk factors. The reduced risk exposure is calculated following the risk reduction activities, using the costs of those activities and the resulting risk exposure for each risk factor (calculated from the probability of occurrence and the cost impact). The resulting total risk exposure is compared with the project budget, profit margin, and commercial exposure for the organization. This can form the basis of effective communication with senior management, financial controllers, and the customer.

However, this approach treats total risk exposure in only its simplest form (a summation assumes that the cost and schedule impacts of each risk factor are independent; this may or may not be a valid assumption). More detailed analysis of interdependencies among risk factors may be required.

Decision makers also need information on the time element. The potential loss caused by a schedule delay may happen as a lump sum at a point in time, it may have a pattern of expenditure, or there may be a choice on the timing of actions, and there will be predictions of occurrence of external events. Similarly, the proposed courses of action to reduce or prevent the loss will have time-based costs and triggers for decisions which themselves will be timed (perhaps related to the reporting and decision-making processes). The combination of possibilities can be expressed as a time-based cash flow. Thus risk exposure may need to be shown as a time-based graph, or a series of graphs.

Risk Mitigation

According to the taxonomy presented in Figure 1, risk mitigation includes risk monitoring, problem resolution, and risk reassessment. If adequate risk assessment and risk reduction are accomplished at the start of a project and on a continuing basis, then, as the project progresses, the action plans and contingency plans actions should, for the most part, have the intended effect of mitigating the risk factors.

Risk monitoring (and reporting) on a regular, continuing basis have the goals of identifying risks that are about to become, or have become, problems, determining whether risks and problems are being successfully resolved, and gaining insight to identify new risk factors as they arise.

Two useful techniques for risk monitoring and reporting are Risk Item Tracking Forms and Top-Ten Risk Lists. Figures 5 and 6 provide an example of a risk item tracking form. This form consists of two parts: the risk item registry and the risk mitigation progress report. As illustrated in Figure 5, the risk registry form provides fields for identifying a risk factor, describing it, assessing it, and developing a mitigation plan to control it. The risk status and date fields provide a mechanism for tracking the progress of risk resolution. As illustrated at the bottom of Figure 5, there are several possible Risk Status Values. Figure 6 illustrates a mechanism for tracking progress on working the mitigation plan identified in Figure 5 by date and the responsible party. As indicated in Figure 6, there are several possible status values for the mitigating action.

RISK NO:	TITLE:		STATUS	DATE
Risk Item Description: Author_____Date_____				
Assessment/Alternatives Considered: Risk Owner_____Date_____				
Mitigation Plan: Planned Manager's Start Date_____Approval_____Date_____				

Possible Risk Status Values: IDENTIFIED
                                           ASSESSED
                                           PLANNED
                                           CONTINGENT
                                           PROBLEM
                                           CRISIS
                                           RESOLVED
                                           CLOSED

Figure 5. Risk Item Tracking Form

DATE	MITIGATION STATUS	ACTIONS COMPLETED	NEXT ACTIONS TO BE TAKEN	BY WHOM

Possible Risk Mitigation Status Values: PLANNED
                                                 CONTINGENT
                                                 AUTHORIZED
                                                 IN PROGRESS
                                                 LATE
                                                 FAILED
                                                 ALTERNATIVE PLAN
                                                 SUCCEEDED
                                                 UNNECESSARY
                                                 OVERTAKEN BY EVENTS
                                                 INCORPORATED IN PROJECT PLAN

Figure 6. A Risk Mitigation Tracking Form

Risk items to be included in the risk registry can be brought to the attention of lead engineers, project managers, and other decision makers using one or more "Top-Ten Risk Item Lists." A Top-Ten List is illustrated in Figure 7. In some organizations, Top-Ten lists are used at all levels, from the individual development team, to the subsystem manager, to the project manager, to the department manager, to the vice-president, to the customer/developer interface. Each group has a different list, depending on their responsibilities; for example, the project manager's list is a prioritized aggregation of top ten reports from the team leaders plus other risks at the project level; the department manager's list includes a prioritized aggregation of project managers' lists and other risks at the department level, and so forth. Reporting is upward through the management chain. If possible, a risk factor is mitigated within the group that identifies it, and reported to the next level. A risk that cannot be mitigated within the bounds of authority of the group that identifies it is promoted to the next level for mitigation.

Each item on a top-ten risk list should have a corresponding risk item tracking form, as illustrated in Figures 5 and 6. The top-ten list should be updated, and the status of risk tracking reviewed weekly at the team and project levels. In the absence of severe risks and problems, the lists at the department level and higher levels should be reviewed and updated monthly.

The term "Top-Ten" implies exactly ten risk items at each reporting level, but in fact, there is no particular best size for the reported list. If the true number of risk items is less than ten, then the report should concentrate on what is important without padding out the list. Ten serious risk items is about as many as a group can cope with, but if there are genuinely more, each should be reported, together with one further item that indicates there are so many risk factors that the project may be in serious trouble.

Communication at the senior management and customer levels using risk, including financial impact in terms of risk exposure, is much more effective than attempting to report progress against deterministic plans. Progress reporting against plans, and updates to plans, must still be done, but that should underpin the dominant theme of reporting in terms of risk. Attempting to communicate with senior management and the customer only on the basis of progress against plans is inadequate for high risk projects (which includes most software projects).

Risk Reassessment is a continuous process. The risk management control loop depends on risk monitoring which leads to corrective action, risk reassessment, and adjustments to risk management plans to stay in control of the evolving risk factors. Further iterations through full risk assessment will be needed on an ad-hoc basis as new risks arise, as well as at regularly scheduled intervals.

Implementation of Risk Management at the Organizational Level

Organizations that deal with advanced technology are increasingly mandating risk management plans on their development projects—the key driver being the use of systematic risk management as a means of relating technical and team/process risks at the project level to company/consortium/customer/commercial/mission risk. Communications with senior management and the customer that are based on risk enables them to understand the financial and strategic implications of risky technical undertakings in a way that they could not before. Understanding risks in financial and strategic terms also provides a basis for risk sharing between the developer and the customer.

Organizations that successfully introduce risk management incorporate:

- Explicit definition of their development and management processes
- Communication based on risk
- Risk reporting to senior management
- A corporate policy for risk management on projects that includes:
  - risk management plans developed at the planning stage of a project and incorporated into the overall project plan
  - project-specific tailoring of the development process and the risk reduction and risk control techniques to be used
  - risks explicitly reviewed on a regular, on-going basis

Deming's principles teach us that improvements must be based on analyzing how the work is done (that is, the development and management processes) rather than merely analyzing the resulting products. This applies not only to quality and productivity, but also to successful risk management [Deming86].

Documenting the development process implies level three of the SEI process maturity model [Humphrey89] and an engineering infrastructure with codes of practice supported by standards, procedures, and training. SEI Level 3 is the first level at which tool support is introduced to support the process (as opposed to tool support for activities within the process). Without tool support, it is only rarely and with difficulty that there is much communication outside

RANK THIS WEEK	RANK LAST WEEK	WEEKS ON LIST	RISK ITEM	POTENTIAL CONSEQUENCE	RISK RESOLUTION PROGRESS
1	4	2	Replacement for sensor-control software team leader	Delay in coding with lower quality - less reliable operation	Desired replacement unavailable
2	6	2	Requested changes in user interface	Will delay delivery date if not finished for demo next week	Two additional people assigned and working
3	2	5	Compiler problem	Delay in completing coding of hardware drivers	New release of compiler appears to solve most problems but must be fully checked out
4	3	6	Availability of work stations for system test	Delay in software system testing	Procurement delay being discussed with vendor
5	5	3	Hardware test-bed definition	Must be completed by end of month to avoid system integration delay	Work being completed; review meeting is scheduled
6	1	3	Fault tolerance requirements impact on performance	Performance problem could require major change to hw/sw architecture with severe impact on schedule and budget	Latest prototype demonstrates performance within specifications but fault tolerance still to be determined
7	-	1	Delay in specification of tele-comm interface	Could delay procurement of hardware subsystem for integration	Meeting scheduled to consider alternatives
8	8	4	Unavailability of technical editor	Insufficient time to produce high quality manuals	Staffing requirement placed with job agency
-	7	4	CM assistant needed	Inadequate support for increasing workload	Experienced CM assistant has joined team on full-time basis
-	9	5	Inability to reuse database software	Increase in planned development effort	Uncertainty resolved in latest prototype

Figure 7. Example of a Top-Ten Risk Item Report

the various project teams on how the work is being done and the risks being identified and mitigated.

Summary

The use of risk management as a common basis for communication at all levels throughout an organization provides for:

- identifying risks
- systematic risk analysis (putting numbers on probabilities and impacts)
- prioritizing risks and evaluating alternative courses of action for risk reduction
- developing risk abatement strategies
- developing action plans and contingency plans for accepted risks
- systematic monitoring and control of accepted risks
- on-going identification of new risk factors
- routine reporting of progress in terms of risk in addition to reporting progress against the project plan
- linkage from project level risks to company/customer/commercial/mission risks

Accepting risk-oriented reporting indicates new corporate attitudes about risk management. Our earlier discussion of the time-based effects of decisions and cash-flow in terms of risk penalty can also be portrayed in terms of probability of benefit as the result of decisions, actions, or expenditures (opportunity being the converse of risk).

In many organizations the effective application of risk management depends on highly motivated individuals who understand risk management and who hold key positions in the organization. It is our hope that, in the future, risk management will become a routine way of doing business at all levels and in all organizations rather than the special domain of a concerned few.

Acknowledgment

The first draft of this paper was prepared by Paul Rook before his untimely death. He is missed as a friend and colleague.

References

[Boehm89] B.W. Boehm, *Tutorial on Software Risk Management*, IEEE Computer Society Press, Los Alamitos, Calif., 1989.

[Boehm93] B.W. Boehm, *Tutorial on Software Process Models and Software Cost Models*, 8th Int'l COCOMO Meeting, Pittsburgh, Oct 1993.

[Charette89] R.N. Charette, *Software Engineering Risk Analysis and Management*, McGraw-Hill, New York, 1989.

[Charette90] R.N. Charette, *Application Strategies for Risk Analysis*, McGraw-Hill, New York, 1990.

[Deming86] W.E. Deming, *Out of the Crisis*, Cambridge, Mass., MIT Center for Advanced Engineering Study, 1986.

[Fairley91] R.E. Fairley, *Risk Management of Software Projects Tutorial*, at 13th ICSE Conference, Austin, 1991.

[Fairley93a] R.E. Fairley, "A Case Study in Managing Technical Risks for Software Projects," *Proc. 2nd SEI Risk Conf.*, 1993.

[Fairley93b] R.E. Fairley, "How Software Cost Models Deal with Risk," *Proc. 4th ESCOM Conf.*, 1993.

[Fairley94] R.E. Fairley, "Risk Management for Software Projects," *IEEE Software*, Vol. 11, No. 3, 1994.

[Humphrey89] W.S. Humphrey, *Managing the Software Process*, Addison Wesley, Reading, Mass., 1989.

Chapter 8

Infrastructure Process

1. Introduction to Chapter

This chapter describes the infrastructure processes. Portions of this text are paraphrased from IEEE/EIA Standard 12207.0-1996, Paragraphs 7.2. Paragraph 2 provides an overview and introduction to the papers contained in this chapter.

1.1 Infrastructure process

The *infrastructure process* is a process used to establish and maintain the infrastructure necessary for any other process. Infrastructure may include hardware, software, tools, techniques, standards, and facilities for development, operation, or maintenance. This process consists of the following activities:

    1. Process implementation

    2. Establishment of the infrastructure

    3. Maintenance of the infrastructure.

1.2 Process implementation

- The infrastructure should be defined and documented to meet the requirements of the process employing this process, considering the applicable procedures, standards, tools, and techniques.

- The establishment of the infrastructure should be planned and documented.

1.3 Establishment of the infrastructure

- The configuration of the infrastructure is planned and documented. Functionality, performance, safety, security, availability, space requirements, equipment, costs, and time constraints are each considered.

- The infrastructure is then installed in time for execution of the relevant process.

1.4 Maintenance of the infrastructure

The infrastructure is maintained, monitored, and modified as necessary to ensure that it continues to satisfy the requirements of the process employing this process. The extent to which the infrastructure is under configuration management is defined as part of maintaining the infrastructure.

2. 0verview of Papers

The first paper presented in this chapter is an overview of life cycle models by Edward Comer, entitled "Alternative Life Cycle Models." The word alternative is used to separate the models discussed by Comer from the conventional or classical models based on Royce's Waterfall model. Comer describes the conventional life cycle models in addition to the original Waterfall model. Because of the growing complexity of software systems, many practitioners feel the need to have different life cycle models available in addition to the conventional requirements, design, implementation, and testing models.

These alternative models are radically different from the conventional model and include such approaches as rapid prototyping, incremental development, evolutionary prototyping, the reuse of previously developed software, and automated software synthesis. Comer points out that many of these alternative models are not yet standardized and are still being developed. It should be noted that the US Mil-Std 498 (now called IEEE/EIA Standard J-STD-016-1995), "Software Development and Documentation," recognizes, among others, three life cycle models: the conventional waterfall, the incremental, and evolutionary development. Comer's paper also discusses in summary form Barry Boehm's spiral model (see the following paper).

The second paper, "A Spiral Model of Software Development and Enhancement," by Barry Boehm, presented, when published, a revolutionary new look at the software development life cycle. An earlier version of this paper was presented by Boehm at a workshop on software requirements in early 1985. The spiral is a more general software development model than those typically in use today and treats the waterfall and other popular software development paradigms as special cases. (Boehm has referred to the spiral model as a "process model generator". Given the conditions and constraints of a particular software development project, the spiral model can be used to generate the correct process for that project.)

Whereas the original waterfall model is "documentation driven," the spiral model focuses on risk management. At the completion of each phase or major activity of software development, the spiral model prompts developers to review objectives, alternatives, and constraints, to evaluate alternatives and risks, and to determine the nature of the next phase (prototyping, specification-driven, etc.).

The third paper in this chapter is titled "Evaluating Software Engineering Standards" and was written by Shari Lawrence Pfleeger, Norm Fenton, and Stella Page of the Center for Software Reliability at the University of London. While not specifically a tutorial paper as described in the Preface, this paper does provide a definition of standards with an overview of the types of standards, their presumed benefits, and a comparison of the characteristics of software standards with those in other fields of specialization. The paper then reports on a study of the effectiveness of standards in industrial practice. The study revealed that in many cases it was impossible to determine whether or not the standards were being followed (because compliance was not testable); that in cases where compliance was testable, management was not aware that compliance was less than complete; and that software standards, far more than those in other fields, apply to the process of development rather than to the final product. The authors also conclude that progress is needed in defining, collecting, and analyzing software metrics before the effectiveness of standards can be adequately judged.

The authors note that the body of software standards is large and growing. As of the date of the article, there were over 250 software engineering standards worldwide, and the IEEE computer society typically completes several new standards or revisions per year. At the time of this writing, the US Department of Defense is in the midst of a major initiative to reduce the use of standards and specifications that are peculiar to the military environment, and to use commercial standards, especially process standards, wherever possible. Thus, the highly dynamic nature of the body of software standards can be expected to continue.

Alfonso Fuggetta authored the fourth chapter of this section, regarding classification of CASE technology. The purpose of this paper is to provide a survey and a classification system to help categorize CASE tools. Several of the tools reviewed by the author are editing tools, programming tools, configuration management tools, verification/validation tools, project management tools, metrics and measurement tools, and miscellaneous tools.

The fifth paper is extracted from IEEE Standard 1074-1997, *Standard for Developing Software Life Cycle Processes*, IEEE, Inc., New York, 1997, which defines a process for creating a software life cycle process. Although this standard is directed primarily at the process architect, it is useful to any organization that is responsible for managing and performing software projects.

This standard is used for the process governing project software development and maintenance. The definition of a user's software life cycle is required. Mapping into typical software life cycles is also illustrated. It is not intended to define or imply a software life cycle of its own.

This standard applies to the management and support activities that continue throughout the entire life cycle, as well as all aspects of the software life cycle from concept exploration through retirement. The utilization of these activities maximizes the benefits to the user when the use of this standard is initiated early in the software life cycle. Software that has proceeded past the initialization phase when this standard is invoked should gradually move into compliance with this standard.

Written for any organization that is responsible for managing and conducting software projects, this standard is useful to project managers, software developers, quality assurance organizations, purchasers, users, and maintainers. It can be used whether software is the total system or is embedded into a larger system.

The reader is again reminded that this copy of the standard is incomplete and cannot be used to cite compliance with the standard in a contractual situation. It is intended to provide the reader and CSDP test taker with a basic understanding of the contents of the lifecycle process standards and an outline of a lifecycle process management plan.

Alternative Software Life Cycle Models

Edward R. Comer

Software Productivity Solutions, Melbourne, Florida

The classic waterfall model for the software life cycle (See Fig. 2.3.1) was defined as early as 1970 by Dr. Winston Royce [1] to help cope with the growing complexity of the aerospace software products being tackled. During the past 5–10 years, alternative, radically different life cycle models have been proposed, including rapid throwaway prototypes, incremental development, evolutionary prototypes, reusable software, and automated software synthesis. Although most of these alternatives are still maturing, many of their aspects have been integrated with the basic life cycle model to form hybrid life cycle models. In fact, the most recent life cycle models are actually hybrid models, including DoD-STD-2167A [2], the NASA Information System Life Cycle [3], and Barry Boehm's Spiral Model [4]. The following sections define a software life cycle model, introduce alternative life cycle models, and present an approach for contrasting and evaluating alternative life cycle models.

Introduction

Software development, for any application, is an expensive and risky endeavor. Critical software errors often remain in deployed software systems. Software maintenance is expensive and, too, error-prone. The software development process is often ad hoc and chaotic.

Aerospace systems offer special challenges for embedded software that make its development even more difficult, such as real-time, multi-mission, distributed, or autonomous.

The classic waterfall model for the software life cycle (see Figure 2.3.1) was defined as early as 1970 by Dr. Winston Royce [1] to help cope with the growing complexity of the aerospace software projects being tackled. With several years of experience with developing software for spacecraft mission planning, commanding and post-mission analysis, Dr. Royce had experienced different degrees of success with respect

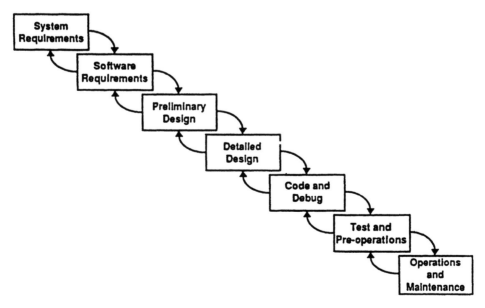

Figure 2.3.1 Waterfall life cycle model of software development

to "arriving at an operational state, on-time, and within costs" [1]. The resulting sequence of steps that he outlined, with various refinements and minor modifications, became the road map for the software development process for the last two decades.

During the past five to ten years, alternative, radically different life cycle models have been proposed, including rapid throwaway prototypes, incremental development, evolutionary prototypes, reusable software, and automated software synthesis. While most of these alternatives are still maturing, many of their aspects have been integrated with the basic life cycle model to form hybrid life cycle models. In fact, the most recent life cycle models are actually hybrid models, including DOD-STD2167A [2], the NASA Information System Life Cycle [3], and Barry Boehm's Spiral Model [4].

The following sections define a software life cycle model, introduce alternative life cycle models, and present an approach for contrasting and evaluating alternative life cycle models.

Definition of a Life Cycle Model

While the concept of a life cycle of software development is well known in the aerospace community, there are numerous misconceptions about its intent and purpose. A life cycle model is not a definition of the process a software development organization follows; the actual process is typically far more complex and includes many activities not depicted in the life cycle model. A life cycle model is not a methodology; it does not provide rules or representations for development.

Instead, we define a software life cycle model to be a *reference model* for a software development process, in the same manner that the Open Systems Interconnection (OSI) model [5] is a reference model for protocols for computer system communication. Such a reference model:

1. provides a common basis for the definition and coordination of specific project and organization software process standards, allowing these standards to be placed into perspective within the overall life cycle reference model;

2. describes the major functions, or activities, involved in software development and the terms used to define those functions;

3. highlights important aspects or features that are deemed to be important for common understanding and focus.

While a life cycle model is insufficient to represent a definition of a software development process, or to describe the methodologies applied for software development, it does serve as a reference model for these processes and methodologies. Indeed, the intent of standard DoD [2] and NASA [3] life cycles is to provide a common framework for contractor-specific processes and methodologies.

Alternative Life Cycle Models

Waterfall Model

The waterfall model documented in 1970 by Royce [1] and later refined by Boehm [6] in 1976 is the most popular and proven of the alternative life cycles. Figure 2.3.1 illustrates a waterfall model, defining the major steps, or phases, and their approximate sequence. A *phase* consists of a set of activities to accomplish the goals of that phase [3]. Additional arrows are added to represent the inherent feedback that occurs between these phases.

Most software development processes in aerospace corporations or mandated by governmental agencies have followed some basic variation of the waterfall model, although there are a variety of different names for each of the phases. Thus, the requirements phase is often called user needs analysis, system analysis, or specification; the preliminary design phase is often called high-level design, top-level design, software architectural definition, or specification; the detailed design phase is often called program design, module design, lower-level design, algorithmic design, or just plain design, etc.

In 1984, McDermid and Ripkin [7] noted that waterfall life cycle models, such as depicted in Figure 2.3.1, are too simple and abstract to deal with an embedded software development project's problem of developing, adopting, or assembling a coherent methodology. Their variant of the waterfall model, shown in Figure 2.3.2, highlights several important issues:

1. The level and purpose of the various representations are identified.

2. Activities are viewed as transformations from high level representations to low level representations.

3. Verification within a representation and between representations is explicitly shown.

4. Iterations around representations occur, as errors are discovered and changes are identified; this includes both fine and coarse iterations.

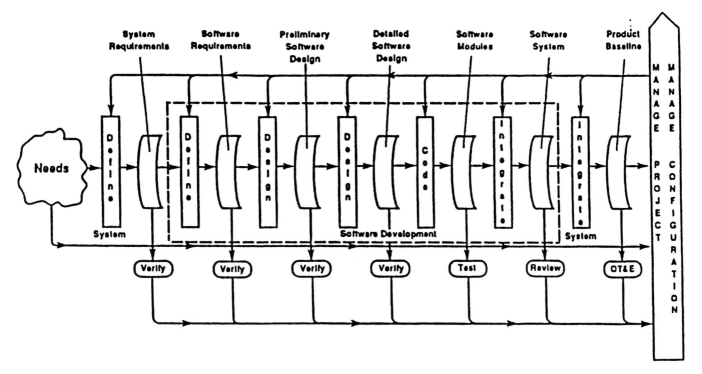

Figure 2.3.2 Another view of the waterfall model [7]

5. Project and configuration control is a special activity; this problem is compounded the presence of iteration.

Development processes based upon the waterfall model have been commonplace for aerospace software development. The use of a waterfall life cycle model:

1. encourages one to specify what the system is supposed to do (i.e., to define the requirements) before thinking about how to build the system (i.e., designing);

2. encourages one to plan how components are going to interact (i.e., designing) before building the components (i.e., coding);

3. enables project managers to track progress more accurately and to uncover possible slippages early;

4. demands that the development process generate a series of documents which can later be utilized to test and maintain the system;

5. enables the organization that will develop the system to be more structured and manageable.

Much of the motivation behind waterfall life cycle models was to provide structure to avoid the problems of the "undisciplined hacker" [6].

Rapid, Throwaway Prototypes

The rapid, throwaway prototype, made popular by Gomaa and Scott [8] in 1981, focuses on ensuring that the software product being proposed really meets the users' needs. Difficulties are often experienced using a waterfall model in the initial step of deriving a requirements specification:

1. Requirements specification documents have problems with correctness, completeness and ambiguity.

2. Errors in requirements specification are usually the last to be detected and the most costly to correct.

3. There is a communication gap between the software system developer and the user. This results in difficulties of the developer truly understanding the user's needs and difficulties of the user in understanding and approving a requirements specification.

Gomaa and Scott found that both the quality of the requirements specification and the communication of user needs can be improved by developing a prototype of the proposed system [8].

The approach is to construct a "quick and dirty" partial implementation of the system prior to (or during) the requirements phase. The potential users utilize this prototype for a period of time and supply feedback to the developers concerning its strengths and weaknesses. This feedback is then used to modify the software requirements specification to reflect the real user needs.

At this point, the developers can proceed with the actual system design and implementation with confidence that they are building the "right" system (except in those cases where the user needs evolve). An extension of this approach uses a series of throwaway prototypes [6], culminating in full-scale development.

Incremental Development

Incremental development [9] is the process for constructing a partial, but deployment-ready, implementation build of a system and incrementally adding increased functionality or performance. Two variants of this approach, shown in Figure 2.3.3, differ only in the level of requirements analysis accomplished at the start. One approach is only to define the requirements for the immediate next build, the other is to initially define and allocate the requirements for all builds.

Incremental development has received government recognition as an acceptable, or even desirable, alternative to the classic waterfall life cycle. Such an approach has been proposed in a 1987 Joint Logistics Commanders (JLC) guidebook for command and control systems [10] and discussed in the NASA Information System Life Cycle and Documentation Standards [3] for their aerospace applications.

An incremental development approach reduces the costs incurred before an initial capability is achieved and defines an approach for the "incremental definition, funding, development, fielding, support and operational testing of an operational capability to satisfy the evolving requirement" [10]. It also produces an operational system more quickly, and it thus reduces the possibility that the user needs will change during the development process.

Experience with the incremental development life cycle for aerospace applications has shown that the approach provides better visibility into the development to better assess progress and has been shown to decrease risk and to increase reliability and productivity in the development process [3]. The approach is compatible with the philosophy of "build a little, test a little" that is popular in the Ada community. Incremental development does require the use of a flexible system architecture to facilitate incremental enhancement and expansion [10] and increases the configuration management support required during the development process [3].

Evolutionary Prototypes

Evolutionary prototyping extends the concept of incremental development to its ultimate conclusion, viewing the software life cycle as a set of numerous prototypes that are evolved through successive experimentation and refinement to meet the user's needs. The approach, described by Giddings in 1984 [11], addresses the inherent problem of truly satisfying user needs and the problem of evolving a software system as the needs of the application domain change. This aspect can be important for many applications, including aerospace systems, that have a very long operational life time, often two or three decades.

In an evolutionary prototyping life cycle, shown in Figure 2.3.4, the developers construct a partial implementation of the system which meets known requirements. The prototype is then experimentally used by its users in order to understand the full requirements better. The usage observations are analyzed and used as the basis for the next evolution of the prototype. This cycle continues until a prototype is considered by the users to be acceptable for operational deployment. Future evolution of the application requirements can be addressed by continuing this evolutionary development process.

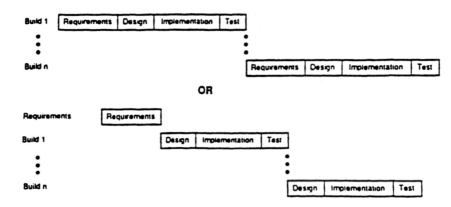

Figure 2.3.3 Incremental development life cycle models

316

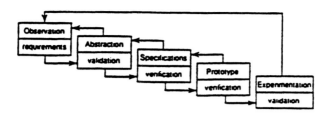

Figure 2.3.4 Evolutionary prototyping life cycle [11]

Whereas incremental development implies a high level of understanding of the requirements up front, implementing subsets of increasing capability, evolutionary prototyping implies that we do not know up front all of our requirements, but need to experiment with an operational system in order to learn them. Note that in the case of throwaway prototypes we are likely to implement only those aspects of the system that are poorly understood, but that in the case of evolutionary prototypes we are more likely to start with those system aspects that are best understood and thus build upon our strengths.

Evolutionary prototyping has challenges in scaling up to very large systems, ensuring process visibility and control, avoiding the negative effects of "information sclerosis," and avoiding the "'undisciplined hacker' approach that the waterfall and other models were trying to correct" [4]. Information sclerosis is a "syndrome familiar to operational information-based systems, in which temporary work-arounds for software deficiencies increasingly solidify into unchangeable constraints on evolution" [4].

For complex aerospace applications, it is not reasonable at this time to expect evolutionary application of prototypes to be particularly "rapid" because reliability, adaptability, maintainability, and performance (RAMP) are major forces behind making such system developments expensive and time-consuming. Since the technology is not yet available to *retrofit* RAMP requirements, they would have to be implemented up front, thus forcing software development costs high and schedules to their limit. Evolutionary prototypes will become more practical in the future as automated techniques for retrofitting RAMP requirements are developed [12].

Reusable Software

Whereas prototyping attempts to reduce development costs through partial implementations leading to a better understanding of requirements, reusable software is the discipline of attempting to reduce development costs by incorporating designs, programs, modules, and data into new software products [13]. Because the emphasis of reusable software is on a dif-

ferent approach for constructing software rather than specifying it, the approach is compatible with prototyping approaches.

The software industry is guilty of continuously reinventing the wheel. Reusability has achieved only limited application, mostly in business applications. There are few tools available to help reuse software designs or code from previous projects. Clearly, what is needed are techniques to analyze application domains for reusability potential, create reusable components, techniques, and tools to store and retrieve reusable components, and component specification and classification techniques to help catalog and locate relevant components. The net effect of reusing components would be shorter development schedules (by using wheels rather than reinventing them) and more reliable software (by using components that been previously "shaken down").

A life cycle incorporating reusable software is a major objective of the government's Ada initiative. Many of the features of the language supporting abstract data types and generics are designed to directly support the development and effective usage of reusable modules.

The most significant work in reusable software for aerospace applications is the Common Ada Missile Packages (CAMP) effort [14]. In a multi-phased Air Force program, McDonnell Douglas provided a comprehensive demonstration of a reusable software life cycle. The effort accomplished a domain analysis of missile software, identified commonalities of that application, specified and constructed a set of over 200 Ada "parts," developed tools to support reusability, and finally accomplished a missile software development using the developed reusable software parts.

Automated Software Synthesis

Automated software synthesis is a term used to describe the automated transformation of formal requirements specifications into operational code [15]. Such an approach, shown in Figure 2.3.5, relies heavily on automated tools. Formal specifications are created and maintained by users using specification tools. The formal specifications become prototypes for the

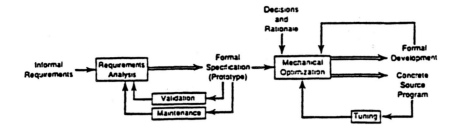

Figure 2.3.5 Automated software synthesis life cycle [15]

desired system that are used to refine the specification. Implementation of a production software system is accomplished using a highly automated transformational programming approach from the formal specification.

Transformational programming [16] is a methodology of program construction by successive application of transformation rules. The individual transitions between the various versions of the program are made by applying correctness-preserving transformation rules, stating with the formal specification. It is guaranteed that the final version of the program will satisfy the initial specification.

Fully automatic transformation clearly is best. Unfortunately, such a solution may not be feasible because of the wide gap between high-level specification languages and implementations. A partially automated solution is more feasible, in the form of an automated assistant. [15]

Automated software synthesis is an active research area [16]. To become practical for aerospace applications, there are two significant technologies that must be matured: tools for derivation of formal specifications using informal specifications and prototyping, and tools for automatic transformation of formal specifications into optimized code. Both are still highly experimental.

User derivation and maintenance of a specification, rather than code, has many advantages. The user as the systems analyst, with the aid of prototyping via an executable specification, can completely and accurately determine what the system will do and evolve the system as the application requirements change. Because implementations can be easily transformed from updated specifications, enhancement can be accomplished easier and more frequently; "it will stay 'soft' and modifiable rather than become ossified and brittle with age" [15].

Evaluation of Alternative Life Cycle Models

It is difficult to compare and contrast these new models of software development because their disciples often use different terminology, and the models often have little in common except their beginnings (marked by a recognition that a problem exists) and ends (marked by the existence of a software solution). This section provides a framework originally described by Davis et al. in 1988 [12] which can serve 1) as a basis for analyzing the similarities and differences among alternative life cycle models; 2) as a tool for software engineering researchers to help describe the probable impacts of a new life cycle model; and 3) as a means to help software practitioners decide on an appropriate life cycle model to utilize on a particular project or in a particular application area.

Life Cycle Model Evaluation Paradigm

For every application beyond the trivial, user needs are constantly evolving. Thus, the system being constructed is always aiming at a moving target. This is the primary reason for delayed schedules (caused by trying to make the software meet a new requirement it was not designed to meet) and software that fails to meet customer expectations (because the developers "froze" the requirements and failed to acknowledge the inevitable changes).

Figure 2.3.6 shows graphically how users' needs evolve over time. It is recognized that the function shown is neither linear nor continuous in reality. Please note that the scale on the X axis is not shown (the units can be either months or years), but could be assumed to be nonuniform, containing areas of compression and expansion. The units of the scale on the Y axis are also not shown, but are assumed to be some measure of the amount of functionality (such as De-Marco's "Bangs for the Buck" [17]). However, none of the observations made are dependent on either the uniformity of the axes or the linearity or continuity of the curve shown in Figure 2.3.6.

Figure 2.3.7 shows what happens during a conventional waterfall life cycle software development. At time t_0, a need for a software system is recognized and a development effort commences with relatively incomplete knowledge of the real user needs. At time

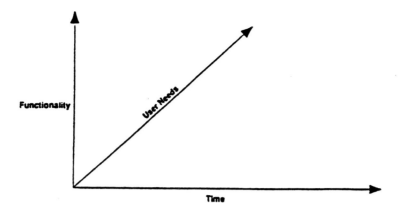

Figure 2.3.6 Constantly evolving user needs [12]

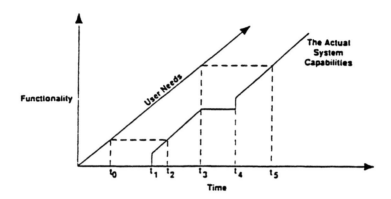

Figure 2.3.7 Evaluation of waterfall model in satisfying evolving user needs [12]

t_1, the development effort has produced an operational product, but not only does it not satisfy the current t_1 needs, it does not even satisfy the old t_0 needs because of a poor understanding of those needs in the first place. The product now undergoes a series of enhancements (between times t_1 and t_3), which eventually enable it to satisfy the original requirements (at t_2) and then some. At some later point in time t_3, the cost of enhancement is so great that the decision is made to build a new system (once again based on poorly understood requirements), development of the product is completed at time t_4, and the cycle repeats itself.

A number of useful metrics can now be defined based on the paradigm defined above. These metrics can later be used to compare and contrast sets of alternative life cycle approaches. These metrics are portrayed graphically in Figure 2.3.8 and are described below [12].

1. A *shortfall is* a measure of how far the operational system, at any time *t*, is from meeting the actual requirements at time *t*. This is

the attribute that most people are referring to when they ask "Does this system meet my needs?"

2. *Lateness is* a measure of the time that elapses between the appearance of a new requirement and its satisfaction. Of course, recognizing that new requirements are not necessarily implemented in the order in which they appear, lateness actually measures the time delay associated with achievement of a level of functionality.

3. The *adaptability* is the rate at which the software solution can adapt to new requirements, as measured by the slope of the solution curve.

4. The *longevity* is the time a system solution is adaptable to change and remains viable, i.e., the time from system creation through the time it is replaced.

5. *Inappropriateness* is the shaded area between the user needs and the solution curves in Figure 2.3.8 and thus captures the behavior of

shortfall over time. The ultimately "appropriate" model would exhibit a zero area, meaning that new requirements are instantly satisfied.

Each of the alternative life cycle models defined earlier is now analyzed with respect to the paradigm described above.

Rapid, Throwaway Prototypes

The use of a rapid throwaway prototype early in the development life cycle increases the likelihood that customers and developers will have a better understanding of the real user needs that existed at time t_0. Thus, its use does not radically affect the life cycle

model per se, but does increase the impact of the resulting system. This is shown in Figure 2.3.9, where the vertical line (i.e., the increase in functionality provided by the system upon deployment) at time t_1 is longer than in the waterfall approach.

Figure 2.3.9 also shows the rapid prototype itself as a short vertical line providing limited and experimental capability soon after time t_0. There is no reason to believe that the length of time during which the product can be efficiently enhanced without replacement is any different than with the waterfall approach. Therefore, this period of time for the rapid prototype-based development (i.e., t_3 minus t_1) is shown in Figure 2.3.9 the same as for the waterfall developed product.

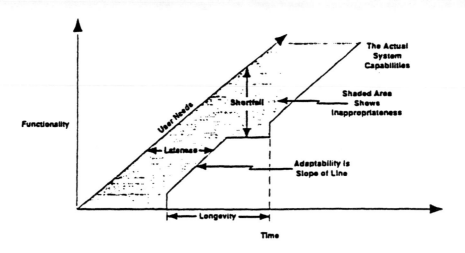

Figure 2.3.8 Life cycle evaluation metrics [12]

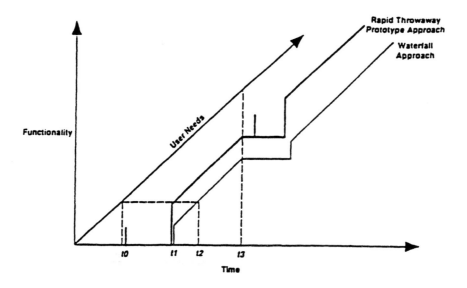

Figure 2.3.9 Comparison of rapid prototyping vs waterfall life cycle [12]

320

Incremental Development

When using incremental development, software is deliberately built to satisfy fewer requirements initially, but is constructed in such a way as to facilitate the incorporation of new requirements and thus achieve higher adaptability. This approach has two effects: 1) the initial development time is reduced because of the reduced level of functionality, and 2) the software can be enhanced more easily and for a longer period of time.

Figure 2.3.10 shows how this approach compares to the waterfall life cycle. Note that the initial development time is less than for the waterfall approach, that the initial functionality (A) is less than for the waterfall approach (B), and that the increased adaptability is indicated by a higher slope of the curve A-C than that for the waterfall approach (line B-D). The stair-step aspect of the graph indicates a series of well-defined, planned, discrete builds of the system.

Evolutionary Prototypes

This approach is an extension of the incremental development. Here, the number and frequency of operational prototypes increases. The emphasis is on evolving toward a solution in a more continuous fashion, instead of by a discrete number of system builds.

With such an approach, an initial prototype emerges rapidly, presumably demonstrating functionality where the requirements are well understood (in contrast to the throwaway prototypes, where one usually implements poorly understood aspects first) and providing an overall framework for the software. Each successive prototype explores a new area of user need,

while refining the previous functions. As a result, the solution evolves closer and closer to the user needs (see Figure 2.3.11). In time, it too will have to be redone or undergo major restructuring in order to continue to evolve.

As with the incremental development approach, the slope (line A-C) is steeper than in the waterfall approach (line B-D) because the evolvable prototype was designed to be far more adaptable. Also, the line A-C in Figure 2.3.7 is not stepped like line A-C in Figure 2.3.6 because of the replacement of well-defined and well-planned system "builds" with a continuous influx of new, and perhaps experimental, functionality.

Reusable Software

Reuse of existing software components has the potential to decrease the initial development time for software significantly. Figure 2.3.12 shows how this approach compares to conventional waterfall development. No parameters are changed, except for the development times.

Automated Software Synthesis

In the ultimate application of this approach, as an engineer recognizes the requirements, these are specified in some type of formal specification and the system is automatically synthesized. This approach has two dramatic effects: 1) the development time is greatly reduced, and 2) the development costs are reduced so much that adapting "old" systems is rarely more meritorious than resynthesizing the entire system. Thus, the longevity of any version is low, and the

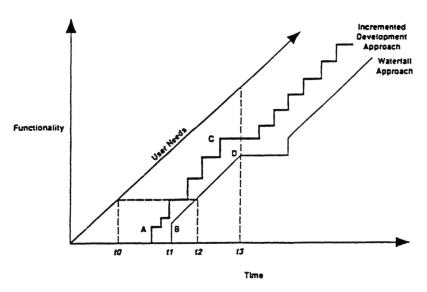

Figure 2.3.10 Comparison of incremental development vs waterfall life cycle [12]

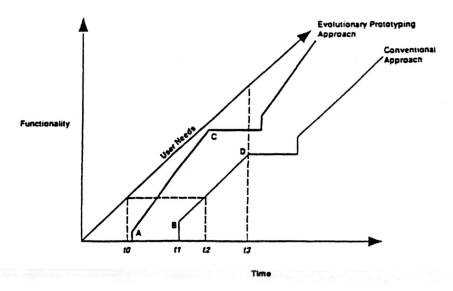

Figure 2.3.11 Comparison of evolutionary prototyping vs waterfall life cycle [12]

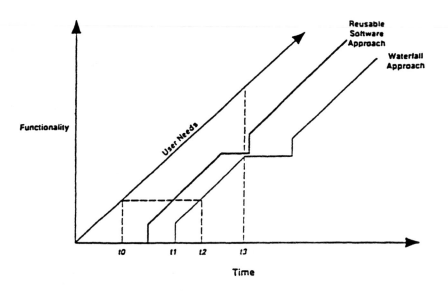

Figure 2.3.12 Comparison of reusable software vs waterfall life cycle [12]

result is a stair-step graph, as shown in Figure 2.3.13, where the horizontal segments represent the time the system is utilized and the time needed to upgrade the requirements. The vertical segments represent the additional functionality offered by each new generation.

Defining, Selecting, or Adapting a Life Cycle Model

The various life cycle alternatives reflect different approaches for improving the software development process. The life cycle model evaluation paradigm [12] provides insight into how we might define, select or adapt a life cycle model to improve our process.

Currently, many project managers make this selection based on fuzzy perceptions and past experiences or blindly follow life cycle standards. The evaluation paradigm presented points to some application aspects that should affect selection of a life cycle approach:

1. requirements volatility (that is, the likelihood that the requirements will change);

2. the "shape" of requirements volatility (such as discrete leaps, based on brand new threats; or gradual changes, as with a need to do things faster);

3. the longevity of the application; and

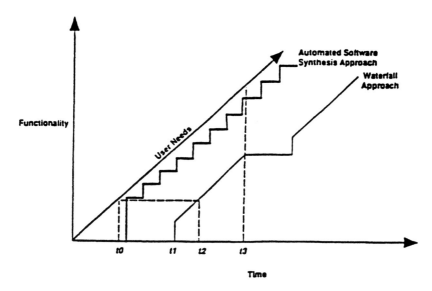

Figure 2.3.13 Comparison of automated software vs waterfall life cycle [12]

4. the availability of resources to develop or effect changes (i.e., it may be easier to get resources up front than to devote significant resources for enhancements).

References

[1] Royce, W.W., "Managing the Development of Large Software Systems: Concepts and Techniques," *1970 WESCON Technical Papers,* Vol. 14, Western Electronic Show and Convention, 1970.

[2] *Defense System Software Development,* DOD-STD-2167A Military Standard, Feb. 29, 1988.

[3] *Information System Life Cycle and Documentation Standards,* Release 4.3, NASA Office of Safety, Reliability, Maintainability, and Quality Assurance, Software Management and Assurance Program (SMAP), Washington, D.C., Feb. 28, 1989.

[4] Boehm, B.W., "A Spiral Model of Software Development and Enhancement," *ACM SIGSOFT Software Eng. Notes,* Vol. 11, No. 4, Aug. 1986, pp. 14–24.

[5] Information Processing Systems—Open Systems Interconnection (OSI)--Basic Reference Model, International Standards Organization ISO-7498-1984, Oct. 15, 1984.

[6] Boehm, B.W., "Software Engineering," *IEEE Trans. Computers,* Vol. C-25, Dec. 1976, pp. 1226–1241.

[7] McDermid, J. and Ripken, K., *Life Cycle Support in the Ada Environment,* Cambridge University Press, Cambridge, UK, 1984.

[8] Gomaa, H. and Scott, D., "Prototyping as a Tool in the Specification of User Requirements," *Proc. 5th IEEE Int'l Conf. Software Eng.,* 1981, pp. 333–342.

[9] Hirsch, E., "Evolutionary Acquisition of Command and Control Systems," *Program Manager,* Nov-Dec 1985, pp. 18–22.

[10] Joint Logistics Commanders Guidance for the Use of an Evolutionary Acquisition (EA) Strategy in Acquiring Command and Control Systems, Defense Systems Management College, Fort Belvoir, VA, 1987.

[11] Giddings, R.V., "Accommodating Uncertainty in Software Design," *Comm. ACM,* Vol. 27, No. 5, May 1984, pp. 428–434.

[12] Davis, A.M., Bersoff, E.H., and Comer, E.R., "A Strategy for Comparing Alternative Software Development Life Cycle Models," *IEEE Trans. Software Eng.,* Vol. 14, No. 10, Oct. 1988, pp. 1453–1461.

[13] Jones, T.C., "Reusability in Programming: A Survey of the State of the Art," *IEEE Trans. Software Eng.,* Vol. SE-10, Sept. 1984, pp. 488–494.

[14] McNicholl, D.G., Palmer, C., and Cohen, S., *Common Ada Missile Packages (CAMP),* Vol. I and II, McDonnell Douglas, AFATL-TR-85-93, May 1986.

[15] Balzer, R., Cheatham, T.E., Jr., and Green, C., "Software Technology in the 1990's: Using a New Paradigm," *Computer,* Nov. 1983, pp. 39–45.

[16] Partsch, H. and Steinbruggen, R., "Program Transformation Systems," *ACM Computing Surveys,* Vol. 16, No. 3, Sept. 1983, pp. 199–236.

[17] DeMarco, T., *Controlling Software Projects,* Yourdon Press, New York, 1982.

A Spiral Model of Software Development and Enhancement

Barry W. Boehm, TRW Defense Systems Group

"Stop the life cycle—I want to get off!"
"Life-cycle Concept Considered Harmful."
"The waterfall model is dead."
"No, it isn't, but it should be."

These statements exemplify the current debate about software life-cycle process models. The topic has recently received a great deal of attention.

The Defense Science Board Task Force Report on Military Software[1] issued in 1987 highlighted the concern that traditional software process models were discouraging more effective approaches to software development such as prototyping and software reuse. The Computer Society has sponsored tutorials and workshops on software process models that have helped clarify many of the issues and stimulated advances in the field (see "Further reading").

The spiral model presented in this article is one candidate for improving the software process model situation. The major distinguishing feature of the spiral model is that it creates a *risk-driven* approach to the software process rather than a primarily *document-driven* or *code-driven* process. It incorporates many of the strengths of other models and resolves many of their difficulties.

This article opens with a short description of software process models and the issues they address. Subsequent sections outline the process steps involved in the

---

This evolving risk-driven approach provides a new framework for guiding the software process.

---

spiral model; illustrate the application of the spiral model to a software project, using the TRW Software Productivity Project as an example; summarize the primary advantages and implications involved in using the spiral model and the primary difficulties in using it at its current incomplete level of elaboration; and present resulting conclusions.

Background on software process models

The primary functions of a software process model are to determine the *order of the stages* involved in software development and evolution and to establish the *transition criteria* for progressing from one stage to the next. These include completion criteria for the current stage plus choice criteria and entrance criteria for the next stage. Thus, a process model addresses the following software project questions:

(1) What shall we do next?

(2) How long shall we continue to do it?

Consequently, a process model differs from a software method (often called a methodology) in that a method's primary focus is on how to navigate through each phase (determining data, control, or "uses" hierarchies; partitioning functions; allocating requirements) and how to represent phase products (structure charts; stimulus-response threads; state transition diagrams).

Why are software process models important? Primarily because they provide guidance on the order (phases, increments, prototypes, validation tasks, etc.) in which a project should carry out its major tasks. Many software projects, as the next section shows, have come to grief because they pursued their various development and evolution phases in the wrong order.

Evolution of process models. Before concentrating in depth on the spiral model, we should take a look at a number of others: the code-and-fix model, the stagewise model and the waterfall model, the evolutionary development model, and the transform model.

The code-and-fix model. The basic model used in the earliest days of software

Reprinted from *Computer*, Vol. 21, No. 5, May 1988, pp. 61–72.

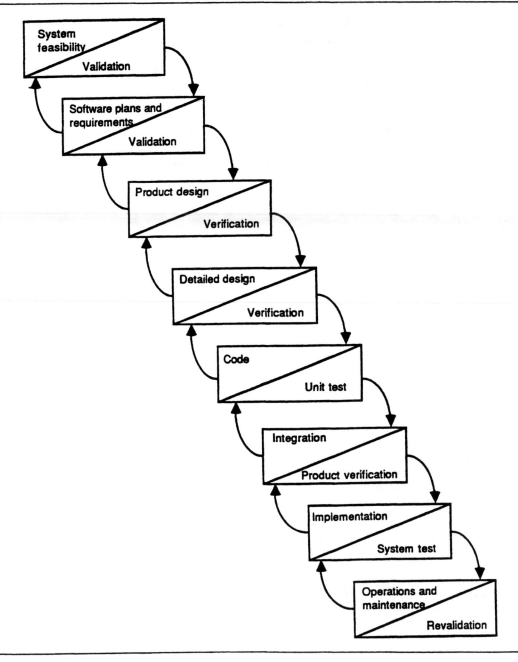

Figure 1. The waterfall model of the software life cycle.

development contained two steps:

(1) Write some code.

(2) Fix the problems in the code.

Thus, the order of the steps was to do some coding first and to think about the requirements, design, test, and maintenance later. This model has three primary difficulties:

(a) After a number of fixes, the code became so poorly structured that subsequent fixes were very expensive. This underscored the need for a design phase prior to coding.

(b) Frequently, even well-designed software was such a poor match to users' needs that it was either rejected outright or expensively redeveloped. This made the need for a requirements phase prior to design evident.

(c) Code was expensive to fix because of poor preparation for testing and modifi-

326

cation. This made it clear that explicit recognition of these phases, as well as test-and-evolution planning and preparation tasks in the early phases, were needed.

The stagewise and waterfall models. As early as 1956, experience on large software systems such as the Semi-Automated Ground Environment (SAGE) had led to the recognition of these problems and to the development of a stagewise model[2] to address them. This model stipulated that software be developed in successive stages (operational plan, operational specifications, coding specifications, coding, parameter testing, assembly testing, shakedown, system evaluation).

The waterfall model,[3] illustrated in Figure 1, was a highly influential 1970 refinement of the stagewise model. It provided two primary enhancements to the stagewise model:

(1) Recognition of the feedback loops between stages, and a guideline to confine the feedback loops to successive stages to minimize the expensive rework involved in feedback across many stages.

(2) An initial incorporation of prototyping in the software life cycle, via a "build it twice" step running in parallel with requirements analysis and design.

The waterfall model's approach helped eliminate many difficulties previously encountered on software projects. The waterfall model has become the basis for most software acquisition standards in government and industry. Some of its initial difficulties have been addressed by adding extensions to cover incremental development, parallel developments, program families, accommodation of evolutionary changes, formal software development and verification, and stagewise validation and risk analysis.

However, even with extensive revisions and refinements, the waterfall model's basic scheme has encountered some more fundamental difficulties, and these have led to the formulation of alternative process models.

A primary source of difficulty with the waterfall model has been its emphasis on fully elaborated documents as completion criteria for early requirements and design phases. For some classes of software, such as compilers or secure operating systems, this is the most effective way to proceed. However, it does not work well for many classes of software, particularly interactive

---

The waterfall model has become the basis for most software acquisition standards.

---

end-user applications. Document-driven standards have pushed many projects to write elaborate specifications of poorly understood user interfaces and decision-support functions, followed by the design and development of large quantities of unusable code.

These projects are examples of how waterfall-model projects have come to grief by pursuing stages in the wrong order. Furthermore, in areas supported by fourth-generation languages (spreadsheet or small business applications), it is clearly unnecessary to write elaborate specifications for one's application before implementing it.

The evolutionary development model. The above concerns led to the formulation of the *evolutionary development* model,[4] whose stages consist of expanding increments of an operational software product, with the directions of evolution being determined by operational experience.

The evolutionary development model is ideally matched to a fourth-generation language application and well matched to situations in which users say, "I can't tell you what I want, but I'll know it when I see it." It gives users a rapid initial operational capability and provides a realistic operational basis for determining subsequent product improvements.

Nonetheless, evolutionary development also has its difficulties. It is generally difficult to distinguish it from the old code-and-fix model, whose spaghetti code and lack of planning were the initial motivation for the waterfall model. It is also based on the often-unrealistic assumption that the user's operational system will be flexible enough to accommodate unplanned evolution paths. This assumption is unjustified in three primary circumstances:

(1) Circumstances in which several independently evolved applications must subsequently be closely integrated.

(2) "Information-sclerosis" cases, in which temporary work-arounds for software deficiencies increasingly solidify into

unchangeable constraints on evolution. The following comment is a typical example: "It's nice that you could change those equipment codes to make them more intelligible for us, but the Codes Committee just met and established the current codes as company standards."

(3) Bridging situations, in which the new software is incrementally replacing a large existing system. If the existing system is poorly modularized, it is difficult to provide a good sequence of "bridges" between the old software and the expanding increments of new software.

Under such conditions, evolutionary development projects have come to grief by pursuing stages in the wrong order: evolving a lot of hard-to-change code before addressing long-range architectural and usage considerations.

The transform model. The "spaghetti code" difficulties of the evolutionary development and code-and-fix models can also become a difficulty in various classes of waterfall-model applications, in which code is optimized for performance and becomes increasingly hard to modify. The transform model[5] has been proposed as a solution to this dilemma.

The transform model assumes the existence of a capability to automatically convert a formal specification of a software product into a program satisfying the specification. The steps then prescribed by the transform model are

- a formal specification of the best initial understanding of the desired product;
- automatic transformation of the specification into code;
- an iterative loop, if necessary, to improve the performance of the resulting code by giving optimization guidance to the transformation system;
- exercise of the resulting product; and
- an outer iterative loop to adjust the specification based on the resulting operational experience, and to rederive, reoptimize, and exercise the adjusted software product.

The transform model thus bypasses the difficulty of having to modify code that has become poorly structured through repeated reoptimizations, since the modifications are made to the specification. It also avoids the extra time and expense involved in the intermediate design, code, and test activities.

Still, the transform model has various

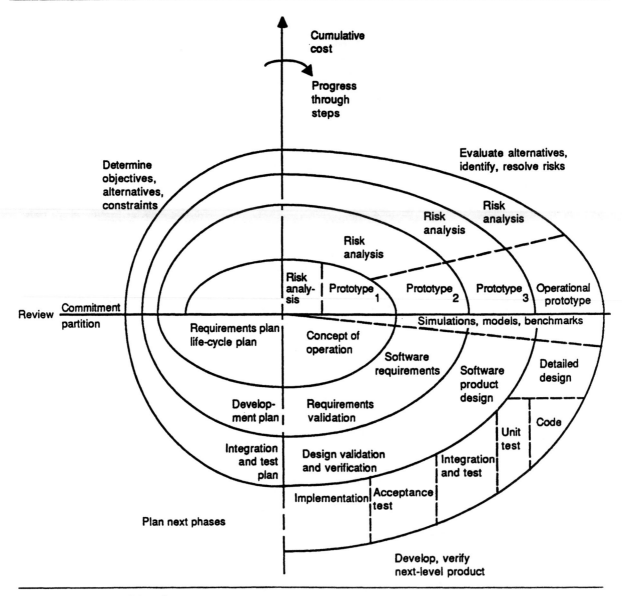

Figure 2. Spiral model of the software process.

difficulties. Automatic transformation capabilities are only available for small products in a few limited areas: spreadsheets, small fourth-generation language applications, and limited computer-science domains. The transform model also shares some of the difficulties of the evolutionary development model, such as the assumption that users' operational systems will always be flexible enough to support unplanned evolution paths.

Additionally, it would face a formidable knowledge-base-maintenance problem in dealing with the rapidly increasing and evolving supply of reusable software components and commercial software products. (Simply consider the problem of tracking the costs, performance, and features of all commercial database management systems, and automatically choosing the best one to implement each new or changed specification.)

The spiral model

The spiral model of the software process (see Figure 2) has been evolving for several years, based on experience with various refinements of the waterfall model as applied to large government software projects. As will be discussed, the spiral model can accommodate most previous models as special cases and further pro-

328

vides guidance as to which combination of previous models best fits a given software situation. Development of the TRW Software Productivity System (TRW-SPS), described in the next section, is its most complete application to date.

The radial dimension in Figure 2 represents the cumulative cost incurred in accomplishing the steps to date; the angular dimension represents the progress made in completing each cycle of the spiral. (The model reflects the underlying concept that each cycle involves a progression that addresses the same sequence of steps, for each portion of the product and for each of its levels of elaboration, from an overall concept of operation document down to the coding of each individual program.) Note that some artistic license has been taken with the increasing cumulative cost dimension to enhance legibility of the steps in Figure 2.

A typical cycle of the spiral. Each cycle of the spiral begins with the identification of

- the objectives of the portion of the product being elaborated (performance, functionality, ability to accommodate change, etc.);
- the alternative means of implementing this portion of the product (design A, design B, reuse, buy, etc.); and
- the constraints imposed on the application of the alternatives (cost, schedule, interface, etc.).

The next step is to evaluate the alternatives relative to the objectives and constraints. Frequently, this process will identify areas of uncertainty that are significant sources of project risk. If so, the next step should involve the formulation of a cost-effective strategy for resolving the sources of risk. This may involve prototyping, simulation, benchmarking, reference checking, administering user questionnaires, analytic modeling, or combinations of these and other risk-resolution techniques.

Once the risks are evaluated, the next step is determined by the relative remaining risks. If performance or user-interface risks strongly dominate program development or internal interface-control risks, the next step may be an evolutionary development one: a minimal effort to specify the overall nature of the product, a plan for the next level of prototyping, and the development of a more detailed prototype to continue to resolve the major risk issues.

If this prototype is operationally useful and robust enough to serve as a low-risk base for future product evolution, the subsequent risk-driven steps would be the evolving series of evolutionary prototypes going toward the right in Figure 2. In this case, the option of writing specifications would be addressed but not exercised. Thus, risk considerations can lead to a project implementing only a subset of all the potential steps in the model.

On the other hand, if previous prototyping efforts have already resolved all of the performance or user-interface risks, and program development or interface-control risks dominate, the next step follows the basic waterfall approach (concept of operation, software requirements, preliminary design, etc. in Figure 2), modified as appropriate to incorporate incremental development. Each level of software specification in the figure is then followed by a validation step and the preparation of plans for the succeeding cycle. In this case, the options to prototype, simulate, model, etc. are addressed but not exercised, leading to the use of a different subset of steps.

This risk-driven subsetting of the spiral model steps allows the model to accommodate any appropriate mixture of a specification-oriented, prototype-oriented, simulation-oriented, automatic transformation-oriented, or other approach to software development. In such cases, the appropriate mixed strategy is chosen by considering the relative magnitude of the program risks and the relative effectiveness of the various techniques in resolving the risks. In a similar way, risk-management considerations can determine the amount of time and effort that should be devoted to such other project activities as planning, configuration management, quality assurance, formal verification, and testing. In particular, risk-driven specifications (as discussed in the next section) can have varying degrees of completeness, formality, and granularity, depending on the relative risks of doing too little or too much specification.

An important feature of the spiral model, as with most other models, is that each cycle is completed by a review involving the primary people or organizations concerned with the product. This review covers all products developed during the previous cycle, including the plans for the next cycle and the resources required to carry them out. The review's major objective is to ensure that all concerned parties are mutually committed to the approach for the next phase.

The plans for succeeding phases may also include a partition of the product into increments for successive development or components to be developed by individual organizations or persons. For the latter case, visualize a series of parallel spiral cycles, one for each component, adding a third dimension to the concept presented in Figure 2. For example, separate spirals can be evolving for separate software components or increments. Thus, the review-and-commitment step may range from an individual walk-through of the design of a single programmer's component to a major requirements review involving developer, customer, user, and maintenance organizations.

Initiating and terminating the spiral. Four fundamental questions arise in considering this presentation of the spiral model:

(1) How does the spiral ever get started?

(2) How do you get off the spiral when it is appropriate to terminate a project early?

(3) Why does the spiral end so abruptly?

(4) What happens to software enhancement (or maintenance)?

The answer to these questions involves an observation that the spiral model applies equally well to development or enhancement efforts. In either case, the spiral gets started by a hypothesis that a particular operational mission (or set of missions) could be improved by a software effort. The spiral process then involves a test of this hypothesis: at any time, if the hypothesis fails the test (for example, if delays cause a software product to miss its market window, or if a superior commercial product becomes available), the spiral is terminated. Otherwise, it terminates with the installation of new or modified software, and the hypothesis is tested by observing the effect on the operational mission. Usually, experience with the operational mission leads to further hypotheses about software improvements, and a new maintenance spiral is initiated to test the hypothesis. Initiation, termination, and iteration of the tasks and products of previous cycles are thus implicitly defined in the spiral model (although they're not included in Figure 2 to simplify its presentation).

Using the spiral model

The various rounds and activities involved in the spiral model are best understood through use of an example. The spiral model was used in the definition and development of the TRW Software Productivity System (TRW-SPS), an integrated software engineering environment.[6] The initial mission opportunity coincided with a corporate initiative to improve productivity in all appropriate corporate operations and an initial hypothesis that software engineering was an attractive area to investigate. This led to a small, extra "Round 0" circuit of the spiral to determine the feasibility of increasing software productivity at a reasonable corporate cost. (Very large or complex software projects will frequently precede the "concept of operation" round of the spiral with one or more smaller rounds to establish feasibility and to reduce the range of alternative solutions quickly and inexpensively.)

Tables 1, 2, and 3 summarize the application of the spiral model to the first three rounds of defining the SPS. The major features of each round are subsequently

discussed and are followed by some examples from later rounds, such as preliminary and detailed design.

Round 0: Feasibility study. This study involved five part-time participants over a two- to three-month period. As indicated in Table 1, the objectives and constraints were expressed at a very high level and in qualitative terms like "significantly increase," "at reasonable cost," etc.

Some of the alternatives considered, primarily those in the "technology" area, could lead to development of a software product, but the possible attractiveness of a number of non-software alternatives in the management, personnel, and facilities areas could have led to a conclusion not to embark on a software development activity.

The primary risk areas involved possible situations in which the company would invest a good deal only to find that

- resulting productivity gains were not significant, or

- potentially high-leverage improvements were not compatible with some aspects of the "TRW culture."

The risk-resolution activities undertaken in Round 0 were primarily surveys and analyses, including structured interviews of software developers and managers, an initial analysis of productivity leverage factors identified by the constructive cost model (Cocomo)[7]; and an analysis of previous projects at TRW exhibiting high levels of productivity.

The risk analysis results indicated that significant productivity gains could be achieved at a reasonable cost by pursuing an integrated set of initiatives in the four major areas. However, some candidate solutions, such as a software support environment based on a single, corporate, maxicomputer-based time-sharing system, were found to be in conflict with TRW constraints requiring support of different levels of security-classified projects. Thus, even at a very high level of generality of objectives and constraints, Round 0 was able to answer basic feasibility questions and eliminate significant classes of candidate solutions.

The plan for Round 1 involved commitment of 12 man-months compared to the two man-months invested in Round 0 (during these rounds, all participants were part-time). Round 1 here corresponded fairly well to the initial round of the spiral model shown in Figure 2, in that its intent was to produce a concept of operation and a basic life-cycle plan for implementing whatever preferred alternative emerged.

Round 1: Concept of operations. Table 2 summarizes Round 1 of the spiral along the lines given in Table 1 for Round 0. The features of Round 1 compare to those of Round 0 as follows:

- The level of investment was greater (12 versus 2 man-months).

- The objectives and constraints were more specific ("double software productivity in five years at a cost of $10,000 a person" versus "significantly increase productivity at a reasonable cost").

- Additional constraints surfaced, such as the preference for TRW products (particularly, a TRW-developed local area network (LAN) system).

- The alternatives were more detailed ("SREM, PSL/PSA or SADT, as requirements tools etc." versus "tools"; "private/shared" terminals, "smart/dumb" terminals versus "workstations").

- The risk areas identified were more specific ("TRW LAN price-performance

Table 1. Spiral model usage: TRW Software Productivity System, Round 0.

Objectives	Significantly increase software productivity
Constraints	At reasonable cost
	Within context of TRW culture
	• Government contracts, high tech., people oriented, security
Alternatives	Management: Project organization, policies, planning, control
	Personnel: Staffing, incentives, training
	Technology: Tools, workstations, methods, reuse
	Facilities: Offices, communications
Risks	May be no high-leverage improvements
	Improvements may violate constraints
Risk resolution	Internal surveys
	Analyze cost model
	Analyze exceptional projects
	Literature search
Risk resolution results	Some alternatives infeasible
	• Single time-sharing system: Security
	Mix of alternatives can produce significant gains
	• Factor of two in five years
	Need further study to determine best mix
Plan for next phase	Six-person task force for six months
	More extensive surveys and analysis
	• Internal, external, economic
	Develop concept of operation, economic rationale
Commitment	Fund next phase

330

within a $10,000-per-person investment constraint'' versus "improvements may violate reasonable-cost constraint'').

• The risk-resolution activities were more extensive (including the benchmarking and analysis of a prototype TRW LAN being developed for another project).

• The result was a fairly specific operational concept document, involving private offices tailored to software work patterns and personal terminals connected to VAX superminis via the TRW LAN. Some choices were specifically deferred to the next round, such as the choice of operating system and specific tools.

• The life-cycle plan and the plan for the next phase involved a partitioning into separate activities to address management improvements, facilities development, and development of the first increment of a software development environment.

• The commitment step involved more than just an agreement with the plan. It committed to apply the environment to an upcoming 100-person testbed software project and to develop an environment focusing on the testbed project's needs. It also specified forming a representative steering group to ensure that the separate activities were well-coordinated and that the environment would not be overly optimized around the testbed project.

Although the plan recommended developing a prototype environment, it also recommended that the project employ requirements specifications and design specifications in a risk-driven way. Thus, the development of the environment followed the succeeding rounds of the spiral model.

Round 2: Top-level requirements specification. Table 3 shows the corresponding steps involved during Round 2 defining the software productivity system. Round 2 decisions and their rationale were covered in earlier work[6]; here, we will summarize the considerations dealing with risk management and the use of the spiral model:

• The initial risk-identification activities during Round 2 showed that several system requirements hinged on the decision between a host-target system or a fully portable tool set and the decision between VMS and Unix as the host operating system. These requirements included the functions needed to provide a user-friendly front-end, the operating system to be used by the workstations, and the functions necessary to support a host-target

operation. To keep these requirements in synchronization with the others, a special minispiral was initiated to address and resolve these issues. The resulting review led to a commitment to a host-target operation using Unix on the host system, at a point early enough to work the OS-dependent requirements in a timely fashion.

• Addressing the risks of mismatches to the user-project's needs and priorities resulted in substantial participation of the user-project personnel in the requirements definition activity. This led to several significant redirections of the requirements, particularly toward supporting the early phases of the software life-cycle into which the user project was embarking, such as an adaptation of the software requirements engineering methodology (SREM) tools

for requirements specification and analysis.

It is also interesting to note that the form of Tables 1, 2, and 3 was originally developed for presentation purposes, but subsequently became a standard "spiral model template" used on later projects. These templates are useful not only for organizing project activities, but also as a residual design-rationale record. Design rationale information is of paramount importance in assessing the potential reusability of software components on future projects. Another important point to note is that the use of the template was indeed uniform across the three cycles, showing that the spiral steps can be and were uniformly followed at successively detailed levels of product definition.

Table 2. Spiral model usage: TRW Software Productivity System, Round 1.

Objectives	Double software productivity in five years
Constraints	$10,000 per person investment Within context of TRW culture • Government contracts, high tech., people oriented, security Preference for TRW products
Alternatives	Office: Private/modular/. . . Communication: LAN/star/concentrators/. . . Terminals: Private/shared; smart/dumb Tools: SREM/PSL-PSA/. . .; PDL/SADT/. . . CPU: IBM/DEC/CDC/. . .
Risks	May miss high-leverage options TRW LAN price/performance Workstation cost
Risk resolution	Extensive external surveys, visits TRW LAN benchmarking Workstation price projections
Risk resolution results	Operations concept: Private offices, TRW LAN, personal terminals, VAX Begin with primarily dumb terminals; experiment with smart workstations Defer operating system, tools selection
Plan for next phase	Partition effort into software development environment (SDE), facilities, management Develop first-cut, prototype SDE • Design-to-cost: 15-person team for one year Plan for external usage
Commitment	Develop prototype SDE Commit an upcoming project to use SDE Commit the SDE to support the project Form representative steering group

Succeeding rounds. It will be useful to illustrate some examples of how the spiral model is used to handle situations arising in the preliminary design and detailed design of components of the SPS: the preliminary design specification for the requirements traceability tool (RTT), and a detailed design rework or go-back on the unit development folder (UDF) tool.

The RTT preliminary design specification. The RTT establishes the traceability between itemized software requirements specifications, design elements, code elements, and test cases. It also supports various associated query, analysis, and report generation capabilities. The preliminary design specification for the RTT (and most of the other SPS tools) looks different from the usual preliminary design specification, which tends to show a uniform level of elaboration of all components of the design. Instead, the level of detail of the RTT specification is risk-driven.

In areas involving a high risk if the design turned out to be wrong, the design was carried down to the detailed design level, usually with the aid of rapid prototyping. These areas included working out the implications of "undo" options and dealing with the effects of control keys used to escape from various program levels.

In areas involving a moderate risk if the design was wrong, the design was carried down to a preliminary-design level. These areas included the basic command options for the tool and the schemata for the requirements traceability database. Here again, the ease of rapid prototyping with Unix shell scripts supported a good deal of user-interface prototyping.

In areas involving a low risk if the design was wrong, very little design elaboration was done. These areas included details of all the help message options and all the report-generation options, once the nature of these options was established in some example instances.

A detailed design go-back. The UDF tool collects into an electronic "folder" all artifacts involved in the development of a single-programmer software unit (typically 500 to 1,000 instructions): unit requirements, design, code, test cases, test results, and documentation. It also includes a management template for tracking the programmer's scheduled and actual completion of each artifact.

An alternative considered during detailed design of the UDF tool was reuse of portions of the RTT to provide pointers to the requirements and preliminary design specifications of the unit being developed. This turned out to be an extremely attractive alternative, not only for avoiding duplicate software development but also for bringing to the surface several issues involving many-to-many mappings between requirements, design, and code that had not been considered in designing the UDF tool. These led to a rethinking of the UDF tool requirements and preliminary design, which avoided a great deal of code rework that would have been necessary if the detailed design of the UDF tool had proceeded in a purely deductive, top-down fashion from the original UDF requirements specification. The resulting go-back led to a significantly different, less costly, and more capable UDF tool, incorporating the RTT in its "uses-hierarchy."

Spiral model features. These two examples illustrate several features of the spiral approach.

• It fosters the development of specifications that are not necessarily uniform, exhaustive, or formal, in that they defer detailed elaboration of low-risk software elements and avoid unnecessary breakage in their design until the high-risk elements of the design are stabilized.

• It incorporates prototyping as a risk-reduction option at any stage of development. In fact, prototyping and reuse risk analyses were often used in the process of going from detailed design into code.

• It accommodates reworks or go-backs to earlier stages as more attractive alternatives are identified or as new risk issues need resolution.

Overall, risk-driven documents, particularly specifications and plans, are important features of the spiral model. Great amounts of detail are not necessary unless the absence of such detail jeopardizes the

Table 3. Spiral model usage: TRW Software Productivity System, Round 2.

Objectives	User-friendly system Integrated software, office-automation tools Support all project personnel Support all life-cycle phases
Constraints	Customer-deliverable SDE ⟹ Portability Stable, reliable service
Alternatives	OS: VMS/AT&T Unix/Berkeley Unix/ISC Host-target/fully portable tool set Workstations: Zenith/LSI-11/. . .
Risks	Mismatch to user-project needs, priorities User-unfriendly system • 12-language syndrome; experts-only Unix performance, support Workstation/mainframe compatibility
Risk resolution	User-project surveys, requirements participation Survey of Unix-using organizations Workstation study
Risk resolution results	Top-level requirements specification Host-target with Unix host Unix-based workstations Build user-friendly front end for Unix Initial focus on tools to support early phases
Plan for next phase	Overall development plan • for tools: SREM, RTT, PDL, office automation tools • for front end: Support tools • for LAN: Equipment, facilities
Commitment	Proceed with plans

project. In some cases, such as with a product whose functionality may be determined by a choice among commercial products, a set of weighted evaluation criteria for the products may be preferable to a detailed pre-statement of functional requirements.

Results. The Software Productivity System developed and supported using the spiral model avoided the identified risks and achieved most of the system's objectives. The SPS has grown to include over 300 tools and over 1,300,000 instructions; 93 percent of the instructions were reused from previous project-developed, TRW-developed, or external-software packages. Over 25 projects have used all or portions of the system. All of the projects fully using the system have increased their productivity at least 50 percent; indeed, most have doubled their productivity (when compared with cost-estimation model predictions of their productivity using traditional methods).

However, one risk area—that projects with non-Unix target systems would not accept a Unix-based host system—was underestimated. Some projects accepted the host-target approach, but for various reasons (such as customer constraints and zero-cost target machines) a good many did not. As a result, the system was less widely used on TRW projects than expected. This and other lessons learned have been incorporated into the spiral model approach to developing TRW's next-generation software development environment.

Evaluation

Advantages. The primary advantage of the spiral model is that its range of options accommodates the good features of existing software process models, while its risk-driven approach avoids many of their difficulties. In appropriate situations, the spiral model becomes equivalent to one of the existing process models. In other situations, it provides guidance on the best mix of existing approaches to a given project; for example, its application to the TRW-SPS provided a risk-driven mix of specifying, prototyping, and evolutionary development.

The primary conditions under which the spiral model becomes equivalent to other main process models are summarized as follows:

• If a project has a low risk in such areas

All of the projects fully using the system have increased their productivity at least 50 percent.

---

as getting the wrong user interface or not meeting stringent performance requirements, and if it has a high risk in budget and schedule predictability and control, then these risk considerations drive the spiral model into an equivalence to the waterfall model.

• If a software product's requirements are very stable (implying a low risk of expensive design and code breakage due to requirements changes during development), and if the presence of errors in the software product constitutes a high risk to the mission it serves, then these risk considerations drive the spiral model to resemble the two-leg model of precise specification and formal deductive program development.

• If a project has a low risk in such areas as losing budget and schedule predictability and control, encountering large-system integration problems, or coping with information sclerosis, and if it has a high risk in such areas as getting the wrong user interface or user decision support requirements, then these risk considerations drive the spiral model into an equivalence to the evolutionary development model.

• If automated software generation capabilities are available, then the spiral model accommodates them either as options for rapid prototyping or for application of the transform model, depending on the risk considerations involved.

• If the high-risk elements of a project involve a mix of the risk items listed above, then the spiral approach will reflect an appropriate mix of the process models above (as exemplified in the TRW-SPS application). In doing so, its risk-avoidance features will generally avoid the difficulties of the other models.

The spiral model has a number of additional advantages, summarized as follows:

It focuses early attention on options involving the reuse of existing software. The steps involving the identification and evaluation of alternatives encourage these options.

It accommodates preparation for life-cycle evolution, growth, and changes of the software product. The major sources of product change are included in the product's objectives, and information-hiding approaches are attractive architectural design alternatives in that they reduce the risk of not being able to accommodate the product-charge objectives.

It provides a mechanism for incorporating software quality objectives into software product development. This mechanism derives from the emphasis on identifying all types of objectives and constraints during each round of the spiral. For example, Table 3 shows user-friendliness, portability, and reliability as specific objectives and constraints to be addressed by the SPS. In Table 1, security constraints were identified as a key risk item for the SPS.

It focuses on eliminating errors and unattractive alternatives early. The risk-analysis, validation, and commitment steps cover these considerations.

For each of the sources of project activity and resource expenditure, it answers the key question, "How much is enough?" Stated another way, "How much of requirements analysis, planning, configuration management, quality assurance, testing, formal verification, etc. should a project do?" Using the risk-driven approach, one can see that the answer is not the same for all projects and that the appropriate level of effort is determined by the level of risk incurred by not doing enough.

It does not involve separate approaches for software development and software enhancement (or maintenance). This aspect helps avoid the "second-class citizen" status frequently associated with software maintenance. It also helps avoid many of the problems that currently ensue when high-risk enhancement efforts are approached in the same way as routine maintenance efforts.

It provides a viable framework for integrated hardware-software system development. The focus on risk-management and on eliminating unattractive alternatives early and inexpensively is equally applicable to hardware and software.

Difficulties. The full spiral model can be successfully applied in many situations, but some difficulties must be addressed before it can be called a mature, universally applicable model. The three primary challenges involve matching to contract software, relying on risk-assessment expertise, and the need for further elaboration of spiral model steps.

Matching to contract software. The spiral model currently works well on internal software developments like the TRW-SPS, but it needs further work to match it to the world of contract software acquisition.

Internal software developments have a great deal of flexibility and freedom to accommodate stage-by-stage commitments, to defer commitments to specific options, to establish minispirals to resolve critical-path items, to adjust levels of effort, or to accommodate such practices as prototyping, evolutionary development, or design-to-cost. The world of contract software acquisition has a harder time achieving these degrees of flexibility and freedom without losing accountability and control, and a harder time defining contracts whose deliverables are not well specified in advance.

Recently, a good deal of progress has been made in establishing more flexible contract mechanisms, such as the use of competitive front-end contracts for concept definition or prototype fly-offs, the use of level-of-effort and award-fee contracts for evolutionary development, and the use of design-to-cost contracts. Although these have been generally successful, the procedures for using them still need to be worked out to the point that acquisition managers feel fully comfortable using them.

Relying on risk-assessment expertise. The spiral model places a great deal of reliance on the ability of software developers to identify and manage sources of project risk.

A good example of this is the spiral model's risk-driven specification, which carries high-risk elements down to a great deal of detail and leaves low-risk elements to be elaborated in later stages; by this time, there is less risk of breakage.

However, a team of inexperienced or low-balling developers may also produce a specification with a different pattern of variation in levels of detail: a great elaboration of detail for the well-understood, low-risk elements, and little elaboration of the poorly understood, high-risk elements. Unless there is an insightful review of such a specification by experienced development or acquisition personnel, this type of project will give an illusion of progress during a period in which it is actually heading for disaster.

Another concern is that a risk-driven specification will also be people-dependent. For example, a design produced by an expert may be implemented by non-experts. In this case, the expert, who does not need a great deal of detailed documentation, must produce enough additional documentation to keep the non-experts from going astray. Reviewers of the specification must also be

Table 4. A prioritized top-ten list of software risk items.

Risk item	Risk management techniques
1. Personnel shortfalls	Staffing with top talent, job matching; teambuilding; morale building; cross-training; pre-scheduling key people
2. Unrealistic schedules and budgets	Detailed, multisource cost and schedule estimation; design to cost; incremental development; software reuse; requirements scrubbing
3. Developing the wrong software functions	Organization analysis; mission analysis; ops-concept formulation; user surveys; prototyping; early users' manuals
4. Developing the wrong user interface	Task analysis; prototyping; scenarios; user characterization (functionality, style, workload)
5. Gold plating	Requirements scrubbing; prototyping; cost-benefit analysis; design to cost
6. Continuing stream of requirement changes	High change threshold; information hiding; incremental development (defer changes to later increments)
7. Shortfalls in externally furnished components	Benchmarking; inspections; reference checking; compatibility analysis
8. Shortfalls in externally performed tasks	Reference checking; pre-award audits; award-fee contracts; competitive design or prototyping; teambuilding
9. Real-time performance shortfalls	Simulation; benchmarking; modeling; prototyping; instrumentation; tuning
10. Straining computer-science capabilities	Technical analysis; cost-benefit analysis; prototyping; reference checking

Table 5. Software Risk Management Plan.

1.	Identify the project's top 10 risk items.
2.	Present a plan for resolving each risk item.
3.	Update list of top risk items, plan, and results monthly.
4.	Highlight risk-item status in monthly project reviews. • Compare with previous month's rankings, status.
5.	Initiate appropriate corrective actions.

sensitive to these concerns.

With a conventional, document-driven approach, the requirement to carry all aspects of the specification to a uniform level of detail eliminates some potential problems and permits adequate review of some aspects by inexperienced reviewers. But it also creates a large drain on the time of the scarce experts, who must dig for the critical issues within a large mass of non-critical detail. Furthermore, if the high-risk elements have been glossed over by impressive-sounding references to poorly understood capabilities (such as a new synchronization concept or a commercial DBMS), there is an even greater risk that the conventional approach will give the illusion of progress in situations that are actually heading for disaster.

Need for further elaboration of spiral model steps. In general, the spiral model process steps need further elaboration to ensure that all software development participants are operating in a consistent context.

Some examples of this are the need for more detailed definitions of the nature of spiral model specifications and milestones, the nature and objectives of spiral model reviews, techniques for estimating and synchronizing schedules, and the nature of spiral model status indicators and cost-versus-progress tracking procedures. Another need is for guidelines and checklists to identify the most likely sources of project risk and the most effective risk-resolution techniques for each source of risk.

Highly experienced people can successfully use the spiral approach without these elaborations. However, for large-scale use in situations where people bring widely differing experience bases to the project, added levels of elaboration—such as have been accumulated over the years for document-driven approaches—are important in ensuring consistent interpretation and use of the spiral approach across the project.

Efforts to apply and refine the spiral model have focused on creating a discipline of software risk management, including techniques for risk identification, risk analysis, risk prioritization, risk-management planning, and risk-element tracking. The prioritized top-ten list of software risk items given in Table 4 is one result of this activity. Another example is the risk management plan discussed in the next section.

Implications: The Risk Management Plan. Even if an organization is not ready to adopt the entire spiral approach, one characteristic technique that can easily be adapted to any life-cycle model provides many of the benefits of the spiral approach. This is the Risk Management Plan summarized in Table 5. This plan basically ensures that each project makes an early identification of its top risk items (the number 10 is not an absolute requirement), develops a strategy for resolving the risk items, identifies and sets down an agenda to resolve new risk items as they surface, and highlights progress versus plans in monthly reviews.

The Risk Management Plan has been used successfully at TRW and other organizations. Its use has ensured appropriate focus on early prototyping, simulation, benchmarking, key-person staffing measures, and other early risk-resolution techniques that have helped avoid many potential project "show-stoppers." The recent US Department of Defense standard on software management, DoD-Std-2167, requires that developers produce and use risk management plans, as does its counterpart US Air Force regulation, AFR 800-14.

Overall, the Risk Management Plan and the maturing set of techniques for software risk management provide a foundation for tailoring spiral model concepts into the more established software acquisition and development procedures.

W e can draw four conclusions from the data presented:

(1) The risk-driven nature of the spiral model is more adaptable to the full range of software project situations than are the primarily document-driven approaches such as the waterfall model or the primarily code-driven approaches such as evolutionary development. It is particularly applicable to very large, complex, ambitious software systems.

(2) The spiral model has been quite successful in its largest application to date: the development and enhancement of the TRW-SPS. Overall, it achieved a high level of software support environment capability in a very short time and provided the flexibility necessary to accommodate a high dynamic range of technical alternatives and user objectives.

(3) The spiral model is not yet as fully elaborated as the more established models. Therefore, the spiral model can be applied by experienced personnel, but it needs further elaboration in such areas as contract-

ing, specifications, milestones, reviews, scheduling, status monitoring, and risk-area identification to be fully usable in all situations.

(4) Partial implementations of the spiral model, such as the Risk Management Plan, are compatible with most current process models and are very helpful in overcoming major sources of project risk. □

Acknowledgments

I would like to thank Frank Belz, Lolo Penedo, George Spadaro, Bob Williams, Bob Balzer, Gillian Frewin, Peter Hamer, Manny Lehman, Lee Osterweil, Dave Parnas, Bill Riddle, Steve Squires, and Dick Thayer, along with the *Computer* reviewers of this article, for their stimulating and insightful comments and discussions of earlier versions of the article, and Nancy Donato for producing its several versions.

References

1. F.P. Brooks et al., *Defense Science Board Task Force Report on Military Software*, Office of the Under Secretary of Defense for Acquisition, Washington, DC 20301, Sept. 1987.
2. H.D. Benington, "Production of Large Computer Programs," *Proc. ONR Symp. Advanced Programming Methods for Digital Computers*, June 1956, pp. 15-27. Also available in *Annals of the History of Computing*, Oct. 1983, pp. 350-361, and *Proc. Ninth Int'l Conf. Software Engineering*, Computer Society Press, 1987.
3. W.W. Royce, "Managing the Development of Large Software Systems: Concepts and Techniques," *Proc. Wescon*, Aug. 1970. Also available in *Proc. ICSE 9*, Computer Society Press, 1987.
4. D.D. McCracken and M.A. Jackson, "Life-Cycle Concept Considered Harmful," *ACM Software Engineering Notes*, Apr. 1982, pp. 29-32.
5. R. Balzer, T.E. Cheatham, and C. Green, "Software Technology in the 1990s: Using a New Paradigm," *Computer*, Nov. 1983, pp. 39-45.
6. B.W. Boehm et al., "A Software Development Environment for Improving Productivity," *Computer*, June 1984, pp. 30-44.
7. B.W. Boehm, *Software Engineering Economics*, Prentice-Hall, 1981, Chap. 33.

Further reading

The software process model field has an interesting history, and a great deal of stimulating work has been produced recently in this specialized area. Besides the references that appear at the end of the accompanying article, here are some additional good sources of insight:

Overall process model issues and results

Agresti's tutorial volume provides a good overview and set of key articles. The three recent *Software Process Workshop Proceedings* provide access to much of the recent work in the area.

Agresti, W.W., *New Paradigms for Software Development*, IEEE Catalog No. EH0245-1, 1986.

Dowson, M., ed., *Proc. Third Int'l Software Process Workshop*, IEEE Catalog No. TH0184-2, Nov. 1986.

Potts, C., ed., *Proc. Software Process Workshop*, IEEE Catalog No. 84CH2044-6, Feb. 1984.

Wileden, J.C., and M. Dowson, eds., Proc. Int'l Workshop Software Process and Software Environments, *ACM Software Engineering Notes*, Aug. 1986.

Alternative process models

More detailed information on waterfall-type approaches is given in:

Evans, M.W., P. Piazza, and J.P. Dolkas, *Principles of Productive Software Management*, John Wiley & Sons, 1983.

Hice, G.F., W.J. Turner, and L.F. Cashwell, *System Development Methodology*, North Holland, 1974 (2nd ed., 1981).

More detailed information on evolutionary development is provided in:

Gilb, T., *Principles of Software Engineering Management*, Addison Wesley, 1988 (currently in publication).

Some additional process model approaches with useful features and insights may be found in:

Lehman, M.M., and L.A. Belady, *Program Evolution: Processes of Software Change*, Academic Press, 1985.

Osterweil, L., "Software Processes are Software, Too," *Proc. ICSE 9*, IEEE Catalog No. 87CH2432-3, Mar. 1987, pp. 2-13.

Radice, R.A., et al., "A Programming Process Architecture," *IBM Systems J.*, Vol. 24, No.2, 1985, pp. 79-90.

Spiral and spiral-type models

Some further treatments of spiral model issues and practices are:

Belz, F.C., "Applying the Spiral Model: Observations on Developing System Software in Ada," *Proc. 1986 Annual Conf. on Ada Technology*, Atlanta, 1986, pp. 57-66.

Boehm, B.W., and F.C. Belz, "Applying Process Programming to the Spiral Model," *Proc. Fourth Software Process Workshop*, IEEE, May 1988.

Iivari, J., "A Hierarchical Spiral Model for the Software Process," *ACM Software Engineering Notes*, Jan. 1987, pp. 35-37.

Some similar cyclic spiral-type process models from other fields are described in:

Carlsson, B., P. Keane, and J.B. Martin, "R&D Organizations as Learning Systems," *Sloan Management Review*, Spring 1976, pp. 1-15.

Fisher, R., and W. Ury, *Getting to Yes*, Houghton Mifflin, 1981; Penguin Books, 1983, pp. 68-71.

Kolb, D.A., "On Management and the Learning Process," MIT Sloan School Working Article 652-73, Cambridge, Mass., 1973.

Software risk management

The discipline of software risk management provides a bridge between spiral model concepts and currently established software acquisition and development procedures.

Boehm, B.W., "Software Risk Management Tutorial," Computer Society, Apr. 1988.

Risk Assessment Techniques, Defense Systems Management College, Ft. Belvoir, Va. 22060, July 1983.

Evaluating Software Engineering Standards

Shari Lawrence Pfleeger, Norman Fenton, and Stella Page
Centre for Software Reliability

Given the more than 250 software engineering standards, why do we sometimes still produce less than desirable products? Are the standards not working, or being ignored?

oftware engineering standards abound; since 1976, the Software Engineering Standards Committee of the IEEE Computer Society has developed 19 standards in areas such as terminology, documentation, testing, verification and validation, reviews, and audits.[1] In 1992 alone, standards were completed for productivity and quality metrics, software maintenance, and CASE (computer-aided software engineering) tool selection. If we include work of the major national standards bodies throughout the world, there are in fact more than 250 software engineering standards. The existence of these standards raises some important questions. How do we know which practices to standardize? Since many of our projects produce less-than-desirable products, are the standards not working, or being ignored? Perhaps the answer is that standards have codified approaches whose effectiveness has not been rigorously and scientifically demonstrated. Rather, we have too often relied on anecdote, "gut feeling," the opinions of experts, or even flawed research, rather than on careful, rigorous software engineering experimentation.

This article reports on the results of the Smartie project (Standards and Methods Assessment Using Rigorous Techniques in Industrial Environments), a collaborative effort to propose a widely applicable procedure for the objective assessment of standards used in software development. We hope that, for a given environment and application area, Smartie will enable the identification of standards whose use is most likely to lead to improvements in some aspect of software development processes and products. In this article, we describe how we verified the practicality of the Smartie framework by testing it with corporate partners.

Suppose your organization is considering the implementation of a standard. Smartie should help you to answer the following questions:

- What are the potential benefits of using the standard?
- Can we measure objectively the extent of any benefits that may result from its use?
- What are the related costs necessary to implement the standard?
- Do the costs exceed the benefits?

Reprinted from *IEEE Software*, Vol. 11, No. 5, Sept. 1994, pp. 71–79.

To that end, we present Smartie in three parts. First, we analyze what typical standards look like, both in software engineering and in other engineering disciplines. Next, we discuss how to evaluate a standard for its applicability and objectivity. Finally, we describe the results of a major industrial case study involving the reliability and maintainability of almost two million lines of code.

Software engineering standards

Standards organizations have developed standards for standards, including a definition of what a standard is. For example, the British Standards Institute defines a standard as

A technical specification or other document available to the public, drawn up with the cooperation and consensus or general approval of all interests affected by it, based on the consolidated results of science, technology and experience, aimed at the promotion of optimum community benefits.[2]

Do software engineering standards satisfy this definition? Not quite. Our standards are technical specifications available to the public, but they are not always drawn up with the consensus or general approval of all interests affected by them. For example, airline passengers were not consulted when standards were set for building the A320's fly-by-wire software, nor were electricity consumers polled when software standards for nuclear power stations were considered. Of course, the same could be said for other standards; for example, parents may not have been involved in the writing of safety standards for pushchairs (strollers). Nevertheless, the intention of a standard is to reflect the needs of the users or consumers as well as the practices of the builders. More importantly, our standards are not based on the consolidated results of science, technology, and experience.[3] Programming languages are declared to be corporate or even national standards without case studies and experiments to demonstrate the costs and benefits of using them. Techniques such as cleanroom, formal specification, or object-oriented design are mandated before we determine under what circumstances they are most beneficial. Even when scientific analysis and evaluation

exist, our standards rarely reference them. So even though our standards are laudably aimed at promoting community benefits, we do not insist on having those benefits demonstrated clearly and scientifically before the standard is published. Moreover, there is rarely a set of objective criteria that we can use to evaluate the proposed technique or process.

Thus, as Smartie researchers, we sought solutions to some of the problems with software engineering standards. We began our investigation by posing three simple questions that we wanted Smartie to help us answer:

- On a given project, what standards are used?
- To what extent is a particular standard followed?
- If a standard is being used, is it effective? That is, is it making a difference in quality or productivity?

What is a standard — and what does it mean for software engineering?

Often, a standard's size and complexity make it difficult to determine whether a particular organization is compliant. If partial compliance is allowed, measurement of the degree of compliance is difficult, if not impossible — consider, for example, the ISO 9000 series and the 14 major activities it promotes.[4] The Smartie project suggests that large standards be considered as a set of smaller "ministandards." A ministandard is a standard with a cohesive, content-related set of requirements. In the remaining discussion, the term *standard* refers to a ministandard.

What is a good standard?

We reviewed dozens of software engineering standards, including international, national, corporate, and organizational standards, to see what we could learn. For each standard, we wanted to know

- How good is the standard?
- What is affected by the standard?
- How can we determine compliance with the standard?
- What is the basis for the standard?

"Goodness" of the standard was difficult to determine, as it involved at least three distinct aspects. First, we wanted to know whether and how we can tell if the standard is being complied with. That is, a standard is not a good standard if there is no way of telling whether a particular organization, process, or piece of code complies with the standard. There are many examples of such "bad" standards. For instance, some testing standards require that all statements be tested "thoroughly"; without a clear definition of "thoroughly," we cannot determine compliance. Second, a standard is good only in terms of the success criteria set for it. In other words, we wanted to know what attributes of the final product (such as reliability or maintainability) are supposed to be improved by using the standard. And finally, we wanted to know the cost of applying the standard. After all, if compliance with the standard is so costly as to make its use impractical, or practical only in certain situations, then cost contributes to "goodness."

We developed a scheme to evaluate the degree of objectivity inherent in assessing compliance. We can classify each requirement being evaluated into one of four categories: reference only, subjective, partially objective, and completely objective. A reference-only requirement declares that something will happen, but there is no way to determine compliance; for example, "Unit testing shall be carried out." A subjective requirement is one in which only a subjective measure of conformance is possible; for example, "Unit testing shall be carried out effectively." A subjective requirement is an improvement over a reference-only requirement, but it is subject to the differing opinions of experts. A partially objective requirement involves a measure of conformance that is somewhat objective but still requires a degree of subjectivity; for example, "Unit testing shall be carried out so that all statements and the most probable paths are tested." An objective requirement is the most desirable kind, as conformance to it can be determined completely objectively; for example, "Unit testing shall be carried out so that all statements are tested."

Clearly, our goal as a profession should be to produce standards with require-

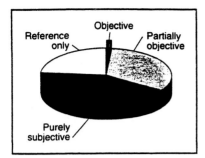

Figure 1. Degree of objectivity in software engineering standards' requirements.

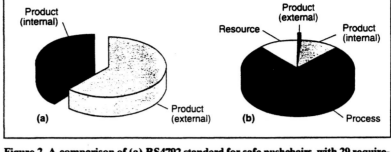

Figure 2. A comparison of (a) BS4792 standard for safe pushchairs, with 29 requirements, and (b) DEF STD 00-55 for safe software, with 115 requirements, shows that software standards place more emphasis on process than on the final product.

ments that are as objective as possible. However, as Figure 1 illustrates, the Smartie review of the requirements in software engineering standards indicates that we are a long way from reaching that goal.

To what do our standards apply?

To continue our investigation, Smartie researchers reviewed software engineering standards to determine what aspect of software development is affected by each standard. We considered four distinct categories of requirements in the standards: process, internal product, external product, and resources. Internal product requirements refer to such items as the code itself, while external product requirements refer to what the user experiences, such as reliability. For examples of these categories, we turn to the British Defence Standard DEF STD 00-55 (interim),[5] issued by the Ministry of Defence (second revision in 1992) for the procurement of safety-critical software in defense equipment. Some are internal product requirements:

- Each module should have a single entry and exit.
- The code should be indented to show its structure.

Others are process requirements:

- The Design Team shall validate the Software Specification against Software Requirements by animation of the formal specification.

while some are resource requirements:

- All tools and support software . . . shall have sufficient safety integrity.
- The Design Authority shall demonstrate . . . that the seniority, authority, qualifications and experience of the staff to be employed on the project are satisfactory for the tasks assigned to them.

Typical of many software standards, DEF STD 00-55 has a mixture of all four types of requirements.

Are software standards like other standards?

Standardization has made life easier in many disciplines. Because of standard voltage and plugs, an electrical appliance from Germany will work properly in Italy. A liter of petrol in one country is the same as a liter in another, thanks to standard measurement. These standards, products of other engineering disciplines, offer lessons that we can learn as software engineers. So the next step in the Smartie process was to examine other engineering standards to see how they differ from those in software engineering. In particular, we asked

- Is the mix of product, process, and resource roughly the same?
- Is the mix of objective and nonobjective compliance evaluation roughly the same?

The answer to both questions is a resounding no. To show just how different software engineering standards are, Figure 2 compares the British standard for pushchair safety with DEF STD 00-55, a

software safety standard.

The figure shows what is true generally: Software engineering standards are heavy on process and light on product, while other engineering standards are the reverse. That is, software engineering standards reflect the implicit assumption that using certain techniques and processes, in concert with "good" tools and people, will necessarily result in a good product. Other engineering disciplines have far less faith in the process; they insist on evaluating the final product in their standards.

Another major difference between our standards and those of other engineering disciplines is in the method of compliance assessment. Most other disciplines include in their standards a description of the method to be used to assess compliance; we do not. In other words, other engineers insist that the proof of the pudding is in the eating: Their standards describe how the eating is to be done, and what the pudding should taste like, look like, and feel like. By contrast, software engineers prescribe the recipe, the utensils, and the cooking techniques, and then assume that the pudding will taste good. If our current standards are not effective, it may be because we need more objective standards and a more balanced mix of process, product, and resource requirements

The proof of the pudding: Case studies

The Smartie framework includes far more than we can describe here — for example, guidelines for evaluating the experiments and case studies on which the standards are based. We address all of these issues in Smartie technical reports, available from the Centre for Software Reliability. For the remainder of this article, we focus on an aspect of Smartie that distinguishes it from other research on standards: its practicality. Because Smartie includes industrial partners, we have evaluated the effectiveness of Smartie itself by applying it to real-life situations. We present here two examples of the Smartie "reality check": (1) applying the framework to written standards for a major company and (2) evaluating the use of standards to meet specified goals.

Both examples involve Company X, a large, nationwide company whose services depend on software. The company is interested in using standards to enhance its software's reliability and maintainability. In the first example, we examine some of the company's programming standards to see if they can be improved. In the second example, we recommend changes to the way data is collected and analyzed, so that management can make better decisions about reliability and maintainability.

Reality check 1: How good are the written standards? We applied the Smartie techniques to a ministandard for using Cobol. The Cobol standard is part of a larger set of mandated standards, called programming guidelines, in the company's system development manual.

Using the guidelines reputedly "facilitate[s] the production of clear, efficient and maintainable Cobol programs." The guidelines were based on expert opinion, not on experiments and case studies demonstrating their effectiveness in comparison with not following the guidelines. This document is clearly designed as a standard rather than a set of guidelines, since "enforceability of the standards is MANDATORY," with "any divergence" being "permanently recorded."

We focused on the layout and naming conventions, items clearly intended to make the code easier to maintain. Layout requirements such as the following can be measured in a completely objective fashion:

- Each statement should be terminated by a full stop.
- Only one verb should appear on any one line.
- Each sentence should commence in

column 12 and on a new line, second and subsequent lines being neatly indented and aligned vertically .... Exceptions are ELSE which will start in the same column as its associated IF and which will appear on a line of its own.

Each line either conforms or does not, and the proportion of lines conforming to all layout requirements represents overall compliance with the standard.

On the other hand, measuring conformance to some naming conventions can be difficult, because such measurements are subjective, as is the case with

- Names must be meaningful.

The Smartie approach recommends that the standard be rewritten to make it

---

The Smartie framework has guidelines for evaluating the case studies on which the standards are based.

---

more objective. For example, improvements might include

- Names must be English or scientific words which themselves appear as identifiable concepts in the specification document(s).
- Abbreviations of names must be consistent.
- Hyphens must be used to separate component parts of names.

Conformance measures can then use the proportion of names that conform to the standard. Analysis of the commenting requirements also led to recommendations that would improve the degree of objectivity in measuring conformance.

Reality check 2: Do the standards address the goals? Company X collects reliability and maintainability data for many of its systems. The company made available to Smartie all of its data relating to a large system essential to its business.

Initiated in November 1987, the system had had 27 releases by the end of 1992. The 1.7 million lines of code for this system involve two programming languages: Cobol (both batch Cobol and CICS Cobol) and Natural (a 4GL). Less than a third of the code is Natural; recent growth (15.2 percent from 1991 to 1992) has been entirely in Cobol. Three corporate and organizational goals are addressed by measuring this system: (1) monitoring and improving product reliability, (2) monitoring and improving product maintainability, and (3) improving the overall development process. The first goal requires information about actual operational failures, while the second requires data on discovering and fixing faults. The third goal, process improvement, is at a higher level than the other two, so Smartie researchers focused primarily on reliability and maintainability as characteristics of process improvement.

The system runs continuously. Users report problems to a help desk whose staff determines whether the problem is a user error or a failure of the system to do something properly. Thus, all the data supplied to Smartie related to software failures rather than to documentation failures. The Smartie team received a complete set of failure information for 1991-92, so the discussion in this section refers to all 481 software failures recorded and fixed during that period. We reviewed the data to see how data collection and analysis standards addressed the overall goal of improving system reliability and maintainability. In many cases, we recommended a simple change that should yield additional, critical information in the future. The remainder of this section describes our findings.

A number is assigned to each "fault" report. We distinguish a fault (what the developer sees) from a failure (what the user sees).[6] Here we use "fault" in quotation marks, since failures are labeled as faults. A typical data point is identified by a "fault" number, the week it was reported, the system area and fault type, the week the underlying cause was fixed and tested, and the actual number of hours to repair the problem (that is, the time from when the maintenance group decides to clear the "fault" until the time when the fix is tested and integrated with the rest of the system). Smartie researchers analyzed this data and made several recommendations about how to improve data collection and analysis to get a better picture of system maintainability. Nevertheless, the depth of data collection practiced at Company X is to be applauded. In particular, the distinction between hours-to-repair and time between problem-open ("week in") and problem-close ("week out") is a critical one that is not usually made in maintenance organizations.

The maintenance group designated 28 system areas to which underlying faults could be traced. Each system area name referred to a particular function of the system rather than to the system architecture. There was no documented mapping of programs or modules to system areas. A typical system area involved 80 programs, with each program consisting of 1,000 lines of code. The fault type indicated one of 11, many of which were overlapping. In other words, the classes of faults were not orthogonal, so it was possible to find more than one fault class appropriate for a given fault. In addition, there was no direct, recorded link between "fault" and program in most cases. Nor was there information about program size or complexity.

Given this situation, we made two types of recommendations. First, we examined the existing data and suggested simple changes to clarify and separate issues. Second, we extracted additional information by hand from many of the programs. We used the new data to demonstrate that enhanced data collection could provide valuable management information not obtainable with the current forms and data.

Issue 1: Faults versus failures. Because the cause of a problem (that is, a fault) is not always distinguished from the evidence to the user of that problem (that is, a failure), it is difficult to assess a system's reliability or the degree of user satisfaction. Furthermore, with no mapping from faults to failures, we cannot tell which particular parts or aspects of the system are responsible for most of the problems users are encountering.

• *Recommendation*: Define fault and failure, and make sure the maintenance staff understands the difference between the two. Then, consider failure reports separate from fault reports. For example, a design problem discovered during a design review would be described in a fault report; a problem in function discovered by a user would be described in a failure report.

Issue 2: Mapping from program to system area. Use of system areas to describe faults is helpful, but a mapping is needed from program name to system area. The current information does not reveal whether code in one system area leads to problems in another system area. The batch reporting and integration into the system of problem repairs compounds this difficulty because there is then no recorded link from program to fault. This information must have existed at some point in the maintenance process in order for the problem to be fixed: capturing it at the time of discovery is much more efficient than trying to elicit it well after the fact (and possibly incorrectly).

• *Recommendation:* Separate the system into well-defined system areas and provide a listing that maps each code module to a system area. Then, as problems are reported, indicate the system area affected. Finally, when the cause of the problem is identified, document the

names of the program modules that caused the problem.

Issue 3: Ambiguity and informality inherent in the incident closure reports. The description of each problem reflects the creativity of the recorder rather than standard aspects of the problem. This lack of uniformity makes it impossible to amalgamate the reports and examine overall trends.

• *Recommendation:* The problem description should include the manifestation, effect, and cause of the problem, as shown in Figure 3. Such data would permit traceability and trend analysis.

Issue 4: Fault classification scheme. Because the scheme contains nonorthogonal categories, it is difficult for the maintainer to decide in which category a particular fault belongs. For this reason, some of the classifications may be arbitrary, resulting in a misleading picture when the faults are aggregated and tracked.

• *Recommendation:* Redefine fault categories so that there is no ambiguity or overlap between categories.

Issue 5: Unrecoverable data. By unrecoverable, we mean that the information we need does not exist in some documented form in the organization. For example, most of the problem report forms related a large collection of faults to a large collection of programs that were changed as a result. What appears to be unrecoverable is the exact mapping of program changes to a particular fault. On the other hand, some information was recoverable, but with great difficulty. For example, we re-created size information

Table 1. Recoverable (documented) data versus nonrecoverable (undocumented) data.

Recoverable	Nonrecoverable
Size information for each module Static/complexity information for each module Mapping of faults to programs Severity categories	Operational usage per system (needed for reliability assessment) Success/failure of fixes (needed to assess effectiveness of maintenance process) Number of repeated failures (needed for reliability assessment)

manually from different parts of the data set supplied to us, and we could have related problem severity to problem cause if we had had enough time.

• *Recommendation:* The data in Table 1 would be useful if it were explicit and available to the analysts.

Figures 4 through 8 show what we can learn from the existing data; Figures 9 through 11 (page 78) show how much more we can learn using the additional data.

Since we have neither mean-time-between-failure data nor operational usage information, we cannot depict reliability directly. As an approximation, we examined the trend in the number of "faults" received per week. Figure 4 shows that there is great variability in the number of "faults" per week, suggesting that there is no general improvement in system reliability.

The chart in Figure 5 contrasts the "faults" received with the "faults" addressed and resolved ("actioned") in a given week. Notice that there is wide variation in the proportion of "faults" that are actioned each week. In spite of the lack-of-improvement trend, this chart provides managers with useful information; they can use it to begin an investigation into which "faults" are handled first and why.

Examining the number of "faults" per system area is also useful, and we display the breakdown in Figure 6. However, there is not enough information to know why particular system areas generate more "faults" than others. Without information such as size, complexity, and operational usage, we can draw no definitive conclusions. Similarly, an analysis of "faults" by fault type revealed that data and program faults dominated user, query, and other faults. However, the fault types are not orthogonal, so again there is little that we can conclude.

Figures 7 and 8 show, respectively,

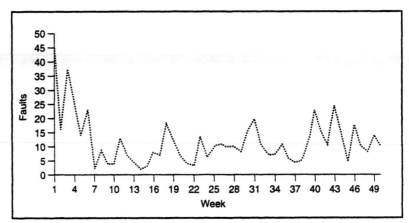

Figure 4. Reliability trend charting the number of faults received per week.

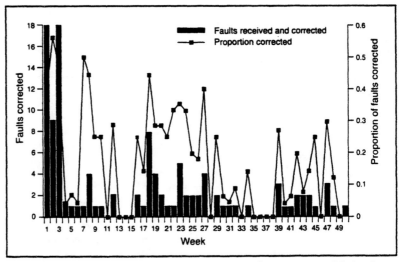

Figure 5. Charting the faults received and acted upon in the same week helps show how Company X deals with software failures.

mean time to repair fault by system area and by fault type. This information highlights interesting variations, but our conclusions are still limited because of missing information about size.

The previous charts contain only the information supplied to us explicitly by Company X. The following charts reflect additional information that was recovered manually. As you can see, this re-

342

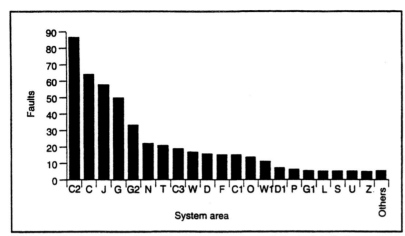

Figure 6. Plotting the number of faults per system area helps isolate fault-prone system areas.

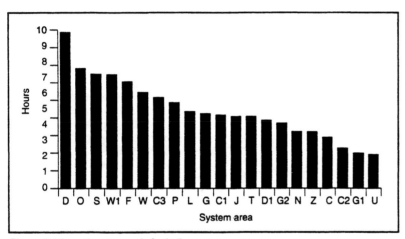

Figure 7. Mean time to repair fault (by system area).

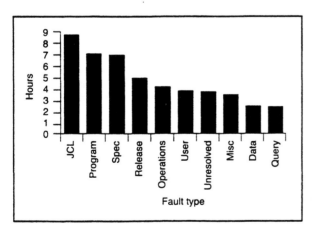

Figure 8. Mean time to repair fault (by fault type).

covered information enriches the management decisions that can be made on the basis of the charts.

By manually investigating the (poorly documented) link between individual programs and system areas, we examined the relationships among size, language, and system area. Figure 9 shows the variation between CICS Cobol and Natural in each of the main system areas

examined. Recall that Figures 4, 5, and 6 revealed limited information about the distribution of "faults" in the overall system. However, by adding size data, the resulting graph in Figure 10 shows the startling result that C2 — one of the smallest system areas (with only 4,000 lines of code) — has the largest number of "faults." If the fault rates are graphed by system area, as in Figure 11, it is easy to see that C2 dominates the chart. In fact, Figure 11 shows that, compared with published industry figures, each system area except C2 is of very high quality; C2, however, is much worse than the industry average. Without size measurement, this important information would not be visible. Consequently, we recommended that the capture of size information be made standard practice at Company X.

These charts represent examples of our analysis. In each case, improvements to standards for measurement and collection are suggested in light of the organizational goals. Our recommendations reflect the need to make more explicit a small degree of additional information that can result in a very large degree of additional management insight. The current amount of information allows a manager to determine the status of the system; the additional data would yield explanatory information that would allow managers to be proactive rather than reactive during maintenance.

Lessons learned in case studies

The Company X case study was one of several intended to validate the Smartie methodology, not only in terms of finding missing pieces in the methodology, but also by testing the practicality of Smartie for use in an industrial environment (the other case studies are not complete as of this writing). The first and most serious lesson learned in performing the case studies involved the lack of control. Because each investigation was retrospective, we could not

- require measurement of key productivity and quality variables,
- require uniformity or repetition of measurement,
- choose the project, team, or staff characteristics that might have eliminated confounding effects,

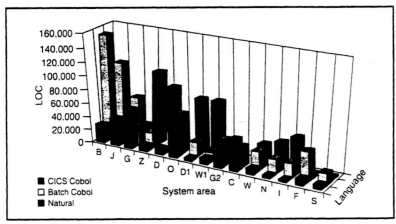

Figure 9. System structure showing system areas with more than 25,000 lines of code and types of programming languages.

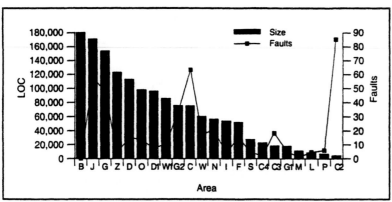

Figure 10. System area size versus number of faults.

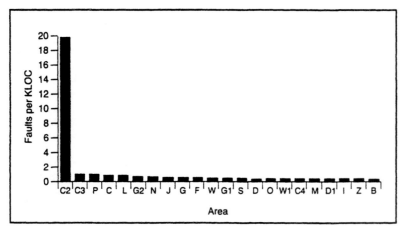

Figure 11. Normalized fault rates.

- choose or rewrite standards so that they were easy to apply and assess,
- choose the type of standard, or
- establish a baseline condition or environment against which to measure change.

The last point is the most crucial. Without a baseline, we cannot describe with confidence the effects of using (or not using) the standards. As a consequence, a great deal of expert (but nevertheless highly subjective) judgment was necessary in assessing the results of the case studies. It is also clear that a consistent level of control must be maintained throughout the period of the case study. There were many events, organizational and managerial as well as technical, that affected the outcome of the case study, and about which we had no input or control. In particular, lack of control led to incomplete or inconsistent data. For example, a single problem report usually included several problems related only by the time period in which the problems occurred. Or the description of a single type of problem varied from report to report, depending on the documentation style of the maintainer and the time available to write the description. With such inconsistency, it is impossible to aggregate the problem reports or fault information in a meaningful way; it is also impossible to evaluate the root causes of problems and relate them to the use of standards. Indeed, the very lack of standards in data collection and reporting inhibits us from doing a thorough analysis.

A final difficulty with our assessment derives from the lack of information about cost. Although we have Company X data on the time required to fix a problem, the company did not keep careful records on the cost of implementation or maintenance at a level that allows us to understand the cost implications of standards use. That is, even if we can show that using standards is beneficial for product quality, we cannot assess the trade-offs between the increase in quality and the cost of achieving that quality. Without such information, managers in a production environment would be loath to adopt standards, even if the standards were certifiably effective according to the Smartie (or any other) methodology.

We learned a great deal from reviewing standards and administering case studies. The first and most startling result of our work is that many standards are not really standards at all. Many "standards" are reference or subjective requirements, suggesting that they are really guidelines (since degree of compliance cannot be evaluated). Organizations with such standards should revisit their goals and revise the standards to address the goals in a more objective way.

We also found wide variety in conformance from one employee to another as well as from one module to another. In one of our case studies, management assured us that all modules were 100 percent compliant with the company's own structured programming standards, since it was mandatory company practice. Our review revealed that only 58 percent of the modules complied with the standards, even though the standards were clearly stated and could be objectively evaluated.

A related issue is that of identifying the portion of the project affected by the standard and then examining conformance only within that portion. That is, some standards apply only to certain types of modules, so notions of conformance must be adjusted to consider only that part of the system that is subject to the standard in the first place. For example, if a standard applies only to interface modules, then 50 percent compliance should mean that only 50 percent of the interface modules comply, not that 50 percent of the system is comprised of interface modules and that all of them comply.

More generally, we found that we have a lot to learn from standards in other engineering disciplines. Our standards lack objective assessment criteria, involve more process than product, and are not always based on rigorous experimental results.

Thus, we recommend that software engineering standards be reviewed and revised. The resulting standards should be cohesive collections of requirements to which conformance can be established objectively. Moreover, there should be a clearly stated benefit to each standard and a reference to the set of experiments or case studies demonstrating that benefit. Finally, software engineering standards should be better balanced, with more product requirements in relation to process and resource requirements. With standards expressed in this way, managers can use project objectives to guide standards' intention and implementation.

The Smartie recommendations and framework are practical and effective in identifying problems with standards and in making clear the kinds of changes that are needed. Our case studies have demonstrated that small, simple changes to standards writing, and especially to data collection standards, can improve significantly the quality of information about what is going on in a system and with a project. In particular, these simple changes can move the project from assessment to understanding. ∎

Acknowledgments

We gratefully acknowledge the assistance of other participants in the SERC/DTI-funded Smartie project: Colum Devine, Jennifer Thornton, Katie Perrin, Derek Jaques, Danny McComish, Eric Trodd, Bev Littlewood, and Peter Mellor.

References

1. *IEEE Software Engineering Technical Committee Newsletter*, Vol. 11, No. 3, Jan. 1993, p. 4.

2. British Standards Institute, *British Standards Guide: A Standard for Standards*, London, 1981.

3. N. Fenton, S.L. Pfleeger, and R.L. Glass, "Science and Substance: A Challenge to Software Engineers," *IEEE Software*, Vol. 11, No. 4, July 1994, pp. 86-95.

4. International Standards Organization, *ISO 9000: Quality Management and Quality Assurance Standards — Guidelines for Selection and Use*, 1987 (with ISO 9001 - 9004).

5. Ministry of Defence Directorate of Standardization, *Interim Defence Standard 00-55: The Procurement of Safety-Critical Software in Defence Equipment, Parts 1-2*, Glasgow, Scotland, 1992.

6. P. Mellor, "Failures, Faults, and Changes in Dependability Measurement," *J. Information and Software Technology*, Vol. 34, No. 10, Oct. 1992, pp. 640-654.

A Classification of CASE Technology

Alfonso Fuggetta, Politecnico di Milano and CEFRIEL

The design, implementation, delivery, and maintenance of software are complex and expensive activities that need improvement and better control. Among the technologies proposed to achieve these goals is CASE (computer-aided software engineering): computerized applications supporting and partially automating software-production activities.[1] Hundreds of CASE products are commercially available, offering a wide spectrum of functionalities.

The evolution and proliferation of such tools has forced CASE researchers to address a new challenging topic: How can they develop more integrated and easier to use CASE tools? In response, they have conceived and introduced new products that extend traditional operating-system functionalities to provide more advanced services, such as sophisticated process-control mechanisms and enhanced database-management functionalities.

Another growing research area is the development of technologies to support formal definition and automation of the software process, the total set of activities, rules, methodologies, organizational structures, and tools used during software production. Developers generally agree it is not possible to identify an optimal, universal, and general-purpose process. Rather, each organization must design and evolve the process according to its own needs, market, and customers. To better manage and support software processes, researchers and practitioners need new means to describe and assess them. Moreover, the descriptions must be usable by a computerized tool to guide, control, and, whenever possible, automate software-process activities. This research has produced its first results, and several industrial products have appeared on the market.

The availability of a large number of products is contributing to the improvement and wide diffusion of software-engineering practice. However, this product proliferation is creating critical problems.

It is more difficult to assess the real capabilities and features of many products on the market, and to understand how they are related to each other functionally and technologically. The terminology is often confusing or misleading. For example, terms such as tool, workbench, toolset, and environment are given very different meanings and interpretations. It is difficult, therefore, to develop a clear and systematic classification of the available technology for effective assessment and acquisition.

The variety of CASE products available today is daunting. This survey provides a classification to help in assessing products ranging from tools and environments to enabling technology.

Reprinted from *Computer*, Vol. 26, No. 12, Dec. 1993, pp. 25–38. Copyright © 1993 by The Institute of Electrical and Electronics Engineers, Inc. All rights reserved.

Critical issues in classification schemes

The basic choices and purpose of the classification scheme for CASE technology I propose in this article can be criticized in many ways. First, the acronym CASE is associated with many different definitions often less general than the one I use here.

Sodhi, for example, proposes the following definition: "Computer-Aided Software Engineering (CASE) encompasses a collection of automated tools and methods that assist software engineering in the phases of the software development life cycle."[1] This definition takes into account only the production-process technology.

Next, Pressman defines CASE as follows: "The workshop for software engineering is called an integrated project support environment, and the toolset that fills the workshop is CASE."[2] The author also includes what he calls framework tools: products supporting infrastructure development. This definition extends the scope of CASE.

And Forte and McCulley define CASE this way: "We take CASE literally, that is, CASE is software engineering enhanced by automated tools (i.e. computer-aided). . . To us, it's all part of a coordinated approach to the design and production of systems and products containing software."[3]

Finally, Sommerville proposes a CASE definition similar to the one I present in this article: "Computer-aided software engineering is the term for software tool support for the software engineering process."[4] These examples show that the term CASE is assuming a wider meaning and becoming associated with the computer-aided support offered to the entire software process.

A second criticism is that the goal of this type of classification and its approaches are shallow. It is not easy to agree on the levels of abstraction of the reference framework used to classify CASE products, or on the products' assignments to the identified classes. Moreover, it is difficult to find the right focus to technically profile the different classes of products.

Nonetheless, the need for a conceptual framework and a classification of available technology is increasing. Practitioners and researchers need to assess and compare existing technology. Customers (software-production organizations) need to have a clear overview of the available technology and its potential benefits. Educators and consultants need a solid conceptual basis for their presentations of the state of the art in the field.

Pressman makes a significant observation on this issue:[2] "A number of risks are inherent whenever we attempt to categorize CASE tools. . . Confusion (or antagonism) can be created by placing a specific tool within one category when others might believe it belongs in another category. Some readers may feel that an entire category has been omitted — thereby eliminating an entire set of tools for inclusions in the overall CASE environment. In addition, simple categorization tends to be flat. . . But even with these risks, it is necessary to create a taxonomy of CASE tools — to better understand the breadth of CASE and to better appreciate where such tools can be applied in the software engineering process."

Pressman's words point to a particularly important problem that deserves some additional comments. An ideal classification should define an equivalence relation on the considered domain. Then it becomes possible to partition the domain in equivalent classes and assign each element in the domain to just one class. An entity's class precisely and unambiguously characterizes it for easy comparison and assessment.

Often, however, it is not possible to find such an equivalence relation, and an entity might span different classes. This risk is particularly real with CASE products. Their functionalities and characteristics are not standardized, so it may be quite difficult to assign a given product to a unique class. Nevertheless, an effective classification should aim at limiting these situations to retain its overall soundness and usefulness.

References

1. J. Sodhi, *Software Eng.: Methods, Management, and CASE Tools*, McGraw-Hill, Blue Ridge Summit, Pa., 1991.

2. R.S. Pressman, *Software Eng. — A Practitioner's Approach*, McGraw-Hill, New York, 1992.

3. *CASE Outlook: Guide to Products and Services*, G. Forte and K. McCulley, eds., CASE Consulting Group, Lake Oswego, Ore., 1991.

4. I. Sommerville, *Software Eng.*, Addison-Wesley, Reading, Mass., 1992.

In this article, I propose a classification with more precise definitions for these terms. To avoid any misunderstanding, I use the term "product" to identify any object in the classification.

Even the development of a precise classification can introduce additional conceptual and practical problems that make such efforts useless or even dangerous. The criteria must clarify the rationale, purposes, and limitations of the proposed approach. The level of abstraction must strike a balance between analysis and synthesis, and avoid the introduction of useless details or vague concepts.

My classification of products supporting the software process is based on a general framework derived from the work of Conradi et al.[2] Figure 1 shows the framework. The software process is decomposed in two subprocesses: a *production process* and a *metaprocess*.

The production process includes all activities, rules, methodologies, organizational structures, and tools used to conceive, design, develop, deliver, and maintain a software product. A production process must be defined, assessed, and evolved through a systematic and continuing metaprocess.

The purpose of the metaprocess is the acquisition and exploitation of new products supporting software-production activities and, more generally, the improvement and innovation of the procedures, rules, and technologies used to deliver the organization's artifacts. In the last decade, efforts aimed at understanding the metaprocess include those of the Software Engineering Institute, whose well-known Capability Maturity Model[3] defines five levels of process maturity and provides guidelines to progressively improve it.

The production process can be supported and partially automated by the *production-process technology* — aids to software developers to specify, build, and maintain a software product. In an organization, the specific technology and related procedures and guidelines used to support the production process are called *production-process support*.

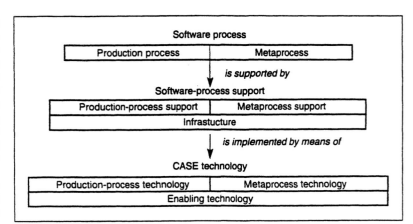

Figure 1. The general framework.

The metaprocess can be automated and supported as well with a *metaprocess technology* used to create the *metapro-* *cess support* — the specific aids used in an organization's metaprocess to automate and guide metaprocess activities.

Related work

One of the first and most important classification attempts was that of Dart et al.,[1] who presented a taxonomy of the trends that have produced state-of-the-art software-development environments. They defined a software-development environment as "an environment that augments or automates *all* the activities comprising the software development cycle." The aim of their classification was to understand the evolution of the principles on which environments have been built.

The taxonomy identified four basic categories:

• *Language-centered environments* built around one language (for example, Interlisp, Smalltalk, or Rational). They are highly interactive, but offer limited support for programming in the large.
• *Structure-centered environments* incorporating the idea of environment generation (for example, Mentor, Cornell Program Synthesizer, and Gandalf). These environments let users directly manipulate the grammar of a programming language to produce structure-oriented tools, such as syntax-directed editors.
• *Toolkit environments* consisting of small tools intended primarily to support the coding phase (for example, Unix PWB and VMS VAX Set). They do not offer any control of the way the tools are applied.
• *Method-based environments* centered around specific methodologies for software development, such as structured analysis and design techniques or object-oriented design (for example, Excelerator, TAGS, and Software Through Pictures).

This pioneering article has several merits, but its scope is limited. It does not offer any finer grained classification of existing products, nor does it take into account the metaprocess and enabling technologies. Moreover, it tends to consider at the same level of abstraction entities that are quite different (for example, complete environments like Interlisp and Smalltalk, and more specialized products like Excelerator).

Forte and McCulley's more recent classification[2] introduces a *tool taxonomy* on two levels. (The term "tool" identifies any product considered in the Forte and McCulley classification.) At the first level, the taxonomy proposes the following classification domains to characterize a tool: application areas targeted by the tool, tasks supported in the development cycle, methods and notations, hardware platforms, operating systems, databases and transaction processing subsystems supported by the tool, network and communication protocols, and programming languages supported by the tool.

At the second level, the authors specify attributes for each domain. Figure A shows the description of the development-tasks domain. This scheme partitions the total set of CASE tools in two main classes: vertical and horizontal tools.

Vertical tools are used in a specific life-cycle phase or activity (for example, testing), while horizontal tools are used throughout the entire software process. The merit of this classification lies in the richness of the domains to characterize tools. Moreover, it is implemented in a tool called Tool Finder, which lets users retrieve product descriptions from an electronic archive.

Unfortunately, the classification does not take into account the conceptual architecture of the software process (as I discuss in the main text). It is not easy to classify tools according to the breadth of support offered to the production process. For instance, Forte and McCulley classify a compiler under the construction task, along with other more complex and sophisticated products (workbenches supporting coding, debugging, and incremental linking). They classify tool integration and process modeling in different horizontal tasks, but provide no hints for understanding their mutual dependencies or their relationships with other classes of products. Moreover, the division between vertical and horizontal tasks becomes unclear if we consider unconventional life cycles not based on the waterfall model.

Production-process and metaprocess supports are based on a common *infrastructure* that provides services and functionalities for their operation in an integrated and homogeneous environment. The infrastructure can be implemented using operating-system services and more advanced and recent products for, say, process control and database management. The products supporting infrastructure implementation are globally identified under the term *enabling technology*. The infrastructure, production-process support, and metaprocess support constitute the *software-process support*.

The classification I propose in this article considers all products in the production-process technology, metaprocess technology, and enabling technology. Globally, these products represent CASE technology.

Refining the reference framework

To refine the framework presented in the previous section, I further classify CASE products used in the production process according to the breadth of support they offer. A production process may be viewed as a set of elementary *tasks* to be accomplished to produce a software application. Examples of tasks are compiling, editing, and generating test cases from requirements specifications.

Tasks are grouped to form *activities*, sets of tasks supporting coarse-grained parts of the software-production process. For example, coding is an activity that includes editing, compiling, debugging, and so on. The activity concept is not to be confused with the phases of a waterfall life cycle. Activities are not necessarily carried out in strict sequence: They can be composed to form any type of life cycle.

According to these definitions, I classify CASE products in the production-process technology in three categories:

(1) *Tools* support only specific tasks in the software process.
(2) *Workbenches* support only one or a few activities.
(3) *Environments* support (a large part of) the software process.

Workbenches and environments are generally built as collections of tools. Tools can therefore be either standalone products or components of workbenches and environments. For exam-

---

Pressman's classification[3] is based on the identification of these different functions supported by CASE products: business systems planning, project management, support (documentation, database, configuration management, and so on), analysis and design, programming, integration and testing, prototyping, maintenance, and framework (support for environment development). Even in this case, however, little help is given for understanding the architecture of the software-process support. Moreover, Pressman does not take metaprocess technology into account.

In another important classification, Sommerville[4] defines CASE tools as the basic building blocks used to create a "software engineering environment." He classifies CASE tools according to the functions they offer and the process activities they support. CASE tools are integrated by an environment infrastructure. Integration can be achieved along four different dimensions: data integration (sharing of information), user-interface integration (common interface paradigms and mechanisms), control integration (mechanisms to control the invocation and execution of tools and applications), and process integration (integration in a defined process model). Environments are collections of tools classified in three different categories:

• *Programming environments* support programming activities, but provide limited support for software analysis and design.
• *CASE workbenches* provide support for analysis and design, but little support for coding and testing.
• *Software-engineering environments* comprise tools for all activities in the software process.

Sommerville proposes a reference framework with two levels of tool aggregations: *stand-alone tools* and *environments*.

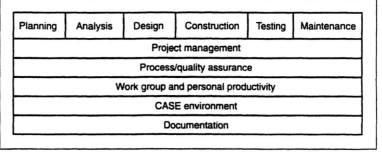

Planning	Analysis	Design	Construction	Testing	Maintenance
Project management					
Process/quality assurance					
Work group and personal productivity					
CASE environment					
Documentation					

Figure A. Development tasks in Forte and McCulley's classification.[2]

Moreover, he relates important concepts such as process integration and environment infrastructure. The classification I present in this article inherits several of these concepts and further refines the idea of a layered classification scheme.

A different type of effort is represented by the *Reference Model for Frameworks of Software Engineering Environments*, jointly developed by the European Computer Manufacturers Association (ECMA) and the National Institute of Standards and Technology.[5,6] This reference model "is a conceptual and functional basis for describing and comparing existing SEEs or SEE components."[6] (SEE stands for software-engineering environment.) Thus, it is not a classification of CASE technology, but it is important because it defines the framework for constructing, operating, and evolving a software-engineering environment. The framework is a set of interrelated services for object management, process management, user interfaces, communication, tools, policy enforcement, framework administration, and configuration.

A software-engineering environment in the ECMA model is similar to the software-process support presented in the main text. The ECMA model's goals and scope, however, are quite different: It is oriented more to the definition of the ideal func-

ple, most computer manufacturers sell tools such as compilers as stand-alone products.[1] They may also integrate compilers with other tools to support both coding and debugging. (In this section, I use "integrate" in its informal and intuitive sense.) In general, these products also include a debugger, an editor, and an incremental linker. Compilers are also very often marketed as standard components of environments (for example, the C compiler in the Unix PWB environment). Some kinds of tools are seldom available as stand-alone products. For example, graphical editors for dataflow or SADT (structured analysis and design technique) diagrams are usually embedded in products also offering other components to support analysis and design.

The distinction among tools, workbenches, and environments further extends Sommerville's classification,[4] which includes only two levels of granularity: tools and environments. Fernström, Närfelt, and Ohlsson[5] advocate a different approach based on four levels of granularity: service, tool, toolset, and environment. In their classification, the term "toolset" is equivalent to workbench, while "service" identifies an operation embedded in a tool.

Production-process support may be built by adopting and integrating one or more tools, workbenches, and environments. In general, it is composed of an environment, which acts as the "backbone." It can be further extended by introducing additional tools and workbenches to fully cover the production process. (All products mentioned in this article are examples. No evaluation is associated with their citation. Readers should refer to specialized publications[1] for a complete presentation of existing products.)

Tools

A CASE tool is a software component supporting a specific task in the software-production process. Table 1 classifies such tools.

Editing tools. Editing tools (editors) can be classified in two subclasses: *textual editors* and *graphical editors*. The first subclass includes traditional text editors and word processors used to produce textual documents such as programs, textual specifications, and documentation. Editors in the second subclass are used to produce documents

---

tionalities to be offered by the infrastructure, so it does not discuss in much detail the characteristics of CASE technology. Also, it does not present a detailed classification of tools (in the ECMA terminology) and does not evaluate the different philosophies adopted by existing environments.

ECMA concepts can be easily recognized in the classification I propose in this article. My infrastructure takes into account all the ECMA services, except for process-management services, which I consider as a separate entity in the production-process and metaprocess supports.

Perry and Kaiser's more general approach[7] for analyzing software-development environments is based on a general model consisting of three components: structures, mechanisms, and policies. Structures are the objects on which mechanisms operate. Mechanisms are the basic functionalities offered by tools. Policies are the procedures, rules, and guidelines offered to and imposed on software developers by environments. An environment can be described by specifying these three components. Classes of environments can be identified by considering analogies and commonalities. For example, toolkit environments[1] can be described by the following model:

```
Toolkit environment =
    (
        {file system/object-management system},
        {assorted construction tools},
        {laissez-faire}
    )
```

To describe the problems of scale in software production, the authors introduce a metaphor that distinguishes four different classes of environments: individual, family, city, and state. Environments in the individual class emphasize software-construction activities and are dominated by mechanisms. Family-class environments address coordination and are dominated by structures. The city class emphasizes cooperation among software developers and is dominated by policies. Finally, environments in the state class address the commonality issue and are dominated by higher order policies.

This classification identifies the components useful in evaluating a software-development environment. Moreover, the metaphor characterizes the different problems that software-development projects must address when scaling up. The model is less useful when applied to classifying the large variety of commercial products, since it considers only environments and does not provide any categorizations for other types of products.

In conclusion, even if the classifications available so far have substantially contributed to the state of the art, they are still incomplete. Much work is needed to provide an effective and comprehensive reference framework and the related classification scheme.

References

1. S.A. Dart et al., "Software Development Environments," *Computer*, Vol. 20, No. 11, Nov. 1987, pp. 18-28.

2. *CASE Outlook: Guide to Products and Services*, G. Forte and K. McCulley, eds., CASE Consulting Group, Lake Oswego, Ore., 1991.

3. R.S. Pressman, *Software Eng. — A Practitioner's Approach*, McGraw-Hill, New York, 1992.

4. I. Sommerville, *Software Eng.*, Addison-Wesley, Reading, Mass., 1992.

5. "Reference Model for Frameworks of Software Engineering Environments," jointly published as ECMA Tech. Report TR/55, European Computer Manufacturers Assoc., Geneva, and NIST Special Publication 500-201, Nat'l Inst. of Standards and Technology, Gaithersburg, Md., 1991.

6. M. Chen and R.J. Norman, "A Framework for Integrated CASE," *IEEE Software*, Vol. 9, No. 2, Mar. 1992. pp. 18-22.

7. D.E. Perry and G.E. Kaiser, "Models of Software Development Environments," *IEEE Trans. Software Eng.*, Vol. 17, No. 3, Mar. 1991, pp. 283-295.

using graphical symbols. Typical examples are general drawing and painting tools (such as MacDraw), tools to enter graphical specifications (for example, those based on dataflow diagrams), and tools to paint the forms and layouts constituting an application's user interface.

Examples of textual and graphical editors are Pmate, a text editor for professional programmers running on MS-DOS personal computers; MacBubbles, a Macintosh-based editing tool for Yourdon-DeMarco diagrams; and DV Draw, an editor that creates several types of graphical output.

Syntax-directed editors are an important category of textual editor. Two examples are Key-one and DEC LSE — Language Sensitive Editor.

Programming tools. These tools are used to support coding and code restructuring. The three main subclasses are *coding and debugging tools*, *code generators*, and *code restructurers*.

The first subclass includes traditional tools used to compile, run, and debug a program. Examples are the numerous traditional compilers and interpreters available on the market, interactive tester/debuggers such as Via/Smartest, and cross-compilers such as HP Cross Compilers, a family of Unix-based C cross-compilers.

The second class includes tools that generate code starting from a high-level description of the application. Typical examples are compiler generators and Cobol generators. Compiler generators (for example, yacc/lex) automatically build lexical analyzers and parsers starting from the formal description of the language syntax. Cobol generators produce Cobol starting from a high-level program description (for example, the VAX Cobol Generator).

The third subclass includes tools used to restructure existing programs. These tools can analyze, reformat, and in some cases improve existing source code by performing actions such as elimination of "gotos" and unreachable portions of code. Examples of such tools are AdaReformat and Via/Renaissance.

Verification and validation tools. This class includes tools that support program validation and verification. Validation aims at ensuring that the product's functions are what the customer really wants, while verification aims at ensuring that the product under construction meets the requirements definition. This class has many subclasses:[6]

- *Static and dynamic analyzers* analyze a computer program without executing the program (static) or by monitoring program execution (dynamic).
- *Comparators* equate two files to identify commonalities or differences. Typically, they are used to compare test results with the expected program outputs.
- *Symbolic executors* simulate program execution using symbols rather than actual values for input data and produce outputs expressed as symbolic expressions.
- *Emulators/simulators* imitate all or part of a computer system. They accept the same data, provide the same functionalities, and achieve the same results as the imitated system.
- *Correctness proof assistants* support formal techniques to prove mathematically that a program satisfies its specifications or that a specification satisfies given properties.
- *Test-case generators* take as input a computer program and a selection of test criteria, and generate test input data that meet these criteria.
- *Test-management tools* support testing by managing test results, test checklists, regression tests, test coverage metrics, and so on.

Examples of such tools are AdaXRef, a cross-reference generator; Q/Auditor, a standards enforcer; lint-Plus, a syntax checker; Instrumentation Tool, a program instrumentor; CICS Simulcast, an execution tracer; Playback, a test-result comparator; and HP Basic Branch Analyzer, a test-coverage tool. (See the detailed classification scheme in Table 1.)

Configuration-management tools. Configuration-management techniques coordinate and control the construction of a system composed of many parts.[7] Software development and management can greatly benefit from configuration

Table 1. Classes of CASE tools.

Class	Subclass
Editing	Graphical editors Textual editors
Programming	Coding and debugging • Assemblers • Compilers • Cross-assemblers • Cross-compilers • Debuggers • Interpreters • Linkage editors • Precompilers/preprocessors Code generators • Compiler generators Code restructurers
Verification and validation	Static analyzers • Cross-reference generators • Flowcharters • Standards enforcers • Syntax checkers Dynamic analyzers • Program instrumentors • Tracers/profilers Comparators Symbolic executors Emulators/simulators Correctness proof assistants Test-case generators Test-management tools
Configuration management	Configuration- and version-management tools Configuration builders Change-control monitors Librarians
Metrics and measurement	Code analyzers Execution monitors/timing analyzers
Project management	Cost-estimation tools Project-planning tools Conference desks E-mail Bulletin boards Project agendas Project notebooks
Miscellaneous tools	Hypertext systems Spreadsheets

management, which can be decomposed into the following tasks:

- *Version management.* During software development, more than one version of each software item is produced. Versions must be managed so subsequent work incorporates the correct version.
- *Item identification.* Each software item must be unambiguously identifiable. Software-process agents (all people working in the software process) must be able to retrieve specific software items to build and rebuild coherent configurations of the product under development.
- *Configuration building.* A software product is a complex collection of versioned software items. Building a product requires invocation of operations such as preprocessing, compiling, and linking on a possibly large set of software items.
- *Change control.* Changes to a software item may have an impact on other components. Moreover, if several programmers can access the same software items, control is necessary to synchronize their activity to prevent the creation of inconsistent or erroneous versions of software items.
- *Library management.* All the software items relevant in a software process must be subject to effective storage and retrieval policies.

Products that support specific configuration-management tasks — such as configuration building (for example, make, MMS, and Pmaker), version management (SCCS and CMS), and library management (Plib86) —

do not offer comprehensive and integrated support to all tasks. Most configuration-management tools in this classification constitute the first generation. The second generation of configuration-management products offers much wider support by integrating into a single product most functionalities offered by the individual tools considered here.

Metrics and measurement tools. Tools that collect data on programs and program execution fall into two subclasses:

- tools to analyze the source code and compute several source-code metrics (for example, to evaluate code complexity according to Halstead's or McCabe's metrics), and
- tools to monitor the execution of programs and collect runtime statistics.

Examples of such tools are Performance Architek and HP Apollo DPAK.

Project-management tools. Several types of products support project management. A first subclass includes products used to estimate software-production costs. These tools typically implement techniques such as Cocomo (Constructive cost model) or function points, and provide user-friendly interfaces to specify project information and analyze estimation results.

A second subclass comprises tools supporting project planning — that is, project scheduling, resource assignment, and project tracking. These tools are based on well-known concepts and notations such as WBS (work breakdown structure), Gantt, and PERT (program

evaluation and review technique) charts.

A third subclass includes tools to support communication and coordination among project team members. Some permit on-line and deferred interaction among people — for example, teleconferencing systems (also called conference desks), e-mail systems, and electronic bulletin boards. Other tools are project agendas used to coordinate activities and meetings.

Examples of these tools are CA-Estimacs (cost estimation), MacProject (project planning), VAX Notes (conference desk), and DateBook (distributed agenda).

Miscellaneous tools. Products difficult to classify include spreadsheets and hypertext systems.

A spreadsheet can be used as a project-management tool to perform what-if analysis or to develop models of the development process (for example, by implementing the Cocomo model). Spreadsheets can also be used for programming. Several applications have been developed using spreadsheet languages, particularly in business administration and marketing. These applications are marketed as add-ons to standard products such as Excel. For example, Computerized Classic Accounting is an integrated accounting system developed for the Macintosh version of Excel.

Hypertext systems can replace desktop publishing systems for authoring advanced documentation. They can also be used as programming tools to develop prototypes or even final applications. Many applications for the Macintosh have been developed using HyperCard — for example, Client, a personal data manager, and MindLink, an idea processor.

Integration in CASE products

The need for integration in CASE technology is increasingly acknowledged by researchers and practitioners.[1] According to Thomas and Nejmeh, integration can be analyzed in four dimensions:[2]

- *Data integration* ensures that all the information in the environment is managed as a consistent whole, regardless of how parts of it are operated on and transformed.
- *Control integration* permits the flexible combination of an environment's functions according to project preferences and the underlying processes and environment supports.
- *Presentation integration* improves user interaction with the environment by reducing users' cognitive load.

- *Process integration* ensures that tools interact effectively in support of a defined process.

We can identify several levels of integration according to the degree of technology exploitation along these four dimensions. For example, Brown and McDermid define five levels of integration, focusing on functionalities and features that support data and control integration.[3]

References

1. *IEEE Software* special issue on integrated CASE, Vol. 9, No. 2, Mar. 1992.

2. I. Thomas and B.A. Nejmeh, "Definition of Tool Integration for Environments," *IEEE Software*, Vol. 9, No. 2, Mar. 1992, pp. 29-35.

3. A.W. Brown and J.A. McDermid, "Learning from IPSE's Mistakes," *IEEE Software*, Vol. 9, No. 2, Mar. 1992, pp. 23-28.

Workbenches

Workbenches integrate in a single application several tools supporting specific software-process activities. Hence, they achieve

- a homogeneous and consistent interface (presentation integration),
- easy invocation of tools and tool chains (control integration), and
- access to a common data set, managed in a centralized way (data integration).

Some products can enforce predefined procedures and policies within the workbench (process integration).

Table 2 shows eight classes of workbenches.

Business planning and modeling workbenches. This class includes products to support the identification and description of a complex business. They are used to build high-level enterprise models to assess the general requirements and information flows, and identify priorities in the development of information systems.

The tools integrated in such products include graphical editors (to provide diagrams and structured charts), report generators, and cross-reference generators. For example, PC Prism integrates tools to create enterprise models and automatically generate documentation from the information stored in its repository.

The borderline between this class of products and analysis and design workbenches is often quite fuzzy.

Analysis and design workbenches. Products for analysis and design activities constitute an important class of workbenches. In fact, very often the term CASE is used to denote just this class of products. Since the term CASE has a wider meaning, "upper" CASE is more properly used to denote this class of tools, which are used in the early stages of the software process. Today's upper CASE workbenches automate most of the analysis and design methodologies developed in the past decades such as SA/SD (structured analysis/structured design), object-oriented analysis and design, and Jackson System Development.

An upper CASE workbench usually includes one or more editors to create and modify specifications, and other tools to analyze, simulate, and transform them. For example, Excelerator has editors to create dataflow diagrams, structure charts, and entity-relationship diagrams. It also includes an editor and a simulator to create and test mock-ups of system inputs and outputs (forms and reports), as well as a code generator to produce skeletal Cobol source code starting from structure charts. Software Through Pictures includes several graphical editors to support the creation, for example, of control-flow diagrams, process-activation tables, and state-transition diagrams. It also includes code- and documentation-generation facilities.

The functionalities these workbenches offer depend heavily on the notations on which they are centered: If the adopted notation is not formally defined, a workbench can provide only editing and document-production facilities. Using a formal notation permits a higher degree of automation.

Table 3 shows a further classification of this class of workbenches according to level of formality, supported application, and activities covered.

Level of formality. Analysis and design workbenches support notations at different levels of formality:

- *Informal.* Structured English and other informal, textual notations, whose syntax and semantics are not formally defined.
- *Semiformal.* Notations for which it is possible to build syntax checkers. Such notations still lack a precise semantics. Dataflow diagrams are a typical example.
- *Formal.* Notations whose syntax and semantics are formally defined. Finite-state machines, Petri nets, and Statecharts are examples.

Supported applications. No notation can universally support the specification of all types of applications. In each project, the software engineer must be allowed to choose the most suitable notation — or combination of notations.

For assessment and selection, notations fall in two main categories:

(1) notations for data-intensive applications, such as banking or accounting systems (for example, dataflow and entity-relationship diagrams), and

Table 2. Classes of CASE workbenches.

Class	Sample Products
Business planning and modeling	PC Prism
Analysis and design	Excelerator Statemate Software Through Pictures
User-interface development	HP Interface Architect DEC VUIT
Programming	CodeCenter
Verification and validation	Battlemap Logiscope
Maintenance and reverse engineering	Recoder Rigi Hindsight SmartSystem
Configuration management	PCMS CCC SCLM DSEE
Project management	Coordinator DEC Plan Synchronize

Table 3. A sampling of "upper" CASE workbenches.

Sample Products	Examples of Notations Supported	Level of Formality	Class of Applications Supported	Activities Covered
Excelerator	Dataflow diagrams Entity-relationship diagrams	Semiformal	General purpose	Both
Teamwork	Dataflow diagrams Ward and Mellor	Semiformal	General purpose	Both
Statemate	Statecharts	Formal	Control intensive	Both
TAGS	Input/Output Requirements Language	Formal	Control intensive	Both
ASA	Integrated System Definition Language Finite State Machine	Formal	Control intensive	Analysis
GEODE	Specification Description Language	Formal	Control intensive	Design
ER-Designer	Entity-relationship diagrams	Semiformal	Data intensive	Both
IEW	Dataflow diagrams Entity-relationship diagrams	Semiformal	General purpose	Both
STP	Dataflow diagrams Object-oriented structured design	Formal and semiformal	General purpose	Both

(2) notations for control-intensive applications, such as avionics and control systems (for example, finite-state machines, Statecharts, and Petri nets).

According to this distinction, analysis and design workbenches can be grouped in three subclasses:

- workbenches for data-intensive applications (for example, Excelerator),
- workbenches for control-intensive applications (for example, Statemate), and
- general-purpose workbenches — products that support notations for both types of applications (for example. Teamwork).

Activities covered. I call these products analysis and design workbenches because most cover both activities. However, some cover only one. Thus, I classify analysis and design workbenches as analysis only, design only, or both.

User-interface-development workbenches. This class of CASE workbenches is distinct from the others already presented. Its products do not help with specific software-process activities but rather with user-interface design and development.

Many authors have suggested that the user interface is the most critical part of some programs. Kay has even argued that in many cases the user interface *is* the program.[8] Effective support for user-interface design and development is important.

The products in this class exploit the capabilities of modern workstations and graphical environments such as Motif or Windows. They let the developer easily create and test user-interface components and integrate them with the application program.

Typically, a user-interface workbench offers

- graphical editors to paint windows, dialog boxes, icons, and other user-interface components;
- simulators to test the developed in-

terface before integrating it with the application;
- code generators to produce the code to be integrated with the application; and
- runtime libraries to support the generation of executable code.

Examples are DEC VUIT and HP Interface Architect, both developed for the Motif standard interface.

Programming workbenches. The workbenches in this class evolved from the basic programming tools and provide integrated facilities supporting programming:

- a text editor to create and modify the source code,
- a compiler and linker to create the executable code, and
- a debugger.

For effective user interaction with the different tools, programming workbenches provide an integrated and consistent interface, and manage all information created during work sessions (source-code files, intermediate files, object- and executable-code files, and so on). Often, the workbench integrates the compiler with an interpreter or an incremental linker to speed the transition from editing to testing.

Examples of programming workbenches are Turbo C++, Turbo Pascal, and CodeCenter.

Verification and validation workbenches. This class of workbenches includes products that help with module and system testing. Products in this class often integrate several tools from both the metrics and measurement class and the verification and validation class. The functionalities offered by both classes jointly analyze the quality of code and support actual verification and validation.

A typical verification and validation workbench includes

- static analyzers to evaluate complexity metrics and call and control graphs,
- cross-reference and report generators,
- a tool to instrument a program and a tracer to support dynamic analysis, and
- a test-case generator and a test-management tool to produce, store, and manage test data, test results, and checklists.

Act and Logiscope are typical products.

Maintenance and reverse-engineering workbenches. In the past, software engineers often assumed that maintenance had only to do with fixing bugs. This approach proved inadequate for evolving software according to changes in the supported business environment, changes in the available technology, and new requirements from the customer. Now maintenance must be a component of the "forward" development process.

For maintenance, software engineers use the same tools and workbenches they normally use for development. They have to modify requirement specifications, designs, and application source code. They have to repeat the testing procedure to verify that the new version of the application can be released into service. And, with appropriate configuration-management techniques, they

have to manage the artifacts of the process (documents, source code, makefiles, and so on).

Even if most maintenance is performed with the same techniques and products used during software development, some more specific tasks must be approached with ad hoc techniques and tools — in particular, techniques identified as *reverse engineering*. Müller et al. describe this discipline as "the process of extracting system abstraction and design information out of existing software systems."[9]

This goal has not been completely fulfilled. Perhaps it will be impossible to fully achieve the automatic derivation of analysis and design information from code. Such an operation requires higher level information to be synthesized from low-level descriptions (the program statements), and it appears that this can be done only by humans with knowledge of the application.

Several available maintenance and reverse-engineering workbenches provide interesting and seemingly effective features. An example is Recoder, one of the first commercial reverse-engineering workbenches. It includes a code restructurer, a flowcharter, and a cross-reference generator. It analyzes unstructured and hard-to-read Cobol programs and produces new, more readable and modifiable versions. Rigi, another reverse-engineering workbench, can build a program's call graph and suggest possible clustering techniques to achieve strong cohesion and low coupling.

Other sample workbenches in this class are Ensemble and Hindsight.

Configuration-management workbenches. The workbenches in this class integrate tools supporting version control, configuration building, and change control. For example, the HP Apollo DSEE workbench integrates a history manager to store versions of source elements, a configuration manager to define and build configurations, and a task manager and monitor manager to control the process of changing a software item. Thus, the single product integrates and substantially extends most features offered by tools such as make, SCCS, and RCS.

A few products in this class also offer more advanced functionalities to support process modeling. For example, software-process managers can tailor

PCMS according to policies and roles they specify. Policies and roles are described through the possible states of a software item and the operations applied to them to change their state.

Other examples of configuration-management workbenches are CCC and SCLM.

Project-management workbenches. There are very few products in this class. Most potential candidates address only specific project-management tasks, and it seems more appropriate to classify them as tools.

Coordinator integrates several project-management functionalities based on an extended theoretical study of how people operate in a structured and complex organization. It lets development team members create typed messages — that is, messages with a precise meaning, requiring a specific action of the addressee (for example, requests for information or submissions of a proposal for approval). Also, Coordinator keeps track of

- the activities a person has to complete,
- temporal relations among significant actions to be completed by the organization, and
- actions that must be scheduled periodically during the project lifetime.

Other examples of project-management workbenches are Synchronize and DEC Plan. Synchronize includes several tools such as a distributed agenda, memo-distribution facilities, distributed to-do lists, and a meeting scheduler. DEC Plan offers functionalities similar to Synchronize, and also addresses project-planning and task-assignment problems.

Environments

An environment is a collection of tools and workbenches that support the software process. Some of the names I use to identify the different classes in Table 4 come from existing terminology — for example, "toolkit and "language-centered environments."[10]

Toolkits. Toolkits are loosely integrated collections of products easily extended by aggregating different tools

Table 4. Classes of CASE environments.

Class	Sample Products
Toolkits	Unix Programmer's Work Bench
Language-centered	Interlisp Smalltalk Rational KEE
Integrated	IBM AD/Cycle DEC Cohesion
Fourth generation	Informix 4GL Focus
Process-centered	East Enterprise II Process Wise Process Weaver Arcadia

and workbenches. Unlike workbenches, toolkits support different activities in the software-production process, but their support is very often limited to programming, configuration management, and project management (and project-management support is generally limited to message handling). Typically, toolkits are environments extended from basic sets of operating-system tools; the Unix Programmer's Work Bench and the VMS VAX Set are two examples.

Toolkits' loose integration requires users to activate tools by explicit invocation or simple control mechanisms such as redirection and pipes in Unix. The shared files users access for data exchange are very often unstructured or in formats that need explicit conversion so different tools can access them (via import and export operations). Because the only constraint for adding a new component is the formats of the files read or created by other tools or workbenches, toolkits can be easily and incrementally extended.

Toolkits do not impose any particular constraint on the process that users follow. Users interact through a general-purpose interface (for example, the shell or the command-language interpreter) that leaves them free to decide which procedures or operations to activate.

Language-centered environments. Examples of environments centered around a specific language are Interlisp, Smalltalk, Rational, and KEE, developed respectively for Lisp, Smalltalk (the language and the environment have the same name), Ada, and Lisp again.[11]

The peculiarity of this class of products is that very often the environment itself is written in the language for which it was developed, thus letting users customize and extend the environment and reuse part of it in the applications under development. The main drawback is that integrating code in different languages may not be feasible. Smalltalk is an environment that suffers from this problem. These environments can hardly be extended to support different programming languages, and they are often concentrated on the edit-compile-debug cycle, with little or no support for large-scale software development.

Language-centered environments offer a good level of presentation and control integration: Users are presented with a consistent interface and are given several mechanisms supporting automatic tool invocation and switching among tools (for example, among the editor, compiler, and debugger). However, these environments suffer from a lack of process and data integration. They are based on structured internal representations (usually abstract trees), but these mechanisms are invisible or hard for users to access for extending or customizing the environment with other products.

Integrated environments. The environments in this class are called "integrated" because, with some limitations, they operate using standard mechanisms so users can integrate tools and workbenches. These environments achieve presentation integration by providing uniform, consistent, and coherent tool and workbench interfaces: All products in the environment are operated through a unique interface concept. They achieve data integration through the *repository* concept: They have a specialized database managing all information produced and accessed in the environment.

The database is structured according to a high-level model of the environment, so users can develop tools and workbenches that access and exchange structured information instead of pure byte streams. This greatly enhances the functionalities and level of integration

offered to the user. Control integration is achieved through powerful mechanisms to invoke tools and workbenches from within other components of the environment.

Such mechanisms can also encapsulate[12] a tool not written to make use of any of the environment framework services. They surround the tool with software that acts as a layer between the tool and the framework. Integrated environments do not explicitly tackle process integration. This distinguishes them from the process-centered environments discussed later.

The infrastructure needed to create an integrated environment is generally more sophisticated than traditional operating-system services. Later, I discuss *integrating platforms* — extensions to operating-system services that provide the tool builder with advanced features.

The DEC Cohesion and IBM AD/Cycle integrated environments provide basic tools and workbenches, and an integrating platform that lets other companies enrich the environment with additional products. For example, DEC Cohesion is based on an integrating platform offering tool encapsulation, a repository, and user-interface-management and tool-integration facilities (ACA Services, CDD Repository, and DEC Fuse). It includes several tools and workbenches to support production-process activities (DEC Set, DEC VUIT, DEC Plan, and DEC Design), and it can be extended with third-party products.

Fourth-generation environments. Fourth-generation environments were precursors to and, in a sense, are a subclass of integrated environments. They are sets of tools and workbenches supporting the development of a specific class of program: electronic data processing and business-oriented applications. At least four characteristics distinguish these applications:

(1) The application's operations are usually quite simple, while the structure of the information to be manipulated is rather complex.

(2) The user interface is critical. Typically, it is composed of many forms and layouts used to input, display, and modify the information stored in the database.

(3) The application requirements are very often not clearly defined and can be

detailed only through the development of prototypes (very often, mock-ups of the user interface).

(4) The software process to produce such applications is generally evolutionary.

Fourth-generation environments were the first integrated environments. In general, they include an editor, an interpreter and/or a compiler for a specialized language, a debugger, database access facilities, a form editor, a simulator, simple configuration-management tools, document-handling facilities, and, in some cases, a code generator to produce programs in traditional languages such as Cobol. Often, these components are integrated through a consistent interface, data are stored in a central, proprietary repository, and built-in triggers activate tools when specific events occur in the environment.

However, fourth-generation environments provide a low degree of process integration, and ad hoc nonstandard mechanisms support the other dimensions of integration. In many cases, for example, programs and other application-related information are stored in proprietary databases. This makes it difficult (or even impossible) for other manufacturers to extend the environment with new products and components. To overcome this problem, most of these environments are migrating to standard platforms for evolution into true integrated environments.

I defined these products as "fourth-generation environments" instead of the more traditional "fourth-generation languages" to emphasize that they are more than compilers or interpreters for specific languages: They are collections of tools to manage the design, development, and maintenance of large electronic data processing applications.

Table 5 presents a more detailed division of fourth-generation environments into three classes. *Production systems* are oriented to the development of banking or accounting systems with strong performance requirements. These environments replace traditional Cobol-based environments and fall into two subclasses: *language-based systems* and *Cobol generators*. The former are based on a language that is directly compiled

Table 5. Fourth-generation environments.

Class	Sample Products
Production systems	
• Language-based systems	Natural 2
	Informix
	4GL/OnLine
• Cobol generators	Pacbase
	Transform
Infocenter systems	Focus
	Ramis
End-user systems	Filemaker

or interpreted. The latter are products that start with a high-level description of the application and generate Cobol source code for new applications to integrate with existing ones. Natural 2 is a language-based system; Pacbase is a Cobol generator.

Infocenter systems support the infocenter department of an organization in extracting and manipulating the information managed by the main electronic data processing application. To ensure high performance, the main system is usually developed using a production system. Typically, infocenter systems do not provide the same level of performance, but offer more flexible facilities to produce, say, nonstandard reports for management, based on the information stored in the main database. A typical example in this class is Ramis.

End-user systems support end users in directly defining their database and access functionalities. They provide predefined functions and forms that users customize easily through interactive facilities, without writing traditional programs. Many products developed for the Macintosh and MS-DOS personal computers can be included in this class. A typical example is Filemaker Pro (running on the Macintosh).

Process-centered environments. A process-centered environment is based on a formal definition of the software process. A computerized application called a *process driver* or *process engine* uses this definition to guide development activities by automating process fragments, automatically invoking tools and workbenches, enforcing specific policies, and assisting programmers, analysts, and project managers in their

work.[13] Thus, these environments focus on process integration. This does not mean they do not address other integration dimensions. Rather, other integration issues are the starting points for process integration.

A process engineer or process modeler (that is, someone who can analyze a process and describe it formally) produces the formal definition of the production process (called the *process model*), using specialized tools with functionalities to define, analyze, and manage it. Thus a process-centered environment operates by interpreting a process model created by specialized tools. Several research prototypes and even products on the market support both the creation and the execution of a process model. These products are therefore *environment generators*, since they can create different, customized environments that follow the procedures and policies enforced by the process model.

Process-centered environments are usually composed of parts to handle two functions:

- *Process-model execution.* The process driver interprets and executes a specific process model to operate the process-centered environment and make it available to software developers.
- *Process-model production.* Process modelers use tools to create or evolve process models.

Because of their process-model-execution function, I classify such products in Table 5 as process-centered environments, concerned with production-process technology. However, their process-model-production capabilities also qualify them as metaprocess technology.

Examples of products and research prototypes are East, Enterprise II, Process Weaver, Arcadia, Process Wise, EPOS, HPSF, Merlin, Marvel, and SPADE/S Lang (Software Process Analysis Design and Enactment/SPADE Language), whose functionalities I discuss in the later section on metaprocess technology. (EPOS, a project at Norges Tekniske Hogskole (NTH) in Trondheim, Norway, is not to be confused with an existing CASE product with the same name.)

358

Metaprocess and enabling technologies

The metaprocess and enabling technologies are important in developing effective software-process support. Metaprocess-technology products let a process manager create, operate, and improve production-process support. Enabling technology provides the basic mechanisms to integrate the different products in both the production-process and the metaprocess technologies.

Metaprocess technology. Toward the beginning of this article, I defined the metaprocess as the set of activities, procedures, roles, and computerized aids used to create, maintain, and further improve the production process. The metaprocess is similar to the software processes. Process managers must conceive, design, verify, use, assess, and maintain a production process (the output of the metaprocess).

To achieve these goals, process managers may be able to use traditional production-process technology — in particular, analysis and design workbenches. For instance, they can create and maintain a process model using Statecharts with the support of Statemate.[14] In this way, however, it is possible to achieve only a quite limited goal: A process model created through traditional CASE products such as Statemate can be used only as a vehicle to communicate process rules and procedures, or to document and assess the existing practice. It cannot automatically generate more advanced environments and production-process supports.

Researchers have tried to develop technologies and methodologies to provide these advanced process supports. The first results were the structure-centered environment generators[10] (for example, Gandalf and the Cornell Program Synthesizer). These meta-environments can produce a set of tools starting from a formal description of the grammar of the language to be supported. Their initial aim was to produce a syntax-directed editor, but their scope has been progressively augmented to support more production-process tasks. These products are therefore environment generators, classified as metaprocess technology.

Recent work on process-centered environments and process modeling (discussed previously) has produced many research prototypes and a few commercial products,[15,16] whose goals I summarize:

- *Process modeling.* The development of notations to describe rules, activities, organizational structures, procedures, deliverables, and CASE products that constitute (or are used in) a software process, and the development of tools to validate and simulate the resulting model.
- *Process instantiation and enactment.* The development of runtime monitors and interpreters to execute or enact a software-process model — that is, to provide guidance to the people, tools, and workbenches involved in the process — and, whenever possible, to automate software-process activities. The resulting support to the production process is called a process-centered environment.
- *Process evolution.* Development of tools to support process-model evolution during the process lifetime.

The results of this research are encouraging, but several problems such as the process-model evolution have not yet been effectively solved. Nevertheless, some commercial products are available and, most important, the industrial community is becoming increasingly aware of the relevance of metaprocess technology.

Enabling technologies. Developing the complex products described in the previous sections requires services more sophisticated than the basic file-system-management and process-control mechanisms traditionally provided by operating systems. CASE products need functionalities such as advanced database-management systems to create and manage the repository, and sophisticated user-interface-management systems to design and develop graphical, easy-to-learn user interfaces for tools and workbenches.

To tackle these problems systematically and effectively, several industries and computer manufacturers are developing a new class of products that provide standard extensions to traditional operating systems (especially Unix). Built on top of the operating system, these products provide the tool developer with runtime libraries implementing several advanced features. Typical examples of this class are the already-mentioned DEC Cohesion Platform, HP SoftBench, and Atherton Software Backplane. Another example is PCTE (Portable Common Tool Environment), which is actually a standard interface definition, not a product. Currently, several existing or forthcoming products comply with this standard: the initial implementation by Emeraude, the Oracle-based version by Verilog, and implementations by DEC and IBM.

A key feature of these *integrating platforms* is their support for the creation of logically integrated but physically distributed systems. The development of personal computers, workstations, and local area network technology has made distributed implementations particularly suitable for advanced software-development environments. Hence, platform designers conceive and implement all the services for a distributed architecture. Moreover, the same services are very often available on different operating systems (for example, Unix, OSF/1, NT, and MS-DOS) to make the creation of heterogeneous architectures possible.

Standardization is a key aspect for such products. CASE developers can embed most of the functionalities offered by a platform in an application by adopting ad hoc components and products already available on the market. However, to develop distributed, highly integrated, and heterogeneous systems, they must identify standard mechanisms that ensure the required degree of product interoperability. (Interoperability is "the ability of two or more systems or components to exchange information and to use the information that has been exchanged."[6])

Besides the repository- and user-interface-management mechanisms, integrating platforms offer (or soon will offer) other key functionalities:

- *Advanced process-control mechanisms.* These let CASE developers encapsulate tools and workbenches, and invoke and control them through standard methods and event-generation mechanisms. Examples are the HP Encapsulator and the ACA Services offered by the DEC Cohesion Platform.
- *Support for the creation of multimedia products.* These features extend the functionalities offered by

traditional user-interface workbenches and let designers create advanced multimedia tools such as video documentation facilities and visual e-mail systems. A product offering these functionalities is the Multimedia Development Kit for Microsoft Windows.

- *Support for the creation of cooperating CASE tools and workbenches.* Typical examples of such applications are on-line agendas and concurrent/distributed editing tools. For example, DEC Fuse, Sun ToolTalk, and HP BMS give the tool developer a message-handling facility to support the integration and cooperation of CASE products.

The total value of the CASE technology market has grown from an estimated $2 billion in 1990 to $5 billion in 1993. Despite the recession Western countries have experienced in recent years, the CASE tool growth rate for the next couple of years is expected to be between 20 and 30 percent.[1]

Such high rates are justified because the total cost for human resources in software production amounts to about $250 billion per year. Therefore, even a modest increase in productivity would significantly reduce costs.[1] For this reason, CASE technology will play a key role in the information technology market, and many new products will appear.

The availability of such a large number of products and the complexity of the technologies used in software-development organizations make a reference framework for market evaluation and technology transfer essential. Moreover, it is important to facilitate comparison and exchange of experiences with other information-technology areas, such as VLSI design, factory automation, and office automation, where there have been similar efforts.

I have proposed concepts to bring in focus the state of the art of CASE technology. Attempts to classify and organize according to complex concepts may lead to extreme simplifications or, conversely, useless details. Moreover, the rapid changes in this area will quickly make some observations obsolete. As a result, this work will need to be updated incrementally as the technology develops. My aim in this article is to provide a reference framework and an initial classification of existing technology as a solid starting point for such a continuous updating. ∎

Acknowledgments

I thank Carlo Ghezzi and the anonymous referees for their stimulating and helpful comments.

References

1. *CASE Outlook: Guide to Products and Services,* G. Forte and K. McCulley, eds., CASE Consulting Group, Lake Oswego, Ore., 1991.

2. R. Conradi et al., "Towards a Reference Framework of Process Concepts," *Proc. Second European Workshop Software Process Technology,* Springer-Verlag, Berlin, 1992.

3. M.C. Paulk et al., "Capability Maturity Model for Software," Tech. Report CMU/SEI-91-TR-24, Software Eng. Inst., Carnegie Mellon Univ., Pittsburgh, 1991.

4. I. Sommerville, *Software Eng.,* Addison-Wesley, Reading, Mass., 1992.

5. C. Fernström, K.-H. Närfelt, and L. Ohlsson, "Software Factory Principles, Architectures, and Experiments," *IEEE Software,* Vol. 9, No. 2, Mar. 1992, pp. 36-44.

6. "Standard Glossary of Software Engineering Terminology," in *Software Eng. Standards,* IEEE, Spring 1991, pp. 7-38.

7. D. Whitgift, *Methods and Tools for Software Configuration Management,* John Wiley, New York, 1991.

8. A. Kay, invited address at the 11th Int'l Conf. Software Eng., 1989.

9. H.A. Müller et al., "A Reverse Engineering Environment Based on Spatial and Visual Software Interconnection Models," *Proc. Fifth ACM SIGSoft Symp. Software Development Environments,* ACM Press, New York, 1992, pp. 88-98.

10. S.A. Dart et al., "Software Development Environments," *Computer,* Vol. 20, No. 11, Nov. 1987, pp. 18-28.

11. *Integrated Programming Environments,* D.R. Barstow, H.E. Shrobe, and E. Sandewall, eds., McGraw-Hill, New York, 1984.

12. "Reference Model for Frameworks of Software Engineering Environments," jointly published as ECMA Tech. Report TR/55, European Computer Manufacturers Assoc., Geneva, and NIST Special Publication 500-201, Nat'l Inst. of Standards and Technology, Gaithersburg, Md., 1991.

13. M.M. Lehman, "Process Models, Process Programs, Programming Support," *Proc. Ninth Int'l Conf. Software Eng.,* IEEE CS Press, Los Alamitos, Calif., Order No. 767, 1987, pp. 14-16.

14. M.I. Kellner, "Software Process Modeling: Value and Experience," *SEI Tech. Rev.,* Software Eng. Inst., Carnegie Mellon Univ., Pittsburgh, 1989, pp. 23-54.

15. C. Liu and R. Conradi, "Process Modeling Paradigms: An Evaluation," *Proc. First European Workshop on Software Process Modeling,* Italian Nat'l Assoc. for Computer Science, Milan, Italy, 1991, pp. 39-52.

16. P. Armenise et al., "A Survey and Assessment of Software Process Representation Formalisms," to be published in *Int'l J. Software Eng. and Knowledge Eng.*

Alfonso Fuggetta is an associate professor of computer science at Politecnico di Milano and a senior researcher at CEFRIEL, the Italian acronym for the Center for Research and Education in Information Technology, established in 1988 by a consortium of universities, public administrations, and information-technology industries. His research interests are software-process modeling and management, CASE products, and executable specifications.

Fuggetta is chairman of the steering committee of the European Software Engineering Conference (ESEC) and a member of the steering committee of the European Workshop on Software Process Technology. He is a member of the board of directors of AICA, the Italian National Society for Computer Science, and of the Technical Committee on Software Quality Certification of Istituto Marchio Qualità. Fuggetta is also a member of IEEE and ACM.

Readers can contact Fuggetta at Dipartimento di Elettronica e Informazione, Politecnico di Milano, P.za Leonardo da Vinci, 32, 20133 Milano, Italy, e-mail fuggetta@IPMEL2.elet.polimi.it.

IEEE Standard 1074-1997
Developing Software Life Cycle Processes

Abstract: A standard for creating a software life cycle process is provided. Although this standard is directed primarily at the process architect, it is useful to any organization that is responsible for managing and performing software projects.

This standard was developed by a working group consisting of the following members who attended two or more meetings, provided text, or submitted comments on more than two drafts of this standard:

David J. Schultz, *Chair*

Dennis E. Nickle, *Vice Chair*

Susan M. Burgess, *Configuration Manager*

John W. Horch, *Editor*

David W. Burnett	Ron Dean	Jean A. Gilmore
Arthur Godin	Daniel Gray	Lynn Ihlenfeldt
Robert J. Kierzyk	Pat Marcinko	Keith Middleton
Robert W. Shillato	Diane Switzer	

Sponsored by

Software Engineering Standards Committee
of the IEEE Computer Society

The Institute of Electrical and Electronic Engineering, Inc.
345 East 47th Street, New York, NY 10017-2394, USA
December 9, 1997

Table of Contents

IEEE Standard 1074-1997
Developing Software Life Cycle Processes

IEEE Standard for Developing
Software Life Cycle Processes

1. Overview

This paragraph presents an overview of this standard.

1.1 Scope

This standard provides a process for creating a software life cycle process (SLCP). It is primarily directed at the process architect for a given software project. It is the function of the process architect to create the SLCP.

This methodology begins with the selection of an appropriate software life cycle model (SLCM) for use on the specific project. It continues through the creation of the software life cycle (SLC), using the selected SLCM and the Activities. The methodology concludes with the augmentation of the SLC with Organizational Process Assets (OPAs) to create the SLCP.

The Activities cover the entire life cycle of a software project, from concept exploration through the eventual retirement of the software system. This standard does not address non-software activities, such as contracting, purchasing, or hardware development. It also does not mandate the use of a specific SLCM, nor does it provide a selection of, or a tutorial on, SLCMs. This standard presumes that the process architect is already familiar with a variety of SLCMs, with the criteria for choosing among them, and with the criteria for determining the attributes and constraints of the desired end system and the development environment that affects this selection. Finally, this standard does not prescribe how to perform software Activities.

1.2 Purpose

This standard defines the process by which an SLCP is created. It is useful to any organization that is responsible for managing and performing software projects. It can be used where software is the total system or where software is part of a larger system.

1.3 Product of standard

The product of this standard is the SLCP that is required for a specific software project. The SLCP is based on the following:

    a)   An SLCM that is selected for the project;

    b)   The Activities; and

    c)   The OPAs that are selected for the project.

While this standard describes the creation of a single, overall SLCP that is to be used for a project, the user of this standard should recognize that an SLCP can itself include lower-level SLCPs. This is the same concept as in configuration management, in which a particular Configuration Item can include subordinate Configuration Items. This standard applies equally to the development of SLCPs at any level.

1.4 Intended audiences

This standard is written to provide direction and guidance to those individuals who are responsible for determining the implementation of this standard's Activities.

1.4.1 Process architect

The primary audience for this standard is the process architect. The process architect is expected to have:

    a)   The authority to develop SLCPs;

    b)   A knowledge of the OPAs;

    c)   A knowledge of SLCMs; and

    d)   An understanding of the Activities that are presented in this standard.

1.4.2 Other interested parties

This standard also can be of use to the performers of the Activities.

1.5 Relationship to other key standards

No standard exists isolated from its associated standards. This standard is related to ISO 9001: 1994 and IEEE/EIA 12207.0-1996.

1.5.1 Relationship to ISO 9001: 1994 and ISO 9000-3: 1994

ISO 9001: 1994, as interpreted by the guidance in Paragraph 5.1 of ISO 9000-3: 1994, recommends organizing a software development project in accordance with a selected life cycle model. It is intended that a conforming application of this standard would satisfy this recommendation; however, it would be the responsibility of the applier to ensure that the created SLCPs satisfy the specific requirements of ISO 9001: 1994 and other applicable standards.

1.5.2 Relationship to IEEE/EIA 12207.0-1996

Paragraph 5.1.2.2 of IEEE/EIA 12207.0-1996 requires an acquirer to "determine which processes, activities, and tasks of IEEE/EIA 12207.0-1996 are appropriate for the project and tailor them accordingly." Paragraph 5.2.4.2 of IEEE/EIA 12207.0-1996 requires a supplier to "define or select a software life cycle model" and map the processes, activities, and tasks of IEEE/EIA 12207.0-1996 onto that model. Paragraph 5.3.1.1 places a similar requirement upon a developer in some situations. It is intended that a conforming application of this standard would satisfy any of these requirements; however, it would be the responsibility of the applier to ensure that the created SLCPs satisfy the other specific requirements of IEEE/EIA 12207.0-1996 and other applicable standards.

1.6 Relationship to process improvement

While process improvement is outside the scope of this standard, this standard can be integrated into an organization's process improvement program through its use as the framework for the OPAs.

Building the OPAs around this standard's structure of Activities and Input and Output Information can:

a) Minimize the effort needed to create an SLCP;

b) Facilitate the reuse of existing OPAs; and

c) Lead to the improvement of the OPAs by incorporating lessons that were learned from the use of the OPAs in projects.

The SLCP for a project, in part or as a whole, can become part of the OPAs for use by future projects.

1.7 Organization of this standard

Paragraphs 1, 2, and 3 of this standard contain required, introductory information. Paragraph 4 provides a brief discussion of the key concepts that are beneficial to the understanding and use of this standard. Paragraph 5 provides the requirements for the creation of an SLCP. Table 1 presents the organization of this standard.

Table 1—Organization of this standard

Element	Title
Paragraph 1	Overview
Paragraph 2	References
Paragraph 3	Definitions
Paragraph 4	Key concepts
Paragraph 5	Implementation of the standard

The components of the SLCP consist of Activities and are organized into Activity Groups. The Activities cover the entire life cycle of a software project, from concept exploration through the eventual retirement of the software system. Activity Groups are further grouped into sections.

The Integral section includes those Activity Groups that are necessary to ensure the successful completion of a project, but are considered as support Activities, rather than those Activities that are directly oriented to the development effort. The Integral Activity Groups contain the following two types of Activities:

a) Activities that are performed discretely and are therefore mapped into an SLCM; and

b) Activities that are invoked (see 4.3.3) by other Activities.

2. References

The supporting references and citations pertaining to this standard can be found in the *Centralized IEEE Software Engineering Standards References* contained in this tutorial. These references provide additional information on developing software life cycle processes to assist in understanding and applying this standard.

3. Definitions

The definitions and acronyms pertaining to this standard can be found in the *Centralized IEEE Software Engineering Standards Glossary* contained in this tutorial. These are contextual definitions serving to augment the understanding of the development of software life cycle process activities as described within this standard.

4. Key concepts

This paragraph provides an explanation of the key concepts that are used throughout this standard.

4.1 Activities

An Activity is a defined body of work that is to be performed, including its required Input and Output Information. Thus, it is a description of the required transformation of Input Information into Output Information. The performance of an Activity is complete when all Input Information has been processed and all Output Information has been generated.

4.1.1 Format

An Activity consists of three parts:

a) *Input Information*—A list of the required information to be transformed and its source(s);

b) *Description*—A discussion of the value-added actions to be performed in order to accomplish the transformation; and

c) *Output Information*—A list of the information that is required to be generated by the transformation, and its destination(s).

4.1.2 Entry and exit criteria

To "enter," or start, an Activity, at least one element of the specified Input Information must be present. To "exit," or complete, an Activity, all Input Information shall have been processed and all Output Information shall be generated. Each project is expected to determine information flow requirements during the mapping of Activities to the SLCM.

4.1.3 "If Applicable" activities

Activities are categorized as either mandatory or "If Applicable." "If Applicable" Activities are marked "If Applicable" in the Activity title. All other Activities are mandatory. Each "If Applicable" Activity contains an explanation of the cases to which it will apply. For example, Design Data Base (If Applicable) applies when a database is to be created as a part of the project. When an "If Applicable" Activity is used, its Output Information becomes "Available" for use by other Activities.

4.1.4 Organizational structure

This standard does not presume or dictate an organizational structure for a software project. Therefore, it is neither implied, nor required that Activities within an Activity Group be performed by the same organizational entity, nor that an organizational entity's involvement be concentrated in only one Activity Group. This standard does, however, presume that persons will be assigned accountability for the performance of the Activities and for the quality of the Input and Output Information sets.

4.2 Elements of the SLCP

Figure 1 depicts the key concepts involved in the development of an SLCP.

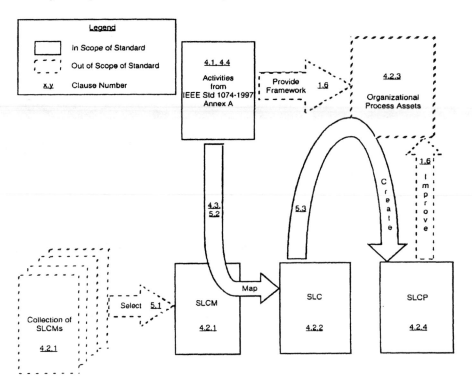

Figure 1—Developing an SLCP

4.2.1 SLCM

The SLCM is the framework on which the Activities of this standard will be mapped to produce the SLC for a project. To use this standard, a SLCM shall be selected for a project. This selection is based on project attributes and organizational capabilities.

This standard does not provide a collection of SLCMs. Providing such a collection of SLCMs is outside the scope of this standard.

4.2.2 SLC

The SLC is the executable sequence of Activities that are to be performed during a project. The SLC is created by mapping the Activities onto the SLCM selected for the project.

4.2.3 OPAs

OPAs are the artifacts that define the environment of an organization for software projects. These artifacts are selected and adapted for a particular project.

The content of the Process Assets collection of an organization will vary from organization to organization. Definition of the collection of OPAs is the responsibility of the using organization. It is recommended, however,

366

that the organization consider including assets such as policies, standards, procedures, existing SLCPs, metrics, tools, methodologies, etc.

4.2.4 SLCP

The SLCP is created by augmenting the SLC with the OPAs that are selected for the project. It provides the specific approach to be used for the project.

4.3 Mapping

Mapping establishes the executable sequence of the Activities in this standard onto a selected SLCM. Activities can be mapped in three ways: Instance, Iteration, and Invocation.

4.3.1 Instance

An Activity is mapped as an Instance if it takes all of its specified inputs, processes them, and produces all of its specified outputs. It is mapped once, and appears as a single event in the SLC.

4.3.2 Iteration

An Activity is mapped as an Iteration if at least some Input Information is processed and some Output Information is created. Iterations are mapped until all Input Information is processed and all Output Information is created.

4.3.3 Invocation

In addition to the Activities that are discretely mapped, there are groups of Activities that are invoked in parallel from many Activities. An Activity is invoked to further process specific information before that information is considered complete and permitted to be output by the creating Activity. When invoked, these Activities perform a distinct function and then return to the invoking Activity.

4.4 Input information and output information

Where Information flows among Activities, it can be traced from its original Activity to the receiving Activity.

Figure 2 depicts the conceptual flow of Input Information and Output Information into and out from an Activity, respectively.

4.4.1 Conventions

The Input Information and Output Information for each Activity need to be standardized as to spelling, capitalization, and grammar.

As a convention of this document, Input and Output Information names are capitalized in the description of an Activity.

4.4.2 External information

External Information sources and destinations are outside the scope of this standard.

External Input Information sources may or may not exist. If an External Input does not exist, the processing listed for it is not required for completion of the Activity. When an External Input does exist, it shall be used.

External Output Information destinations will receive the information sent, if they exist. No assumption about the use of the Output Information by external destinations is made by this standard.

4.4.3 Generic information

In most cases, the Input Information and Output Information designate the specific Information that enters or exits the Activity.

4.4.4 Information vs. documents

This standard prescribes the Activities of the SLC, not the products of that life cycle. Therefore, this standard does not require the creation of specific documents. The information that results from the execution of the Activities is expected to be collected in whatever manner and form are consistent with the selected SLCM and OPAs.

5. Implementation of the standard

This paragraph presents a description of the way in which implementation of this standard is to be approached. The process architect has primary responsibility for creating and maintaining the SLCP. This responsibility is implemented in three steps, as described below.

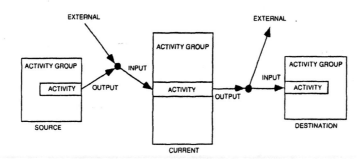

Figure 2 — Information Flow

5.1 Select an SLCM

Initially, the process architect shall identify the SLCM to which the Activities will be mapped. This step encompasses locating, evaluating, selecting, and acquiring an SLCM. It is possible for an organization to have multiple SLCMs; however, only one model is to be selected for a project.

The process architect shall follow the following five steps in order to evaluate and select an SLCM:

    a)   Identify all the SLCMs that are available to the development project;

    b)   Identify the attributes that apply to the desired end system and the development environment;

    c)   Identify any constraints that might be imposed on the selection;

    d)   Evaluate the various SLCMs based on past experience and organizational capabilities; and

    e)   Select the SLCM that will best satisfy the project attributes and constraints.

5.2 Create an SLC

The Activities shall be mapped onto the SLCM. It should be noted, however, that failure to map one or more of the mandatory Activities will result in an SLC and, therefore, an SLCP that are not compliant with this standard. The components of mapping are as follows.

5.2.1 Place the activities in executable sequence

The order in which Activities will be performed will be determined by three major factors:

    a)   The selected SLCM will dictate an initial ordering of Activities. As mapping progresses, the actual order in which Activities will be performed will be established.

    b)   Schedule constraints may require the overlapping of Activities in the SLCM and may thus impact the ordering. In this case, Activities may be mapped for parallel execution rather than for serial execution.

    c)   The ordering of Activities may be impacted by the entry and exit criteria of associated Activities. The availability of Output Information from one Activity could affect the start of another Activity. The second Activity may require, as inputs, one or more of the outputs of the first Activity. For example, no software design of any kind can be done unless some minimum information is available about software requirements. Another example is that no Evaluation Activities can be performed unless there is some output product upon which to work.

5.2.2 Develop and justify a list of activities not used

All "If Applicable" Activities that do not apply to this project shall be identified and explained in the List of Activities Not Used.

5.2.3 Verify the map

The process architect shall ensure that the Activities are fully mapped onto the selected SLCM and that the resulting SLC contains all of the Activities that are necessary to successfully complete a software project.

The process architect shall also verify that the information flow into and out of the Activities will support the relative order into which they have been mapped.

5.3 Establish an SLCP

The preceding steps develop the SLC. As the next step, the available OPAs shall be applied to the SLC Activities, and the known constraints shall be reconciled. The Output Information that is generated by each Activity shall be assigned to the appropriate document(s). The result is the established SLCP.

Chapter 9

Improvement and Training Processes

1. Introduction to Chapter

This chapter describes both the improvement and training processes. Paragraph 2 describes the improvement process, and Paragraph 3 describes the audit process. Portions of this text are paraphrased from IEEE/EIA Standard 12207.0-1996, Paragraphs 7.3 and 7.4. Paragraph 4 provides an overview and introduction to the papers contained in this chapter.

2. Improvement process

The *improvement process* is a process for establishing, assessing, measuring, controlling, and improving a software life cycle process. This process consists of the following activities:

1. Process establishment

2. Process assessment

3. Process improvement.

2.1 Process establishment

The organization establishes a suite of organizational processes for all software life cycle processes as they apply to its business activities. The processes and their application to specific cases are documented in the organization's publications. As appropriate, a process control mechanism should be established to develop, monitor, control, and improve the process(es).

2.2 Process assessment

- A *process assessment procedure* is developed, documented, and applied. Assessment records should be kept and maintained.

- The organization plans and executes review of the processes at appropriate intervals to assure their continuing suitability and effectiveness in light of assessment results.

2.3 Process improvement

- The organization shall effect such improvements to its processes as it determines to be necessary as a result of process assessment and review. Process documentation is updated to reflect improvement in the organizational processes.

- Historical, technical, and evaluation data are collected and analyzed to gain an understanding of the strengths and weaknesses of the employed processes. These analyses are in turn used as feedback to improve these processes, to recommend changes in the direction of the projects (or subsequent projects), and to determine technology advancement needs.

- Quality cost data are collected, maintained, and used to improve the organization's processes as a management activity. These data serve the purpose of establishing the cost of both the prevention and resolution of problems and non-conformity in software products and services.

3. Training Process

The *training process* is a process for providing and maintaining trained personnel. The acquisition, supply, development, operation, or maintenance of software products is largely dependent upon knowledgeable and skilled personnel. For example: developer personnel should have essential training in software management and software engineering. It is, therefore, imperative that personnel training be planned and implemented early so trained personnel are available as the software product is acquired, supplied, developed, operated, or maintained. This process consists of the following activities:

1. Process implementation

2. Training material development

3. Training plan implementation.

3.1 Process implementation

A review of the project requirements is conducted to establish and make timely provisions for acquiring or developing resources and skills required by the management and technical staff. The types and levels of training and categories of personnel requiring training shall be determined. A *training plan*, addressing implementation schedules, resource requirements, and training needs, should be developed and documented.

3.2 Training material development

- Development of training manuals, including presentation materials used in providing training.

3.3 Training plan implementation

- The training plan is implemented to provide training to personnel. Regularly maintain training records.

- Ensure that the necessary mix and categories of appropriately trained personnel are available for planned activities and tasks in a timely manner.

4. Overview of Papers

The first paper in this chapter is authored by Mark Paulk, Bill Curtis, and Mary Beth Chrissis of the Software Engineering Institute (SEI) and Charles Weber of Loral Federal Systems (formerly IBM Federal Systems and now part of Lockheed Martin). This paper is an update of a 1993 article [1] that introduced the SEI's Capability Maturity Model for Software (CMM), Version 1.1, in which its rationale and contents were described. During development of CMM Version 1.1, Weber was a resident affiliate at the SEI.

The CMM, and the process improvement efforts it fostered, represent perhaps the most important real change in the development of large-scale, mission-critical software during the past 20 years. Until the mid-1980s, efforts to improve the quality of software products and the cost and schedule of developing the products focused almost entirely on technology (methods and tools) and personnel (hiring, educating, and training). A third aspect, the process by which software is developed and maintained, was neglected; its recognition as a factor of equal importance to the other two is largely due to the SEI.

The CMM is the result of approximately seven years of work on quantitative methods by which a software developer, or a potential customer of that developer, could determine the maturity of the developer's process. The US Department of Defense (DoD) sponsored the SEI's work; the SEI in turn convinced the DoD that process maturity should be a factor in the selection of contractors to develop software for DoD.

The CMM defines five levels of process maturity through which a software developer must move in order to become truly effective:

1. Initial (ad hoc, chaotic; process not defined and followed)

2. Repeatable (basic software management processes in place, defined and followed at the project level)

3. Defined (standard process defined at organization [company or division] level and tailored for use by projects)

4. Managed (measurements taken and used to improve product quality)

5. Optimizing (measurements used to improve process; error prevention).

The CMM has become a driving force in the US and elsewhere in the world for the improvement of software development processes. Many companies and US government agencies strive to improve their software engineering through the use of the goals and activities associated with this model. At the present time, achievement of Level 3 is the goal of many development organizations, although some have achieved Level 4 and a handful are reported to be operating at Level 5.

The second paper in this chapter discusses training. The author, Paula Shafer, emphasizes that the cost of good training is cheaper than the cost of poor training or lack of training. She points out that it can be costly in staff hours and lost productivity when a company or software development organization attempts to upgrade its process or tools or to move to a different business line without the benefit of training. Poor training or poorly planned training wastes money and time while lowering moral.

To provide a contrast to training, a third paper is included on software engineering education. The paper, authored by the well-known computer scientist David Parnas, addresses a broader topic, "Education for Computer Professionals." Dr. Parnas developed the concept of information hiding and has a large number of other noteworthy achievements [2, 3, 4.]

Parnas believes that present-day computer science education is inadequate. He discusses the fact that computer science graduates are employed to produce useful artifacts, often software systems. Their education must therefore emphasize classical engineering and other fundamentals such as mathematics and science, rather than programming languages and compiler theory (topics of interest when computer science first became an independent discipline) and the research interests of computer science faculty. Computer science graduates do not possess the fundamental knowledge needed to sustain them during their professional careers. The material they learn quickly becomes obsolete. He cites computer system researchers and implementers who would prefer to take graduates in engineering, mathematics, or even history and train them in programming rather than hire computer science graduates.

Based on the above assertions and beliefs, Parnas outlines a curriculum for computing professionals.

He also believes in the value of cooperative education, in which students spend time in industry developing "a real product and getting feedback from interested users."

While Parnas does not propose a course or courses called "Software Engineering" as part of an undergraduate program, many elementary aspects of the material in this *Tutorial* appear in the computing science courses he does recommend. Other topics, such as system engineering, requirements, configuration management, quality assurance, and management topics, are, in Parnas' view, not part of an undergraduate education in computer science.

1. Paulk, Mark C., Bill Curtis, Mary Beth Chrissis, and Charles V. Weber, "Capability Maturity Model, Version 1.1," *IEEE Software*, Vol. 10, No. 4, July 1993, pp. 18-27.

2. Parnas, D. L., and P. C. Clements, "A Rational Design Process: How and Why to Fake It," IEEE Transactions on Software Engineering, Vol. SE-12, No. 2, February 1986, pp. 251-257.

3. Parnas, D. L., "On the Criteria to be Used in Decomposing Systems into Modules," *Communications of the ACM*, Vol. 15, No. 12, December 1972, pp. 1053-1058.

4. Parnas, David L., "Software Aspects of Strategic Defense Systems," *American Scientist*, Vol. 73, September-October 1985, pp. 432-440.

The Capability Maturity Model for Software

Mark C. Paulk

Software Engineering Institute
Carnegie Mellon University
Pittsburgh, PA 15213-3890

Bill Curtis

TeraQuest Metrics, Inc.
P.O. Box 200490
Austin, TX 78720-0490

Mary Beth Chrissis

Software Engineering Institute
Carnegie Mellon University
Pittsburgh, PA 15213-3890

Charles V. Weber

Lockheed Martin Federal Systems Company
6304 Spine Road
Boulder, CO 80301

Abstract

This paper provides an overview of the latest version of the Capability Maturity Model[SM] for Software, CMM[SM] v1.1. CMM v1.1 describes the software engineering and management practices that characterize organizations as they mature their processes for developing and maintaining software. This paper stresses the need for a process maturity framework to prioritize improvement actions, describes the five maturity levels, key process areas, and their common features, and discusses future directions for the CMM.

Keywords: capability maturity model, CMM, software process improvement, process capability, maturity level, key process area, software process assessment, software capability evaluation.

1   Introduction

After decades of unfulfilled promises about productivity and quality gains from applying new software methodologies and technologies, organizations are realizing that their fundamental problem is the inability to manage the software process. In many organizations, projects are often excessively late and over budget, and the benefits of better methods and tools cannot be realized in the maelstrom of an undisciplined, chaotic project.

In November 1986, the Software Engineering Institute (SEI), with assistance from the Mitre Corporation, began developing a process maturity framework that would help organizations improve their software process. In September 1987, the SEI released a brief description of the process maturity framework, which was later expanded in Watts Humphrey's book, *Managing the Software Process* [Humphrey89]. Two methods, software process assessment[1] and software capability evaluation[2] were developed to appraise software process maturity.

After four years of experience with the software

---

[1] A software process assessment is an appraisal by a trained team of software professionals to determine the state of an organization's current software process, to determine the high-priority software process-related issues facing an organization, and to obtain the organizational support for software process improvement.

[2] A software capability evaluation is an appraisal by a trained team of professionals to identify contractors who are qualified to perform the software work or to monitor the state of the software process used on an existing software effort.

process maturity framework, the SEI evolved the maturity framework into the Capability Maturity Model for Software (CMM or SW-CMM[3]). The CMM presents sets of recommended practices in a number of key process areas that have been shown to enhance software process capability. The CMM is based on knowledge acquired from software process assessments and extensive feedback from both industry and government.

The CMM provides software organizations with guidance on how to gain control of their processes for developing and maintaining software and how to evolve toward a culture of software engineering and management excellence. The CMM was designed to guide software organizations in selecting process improvement strategies by determining current process maturity and identifying the most critical issues for software quality and process improvement. By focusing on a limited set of activities and working aggressively to achieve them, an organization can steadily improve its organization-wide software process to enable continuous and lasting gains in software process capability.

The initial release of the CMM, version 1.0, was reviewed and used by the software community during 1991 and 1992. The current version of the CMM, version 1.1, was released in 1993 [Paulk95a] and is the result of extensive feedback from the software community. The CMM has evolved significantly since 1986 [Paulk95b], and the SEI is currently working on version 2.

1.1 Immature Versus Mature Software Organizations

Setting sensible goals for process improvement requires an understanding of the difference between immature and mature software organizations. In an immature software organization, software processes are generally improvised by practitioners and their management during the course of the project. Even if a software process has been specified, it is not rigorously followed or enforced. The immature software organization is reactionary, and managers are usually focused on solving immediate crises (better known as fire fighting). Schedules and budgets are routinely exceeded because they are not based on realistic estimates. When hard deadlines are imposed, product functionality and quality are often compromised to meet the schedule.

In an immature organization, there is no objective basis for judging product quality or for solving product or process problems. Therefore, product quality is difficult to predict. Activities intended to enhance quality such as reviews and testing are often curtailed or eliminated when projects fall behind schedule.

On the other hand, a mature software organization possesses an organization-wide ability for managing software development and maintenance processes. The software process is accurately communicated to both existing staff and new employees, and work activities are carried out according to the planned process. The mandated processes are usable and consistent with the way the work actually gets done. These defined processes are updated when necessary, and improvements are developed through controlled pilot-tests and/or cost benefit analyses. Roles and responsibilities within the defined process are clear throughout the project and across the organization.

In a mature organization, managers monitor the quality of the software products and the process that produced them. There is an objective, quantitative basis for judging product quality and analyzing problems with the product and process. Schedules and budgets are based on historical performance and are realistic; the expected results for cost, schedule, functionality, and quality of the product are usually achieved. In general, a disciplined process is consistently followed because all of the participants understand the value of doing so, and the necessary infrastructure exists to support the process.

1.2 Fundamental Concepts Underlying Process Maturity

A *software process* can be defined as a set of activities, methods, practices, and transformations that people use to develop and maintain software and the associated products (for instance, project plans, design documents, code, test cases, and user manuals). As an organization matures, the software process becomes better defined and more consistently implemented throughout the organization.

Software process capability describes the range of expected results that can be achieved by following a software process. An organization's software process capability is one way of predicting the most likely outcome to expect from the next software project the organization undertakes.

Software process performance represents the actual results achieved by following a software process. Thus, software process performance focuses on

---

[3] A number of CMMs inspired by the CMM for Software have now been developed, including the Systems Engineering CMM [Bate95] and the People CMM [Curtis95]. Additional CMMs are being developed on software acquisition and integrated product development. To minimize confusion, we are starting to use SW-CMM to distinguish the original CMM for Software, but since this paper focuses on software engineering, we will use the CMM acronym.

the results achieved, while software process capability focuses on results expected.

Software process maturity is the extent to which a specific process is explicitly defined, managed, measured, controlled, and effective. Maturity implies a potential for growth in capability and indicates both the richness of an organization's software process and the consistency with which it is applied in projects throughout the organization.

As a software organization gains in software process maturity, it institutionalizes its software process via policies, standards, and organizational structures. Institutionalization entails building an infrastructure and a corporate culture that supports the methods, practices, and procedures of the business so that they endure after those who originally defined them have gone.

2   The Five Levels of Software Process Maturity

Continuous process improvement is based on many small, evolutionary steps rather than revolutionary innovations. The staged structure of the CMM is based on principles of product quality espoused by Walter Shewart, W. Edwards Deming, Joseph Juran, and Philip Crosby. The CMM provides a framework for organizing these evolutionary steps into five maturity levels that lay successive foundations for continuous process improvement. These five maturity levels define an ordinal scale for measuring the maturity of an organization's software process and for evaluating its software process capability. The levels also help an organization prioritize its improvement efforts.

A *maturity level* is a well-defined evolutionary plateau toward achieving a mature software process. Each maturity level comprises a set of process goals that, when satisfied, stabilize an important component of the software process. Achieving each level of the maturity framework establishes a higher level of process capability for the organization.

Organizing the CMM into the five levels shown in Figure 2.1 prioritizes improvement actions for increasing software process maturity. The labeled arrows in Figure 2.1 indicate the type of process capability being institutionalized by the organization at each step of the maturity framework.

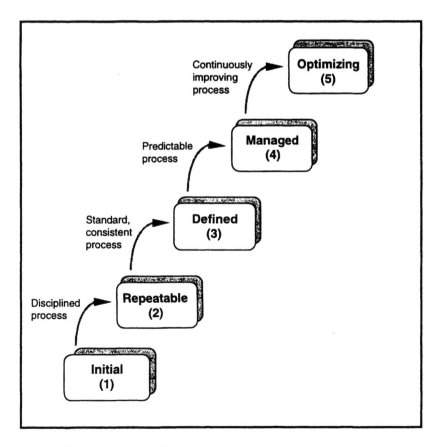

Figure 2.1   *The five levels of software process maturity*

377

The five levels can be briefly described as:

1) Initial The software process is characterized as ad hoc, and occasionally even chaotic. Few processes are defined, and success depends on individual effort and heroics.

2) Repeatable Basic project management processes are established to track cost, schedule, and functionality. The necessary process discipline is in place to repeat earlier successes on projects with similar applications.

3) Defined The software process for both management and engineering activities is documented, standardized, and integrated into a standard software process for the organization. All projects use an approved, tailored version of the organization's standard software process for developing and maintaining software.

4) Managed Detailed measures of the software process and product quality are collected. Both the software process and products are quantitatively understood and controlled.

5) Optimizing Continuous process improvement is enabled by quantitative feedback from the process and from piloting innovative ideas and technologies.

These five levels reflect the fact that the CMM is a model for improving the capability of software organizations. The priorities in the CMM, as expressed by these levels, are not directed at individual projects. A project that is in trouble might well prioritize its problems differently than the taxonomy given by the CMM. Its solutions might be of limited value to the rest of the organization, because other projects might have different problems or because other projects could not take advantage of its solutions if they lack the necessary foundation to implement the solutions. The CMM focuses on processes that are of value across the organization.

2.1 Behavioral Characterization of the Maturity Levels

Maturity Levels 2 through 5 can be characterized through the activities performed by the organization to establish or improve the software process, by activities performed on each project, and by the resulting process capability across projects. A behavioral characterization of Level 1 is included to establish a base of comparison for process improvements at higher maturity levels.

2.1.1 Level 1—The Initial Level

At the Initial Level, the organization typically does not provide a stable environment for developing and maintaining software. Over-commitment is a characteristic of Level 1 organizations, and such organizations frequently have difficulty making commitments that the staff can meet with an orderly engineering process, resulting in a series of crises. During a crisis, projects typically abandon planned procedures and revert to coding and testing. Success depends on having an exceptional manager and a seasoned and effective software team. Occasionally, capable and forceful software managers can withstand the pressures to take shortcuts in the software process; but when they leave the project, their stabilizing influence leaves with them. Even a strong engineering process cannot overcome the instability created by the absence of sound management practices.

In spite of this ad hoc, even chaotic, process, Level 1 organizations frequently develop products that work, even though they may exceed the budget and schedule. Success in Level 1 organizations depends on the competence and heroics of the people in the organization[4] and cannot be repeated unless the same competent individuals are assigned to the next project. Thus, at Level 1, capability is a characteristic of the individuals, not of the organization.

2.1.2 Level 2—The Repeatable Level

At the Repeatable Level, policies for managing a software project and procedures to implement those policies are established. Planning and managing new projects is based on experience with similar projects. Process capability is enhanced by establishing basic process management discipline on a project by project basis. Projects implement effective processes that are defined, documented, practiced, trained, measured, enforced, and able to improve.

Projects in Level 2 organizations have installed basic software management controls. Realistic project commitments are made, based on the results observed on previous projects and on the requirements of the current project. The software managers for a project

---

[4] Selecting, hiring, developing, and retaining competent people are significant issues for organizations at all levels of maturity, but they are largely outside the scope of the CMM.

track software costs, schedules, and functionality; problems in meeting commitments are identified when they arise. Software requirements and the work products developed to satisfy them are baselined, and their integrity is controlled. Software project standards are defined, and the organization ensures they are faithfully followed. The software project works with its subcontractors, if any, to establish an effective customer-supplier relationship.

Processes may differ among projects in a Level 2 organization. The organizational requirement for achieving Level 2 is that there are policies that guide the projects in establishing the appropriate management processes.

The software process capability of Level 2 organizations can be summarized as disciplined because software project planning and tracking are stable and earlier successes can be repeated. The project's process is under the effective control of a project management system, following realistic plans based on the performance of previous projects.

2.1.3   Level 3—The Defined Level

At the Defined Level, a standard process (or processes) for developing and maintaining software is documented and used across the organization. This standard process includes both software engineering and management processes, which are integrated into a coherent whole. This standard process is referred to throughout the CMM as the *organization's standard software process*. Processes established at Level 3 are used (and changed, as appropriate) to help the software managers and technical staff perform more effectively. The organization exploits effective software engineering practices when standardizing its software processes. A group such as a software engineering process group or SEPG is responsible for the organization's software process activities. An organization-wide training program is implemented to ensure that the staff and managers have the knowledge and skills required to fulfill their assigned roles.

Projects tailor the organization's standard software process to develop their own defined software process, which accounts for the unique characteristics of the project. This tailored process is referred to in the CMM as the *project's defined software process*. It is the process used in performing the project's activities. A defined software process contains a coherent, integrated set of well-defined software engineering and management processes. A well-defined process includes readiness criteria, inputs, standards and procedures for performing the work, verification mechanisms (such as peer reviews), outputs, and completion criteria. Because the software process is well defined,

management has good insight into technical progress on the project.

The software process capability of Level 3 organizations can be summarized as standard and consistent because both software engineering and management activities are stable and repeatable. Within established product lines, cost, schedule, and functionality are under control, and software quality is tracked. This process capability is based on a common, organization-wide understanding of the activities, roles, and responsibilities in a defined software process.

2.1.4   Level 4—The Managed Level

At the Managed Level, the organization sets quantitative quality goals for both software products and processes. Productivity and quality are measured for important software process activities across all projects as part of an organizational measurement program. An organization-wide software process database is used to collect and analyze the data available from the projects' defined software processes. Software processes are instrumented with well-defined and consistent measurements. These measurements establish the quantitative foundation for evaluating the projects' software processes and products.

Projects achieve control over their products and processes by narrowing the variation in their process performance to fall within acceptable quantitative boundaries. Meaningful variations in process performance can be distinguished from random variation (noise), particularly within established product lines. The risks involved in moving up the learning curve of a new application domain are known and carefully managed.

The software process capability of Level 4 organizations can be summarized as being quantified and predictable because the process is measured and operates within quantitative limits. This level of process capability allows an organization to predict trends in process and product quality within the quantitative bounds of these limits. Because the process is both stable and measured, when some exceptional circumstance occurs, the "special cause" of the variation can be identified and addressed. When the pre-defined limits are exceeded, actions are taken to understand and correct the situation. Software products are of predictably high quality.

2.1.5   Level 5—The Optimizing Level

At the Optimizing Level, the entire organization is focused on continuous process improvement. The organization has the means to identify weaknesses and strengthen the process proactively, with the goals of preventing defects and improving efficiency. Data on process effectiveness are used to perform cost/benefit analyses of new technologies and proposed changes to the organization's software process. Innovations that exploit the best software engineering practices are identified and transferred throughout the organization.

Software teams in Level 5 organizations analyze defects to determine their causes, evaluate software processes to prevent known types of defects from recurring, and disseminate lessons learned throughout the organization.

There is chronic waste, in the form of rework, in any system simply due to random variation. Organized efforts to remove waste result in changing the system by addressing "common causes" of inefficiency. While efforts to reduce waste occur at all maturity levels, it is the focus of Level 5.

The software process capability of Level 5 organizations can be characterized as continuously improving because Level 5 organizations are continuously striving to improve the range of their process capability, thereby improving the process performance of their projects. Improvements occur both by incremental advancements in the existing process and by innovations using new technologies and methods. Technology and process improvements are planned and managed as ordinary business activities.

2.2   Process Capability and the Prediction of Performance

An organization's software process maturity helps predict a project's ability to meet its goals. Projects in Level 1 organizations experience wide variations in achieving cost, schedule, functionality, and quality targets. Figure 2.2 illustrates the kinds of improvements expected in predictability, control, and effectiveness in the form of a probability density for the likely performance of a particular project with respect to targets, such as cycle time, cost, and quality.

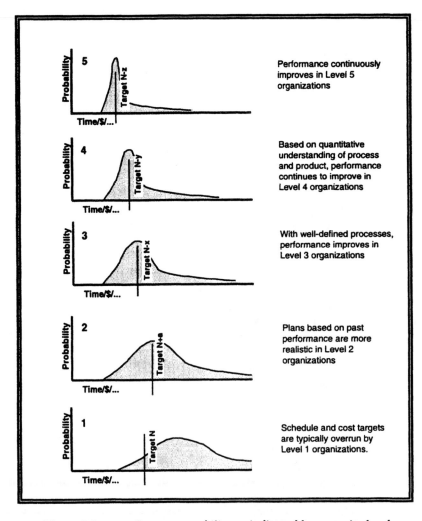

Figure 2.2   Process capability as indicated by maturity level

380

The first improvement expected as an organization matures is in predictability. As maturity increases, the difference between targeted results and actual results decreases across projects. For instance, Level 1 organizations often miss their originally scheduled delivery dates by a wide margin, whereas higher maturity level organizations should be able to meet targeted dates with increased accuracy.

The second improvement is in control. As maturity increases, the variability of actual results around targeted results decreases. For instance, in Level 1 organizations delivery dates for projects of similar size are unpredictable and vary widely. Similar projects in a higher maturity level organization, however, will be delivered within a smaller range.

The third improvement is in effectiveness. Targeted results improve as the maturity of the organization increases. That is, as a software organization matures, costs decrease, development time becomes shorter, and productivity and quality increase. In a Level 1 organization, development time can be quite long because of the amount of rework that must be performed to correct mistakes. In contrast, higher maturity level organizations have increased process effectiveness and reduced costly rework, allowing development time to be shortened.

The improvements in predicting a project's results represented in Figure 2.2 assume that the software project's outcomes become more predictable as noise, often in the form of rework, is removed from the software process. Unprecedented systems complicate the picture since new technologies and applications lower the process capability by increasing variability. Even in the case of unprecedented systems, the management and engineering practices characteristic of more mature organizations help identify and address problems earlier than for less mature organizations. In some cases a mature process means that "failed" projects are identified early in the software life cycle and investment in a lost cause is minimized.

The documented case studies of software process improvement indicate that there are significant improvements in both quality and productivity as a result of the improvement effort [Herbsleb94, Lawlis95, Goldenson95, Hayes95]. The return on investment seems to typically be in the 4:1 to 8:1 range for successful process improvement efforts, with increases in productivity ranging from 9-67 percent and decreases in cycle time ranging from 15-23 percent reported [Herbsleb94].

2.3 Skipping Maturity Levels

Trying to skip maturity levels may be counterproductive because each maturity level in the CMM forms a foundation from which to achieve the next level. The CMM identifies the levels through which an organization should evolve to establish a culture of software engineering excellence. Organizations can institute specific process improvements at any time they choose, even before they are prepared to advance to the level at which the specific practice is recommended. However, organizations should understand that the stability of these improvements is at greater risk since the foundation for their successful institutionalization has not been completed. Processes without the proper foundation fail at the very point they are needed most—under stress.

For instance, a well-defined software process that is characteristic of a Level 3 organization, can be placed at great risk if management makes a poorly planned schedule commitment or fails to control changes to the baselined requirements. Similarly, many organizations have collected the detailed data characteristic of Level 4, only to find that the data were uninterpretable because of inconsistent software processes.

At the same time, it must be recognized that process improvement efforts should focus on the needs of the organization in the context of its business environment, and higher-level practices may address the current needs of an organization or project. For example, when prescribing what steps an organization should take to move from Level 1 to Level 2, one frequent recommendation is to establish a software engineering process group (SEPG), which is an attribute of Level 3 organizations. While an SEPG is not a necessary characteristic of a Level 2 organization, they can be a useful part of the prescription for achieving Level 2.

3 Operational Definition of the Capability Maturity Model

The CMM is a framework representing a path of improvements recommended for software organizations that want to increase their software process capability. The intent is that the CMM is at a sufficient level of abstraction that it does not unduly constrain how the software process is implemented by an organization. The CMM describes what we would normally expect in a software process, regardless of how the process is implemented.

This operational elaboration of the CMM is designed to support the many ways it will be used. There are at least five uses of the CMM that are supported:

- Senior management will use the CMM to understand the activities necessary to launch a software process improvement program in their organization.

- Appraisal method developers will use the CMM to develop CMM-based appraisal methods that meet specific needs.

- Evaluation teams will use the CMM to identify the risks of selecting among different contractors for awarding business and to monitor contracts.

- Assessment teams will use the CMM to identify strengths and weaknesses in the organization.

- Technical staff and process improvement groups, such as an SEPG, will use the CMM as a guide to help them define and improve the software process in their organization.

Because of the diverse uses of the CMM, it must be decomposed in sufficient detail that actual process recommendations can be derived from the structure of the maturity levels. This decomposition also indicates the key processes and their structure that characterize software process maturity and software process capability.

3.1   Internal Structure of the Maturity Levels

Each maturity level, with the exception of Level 1, has been decomposed into constituent parts. The decomposition of each maturity level ranges from abstract summaries of each level down to their operational definition in the key practices, as shown in Figure 3.1. Each maturity level is composed of several key process areas. Each key process area is organized into five sections called common features. The common features specify the key practices that, when collectively addressed, accomplish the goals of the key process area.

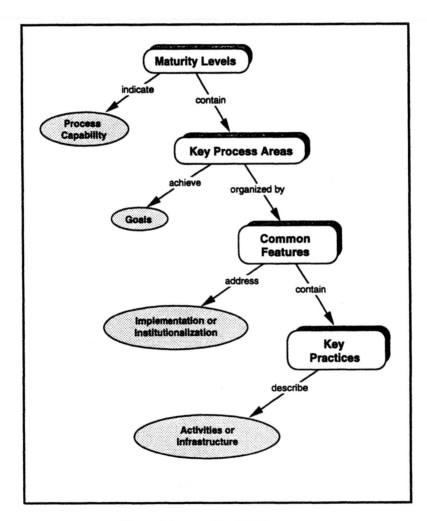

Figure 3.1   *The CMM structure*

3.2 Maturity Levels

A maturity level is a well-defined evolutionary plateau toward achieving a mature software process. Each maturity level indicates a level of process capability, as was illustrated in Figure 2.2. For instance, at Level 2 the process capability of an organization has been elevated from ad hoc to disciplined by establishing sound project management controls.

3.3 Key Process Areas

Except for Level 1, each maturity level is decomposed into several key process areas that indicate where an organization should focus on to improve its software process. Key process areas identify the issues that must be addressed to achieve a maturity level.

Each *key process area* identifies a cluster of related activities that, when performed collectively, achieve a set of goals considered important for enhancing process capability. The key process areas have been defined to reside at a single maturity level as shown in Figure 3.2. The path to achieving the goals of a key process area may differ across projects based on differences in application domains or environments. Nevertheless, all the goals of a key process area must be achieved for the organization to satisfy that key process area.

The adjective "key" implies that there are process areas (and processes) that are not key to achieving a maturity level. The CMM does not describe in detail all the process areas that are involved with developing and maintaining software. Certain process areas have been identified as key determiners of process capability, and these are the ones described in the CMM.

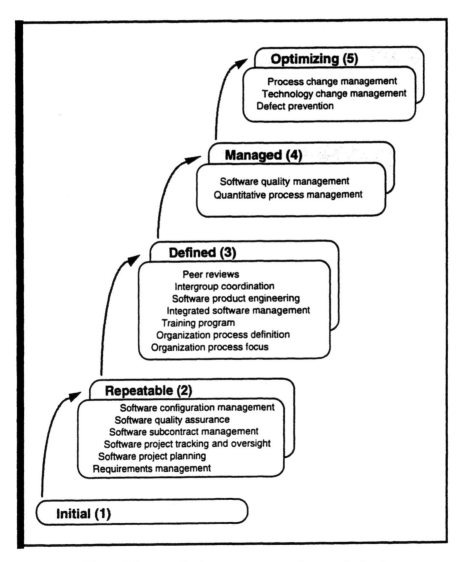

Figure 3.2   *The key process areas by maturity level*

The key process areas are the requirements for achieving a maturity level. To achieve a maturity level, the key process areas for that level and the lower levels must be satisfied (or not applicable, such as Software Subcontract Management when there are no subcontractors).

The specific practices to be executed in each key process area will evolve as the organization achieves higher levels of process maturity. For instance, many of the project estimating capabilities described in the Software Project Planning key process area at Level 2 must evolve to handle the additional project data available at Level 3, as described in Integrated Software Management.

The key process areas at Level 2 focus on the software project's concerns related to establishing basic project management controls.

- **Requirements Management:** establish a common understanding between the customer and the software project of the customer's requirements that will be addressed by the software project. This agreement with the customer is the basis for planning and managing the software project.

- **Software Project Planning:** establish reasonable plans for performing the software engineering and for managing the software project. These plans are the necessary foundation for managing the software project.

- **Software Project Tracking and Oversight:** establish adequate visibility into actual progress so that management can take effective actions when the software project's performance deviates significantly from the software plans.

- **Software Subcontract Management:** select qualified software subcontractors and manage them effectively.

- **Software Quality Assurance:** provide management with appropriate visibility into the process being used by the software project and of the products being built.

- **Software Configuration Management:** establish and maintain the integrity of the products of the software project throughout the project's software life cycle.

The key process areas at Level 3 address both project and organizational issues, as the organization establishes an infrastructure that institutionalizes effective software engineering and management processes across all projects.

- **Organization Process Focus:** establish the organizational responsibility for software process activities that improve the organization's overall software process capability.

- **Organization Process Definition:** develop and maintain a usable set of software process assets that improve process performance across the projects and provides a basis for defining meaningful data for quantitative process management. These assets provide a stable foundation that can be institutionalized via mechanisms such as training.

- **Training Program:** develop the skills and knowledge of individuals so they can perform their roles effectively and efficiently. Training is an organizational responsibility, but the software projects should identify their needed skills and provide the necessary training when the project's needs are unique.

- **Integrated Software Management:** integrate the software engineering and management activities into a coherent, defined software process that is tailored from the organization's standard software process and related process assets. This tailoring is based on the business environment and technical needs of the project.

- **Software Product Engineering:** consistently perform a well-defined engineering process that integrates all the software engineering activities to produce correct, consistent software products effectively and efficiently. Software Product Engineering describes the technical activities of the project, for instance requirements analysis, design, code, and test.

- **Intergroup Coordination:** establish a means for the software engineering group to participate actively with the other engineering groups so the project is better able to satisfy the customer's needs effectively and efficiently.

- **Peer Reviews:** remove defects from the software work products early and efficiently. An important corollary effect is to develop a better understanding of the software work products and of the defects that can be prevented. The peer review is an important and effective engineering method that can be implemented via inspections, structured walkthroughs, or a number of other collegial review methods.

The key process areas at Level 4 focus on establishing a quantitative understanding of both the software process and the software work products being built.

- Quantitative Process Management: control process performance of the software project quantitatively. Software process performance represents the actual results achieved from following a software process. The focus is on identifying special causes of variation within a measurably stable process and correcting, as appropriate, the circumstances that drove the transient variation to occur.

- Software Quality Management: develop a quantitative understanding of the quality of the project's software products and achieve specific quality goals.

The key process areas at Level 5 cover the issues that both the organization and the projects must address to implement continuous and measurable software process improvement.

- Defect Prevention: identify the causes of defects and prevent them from recurring. The software project analyzes defects, identifies their causes, and changes its defined software process.

- Technology Change Management: identify beneficial new technologies (such as tools, methods, and processes) and transfer them into the organization in an orderly manner. The focus of Technology Change Management is on performing innovation efficiently in an ever-changing world.

- Process Change Management: continually improve the software processes used in the organization with the intent of improving software quality, increasing productivity, and decreasing the cycle time for product development.

3.4 Goals and Key Practices

Goals summarize the key practices of a key process area and can be used to determine whether an organization or project has effectively implemented the key process area. The goals signify the scope, boundaries, and intent of each key process area. Satisfaction of a key process area is determined by achievement of the goals.

Key practices describe the activities and infrastructure that contribute most to the effective imple-

mentation and institutionalization of the key process area. Each key practice consists of a single sentence, often followed by a more detailed description, which may include examples and elaboration. These key practices, also referred to as the top-level key practices, state the fundamental policies, procedures, and activities for the key process area. The components of the detailed description are frequently referred to as subpractices. The key practices describe "what" is to be done, but they should not be interpreted as mandating "how" the goals should be achieved. Alternative practices may accomplish the goals of the key process area. The key practices should be interpreted rationally to judge whether the goals of the key process area are effectively, although perhaps differently, achieved.

4 Future Directions of the CMM

Achieving higher levels of software process maturity is incremental and requires a long-term commitment to continuous process improvement. Software organizations may take ten years or more to build the foundation for, and a culture oriented toward, continuous process improvement. Although a decade-long process improvement program is foreign to most U.S. companies, this level of effort is required to produce mature software organizations.

The CMM is not a silver bullet and does not address all of the issues that are important for successful projects. For example, it does not currently address expertise in particular application domains, advocate specific software technologies, or suggest how to select, hire, motivate, and retain competent people. Although these issues are crucial to a project's success, they have not been integrated into the CMM.

The CMM has evolved since 1986 [Paulk95b] and will continue to evolve. Feedback from the use of the CMM in software process assessments, software capability evaluations, and process improvement programs, the continuing evolution of the field of software engineering, and the changing business environment all contribute to the need for a "living CMM." To achieve a reasonable balance between the need for stability by organizations using the CMM in software process improvement and the need for continual improvement, we anticipate a 5-year cycle for major revisions of the CMM. Version 2 of the CMM is planned for the 1997 time frame.

The SEI is also working with the International Standards Organization (ISO) in its efforts to build international standards for software process assessment, improvement, and capability determination [Dorling93, Konrad95]. This effort will integrate concepts from many different process improvement methods. The development of the ISO standards (and the contributions of other methods) will influence CMM v2, even as the SEI's process work will influence the activities of the ISO.

5   Conclusion

The CMM represents a "common sense engineering" approach to software process improvement. The maturity levels, key process areas, common features, and key practices have been extensively discussed and reviewed within the software community. While the CMM is not perfect, it does represent a broad consensus of the software community and is a useful tool for guiding software process improvement efforts.

The CMM provides a conceptual structure for improving the management and development of software products in a disciplined and consistent way. It does not guarantee that software products will be successfully built or that all problems in software engineering will be adequately resolved. However, current reports from CMM-based improvement programs indicate that it can improve the likelihood with which a software organization can achieve its cost, quality, and productivity goals.

The CMM identifies practices for a mature software process and provides examples of the state-of-the-practice (and in some cases, the state-of-the-art), but it is not meant to be either exhaustive or dictatorial. The CMM identifies the characteristics of an effective software process, but the mature organization addresses all issues essential to a successful project, including people and technology, as well as process.

6   References

Bate95   Roger Bate, et al, "A Systems Engineering Capability Maturity Model, Version 1.1," Software Engineering Institute, CMU/SEI-95-MM-003, Nov. 1995.

Dorling93   Alec Dorling, "Software Process Improvement and Capability dEtermination," Software Quality J., Vol. 2, No. 4, Dec. 1993, pp. 209–224.

Curtis95   Bill Curtis, William E. Hefley, and Sally Miller, "People Capability Maturity Model," Software Engineering Institute, CMU/SEI-95-MM-02, Sept. 1995.

Goldenson95   Dennis R. Goldenson and James D. Herbsleb, "After the Appraisal: A Systematic Survey of Process Improvement, Its Benefits, and Factors that Influence Suc

cess," Software Engineering Institute, CMU/SEI-95-TR-009, Aug. 1995.

Hayes95   Will Hayes and Dave Zubrow, "Moving On Up: Data and Experience Doing CMM-Based Process Improvement," Software Engineering Institute, CMU/SEI-95-TR-008, Aug. 1995.

Herbsleb94   James Herbsleb, et al., "Benefits of CMM-Based Software Process Improvement: Initial Results," Software Engineering Institute, CMU/SEI-94-TR-13, Aug. 1994.

Humphrey89   W.S. Humphrey, Managing the Software Process, Addison-Wesley, Reading, Mass., 1989.

Konrad95   Michael D. Konrad, Mark C. Paulk, and Allan W. Graydon, "An Overview of SPICE's Model for Process Management," Proc. 5th Int'l Conf. Software Quality, 1995.

Lawlis95   Patricia K. Lawlis, Robert M. Flowe, and James B. Thordahl, "A Correlational Study of the CMM and Software Development Performance," Crosstalk: The Journal of Defense Software Engineering, Vol. 8, No. 9, Sept. 1995, pp. 21–25.

Paulk95a   Carnegie Mellon University, Software Engineering Institute (Principal Contributors and Editors: Mark C. Paulk, Charles V. Weber, Bill Curtis, and Mary Beth Chrissis), The Capability Maturity Model: Guidelines for Improving the Software Process, Addison-Wesley Publishing Company, Reading, Mass., 1995.

Paulk95b   Mark C. Paulk, "The Evolution of the SEI's Capability Maturity Model for Software," Software Process: Improvement and Practice, Pilot Issue, Spring 1995.

For Further Information

For further information regarding the CMM and its associated products, including training on the CMM and how to perform software process assessments and software capability evaluations, contact:

SEI Customer Relations
Software Engineering Institute
Carnegie Mellon University
Pittsburgh, PA 15213-3890
(412) 268-5800
Internet: customer-relations@sei.cmu.edu

Software Process Improvement

Robin B. Hunter, Ph.D.
University of Strathclyde

1. Introduction

The process approach to the production of quality software on time and within budget is based on the following premise:

> *The quality of a software system is governed by the quality of the process used to develop and maintain it.*

Thus, improvement to the software process will lead to better quality software being produced in a timely manner and at a predictable cost. Process improvement requires process assessment, and process assessment is normally based on an assessment model, a number of which are in existence. One of the first such models to be produced, is known as the capability maturity model for software (SW-CMM), and was developed by the Software Engineering Institute (SEI) in Pittsburgh, Pennsylvania. This model has evolved from its original form in 1987 and has been the inspiration for other software process assessment and improvement models. The generic process assessment standard ISO 9001 has also been used to assess software processes, particularly in the United Kingdom, though also in other parts of the world.

The SW-CMM has not been standardized at either the national or international level. However, to bring together the many approaches to software process assessment and improvement in existence, the SPICE (Software Process Improvement and Capability dEtermination) project was set up to assist in the production of an international standard for software process assessment, capability determination, and software process improvement. This resulted in the production of the emerging standard ISO/IEC TR 15504. In this chapter, the ideas of *software process assessment, capability determination,* and *software process improvement* are introduced. A number of the models used for software process assessment, capability determination, and software process improvement are described, along with related standards such as ISO/IEC 15504, ISO/IEC 12207, and the ISO 9000 series. The benefits of software process improvement, both qualitative and quantitative, are described, and the prospects for convergence between the various assessment and improvement methods are discussed.

2. Objectives

In this chapter you will learn:

- Why many experts believe that management of the software process is the key to developing quality software on time and within budget.

- The relative advantages of process and product approaches to achieving quality in software.

- How the development of the capability maturity model for software at the Software Engineering Institute was the foundation for software process improvement.

- The details of other assessment and improvement models inspired by the SW-CMM.

- The role that ISO 9000 can play in software process assessment and software process improvement.

- How the SPICE project is contributing to an international standard in capability determination and software process improvement.

- What qualitative and quantitative benefits can be derived from software process improvement?

- What current or emerging international standards are relevant to software process improvement?

- How many of the current approaches to software process improvement are converging.

3. Background

3.1 Software Quality

The production of quality software on time and within budget has largely eluded the worldwide software industry for several decades now. Consideration of software development and maintenance as an engineering discipline has helped to alleviate the situation and offers hope for the future. When the term *software engineering* was coined in 1969 [Naur & Randell 1969], it was hailed as identifying an approach to software production that would lead to an engineering type process for developing (and maintaining) software. Since then contributions in this direction have been made, including the following:

- The use of structured analysis and design,

- The introduction of the object-oriented approach to software development, and

- The application of software measurement

While the benefits of the engineering approach have been real and significant, the software "crisis," as it has become known, has refused to go away. Software "disasters" continue to occur and according to Curtis [Curtis 1995] 25 percent of software projects still do not reach fruition, many projects are up to 40 percent over budget, and project schedules are only met about half of the time.

3.2 Process and Product Approaches

The emphasis on the engineering aspects of software development and maintenance can lead to an overemphasis on the use of *methods* and *tools* to produce software products, whereas it is now being realized that *process* and *people issues* also have to be addressed if quality products are to be produced.

The *process* approach to software development and maintenance attempts to model all significant aspects of software development and maintenance. The ultimate aim of this approach is to produce software in a controlled way that will be on time, within budget, and of appropriate quality. The process approach is not so much about using particular methods or tools but more about using a well-defined and controlled process, which may of course be supported by appropriate methods and tools.

According to Humphrey [Humphrey 1989] the software process is defined as "the set of tools, methods and practices we use to produce a software product." An alternative to focusing on the process in order to produce quality software is to focus on the product. This approach involves monitoring the product from early stages of development through industrial use. The product is tested with an emphasis on functional testing, including statistical testing, and measurement of various process outputs are used in order to spot anomalies.

Although the product approach would appear to give a more direct assessment of product quality (rather than inferring it from characteristics of the process) it is generally believed to be of less predictive value than the process approach to achieving software quality. In addition, as we shall see, the process approach has more to offer in terms of controlling the cost of a software project and ensuring adherence to schedule than the product approach.

3.3 Software Process Improvement

3.3.1 Software Process Assessment

At the heart of the process approach to software development and maintenance/evolution is the concept of *software process assessment*, which is concerned with assessing a software process against a process standard or framework. Standards are used in two ways, first as a reference model and second as a gauge of compliance. In the first case, the standard is used internally by an organization to guide its process improvement efforts. In the second situation a standard is used in a normative manner to determine whether or not the organization is in compliance with the standard or not. Frameworks, on the other hand, normally incorporate a number of capability levels of increasing severity, with the framework serving as a road map for long-term improvement efforts. The SW-CMM, for example, has five levels of achievement, each based on increasing capability in key process areas.

3.3.2 Uses of Software Process Assessment

Software process assessment can be used for a number of purposes, the two principal ones being (1) *capability determination*, which is used by software procurers to determine the capability of potential contractors (software producers) and (2) *software process improvement*, which is used by software producers to improve their software processes in line with their business aims.

In addition, the results of process assessments are sometimes used to represent the state of the practice in software development and maintenance, though this should only be done with care, because the sample used for this purpose is rarely representative of the industry as a whole.

3.4 The Need for Software Process Improvement

The need for software process improvement follows from the premise first enunciated by Humphrey [Humphrey 1987]: "The quality of a software system is governed by the quality of the process used to develop and maintain it." From this statement, it follows that investment in the software process will be repaid in terms of increased quality in the software product developed and maintained by the process. Further benefits from process improvement follow from the increased quantitative and qualitative control over the process that can be achieved by high-quality processes.

According to Paulk, Weber, Curtis, and Chrissis [Paulk et al. 1995] the control, predictability, and effectiveness of software processes all increase as processes are improved. The ultimate test of whether software process improvement is a worthwhile endeavor rests on *return on investment* (ROI) arguments. ROI arguments compare the costs involved with process improvement with the financial benefits that ensue from improved processes. ROI arguments are considered later in Section 6.3.

4. Models for Software Process Improvement

During the last decade or so a large number of models for software process assessment and improvement have been developed. The best known of these is the SW-CMM, which first appeared in 1987 and is described in Section 4.1. Other models derived from the SW-CMM are described in Section 4.2, and Section 4.3 describes a complementary approach to software process assessment based on the application of ISO 9000 to the production and maintenance of software. Finally, Section 4.4 describes the activities of the SPICE project in developing an international standard for capability determination and software process improvement.

4.1 The Capability Maturity Model for Software

By far the best-known model for software process improvement, based on software process assessment, is the SW-CMM. In this section, its development is traced and some experiences gained through its use are described.

The SW-CMM has a history going back about 15 years and has evolved from a relatively simple model to a more complex one capable of providing a rich characterization of the current state of a software process.

The first public version of SW-CMM, known then as the software process maturity framework, was developed in 1987. It was based on two sets of questionnaires, a maturity questionnaire and a technology questionnaire. The maturity questionnaire was concerned with the maturity of the software process (principally how well it was defined and managed), whereas the technology questionnaire was concerned with the extent to which advanced technology was used in the process. The result of a process assessment depended on the answers to the questions in both sets of questionnaires, and was two dimensional, with low-maturity, low-technology processes being represented on the bottom left of a two-dimensional grid and high-maturity, high-technology processes on the top right of the grid. It was also suggested that an organization might progress from the bottom left position of the grid to the top right position of the grid in a period of around 4 years, though this rate of progress would now be considered rather ambitious.

As far as the route that an organization might take to go from the bottom left to the top right of the grid was concerned, it was strongly suggested that priority should be given to getting the process to mature in the first instance, followed by increasing the level of technology to support the mature aspects of the process. At the time, this was seen as radical thinking in a context where many software producers were trying to "buy their way out of trouble" by investing in the latest technology.

4.1.1 Development of the SW-CMM

Later versions of the SW-CMM were one (rather than two) dimensional, the emphasis now being on *maturity* rather than use of advanced *technology*. However, the original two-dimensional framework is still reflected in the diagonal layout of the five capability levels defined in the SW-CMM, as shown in Figure 1.

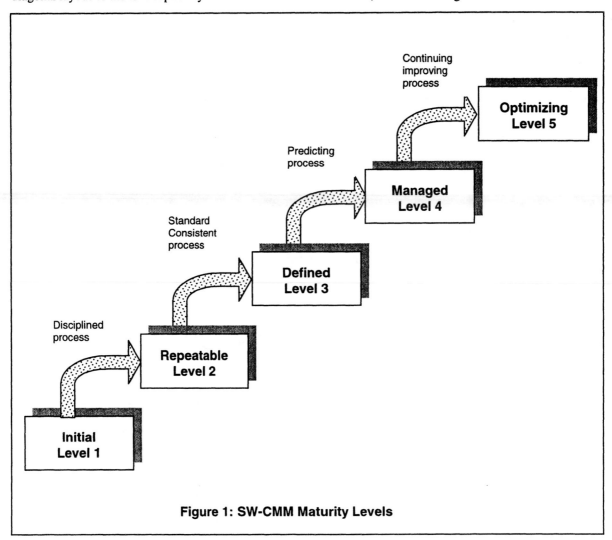

Figure 1: SW-CMM Maturity Levels

The following description of the five levels of the SW-CMM appear on the SEI Web pages (http://www.sei.cmu.edu):

1. *Initial.* The software process is characterized as ad hoc, and occasionally even chaotic. Few processes are defined, and success depends on individual effort and heroics.

2. *Repeatable.* Basic project management processes are established to track cost, schedule, and functionality. The necessary process discipline is in place to repeat earlier successes on projects with similar applications.

3. *Defined.* The software process for both management and engineering activities is documented, standardized, and integrated into a standard software process for the organization. All projects use an

approved, tailored version of the organization's standard software process for developing and maintaining software.

4. *Managed.* Detailed measures of the software process and product quality are collected. Both the software process and products are quantitatively understood and controlled.

5. *Optimizing.* Continuous process improvement is enabled by quantitative feedback from the process and from piloting innovative ideas and technologies.

Figure 2 shows the detailed structure of Version 1.1 of the SW-CMM. All software processes are at Level 1 at least, by default. In general, any process at level n ($1 \leq n \leq 4$) is deemed to be at level n+1 if certain *key process areas* satisfy their *goals* (defined by the model). For example, whether a Level 1 process is a Level 2 process depends on assessing whether the process is *disciplined*, which in turn depends on assessing whether the goals of the following key process areas have been satisfied:

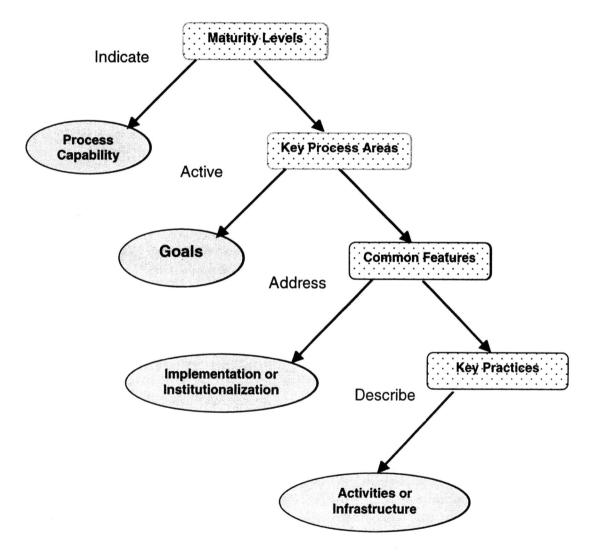

Figure 2: Structure of SW-CMM

- Requirements management,

- Software project planning,

- Software project tracking and oversight,

- Software subcontract management,

- Software quality assurance, and

- Software configuration management

As an example, here is one of the goals of *requirements management*: Software plans, products, and activities are kept consistent with the system requirements allocated to software.

The key process areas corresponding to the various transitions between adjacent levels are given in Table 1. The key process areas are further refined into *key practices* capable of direct observation and measurement. The refinement is performed using five *common features*, namely: (1) commitment to perform, (2) ability to perform, (3) activities performed, (4) measurement and analysis, and (5) verification of implementation.

Each *common feature* (CF) applied to a *key process area* (KPA) produces one or more *key practices* (KPs). In a more mathematical notation this might be written

$$CF(KPA) \Rightarrow KPs.$$

As an example,

The ability to perform (Software subcontract management)

produces

Periodic technical reviews and interchanges are held with the software subcontractor

as well as several other key practices.

Table 1: Key Process Areas

Level 1–Level 2: disciplined process	Requirements management Software project planning Software project tracking and oversight Software subcontract management Software quality assurance Software configuration management
Level 2–Level 3: standard consistent process	Organization process focus Organization process definition Training program Integrated software management Software product engineering Intergroup coordination Peer reviews
Level 3–Level 4: predictable process	Quantitative process management Software quality management
Level 4–Level 5: continuously improving process	Defect prevention Technology change management Process change management

4.1.2 Using the SW-CMM

Considerable experience has been gained, especially within the United States, in using the SW-CMM, and this experience has had considerable influence over the various revisions to the model, especially the creation of Version 1.1. One of the best sources of advice on how to use the SW-CMM and what to expect from it remains Humphrey's original book [Humphrey 1989]. Assessments can be performed using internal or external resources. The SEI trains and licenses individuals and organizations to conduct assessments. Some larger organizations have chosen to have individuals trained by the SEI, whereas others contract with licensed contractors. The SEI Web site maintains a list of licensed assessors. Note that the SEI itself does not "certify" assessments. It only trains and licenses the individuals and the organizations who conduct the assessments.

4.1.3 Humphrey's Principles

In his book *Managing the Software Process*, Humphrey [Humphrey 1989] lists six basic principles of software process change:

1. Major changes to the software process must start at the top. Senior management leadership is required.

2. Ultimately everyone must be involved. Software engineering is a team effort.

3. Effective change requires a goal and a knowledge of the current process. To use a map, you must know where you are.

4. Change is continuous. Software process improvement involves continual learning and growth.

5. Software process changes will not be retained without conscious effort and periodic reinforcement.

6. Software process improvement requires investment. It takes time, skill, and money to improve the software process. Each of these principles is expanded in the sections of Humphrey's book, which follow the statement of these principles.

4.1.4 Experience in Use

Many papers have been published describing successful (and occasionally less successful) use of the SW-CMM [Paulish & Carleton 1994, Grady 1996, Lowe& Cox 1996]. In particular, these authors point out the requirements for software process improvement and some of the benefits of SPI.

The principal requirements for successful software process improvement (SPI) would appear to be as follows:

- Engineers need to be convinced of the need for a standard process.

- Appropriate training is essential.

- A clearly defined improvement model is required.

- Fault and failure analysis is important.

The principal benefits identified were

- Increased ability to respond to change,

- Possible reduction of times spent on the investigation phase of a project, and

- Higher maturity levels, which lead to accelerated spread of proven best practices across an organization.

4.2 Other Models Inspired by the SW-CMM

The SW-CMM was the first *staged* model used for process assessment, where the term *staged* refers to the discrete levels inherent in the model. In due course, other staged models appeared mainly for use in particular industries, in particular regions of the world, or for particular types of software. BOOTSTRAP [Kuvaja & Bicego

1994], which started off as an ESPRIT project, was designed particularly for use in Europe, whereas TRILLIUM [Coallier 1995], designed in Canada, was intended for use in the telecom industry.

In parallel with these developments, Humphrey developed two new models, clearly inspired by the SW-CMM but serving slightly different purposes, the personal software process (PSP), which, according to Humphrey [Humphrey 1995] was "a self-improvement process designed to help you control, manage, and improve the way you work" and the team software process (TSP), which was designed to perform a similar role for teams of software developers as the PSP performs for individuals. These models are briefly described in the sections that follow.

4.2.1 BOOTSTRAP

The BOOTSTRAP model [Kuvaja & Bicego 1994] was originally developed as a European ESPRIT project. BOOTSTRAP is clearly based on the SW-CMM, with additional features added, in order to adapt it to the European environment. These features included aspects of the ISO 9001 approach to process assessment (see Section 4.3) and of the European Space Agency's process model standard (PSS-05).

The phases of a BOOTSTRAP assessment are similar to those of a SW-CMM assessment: (1) preparation, (2) assessment, and (3) action plan derivation.

Since the end of the ESPRIT project, which originally developed it, the BOOTSTRAP model has been in the care of the BOOTSTRAP Institute, an independent body set up by the BOOTSTRAP partners. The model is under continual development and has now been brought in line with ISO/IEC 12207 (*Software Life Cycle Processes*) and ISO/IEC 15504 (see Section 4.4).

4.2.2 TRILLIUM

TRILLIUM [Coallier 1995] was developed around 1991 through a partnership among Bell Canada, Northern Telecom, and Bell Northern Research. It was clearly inspired by the SEI's SW-CMM and can be used as a customer-focused benchmark for one of two purposes: (1) assessment of a supplier's development process or (2) internal process improvement.

TRILLIUM (unlike the SW-CMM) has a clear product focus, where the product is defined to be the software that is delivered to the customer including, in the case of embedded software, the system of which the software is a part. TRILLIUM emphasizes *road maps* that lead from one level to another, as distinct from the *key process areas* emphasized in the SW-CMM.

4.2.3 PSP/TSP

Humphrey's major contributions since his development of the SW-CMM at the SEI have been (1) the personal software process (PSP) and (2) the team software process (TSP).

The PSP is described in Humphrey's 1995 book, *A Discipline for Software Engineering*. The purpose of the PSP is to improve the effectiveness of software engineers by encouraging them to plan, track, and measure their personal performance as part of the software process.

According to Humphrey, the basic steps taken by the PSP are as follows:

1. Identify those large-system software methods and practices that can be used by individuals.

2. Define the subset of these methods and practices that can be applied while developing small programs.

3. Structure these methods and practices so they can be gradually introduced.

4. Provide exercises suitable for practicing these methods in an educational setting.

The PSP has a framework similar to the SW-CMM. Clearly some of the key process areas of the SW-CMM such as software project planning, peer reviews, and defect prevention may reasonably be addressed by the PSP while others, such as software quality assurance and software subcontract management, may not.

Humphrey suggests that the ideas inherent in the PSP may be sufficient to build programs up to 10K lines of code (LOC), but not larger. For larger programs, the TSP may be used to supplement the PSP.

The TSP [Humphrey 1999a] builds on PSP training and focuses on structured weekly team meetings including a 3-day meeting at the start of each new project and 2-day relaunch meetings at the start of each project milestone. The initial meeting for each project is used to (1) develop team-working practices, (2) establish goals, (3) select roles, (4) define processes, and (5) make plans.

TSP provides forms, scripts, and standards that lead the PSP trained team through the process steps.

4.2.4 CMM Integration

The SW-CMM, originally just the CMM, has inspired other CMMs to be developed at the SEI including people CMM, systems engineering CMM, software acquisition CMM, and integrated product management CMM, each of which is used for a distinct, but complementary, purpose to the SW-CMM. Further information on each of the above CMMs can be obtained from the SEI web site (http://www.sei.cmu.edu).

Around 1997 it was decided that the SW-CMM, currently in Version 1.1, was due for major revision and a project was set up at the SEI to produce Version 2 of the SW-CMM by around 1999. It was also envisioned that a further version of SW-CMM (2.1), a relatively minor revision of Version 2, would appear about 2 years later. Extensive industrial consultation took place over the form of Version 2 of SW-CMM, but Version 2 was never released. Instead, the SEI launched a new project to integrate three of the key CMMs that had been developed, namely, SW-CMM (CMM for software), SE-CMM (systems engineering CMM), and IPD-CMM (integrated product development CMM). The new project was titled *CMM integration* or *CMMI* and further information concerning it can be found at the CMMI Web site (http://www.sei.cmu.edu/cmm/cmms/cmms.integration.html).

The reasons for not proceeding with Version 2 of the SW-CMM have been explained by Schaeffer [Schaeffer 1998]. According to Schaeffer, they resulted from acquisition reform within the Department of Defense (DoD) creating a significant paradigm shift from a "how to" mentality approach to an approach based on statements of objectives and performance based requirements. This and the clear commonality between the SW-CMM, the SE-CMM, and the IPD-CMM in terms of configuration, quality, and requirements management, led to the abandonment of SW-CMM Version 2 and the creation of the CMMI project.

4.3 ISO 9001 and TickIT

An approach toward software process quality that is quite distinct from the SW-CMM approach, and developed independently from it, is the use the ISO 9000 series of standards, a series of generic process standards that can be applied to a wide range of service and manufacturing industries. The current version of the ISO 9000 series, ISO 9000:2000, has a number of principal components:

- ISO 9000 Quality Management Systems—Fundamentals and Vocabulary,

- ISO 9001 Quality Management Systems—Requirements,

- ISO9004 Quality Management Systems—Guidelines for Performance Improvements, and

- ISO 19011: Guidelines on Quality and/or Environmental Management Systems Auditing.

4.3.1 Basic Ideas

The use of the ISO 9000 series (also known as BS 5750 and EN 29000) was basically a British initiative based on the original version of ISO 9000. The United Kingdom scheme, which was launched in 1989, was known as TickIT. (A *tick* is a check in the United States. Therefore, TickIT would be CheckIT in American!).

One of the issues involved in the use of TickIT was the extent to which software products and the processes used to develop and maintain them are similar to other manufactured products. Earlier studies commissioned by the U.K. government found that (1) it was appropriate to apply ISO 9000 to software (the Logica report [Logica 1988]) and (2) the anticipated costs and benefits of applying ISO 9000 to software suggested that it was cost effective to do so (the Price Waterhouse report [Price Waterhouse 1988]).

The part of the original ISO 9000 series considered most appropriate for application to software was ISO 9001 (equivalent to BS 5750 part 1, which preceded it, and EN 29001, the European version of the standard) and a guide to the application of ISO 9001 to software entitled *Guidelines for the Application of ISO 9001 to the Development Supply and Maintenance of Software* was produced. This guide is known as ISO 9000-3.

TickIT is supported by a guide subtitled *Making a Better Job of Software*, now in its fourth edition and recently updated to bring it into line with the 1997 revision of ISO 9000-3 and the 1995 edition of the standard ISO/IEC 12207 on software life cycle processes. The guide defines the scope of TickIT and describes the organization behind it. It provides guidance for software customers and software suppliers as well as for auditors. It also contains listings of other relevant standards and relevant reading as well as guidance to relevant standards information on the web. Information concerning the guide is available at the TickIT Web site (http://www.tickit.org). Information concerning other support material for TickIT including a video, details of case studies, and a quarterly international journal entitled *TickIT International*, are also available at the Web site.

The TickIT scheme certifies software organizations for compliance with ISO 9001. The bulk of TickIT certifications have taken place in the United Kingdom. In June 1998, 70 percent of the 1,486 active certificates were held in the United Kingdom. However, at that time only half of the certificates being granted were in the United Kingdom, suggesting a gradual spread of TickIT toward other countries. Approximately 10 percent of certificates are held in North America (United States and Canada), and the European countries where TickIT has made the most impact are Ireland and Sweden. Elsewhere in the world TickIT has made the largest impact in India, South Korea, and Japan. Overall, the number of TickIT certificates held has grown steadily during the last few years from just over 600 in 1994 to nearly 1,500 in 1998.

A list is maintained (accessible over the Internet) of bodies able to award TickIT certificates, all of which have been approved for the purpose by UKAS (United Kingdom Accreditation Service). UKAS lays down detailed criteria to which certification bodies should conform in the areas of impartiality, confidentiality, competence, maintenance of records, and appeal procedures.

Although TickIT has clearly had its greatest impact in the United Kingdom, there is no doubt that it has also had considerable influence worldwide.

4.3.2 Experience in Use

A number of studies have been made of ISO 9001 applied to software. One of these [Stelzer et al. 1998] entitled *Benefits and Prerequisites of ISO 9000 Based Software Quality Management*, presents a study of the experiences of 12 European software organizations who have sought ISO 9001 certification. In particular, it summarizes the benefits of seeking such certification, and the prerequisites for seeking certification, as seen by the 12 organizations.

The *benefits* are much as would be expected under the circumstances:

- Improved project management,

- Improved productivity,

- Improved customer satisfaction,

- Improved product quality, and so on.

In 26 percent of cases, a positive return on investment was also indicated.

The two top prerequisites, *management commitment and support* and *staff involvement*, were also fairly predictable. However, the next two prerequisites, *providing enhanced understanding* (acquiring and transferring knowledge of current practices) and *tailoring improvement initiatives* (adapting quality management practices to the specific strengths and weaknesses of different teams and departments) are perhaps less obvious.

In another paper entitled *How ISO 9001 Compares with the CMM* [Paulk 1995], the use of ISO 9001 for software is compared to the SW-CMM. The paper answers these two questions:

1. At what level in the SW-CMM would an ISO 9001-compliant organization be?

2. Can a SW-CMM Level 2 (or 3) organization be considered compliant with ISO 9001?

The SW-CMM and ISO 9001/TickIT differ from each other in a number of ways. One difference is seen in their scopes. For example, certain aspects of ISO 9001 are not addressed at all by the SW-CMM. However, a mapping can be made from the ISO 9001 requirements onto the key process areas at each level of the SW-CMM and from this a reasonable level of equivalence can be established. This mapping suggests that an organization that is ISO 9001 compliant for software would be at least equivalent to one gaining somewhere between levels 2 and 3 of the SW-CMM. However, it is possible for a SW-CMM Level 1 organization to satisfy the requirements of ISO 9001.

Another difference between the SW-CMM and TickIT in practice is in the frequency and cost of repeat (formal) assessments (called *surveillance audits* in ISO terminology). TickIT certificates last for 3 years, and brief unannounced surveillance visits take place two or three times per year during this period. The SEI does not specify a time period after which assessment results are invalid, although 2 years is a commonly accepted time period in the industry.

Finally, the cost of performing a CMM assessment for an organization of between 100 and 300 software engineers can be in the range of $100,000 to $300,000 when the total cost of the assessment is included [Christensen 2000]. These costs include the following:

- Employee training (needed to ensure that the employees use terminology in a manner consistent with the assessment team; this does not include training in the processes themselves),

- Payment to the assessment contractor, and

- Employee time during the assessment itself.

For smaller organizations, the costs can be lower, although they would not typically decrease in a linear manner.

Internal assessments can, of course, be conducted on a much more economic basis and, in practice, for many organizations this is all that is needed. Finally, always keep in mind that an ISO 9001 certification is binary (certification is either awarded or it is not), whereas the SW-CMM model is staged. As a result, SW-CMM assessments can be used to motivate and document continuous process improvement explicitly.

4.4 SPICE/ISO/IEC 15504

The plethora of models and standards for software process assessment and improvement led to an international initiative to create an international standard in the area. The project associated with this initiative is known as the *SPICE project*. Descriptions of the early work on SPICE and some of the work that led up to it can be found in Dorling [Dorling & Simms 1991] and El Emam et al. [El Emam et al. 1998].

4.4.1 Development of the Standard

As an international standardization project, SPICE is unique in two ways:

1. During its development, the standard is being subjected to extensive trials (or "pilot tested" in U.S. terminology) throughout the world (the SPICE trials).

2. It is using a fast-track route to standardization via a series of technical reports.

The SPICE trials have a number of objectives including these:

- To promote process improvement in general and the SPICE approach to process improvement in particular.

- To identify weaknesses in the early versions of the SPICE model and their associated documentation.

- To ensure the applicability of the emerging standard throughout the world and throughout a wide range of industries and product type.

The normal route to ISO/IEC standardization goes through the following stages:

- New work item,

- Working draft,

- Committee draft,

- Draft international standard, and, finally,

- International standard.

The technical report route, however, has different stages after the working draft stage: proposed draft technical report, then a draft technical report, and finally a technical report.

The technical report route is sometimes used by a standards working group when it is not sure that the degree of consensus required for an international standard is present. The set of documents produced by the working group is known as a *technical report type 2* or a *TR-2* and is expected to be replaced by a full international standard within 2 years of its publication. The standard being produced by the SPICE project is currently at the TR-2 stage and is known as ISO/IEC TR 15504:1998.

To manage the SPICE project, a regional structure was adopted and technical centers were set up for four (later five) regions of the world, initially, the United States; Canada and Latin America; Europe and Africa; and the Asia Pacific region. Later the Asia Pacific region was split into two parts: Northern Asia Pacific (mainly Japan and Korea) and Southern Asia Pacific (centered on Australia). More details about the development of the 15504 standard can be found in El Emam et al. [El Emam et al. 1998].

4.4.2 Comparison of ISO/IEC TR 15504 and SW-CMM

A number of significant differences exist between ISO/IEC 15504 and the SW-CMM, the principal one being that 15504 is a *continuous model*, whereas the SW-CMM is a *staged model*. The difference between the two is that in 15504 (a continuous model) each of the 40 processes is assessed at each of the capability levels, whereas in the SW-CMM (a staged model) only the relevant key process areas are assessed at each level. Thus, while the 15504 *capability levels* measure process capability, the SW-CMM *maturity levels* are a measure of organization maturity. Paulk, Konrad, and Garcia [Paulk, Konrad, &Garcia 1995] discuss the differences in the two architectures in more detail.

Clearly, the amount of data produced by a 15504 assessment will tend to be greater than for a SW-CMM assessment because, potentially, each process is assessed at each level in a 15504 assessment, whereas in a SW-CMM assessment only processes within the key process area are assessed at each level.

Another important difference between 15504 and the SW-CMM is that SPICE uses a four-valued logic for measurement, each process attribute having one of the values *fully, largely, partially*, or *not* present. In the SW-CMM, on the other hand a two-valued logic is used, each key process area being *fully* or *not* implemented, although some assessors will indicate partial implementation if a significant number of the practices of a KPA are implemented by the organization. Handling the results of a process assessment (whether based on 15504 or SW-CMM) is a nontrivial task and one that can certainly benefit from tool support [Hunter et al. 1997].

5. Capability Determination

Although the main theme of this chapter is software process improvement, another application of software process assessment should be borne in mind, namely, *capability determination*. In fact, the SW-CMM was originally developed for procurement purposes by the DoD and capability determination was the main aim of the model at this stage rather than process improvement. Part 8 of ISO/IEC TR 15504 defines process capability determination as

A systematic assessment and analysis of selected software processes within an organization, carried out with the aim of identifying the strengths, weaknesses and risks associated with deploying the processes to meet a particular specified requirement.

Capability determination is normally carried out in connection with a procurement-related decision. A software procurer may be interested in assessing the risk of placing a contract with a particular software supplier, or a contractor may be interested in assessing its own capability before deciding whether to bid for a particular contract.

A software procurer may specify a target capability for potential contractors and may identify areas in which a contractor's capability falls short of the target capability as areas of risk for the proposed project. The process-oriented risks identified would then be considered as part of the overall risks involved in completing the project on time and within budget. In some cases, the procurer may take into consideration the current capability of a potential contractor and its current process improvement plans in order to identify the risk in placing a contract with that contractor.

The topic of software acquisition has led to the production of the software acquisition CMM (SA-CMM) through collaboration between the DoD, federal agencies, and the SEI. Despite the existence and growing experience of the SW-CMM, the immaturity of the procurement process itself has, in many cases, limited the effectiveness of the procurement function. The SA-CMM [Kind & Ferguson 1997] has five levels similar to those of the SW-CMM ranging from Level 1 (competent people and heroics) to Level 4 (quantitative management) and Level 5 (continuous process improvement). The SA-CMM builds on the experiences and success of the SW-CMM and is applicable to large and small procurements, and for both large and small projects

In 1997, Volume 10, issue 3, of *Crosstalk, The Journal of Defense Software Engineering*, was devoted to software acquisition management, emphasizing that this is a live topic and not an issue that has been completely solved through the existence of the SW-CMM.

6. Software Process Improvement

Part 7 of ISO/IEC TR 15504 defines the eight steps of software process improvement as follows:

1. Examine an organization's needs.

2. Initiate process improvement.

3. Prepare and conduct process assessment.

4. Analyze results and prepare action plan.

5. Implement improvements.

6. Confirm improvements.

7. Sustain improvement gains.

8. Monitor performance.

Once all eight steps have been executed, the organization should start again at step 2 and so on.

The SPIRE Handbook [Sanders 1998] was produced by a European research project and provides sound advice for organizations involved in process improvement based on the preceding eight steps. The handbook aims to "help management and staff in small software development organizations to improve their businesses by systematic software process improvement," though this is not to say that much of the advice given is not equally applicable to large or medium-sized organizations.

Expanding on the eight steps, the handbook emphasizes these aspects of the process:

- To be effective, a process improvement initiative should be conducted as a project in its own right.

- An external "mentor" should be used where appropriate.

- Planning an assessment includes defining the purpose, scope, constraints, resources, and timescale for the formal process assessment.

- Prioritizing processes for improvement is a necessary, but not trivial, task.

- Experimenting with improvements on a pilot project may be useful.

- When the process improvement plan has been completed, it is necessary to check whether the anticipated benefits have been realized.

- Systematic data collection and analysis should be used to ensure that process improvements are sustained.

Under the heading of "Managing Process Improvement," the handbook describes how the eight steps might be executed for a typical software process improvement project.

Many cultural and interpersonal issues arise in the context of software process improvement [Jansen & Sanders 1998]. These include the following:

- The need for leadership and support from all levels of management;

- The effect of software process improvement on staff values, attitudes, and behavior;

- The need to motivate staff in order to ensure that process improvement goals are achieved;

- The need for effective communication and teamwork among those involved in process improvement; and

- Identification of the role of education and training for effective process improvement.

Not all software process improvement plans are successful; some may even have a totally negative effect. To maximize the chances of a successful outcome of a software process improvement project, it is important to plan well, allocate sufficient and appropriate resources, and build on the experiences described in the literature. As we will see in the next section, the benefits of a successful software process improvement project are significant and, in the right circumstances, even substantial.

6.1 Benefits of Software Process Improvement

The practice of SPI in the first instance was based on intuition and experience rather than on sound empirical evidence. However, now that considerable amounts of data concerning the effects of SPI have been collected, we can deduce many positive benefits that arise from using SPI. The benefits fall into two categories: qualitative benefits and quantitative benefits.

The following organizations systematically collect software process assessment data from which the benefits of software process improvement can be deduced:

- SEI (http://www.sei.cmu.edu),

- European Software Institute, from process improvement experiments conducted under the European Systems and Software Initiative (http://www.esi.es), and

- The SPICE project, from its trials activities (http://www.sqi.gu.edu.au/spice/).

6.2 Qualitative Benefits

Among others, the organization responsible for the space shuttle software (originally part of IBM Federal Systems but now owned by the Lockheed Martin Corporation) has reported that extremely favorable results were obtained through software process improvement. Billings et al. [Billings et al. 1994] describe experiences with SPI over many years. They also confirm, from their own experiences, the importance of many widely acknowledged prerequisites for producing good software such as attention to requirements, good customer relations, and collection of fault data.

An SEI report [Herbsleb & Goldenson 1996] follows up SEI assessments that were performed between 1 and 3 years after the original assessment. The survey performed supported the view that successful SPI led to the following:

- Increased product quality,

- Increased productivity,

- Increased staff morale,

- Increased customer satisfaction, and

- Increased ability to meet budget.

In addition, 74 percent of those questioned agreed that the SW-CMM assessment was worth the money and effort expended on it.

The SEI study was also used to identify the prerequisites for successful SPI. These included (perhaps not surprisingly) having clear, well-understood goals and having minimal organizational politics.

Results of phases 1 and 2 of the SPICE trials have been published [SPICE 1996,SPICE 1998] and tend to show general support for the effectiveness of software process improvement and for testing of the various versions of the SPICE model involved and their associated documentation. Other SPICE studies [Simon et al. 1997] on the reliability of process assessments, based on inter-rater agreements, have produced generally positive results.

6.3 Quantitative Benefits

Quantitative benefits of SPI are more difficult to show. In this section, we discuss how economic arguments can be made in favor of software process improvement. Readers will also find two articles by Watts Humphrey [Humphrey 1999b,Humphrey 2000] relevant to this issue.

The costs of SPI are not too hard to itemize and include the following:

- Costs of staff training,

- Costs of regular process assessments,

- Cost of staff responsible for the process,

- Costs of data collection for process monitoring, and

- Costs of assessments.

According to a SEI guideline, these costs should amount to between 3 and 5 percent of software development costs [Krasner 1994]. Clearly, the lower these costs are kept, the greater the opportunity there is for recouping them from the benefits of software process improvement.

The financial benefits of software process improvement initiatives are harder to measure and predict than the costs. Some of the benefits are more qualitative than quantitative and can only be estimated from appropriate indicators. For example, increased staff morale can be indicated by lower staff turnover, and the consequent savings measured in terms of lower staff training costs and avoidance of additional project costs following from lack of staff continuity. In a similar way, increased customer satisfaction can be inferred from increased repeat orders, and quantified in terms of the value of these orders.

Increased maturity of the process should lead to fewer faults appearing in the software due to human error and, hence, reduced rework. This is just one of the reasons why productivity should increase as the software process is improved. It is interesting to note that COCOMO II (http://sunset.usc.edu/COCOMOII/cocomo.html) includes a process maturity factor to evaluate the effort required to complete a software project. Applying this model to moderately sized efforts (100K LOC) produces an 8 percent decrease in predicted software development costs for a one-step increase in process maturity. Clark [Clark 2000] reports that a one-step increase in maturity results in a 15 to 21 percent decrease in total project cost.

We can see, therefore, that over a period of time it is possible, based on some reasonable assumptions, to measure the effects of software process improvement, and to estimate the return on investment over the period.

A number of detailed case studies on the return on investment from SPI have been conducted and are described by Krasner [Krasner 1994]. Among the organizations and activities involved are the Software Engineering Laboratory at the University of Maryland, the space shuttle program, and Hewlett Packard. The general conclusion drawn from the case studies is that ROI benefits of between 5 to 1 and 9 to 1 may be expected over a 2-year period.

Additional information on ROI can be found at the SEI web site (http://www.sei.cmu.edu) and at the University of Southern California Web site (http://www.usc.edu). See also the doctoral dissertation of Clark [Clark 1997].

7. Existing and Emerging Standards

7.1 ISO/IEC 12207

ISO/IEC 12207, Software Life Cycle Processes—1995, describes the major component processes of a complete' software life cycle and is based on earlier military standards. It does not assume any particular life cycle model, but it has been suggested that it suits the waterfall model particularly well. It has been adopted as an IEEE standard, IEEE/EIA 12207. This standard was expanded to include:

- IEEE/EIA12207.0-1996, *Industry Implementation of International Standard ISO/IEC 12207:1995 Standard for Information Technology—Software Life Cycle Processes*, contains ISO/IEC 12207 in its original form and six additional annexes (E through J): basic concepts, compliance, life cycle process objectives, life cycle data objectives, relationships, and errata.

- IEEE/EIA12207.1-1997, *Industry Implementation of International Standard ISO/IEC 12207:1995 Standard for Information Technology—Software Life Cycle Processes— Life Cycle Data*, provides additional guidance on recording life cycle data.

- IEEE/EIA12207.2-1997, *Industry Implementation of International Standard ISO/IEC 12207:1995 Standard for Information Technology—Software Life Cycle Processes— Implementation Considerations*, provides additions, alternatives, and clarifications to the ISO/IEC 12207's life cycle processes as derived from U.S. practices.

ISO/IEC 12207 groups the activities that may be performed during the life cycle of a software into five primary processes, eight supporting processes, and four organizational processes.

- *Primary processes:* acquisition, supply, development, operation, and maintenance.

- *Supporting processes:* documentation, configuration management, quality assurance, verification, validation, joint review, audit, and problem resolution.

- *Organization Processes:* management, infrastructure, improvement, and training. Each process is further divided into a set of activities and each activity is divided into a set of tasks. As of 2000, ISO/IEC 12207 was undergoing revision.

7.2 ISO/IEC 15504

As already described in Section 4.4, the emerging standard ISO/IEC 15504 is currently at the technical report (TR) stage and is expected to become a full standard around mid-2002. The development of 15504 has been supported by the SPICE project and the standard is sometimes known (informally) as the SPICE standard or SPICE99. Standard 15504 has been developed in parallel with ISO/IEC 12207 and the current (TR) version is described in Section 4.4. Like 12207, 15504 defines the software process to consist of component processes.

According to 15504 these processes are grouped into five categories: customer supplier, engineering, support, management, and organization. The categories are not dissimilar to those used in 12207. However, a strong case has been made that they should not just be similar to those of 12207 but they should be identical; and successive versions of what is now known as 15504 have brought the two sets of component processes more closely together.

As far as the current (TR) version of 15504 is concerned, it is possible to impose a higher-level structure on the process categories to bring them close to the 12207 categories. Thus, we can group the 15504 processes as follows:

- *Primary processes:* all processes in the customer supplier and engineering categories.

- *Supporting processes:* all processes in the support process category.

- *Organizational processes:* all processes in the management and organization process categories.

Further discussion about the convergence of ISO/IEC 12207 and ISO/IEC 15504 is given in the next section.

7.3 Convergence

The areas of software process assessment and software process improvement are clearly now ready for convergence and consolidation. Several issues need to be addressed:

- The fact that ISO/IEC 15504 is a continuous model, whereas the SW-CMM is a staged model;

- The fact that the process architectures of ISO/IEC 12207 and ISO/IEC 15504 are not the same; and

- The fact that ISO 9001 as applied to software is not compatible with any of the software process standards.

Fortunately, it appears that the desired convergence may well take place within the next few years. As far as the continuous versus staged model choice is concerned, it seems likely that the CMM integration project will define one or more mappings between the results of a CMMI mapping (which is staged) onto the format of the output from a SPICE assessment (which is continuous), thus making CMMI assessments 15504 compatible.

As far as the process architectures of ISO/IEC 12207 and ISO/IEC 15504 are concerned, their incompatibility is seen as a major issue within ISO/IEC JTC1/SC7, the parent committee of WG7. Which is responsible for 12207, and WG10, which is responsible for 12207. As of 2000, WG7 and WG10 were planning a series of joint meetings to resolve the issues. One possible outcome of these meetings would be a new process architecture standard on which both 12207 and 15504 could build.

The remaining issue of compatibility between ISO 9000 is not so great now that ISO 9000:2000, which is more supportive of process improvement than previous versions of the ISO 9000 series, has been published. Although the standards world may at times seem to be slow moving, it is in fact constantly changing, always seeking consensus, consistency, and—where appropriate—change!

8. Summary

Software process improvement is a well-established and accepted method of controlling the software process in order to deliver high-quality software products on time and within budget. Software process improvement is normally dependent on a software process assessment model of which a number exist. The best known, and longest standing, such model is the SW-CMM, which is widely used for two purposes: (1) determining the capability of software contractors and (2) software process improvement. A number of alternative models of process assessment have been developed based on, or inspired by, the SW-CMM.

Although most methods of process assessment are software specific, the generic standard ISO 9001 is also used for software process assessment. In recent years, an international standard, ISO/IEC 15504 (sometimes known as SPICE), has emerged based on virtually all of the existing software assessment methods, and many of these methods have become 15504 compliant. There are also indications of a general convergence in the area of software process assessment.

The benefits of software process assessment are now being realized and may now be quantified so that while software process improvement may have begun as an act of faith, it is now beginning to be possible to predict the benefits that can be obtained from it.

Applicable Standards

IEEE Std 610.12-1990. *IEEE Standard Glossary of Software Engineering Terminology.* IEEE, New York.

ISO 9000-3 (1991/7). *Quality Management and Quality Assurance Standards—Part 3: Guidelines for the Application of ISO 9001 to the Development, Supply and Maintenance of Software (also known as BS 5750, Part 13).* International Standards Organization, Geneva.

ISO 9000:2000. *Quality Management Systems.* International Standards Organization, Geneva.

ISO 9001 (1991). *Quality Systems—Model for Quality Assurance in Design, Development, Production, Installation and Servicing.* International Standards Organization, Geneva. ISO/IEC 9126 (1995). *Information Technology—Software Quality Characteristics and Metrics*, ISO/IEC JTC1/SC7 WG 6. International Standards Organization, Geneva.

ISO/IEC 12207 (1995). *Information Technology—Software Life Cycle Processes*, ISO/IE C JTC1/SC7 WG 7. International Standards Organization, Geneva.

ISO/IEC TR15504-9, 1–9 (1998). *Information Technology—Software Process Assessment— Parts 1–9*, ISO/IEC JTC1/SC7WG 10. International Standards Organization, Geneva.

Additional References

[Billings et al. 1994] Billings, C., Clifton, J., Kolkhorst, B., Lee, E., and Wingert, W. B. (1994). "Journey to a Mature Software Process." IBM Systems Journal, vol. 33, no. 1, pp. 46–61.

[Christensen 2000] Christensen, M. J. (2000). "The Cost of SW-CMM Call Backs." Private correspondence.

[Clark 1997] Clark, B. K. (1997). *The Effects of Software Process Maturity on Software Development Effort.* PhD dissertation, Computer Science Department, University of Southern California, August. Available at http://www.usc.edu/ bclark/research.

[Clark 2000] Clark, B. K. (2000). "Quantifying the Effects on Effort of Software Process Maturity." *IEEE Software*, vol. 17, no. 6, November/December, pp. 65–70.

[Coallier 1995] Coallier, F. (1995). "TRILLIUM: A Model for the Assessment of Telecom Product Development and Support Capability." *IEEE Software Process Newsletter*, vol. 3, pp. 3–8.

[Craigyle & Fletcher 1993] Craigmyle, M., and Fletcher, I. (1993). "Improving IT Effectiveness through Software Process Assessment." *Software Quality Journal*, vol. 2, pp. 257–264.

[Curtis 1995] Curtis, B. (1995). "Building a Cost Benefit Case for Software Process Improvement." Tutorial presented at 7th Software Engineering Process Group Conference, Boston.

[Dorling & Simms 1991] Dorling, A., and Simms, P. (1991). *Improve IT Study Report*, U.K. Ministry of Defence.

[El Emam et al. 1998] El Emam, K., Drouin, J. -N., and Melo, W., eds. (1998). *SPICE: The Theory and Practice of Software Process Improvement and Capability Determination.* IEEE Computer Society Press, Los Alamitos, CA.

[Grady 1996] Grady, R. B. (1996). "Software Failure Analysis for High-Return Process Improvement Decisions." *Hewlett- Packard Journal*, vol. 47, no 3, pp. 15–24.

[Herbsleb & Goldenson 1996] Herbsleb, J., and Goldenson, D. (1996). "A Systematic Survey of CMM Experience and Results." *Proceedings International Conference on Software Engineering, ICSE- 18.* IEEE Computer Society Press, Los Alamitos, CA, pp. 323–330.

[Humphrey 1987] Humphrey, W. S. (1987). "Software Process Program." Presented at SEI Affiliate Symposium, Pittsburgh, PA.

[Humphrey 1989] Humphrey, S. (1989). *Managing the Software Process.* Addison-Wesley, Reading, MA.

[Humphrey 1995] Humphrey, W. S. (1995). *A Discipline for Software Engineering.* Addison-Wesley, Reading, MA.

[Humphrey 1999a] Humphrey, W. S. (1999a). *Introduction to the Team Software Process.* Addison-Wesley-Longman, Reading, MA.

[Humphrey 1999b] Humphrey, W. S. (1999b). "Making the Strategic Case for Process Improvement." *SEI Interactive*, vol. 2, no. 4, December 1999. http://interactive.sei.cmu.edu/news@sei/columns/watts_new/1999/December/watts-dec99.htm

[Humphrey 2000] Humphrey, W. S. (2000). "Justifying a Process Improvement Proposal." *SEI Interactive*, vol. 3, no. 1, March 2000. http://interactive.sei.cmu.edu/news@sei/columns/watts_new/2000/March/watts-mar00.htm

[Hunter et al. 1997] Hunter, R., Robinson, G., and Woodman, I. (1997). "Tool Support for Software Process Assessment and Improvement." *Software Process: Improvement and Practice*, vol. 3, pp. 213–223.

[Jansen & Sanders 1998] Jansen, P., and Sanders, J. (1998). "Guidelines for Process Improvement." *SPICE: The Theory and Practice of*

Software Process Improvement and Capability Determination, K. El Emam, J.N. Drouin, and W. Melo, eds. IEEE Computer Society Press, Los Alamitos, CA, pp. 171–192.

[Kind & Ferguson 1997] Kind, P.A., and Ferguson, J. (1997). "The Software Acquisition Capability Maturity Model." *Crosstalk*, vol. 10, no. 3, pp. 13–17.

[Krasner 1994] Krasner, H. (1994). "The Payoff for Software Process Improvement (SPI): What Is It and How to Get It." *IEEE Software Process Newsletter*, no. 1, pp. 3–8.

[Kuvaja & Bicego 1994] Kuvaja, P., and Bicego, A. (1994). "A European Assessment Methodology." *Software Quality Journal*, vol. 3, pp. 117–127.

[Logica 1988] Logica Consultancy Ltd. (1988). *Quality Management Standards for Software.* Author, London.

[Lowe & Cox 1996] Lowe, D. E., and Cox, G. M. (1996). "Implementing the Capability Maturity Model for Software Development." *Hewlett-Packard Journal*, vol. 47, no. 3.

[Naur & Randell 1969] Naur, P., and Randell, B., eds. (1969). *Software Engineering: A Report on a Conference Sponsored by the NATO Science Committee*, NATO, Brussels.

[Paulish & Carleton 1994] Paulish, D. J., and Carleton, A. D. (1994). "Case Studies of Software Process Improvement Measurement." *IEEE Computer.* vol. 27, no. 9, pp. 50–57.

[Paulk 1995] Paulk, M. C. (1995). "How ISO 9001 Compares with the CMM." *IEEE Software*, vol. 12.

[Paulk, Konrad, & Garcia 1995] Paulk, M. C., Konrad, M. D., and Garcia, S. M. (1995). "CMM Versus SPICE Architectures." *IEEE Software Process Newsletter*, no. 3, pp. 7–11.

[Paulk et al. 1995] Paulk, M. C., Weber, C. V., Curtis, B., and Chrissis, M. B. (1995). *The Capability Maturity Model: Guidelines for Improving the Software Process.* Addison Wesley, Reading, MA.

[Price Waterhouse 1988] Price Waterhouse (1988). *Software Quality Standards: The Costs and Benefits.* Author, London.

[Sanders 1998] Sanders, M., ed., and the SPIRE Project Team. (1998). *The SPIRE Handbook.* Centre for Software Engineering, Dublin, Ireland.

[Schaeffer 1998] Schaeffer, M.D. (1998). "Capability Maturity Model Process Improvement." *Crosstalk*, May 1998, vol. 11, pp. 4– 5.

[Simon et al. 1997] Simon, J. -M., El Emam, K., Rousseau, S., Jacquet, E., and Babey, F. (1997). "The Reliability of ISO/IEC PDTR 15504 Assessments." *Software Process: Improvement and Practice*, vol. 3, pp. 177–188.

[Stelzer et al. 1998] Stelzer, D., Reibnitz, M., and Mellis, W. (1998). "Benefits and Prerequisites of ISO 9000 Based Software Quality Management." *IEEE Software Process Newsletter*, no. 12, pp. 3–7.

[SPICE1996] SPICE Project. (1996). *SPICE Trials Phase 1 Report.* The SPICE Project, http://www.sqi.gu.edu.au/spice.

[SPICE1998] SPICE Project (1998). *SPICE Trials Phase 2 Interim Report.* The SPICE Project, http://www.sqi.gu.edu.au/spice.

[Webb & Humphrey 1999] Webb, D., and Humphrey, W. S. (1999). "Using the TSP on the Task View Project." *Crosstalk*, February, pp. 3–10.

Planning an Effective Training Program

Paula S. Shafer
Independent Consultant

In Quality Is Free, *Bill Corsby notes that the cost to build a product correctly (cost of conformance) is lower than the cost to fix the product after delivery to clients (cost of nonconformance). The same concept is true in training: the cost of good training is lower than the cost of not training or of training poorly. Organizations stand to lose significant amounts of money from lost productivity when there are changes in process, technology, or culture and employees are not properly trained to handle them. Some organizations report a 3,000 percent to 6,000 percent return on investment from good training [1]. By contrast, poor training or poorly planned training wastes money and time and lowers morale. A properly planned training program is required to ensure success and return on investment for training dollars.*

THE FIRST THING TO ASK when planning a training program is "What do people need to do their jobs?" The answers to this question usually fall into the following categories:

- Process – a way to work.
- Technology – the tools with which to work.
- Management support – a reason for the work.
- Skills – ability to do the work.

Process addresses what work to do, how to perform the task, when to do it, what resources are required, who has the inputs, and who gets the results. Without process, there is chaos. Training alone cannot establish process, but process improvement is at best transitory without good training. Also, ineffective, inconsistent, or undocumented processes require more training to overcome the confusion or miscommunication that is rife in immature organizations. Employees who attend training and return to an undisciplined environment will often not use the skills learned. The money spent on the training will have been wasted and morale will suffer.

Technology. People need appropriate tools and technology to perform their jobs. An organization and its management select, purchase, and make available the appropriate technology. The company's process indicates appropriate uses for the technology. Training tells the employee how to successfully use new technology.

Management support is needed to provide the motivation for effective organizational change. An effective reward system reinforces desired behavior and corrects undesired behavior. Although some organizations try to *motivate* through training, there is little or no lasting impact with this approach. Courses that attempt to motivate have objectives that use phrases such as "understand" or "provide an overview" or "gain an appreciation." Participants may leave this kind of training enthused, but a week later they are back to old work patterns. Training cannot be effective without management support consistent with the messages in the training program.

Skills and knowledge are where training can have the most impact in an organization. Skills that people need overlap with process and technology and are reinforced through effective management support. Training is not the solution to problems that businesses have today; however, without training, an organization will fail in its process improvement program.

This article defines effective training, discusses various means to deliver training, and suggests possible metrics to evaluate training effectiveness.

Training Goals

Effective training is integrated and consistent with many aspects of a software development group. It must be consistent with the following:

- *Organizational goals and strategy.* Although training does not define or establish business strategy, it is important to reinforce that strategy at every opportunity, including during training. Training developed and delivered within the organization should always begin with the business goals. Any training purchased from outside can be aligned with those goals if it is introduced by senior management, who reinforce the mission and vision.
- *Project planning.* The Organization Standard Software Process (OSSP) software project planning procedures need to address project training needs. For example, software development planning standards should account for training to encourage the planners to consider what skills and abilities their project team members will require.
- *Software quality assurance (SQA).* An independent SQA program must be highly involved in training. Independent SQA can perform multiple roles for a software development organization: verifying the implementation of processes, mentoring projects in the use of processes, and collecting and analyzing data on the quality of product and process. Integrating training and SQA means several things. First, some training may be delivered by the SQA organization. Second, SQA participates in the review of training materials to ensure that the messages of the training are consistent with the organization's standard software process. Third, SQA ensures that

project teams receive the training that had been planned. Finally, as SQA analyzes process and product quality, it may propose additional training or improvement of existing training.

- *Software process improvement (SPI) initiatives.* The organization's SPI program should address training in multiple places. The Software Process Engineering Group (SEPG) ensures that process training is integrated into the OSSP. It defines a process to plan, to make available, to track, and to measure quality of training. The SEPG also coordinates or delivers training on topics related to process. Examples of training that the SEPG addresses are the Capability Maturity Model, process analysis, process modeling, or using specific processes during pilots and implementation.

Theory vs. Practice

Effective training focuses on skills or competence in the software development organization. It is specific, timely, and result oriented. People learn by doing, but many trainers do not seem to realize this. Many training techniques do not include active involvement by participants; instead, participants spend most of their time listening to an expert lecture on the theory of topics like SQA or project planning. Precious little time is devoted to practicing these theories. One colleague of mine calls this the "spray-and-pray" approach: the lecturer disperses knowledge, and management hopes it will somehow be absorbed. What usually happens instead? If the participants can stay awake, they may learn something, but there is no way to test what they learned until they return to the workplace. When the real world collides with the theory, the theory will not be applied, no one is available to help the employees apply it, and old methods or habits are perpetuated. The training dollar is wasted, and the employees become discouraged.

In an effective training course, real-world experience and applying skills are more important than theory. The goal

is *not* to put employees through training; the goal is for employees to learn and begin to apply new skills. Less time is spent in lecture and more time is spent practicing the skill. A good approach is the case study. For example, a course on peer reviews could provide participants with the experience of a peer review through sample materials for a simulated software inspection. A better approach is to use actual materials from the trainees' projects. For example, a former colleague of mine delivered analysis and design principles training to an entire project team using its own project rather than a case study. The training was spaced over a period of time as well: teach a little, then work a little. The skills could then be used in "real life," and the trainer could be questioned upon returning to the classroom after the trainees tried out the concepts. When the team completed this training, it had draft work products that were used as they progressed in the project.

Methods of Training

Once a careful analysis of the training needs has been accomplished, appropriate training can be developed. Several methods of delivering the training are viable in today's environment.

- Classroom.
- Teletraining.
- Videotape presentations.
- Job aids or just-in-time training.
- Mentoring.
- Computer-based training.

All have value when used appropriately. To gain the most out of training, use all the methods that make sense for the organization's needs.

Classroom training is the traditional delivery approach and may also be called a workshop, lecture, or laboratory. This approach relies on an instructor who leads a participant discussion and usually a case study or exercises. This mechanism is the most flexible and easiest to adapt. It can be developed comparatively quickly and inexpensively. Drawbacks are lost work time for the participants, scheduling difficulties, travel costs, and the lack of skilled instructors.

A close approximation to training in the classroom is **teletraining** or using teleconferencing facilities for a lecture or laboratory-type course. This is useful in the same ways as classroom-led training. Additionally, it can be delivered to isolated or dispersed locations while minimizing travel costs. This does, however, require a significant investment in technology, and it still requires that people leave their work site. Also, teletraining can present scheduling problems, especially when the participants are located in different time zones. Teletraining also is difficult to make interactive and limits the instructor's available techniques. It is best used for short, clear, and concise training.

Videotaped training is gaining popularity in some organizations. This has some of the same advantages of teletraining in that the training can be delivered to remote locations but does not require the significant investment in technology required by teletraining. It is excellent for delivering short, clear messages and can incorporate interviews or demonstrations from managers or staff, especially when used in conjunction with other forms of training. The disadvantages are the high development and production costs and the lack of participant interaction. Generally, this form has limited utility if used without on-site support.

Job aids, also called just-in-time training, are items such as cards or trifold brochures that outline a procedure succinctly. These are a useful means of training—relatively inexpensive to develop, and easily modified when needed. This form of training does not require that participants leave the job, thus minimizing costs such as lost productivity or travel. These aids can be used to supplement any other form of training, especially for topics like procedures and technology. They are not effective stand-alone, especially for complex skills like project planning. Additionally, unless carefully designed, they can be complex and difficult to comprehend.

Highly skilled people who guide the learner in the workplace perform mentoring. This approach is inexpensive to develop because the expert already has the skills. It is provided at the time the participant needs it and does not require leaving the workplace. It does require some investment, though. The mentor's instructional skills need to be developed, and a structure for the training, such as a "lesson plan," needs to be developed. Quality control is difficult because there is usually no evaluation of it. This form of training works only when properly planned to ensure that the mentor is available, able, and motivated. To merely give training participants the name and telephone number of the expert to call if they have problems is *not* mentoring. The danger in this approach is the potential to propagate bad practices if the mentors do not apply best practices.

Computer-based training is useful in some situations. If well designed, it can be interactive, be used in dispersed geography, minimize travel costs, and reach a wide audience quickly. It is especially useful in simulating dangerous or costly situations, such as landing a jet on an aircraft carrier. However, it requires significant development costs and lead time and can have significant delivery costs when simulating complex environments. It is good for learning basic skills but falls short when used to teach advanced skills. Eventually, the "pilot" has to try to "land a real airplane." This form of training is usually difficult to maintain, update, and redistribute.

All of these forms of training have strengths and weaknesses. When appropriately integrated, they can capitalize on the strengths of each while overcoming their individual weaknesses. The result will be the development of a coherent and comprehensive training capability.

Measuring the Quality of Training

There are at least four ways to measure the quality of a training class or program: post-course evaluations, testing, follow-up surveys, and the organization's metrics program.

Most training courses end with a post-course evaluation completed by the participants. These forms ask the participant's opinion of the course materials, the instructor, and the classroom environment. But it can be difficult to know precisely what these evaluations measure. Do they evaluate whether the participants learned anything or whether they merely enjoyed the training? For example, studies show that these evaluations show high marks when the instructor tells jokes. However, studies also show that when participants enjoy the experience, they open their minds to the new process or procedure, which is a key step to change behavior. Unfortunately, post-course evaluations do not measure the effectiveness of the training in changing behavior in the workplace.

Testing is an effective means to evaluate whether a participant learned. However, this form of evaluation requires investment in developing good tests. This form of evaluation is needed in certain circumstances, such as maintaining accreditation with an organization like the American Council on Education. The tests allow employees to achieve credit for the training in a university environment. However, many organizations find the value of the credit is not worth the expense.

Follow-up surveys are an improvement on the post-course evaluation. The approach is to send an evaluation to participants some time after the training was delivered, e.g., six to nine months later. These surveys are generally more in-depth than most end-of-course evaluations and are targeted to the goals of the training course. Such a survey would ask questions such as "Have you defined and are you using the procedure for making the software project size estimates?" These surveys only secondarily seek to determine the participant's opinion of the training. The focus is on the behavioral change in the work environment. These surveys also can gather data concerning other factors discussed earlier, such as process, technology, or management support. The chief drawback to follow-up surveys is the cost to develop and conduct

the survey. It also is difficult to get people to respond to surveys; those who do respond may not represent the average participant.

The best way to judge a training program is in conjunction with the organization's metrics program. Collect appropriate data before and after conducting training. Effective training will result in improvement in the data. As an example, software inspection data reveals that 75 percent of defects found in design, code, and test phases of the software lifecycle relate to defects in requirements. Six months after implementing a training program in requirements elicitation and analysis, the defect rate goes down to 35 percent, and the training can be declared a success.

Summary

Training is necessary to improve process, but it costs money. Poor training potentially wastes money, lowers morale, and reduces productivity. Good training achieves significant returns on investment. To get the most out of your training investment,

- Deliver training aligned with business strategy.
- Focus on skills that people need.
- Emphasize interactive training.
- Provide multiple forms of training.
- Reinforce through management support. ◆

About the Author

Paula S. Shafer is a freelance consultant and trainer specializing in software project management and software process improvement. She has nearly 25 years software development experience. She is currently developing a course in requirements management.

220-K Stony Run Lane
Baltimore, MD 21210
Voice and Fax: 410-366-6430
E-mail: psshafer@erols.com

Reference

1. Wiggenhorn, William, "Motorola U: When Training Becomes an Education," *Harvard Business Review*, July-August 1990, p. 75.

Education for Computing Professionals

David Lorge Parnas

Queen's University

E ngineering is often defined as the use of scientific knowledge and principles for practical purposes. While the original usage restricted the word to the building of roads, bridges, and objects of military use, today's usage is more general and includes chemical, electronic, and even mathematical engineering. All use science and technology to solve practical problems, usually by designing useful products.

Most engineers today have a university-level education. Government and professional societies enforce standards by accrediting educational programs and examining those people who seek the title "Professional Engineer." Certification is intended to protect public safety by making certain that engineers have a solid grounding in fundamental science and mathematics, are aware of their professional responsibilities, and are trained to be thorough and complete in their analysis. In each of these aspects, engineers differ sharply from technicians, who are trained to follow established procedures but do not take responsibility for the correctness of those procedures.

Engineering education differs from traditional "liberal arts" education as well. Engineering students are much more restricted in their choice of courses; this en-

Computing science graduates are ending up in engineering jobs. CS programs must therefore return to a classical engineering approach that emphasizes fundamentals rather than the latest fads.

sures that all graduate engineers have had exposure to those fields that are fundamental to their profession. Engineering education also stresses finding good, as contrasted with workable, designs. Where a scientist may be happy with a device that validates his theory, an engineer is taught to make sure that the device is efficient,

reliable, safe, easy to use, and robust. Finally, engineers learn that even the most intellectually challenging assignments require a great deal of boring "dog work."

It has been a quarter century since universities began to establish academic programs in computing science. Graduates of these programs are usually employed by industry and government to build useful objects, often computer programs. Their products control aircraft, automobile components, power plants, and telephone circuits. Their programs keep banking records and assist in the control of air traffic. Software helps engineers design buildings, bridges, trucks, etc. In other words, these nonengineering graduates of CS programs produce useful artifacts; their work is engineering. It is time to ask whether this back door to engineering is in the best interests of the students, their employers, and society.

I have written this article to discuss a trend, not to single out any particular department's curriculum or any particular committee report. Each new curriculum proposal includes more "new" computer science and, unavoidably, less "classical" material. In this article I reject that trend and propose a program whose starting point is programs that were in place when computing science began.

Reprinted from *Computer*, Vol. 23, No. 1, Jan. 1990, pp. 17–22.

411

An historical debate

In the early 1960s, those of us who were interested in computing began to press for the establishment of computing science departments. Much to my surprise, there was strong opposition, based in part on the argument that graduates of a program specializing in such a new (and, consequently, shallow) field would not learn the fundamental mathematical and engineering principles that should form its basis. Both mathematicians and electrical engineers argued that computing science was an integral part of their own fields. They felt that students should major in one of those fields and take some computing courses near the end of their academic careers, rather than get an education in computing science as such. They predicted that graduates of CS programs would understand neither mathematics nor engineering; consequently, they would not be prepared to apply mathematical and engineering fundamentals to the design of computing systems.

My colleagues and I argued that computing science was rapidly gaining importance and that computing majors would be able to study the older fields with emphasis on those areas that were relevant to computing. Our intent was to build a program incorporating many mathematics and engineering courses along with a few CS courses. Unfortunately, most departments abandoned such approaches rather early. Both faculty and students were impatient to get to the "good stuff." The fundamentals were compressed into quick, shallow courses that taught only those results deemed immediately relevant to computing theory.

The state of graduate CS education

Nearly 25 years later, I have reluctantly concluded that our opponents were right. As I look at CS departments around the world, I am appalled at what my younger colleagues — those with their education in computing science — don't know. Those who work in theoretical computing science seem to lack an appreciation for the simplicity and elegance of mature mathematics. They build complex models more reminiscent of programs written by bad programmers than the elegant models I saw in my mathematics courses. Computing scientists often invent new mathemat-

> ## As I look at computing science departments around the world, I am appalled at what my younger colleagues don't know.

ics where old mathematics would suffice. They repeatedly patch their models rather than rethink them when new problems arise.

Further, many of those who work in the more practical areas of computing science seem to lack an appreciation for the routine systematic analysis that is essential to professional engineering. They are attracted to flashy topics that promise revolutionary changes and are impatient with evolutionary developments. They eschew engineering's systematic planning, documentation, and validation. In violation of the most fundamental precepts of engineering design, some "practical" computing scientists advocate that implementors begin programming before the problem is understood. Discussions of documentation and practical testing issues are considered inappropriate in most CS departments.

Traditional engineering fosters cooperation between theory and practice. The theory learned in mathematics and science classes is applied in engineering classes. In computing science, though, theory and practice have diverged. While classical mathematical topics, such as graph theory, continue to have applications in computing, most of the material in CS theory courses is not relevant in practice. Much theory concentrates on machines with infinite capacity, although such machines are not, and never will be, available. Academic departments and large conferences are often battlegrounds for the "theoretical" and "applied" groups. Such battles are a sure sign that something is wrong.

As the opponents of computing science predicted, most CS PhDs are not scientists; they neither understand nor apply the methods of experimental science. They are neither mathematicians nor engineers. There are exceptions, of course, but they stand out so clearly that they "prove the rule."

The state of undergraduate CS education

The preparation of CS undergraduates is even worse than that of graduate students. CS graduates are very weak on fundamental science; their knowledge of technology is focused on the very narrow areas of programming, programming languages, compilers, and operating systems. Most importantly, they are never exposed to the discipline associated with engineering. They confuse existence proofs with products, toys with useful tools. They accept the bizarre inconsistencies and unpredictable behavior of current tools as normal. They build systems of great complexity without systematic analysis. They don't understand how to design a product to make such analysis possible. Whereas most engineers have had a course in engineering drawing (also known as engineering graphics), few CS graduates have had any introduction to design documentation.

Most CS graduates are involved in the construction of information and communications systems. These systems are highly dependent on information representation and transmission, but the graduates working on them are almost completely ignorant of information theory. For example, CS graduates are not conscious of the difference between the information unit "bit" and the storage unit, which is properly called a "binary digit." As a result, conversations on important practical issues, such as the design of data representations, proceed on an intuitive ad hoc level that engineers would consider unprofessional.

Although most CS graduates have been exposed to logic, the topic's treatment is usually quite shallow. The students are familiar with the symbol manipulation rules of predicate calculus but are usually unable to apply logic in practical circumstances. For example, most graduates cannot use quantifiers properly to "translate" informal statements into formal ones, perhaps because their instructors prefer inventing new logics to applying conventional ones. Mathematicians can successfully invent formalisms, but engineers usually succeed by finding new ways to use existing formalisms.

Because they lack knowledge of logic and communications concepts, CS graduates use fuzzy words like "knowledge" without the vaguest idea of how to define such a term or distinguish it from older concepts like "data" and "information." They talk of building "reasoning" systems without being able to distinguish reasoning from mechanical deduction or simple search techniques. The use of such fuzzy terms is not merely sloppy wording; it prevents the graduate from doing the systematic analyses made possible by precise definitions.

Reliability requirements are forcing the introduction of redundancy in computer systems. Unfortunately, current CS graduates are usually unfamiliar with all but the most naive approaches to redundancy. They often build systems that are needlessly expensive but allow common mode failures. Many CS graduates have not been taught the fundamentals needed to perform reliability analyses on the systems they design. Few of them understand concepts such as "single error correction/double error detection." Familiarity with such concepts is essential to the design of reliable computing systems.

Public safety is seriously affected by the fact that many CS graduates program parts of such control systems as those that run nuclear plants or adjust flight surfaces on aircraft. Unfortunately, I do not know of a single CS program that requires its students to take a course in control theory. The basic concepts of feedback and stability are understood only on an intuitive level at best. Neither the graduates nor most of their teachers know of the work in control theory that is applicable to the design of real-time systems.

Some graduates work in the production of signal processing systems. Unfortunately, signal processing is not offered in most CS programs; in fact, many departments will not allow a student to take such a course for CS credit. Signal processing deals with issues that are fundamental to the science and application of computing, but it is neglected in most programs.

Although many CS programs began with numerical analysis, most of our graduates have no understanding of the problems of arithmetic with finite representations of real numbers. Numerical analysis is, at best, an option in most CS programs.

What went wrong?

Most CS departments were formed by multidisciplinary teams comprising mathematicians interested in computing, electrical engineers who had built or used

---

The manager of one safety-critical project stated with evident pride that his product was produced by engineers, "not just computer scientists."

---

computers, and physicists who had been computer users. Each had favorite topics for inclusion in the educational program, but not everything could be included. So, the set of topics was often the intersection of what the founders knew, not the union. Often, several topics were combined into a single course that forced shallow treatment of each.

The research interests of the founding scientists distorted the educational programs. At the time computing became an academic discipline, researchers were preoccupied with language design, language definition, and compiler construction. One insightful paper speculated that the next 1,700 PhD theses would introduce the next 1,700 programming languages. It might have been more accurate to predict 700 languages, 500 theories of language semantics, and 500 compiler-compilers.

Soon, "artificial intelligence" became a popular term with American funding agencies, and the CS field expanded to include a variety of esoteric topics described by anthropomorphic buzzwords. Cut off from the departments of mathematics and electrical engineering by the usual university divisions, CS graduates came to view their field as consisting primarily of those topics that were research interests in their department. The breadth that would have come from being in one of the older, broader departments was missing.

Today, it is clear that CS departments were formed too soon. Computing science focuses too heavily on the narrow research interests of its founding fathers. Very little computing science is of such fundamental importance that it should be taught to undergraduates. Most CS programs have replaced fundamental engineering and mathematics with newer material that quickly becomes obsolete.

CS programs have become so inbred that the separation between academic computing science and the way computers

---

are actually used has become too great. CS programs do not provide graduates with the fundamental knowledge needed for long-term professional growth.

What is the result?

In recent years, I have talked to a number of top industry researchers and implementors who are reluctant to hire CS graduates at any level. They prefer to take engineers or mathematicians, even history majors, and teach them programming. The manager of one safety-critical programming project stated with evident pride that his product was produced by engineers, "not just computer scientists." The rapid growth of the industry assures that our graduates get jobs, but experienced managers are very doubtful about the usefulness of their education.

As engineers in other fields are becoming more dependent on computing devices in their own professional practice, they are also becoming more concerned about the lack of professionalism in the products they use. They would rather write their own programs than trust the programs of our graduates.

As awareness of the inadequacies of CS education grows, as people begin to realize that programming languages and compiler technology are not relevant background for the people they hire, our students may have trouble getting jobs. The main problem now is that their education has not prepared them for the work they actually do.

A new program for computing professionals

While the critics of the original CS programs were quite accurate in their predictions, I still believe that a special educational program for computing professionals is needed. When we look at the programs produced by engineers and scientists who did not have such an education, we see that they are quite naive about many of the things we have learned in 25 years of computing science. For example, new programs in the defense industry are written in the same unsystematic style found in programs written in the 1950s and 1960s. Our graduates should be able to do better.

I believe the program proposed below would provide a good education for computing professionals. It is designed to draw heavily on the offerings of other departments, and it emphasizes mature fundamentals to prepare our graduates for a life of learning in a dynamic field. Wherever possible, the courses should be existing courses that can be shared with mathematicians and engineers. Students should meet the strict requirements of engineering schools, and the programs should be as rigid as those in other engineering disciplines.

Basic mathematics. The products of most computing professionals are so abstract that the field could well be called "mathematical engineering." In fact, this is the title used at some Dutch universities. Computing professionals need to know how to use mathematics, although they rarely need to invent it. Some computer scientists have suggested that their students need only discrete mathematics, not the mathematics of continuous functions. However, while discrete mathematics is used in theoretical computing science, many practical applications use computers to approximate piecewise continuous functions. Computer professionals need a full introduction to mathematics; they should not be restricted to those items taught as theoretical computing science.

Calculus. All computing professionals should take the standard two- or four-semester calculus sequence taken by other engineers. This is the basic preparation for understanding how to deal with dynamic systems in the continuous domain. Many computer applications are best understood as approximations or improvements of dynamic analog systems. Computer professionals require the full sequence.

Discrete mathematics. CS students should join mathematics students in a course on such fundamentals as set theory, functions, relations, graphs, and combinatorics. In current computing courses, students view these topics as notations for describing computations and do not understand mathematics as an independent deductive system.

Logic. Logic is fundamental to many of the notations and concepts in computing science. Students should have a deeper understanding than that usually provided by CS logic courses or a few lectures on logic in some other course. I propose a two-semester sequence, taken with mathematics students, covering such advanced topics as decision procedures and higher order logics. The relationship between

logic, set theory, lambda calculus, etc. should be thoroughly explored. Applications to computing should not be discussed.

Linear algebra. This should be covered in the standard one-semester course for engineers offered by the mathematics department.

Graph theory. Graphs offer useful representations of a wide variety of computing problems. Students who understand graph theoretic algorithms will find them useful in a variety of fields. An optional second course could deal with the application of this theory in computing practice.

Differential equations. This also should be covered in the usual one-semester course offered by mathematics departments for engineers. Many modern computer systems are approximations to analog circuits, for which this analysis is essential.

Probability and applied statistics. The reliability and adequacy of testing is a major concern in modern computing applications. Probability theory is also a fundamental tool in situations where random noise is present in communications. Everyone who works as an engineer should have at least a one-semester course on this topic; a two-semester sequence would be better for many.

Optimization. Linear and nonlinear programming are major applications for large computers. A course in this area would make students aware of the complexity of search spaces and the need to precisely define objective functions. One need not look very far into the class of programs known as "expert systems" to find areas where optimization concepts should have been applied.

Numerical analysis. This topic could be taught as either computing science or mathematics. (It is described below under "Computing science.")

Basic science. Computing professionals need the same knowledge of basic science as engineers. A basic course in chemistry and a two-semester sequence in physics should be the minimal requirement for all technical students.

Engineering topics. Computing professionals are engineers and should be educated as such. Computers and software are now replacing more conventional technologies, but the people who design the new systems need to understand fundamental engineering systems as well as did the engineers who designed those older systems.

Engineering electricity and magnetism. This topic should be covered in the standard one-semester course taken by electrical engineers.

Electric circuits. This also should be covered in the standard one-semester course for electrical engineers.

Mechanics. An understanding of mechanics is essential to a study of practical robotics, automated manufacturing, etc. This topic, too, should be covered in the standard, one-semester, electrical engineering course.

Systems and control theory. This standard two-semester sequence for electrical engineers should emphasize the use of differential equations, transforms, and complex analyses to predict the behavior of control systems. The course should also discuss the discrete analogues of methods for dealing with continuous functions.

Information theory. This is one of the most fundamental and important areas for computing professionals. In addition to the standard one-semester course for electrical engineers, a second course on applications in computer design would be useful as an elective.

Digital system principles/logic design. This topic could be covered under either computing science or electrical engineering. (It is described below under "Computing science.")

Signal processing. This area should be examined in a one-semester course introducing the concepts of noise, filters, signal recognition, frequency response, digital approximations, highly parallel algorithms, and specialized processors.

Computing science. Before the advent of CS departments, engineering and science students were expected to learn programming and programming languages on their own or through noncredit courses. Computers were compared to slide rules and calculators: tools that university students could learn to use. Engineering and

---

> **Very little computing science is of such fundamental importance that it should be taught to undergraduates.**

science faculty felt that courses in programming and programming languages would not have the deep intellectual content of mathematics or physics courses. We responded that we would teach computing science, not programming or specific languages.

Unfortunately, many of today's courses prove the critics correct. The content of many courses would change dramatically if the programming language being used underwent a major change. The courses proposed below assume that students are capable programmers and avoid discussions of programming languages.

Systematic programming. This would be taught in a two-semester sequence covering finite-state machines, formal languages and their applications, program state spaces, the nature of programs, program structures, partitioning the state space, program composition, iteration, program organization, program design documentation, systematic verification, etc. Students should be competent programmers as a prerequisite to this course.

Computer system documentation. This one-semester course would teach formal methods to document computer system designs, with emphasis on methods that apply to both digital and integrated digital/analog systems.

Design and analysis of algorithms and data structures. This course would discuss comparative analysis of algorithms and data structures as well as theoretical models of problem complexity and computability. Students would learn to predict the performance of their programs and to chose algorithms and data structures that give optimal performance.

Process control. This integrated treatment of the theoretic hardware, software, and control problems of process control systems would include hardware characteristics, operating systems for real-time applications, the process concept, synchronization, and scheduling theory. Students would learn how to prove that their systems will meet deadlines and how to design for fail-safe behavior. A course in control theory should be a prerequisite.

Computing systems architecture and networks. This fairly standard course, now taught in both electrical engineering and CS departments, would cover the structure of a computer and multicomputer networks, communications bus design, network performance analysis, etc. A knowledge of assembly language should be assumed. Students should be

---

> **Inadequate analyses and unsystematic work are often rewarded and reinforced by high grades.**

---

taught to avoid buzzwords and discuss the quantitative characteristics of the systems they study.

Numerical analysis. This course, which could be taught as either computing science or mathematics, would cover the study of calculations using finite approximations to real numbers and would teach round-off, error propagation, conditioning of matrices, etc.

Digital system principles/logic design. This standard one-semester course for electrical engineers should cover the basics of combinational circuit design, memory design, error correction, error detection, and reliability analysis. The emphasis should be on systematic procedures. The course could be offered as either computing science or electrical engineering.

As in any academic program, the above program includes compromises. Many topics, such as databases, compilers, and operating systems, were considered and omitted because of time limitations. It is not that these areas are uninteresting, but rather that I have chosen the oldest, most mature, most fundamental topics over those that are relatively recent and likely to be invalidated by changes in technology. Some may find the program old-fashioned. I prefer to call it long-lasting.

One obvious exception to the "older is better" rule is the course on computer system documentation. I would like to think that its inclusion reflects its importance, but it may simply reflect my own research interests.

The program is rather full and far more closely resembles a heavily packed engineering program than the liberal arts program to which CS educators have become accustomed. The educational philosophy issues behind this traditional split are clearly outside the scope of this article. Personally, I would welcome a five-year undergraduate engineering degree to allow a broader education, but would find it

---

irresponsible to make substantial reductions in the technical content of four-year programs.

Projects versus cooperative education

CS students are burdened by many courses that require hours of struggle with computing systems. Programming assignments include small programs in introductory courses, larger programs in advanced courses, and still-larger projects that comprise the main content of entire courses. This "practical content" is both excessive and inadequate. Much effort is spent learning the language and fighting the system. A great deal of time is wasted correcting picayune errors while fundamental problems are ignored. "Practical details" consume time better spent on the theoretical or intellectual content of the course.

Also, the programs that students write are seldom used by others and rarely tested extensively. Students do not get the feedback that comes from having a product used, abused, rejected, and modified. This lack of feedback is very bad education. Students and faculty often believe they have done a very good job when they have not. Inadequate analyses and unsystematic work are often rewarded and reinforced by high grades.

There is no doubt that students cannot learn programming without writing programs, but we should not be teaching programming. Small assignments should have the same role as problems in a mathematics class and often should be graded the same way. The computer and the person grading the program both provide feedback, but the computer is often quite demanding about arbitrary details while ignoring substantial weaknesses in the program. The person who grades the program should be tolerant on matters of arbitrary conventions but should pay attention to the fundamental issues.

Properly run cooperative education programs provide the desired transition between academia and employment. Students produce a real product and get feedback from interested users. Review and guidance from faculty advisors is essential to integrate the work experience with the educational program. Project courses can and should be replaced by such a program. The use of the computer in academic courses can be greatly reduced.

Student needs versus faculty interests

I do not expect these remarks and proposals to be popular with the faculty of CS departments. We all have considerable emotional investment in the things we have learned and intellectual investment in the things we teach. Many faculty want to teach courses in their research areas in the hope of finding students to work on their projects. Moreover, my criticism of the education we now provide is unavoidably a criticism of the preparation of my younger colleagues.

A university's primary responsibilities are to its students and society at large. It is unfortunate that they are often run for the comfort and happiness of the teachers and administrators. In this matter, the interests of our students and society coincide. It is not in the students' interest to make them perform engineering without being prepared for that responsibility. Nor is it in their interest to give them an education that prepares them only to be technicians. Too many graduates end up "maintaining"

commercial software products, which is analogous to electrical engineers climbing poles to replace cables on microwave towers.

My industrial colleagues often complain that CS students are not prepared for the jobs they have to do. I must emphasize that my proposals will not produce graduates who can immediately take over the responsibilities of an employee who has left or been promoted. That is not the role of a university. Universities should not be concerned with teaching the latest network protocol, programming language, or operating system feature. Graduates need the fundamentals that will allow a lifetime of learning new developments; the program I have proposed provides those fundamentals better than most current CS programs.

CS departments should reconsider the trade-off in their courses between mature material and new developments. It is time for them to reconsider their role, to ask whether the education of computing professionals should not be the responsibility of engineering schools. ∎

Acknowledgments

I have developed these views through a great many conversations with engineers, mathematicians, and computer professionals around the world. The contributors are too numerous to mention. Selim Akl, David Lamb, and John van Schouwen made helpful suggestions about earlier drafts. The referees made several helpful comments.

Appendix A

Centralized IEEE Software Engineering Standards Glossary

acceptance testing: Testing conducted in an operational environment to determine whether a system satisfies its acceptance criteria (e.g., initial requirements and current needs of its user) and to enable the customer to determine whether to accept the system.

activity: A defined body of work to be performed, including its required input and output information. *See also activity group.*

activity group: A set of related activities. *See also activity.*

adaptive maintenance: Modification of a software product performed after delivery to keep a computer program usable in a changed or changing environment.

anomaly: Any condition that deviates from the expected based on requirements, specifications, design, documents, user documents, standards, etc., or from someone's perceptions or experiences. Anomalies may be found during, but not limited to, the review, test, analysis, compilation, or use of software products or applicable documentation.

CARE: Acronym for computer-assisted re-engineering.

CASE: Acronym for computer-aided software engineering.

CCB: Acronym for configuration control board.

CI: Acronym for configuration item.

CM: Acronym for configuration management.

component testing: Testing conducted to verify the correct implementation of the design and compliance with program requirements for one software element (e.g., unit, module) or a collection of software elements.

constraint: A restriction on software life cycle process (SLCP) development. *See also software life cycle process* (SLCP).

control point (project control point): A project agreed on point in time or times when specified agreements or controls are applied to the software configuration items being developed, e.g., an approved baseline or release of a specified document/code.

corrective maintenance: Reactive modification of a software product performed after delivery to correct discovered faults.

COTS: Acronym for commercial-off-the-shelf.

CPU: Acronym for central processing unit.

criticality: A subjective description of the intended use and application of the system. Software criticality properties may include safety, security, complexity, reliability, performance, or other characteristics.

criticality analysis: A structured evaluation of the software characteristics (e.g., safety, security, complexity, performance) for severity of impact of system failure, system degradation, or failure to meet software requirements or system objectives.

CSA: Acronym for configuration status accounting.

customer: The person, or persons, for whom the product is intended, and usually (but not necessarily) who decides the requirements.

design level: The design decomposition of the software item (e.g., system, subsystem, program, or module).

emergency maintenance: Unscheduled, corrective maintenance performed to keep a system operational.

external: An input information source or output information destination that is outside the scope of this standard and, therefore, may or may not exist.

FCA: Acronym for functional configuration audit.

FR: Acronym for feasibility report.

hazard: A source of potential harm or a situation with a potential for harm in terms of human injury, damage to health, property, or the environment, or some combination of these.

hazard analysis: A systematic qualitative or quantitative evaluation of software for undesirable outcomes resulting from the development or operation of a system. These outcomes may include injury, illness, death, mission failure, economic loss, property loss, environmental loss, or adverse social impact. This evaluation may include screening or analysis methods to categorize, eliminate, reduce, or mitigate hazards.

hazard identification: The process of recognizing that a hazard exists and defining its characteristics.

IDD: Acronym for interface design document. *See also interface design document (IDD).*

IEC: Acronym for International Electrotechnical Commission.

independent verification and validation (IV&V): V&V processes performed by an organization with a specified degree of technical, managerial, and financial independence from the development organization.

instance: The mapping of an activity that processes all of its input information and generates all of its output information. Contrast with invocation; iteration. *See also mapping.*

integral activity group: An activity group that is needed to complete project activities, but is outside the management and development activity groups.

integration testing: An orderly progression of testing of incremental pieces of the software program in which software elements, hardware elements, or both are combined and tested until the entire system has been integrated to show compliance with the program design, and capabilities and requirements of the system.

integrity level: A denotation of a range of values of a property of an item necessary to maintain system risks within acceptable limits. For items that perform mitigating functions, the property is the reliability with which the item must perform the mitigating function. For items whose failure can lead to a threat, the property is the limit on the frequency of that failure.

interface design document (IDD): Documentation that describes the architecture and design of interfaces between system and components. These descriptions include control algorithms, protocols, data contents and formats, and performance.

interface requirement specification (IRS): Documentation that specifies requirements for interfaces between systems or components. These requirements include constraints on formats and timing.

interoperability testing: Testing conducted to ensure that a modified system retains the capability of exchanging information with systems of different types, and of using that information.

invocation: The mapping of a parallel initiation of activities of an integral activity group that perform a distinct function and return to the initiating activity. Contrast with instance; iteration. *See also mapping.*

I/O: Acronym for input/output.

IOS: Acronym for International Organization for Standardization.

IRS: Acronym for interface requirements specification. *See also interface requirements specification (IRS).*

iteration: The mapping of any execution of an activity where at least some input information is processed and some output information is created. One or more iterations comprise an instance. Contrast with instance; invocation. *See also mapping.*

IV&V: Acronym for independent verification and validation. *See also independent verification and validation (IV&V).*

LC: Acronym for linear circuit.

life cycle process: A set of interrelated activities that result in the development or assessment of software products. Each activity consists of tasks. The life cycle processes may overlap one another. For V&V purposes, no process is concluded until its development products are verified and validated according to the defined tasks in the SVVP.

mapping: Establishing a sequence of the activities in this standard according to a selected software life cycle model (SLCM). *See also instance; invocation; iteration; software life cycle model (SLCM).*

minimum tasks: Those V&V tasks required for the software integrity level assigned to the software to be verified and validated.

modification request (MR): A generic term that includes the forms associated with the various trouble/problem-reporting documents (e.g., incident report, trouble report) and the configuration change control documents [e.g., software change request (SCR)].

MP: Acronym for maintenance plan.

MR: Acronym for modification request. *See also modification request (MR).*

OPA: Acronym for organizational process asset. *See also organizational process asset (OPA).*

optional tasks: Those V&V tasks that may be added to the minimum V&V tasks to address specific application requirements.

organizational process asset (OPA): An artifact that defines some portion of an organization's software project environment.

pass/fail criteria: Decision rules used to determine whether a software item or a software feature passes or fails a test.

PCA: Acronym for physical configuration audit.

PDL: Acronym for program design language.

perfective maintenance: Modification of a software product after delivery to improve performance or maintainability.

PR&RPI: Acronym for problem reporting and resolution planned information.

process architect: The person or group that has primary responsibility for creating and maintaining the software life cycle process (SLCP). *See also software life cycle process (SLCP).*

product: Any output of the software development activities (e.g., document, code, or model). *See also activity.*

project: A subsystem that is subject to maintenance activity.

regression test: Retesting to detect faults introduced by modification.

release: The formal notification and distribution of an approved version.

repository: (A) A collection of all software-related artifacts (e.g., the software engineering environment) belonging to a system, or (B) The location/format in which such a collection is stored.

required inputs: The set of items necessary to perform the minimum V&V tasks mandated within any life cycle activity.

required outputs: The set of items produced as a result of performing the minimum V&V tasks mandated within any life cycle activity.

reverse engineering: The process of extracting software system information (including documentation) from source code.

RFP: Acronym for request for proposal (tender).

risk: The combination of the frequency, or probability, and the consequence of a specified hazardous event.

risk analysis: The systematic use of available information to identify hazards and to estimate the risk to individuals or populations, property or the environment.

SCA: Acronym for software change authorization.

SCM: Acronym for software configuration management.

SCMPI: Acronym for software configuration management planned information.

SCR: Acronym for system/software change request.

SDD: Acronym for software design description. *See also software design description (SDD).*

SE: Acronym for software engineering.

SLC: Acronym for software life cycle. *See also software life cycle (SLC).*

SLCM: Acronym for software life cycle model. *See also software life cycle model (SLCM).*

SLCP: Acronym for software life cycle process. *See also software life cycle process (SLCP).*

SLOC: Acronym for source lines of code.

software design description (SDD): A representation of software created to facilitate analysis, planning, implementation, and decision-making. The software design description is used as a medium for communicating software design information, and may be thought of as a blueprint or model of the system.

software feature: A distinguishing characteristic of a software item (e.g., performance, portability, or functionality).

software integrity level: The integrity level of a software item.

software item: Source code, object code, job control code, control data, or a collection of these items.

software life cycle (SLC): The project-specific sequence of activities that is created by mapping the activities of this standard onto a selected software life cycle model (SLCM). Contrast with software life cycle model (SLCM); software life cycle process (SLCP).

software life cycle model (SLCM): The framework, selected by each using organization, on which to map the activities of this standard to produce the software life cycle (SLC). Contrast with software life cycle (SLC); software life cycle process (SLCP).

software life cycle process (SLCP): The project-specific description of the process that is based on a project's software life cycle (SLC) and the organizational process assets (OPA). Contrast with software life cycle (SLC); software life cycle model (SLCM). *See also organizational process asset (OPA).*

software maintenance: Modification of a software product after delivery to correct faults, to improve performance or other attributes, or to adapt the product to a modified environment.

software requirements specification (SRS): Documentation of the essential requirements (e.g., functions, performance, design constraints, and attributes) of the software and its external interfaces. The software requirements are derived from the system specification.

software verification and validation plan (SVVP): A plan describing the conduct of software V&V.

software verification and validation report (SVVR): Documentation of V&V results and software quality assessments.

SPMPI: Acronym for software project management planned information.

SQA: Acronym for software quality assurance.

SRS: Acronym for software requirements specification. *See also software requirements specification (SRS).*

SVVP: Acronym for software verification and validation plan. *See also software verification and validation plan (SVVP).*

SVVR: Acronym for software verification and validation report. *See software verification and validation report (SVVR).*

system: A set of interlinked units organized to accomplish one or several specific functions.

system testing: The activities of testing an integrated hardware and software system to verify and validate whether the system meets its original objectives.

test: (A) A set of one or more test cases, (B) A set of one or more test procedures, or (C) A set of one or more test cases and procedures.

test case: Documentation that specifies inputs, predicted results, and a set of execution conditions for a test item.

test case specification: A document specifying inputs, predicted results, and a set of execution conditions for a test item.

test design: Documentation that specifies the details of the test approach for a software feature or combination of software features and identifying the associated tests.

test design specification: A document specifying the details of the test approach for a software feature or combination of software features and identifying the associated tests.

test incident report: A document reporting on any event that occurs during the testing process, which requires investigation.

test item: A software item that is an object of testing.

test item transmittal report: A document identifying test items. It contains current status and location information.

test log: A chronological record of relevant details about the execution of tests.

test plan: A document describing the scope, approach, resources, and schedule of intended testing activities. It identifies test items, the features to be tested, the testing tasks, who will do each task, and any risks requiring contingency planning.

test procedure: Documentation that specifies a sequence of actions for the execution of a test.

test procedure specification: A document specifying a sequence of actions for the execution of a test.

test summary report: A document summarizing testing activities and results. It also contains an evaluation of the corresponding test items.

testing: The process of analyzing a software item to detect the differences between existing and required conditions (that is, bugs) and to evaluate the features of the software item.

user: The person or persons operating or interacting directly with the system.

V&V: Acronym for verification and validation. *See also validation, and verification.*

validation: Confirmation by examination and provisions of objective evidence that the particular requirements for a specific intended use are fulfilled. In design and development, validation concerns the process of examining a product to determine conformity with user needs.

VDD: Acronym for version description document.

verification: Confirmation by examination and provisions of objective evidence that specified requirements have been fulfilled. In design and development, verification concerns the process of examining the result of a given activity to determine conformity with the stated requirement for that activity.

Appendix B
Centralized IEEE Software Engineering Standards References

The reader is cautioned to always use the most recent IEEE Software Engineering Standard.

[Bass, Clements & Kazman, 1998] Bass, L., Clements, P., and Kazman, R., *Software Architecture in Practice*, Reading, MA: Addison-Wesley, 1998.

[British Standard BS7649:1993] *Guide to the design and preparation of documentation for users of application software.*

[British Standard BS7830:1996] *Guide to the design and preparation of on-screen documentation for users of application software.*

[Brockmann, 1990] Brockmann, R.J., *Writing Better Computer Documentation: From Paper to Hypertext*, John Wiley & Sons, New York, 1990.

[Dumas & Redish, 1999] Dumas, J.S., and Redish, J.C., *A Practical Guide to Usability Testing*, rev. ed., Intellect, 1999.

[EIA/IEEE J-Std-016-1995] EIA/IEEE Interim Standard for Information Technology—Software Life Cycle Processes—Software Development: Acquirer- Supplier Agreement.

[Hackos, 1990] Hackos, J.T., *Managing Your Documentation Projects*, John Wiley & Sons, New York, 1990.

[Hackos & Redish, 1998] Hackos, J.T., and Redish, J.C., *User and Task Analysis for Interface Design*, John Wiley & Sons, New York, 1998.

[Hackos & Stevens, 1997] Hackos, J.T., and Stevens, D.M., *Standards for Online Communication: Publishing Information for the Internet/World Wide Web/Help Systems/Corporate Internets*, John Wiley & Sons, New York, 1997.

[Horton, 1994] Horton, W., *Designing and Writing Online Documentation: Hypermedia for Self-Supporting Products*, 2nd ed., John Wiley & Sons, New York, 1994.

[IEC 60300-3-9 (1995)] Dependability management—Part 3: Application guide—Section 9: Risk analysis of technological systems.

[IEEE Std 100-1997] The IEEE Standard Dictionary of Electrical and Electronics Terms, 6th Edition.

[IEEE Std 100-2000] The Authoritative Dictionary of IEEE Standards Terms, 7th Edition.

[IEEE Std 610.12-1990] IEEE Standard Glossary of Software Engineering Terminology.

[IEEE Std 730-1989] IEEE Standard for Software Quality Assurance Plans.

[IEEE Std 730-1998] IEEE Standard for Software Quality Assurance Plans.

[IEEE Std 730.1-1995] IEEE Guide for Software Quality Assurance Planning.

[IEEE Std 828-1990] IEEE Standard for Software Configuration Management Plans.

[IEEE Std 828-1998] IEEE Standard for Software Configuration Management Plans.

[IEEE Std 829-1983 (R1991)] IEEE Standard for Software Test Documentation.

[IEEE Std 829-1998] IEEE Standard for Software Test Documentation.

[IEEE Std 830-1993] IEEE Recommended Practice for Software Requirements Specifications.

[IEEE Std 830-1998] IEEE Recommended Practice for Software Requirements Specifications.

[IEEE Std 982.1-1988] IEEE Standard Dictionary of Measures to Produce Reliable Software.

[IEEE Std 982.2-1988] IEEE Guide for the Use of IEEE Standard Dictionary of Measures to Produce Reliable Software.

[IEEE Std 990-1987 (R1992)] IEEE Recommended Practice for Ada as a Program Design Language.

[IEEE Std 1002-1987 (R1992)] IEEE Standard Taxonomy for Software Engineering Standards.

[IEEE Std 1008-1987 (R1993)] IEEE Standard for Software Unit Testing.

[IEEE Std 1012-1986 (R1992)] IEEE Standard for Software Verification and Validation Plans.

[IEEE Std 1012-1998] IEEE Standard for Software Verification and Validation.

[IEEE Std 1012a-1998] IEEE Standard for Software Verification and Validation – Supplement to 1012-1998 – Content Map to IEEE 12207.1.

[IEEE Std 1016-1987 (R1993)] IEEE Recommended Practice for Software Design Descriptions.

[IEEE Std 1016-1998] IEEE Recommended Practice for Software Design Descriptions.

[IEEE Std 1016.1-1993] IEEE Guide to Software Design Descriptions.

[IEEE Std 1028-1997] IEEE Standard for Software Reviews.

[IEEE Std 1042-1987 (R1993)] IEEE Guide to Software Configuration Management.

[IEEE Std 1044-1993] IEEE Standard Classification for Software Anomalies.

[IEEE Std 1044.1-1995] IEEE Guide to Classification for Software Anomalies.

[IEEE Std 1045-1992] IEEE Standard for Software Productivity Metrics.

[IEEE Std 1058-1987 (R1993)] IEEE Standard for Software Project Management Plans.

[IEEE Std 1058-1998] IEEE Standard for Software Project Management Plans.

[IEEE Std 1059-1993] IEEE Guide for Software Verification and Validation Plans.

[IEEE Std 1061-1992] IEEE Standard for a Software Quality Metrics Methodology.

[IEEE Std 1061-1998] IEEE Standard for a Software Quality Metrics Methodology.

[IEEE Std 1062 1998] IEEE Recommended Practice for Software Acquisition.

[IEEE Std 1063-1987 (R1993)] IEEE Standard for Software User Documentation.

[IEEE Std 1074-1995] IEEE Standard for Developing Software Life Cycle Processes.

[IEEE Std 1074-1997] IEEE Standard for Developing Software Life Cycle Processes.

[IEEE Std 1175-1991] IEEE Standard Reference Model for Computing System Tool Interconnections.

[IEEE Std 1209-1992] IEEE Recommended Practice for the Evaluation and Selection of CASE Tools.

[IEEE Std 1219-1992] IEEE Standard for Software Maintenance.

[IEEE Std 1219-1998] IEEE Standard for Software Maintenance.

[IEEE Std 1220-1994] IEEE Trial Use Standard for Application and Management of the Systems Engineering Process.

[IEEE Std 1220-1998] IEEE Standard for the Application and Management of the Systems Engineering Process.

[IEEE Std 1228-1994] IEEE Standard for Software Safety Plans.

[IEEE Std 1233 1998] IEEE Guide for Developing System Requirements Specifications.

[IEEE Std 1298-1992] IEEE Software Quality Management System, IEEE Part 1 Requirements.

[IEEE Std 1348-1995] IEEE Recommended Practice for the Adoption of Computer-Aided Software Engineering (CASE) Tools.

[IEEE Std 1465-1998 (12119:1998 ISO/IEC)] Information Technology- Software Packages - Quality Requirements and Testing.

[IEEE/EIA 12207.0-1996] IEEE/EIA Standard: Industry Implementation of International Standard ISO/IEC 12207:1995, Standard for Information Technology—Software Life Cycle Processes.

[IEEE/EIA 12207.0-1997] Information Technology—Software Life Cycle Processes.

[IEEE/EIA 12207.1-1997] IEEE/EIA Standard: Industry Implementation of International Standard ISO/IEC 12207:1995 Standard for Information Technology—Software Life Cycle Processes—Life Cycle Data.

[IEEE/EIA 12207.2-1997] IEEE/EIA Standard: Industry Implementation of International Standard ISO/IEC 12207:1995 Standard for Information Technology—Software Life Cycle Processes—Implementation considerations.

[ISO 8402:1994] Quality management and quality assurance—Vocabulary.

[ISO 9001:1994] Quality systems—Model for quality assurance in design, development, production, installation, and servicing.

[ISO 9003:1994] Quality systems—Model for quality assurance in final inspection and test.

[ISO 10011-1:1990] Guidelines for auditing quality systems—Part 1: Auditing.

[ISO/IEC 10746-2:1996] Information technology. Open distributed processing. Reference model: Foundations.

[ISO/IEC 10746-3:1996] Information technology. Open distributed processing. Reference model: Architecture.

[ISO/IEC 12207:1995] Information technology—Software life cycle processes.

[ISO/IEC DIS 15026:1996] Information technology—System and software integrity levels.

[ISO/IEC TR 9294-1990] Information Technology—Guidelines for the Management of Software Documentation.

[Nagle, 1996] Nagle, J.G., *Handbook for Preparing Engineering Documents: From Concept to Completion*, IEEE Press, New York, 1996.

[OMG AD/97-08-05 1997] *Unified Modeling Language Specification*, version 1.1, Object Management Group.

[Perry & Wolf, 1992] Perry, D.E., and Wolf, A.L., Foundations for the Study of Software Architecture. *ACM SIGSOFT Software Engineering Notes*, Vol. 17, No. 4, 1992.

[Price & Korman, 1993] Price, J., and Korman, H., *How to Communicate Technical Information: A Handbook of Software and Hardware Documentation*, Benjamin/Cummings, Redwood City, CA, 1993.

[Proakis, 1995] Proakis, J.G., *Digital Communications*. New York: McGraw-Hill, 1995.

[Schriver, 1994] Schriver, K.A., *Dynamics in Document Design: Creating Texts for Users*, John Wiley & Sons, New York, 1994.

[Shaw & Garlan, 1993] Shaw, M., and Garlan, D., An Introduction to Software Architecture. In *Advances in Software Engineering and Knowledge Engineering*, V. Ambriola and G. Tortora (eds.), River Edge, NJ: World Scienti.c Publishing Company, 1993.

[Zachman, 1987] Zachman, J. A., A Framework for Information Systems Architecture. *IBM Systems Journal*, Vol. 26, No. 3, 1987.

Appendix C: CSDP Examination Specifications

I. Professionalism and Engineering Economics (3-4% questions)

    A. Engineering Economics
    B. Ethics
    C. Professional Practice (e.g., legal issues)
    D. Standards

II. Software Requirements (13-15% questions)

    A. Requirements Engineering Process
    B. Requirements Elicitation
    C. Requirements Analysis (e.g., system definition techniques)
    D. Software Requirements Specification
    E. Requirements Validation
    F. Requirements Management

III. Software Design (22-24% questions)

    A. Software Design Concepts
      - general design concepts
      - software design context
      - software design process
      - real-time concepts
      - fault tolerance
      - distributed computing
      - disaster recovery
    B. Software Architecture
      - architectural structures and viewpoints
      - architectural styles and patterns
      - design patterns
      - design of families of programs and frameworks
    C. Software Design Quality Analysis and Evaluation
      - product attributes and measures
      - quality analysis and evaluation tools
      - performance analysis techniques and tools
    D. Software Design Notations and Documentation
    E. Software Design Strategies and Methods
      - general strategies
      - function-oriented design
      - object-oriented design
      - data-structure-oriented design
    F. Human Factors in Software Design (e.g., human-computer interaction)
    G. Software and System Safety (e.g., hazard analysis)

IV. Software Construction and Implementation (10-12% questions)

A. Construction planning
B. Code design
C. Data design and management
D. Error processing
E. Source code organization
F.Code documentation
G.Construction QA
H.System integration and deployment
I.Code tuning
J.Construction tools

V. Software Testing (15-17% questions)

A. Types of Tests
B. Test Levels
C. Testing Strategies
D. Test Design
E. Test Coverage of Code
F. Test Coverage of Specifications
G. Test Execution H. Test Documentation
I. Test Management

VI. Software Maintenance (3-5% questions)

A. Software Maintainability (e.g., software evolution)
B. Software Maintenance Process (e.g., maintenance types, change impact analysis and regression tesitng)
C. Software Maintenance Measurement
D. Software Maintenance Planning
E. Software Maintenance Management
F. Software Maintenance Documentation

VII. Software Configuration Management (3-4% questions)

A. Management of SCM Process
B. Software Configuration Identification
C. Software Configuration Control
D. Software Configuration Status Accounting
E. Software Configuration Auditing
F. Software Release Management and Delivery

VIII. Software Engineering Management (10-12% questions)

A. Measurement
  - measurement program goals
  - measurement of software and its development
  - selection of measurement
  - data collection
  - software metric model
B. Organizational Management and Coordination

- policy management
- personnel management
- communication
- customer relations
- asset protection

C. Initiation and Scope Definition
D. Planning
- process planning
- deliverable determination
- quality management
- schedule and cost estimates
- resource allocation
- task and responsibility allocation
- metric process implementation

E. Software Acquisition
F. Enactment
- plan implementation
- monitor process
- control process (e.g., problem tracking and resolution techniques)
- feedback

G. Risk Management
H. Review and Evaluation
I. Project Close Out
J. Post-closure Activities

IX. Software Engineering Process (2-4% questions)

A. Process Infrastructure (e.g., life cycle models)
B. Process Measurement
C. Process Definition
D. Qualitative Process Analysis
E. Process Implementation and Change

X. Software Engineering Tools and Methods (2-4% questions)

A. Management Tools and Methods (e.g., statistical process control)
B. Development Tools and Methods
C. Maintenance Tools and Methods
D. Support Tools and Methods

XI. Software Quality (6-8% questions)

A. Software Quality Concepts
B. Planning for SQA and V&V
C. Methods for SQA and V&V
- audits, reviews and inspections
- analytic techniques
- dynamic techniques

D. Measurement Applied to SQA and V

Appendix D: CSDP Recommended References (Books)

The following books were an early recommended to candidates preparing for the IEEE Computer Society Certified Software Development Professional (CSDP) <u>beta</u> examination. They are still applicable to current exam takers.

Software Engineering Overview

Either of the following books is recommended as an overview of software engineering:

- **Software Engineering: A Practitioner's Approach**, 5th ed., Pressman, Roger S., New York, New York: McGraw-Hill, 2000.
- **Software Engineering**, Sommerville, I., 6th ed. Reading, Massachusetts: Addison-Wesley, 2000.

The following books are suggested as supplemental reading in this area:

- <u>Software Engineering</u>. Dorfman, M. & Thayer, R., eds., Los Alamitos, California: IEEE Computer Society Press, 1997.
- **Software Engineering – Theory and Practice**, Pfleeger, Shari Lawrence, Upper Saddle River, NJ: Prentice Hall, 1998.
- <u>IEEE Software Engineering Collection</u>, 1999, vols. 1-4.

Software Configuration Management

No book-length references are recommended for this topic. Please refer to the "IEEE Exam Preparation Guide" for recommended reading.

Software Construction

The following book is recommended on this topic:

- **Code Complete**, McConnell, Steve, Microsoft Press, 1993.

The following books are suggested as supplemental reading in this area:

- **The Practice of Programming**, Kernighan, Brian W. and Rob Pike, Reading, Mass.: Addison Wesley, 1999.
- **The Pragmatic Programmer: From Journeyman to Master**, Hunt, Andrew, David Thomas, and Ward Cunningham, Reading, Mass.: Addison Wesley, 1999.

Software Design

Any one of the following books is recommended in this area:

- **Software Architecture in Practice**, Bass, Len, Paul Clements and Rick Kazman. Reading, Massachusetts: Addison-Wesley, 1998.
- **Pattern Oriented Software Architecture: A System of Patterns**, Buschmann, Frank, et al, John Wiley & Sons, 1996.
- **Fundamentals of Object-Oriented Design in UML**, Page-Jones, Meilir, Addison-Wesley, 1999.

The following books are suggested as supplemental reading in this area:

- **Fundamentals of Database Systems**, Elmasri, Ramez and Shamkant Navathe, 3d Ed., Reading, Mass.: Addison Wesley, 2000.
- **Software Reuse: Architecture, Process and Optimization for Business Success**, Jacobsen, Ivar, Martin Griss, and Patrik Jonson, Reading, Massachusetts: Addison-Wesley, 1997.

Software Engineering Tools & Methods

No book-length references are recommended for this topic. See the "IEEE Exam Preparation Guide" for recommended reading.

Software Engineering Management

Any one of the following books is recommended in this area:

- **Principles of Software Engineering Management**, Gilb, Tom, Reading, Mass.: Addison Wesley, 1988.
- **Rapid Development**, McConnell, Steve, Microsoft Press, 1996.
- **Software Engineering Project Management**, 2d ed, Thayer, Richard H., IEEE Computer Society Press, Los Alamitos, CA 1997
- **Quality Software Management, Vol. 1, Systems Thinking**, Weinberg, Gerald M.. New York: Dorset House, 1992.

The following book is suggested as supplemental reading in this area:

- **Developing Managerial Skills in Engineering and Scientist**, Badawy, Michael K. Van Hostrand, NY, 1995

Software Engineering Process

Either of the following books is recommended in this area:

- **The Capability Maturity Model: Guidelines for Improving the Software Process**, Paulk, Mark, et al (Carnegie Mellon University / Software Engineering Institute). Reading, Mass.: Addison Wesley, 1995.
- **Managing the Software Process**, Humphrey, Watts S. Reading, Massachusetts, Addison-Wesley, 1989.

Software Maintenance

The following book is recommended on this topic:

- **Practical Software Maintenance**, Pigoski, Thomas M. New York, Wiley Computer Publishing, 1997.

Software Quality

No book-length references are recommended for this topic. See the "IEEE Exam Preparation Guide" for recommended reading.

The following books are suggested as supplemental reading in this area:

- **Software Engineering**, Dorfman, M. & Thayer, R., eds. Los Alamitos, California: IEEE Computer Society Press, 1997.
- **Software Inspection**, Gilb, Tom., and Dorothy Graham, Reading, MA, Addison-Wesley, 1994.
- **Practical Guide to Software Quality Management**, Horch, John, Artech House, 1996.
- **A Discipline for Software Engineering**, Humphrey, Watts S. Reading, Massachusetts: Addison-Wesley, 1995.
- **Metrics and Models in Software Quality Engineering**, Kan, Stephen H. Addison Wesley, 1995.

Software Requirements Engineering

Any one of the following books is recommended in this area

- **Software Requirements: Objects, Functions, & States**, Davis, Alan. Upper Saddle River, New Jersey: Prentice Hall, 1993.
- **Practical Software Requirements: A Manual of Content and Style**, Kovitz, Benjamin L., Manning Publications Company, 1998.
- **Mastering the Requirements Process**, Robertson, James and Suzanne Robertson, New York: Dorset House, 2000.
- **Requirements Engineering: A Good Practice Guide**, Sommerville, Ian, New York: John Wiley & Sons, 1997.
- **Software Requirements**, Wiegers, Karl. Microsoft Press, 1999.

The following book is suggested as supplemental reading in this area:

- **<u>Software Requirements Engineering</u>**, 2nd ed., Thayer, Richard H., and Merlin Dorfman, eds., IEEE Computer Society Press, Los Alamitos, CA 1997

Software Testing

Any one of the following books is recommended in this area:

- **Testing Object-Oriented Systems**, Binder, Robert V. Reading, Massachusetts: Addison-Wesley, 2000.
- **Complete Guide to Software Testing**, 2nd Ed., Hetzel, Bill, New York, New York: John Wiley & Son, 1993.
- **Software Testing : A Craftsman's Approach**, Jorgensen, Paul C. CRC Press, 1995.
- **Testing Computer Software**, 2nd Ed., Kaner, Clem, Jack Falk, and Hung Quoc Nguyen, New York, New York: John Wiley and Sons, 1999.
- **Software Testing and Continuous Quality Improvement**, Lewis, William. CRC Press 2000.
- **The Craft of Software Testing: Subsystems Testing Including Object-Based and Object-Oriented Testing**, Marick, Brian. Prentice Hall, 1997.

Professionalism and Engineering Economics

No book-length references are recommended for this topic. See the "IEEE Exam Preparation Guide" for recommended reading.

The following books are suggested as supplemental reading in this area:

- **Morality and Machines: Perspectives on Computer Ethics**, Edgar, S. L., Sudbury, Massachusetts: Jones and Bartlett, 1997.
- **Computer Ethics**, 2d Ed., Johnson, Deborah G, Upper Saddle River, NJ: Prentice-Hall, 1994
- **Smith and Roberson's Business Law**, 11th ed., Mann, Richard A., & Barry S. Roberts, Cincinnati, OH: West Thomson Learning, 2000.
- **Engineering Economy**, Thusen, G.J., Prentice-Hall, 2000

Appendix E: CSDP Online Preparation Guide (Papers)

This guide contains the articles needed to prepare for the *IEEE Computer* Society Certified Software Development Professional (CSDP) examination.

Software Engineering Overview

Boehm, Barry. "Unifying Software Engineering and Systems Engineering," *IEEE Computer*, March 2000. (PDF 102KB)

Lethbridge, Timothy C. "What Knowledge Is Important to a Software Professional?" *IEEE Computer*, May 2000. (PDF 193KB)

McConnell, Steve, "Cargo Cult Software Engineering," *IEEE Software*, March/April 2000. (PDF 71KB)

McConnell, Steve, ed. "The Best Influences on Software Engineering," *IEEE Software*, January 2000. (PDF 327KB)

McConnell, Steve. "Software's Ten Essentials," *IEEE Software*, Vol. 14, No. 2, March/April 1997.(PDF 118KB)

Reel, John S. "Critical Success Factors In Software Projects," *IEEE Software*, May 1999. (PDF 113KB)

Software Configuration Management

Bersoff, Edward H. "Elements of Software Configuration Management," IEEE Transactions on Software Engineering, vol. SE-10, no. 1 (January 1984). (PDF 1,888KB)

Forte, Gene. "Managing Change for Rapid Development," *IEEE Software*, March/April 1997. (PDF 86KB)

Jones, Capers. "Software Change Management," *IEEE Computer*, February 1996. (PDF 1,582KB)

Phillips, Dwayne. "Project Management: Filling in the Gaps," *IEEE Software*, July 1996. (PDF 380KB)

Software Construction and Implementation

McConnell, Steve. "Who Cares about Software Construction?" *IEEE Software*, January 1996 (PDF 369KB). HTML

McConnell, Steve. "Daily Build and Smoke Test," *IEEE Software*, July 1996 (PDF 340KB).

Software Design

Focus on Advances in Software Architecture: *IEEE Software*, September 1999.

Focus on Software Architecture, *IEEE Software*, November 1995.

Focus on Object Methods, Patterns, and Architectures, *IEEE Software*, January 1997.

Focus on Component Based Software Engineering, *IEEE Software*, September 1998

Focus on Component Based Development, *IEEE Computer*, July 1999

Budgen, David. "Software Design Methods: Life Belt or Leg Iron?" *IEEE Software*, September 1999. (PDF 97KB)

Jackson, Daniel and John Chapin. "Redesigning Air Traffic Control: An Exercise in Software Design," *IEEE Software*, May 2000. (PDF 101KB)

McCabe, Tom, 1976. "A Complexity Measure," IEEE Transactions on Software Engineering, Volume SE-2, Number 12 (December 1976), pp. 308-320. (PDF 1,722KB)

McConnell, Steve. "Keep It Simple," *IEEE Software*, November 1996. (PDF 418 KB)

McConnell, Steve. "Missing in Action: Information Hiding," *IEEE Software*, March 1996.

Parnas, David L. "On the design and development of program families," IEEE Transactions on Software Engineering, SE-2, 1 (March 1976), pp. 1-9. (PDF 1,218KB)

Parnas, David L. "Designing Software for Ease of Extension and Contraction," IEEE Transactions on Software Engineering, v. SE-5, March 1979, pp. 128-138. (PDF 1,568KB)

Parnas, David L., Paul C. Clements, and D. M. Weiss, 1985. "The Modular Structure of Complex Systems," IEEE Transactions on Software Engineering, March 1985, pp. 259-266. (PDF 1,105KB)

Parnas, David L., Paul C. Clements, 1986. "A Rational Design Process: How and Why to Fake It," IEEE Transactions on Software Engineering, vol. SE-12, no. 2, February 1986, pp. 251-257. (PDF 1,011KB)

Wirth, Niklaus. "A Plea for Lean Software," *IEEE Computer*, February 1995, pp. 64-68. (PDF 515 KB)

Software Engineering Tools and Methods

[TBD]

Software Engineering Management

Focus on Software Estimation: *IEEE Software*, November 2000.

Focus on Software Risk Management, *IEEE Software*, May 1997.

Focus on Software Measurement, *IEEE Software*, March 1997.

Focus on Managing Large Software Projects, *IEEE Software*, July 1996.

Boehm, Barry. "Project Termination Doesn't Equal Project Failure," *IEEE Computer*, September 2000. (PDF 46KB)

Boehm, Barry. "Managing Software Productivity and Reuse," *IEEE Computer*, September 1999. (PDF 192KB)

Boehm, Barry. "The Art of Expectations Management," *IEEE Computer*, January 2000. (PDF 170KB)

Boehm, Barry. "COTS Integration: Plug and Pray?" *IEEE Computer*, January 1999. (PDF 28KB)

Boehm, Barry W. "Safe and Simple Software Cost Analysis," *IEEE Software*, September 2000. (PDF 131KB)

Gilb, Tom. "Level 6: Why We Can't Get There from Here," *IEEE Software*, January 1996. (PDF 445KB)

Hall, Tracy and Norman Fenton. "Implementing Effective Software Metrics Programs," *IEEE Software*, March 1997 (PDF 177KB)

Hendersen-Sellers, Brian. "OO Project Management: The Need for Process," *IEEE Software*, July 1997. (PDF 75KB)

Jones, Capers. "How office space affects programming productivity," *IEEE Computer*, Vol. 28, No. 1: January 1995, pp. 76-76. (PDF 172KB)

Jones, Capers. "Patterns of Large Software Systems: Failure and Success," *IEEE Computer*, Vol. 28, No. 3: March 1995, pp. 86-87 (PDF 196KB)

Jones, Capers. "Software Specialization," *IEEE Computer*, July 1995. (PDF 178KB)

Jones, Capers. "Our Worst Current Development Practices," *IEEE Software*, March 1996. (PDF 533KB)

McConnell, Steve. "The Software Manager's Toolkit," *IEEE Software*, July 2000. (PDF 149KB)

McConnell, Steve. "Feasibility Studies," *IEEE Software*, May 1998. (PDF 79KB)

McConnell, Steve. "Sitting on the Suitcase," *IEEE Software*, May/June 2000. (PDF 69KB)

Putnam, Lawrence H. and Ware Myers, "How Solved Is the Cost Estimation Problem?" *IEEE Software*, November 1997. (PDF 190KB)

Tacket, Buford D. III and Buddy Van Doren. "Process Control for Error Free Software: A Software Success Story," *IEEE Software*, May 1999 (PDF 371KB)

van Genuchten, Michiel. "Why is Software Late? An Empirical Study of Reasons for Delay in Software Development." IEEE Transactions on Software Engineering, vol. 17, no. 6 (June 1991), pp. 582-590. (PDF 1,448KB)

Software Engineering Process

Focus on the Personal Software Process: *IEEE Software*, November 2000.

Focus on Process Diversity: *IEEE Software*, July 2000.

Focus on Process Maturity, *IEEE Software*, July 2000.

Basili, Victor, et al. "SEL's Software Process Improvement Program," *IEEE Software*, November 1995. (PDF 449KB)

Bollinger, Terry B. and Clement McGowan, "A Critical Look at Software Capability Evaluations," *IEEE Software*, July 1991, pp. 25-41. (6,359KB)

Cockburn, Alistair. "Selecting a Project's Methodology," *IEEE Software*, July 2000. (PDF 141KB)

Curtis, Bill. "Which Comes First, the Organization or Its Processes?" *IEEE Software*, November 1998. (PDF170KB)

Glass, Robert L. "Process Diversity and a Computing Old Wives'/Husbands' Tale," *IEEE Software*, July 2000. (PDF152 KB)

McConnell, Steve. "Quantifying Soft Factors," *IEEE Software*, November 2000. (PDF 258KB)

Paulk, Mark C. "How ISO 9001 Compares with the CMM," *IEEE Software*, January 1995. (PDF 1,099KB)

Roberts, Tom. "Why Can't We Implement This SDM?" *IEEE Software*, November 1999. (PDF 100KB)

Weller, Edward F. "Practical Applications of Statistical Process Control," *IEEE Software*, May 2000. (PDF 92KB)

Software Maintenance

Focus on Legacy Systems, *IEEE Software*, July 1998.

Focus on Legacy Systems, *IEEE Software*, January 1995.

Software Quality

Focus on Software Quality, *IEEE Software*, January 1996.

Focus on Reliability, *IEEE Software*, May 1995.

Jones, Capers. "Software Defect Removal Efficiency," *IEEE Computer*, April 1996. (PDF 913 KB)

McConnell, Steve. "Gauging Software Readiness with Defect Tracking," *IEEE Software*, May 1997. (PDF 117KB)

Nuseibeh, Bashar. "Ariane 5: Who Dunnit?" *IEEE Software*, May/June 1997, pp. 15-16. (PDF 128KB)

Porter, Adam and Lawrence Votta. "What Makes Inspections Work?" *IEEE Software*, November 1997. (PDF 133KB)

Voas, Jeff. "Software Quality's Eight Greatest Myths," *IEEE Software*, September 1999. (PDF 96KB)

Software Requirements

Focus on Software Requirements Engineering, *IEEE Software*, March, 1996.

Bach, James. "Reframing Requirements Analysis," *IEEE Computer*, February 1999. (PDF 254KB)

Boehm, Barry. "Requirements that Handle IKIWISI, COTS, and Rapid Change," *IEEE Computer*, July 2000. (PDF 130KB)

Davis, Alan M. "Tracing: A Simple Necessity Neglected," *IEEE Software*, September 1995. (PDF 437KB)

Gordon, V. Scott and James M. Bieman. "Rapid Prototyping: Lessons Learned," *IEEE Software*, January 1995, pp. 85-95. (PDF 1,081KB)

Jones, Capers. "Strategies for Managing Requirements Creep," *IEEE Computer*, June 1996, pp. 92-94.(PDF 319KB)

McConnell, Steve. "Achieving Leaner Software," *IEEE Software*, November 1997. (PDF 119KB)

Software Testing

Bach, James, "Risk and Requirements-Based Testing," *IEEE Computer*, June 1999. (PDF 190KB)

Berard, Edward. "Bringing Testing Into the Fold," *IEEE Software*, May 1996. (PDF 493KB)

Whitaker, James A. "What Is Software Testing? And Why Is It So Hard?" *IEEE Software*, January 2000. (PDF 120KB)

Yamaura, Tsuneo. "How to Design Practical Test Cases," *IEEE Software*, November 1998. (PDF 138KB)

Software Professionalism and Engineering Economics

Focus on Professional Software Engineering: *IEEE Software*, November 1999.

Focus on Future Directions in Software Engineering "A Tale of Two Futures," *IEEE Software,* **January 1998**

<u>IEEE-CS/ACM Code of Ethics and Professional Conduct</u>

Boehm, B. W. "<u>Software Engineering Economic</u>s," *IEEE Transactions on Software Engineering,* v. SE-10, pp. 4-21, January 1984. (PDF 3,155KB)

Boehm, Barry W. and Philip N. Papaccio. "<u>Understanding and Controlling Software Costs</u>," *IEEE Transactions on Software Engineering,* v. 14, no. 10, October 1988, pp. 1462-1477. (PDF 2,770KB)

Charette, Bob. "<u>Are We Liars or Just Fools?</u>" *IEEE Software,* July 1995. (PDF 375KB)

Davis, Alan M. "<u>Software Lemminginerring</u>," *IEEE Software,* September 1993. (PDF 1,805KB)

Ebert, Christof, et al. "<u>The Road to Maturity: Navigating Between Craft and Science</u>," *IEEE Software,* November 1997. (PDF 322KB)

Jones, Capers. "<u>Activity Based Software Costing</u>," *IEEE Computer,* May 1996. (PDF 220KB)

Parnas, David L. "<u>Software Engineering Programmes are not Computer Science Programmes</u>," *IEEE Software,* Nov/Dec 1999. (PDF 245KB)

Pour, Gilda, Martin L. Griss, and Michael Lutz. "<u>The Push to Make Software Engineering Respectable</u>," *IEEE Computer,* May 2000. (PDF 197KB)

Tockey, Steve. "<u>A Missing Link in Software Engineering</u>," *IEEE Software,* November 1997. (PDF 182KB)

Appendix F:
Certified Software Development Professional (CSDP) Examination Preparation Glossary

Richard H. Thayer, Steve McConnell, and Steve Seidman

Scope

This glossary defines the terms used in the field of *software engineering, project management,* and supporting disciplines. These definitions have their roots in several management and technical domains: system and hardware engineering, general (mainstream) management, and project management. In addition, new definitions and old terms with new meanings are included. Therefore, read the definitions carefully.

The domain of the definition should be understood or identified in the first sentence of the definition. The domain was added to definitions taken from another source and to definitions without an obvious demain.

Glossary Structure

The purpose of this glossary is to provide a definition and understanding of the Certified Software Engineering Professional Exam specifications. Maximum use was made of the definitions from IEEE Standard 610.12-1990, *Standard Glossary of Software Engineering Terminology.*

Entries in the glossary are arranged alphabetically. An entry may consist of a single word, such as *quality;* a phrase, such as *software quality analysis* or an acronym such as *SQA.* Phrases are given in their natural order *(requirements engineering)* rather than reversed order *(engineering, requirements).*

Blank spaces are taken into account in alphabetizing. They precede all other characters. For example, *test report* precedes *testability.* Hyphens and slashes follow blanks. Alternative spellings are shown as separate glossary entries with cross-references to the preferred spelling.

The singular version of nouns is always used except when the exam preparation outline uses a plural noun. Proper names are always capitalized; non-proper nouns are not capitalized.

No distinction is made between acronyms and abbreviations (an acronym is an abbreviation). Where appropriate, a term with a common acronym or abbreviation follows the term in parentheses.

Terms with multiple definitions are listed with numerical prefixes. This ordering does not imply preference. Where necessary, examples and notes have been added to clarify the definitions.

The following cross-references are used to show a term's relationship to other terms in the glossary:

- *See* refers to a preferred term or to a term whose definition serves to define the term that has been looked up.

- *See also* refers to a related term, or a term which expands the understanding of the definition.

- *Synonymous with* refers to a term that is always or nearly always synonymous with the defined term.

- *Sometimes synonymous with* refers to a term that may or may not be synonymous with the defined term; i.e., a non-standard usage.

- *Contrast with* refers to a term with an opposite or substantially different meaning.

In a few cases, nonstandard cross-references are used to clarify a particular definition.

Sources

When a definition is taken or paraphrased from another source or paper, the source is designated in brackets following the definition; for example, [Smith, 1998] or [ANSI/ANSI/IEEE-Standard 610.12-1990]. The use of a source reference does not imply an exact quote, but is an acknowledgment of the source of the definition. A list of all sources used in this glossary appears at the end of the glossary.

Glossary

adaptive maintenance -- Modification of a software product performed after delivery to keep a computer program usable in a changed or changing environment.

allocation -- (1) The process of distributing requirements, resources, or other entities among the components of a system or program. (2) The result of the distribution in (1). [IEEE Standard 610.12-1990]

analysis -- In system/software engineering, the process of studying a system by partitioning the system into parts (functions or objects) and determining how the parts relate to each other to understand the whole.

analytic technique -- *See analysis. See also technique.*

application frameworks -- A sub-system design made up of a collection of *abstract and concrete classes* and interfaces between them. Frameworks are often instantiation of a number of patterns.

architectural design -- (1) The process of defining a collection of hardware and software components and their interfaces to establish the framework for the development of a computer system. (2) The result of the process in (1) [IEEE Standard 610.12-1990]

architectural structure -- Synonym for architecture. See *architecture.*

architectural structures and viewpoints -- *See architectural structure, architectural view, architectural viewpoint.*

architectural style -- (1) Defines a family of systems in terms of a pattern of structural organization. Commonly used styles include pipes and filters, layers, rule-based systems, and blackboards. [Shaw and Garlan, 1996] (2) Characterizes a family of systems that are related by sharing structural and semantic properties.

architectural styles and patterns -- *See architectural styles, design patterns.*

architectural view -- A representation of a whole system from the perspective of a related set of concerns. [IEEE Standard 1471-2000]

architectural viewpoint -- A specification of the conventions for constructing and using a view. A pattern or template from which to develop individual views by establishing the purposes and audience for a view and the techniques for its creation and analysis. [IEEE Standard 1471-2000]

architecture --- The fundamental organization of a system embodied in its components, their relationships to each other, and to the environment and the principles guiding its design and evolution. [IEEE Standard 1471-2000]

asset -- Anything owned having monetary value; property both real and personal. [Cleland and Kerzner, 1985]

asset protection -- See *asset, protection.*

audit -- An independent examination of a work product or set of work products to assess compliance with specifications, standards, contractual agreements, or other criteria. [IEEE Standard 610.12-1990]

audit, reviews, and inspections -- *See audit, reviews, and inspections.*

change impact analysis -- Concerned with assessing the impact on work products, schedules, and budgets of the proposed change. *Also called impact analysis*

code -- (1) In software engineering, computer instructions and data definitions expressed in a programming language or in a form output by an assembler, compiler, or other translator. (2) To express a computer program in a programming language. (3) A character or bit pattern that is assigned a particular meaning; for example, a status code. [IEEE Standard 610.12-1990]

code design -- Design of code. *See also code, design.*

code documentation -- *See documentation.*

code of ethics standard -- A standard that describes the characteristics of a set of moral principles dealing with accepted standards of conduct by, within, and among professionals. [IEEE Standard 610.12-1990]

code tuning -- Changes made to program source code for the purpose of optimizing performance; usually to increase speed or reduce memory usage.

coding -- (1) In software engineering, the process of expressing a computer program in a programming language. (2) The transformation of logic and data from design specifications (design descriptions) into a programming language. [IEEE Standard 610.12-1990]

communication -- In management, the process of transferring information from one person or group to another person or group with the understanding that the message being transmitted was understood by both groups or by both individuals. [Thayer & Thayer, *Project Management*, 1997]

configuration auditing -- In configuration management, this is an independent examination of the configuration status to be compared with the physical configuration. *See also audit.*

configuration control -- An element of configuration management consisting of evaluation, coordination, approval or disapproval, and implementation of changes to configuration items after formal establishment of their configuration identification. [IEEE Standard 610.12-1990]

configuration identification -- In configuration management, (1) An element of configuration management consisting of selecting the configuration items for a system and recording their functional and physical characteristics in technical documentation. (2) The current approved technical documentation for a configuration item as set forth in specifications, drawings, associated lists, and documents referenced therein. [IEEE Standard 610.12-1990]

configuration management (CM) -- In system/software engineering, a discipline applying technical and administrative direction and surveillance to: identify and document the functional and physical characteristics of a configuration item, control changes to those characteristics, record and report change processing and implementation status, and verify compliance with specified requirements. [IEEE Standard 610.12-1990]

configuration status accounting -- In configuration management, an element of configuration management consisting of the recording and reporting of information needed to manage a configuration effectively. This information includes a listing of the approved configuration identification, the status of proposed changes to the configuration, and the implementation status of approved changes. [IEEE Standard 610.12-1990]

construction -- The general name for detailed design, coding, unit testing, and related activities — the collection of activities focused on creating source code.

construction planning -- *See construction, planning.*

construction QA -- *See construction, software quality assurance.*

construction tools -- Tools used during construction. *See also tool.*

control -- (1) In management, all the activities that ensure that actual work goes according to plan. It measures performance against goals and plans, reveals when and where deviation exists, and, by putting in motion actions to correct deviations, helps ensure the accomplishment of plans [Thayer & Thayer, *Project Management*, 1997] (2) In engineering, the monitoring of system output to compare with expected output and taking corrective action when the actual output does not match the expected output. *Also known as feedback control.*

control process -- *See control.*

coordination -- The combining of diverse parts or groups to make a unit, or the way these parts work together. [MSN Encarta, 2000]

corrective maintenance -- Reactive modification of a software product performed after delivery to correct discovered faults.

cost estimate -- (1) The estimated cost to perform a stipulated task or acquire an item. (2) The product of a cost-estimation method or model. [Thayer & Thayer, *Project Management*, 1997]

customer -- (1) In system/software system engineering, an individual or organization who specifies the requirements for and formally accepts delivery of a new or modified hardware/software product and its documentation. The customer may be internal or external to the parent organization of the project and does not necessarily imply a financial transaction between customer and developer. (2) The person or persons who pay for the project and usually (but not necessarily) decide the requirements; the customer may or may not be the user. [IEEE Standard 830-1998]

customer relations -- In system/software engineering, a set of agreements, both formal and informal, detailing how the customer will be treated by the developer. [Thayer & Thayer, European Perspective, 1993] *See also customer.*

data -- In system/software engineering, a representation of facts, concepts, or instructions in a manner suitable for communication, interpretation, or processing by humans or by automatic means. [IEEE Standard 610.12-1990]

data collection -- The process of combining data from different sources to a central point for the purpose of being processed by a computer. [Thayer & Thayer, *European Perspective, 1993*] *See also data.*

data design -- Design of a program's data, especially table design in database applications.

data design and management -- *See data design, data management.*

data management -- In software development, a term referring to systems offering users an interface that blocks the majority of file handling details. This leaves the user free to concentrate on the logical properties of the data. [Oxford Dictionary, 1990]

data-structured design -- A software system engineering design methodology used for business applications and other systems with well-understood data structures. It produces a program structure by designing input/output data structures and relies on decomposition based on the higher-level nature of these data structures. [Thayer & Thayer, *Software Requirements, 1997*] *Contrast with object-oriented design, functional design.*

data–structure-oriented design -- *See data-structured design.*

deliverable determination -- *See deliverable document.*

deliverable document -- In software system engineering, a document that is deliverable to a customer. Examples are user manuals, operator manuals, and programmer maintenance manuals. [Thayer & Thayer, *Software Requirements, 1997*] *See also documentation.*

design -- (1) The process of defining the architecture, components, interfaces, and other characteristics of a system or component. (2) The result of the process in (1). [ANSI/IEEE Standard 610.12 1990]

design framework -- *Synonym for architecture or design.*

design of families of programs and frameworks -- *See families of programs, design frameworks*

design patterns -- A description of the problem and the essence of its solution so the solution may be reused in different settings. The pattern is not a detailed specification, but a description of accumulated wisdom and experience. [Buschmann et al, 1996]

development tools and methods -- *See tool, method.*

disaster -- In software engineering, a system crash caused by software, database corruption, or erroneous logical processes caused by degraded software.

disaster recovery -- In computer system operations, the return to normal operation after a hardware or software failure. *See also disaster, recovery.*

distributed computing -- The spreading of computation and data across a number of computers connected by a network.

documentation -- (1) A collection of documents on a given subject. (2) Any written or pictorial information describing, defining, specifying, reporting, or certifying activities, requirements, procedures, or results. (3) The process of generating or revising a document. (4) The management of documents, including identification, acquisition, processing, storage, and dissemination. [IEEE Standard 610.12-1990]

dynamic -- Pertaining to an event or process that occurs during computer program execution; for example, dynamic analysis, dynamic binding. *Contrast with static.* [IEEE Standard 610.12-1990]

dynamic techniques -- *See dynamic.*

economics -- The study of the production, distribution, and consumption of goods and services. [MSN Encarta, 2000]

enactment -- The establishment of something by law, ruling, or other authoratative acts.

engineering -- The application of science in the design, planning, construction, and maintenance of buildings, machines, and other manufactured things. [MSN Encarta, 2000]

engineering economics -- The methods and models for analyzing choices that software projects must make related to project costs and cost impacts. *See also economics, engineering.*

error -- (1) The difference between a computed, observed, or measured value or condition and the true, specified, or theoretically correct value or condition. For example, a difference of 30 meters between a computed result and the correct result. (2) An incorrect step, process, or data definition. For example, an incorrect instruction in a computer program. (3) An incorrect result. For example, a computed result of 12 when the correct result is 10. (4) A human action that produces an incorrect result. For example, an incorrect action on the part of a programmer or operator. [IEEE Standard 610.12-1990]

error processing -- The detection of and responses to errors in a program. *See also error.*

ethics -- A system of moral principles governing the appropriate conduct for an individual or group. [MSN Encarta, 2000] *See also code of ethics standard.*

evaluation -- (1) Determination of fitness for use. (2) The process of determining whether an item or activity meets specified criteria.

evaluation tools -- An automatic or manual tool used for the evaluation of a software product or process. *See also evaluation, tool.*

execute --- To carry out an instruction, process, or computer program. [IEEE Standard 610.12-1990]

families of programs -- Sets of programs that are related by sharing significant portions of requirements, design, and code; e.g., a program family might include one version of a program developed for an English-speaking audience, a second version of a program developed for a German-speaking audience, and a third version for a Japanese-speaking audience .

fault tolerance -- (1) The ability of a system or component to continue normal operation despite the presence of hardware or software faults. (2) The number of faults a system or component can withstand before normal operation is impaired. (3) Pertaining to the study of errors, faults, and failures, and of methods for enabling systems to continue normal operation in the presence of faults. [IEEE Standard 610.12-1990]

feedback --- (1). In project, management reports that provide information or a project's current status as measured against original plans . It also includes the degree and cause of the deviation. (2). In electrical circuits, signals, or information that is taken from the output stage of a system and is feedback to the input stage of the same system to provide control. [Thayer & Thayer, *European Perspective, 1993*]

functional decomposition -- In software engineering, the partitioning of higher-level system functions into smaller and smaller pieces to render them more manageable and understandable.

functional design --- (1) The process of defining the working relationships among the components of a system. (2) The result of the process in (1). [IEEE Standard 610.12-1990] *Contrast with object-oriented design, data-structure design.*

function-oriented design -- *See functional design, architectural design.*

general design concepts -- A fundamental idea that can be applied to designing a system. For example, information hiding is a software design concept. [Gomaa, 1997] *See also design.*

general strategies -- The overall plan and direction for performing design. For example, *functional decomposition* is a software design strategy. [Gomaa, 1997]

hazard analysis -- The process of studying actual or potential hazards to determine their impact on a software system. The impact of the hazard may include delays, costly repairs, danger to properity or human life, or failure to meet the required functionality.

human factors in software design -- *See human-engineering, user interface.*

human-computer interaction -- *See human-engineering, user interface*

446

human-engineering -- In system/software system engineering, a multidisciplinary activity that applies the knowledge, derived from psychology and technology, to specify and design high quality human-machine interfaces. The human engineering process encompasses the following steps: activity analysis, semantic analysis and design, syntactic and lexical design, user environment design, and prototyping. [Thayer & Thayer, *Software Requirements,* 1997]

implementation -- (1) The process of translating a design into hardware components, software components, or both. (2) The result of the process in (1). [IEEE Standard 610.12-1990]

implementation plan -- *See implementation, coding.*

initiation and scope definition -- A non-specific term for work performed early in a software project that includes high-level statements of requirements and rough estimates of project cost and schedule.

inspections --- A static analysis technique that relies on visual examination of development products to detect errors, violations of development standards, and other problems. Types include code inspections and design inspections. [IEEE Standard 610.12-1990]

maintenance -- (1) The process of modifying a software system or component after delivery to correct faults, improve performance or other attributes, or adapt to a changed environment. (2) The process of retaining a hardware system or component in, or restoring it to, a state in which it can perform its required functions. [IEEE Standard 610.12-1990]

maintenance tools and methods -- *See tool, method.*

maintenance type -- One of a category of maintaince activities such as adaptative maintenance, corrective maintenance, and perfective maintenance. *See adaptative maintenance, corrective maintenance, and perfective maintenance.*

management -- All activities and tasks undertaken by one or more persons to plan and control the activities of others to achieve an objective or complete an activity that could not be achieved by the others acting independently. [Thayer & Thayer, *Project Management,* 1997]

management of SCM process -- *See configuration management (CM).*

management tools and methods -- *See management, tools, methods.*

measurement applied to SQA and V&V -- *See SQA measurement, V&V measurement.*

measurement of program goals -- *See measurement, program goals.*

measurement of software and its development -- *See software measurement.*

measurement -- The process by which numbers or symbols are assigned to attributes of entities in the real world in such a way as to describe them according to clearly defined rules. [Fenton & Pfleeger, 1996]

methods -- A systematic and regular way of accomplishing a given task.

methods for SQA and V&V -- *See SQA methods, V&V methods.*

metric -- A quantitative measure of the degree to which a system, component, or process possesses a given attribute. [IEEE Standard 610.12-1990]

metric process implementation -- *See process implementation metric.*

monitor process --- *See control.*

object-oriented design --- A software development technique in which a system or component is expressed in terms of objects and connections between those objects. [IEEE Standard 610.12-1990] *Contrast with functional design, data-structure design.*

organization -- In management, a formal or informal framework of tasks, groups of tasks, and the line of authority between tasks for the purpose of focusing the efforts of many on a goal or objective. [Thayer & Thayer, *Project Management*, 1997]

organizational management -- All management activities that result in the design of a formal structure of tasks and authority. Organizing involves the determination and enumeration of the activities required to achieve the objects of the organization, the grouping of these activities, the assignment of such groups of activity to an organizational entity or group identifiers, the delegation of responsibilities and authority to carry them out, and the provisions for coordination of authoritative relationships. [Thayer & Thayer, *Project Management*, 1997]

organizational management and coordination -- *See organizational management, coordination.*

pattern -- An abstraction from a concrete form that recurs in specific non-arbitrary contexts; within software, a "pattern" most often refers to solving problems in design; i.e., a solution to a recurring design problem. [Buschmann et al, 1996]

perfective maintenance -- Modification of a software product after delivery to improve performance or maintainability.

performance -- The degree to which a system or component accomplishes its designated functions within given constraints, such as speed, accuracy, or memory usage. [IEEE Standard 610.12-1990]

performance analysis techniques and tools -- Techniques and tools to measure and evaluate the performance of a software system. *See also performance, tools and techniques.*

personnel -- In management, persons employed in any work, enterprise, service, or establishment. [Thayer & Thayer, *Software Requirements, 1997*]

personnel management -- The management of activities involving the hiring, retaining, promoting, training, and terminating of personnel. *See also personnel.*

plan implementation -- To initiate and put the plan into action. *See also execute.*

planning -- All management activities that lead to the selection, from among alternatives, of future courses of action for the enterprise. Planning involves selecting the objectives of the enterprise and the strategies, policies, programs and procedures for achieving them, either for the entire enterprise or for any organized part thereof. [Thayer & Thayer, *Project Management*, 1997]

planning -- *See planning.*

planning for SQA and V&V -- *See SQA planning, V&V planning.*

policy -- .1. In management, policies are concerned with predetermined management decisions. They are general statements or understandings that guide decision-making activities. Policies limit the freedom in making decisions but allow for some discretion. 2. In software engineering (structured analysis methodology), a tool of the structured specifications methodology. [Thayer & Thayer, *Project Management*, 1997]

policy management -- *See policy.*

post-closure activities -- Activities that occur after a software system has been formally accepted by its customer; these activities include but are not limited to post mortem reviews and archiving project materials. *See also project close out.*

process -- (1) A sequence of steps performed for a given purpose; for example, the software development process. (2) An executable unit managed by an operating system scheduler. (3) To perform operations on data. [IEEE Standard 610.12-1990]

process definition – *See process.*

process implementation and change -- *See process management.*

process infrastructure -- In software engineering, the internal structure of the software develoment process, to include lifecycle phases, documentation, baselines, reviews, and products.

process management --- The direction, control, and coordination or work performed to develop a product or perform a service. An example is quality assurance. [IEEE Standard 610.12-1990]

process measurement -- Those measurements established for each step in the software engineering process that are used to determine its effectiveness. The metrics define the results of each process stage and relate them to the resources expended, errors introduced, errors removed, and various coverage, efficiency, and productivity indicators. [Gray, Survey Tools 1992]

process planning -- Planning the development and use of a software process. *See also process, planning.*

product attributes -- Characteristics of a software product. Can refer either to general characteristics such as reliability, maintainability, and usability or to specific features of a software product.

product attributes and measure -- *See product attributes, product measures, quality attributes.*

product measures -- In software engineering, a metric that can be used to measure the characteristics of the delivered documents and software.

professional practice -- Non-technical elements of a software engineer's work practices including responsibility to the public, responsibility to clients and employers, legal and ethical conduct, independence of judgment, and professional development.

project close out -- A plan to ensure orderly closeout of the software project. Items in the closeout plan should include a staff reassignment plan, a plan for archiving project materials, a plan for post-mortem debriefings of project personnel, and preparation of a final report to include lessons learned and analysis of project objectives achieved. [IEEE Standard 1058-1998]

project management -- A system of procedures, practices, technologies, and know-how that provides the planning, organizing, staffing, directing, and controlling necessary to successfully manage an engineering project. Know-how in this case means the skill, background, and wisdom to apply knowledge effectively in practice. *See also software engineering project management.* [Thayer & Thayer, *Project Management*, 1997]

project plan -- A document that describes the technical and management approach to be followed for a project. The plan typically describes the work to be done, the resources required, the methods to be used, the procedures to be followed, the schedules to be met, and the way that the project will be organized. For example, a software development plan. [IEEE Standard 610.12-1990]

protection -- A process that prevents somebody or something from being harmed or damaged.

qualitative process analysis -- Evaluation of software processes that are based on subjective, qualitative information rather than quantitative information.

quality analysis -- (1) A planned and systematic pattern of all actions necessary to provide adequate confidence that an item or product conforms to established technical requirements. (2) A set of activities designed to evaluate the process by which products are developed or manufactured. [IEEE Standard 610.12-1990]

quality analysis and evaluation tools -- *See quality analysis, evaluation tools.*

quality attribute -- A feature or characteristic that affects an item's quality. <u>Note</u>: In a hierarchy of quality attributes, higher-level attributes may be called quality factors, and lower level attributes called quality attributes. [IEEE Standard 610.12-1990]

quality management -- That aspect of the overall management function that determines and implements the quality policy. [IEEE-Standard 1074]

real-time -- Pertaining to a system or mode of operation in which computation is performed during the actual time that an external process occurs, in order that the computation results can be used to control, monitor, or respond to the external process in a timely manner. [IEEE Standard 610.12-1990]

real-time concepts -- *See real-time.*

recovery -- The return of something to a normal or improved state after a setback or loss.

regression testing -- Retesting to detect faults introduced by modification.

requirement -- (1) A condition or capability needed by a user to solve a problem or achieve an objective. (2) A condition or capability that must be met or possessed by a system or system component to satisfy a contract, standard, specification, or other formally imposed document. (3) A documented representation of a condition or capability as in (1) or (2). [IEEE Standard 610.12-1990]

requirements analysis -- *See software requirements analysis.*

requirements elicitation -- The process through which the customers (buyers and/or users) and developer (contractor) of a software system discover, review, articulate, and understand their requirements. [Thayer, 2001]

requirements engineering -- (1) A method of obtaining a precise formal specification from the informal and often vague requirements of a customer. (2) In system engineering, the science and discipline concerned with analyzing and documenting requirements. It comprises needs analysis, requirements analysis, and requirements specifications. [Sannella, 1988], [Thayer & Thayer, *European Perspective, 1993*]

requirements engineering process – *See requirements engineering.*

requirements management -- *See software requirements management.*

requirements validation – *See validation. See also software requirements verification.*

requirements verification -- *See software requirements verification.*

resource allocation -- The assignment or allocating of computer resources to different activities or tasks.

responsibility -- In management, the accountability for actions taken, resources used, compliance with policy, and the attainment of results. It is "the obligation owed by subordinates to their supervisors for exercising authority delegated to them in a way to accomplish results expected." [Koontz and O'Donnell, 1972]

responsibility allocation -- The allocation (partitioning) of responsibility to different organizational units. *See also responsibility, allocation.*

review and evaluation -- *See reviews, evaluation.*

reviews -- A process or meeting during which a work product or set of work products, is presented to project personnel, managers, users, customers, or other interested parties for comment or approval. Types include code reviews, design reviews, formal qualification reviews, requirements reviews, and test readiness reviews. [IEEE Standard 610.12-1990]

risk management -- In system/software engineering, an "umbrella" title for the processes used to manage risk.. It is an organized means of identifying and measuring risk (risk assessment) and developing, selecting, and managing options (risk analysis) for resolving (risk handling) these risks. The primary goal of risk management is to identify and respond to potential problems with sufficient lead-time to avoid a crisis situation.

schedule -- A management device used to plan future events. [Thayer & Thayer, *European Perspective, 1993*]

schedule and cost estimates -- The management activity of determining the probable cost of an activity or product and the time to complete the activity or deliver the product. *See also schedule.*

selection of measurement --- The selection process of appropriate measurements to aid in the management of software development. *See also measurement.*

SEPM -- Acronym for software engineering project management.

software -- Computer programs, procedures, and possibly associated documentation and data pertaining to the operation of a computer system. *Contrast with hardware.* [IEEE Standard 610.12-1990]

software acquisition -- The process of obtaining a system, software product or software service. [IEEE/EIA Standard 12207.0-1996] *See also software.*

software and system safety -- In safety-critical systems, freedom from unacceptable risk of personal harm. The likelihood that a system does not lead to a state in which human life or environment are endangered. Note: safety relates to all aspects of a system, sub-systems, environment, and to human factors such as operator error, wrongdoing, and incorrect data. [IEE/BCS Safety-Related Systems, 1989]

software architecture -- *See architecture. See also software*

software configuration auditing -- In configuration management, an independent examination of the configuration status to compare with the physical configuration. *See also audit.*

software configuration control -- In configuration management, an element of configuration management consisting of the evaluation, coordination, approval or disapproval, and implementation of changes to configuration items after formal establishment of their configuration identification. [IEEE Standard 610.12-1990]

software configuration identification -- In configuration management, (1) An element of configuration management consisting of selecting the configuration items for a system and recording their functional and physical characteristics in technical documentation. (2) The current approved technical documentation for a configuration item as set forth in specifications, drawings, associated lists, and documents referenced therein. [IEEE Standard 610.12-1990]

software configuration management -- In system/software engineering, a discipline applying technical and administrative direction and surveillance to: identify and document the functional and physical characteristics of a configuration item, control changes to those characteristics, record and report change processing and implementation status, and verify compliance with specified requirements. [IEEE Standard 610.12-1990]

software configuration status accounting -- In configuration management, an element of configuration management consisting of the recording and reporting of information needed to manage a configuration effectively. This information includes a listing of the approved configuration identification, the status of proposed changes to the configuration, and the implementation status of approved changes. [IEEE Standard 610.12-1990]

software design -- In software engineering, the process of defining the software architecture (structure), components, modules, interfaces, test approach, and data for a software system to satisfy specified requirements. [ANSI/IEEE Standard 729-1983]

software design concepts -- In software engineering, a fundamental idea that can be applied to designing a system. For example, information hiding is a software design concept

software design context -- The framework and the environment in which the software design is developed.

software design notation --- Software design notation or representation is a means of describing a software design. It may be diagrammatic, symbolic, or textual. For example, structure charts and pseudocode are software design notations. [Gomaa, 1997]

software design notation and documentation -- *See software design notation, software documentation.*

software design process -- A systematic approach for carrying out design. It typically describes a sequence of steps for producing a design. [Gomaa, 1997]

software design quality analysis and evaluation -- *See quality analysis, evaluation tools.*

software design strategies and methods -- The overall plan and direction for performing design.

software development methodology -- In software engineering: (1) An integrated set of software engineering methods, policies, procedures, rules, standards, techniques, tools, languages, and other methodologies for analyzing, designing, implementing, and testing software; (2) A set of rules for selecting the correct methodology, process, or tools. [Thayer & Thayer, *Project Management*, 1997]

software documentation -- *See documentation.*

software engineering management -- *See software engineering project management.*

software engineering process --- The total set of software engineering activities needed to transform a user's requirements into software. [Humphrey, 1989] *See also software development methodology.*

software engineering project management (SEPM) -- A system of procedures, practices, technologies, and know-how that provides the planning, organizing, staffing, directing, and controlling necessary to successfully manage a software engineering project. Know-how in this case means the skill, background, and wisdom to apply knowledge effectively in practice. [Thayer & Thayer, *Project Management*, 1997]

software engineering tools and methods -- *See tool, method, software development methodology.*

software maintenance -- *See maintenance (1).*

software maintenance documentation -- *See support manual.*

software maintenance management -- *See management.*

software maintenance measurement -- *See measurement.*

software maintenance planning -- *See planning.*

software maintenance process -- *See process.*

software management process -- *See software configuration management.*

software measurement -- *See measurement. See also software metric.*

software metric -- A quantitative measure of the degree to which a system, component, or process possesses a given attribute. [IEEE Standard 610.12-1990

software metric model -- *See software metric.*

software quality -- In software engineering: (1) The totality of features and characteristics of a software product that affects its ability to satisfy given needs (for example, to conform to specifications). (2) The degree to which software possesses a desired combination of attributes. (3). The degree to which a customer or user perceives that his or her composite expectations are met. (4) The composite characteristics of software that determine the degree to which the software will meet the expectations of the customer. [ANSI/IEEE Standard 729-1983] (5) Attributes of software that affect its perceived value; for example, correctness, reliability, maintainability, and portability. (6) Software quality includes fitness for purpose, reasonable cost, reliability, ease of use in relation to those who use it, design of maintenance and upgrade characteristics, and compares well against reliable products. [Thayer & Thayer, *European Perspective, 1993*]

software quality assurance -- *See quality assurance.*

software quality assurance -- See SQA.

software quality concepts -- *See software quality.*

software quality metric -- *See quality metric.*

software release management -- Management of activities surrounding release of one or more versions of software to one or more customers. Release management includes defining acceptable quality levels for release, authority to authorize the release, release procedures, etc. *See also version.*

Software Requirements -- *See requirement, requirements engineering.*

Software Requirements analysis -- (1) The process of studying user needs to arrive at a definition of system, hardware, or software requirements. (2) The process of studying and refining system, hardware, or software requirements. [IEEE Standard 610.12-1990] (3) Reasoning and analyzing the customer and user needs to arrive at a definition of software requirements. [Thayer, 2001]

software requirements management -- In system/software system engineering, the process of controlling the identification, allocation, and flowdown of requirements from the system level to the module or part level, including interfaces, verification, modifications, and status monitoring. [Thayer & Thayer, *Software Requirements, 1997*]

software requirements specification -- (1) A document that specifies the requirements for a system or component. Typically included are functional requirements, performance requirements, interface requirements, design requirements, and development standards. [IEEE Standard 610.12-1990] 2. A document that clearly and precisely records each of the requirements of the software system. [Thayer, 2001]

software requirements verification -- Ensuring that the software requirements specification is in compliance with the system requirements, conforms to document standards of the requirements phase, and is an adequate basis for the architectural (preliminary) design phase. [Thayer, 2001] *See also verification, requirements validation.*

software testing --- *See testing.*

software tool -- A computer program used in the development, testing, analysis, or maintenance of a program or its documentation. Examples include comparator, cross-reference generator, decompiler, driver, editor, flowcharter, monitor, test case generator, and timing analyzer. [IEEE Standard 610.12-1990]

source code organization -- Arrangement of source code including layout of code within a single file and packaging of source code into modules, classes, physical files, etc.

SQA (software quality assurance) -- (1) A planned and systematic pattern of all actions necessary to provide adequate confidence that an item or product conforms to established technical requirements. (2) A set of activities designed to evaluate the process by which products are developed or manufactured. [IEEE Standard 610.12-1990]

SQA measurement -- *See SQA, measurement.*

SQA methods -- *See SQA, methods.*

SQA planning -- *See SQA, planning.*

standards -- Mandatory requirements employed and enforced to prescribe a disciplined uniform approach to software development, that is, mandatory conventions and practices are in fact standards. [IEEE Standard 610.12-1990]

style -- A way of doing something; a particular technique or method to perform an activity.

support manual -- A document that provides the information necessary to service and maintain an operational system or component throughout its life cycle. Typically described are the hardware and software that make up the system or component, and procedures for servicing, repairing, or reprogramming it. [IEEE Standard 610.12-1990]

support methods -- Software methods that provide support to the development of a software system. *See also methods, support software.*

support software -- Software that aids in the development or maintenance of other software; for example, compilers, loaders, and other utilities. [IEEE Standard 610.12-1990]

support tools and methods -- *See support software, support methods.*

system deployment -- (1) Release of software to end users or customers; i.e., "release." (2) Phase of a project in which software is put into operation and cutover issues are resolved.

system integration --- In system/software system engineering, this ensures that the various segments and elements of the total system can interface with each other and with the external environment. [Thayer & Thayer, *European Perspective, 1993*]

system integration and deployment -- *See system integration, system deployment.*

task -- The smallest unit of work subject to management accountability. A task is a well-defined work assignment for one or more project members. Related tasks are usually grouped to form activities. [IEEE-Standard 1074-1997]

task and responsibility allocation -- *See task assignment, responsibility allocation.*

task assignment -- *See task.*

technique -- Technical and managerial procedures that aid in the evaluation and improvement of the software development process. [IEEE Standard 610.12-1990]

test coverage -- The degree to which a given test or set of tests addresses all specified requirements for a given system or component. [IEEE Standard 610.12-1990]

test coverage of code -- The amount of code actually executed during the test process. It is stated as a percentage of the total instructions executed or paths traversed.

test coverage of specifications – *See test coverage.*

test design -- Documentation specifying the details of the test approach for a software feature or combination of software features and identifying the associated tests. [IEEE Standard 610.12-1990]

test documentation -- Documentation describing plans for, or results of, the testing of a system or component. Types include test case specification, test incident report, test log, test plan, test procedure and test report. [IEEE Standard 610.12-1990]

test execution -- Act of performing one or more test cases.

test level -- In software engineering, the effort associated with the execution of a set of tests governed by a common test plan, test specification, and/or test procedures document.

test management -- *See management.*

testing strategies -- In software engineering, one of a number of approaches used for testing software. For example, functional versus structural testing, static versus dynamics testing, etc. [Thayer & Thayer, *European Perspective, 1993*]

tool -- (1) An item either used in performing an operation or necessary in the practice of a vocation or profession. (2) In engineering, a step-by-step formalized, manual, or automated process for solving engineering problems. (3) In software engineering, a process or method sometimes used in the performance of a task or procedure used by programmers, software engineers, or managers in the performance of their tasks. [Thayer & Thayer, *European Perspective, 1993*] *See also software tool.*

types of tests -- In system/software engineering, a description of different testing techniques and strategies; for example, unit, integration, system, and acceptance tests. Other descriptions are alpha (factory) and beta tests.

user interface -- An interface that enables information to be passed between a human user and hardware or software components of a computer system. [IEEE Standard 610.12-1990]

V&V (verification and validation) -- The process of determining whether the requirements for a system or component are complete and correct, the products of each development phase fulfill the requirements or conditions imposed by the previous phase, and the final system or component complies with specified requirements. [IEEE Standard 610.12-1990]

V&V measurement -- *See V&V, measurement.*

V&V methods -- *See V&V, methods.*

V&V planning -- *See V&V, planning.*

Validation -- (1) The process of evaluating a system or component during or at the end of the development process to determine whether it satisfies specified requirements. *Contrast with verification.* [IEEE Standard 610.12-1990] (2) The process for determining whether the requirements and the final, as-built system or software product fulfills its specific intended use [IEEE/EIA Standard 12207.2, Paragraph 6.5-1997]

verification -- (1) The process of evaluating a system or component to determine whether the products of a given development phase satisfy the conditions imposed at the start of that phase. *Contrast with validation.* [IEEE Standard 610.12-1990] (2) The verification process is a process for determining whether the software products of an activity fulfill the requirements or conditions imposed on them in the previous activities [IEEE/EIA Standard12207.2, Paragraph 6.4-1997]

version -- (1) An initial release or re-release of a computer software configuration item, associated with a complete compilation or recompilation of the computer software configuration item. (2) An initial release or complete re- release of a document, as opposed to a revision resulting from issuing change pages to a previous release. *See also configuration control; version description document.* [IEEE Standard 610.12-1990]

References

[**ANSI/IEEE Standard 729-1983**] IEEE Standard Glossary of Software Engineering Terminology, The Institute of Electrical and Electronics Engineers, Inc., NY, approved by American National Standards Institute August 9, 1983.

[**Buschmann et al, 1996**] Buschmann, Frank, Regine Meunier, Hans Rohnert, Peter Sommerlad, Michael Stal, Pattern-Oriented Software Architecture: A System of Patterns, Wiley, Chichester, 1996.

[**Cleland and Kerzner, 1985**] Cleland, D.I., and H. Kerzner, *The Project Management Dictionary of Terms,* Van Nostrand Reinhold Company, New York, 1985.

[**Fenton & Pfleeger, 1996**] Fenton, Norman E., Shari L. Pfleeger, *Software Metrics: A Rigorous & Practicle Approach,* 2nd ed., PWS Publishing Company, International Thompson Computer Press, London, 1996.

[**Gomaa, 1997**] Gomaa, Hassan, "Design Methods for Concurrent and Real-Time Systems," in Dorfman, M, and R.H. Thayer (eds.), *Software Engineering,* IEEE Computer Society Press, Los Alamitos, CA, 1997.

[**Humphrey, 1989**] Humphrey, W.S., *Managing the Software Process*, Addison-Wesley, Reading, MA, 1989

[IEE/BCS Safety-Related Systems 1989] IEE/BCS, Software in Safety-Related Systems, The Institution of Electrical Engineering and The British Computer Society, October 1989.

[IEEE Standard 1058-1998] *IEEE Standard for Software Project Management Plans*, The Institute of Electrical and Electronics Engineers, Inc., NY.

[IEEE Standard 610.12-1990] Standard Glossary of Software Engineering Terminology, The Institute of Electrical and Electronics Engineers, Inc., NY.

[IEEE Standard 830-1998] *IEEE Recommended Practice for Software Requirements Specifications*, The Institute of Electrical and Electronics Engineers, Inc., NY.

[IEEE/EIA Standard 12207.0-1996] *Standard for Information Technology Software Life Cycle Processes*, The Institute of Electrical and Electronics Engineers, Inc., NY.

[IEEE/EIA Standard 12207.2-1997] *Guide for ISO/IEC 12207 Life Cycle Processes Implementation Considerations*, The Institute of Electrical and Electronics Engineers, Inc., NY.

[IEEE-Standard 1074-1997] IEEE Standard for Developing Software Life Cycle Processes, The Institute of Electrical and Electronics Engineers, Inc., NY.

[IEEE-Standard 1471-2000] IEEE Recommended Practice for Architectural Description for Architectural Description of Software-Intensive Systems, The Institute of Electrical and Electronics Engineers, Inc., NY.

[Koontz and O'Donnell, 1972] H. Koontz and C. O'Donnell, *Principles of Management: An Analysis of Managerial Functions*, 5th ed., McGraw-Hill Book Company, NY, 1972.

[MSN Encarta, 2000] http://dictionary.msn.com

[Oxford Dictionary, 1990] *Dictionary of Computing*, 3rd edition, Oxford University Press, Oxford, 1990

[Sannella, 1988] Sannella, D., "A Survey of Formal Software Development Methods," in R.H. Thayer and A.D. McGettrick (eds.), Software Engineering: A European Prospective," IEEE Computer Society Press, Los Alametos, CA, 1992.

[Shaw and Garlan, 1996] Shaw, M. and D. Garlan, *Software Architecture: Perspectives on an Emerging Discipline*, Prentice-Hall, Upper Saddle River, NJ, 1996.

[Thayer & Thayer *European Perspective, 1993***]** Thayer, R.H. and M.C. Thayer, "European Perspective Glossary" in Thayer, R.H., and A.D. McGettrick (eds.), *Software Engineering: A European Perspective*, IEEE Computer Society Press, Los Alamitos, CA, 1993, IEEE-CS Press catalog number 2117.

[Thayer & Thayer *Software Requirements, 1997***]** Thayer, R.H. and M.C. Thayer, "Software Requirements Engineering Glossary" in Thayer, R.H., and M. Dorfman (eds.), *Software Requirements Engineering*, 2nd ed., IEEE Computer Society Press, Los Alamitos, CA, 1997, IEEE-CS Press catalog number 7738.

[Thayer & Thayer, *Project Management***, 1997]** Thayer, R.H. and M.C. Thayer, "Project Management Glossary" in Thayer, R.H. (ed.), *Software Engineering Project Management*, 2nd ed., IEEE Computer Society Press, Los Alamitos, CA, 1997, IEEE-CS Press catalog number 8000.

[Thayer, 2001] Thayer, R.H. "Software Requirements Engineering," in supplement to Dorfman, M, and R.H. Thayer (eds.), Software Engineering, IEEE Computer Society Press, Los Alamitos, CA, 2001, IEEE-CS Press catalog number 7609.